AMERICAN GOVERNMENT

BRIEF VERSION

TENTH EDITION

James Q. Wilson

University of California, Los Angeles
Pepperdine University
Boston College

WADSWORTH
CENGAGE Learning™

Australia • Brazil • Japan • Korea • Mexico • Singapore • Spain • United Kingdom • United States

WADSWORTH
CENGAGE Learning

American Government, Brief Version,
Tenth Edition
James Q. Wilson

Publisher: Suzanne Jeans

Executive Editor: Carolyn Merrill

Development Editor: Rebecca Green

Associate Development Editor: Katherine
Hayes

Editorial Assistant: Angela Hodge

Media Editor: Laura Hildebrand

Marketing Manager: Lydia LeStar

Marketing Coordinator: Josh Hendrick

Senior Marketing Communications
Manager: Heather Baxley

Associate Content Project Manager:
Sara Abbott

Art Director: Linda Helcher

Print Buyer: Fola Orekoya

Rights Acquisition Specialist, Image:
Amanda Groszko

Senior Rights Acquisition Specialist, Text:
Katie Huha

Production Service/Compositor:
MPS Limited, a Macmillan Company

Text Designer: Lou Ann Thesing

Cover Designer: Riezebos Holzbaur/
Brie Hattey

Cover Image: Palmi Einarsson/Photolibrary

> For product information and technology assistance, contact us at
> **Cengage Learning Customer & Sales Support, 1-800-354-9706**
>
> For permission to use material from this text or product,
> submit all requests online at **www.cengage.com/permissions**
> Further permissions questions can be emailed to
> **permissionrequest@cengage.com**

Library of Congress Control Number: 2010936586

ISBN-13: 978-0-495-90678-0

ISBN-10: 0-495-90678-6

Wadsworth
20 Channel Center Street
Boston, MA 02210
USA

Cengage Learning is a leading provider of customized learning solutions
with office locations around the globe, including Singapore, the United
Kingdom, Australia, Mexico, Brazil and Japan. Locate your local office at
international.cengage.com/region

Cengage Learning products are represented in Canada by
Nelson Education, Ltd.

For your course and learning solutions, visit **www.cengage.com**

Purchase any of our products at your local college store or at our preferred
online store **www.cengagebrain.com.**

Printed in the United States of America
2 3 4 5 6 7 14 13 12 11

To Diane

Contents

PREFACE

American Government, Brief Version explains not only how the federal government works but also clarifies how its institutions have developed over time and their effects on public policy. Students will gain a deeper understanding about the subject's enduring historical, constitutional, and institutional dimensions within a concise framework. This book is thoroughly revised and redesigned to excite students' interest about the latest in American politics and encourage critical thinking.

In response to suggestions from readers, I have added the following features:

- **So What?** sections in each chapter pose a question to students about the content ahead, ask them to brainstorm about possible answers, and then offer an alternate answer that may not be so apparent. The goal is to make the chapter immediately accessible to students and help them see why it's so important to learn about our government.
- **What Would You Do?** boxes further enhance the critical thinking emphasis of the book, challenging students to explore their opinions on controversial topics and generating classroom discussion and debate.
- **How We Compare** features show how other nations around the world structure their governments and policies in relation to the United States and ask students to think about the results of these differences.

In addition to updates on statistics, tables, figures, and photos throughout, new topics include:

- Chapter 1: A look at why it's important to study American government in light of how we differ from other countries and how our nation deals with times of crisis, such as war and the current economic downturn.
- Chapter 2: How our Constitution differs from those around the world and what that means for us as citizens.

- Chapter 3: *Citizens United* v. *Federal Election Commission*, a discussion of church and state in the United States and other countries, and the issues of trying terrorists in civilian courts and the closing of Guantanamo prison.
- Chapter 4: A new introduction looks at the difference between minimum, intermediate, and strict scrutiny, and a How We Compare box looks at same-sex marriages at home and abroad.
- Chapter 5: State and federal relations in regard to the 2010 Health Care and Education Reconciliation Act, forms of Federalism around the world, and updates on grants and the intergovernmental lobby.
- Chapter 6: The increased role of the Internet and other technology in today's political world, the role of genetics in our political ideology, the world's opinions on America, a new table examining the policy positions of politically engaged Republicans and Democrats, and a new discussion about media bias in newspapers.
- Chapter 7: New updates on party preferences and delegates' representativeness to their voters, a look at political parties in other countries, and a new section on interest groups at work.
- Chapter 8: Updates on voter participation in the recent elections and an examination of how to increase voter turnout, a look at voting laws and turnout around the world compared to the United States, the role of the Internet, blogs, and social networking in campaigns, "narrowcasting" and "astroturfing," and an updated section on campaign financing.
- Chapter 9: A look at the recent party polarization of Congress, the 2010 elections, and how our number of legislators compares to other governments.
- Chapter 10: New coverage of the Obama administration and his policy toward issues such as the recession, health care, and war, a new section

on signing statements, and a look at presidential systems in other countries.

- Chapter 11: A new discussion helping students see why the bureaucracy matters and how the public and private sectors differ, and a How We Compare box on Outsourcing Government.
- Chapter 12: A revised discussion of the confirmation process, including Elena Kagan's hearing; an expanded and clarified look at activist and strict constructionist approaches, and a comparison of judicial review in the United States and the rest of the world.
- Chapter 13: The economic downturn and new policies to combat the crisis, health care reform, the BP oil spill, and how our Social Security system compares to those in other countries.
- Chapter 14: Updates on the war in Afghanistan and how our opinions on global issues compare to the rest of the world.
- Chapter 15: A new discussion about the current issues facing our government and those that lie ahead.

Instructor and Student Ancillaries

On **cengagebrain.com** students will be able to save up to 60% on their course materials through our full spectrum of options. Students will have the option to rent their textbooks, purchase print textbooks, e-textbooks, or individual e-chapters and audio books all for substantial savings over average retail prices. CengageBrain.com also includes access to Cengage Learning's broad range of homework and study tools, including the student resources discussed here.

Instructors should contact their Cengage sales representative for supplements and packaging options.

PowerLecture DVD with JoinIn™ and ExamView®

This instructor DVD includes two sets of PowerPoint® slides—a book-specific and a media-enhanced set; a Test Bank in both Microsoft® Word

and Exam View® formats; an Instructor's Manual; JoinIn clicker questions; videos; animated learning modules; and a Resource Integration Guide.

 Go to **cengagebrain.com/ shop/ISBN/0495906786** to access your Political Science CourseMate resources.

CourseMate

The CourseMate for *American Government, Brief Version, Tenth Edition* offers a variety of rich online learning resources designed to enhance the student experience. These resources include video activities, audio summaries, critical thinking activities, simulations, animated learning modules, interactive timelines, primary source quizzes, flashcards, learning objectives, glossaries, and crossword puzzles. Chapter resources are correlated with key chapter learning concepts, and users can browse or search for content in a variety of ways. It also contains an interactive **eBook** that has highlighting and search capabilities along with links to the chapters' study tools.

NewsNow on CourseMate brings current events to life for the student through weekly news stories from the Associated Press, videos, and images. For instructors, NewsNow includes an additional set of multimedia-rich PowerPoint slides posted each week to the password-protected area of the text's instructor companion website. Instructors may use these slides to take a class poll or trigger a lively debate about the events that are shaping the world right now. No Internet connection is required! Instructors also have access to the **Instructor's Guide to YouTube**, which shows American government instructors where on the Internet to find videos that can be used as learning tools in class.

Engagement Tracker lets instructors assess student preparation and engagement on CourseMate. Use the tracking tools to see progress for the class as a whole or for individual students.

WebTutor on Blackboard and WebCT

This web-based teaching and learning tool includes course management, study/mastery, and communication tools. Use WebTutor to provide virtual office hours, post your syllabus, and track student progress with WebTutor's quizzing material. For students, WebTutor offers real-time access to interactive online tutorials and simulations, practice quizzes, and Web links—all correlated to *American Government, Brief Version, Tenth Edition.*

Political Theatre 2.0 DVD

Available to adopters of Cengage textbooks and up-to-date through the 2008 election season, this 3-DVD series includes both classic and contemporary video clips, political advertisements, speeches, interviews, and more. JoinIn™ on Turning Point® for Political Theatre is available to accompany the videos.

The Wadsworth News Videos for American Government 2012 DVD

This collection of three- to six-minute video clips on relevant political issues serves as a great lecture or discussion launcher.

Great Speeches Collection

The Great Speeches Collection includes the full text of over sixty memorable orations for you to incorporate into your course for tremendous insight into historical, political, and cultural events. Speeches can be collated in a printed reader to supplement your course materials or bound into a core textbook.

ABC Video: Speeches by President Barack Obama

This DVD of nine famous speeches by President Barack Obama, from 2004 through his inauguration, also features critical-thinking questions and answers for each speech, designed to spark classroom discussion.

Election 2010: An American Government Supplement

Written by John Clark and Brian Schaffner, this booklet addresses the 2010 congressional and gubernatorial races, with real-time analysis and references.

The Obama Presidency—Year One Supplement

This full-color, sixteen-page supplement by Kenneth Janda, Jeffrey Berry, and Jerry Goldman analyzes such issues as healthcare, the economy and stimulus package, changes in the U.S. Supreme Court, and the effect Obama's policies have had on global affairs.

American Government CourseReader: Politics in Context

This database of readings enables instructors to create a customized reader, available to their students online or in print format. Hundreds of documents, readings, and videos can be searched by various criteria or browsed by collection, previewed, and then selected for a customized collection. The sources are edited to an appropriate length and include headnotes describing the document and critical-thinking and multiple-choice questions. Students can take notes, highlight, and print content. The e-Reader gives instructors easy-to-use assignment and assessment tools.

Acknowledgments

In preparing this edition, I was greatly aided by advice from the following colleagues and the reviewers of this and previous editions:

John J. DiIulio, Jr., University of Pennsylvania
Zach Courser, Boston College
Carl D. Cavalli, North Georgia College and State University
Brian DiSarro, California State University – Sacramento
Alejandro Gancedo, Miami Dade College
Stewart Gardner, Boise State University
Kenneth L. Grasso, Texas State University
Baogang Guo, Dalton State College
A. Michael Kinney, Calhoun Community College

David E. Marion, Hampden-Sydney College
John A. Murley, Rochester Institute of Technology
Robert P. Saldin, University of Montana
Justin S. Vaughn, Cleveland State University
Vernon Wilder, Texarkana College
Melanie Young, University of Nevada – Las Vegas
Scott Buchanan, Columbus State University
Damon Cann, University of Georgia

Martin Saiz, California State University, Northridge
Drew Lanier, University of Central Florida
Shari MacLachlan, Palm Beach Community College
Dana Morales, Montgomery College
Robert Locander, North Harris College
Kate Scheurer, University of North Dakota

J. Q. W.

ABOUT THE AUTHOR

James Q. Wilson is an emeritus professor of management and public policy at the University of California, Los Angeles. He lectures at Boston College and Pepperdine University, where he is the Ronald Reagan professor. From 1961 to 1987, he was a professor of government at Harvard University. Raised in California, he received a B.A. degree from the University of Redlands and a Ph.D. from the University of Chicago.

He is the author or coauthor of fifteen books, including *The Marriage Problem* (2002), *Moral Judgment* (1997), *The Moral Sense* (1993), *Bureaucracy* (1989), *Crime and Human Nature* (1985, with Richard J. Herrnstein), and *Political Organizations* (revised edition, 1995).

Wilson has served on a number of advisory posts in the federal government. He was chairman of the White House Task Force on Crime in 1967, chairman of the National Advisory Council on Drug Abuse Prevention in 1972–1973, a member of the President's Foreign Intelligence Advisory Board in 1986–1990, and a member of the President's Council on Bioethics (2002).

He has received three lifetime achievement awards from the American Political Science Association: the Charles E. Merriam Award for advancing government through social science knowledge; the John Gaus Award for scholarship on public administration; and the James Madison Award for distinguished scholarship. In 1991–1992, he was president of the Association.

He is a fellow of the American Academy of Arts and Sciences and of the American Philosophical Society. During his free time, he rides horses and goes scuba diving. In 2003, he received at the White House the Presidential Medal of Freedom, this nation's highest civilian award.

What Should We Know About American Government?

ENDURING QUESTIONS

1. **If citizens are fit to select their leaders, why may they be unfit to decide public policies?**

2. **What is democracy, and why is democracy alone not sufficient to protect personal freedom?**

If you are like most Americans, you may not have much confidence in the federal government. Many of us worry that it is too remote from the people, spends more money than it takes in from taxes, can't solve social problems, and never seems to serve as a remedy for disasters such as Hurricane Katrina.

Some people believe that government works that way because it is run by self-seeking politicians and dominated by special interest groups. I think that view is an exaggeration. Every government in the world will be influenced by politicians and interest groups. Yet government is necessary to protect the people, manage conflict, and provide essential services. What is striking about American government is that the same people who criticize its actions defend its principles: they like the way our Constitution protects personal freedom, sets limits to what government can do, and manages a capitalist economy. Winston Churchill, the British statesman, put it this way: "Democracy is the worst form of government except for all those other forms that have been tried."

CourseMate

AP Photo/J. Scott Applewhite

Why Have a Government?

It may seem obvious that every nation has a government, but it is important to understand why. One reason is that there are many things that people acting by themselves or through the economic market cannot achieve. When we buy a television set or an automobile, we have to pay for it; but a military force that protects the country affects everybody, whether they pay or not, and as a result nobody has any reason to fund it voluntarily. An environmental law that safeguards the quality of the air we breathe helps everybody, so no one has any incentive to pay its costs. We need government to compel people to pay for those things that they need but that cannot be supplied by the market.

A second reason is that people disagree about what should be done in society. They will argue about how a military force should be employed or whether we need an environmental law. Because these are important issues, there must be a way to settle the argument. **Politics** exists because people disagree about who should have power and what decisions they should make. Politics is inevitable. When people say that the government should "do the right thing" and ignore "politics," they are making a nonsensical statement. Taking politics out of government would be like taking religion out of church. **Government** exists to manage disagreements; it consists of those institutions that have the right to make decisions binding on the whole society.

Of course, politics exists in clubs, families, unions, and business firms, but this book is not about those entities. It is about disagreements that affect us all and so can be managed only by an institution—the government—that controls the lawful use of power. A business firm or labor union may change your behavior, but only the government can send you to jail or tax away your money.

Politics *The management of conflict over who shall rule and what policies shall be made.*

Government *The institution that, with a monopoly on the lawful use of power, can make decisions binding the whole society.*

The Meanings of Democracy

A **democracy** is government by the people. But what does "by the people" mean? It could mean **direct democracy**, in which all or most citizens make government decisions by themselves. They might do so by coming together in meetings to debate and vote on various issues, as happens in many town meetings in New England. Or they could vote on major issues that are put on the ballot, as is done in California and several other states.

However, our nation's government is not like this; it is a **representative democracy**. Voters do not decide policies; they choose leaders. If there is free competition among people who want to hold office and the election process is fair, it is democratic. The framers of our Constitution called a representative democracy a **republic**.

But it is not enough for a government to be democratic. After all, the people could elect rulers who would ignore or repress a minority of the population. Americans want not only democracy but also freedom. Americans believe their freedom can be protected by having a government with limited powers, access to courts where they can challenge government decisions, and a clear right to demand new policies or complain about existing ones. As we shall see in the next chapter, the Constitution and its chief amendments were written to do just that.

Democracy *Political system where the people rule.*

Direct democracy *Political system in which most citizens make policy, as in a town meeting.*

Representative democracy *Political system in which policy is made by officials elected by the people.*

Republic *A form of democracy in which power is vested in representatives selected by means of popular competitive elections.*

Citizens cast their votes electronically at a polling place in Austin, Texas.

Because Americans like these arrangements (even though they may not really understand them), our national government is regarded by them as **legitimate**. A legitimate government is one whose decisions most people will obey because they think the government has the right to make them. Of course, some people will not obey; a few refuse to pay their income taxes or hope to overthrow the government. But if the vast majority obeys the laws, then the government is legitimate.

Legitimate *Political authority supported by public opinion.*

Two Kinds of Democracy

There are two ways of organizing a democracy. One is a **parliamentary system**, in which all national authority is vested in an elected national legislature that then chooses the chief executive (usually called the prime minister). Parliamentary systems are common in Europe. The prime minister can rule as long as he or she is supported by a majority of the parliament, elections to which must be held every few (often 5) years. In a parliamentary system, political power is centralized in the prime minister and his or her cabinet. The bureaucracy works only for the cabinet. The courts usually do not interfere. The theory behind this system is that the government should be free to do whatever it wishes so long as it is consistent with the constitution and then is accountable to the voters in the next election.

Parliamentary system *A government that vests power in an elected legislature that chooses the chief executive.*

America, by contrast, has a **presidential system**, in which power is divided between a separately elected president and Congress and there are courts that can declare a law to be unconstitutional. The president proposes legislation but cannot be confident Congress will approve it. Indeed, Congress itself may pass laws it likes and the president dislikes; they will go into effect unless the president vetoes them. The bureaucracy reports to two masters, the president and Congress. Because its loyalties are divided, its actions may make the president unhappy. The theory underlying this system is that policies should be tested for their political acceptability at every stage of the policy-making process and not just at election time.

Presidential system *A government that vests power in a separately elected president and legislature.*

Mark Wilson/Getty Images News/Getty Images

RAINER JENSEN/Newscom

The chief executives of two different democracies: America's Barack Obama (left) heads a presidential system; England's David Cameron (right), a parliamentary one.

 ## So What?

America has a national government. Some of you are probably saying, "I only have to study it because my teacher wants me to. So what?"

The answer is that unless we study it, we might form some strange ideas about how the government works. And since the government affects almost every part of our lives, we might form some negative impressions about its ability to help us. Here is one view:

The president gets elected because of some slick television ads. The party platform is a meaningless set of words that gives you no idea of what its members will do once in office. Congress and the president pass laws, not to solve problems but to reward interest groups that have spent the most money getting them elected. Once passed, the laws are administered by an all-powerful bureaucracy that pretty much does what it wants. If you challenge these laws in court, the judges will decide matters on the basis of their party affiliation with little regard for standards of justice and fair play. No wonder our national problems don't get solved.

Now, there is some truth in all of these statements, but they do not give a full and accurate picture of how our government works. The purpose of this book is to provide that picture. As you read it, you will discover that politics is a lot more complicated than the above paragraph suggests. Getting elected involves much more than slick ads; the president and Congress often work hard to solve serious problems; the bureaucracy is scarcely all powerful; the courts worry a great deal about justice and fair play. But they do these things in a complex, politically charged world in which compromise is often as important as commitment.

Consider how other democratic nations are governed. In many, the national government is very powerful, with few opportunities for people to get involved at the local level. Interest groups may be weak, but only because political parties are strong. Courts exist; but in many nations you cannot use them to challenge the government. And many of these governments impose heavier taxes than does America. Strong governments and weak courts have advantages—it is easier to enact bold new policies. But they also have disadvantages—it is harder to stop what you don't like.

When you think about how this country differs from others, you might well decide that it is worth learning who really governs and what ends they seek.

Who Governs?

People who are unhappy about our government often say that it is run by big business, labor unions, Wall Street, the military, right-wing nuts, or crackpot liberals. In later chapters you will learn that these views are much too simple. Competing groups now have so much access to government that decisions about public policy usually emerge out of a complicated struggle among many different interests. Over the last several decades, our government has become what political scientists call pluralist; that is, political resources (money, prestige, expertise, and access to the media) are so widely available that only rarely can any single group dominate decisions.

 How We Compare

Academic Freedom

You are reading a textbook on American government, but how is the freedom to study, teach, or do research protected from undue government interference? And how do European democracies protect academic freedom?

The U.S. Constitution does not mention academic freedom. Rather, in America, the federal and state courts have typically treated academic freedom as "free speech" strongly protected under the First Amendment.

In each of nine European nations, the constitution is silent on academic freedom, but various national laws protect it. In 13 other European nations, academic freedom is protected both by explicit constitutional language and by national legislation. But is academic freedom better protected in these nations than in either the United States or elsewhere in Europe?

Not necessarily. Germany's constitution states that "research and teaching are free" but subject to "loyalty to the constitution." Italy's constitution offers lavish protections for academic freedom, but its national laws severely restrict those same freedoms.

The United Kingdom has no written constitution, but its national laws regarding academic freedom (and university self-governance) are quite restrictive by American standards.

Source: Terence Karran, "Freedom in Europe: A Preliminary Analysis," *Higher Education Policy,* Vol. 20, 2007: 289–313.

Moreover, national politics is not the only kind that counts. State and local governments play a much larger role in American politics than is true in most other democracies. Our Constitution and political culture ensure that the desires of local groups make a difference. In many democracies, education, law enforcement, and planning land use are done by the national government; here they are (largely) done by local governments.

To What Ends?

There have been big changes in what the national government does, changes that are summarized in the final chapter. Consider: In 1935, 96 percent of all Americans paid no federal income tax, and for those who did pay the average rate was only 4 percent of their income. Today, almost every family pays federal taxes, and the average income tax rate is over 20 percent. Or consider: In 1960, many African Americans had to ride in the back of buses, could only send their children to all-black schools, and would not be served in many public restaurants. Today these legal barriers have vanished. Consider again: In 1970, there was not much in the way of federal environmental legislation, but today federal (and state) rules powerfully affect how land is used, factories are operated, air is kept clean, and endangered species are protected.

The two questions—who governs and to what ends—cannot be given the same answer. Most people holding elective national office are white, affluent, middle-aged men, but that does not mean that national policies benefit that demographic alone. The affluent are taxed more heavily than the less well off, and blacks and women have had their rights dramatically increased.

What American Politics Means for Us

Our Constitution and habits have four effects on how we make policies. In this book you will read about:

1. *The separation of powers.* The president and Congress are rivals, even when they are from the same political party. As a result, stalemates are the rule, not the exception, and they can only be overcome by a national crisis, a powerful tide of public opinion, or tough political bargaining.
2. *Federalism.* The states have an independent political position, and members of Congress think of themselves as representing these localities. Hardly any policy becomes law without adjusting it to meet the needs of states, and so they play a large role in managing welfare programs, enforcing pollution-control laws, and building major highways even though most of the money comes from Washington. States dominate education, law enforcement, and land-use planning.
3. *Judicial review.* Not only can the federal courts declare a presidential action or a federal law to be unconstitutional, but also they may hear lawsuits brought by people who claim that federal agencies have not acted properly.

WHAT WOULD YOU DO?

MEMORANDUM

To: Governor Steve Finore

From: Edward Heron, chief policy adviser

Subject: Initiative Repeal

You have supported several successful initiatives (life imprisonment for thrice-convicted violent felons, property tax limits), but you have never publicly stated a view on the initiative itself, and the repeal proposal will probably surface during tomorrow's press briefing.

Arguments for a ban:

1. Ours is a representative, not a direct, democracy in which voters elect leaders and elected leaders make policy decisions subject to review by the courts.

2. Voters often are neither rational nor respectful of constitutional rights. For example, many people demand both lower taxes and more government services, and polls find that most voters would prohibit people with certain views from speaking and deprive all persons accused of a violent crime from getting out on bail while awaiting trial.

3. Over the past 100 years, about 800 statewide ballot initiatives have been passed in 24 states. Rather than giving power to the people, special-interest groups have spent billions of dollars manipulating voters to pass initiatives that enrich or benefit them, not the public at large.

Arguments against a ban:

1. When elected officials fail to respond to persistent public majorities favoring tougher crime measures, lower property taxes, and other popular concerns, direct democracy via the initiative is legitimate, and the courts can still review the law.

2. More Americans than ever have college degrees and easy access to information about public affairs.

Friday,

Legal and Policy Experts Call for a Ban on Ballot Initiatives

December 11
SACRAMENTO, CA

A report released yesterday and signed by more than 100 law and public policy professors statewide urges that the state's constitution be amended to ban legislation by initiative. The initiative allows state voters to place legislative measures directly on the ballot by getting enough signatures. The initiative "has led to disastrous policy decisions on taxes, crime, and other issues," the report declared . . .

Studies find that most average citizens are able to figure out which candidates, parties, or advocacy groups come closest to supporting their own economic interests and personal values.

3. All told, the 24 states that passed 35 laws by initiative also passed more than 14,000 laws by the regular legislative process (out of more than 70,000 bills they considered). Studies find that special-interest groups are severely limited in their ability to pass new laws by initiative, while citizens' groups with broad-based public support are behind most initiatives that pass.

Your Decision:

Favor ban _____

Oppose ban _____

4. *Freedom of speech and assembly.* The First Amendment guarantees the right of people not only to speak their minds but also to lobby Congress. You may dislike lobbyists, but you cannot silence them.

The result of these four factors is that American politics is adversarial; it is a system that by encouraging participation stimulates disagreement. You can see adversarial politics in action in almost any policy area. Business and government fight over environmental rules, pro-life groups attack pro-choice groups (and vice versa), and many citizens complain about the number of special benefits Congress hands out to other people while insisting that they get benefits of their own. When the government does something unpopular, we often threaten to sue it or hold a protest march. Our Constitution so empowers us.

And from time to time our government faces a crisis. It did during the struggle to win the Second World War and in Vietnam, in the long competition between this country and the old Soviet Union, and most recently in the deep recession that caused massive unemployment and led the government to try new ways of stimulating economic growth. When you ask "So what?" about studying politics, one answer is this: Why did the government manage the Second World War effectively and the war in Vietnam unsuccessfully? Why did the government try to end the current recession while at the same time attempting to put in place big and expensive new programs? And since we will soon run out of money to pay for Medicare and Social Security, how do you think the government will respond to these problems?

RECONSIDERING THE ENDURING QUESTIONS

1. If citizens are fit to select political leaders, why might they be unfit to make policies?

One obvious reason is that there are too many (over 300 million) Americans to come together and make decisions. A deeper answer is that citizens who are largely concerned about earning a living and maintaining a family may have little time or interest in politics, and thus be less able to reason carefully than are people who make politics a career.

2. What is a democracy, and why is democracy alone not sufficient to protect freedom?

Democracy means rule by the people, either directly (as in a town meeting) or indirectly (by selecting leaders). But democracy without guarantees of personal liberty may allow popularly elected officials to oppress a minority.

Online Resources: What Should We Know About American Government?

Suggested Readings

King, Anthony. *The New American Political System.* Washington, D.C.: American Enterprise Institute, 1990. This book, edited by a British scholar, gives an intelligent overview of how American national government operates.

O'Rourke, P. J. *Parliament of Whores: A Lone Humorist Attempts to Explain the Entire U. S. Government.* New York: Grove Press, 1991. O'Rourke, a conservative version of Monty Python, offers a funny, outrageous, and sometimes insightful account of our politics.

Schumpeter, Joseph A. *Capitalism, Socialism, and Democracy.* 3d ed. New York: Harper, 1950, chs. 20–23. A lucid statement of the theory of representative democracy.

ENDURING QUESTIONS

1. **What was wrong with the Articles of Confederation?**

2. **How did the authors of the Constitution view human nature?**

3. **How can a government be strong enough to govern without threatening freedom?**

4. **Has the system of separated powers and checks and balances protected liberty?**

CourseMate

The Problem of Liberty

The goal of the American Revolution was liberty. The rebellion was perhaps the first, and certainly was the clearest, case of a people altering the political order violently simply to protect their liberties. The French Revolution in 1789 sought

Michael Ventura/Alamy

not only liberty but also "equality and fraternity"; the Russian Revolution in 1917 and the Chinese Revolution in 1949 chiefly sought equality and were little concerned with liberty.

Americans sought to protect the traditional liberties to which they thought they were entitled as British subjects. These included the right to bring cases before independent judges rather than those subordinate to the king; to be free of the burden of having British troops quartered in their homes; to engage in trade without costly restrictions; and to pay no taxes levied by the British Parliament, in which Americans had no direct representation.

Many Americans thought these liberties could be protected while remaining part of Great Britain, but those who supported the American Revolution were convinced that only independence would guarantee freedom. They had lost confidence in the British government and the unwritten constitution on which it was based. Their explanation for the inadequacy of British government was human nature.

Human Nature

"A lust for domination is more or less natural to all parties," one anonymous American wrote in 1775, and his views were widely shared. Men, Americans thought, seek power because they are ambitious, greedy, and easily corrupted. John Adams denounced the "luxury, effeminacy, and venality" of British politicians; Patrick Henry spoke scathingly of the "corrupt House of Commons"; and Alexander Hamilton described Great Britain as "an old, wrinkled, withered, worn-out hag." This flamboyant language may have been useful in whipping up enthusiasm for the war, but most leaders believed it. When the American Constitution was being debated by the states, the chief issue was whether it went far enough in protecting people from self-seeking politicians.

The liberties that Britain threatened and that the colonists cherished did not exist because a king had granted them or a statute had authorized them, but because they were supported by a "higher law" embodying "natural rights" that were ordained by God, discoverable by reason, and essential to progress. These rights, John Dickinson wrote, "are born with us; exist with us; and cannot be taken away from us by any human power." These rights, most people agreed, included life, liberty, and property. Thomas Jefferson changed "property" to "the pursuit of happiness" when he wrote the Declaration of Independence, but others went on talking about property.

This interest in property did not mean that the American Revolution was initiated by the rich to protect their interests or that the debate over the Constitution was between property owners and the propertyless. In late-eighteenth-century America, most people (except black slaves) had property of some kind because they worked as farmers or artisans. Nor did the Revolution enrich Americans. Taxes rose, trade was disrupted, and debts increased. There were, of course, war profiteers and those who tried to manipulate the currency to their own advantage. For most Americans, however, the Revolution was not about money but about ideology.

Everyone remembers the glowing language with which Jefferson set out the case for independence in the second paragraph of the Declaration:

> We hold these truths to be self-evident, that all men are created equal, that they are endowed by their Creator with certain unalienable Rights, that among these are Life, Liberty, and the pursuit of Happiness.—That to secure these rights, Governments are instituted among Men, deriving their just powers from the consent of the governed—That whenever any Form of Government becomes destructive of these ends, it is the right of the People to alter or abolish it, and to institute new Government, laying its foundation on such principles, and organizing its powers in such form, as to them shall seem most likely to effect their Safety and Happiness.

However, most people do not remember the next twenty-seven paragraphs, in which Jefferson listed the colonists' specific complaints against George III and his ministers. None of these referred to social or economic conditions in the colonies; all spoke instead of political liberties. Jefferson in his draft added a twenty-eighth complaint—that the king had allowed the slave trade to continue and was inciting slaves to revolt against their masters. So contradictory was this argument that Congress dropped it.

Indeed, many British critics (and probably some Americans) felt that the Declaration was an unconvincing document. "All men" could not be created equal if most blacks were held in slavery. For whites, what did "equal" mean? Since people differ in ability, interests, and energy, how could they be called equal?

The Declaration set out an ideal, but it was one with a history. Nearly a century earlier, in 1690, the English philosopher John Locke wrote *Two Treatises of Government.* In it he argued against the ancient view that no man is born free, that people cannot rule themselves because they lack the talents true rulers will have, and that tradition or God will select those rulers. Locke said that all men are in fact born equal in rights; that when in "the state of nature" they will live together without a common superior; that to avoid the conflicts and inconvenience that will occur in a state of nature they will form a government; that this government must rest on the voluntary consent of the governed; that the government exists to protect life, liberty, and property; and that it can do so only on the basis of majority rule. This "state of nature" once existed, for "in the beginning all the world was America."[1]

The Real Revolution

The Revolution was more than the Declaration or the War of Independence. It began before the war, continued after it, and involved more than defeating British soldiers. John Adams explained afterward that the real revolution was the "radical change in the principles, opinions, and sentiments, and affections of the people." The new sentiment was that political authority could not rest on tradition but only on consent.

At the time these were remarkable views. No government then existing had been organized on such a basis. In 1778, eight states adopted written constitutions; within a few years, every state but Connecticut and Rhode Island had such documents. (These two states relied on their old colonial charters.) The constitutions spelled out rights and tended to concentrate authority in the hands of elected representatives.

Written constitutions, elected leaders, and a bill of rights are now so familiar to us that we take them for granted. But when they were produced, many Americans did not think they would succeed: such arrangements would be either so strong that they would threaten liberty or so weak that they would permit chaos.

The Articles of Confederation

After declaring their independence, each of the thirteen former colonies formed a loose alliance under the **Articles of Confederation**. This alliance (barely) allowed the colonies to wage the War of Independence.

Turmoil, uncertainty, and fear permeated the eleven years between the Declaration of Independence in 1776 and the signing of the Constitution in 1787. General George Washington had to wage a bitter, protracted war against a world power with only the support the state governments chose to give. When peace finally came, many parts of the nation were a shambles. The British were still a powerful force in North America, with an army available in Canada (where many Americans loyal to Britain had fled) and a large navy at sea. Spain claimed the Mississippi River valley and occupied Florida. Soldiers returning to their farms found themselves heavily in debt but with no money to pay it or their taxes. The paper money printed to finance the war was now virtually worthless.

The thirteen states had only a faint semblance of a national government with which to bring order and stability to the nation. The Articles of Confederation, which had gone into effect in 1781, created little more than a "league of friendship" that lacked the power to levy taxes or regulate commerce. Each state retained its **sovereignty** and independence; each state (regardless of size) had one vote in Congress; nine (of thirteen) votes were required to pass any measure; and the delegates who cast these votes were picked and paid by the state legislatures. Several states claimed the unsettled lands in the West and occasionally pressed those claims with guns, but there was no national judicial system to settle these or other disputes among the states. To amend the Articles of Confederation, all thirteen states had to agree.

Many leaders of the Revolution, such as George Washington and Alexander Hamilton, believed that a stronger national government was essential. A small group, conferring at Washington's home at Mount Vernon in 1785, decided to call a meeting to discuss trade regulation, one of the many seemingly insoluble problems facing Congress. That meeting, held at Annapolis, Maryland, in September 1786, was not well attended, so another meeting was called for May 1787 in Philadelphia—this time for the more general purpose of considering ways to remedy the defects of the Confederation.

Articles of Confederation *A constitution drafted by the newly independent states in 1777 and ratified in 1781. It created a weak national government that could not levy taxes or regulate commerce. In 1789, it was replaced by our current constitution in order to create a stronger national government.*

Sovereignty *A governmental unit that has supreme authority and is accountable to no higher institution.*

The Constitutional Convention

The delegates assembled in Philadelphia for what was advertised (and authorized by Congress) as a meeting to revise the Articles; they adjourned four months later having written a wholly new constitution. When they met, they were keenly aware of the problems of the confederacy but far from agreement on remedies. As in 1776, their objectives were still the protection of life, liberty, and property, but they had no accepted political theory that would tell them what kind of national government, if any, would serve that goal.

The Lessons of Experience

James Madison, who was to be one of the leading framers of the new constitution, spent a good part of 1786 studying books sent to him by Thomas Jefferson, then in Paris, in hopes of finding some model for a workable American republic—but concluded that no model existed. History showed that confederacies were too weak to govern and tended to collapse from internal dissension, whereas all stronger forms of government were so powerful as to trample the liberties of the citizens. At home, the state governments of Pennsylvania and Massachusetts vividly illustrated the dangers of excessively strong and excessively weak governments.

The Pennsylvania constitution, adopted in 1776, created the most radically democratic of the new state regimes. All power was given to a one-house (or **unicameral**) **legislature**, the members of which were elected for one-year terms. No legislator could serve for more than four years. There was no real executive. The radical pamphleteer Thomas Paine and various French philosophers hailed the Pennsylvania constitution as the very embodiment of the principle of rule by the people, but it was a good deal less popular in Philadelphia. The legislature disfranchised the Quakers, persecuted conscientious objectors to the war, ignored the requirement of trial by juries, and manipulated the judiciary.[2] To Madison and his friends, the Pennsylvania constitution demonstrated how a government, though democratic, could be tyrannical by concentrating all powers in one set of hands, in this case the legislature.

The Massachusetts constitution of 1780, in contrast, was a good deal less democratic. There was a clear separation of powers among the branches of government; the directly elected governor could veto acts of the legislature; and judges served for life. But if the government of Pennsylvania was thought too strong, that of Massachusetts seemed too weak, despite its "conservative" features. In 1787, a group of ex-Revolutionary War soldiers and officers led by one Daniel Shays, plagued by debt and high taxes, forcibly prevented the courts in western Massachusetts from sitting. The governor of Massachusetts asked the Congress of the Confederation to send troops, but it could not raise the money or the manpower; the governor then discovered that he had no state militia. In desperation, private funds were collected to hire a volunteer army that, with the firing of a few shots, dispersed the rebels.

Shays's Rebellion, occurring between the aborted Annapolis convention and the upcoming Philadelphia convention, had a powerful effect on public opinion.

Unicameral legislature *A lawmaking body with only one chamber, as in Nebraska.*

Shays's Rebellion *A rebellion in 1787 led by Daniel Shays and other ex–Revolutionary War soldiers and officers to prevent foreclosures of farms as a result of high interest rates and taxes. The revolt highlighted the weaknesses of the Confederation and bolstered support for a stronger national government.*

Far away in Paris, Thomas Jefferson took a detached view: "A little rebellion now and then is a good thing," he wrote. "The tree of liberty must be refreshed from time to time with the blood of patriots and tyrants."[3] But many other leaders were aghast at the rebellion. Delegates who might otherwise have been reluctant to attend the Philadelphia meeting were galvanized by the fear that state governments were about to collapse from internal dissension. George Washington wrote to a friend despairingly: "For God's sake . . . , if they [the rebels] have *real* grievances, redress them; if they have not, employ the force of government against them at once."[4]

The Framers

The Philadelphia convention attracted fifty-five delegates, only about thirty of whom participated regularly in the proceedings. Pledged to keep their deliberations secret, the delegates had to keep an eye on the talkative, party-loving Benjamin Franklin. The delegates were not bookish intellectuals, but men of practical affairs. Most were young but experienced in politics: eight had signed the Declaration of Independence, seven had been governors, thirty-four were lawyers; a few were wealthy. Thirty-nine had served in the ineffectual Congress of the Confederation; a third were veterans of the Continental army.

The key men at the convention were an odd lot. George Washington was a very tall, athletic man who was the best horseman in Virginia and who impressed everyone with his dignity despite decaying teeth and big eyes. James Madison was the very opposite: quite short, with a frail body, and not much of an orator, but possessed of one of the best minds in the country. Benjamin Franklin, though old and ill, was the most famous American in the world as a scientist and writer; he always displayed shrewd judgment, at least when sober. Alexander Hamilton was the illegitimate son of a French woman and a Scottish merchant who had so strong a mind and so powerful a desire that he succeeded in everything he did, from being Washington's aide during the Revolution to making a splendid secretary of the treasury during Washington's presidency.

The convention produced not a revision of the Articles of Confederation, as it had been authorized to do, but instead a wholly new written constitution creating a true national government unlike any that had existed before. That document is today the world's oldest written national constitution. The deliberations that produced it were not always lofty or

Bettmann/Corbis

James Madison, often described as the "Father of the Constitution," prepared the Virginia Plan that formed the basis for the deliberations at the 1787 convention.

philosophical; much hard bargaining, not a little confusion, and accidents of time and personality helped shape the final product. But though the leading political philosophers were only rarely mentioned, the debate was profoundly influenced by philosophical beliefs, some of which were formed by the revolutionary experience and others by the eleven-year attempt at self-government.

When the Constitutional Convention met in Philadelphia in May 1787, its members were in general agreement that liberty must be preserved, that government should have the consent of the governed, and that the powers of the national government should be separated among several branches. But this agreement left much room for debate. How strong should the government be? How much power should the states have? Some leaders, such as James Madison, wanted to give to the national government the right to veto actions of state legislatures, while other leaders wanted the states to yield only a few limited powers to the national government. These were tough questions, but unlike government meetings held today, the Philadelphia convention was small in size, met in secret, issued no press releases, and supplied no media leaks.

Americans are proud of the Constitution that was produced. But they should remember that it was the result not of wise philosophers discussing large principles but of a happy accident: It was written in secret by a small number of practical men who met at a time when most people realized that they needed a new government.

The Challenge

American experience since 1776, as well as the history of British government, led the Framers to doubt whether popular consent alone would be a sufficient guarantor of liberty. A popular government might prove too weak to prevent one faction from abusing another (as in Massachusetts), or a popular majority could turn tyrannical (as in Pennsylvania). In fact, the tyranny of the majority could be an even greater threat than rule by the few: facing the will of the majority, the lone person could not count on the succor of popular opinion or the possibility of popular revolt. The problem, then, was a delicate one: how to frame a government strong enough to rule effectively but not too strong to overrun the liberties of its citizens. The answer, the delegates believed, was not "democracy" as it was then understood—that is, mob rule, such as Shays's Rebellion. Aristocracy—the rule of the few—was no solution either, because the few were as likely to be corrupted by power as the many. Nor could liberty be assured, Madison believed, by simply writing a constitution that limited government.

The chief problem faced by the Framers, as they came to be called, was that of liberty: how to devise a government strong enough to preserve order but not so strong that it would threaten liberty. In one of his most famous essays in defense of the Constitution, James Madison explained their delicate task:

> In framing a government which is to be administered by men over men, the great difficulty lies in this: You must first enable the government to control the governed; and in the next place oblige it to control itself.[5]

Some Key Political Concepts

Constitution

A constitution, whether written or unwritten, is the fundamental law of a nation. It defines the powers of government, specifies the offices to be filled and the authority each is to exercise, and sets the limits to governmental authority.

Note: True constitutional government is limited government. Nations may have documents called "constitutions," but if they are ruled by tyrants or dictators who recognize no limits to their authority, then the "constitution" is only a piece of paper, not a fundamental law.

Majority Rule

The doctrine of majority rule states that offices will be filled by those candidates who win the most votes and that laws will be made by whichever side in a legislature has the most votes.

Minority Rights

Minority rights set two kinds of limits on the power of the majority:

1. *Absolute:* There are certain things that the majority, no matter how large, cannot do. For example, Congress may not pass a law that makes an individual guilty of a crime without a trial.
2. *Conditional:* There are certain things that the majority can do only if it is an "extraordinary majority"—that is, contains some percentage of the votes greater than 50 percent. For example, Congress may propose a constitutional amendment only if two-thirds of each house vote in favor of it.

History has taught us, Madison and the other Framers believed, that people will seek power because they are by nature ambitious, greedy, and easily corrupted. As Madison wrote:

> But what is government itself but the greatest of all reflections on human nature? If men were angels, no government would be necessary. If angels were to govern men, neither external nor internal controls on government would be necessary.[6]

Madison's views captured nicely the experience of the convention delegates and the later state ratifying meetings. To solve the problem he had identified, Madison became the author of the outline for a new constitution called the *Virginia Plan.* It was introduced to the convention shortly after it had organized itself and chosen George Washington as its presiding officer. The Virginia Plan quickly became the meeting's major item of business.

Large States versus Small States

By agreeing to consider the Virginia Plan, the convention fundamentally altered its task from amending the Articles to designing a true national government. The Virginia Plan called for a strong national union organized into three governmental branches: legislative, executive, and judicial. It had two key features: (1) a

The Structure of the National Government

AS DESCRIBED IN THE CONSTITUTION OF 1787

A Congress, Made Up of Two Houses:

A HOUSE OF REPRESENTATIVES

- Composed of members apportioned roughly in accordance with the population of each state; initially, the number varied from one (Rhode Island) to eight (Pennsylvania)
- Representatives to be elected every two years by those people in each state eligible to vote for the members of the "most populous" (usually, the lower house) of their state legislatures

A SENATE

- Composed of two members from each state
- Senators to be elected by state legislatures for staggered six-year terms

A President

- To be elected for a four-year term by "electors" chosen in each state as directed by the state legislature
- Each state to have electors equal to the number of senators and representatives from that state. (No senator or representative may serve as an elector.)

The Judiciary

- One Supreme Court
- Such lower courts as Congress may create
- All judges to be nominated by the president and confirmed by the Senate. The judges are to hold office during good behavior (that is, without fixed terms and without being removable except by impeachment)

Great (or **Connecticut**) **Compromise** *A compromise at the Constitutional Convention in 1787 that reconciled the interests of small and large states by allowing the former to predominate in the Senate and the latter in the House. Under the agreement, each state received two representatives in the Senate, regardless of size, but was allotted representatives on the basis of population in the House.*

national legislature would have supreme power over all matters on which the separate states were not competent to act, as well as the power to veto any and all state laws; and (2) the people would directly elect at least one house of the legislature.

As the debate went on, the representatives of New Jersey and other small states became increasingly worried that the convention was going to write a constitution in which the states would be represented in both houses of Congress on the basis of population. If this happened, the smaller states feared they would always be outvoted by the larger states. A substitute idea, the *New Jersey Plan*, was submitted to the convention by William Paterson. It would have amended, not replaced, the Articles of Confederation, giving the central government somewhat stronger powers than it had but retaining the Articles' one-state, one-vote system of representation. The key feature of the New Jersey Plan was a unicameral Congress in which each state would have an equal vote.

The Compromise

The small states' demand for equal representation embodied in the New Jersey Plan led to the **Great** (or **Connecticut**) **Compromise**. That compromise, hammered out by a committee headed by Benjamin Franklin, was adopted by the narrowest of margins on July 16, 1787. The structure of the national legislature was set as follows:

- A House of Representatives consisting initially of sixty-five members apportioned among the states roughly on the basis of population and elected by the people.
- A Senate consisting of two senators from each state to be chosen by the state legislatures.

The Great Compromise reconciled the interests of small and large states by allowing the former to predominate in the Senate and the latter in the House. This reconciliation was necessary to ensure support for a strong national government in small and large states alike, but it represented major concessions on both sides. In time, most of the delegates from the dissenting states accepted it.

After the Great Compromise, many more issues had to be resolved, but by now a spirit of accommodation had developed, and other compromises were reached providing for the election of the president by an electoral college, establishing

So What?

Studying a constitution probably strikes you as a pretty dull affair. Everyone knows this country is a democracy, but aren't all democracies pretty much alike? No. American democracy is unique in the world, and you cannot understand why without paying close attention to our Constitution. In fact, a good place to begin is to wonder whether its authors really meant to create a democracy.

The answer is complex. The Framers did not intend to create a "pure" or "direct" democracy—one in which the people rule directly. For one thing, the size of the country and the distances between settlements would have made that physically impossible. But for another, the Framers worried that a government in which all citizens directly participate, as in the New England town meeting, would be excessively subject to temporary popular passions and could not ensure minority rights.

The Framers put in place many features that do not appear to be democratic. The president would be chosen by an electoral college, not by the voters. Members of the Senate, as originally designed, would be picked by state legislatures, not by the people. A Supreme Court would exist that might decide that a law passed by Congress could not go into effect because it was unconstitutional.

The Framers intended to create a republic: a government in which a system of representation operates. In designing that system, there was an intense dispute over whether the members of the House of Representatives would be elected directly by the people. After arguing, the Framers decided that they would be. Supporters of this provision contended that "no government could long subsist without the confidence of the people."

Ways of Amending the Constitution

Under Article V, there are two ways to *propose* amendments to the Constitution and two ways to *ratify* them.

To Propose an Amendment

1. Two-thirds of both houses of Congress vote to propose an amendment, *or*
2. Two-thirds of the state legislatures ask Congress to call a national convention to propose amendments

To Ratify an Amendment

1. Three-fourths of the state legislatures approve it, *or*
2. Ratifying conventions in three-fourths of the states approve it

Some Key Facts

- Only the first method of proposing an amendment has been used.
- The second method of ratification has been used only once, to ratify the Twenty-first Amendment (repealing Prohibition).
- Congress may limit the time within which a proposed amendment must be ratified. The usual limitation has been seven years, but the Twenty-seventh Amendment took 202 years to ratify.
- Thousands of proposals have been made, but only thirty-three have obtained the necessary two-thirds vote in Congress.
- Twenty-seven amendments have been ratified.
- The first ten amendments, ratified on December 15, 1791, are known as the Bill of Rights.

the president's term of office, and deciding who would select the members of the Supreme Court. Finally, on July 26, those proposals that were already accepted, together with a bundle of unresolved issues, were handed over to a "Committee of Detail"—five delegates, including James Madison and the chief draftsman of the final document, Gouverneur Morris. The committee hardly contented itself with mere "details," however. It inserted some new proposals and made changes in old ones, drawing on existing state constitutions and the members' beliefs as to what the other delegates might accept. On August 6, the first complete draft of the Constitution was submitted to the convention. There it was debated item by item, revised, amended, and finally, on September 17, approved by all twelve states in attendance (Rhode Island had never sent a delegation).

Thus, popular rule was only one element of the new government. State legislatures, not the people, would choose the senators; electors, not the people directly, would choose the president. As we have seen, without these arrangements, there would have been no Constitution at all, for the small states adamantly opposed any proposal that would have given undue power to the large ones—direct popular election would clearly have made the populous states dominant. In short, the Framers wished to observe the principle of majority rule, but they felt that, on the most important questions, two kinds of majorities were essential: a majority of the voters and a majority of the states.

The power of the Supreme Court to declare an act of Congress unconstitutional—**judicial review**—is also a way of limiting the power of popular majorities. It is not clear whether the Framers intended that there be judicial review, but there is little doubt that in the Framers' minds, the fundamental law, the Constitution, had to be safeguarded against popular passions. They made the process for amending the Constitution easier than it had been under the Articles but still relatively difficult (see the box on page 20).

In short, the answer to the question of whether the Constitution brought about a democratic government is yes if by *democracy* we mean a system of representative government based on popular consent. The degree of that consent has changed since 1787; for example, the people—not state legislatures—now elect the Senate.

Judicial review *The power of the courts to declare acts of the legislature and of the executive to be unconstitutional and, hence, null and void.*

Two Key Principles: Separation of Powers and Federalism

The American version of representative democracy was based on two major principles, both of which distributed power. The **separation of powers** ensured that in America political power would be shared by three separate branches of government, unlike parliamentary democracies where power was concentrated in a single supreme legislature. In America, political authority was divided between a national government and the state governments—a division called **federalism**—whereas in most European systems, authority was centralized in the national government. Neither of these principles was especially controversial at Philadelphia. The delegates began their work in broad agreement that separated powers and some measure of federalism were necessary, and both the Virginia Plan and the New Jersey Plan contained a version of each. How much of each should be written into the Constitution was quite controversial, however.

Chapter 5 describes how federalism developed and how it works today. Here we review the key features of the separation of powers system. The first point to bear in mind is that the powers of the three branches of government are not actually separated; rather they are *shared*. The checks and balances built into the constitutional system exist because three branches of government share all the powers of that system, as shown in the box on page 22.

Separation of powers *A principle of American government whereby constitutional authority is shared by three separate branches of government— the legislative, the executive, and the judicial.*

Federalism *A political system in which ultimate authority is shared between a central government and state or regional governments.*

Government and Human Nature

These checks and balances were based on a theory of human nature. The Framers believed that men and women were good enough to make it possible to have a free government, but they were not good enough to make it inevitable. People would pursue their self-interest, and no "parchment barrier," like a constitution or a bill of rights, would be a sufficient check on those self-seeking tendencies. Some Revolutionary War leaders felt that republican government was possible only if human character were to improve, but James Madison disagreed. To him and others at the Philadelphia convention, the proper way to keep government in check while still leaving it strong enough to perform its essential tasks was to allow the self-interest of one person to check the self-interest of another. This would make republican government possible, Madison thought, "even in the absence of virtue."

Checks and Balances

The Constitution created a system of *separate institutions that share powers*. Because the three branches of government share powers, each can (partially) check the powers of the others. This is the system of **checks and balances**. The major checks possessed by each branch are listed below.

Congress

1. Can check the president in these ways:
   a. By refusing to pass a bill the president wants
   b. By passing a law over the president's veto
   c. By using impeachment powers to remove the president from office
   d. By refusing to approve a presidential appointment (Senate only)
   e. By refusing to ratify a treaty the president has signed (Senate only)
2. Can check the federal courts in these ways:
   a. By changing the number and the jurisdiction of the lower courts
   b. By using impeachment powers to remove a judge from office
   c. By refusing to approve a person nominated to be a judge (Senate only)

   d. By proposing constitutional amendments (must be ratified by the states)

President

1. Can check Congress by vetoing a bill it has passed
2. Can check the federal courts by nominating judges

Courts

1. Can check Congress by declaring a law unconstitutional
2. Can check the president by declaring actions by him or his subordinates to be unconstitutional or not authorized by law

In addition to these checks provided for in the Constitution, each branch has informal ways of checking the others. For example, the president can try to withhold information from Congress (on the grounds of "executive privilege"), and Congress can try to get information by mounting an investigation.

The exact meaning of the various checks is explained in Chapter 9 on Congress, Chapter 10 on the president, and Chapter 12 on the courts.

Checks and balances *The power of the legislative, executive, and judicial branches of government to block some acts by the other two branches.*

Madison argued that the very self-interest that leads people toward factionalism and tyranny might, if properly harnessed by appropriate constitutional arrangements, provide a source of unity and a guarantee of liberty. This harnessing was to be accomplished by dividing the offices of the new government among many people and by giving to the holder of each office the "necessary means and personal motives to resist encroachments of the others." Thus self-interest could prevent one set of officeholders from gathering all the political power into its hands. The separation of powers would work, not in spite of the imperfections of human nature, but because of them.

So also with federalism. By dividing power between the states and the national government, one level of government can be a check on the other. This should provide a "double security" to the rights of the people—especially in America,

Madison thought, because it was a large country with diverse interests. Each interest would constitute a **faction*** that would seek its own advantage. One faction might come to dominate government, or part of government, in one place; a different one might come to dominate it in another. The pulling and pushing among these factions would prevent any one faction from dominating all of government. The division of powers among several portions of the government would give to virtually every faction an opportunity to gain some—but not full—power.

The Constitution and Liberty

A more difficult question to answer is whether the Constitution created a system of government that would respect personal liberties. And that, in fact, was the question debated in the thirteen states when the document was presented for ratification by special conventions elected by the people. These conventions bypassed the existing Congress and the state legislatures, which were still operating under the Articles of Confederation.

The Antifederalist View

The great issue before the state conventions was liberty, not democracy. The proponents of the new government called themselves the **Federalists**, implying that they, like many other people, strongly favored states' rights. This left opponents of the new system with the unhappy choice of calling themselves **Antifederalists**, even though they were much more committed to strong states and a weak national government. The Antifederalists had a variety of objections, but they were united by the belief that liberty could be secure only in a small republic in which the rulers were physically close to—and closely checked by—the ruled. A strong national government, they felt, would be distant from the people and would use its powers to annihilate or absorb functions that properly belonged to the states. (Many of their fears have in fact been realized. Congress taxes heavily; the Supreme Court overrules state courts; the president heads a large standing army, and so forth. Thus we cannot dismiss the Antifederalists as cranks who opposed the Framers' wise plans.) Hoping to limit the national government to a loose confederation of states, the Antifederalists wanted most of the powers of government kept firmly in the hands of state legislatures and state courts.

James Madison answered these Antifederalist objections in the **Federalist Papers** 10 and 51 (see Appendix for text). It was a bold answer, for it flew squarely in the face of widespread popular sentiment and traditional political philosophy, which held that liberty was safe only in small societies governed either by direct

Faction *According to James Madison, a group of people who seek to influence public policy in ways contrary to the public good.*

Federalists *Supporters of a stronger central government who advocated ratification of the Constitution. After ratification they founded a political party supporting a strong executive and Alexander Hamilton's economic policies.*

Antifederalists *Opponents of a strong central government who campaigned against ratification of the Constitution in favor of a confederation of largely independent states. Antifederalists successfully marshaled public support for a federal bill of rights. After ratification, they formed a political party to support states' rights.*

Federalist Papers *A series of eighty-five essays written by Alexander Hamilton, James Madison, and John Jay (all using the name "Publius") that were published in New York newspapers in 1787–1788 to convince New Yorkers to adopt the newly proposed Constitution. They are classics of American constitutional and political thought.*

---

*Today we often think of a faction as a special interest group, but originally it had a broader meaning. Madison defined a faction as "a number of citizens, whether amounting to a majority or a minority of the whole, who are united and actuated by some common impulse of passion, or of interest, adverse to the rights of other citizens, or to the permanent and aggregate interests of the community" (*Federalist* No. 10).

democracy or by large legislatures with small districts and frequent turnover among members. Madison argued quite the opposite—that liberty is safest in *large* republics, where there are many opinions and interests rather than the uniformity characteristic of small communities. People with unpopular views find it easier to acquire allies in a larger, more diverse society.

By favoring a large republic, Madison was not trying to stifle democracy. Rather, he was attempting to show how democratic government really works and what can make it work better. To rule, different interests must come together and form a **coalition**—that is, an alliance. Coalitions that would form in a larger republic would be more diverse, and hence more moderate, than those that would form in a smaller republic. He concluded that in a nation the size of the United States, with its enormous variety of interests, "a coalition of a majority of the whole society could seldom take place on any other principles than those of justice and the general good."

The implication of Madison's argument was daring. He was suggesting that the national government should be at some distance from the people and insulated from their momentary passions because the people did not always want to do the right thing. Liberty was threatened as much or more by public passions and popularly based factions as by strong governments. Thus the government had to be designed to prevent both the politicians and the people from using it for ill-considered or unjust purposes.

Arguing in 1787 against the virtues of small democracies was akin to arguing against motherhood, but the argument prevailed. Many citizens had become convinced that a reasonably strong national government was essential. The political realities of the moment and the recent bitter lessons with the Articles of Confederation probably counted for more in ratifying the Constitution than did Madison's arguments. His cause was helped by the Antifederalists who, for all their legitimate concerns and their uncanny instinct for what the future might bring, could offer no agreed-upon alternative to the new Constitution. In politics, then as now, you cannot beat something with nothing.

Coalition *An alliance among different interest groups (factions) or parties to achieve some political goal. An example is the coalition sometimes formed between Republicans and conservative Democrats.*

How We Compare

Does a Constitution Guarantee Freedom?

You may think that the best protection for individual freedom is for a nation to have a written constitution. After all, a constitution is supposed to limit governmental action. But if you look around the world you will see that a constitution is not enough.

Here are three nations that do not have a written constitution and yet personal freedom is well established:

Israel   New Zealand   United Kingdom

And here are three nations with a written constitution where personal freedom is rare:

Iran   North Korea   Russia

What else must nations have in order to insure personal freedom?

Constitutional Protections

The Bill of Rights

The first ten amendments to the Constitution gave American citizens important guarantees of individual liberty. But the unamended Constitution also contained such protections. Among those protections listed under Article I, sections 9 and 10, are the following:

Ex Post Facto Law

Any law that makes an act a crime that was not a crime at the time it was committed, or that increases penalties or renders conviction easier after the fact, was outlawed by the Constitution.

Writ of Habeas Corpus

Intended as a check against arbitrary arrest or imprisonment, it is a legal order requiring that a person in custody be brought to court in order that just cause be shown for the person's detention. Habeas corpus can be suspended only under emergency conditions.

Bill of Attainder

Any act of a legislature that declares a person guilty and sets the punishment without benefit of a judicial trial was outlawed by the Constitution.

But this does not explain why the original Constitution had no bill of rights, which was the Antifederalists' most important objection. If the Framers were so preoccupied with liberty, why didn't they take this most obvious step toward protecting liberty, especially since the Antifederalists were demanding it? There appear to have been several reasons.

First, the Constitution, as written, *did* contain a number of specific guarantees of individual liberty: the right of trial by jury in criminal cases; the privilege of the writ of habeas corpus (see the above box for a definition); prohibitions against bills of attainder and ex post facto laws; bans on religious tests for holding federal office and on laws interfering with contracts; and promises that citizens of each state would enjoy the same rights enjoyed by citizens of every other state. Second, most states in 1787 already had bills of rights, and the delegates at the convention thought that these were sufficient to guarantee individual liberties.

Third, and perhaps most important, the Framers thought they were creating a government with specific, limited powers. They thought it could do only what the Constitution gave it power to do, and nowhere in that document was there permission to infringe upon freedom of speech or of the press or to impose cruel and unusual punishments. Some delegates probably feared that if any serious effort were made to list the rights that were guaranteed, later officials might assume that they had the power to do anything not explicitly forbidden.

Need for a Bill of Rights

Whatever their reasons, the Framers made at least a tactical and perhaps a fundamental mistake. It quickly became clear that without at least the promise of a bill of rights, the Constitution would not be ratified. Though most small states, pleased by their equal representation in the Senate, quickly ratified, the battle in the large states was intense, and supporters of the new Constitution won only by narrow margins (often, as in Massachusetts, only after promising to add a bill of rights). Indeed, conventions in North Carolina and Rhode Island initially rejected the Constitution. By June 21, 1788, however, the ninth state—New Hampshire— had ratified, and the Constitution was law.

Despite the bitterness of the ratification struggle, the new government that took office in 1789–1790, headed by President Washington, was greeted enthusiastically. By the spring of 1790, all thirteen states had ratified. But there remained the task of fulfilling the promise of a bill of rights. To that end, James Madison introduced into the first session of the First Congress a set of proposals, many based on the existing Virginia bill of rights. Twelve were approved by Congress; ten of these were ratified by the states and went into effect in 1791. These amendments limited the power of the federal government over citizens. Later, the Fourteenth Amendment (1868), as interpreted by the Supreme Court, extended many of the guarantees of the Bill of Rights so as to limit state governmental actions.

The Constitution and Slavery

Though black slaves accounted for one-third of the population of the five southern states, nowhere in the Constitution can one find the words *slave* or *slavery*. Three provisions bear on the matter, all designed to placate the slave-owning states. First, the apportionment of seats in the House of Representatives was to be made by counting all free persons and three-fifths of all "other persons." This meant giving a few extra seats in the House to those states that had many "other persons"—that is, slaves. Second, Congress was forbidden from prohibiting the "importation" of "persons" (that is, slaves) before the year 1808. And third, if any "person held to service or labour" (that is, any slave) were to escape from a slave-owning state and get to a free state, that person would not become free but would have to be returned to his or her master.

To some, the failure of the Constitution to address the question of slavery was a great betrayal of the promise of the Declaration of Independence that "all men are created equal."[7] Even though criticism of slavery mounted during the Revolutionary period—especially in the North, where most states adopted some form of emancipation—it is easy to accuse the signers of the Declaration of Independence and the Constitution of hypocrisy. They knew of slavery, many of them owned slaves, and yet they were silent. Slavery continued unabated in the South, defended by some whites because they thought it was right, and by others because they found it useful. Even in the South, however, there were opponents, though rarely conspicuous ones. Washington, Madison, Jefferson, and George Mason (a prominent Virginia slave owner and a delegate to the convention) were among numerous Southerners who deplored slavery without knowing how it could safely be abolished.

Chicago Historical Society

The Constitution was silent about slavery, so buying and selling slaves continued
for many years.

The blunt fact was that any effort to use the Constitution to end slavery would have meant the end of the Constitution. The southern states would never have signed a document that seriously interfered with slavery. Without the southern states, the Articles of Confederation would have continued in effect, which would have left each state entirely sovereign and thus entirely free of any prospective challenge to slavery.

The unresolved issue of slavery was to prove the most explosive question of all and led to a great civil war. Those who opposed abolishing slavery argued that, because the Constitution was silent on the subject, the federal government had no power to free slaves. Those who favored abolishing it argued that the Constitution had to be interpreted in light of the Declaration of Independence, signed eleven years earlier. The Declaration states that "all men are created equal" and are "endowed by their Creator with certain unalienable rights"—"all men," not "all white men." In the first view, the Constitution stands alone as the charter of the nation; in the second, the Constitution is a charter designed to put into effect the political and moral principles of the Declaration.

The slaves were emancipated in 1863, but the legacy of slavery remains with us to this day. However one interprets the relationship between the Declaration and the Constitution, the authors of the latter clearly tabled the issue of slavery in order to create a union strong enough to handle the issue when it could no longer be postponed.

The Bill of Rights

THE FIRST TEN AMENDMENTS TO THE CONSTITUTION, GROUPED BY TOPIC AND PURPOSE

Protections Afforded Citizens to Participate in the Political Process

AMENDMENT 1
Freedom of religion, speech, press, assembly, and of the right to petition the government.

Protections Against Arbitrary Police and Court Action

AMENDMENT 4
No unreasonable searches or seizures.

AMENDMENT 5
- Grand jury indictment required to prosecute a person for a serious crime.
- No "double jeopardy" (being tried twice for the same offense).
- No one can be forced to testify against oneself.
- No loss of life, liberty, or property without due process.

AMENDMENT 6
Right to speedy, public, impartial trial with defense counsel and right to cross-examine witnesses.

AMENDMENT 7
Jury trials in civil suits where value exceeds $20.

AMENDMENT 8
No excessive bail or fines; no cruel and unusual punishment.

Protections of States' Rights and Unnamed Rights of People

AMENDMENT 9
Unlisted rights are not necessarily denied.

AMENDMENT 10
Powers not delegated to the United States or denied to states are reserved to the states.

Other Protections

AMENDMENT 2
Right to bear arms.

AMENDMENT 3
Troops may not be quartered in homes in peacetime.

Political Ideals or Economic Interests?

In another respect, some modern scholars have questioned the Framers' candor. Some critics find the words and writings of the Framers an unpersuasive guide to their true intentions. To these critics, the Framers' intentions are better revealed by trying to analyze their underlying economic interests.

Scholars have debated at length whether the Constitutional Convention was made up of opposed factions that spoke and voted in ways that would protect their own economic interests. Charles A. Beard was the first and most influential historian to argue that such was the case in his widely read book, *An Economic Interpretation of the Constitution* (1913). Beard attempted to show that the convention and the subsequent ratification process were dominated by well-off urban and commercial leaders, to the disadvantage of small farmers, debtors, and the propertyless masses.

This argument has been subjected to searching analysis by many historians and, by and large, disproved. The economic interests of the Federalists and Anti-federalists were so complex and diverse as to offset one another, and though they played a role in the adoption of the Constitution, they did not follow any neat class lines. Creditors tended to favor the Constitution; debtors to oppose it. Urban dwellers involved in commerce, whether merchants or workers, favored the Constitution more than rural folk. But there were plenty of exceptions even among these groups. Though in some states, such as Massachusetts, economic issues were explicitly raised in the debate over ratification of the new Constitution, in most states the debate centered on *political* questions—chiefly, on whether liberty could prosper under a large national government as well as under small local governments.

Liberty and Equality

Today some people look back at the struggle to ratify the Constitution and wonder whether the Framers, in their concern to preserve liberty from tyrannical rulers, did not end up creating a government too weak to reduce social inequality. Even asking this question shows how much our understanding of liberty and equality has changed since the founding. To Jefferson and Madison, citizens, in the natural order of things, differed in their talents and qualities. It was the use of governmental power to create *un*natural and undesirable inequalities—for example, by concentrating political power in a few individuals (who could then obtain special privileges) or by permitting some private parties to acquire exclusive charters and monopolies—that had to be guarded against. To prevent the inequality that might result from having too strong a government, its powers must be kept strictly limited.

Modern Americans often think of inequality quite differently. They believe that the natural social order—the marketplace and the acquisitive talents of people operating in that marketplace—leads to undesirable inequalities, especially in economic power. The government should be powerful enough to restrain these natural tendencies and produce, by law, a greater degree of equality than society allows when left alone.

To the Framers, government had to be kept limited enough to prevent it from creating the worst kind of inequality: political privilege. To some modern observers, government must be strong enough to reduce the worst kind of inequality: differences in wealth.

A Recipe for Moderation

Many people would like the American government to act boldly and decisively. Some want it to cut taxes dramatically; others wish it would abolish private contributions to political campaigns. Some hope it would ban handguns, while others wish it would ban abortions. Some would like illegal drugs to be made legal, while others hope that the government would crack down on all drug abusers.

Were Women Left Out of the Constitution?

In One Sense, Yes

Women were nowhere mentioned in the Constitution when it was written in 1787. Moreover, Article I, which set forth the provisions for electing members of the House of Representatives, granted the vote to those people who were allowed to vote for members of the lower house of the legislature in the states in which they resided. In no state could women vote in any elections or hold any offices. Furthermore, wherever the Constitution uses a pronoun, it uses the masculine form—he or him.

In Another Sense, No

The Constitution and the Bill of Rights grant rights to "persons" or "citizens"—not to "men"—or it makes no mention at all of gender. For example:

- "The *citizens* of each State shall be entitled to all privileges and immunities of citizens in the several States." [Art. IV, sec. 2]
- "No *person* shall be convicted of treason unless on the testimony of two witnesses to the same overt act, or on confession in open court." [Art. III, sec. 3]
- "No bill of attainder or ex post facto law shall be passed." [Art. I, sec. 9]
- "The right of the *people* to be secure in their persons, houses, papers, and effects, against unreasonable searches and seizures, shall not be violated. . . ." [Amend. IV]
- "No *person* shall be held to answer for a capital, or otherwise infamous crime, unless on a presentment or indictment of a grand jury . . . nor shall any *person* be subject for the same offense to be twice put in jeopardy of life or limb; . . . nor be deprived of life, liberty, or property, without due process of law. . . ." [Amend. V]
- "In all criminal prosecutions, the *accused* shall enjoy the right to a speedy and public trial, by an impartial jury. . . ." [Amend. VI]

Moreover, when the qualifications for elective office are stated, the word *person*, not *man*, is used:

- "No *person* shall be a Representative who shall not have attained to the age of twenty-five years. . . ." [Art. I, sec. 2]
- "No *person* shall be a Senator who shall not have attained to the age of thirty years. . . ." [Art. I, sec. 3]
- "No *person* except a natural born citizen . . . shall be eligible to the office of president; neither shall any *person* be eligible to that office who shall not have attained to the age of thirty-five years. . . ." [Art. II, sec. 1]

In places such as Article II, section 1 of the Constitution, the pronoun *he* was used but always in the context of referring back to a *person* or *citizen*. At the time, and still today, the male pronoun was often used in legal documents to refer generically to both men and women.

Thus, though the Constitution did not give women the right to vote until the Nineteenth Amendment was ratified in 1920, it did use language that extended fundamental rights and access to office to women and men equally.

Of course what the Constitution permitted did not necessarily occur. State and local laws denied women many rights that men enjoyed. No women voted in state elections until 1838, and then only in school board elections in Kentucky. It was not until 1869 that women voted on an equal basis with men anywhere—in territorial elections in Wyoming.

When Amendment XIX gave women the right to vote, that document did not amend any existing language in the Constitution because nothing in the Constitution itself denied women the right to vote; the amendment simply added a new right:

- "The right of citizens of the United States to vote shall not be denied or abridged by the United States or by any state on account of sex." [Amend. XIX]

Source: Adapted from Robert Goldwin, "Why Blacks, Women and Jews Are Not Mentioned in the Constitution," Commentary (May 1987): 28–33.

WHAT WOULD YOU DO?

MEMORANDUM

To: Elizabeth Anthony, Arkansas state senate majority leader

From: George Morris, chief of staff

Subject: Proposal for a New Constitutional Convention

In the 1990s, Arkansas and several other states approved term limits for their members of Congress, but the Supreme Court ruled in 1995 that states do not have this authority. Now term-limit advocates are pursuing a broader strategy, calling for states to approve legislation that would require Congress to consider several amendment proposals, including term limits and abolishing the electoral College to permit the direct popular election of the president. The Arkansas General Assembly passed such a bill last week, and several senators in your party have declared their support.

Arguments for:

1. Since the Twenty-second Amendment restricts the president to two terms, that members of Congress should face similar limits.

2. Term limits will ensure that national leaders do not become career politicians.

3. The public favors the direct popular election of the president; this constitutional convention would make possible abolishing the electoral College.

Arguments against:

1. Limiting members of Congress to two terms would increase the power of lobbyists, congressional staffers, and administrative officials.

+

Friday,

Twenty-Eight States Back Proposal for Constitutional Convention

March 13
LITTLE ROCK

Yesterday Pennsylvania's legislature approved a proposal for a constitutional convention, becoming the twenty-eighth state to do so. The Constitution states that Congress shall hold a convention for proposing amendments at the request of two-thirds of the state legislatures, but it has never happened in U.S. history. Six more states must approve for Congress to take action, and two announced yesterday that they plan to review similar proposals this week. . . .

2. The Electoral College encourages a two-party system; a direct popular vote for the president would require runoff elections if no candidate won a majority.

3. The Constitutional Convention of 1787 was held in secret and involved only a few dozen people; today it would be heavily covered by the press and involve hundreds, perhaps thousands, of people. No one knows what changes it might make.

Your Decision:

Favor legislation: _____

Oppose legislation: _____

Our Constitution does not allow for much in the way of dramatic or bold action. Though there have been significant changes in how it operates—changes described in Chapter 15—most have been the result of the slow accumulation of new ways of thinking and acting. A parliamentary democracy, by contrast, often allows for dramatic or bold action. Great Britain, for example, nationalized some industries and then, later on, privatized them. It adopted in short order a national health-care scheme and a large social welfare plan. The United States does this infrequently, not because American politicians are weak and British ones strong, but because the American Constitution requires that a broad coalition of interests be mobilized behind almost any change. Except in times of crisis—say, during war or in the midst of a great depression—broad coalitions are, of necessity, moderate coalitions.

The American Constitution contains only 4,553 words and was ratified over two centuries ago to govern thirteen states with a few million inhabitants. Today, after only twenty-seven amendments, it governs fifty states with over 300 million people. Not bad.

SUMMARY

The Framers of the Constitution sought to create a government capable of protecting both liberty for citizens and order in government. The solution they chose—one without precedent at that time—was a government based on a written constitution that combined the principles of popular consent, the separation of powers, and federalism.

Popular consent was embodied in the procedure for choosing the House of Representatives but limited by the indirect election of senators (initially) and by the electoral college system for selecting a president. Power was to be distributed by a separation of powers: political authority was to be shared by three branches of government in a manner deliberately intended to produce conflict among these branches. This conflict, motivated by the self-interest of the individuals occupying each branch, would, it was hoped, prevent tyranny, even by a popular majority.

Federalism came to mean a system in which both the national and state governments had independent authority. Allocating powers between the two levels of government and devising means to ensure that neither large nor small states would dominate the national government required the most delicate compromises at the Philadelphia convention. The decision to do nothing about slavery was another such compromise.

In the drafting of the Constitution and the struggle over its ratification in the states, the positions people took were not chiefly determined by their economic interests but by a variety of political opinions. Among these were profound differences of opinion over whether state governments or a national government would be the best protector of personal liberty.

RECONSIDERING THE ENDURING QUESTIONS

1. What was wrong with the Articles of Confederation?

The Articles did not allow for effective government. The Continental Congress could not levy taxes or pay soldiers without the consent of most state governments. General George Washington was often left with few soldiers and little money, for example.

2. How did the authors of the Constitution view human nature?

They were not optimistic. They thought people had enough virtue to make government possible, but government would not protect freedom without restricting the ability of any politician to acquire power.

3. How can a government be strong enough to govern without threatening freedom?

It must put limits on the ability of politicians to govern. These limits were federalism, the separation of powers, and checks and balances.

4. Has the system of separated powers and checks and balances protected liberty?

So far, the system has protected liberty better than anyone could have expected. But the United States pays a price for weak central authority. It took almost a century to abolish slavery, and it took even longer to mount programs to address human welfare or to play an effective international role. As we shall see, weak central authority not only makes it hard to start new programs, but also hard to get rid of bad ones.

Online Resources: The Constitution

 CourseMate

To find historical and legal documents:

- Emory University Law School: www.law.emory.edu/FEDERAL/conpict.html
- National Constitution Center: www.constitutioncenter.org
- Congress: http://thomas.loc.gov/ (choose More Historical Documents)

To look at court cases about the Constitution:

- Yale University Law School: www.yale.edu/lawweb/avalon/avalon.htm

Suggested Readings

Bailyn, Bernard. *The Ideological Origins of the American Revolution.* Cambridge, Mass.: Harvard University Press, 1967. A brilliant account of how the American colonists formed and justified the idea of independence.

Becker, Carl L. *The Declaration of Independence.* New York: Vintage, 1942. The classic account of the meaning of the Declaration.

Beeman, Richard. *Plain, Honest Men: The Making of the American Constitution.* New York: Random House, 2009. The best account of the constitutional convention yet written.

Farrand, Max. *The Framing of the Constitution of the United States.* New Haven, Conn.: Yale University Press, 1913. A good, brief account of the Philadelphia convention, by the editor of Madison's notes on the convention.

Federalist Papers. By Alexander Hamilton, James Madison, and John Jay. The best edition was edited by Jacob E. Cooke. Middletown, Conn.: Wesleyan University Press, 1961.

Goldwin, Robert A., and William A. Schambra, eds. *How Capitalistic Is the Constitution?* Washington, D.C.: American Enterprise Institute, 1982. Essays from different viewpoints discussing the relationship between the Constitution and the economic order.

———. *How Democratic Is the Constitution?* Washington, D.C.: American Enterprise Institute, 1980. A collection of essays offering different interpretations of the political meaning of the Constitution.

Storing, Herbert J. *What the Anti-Federalists Were For.* Chicago: University of Chicago Press, 1981. A close analysis of the political views of those opposed to the ratification of the Constitution.

Wood, Gordon S. *The Creation of the American Republic.* Chapel Hill: University of North Carolina Press, 1969. A detailed study of American political thought before the Philadelphia convention.

———. *The Radicalism of the American Revolution.* New York: Knopf, 1992. A penetrating account of the nature and effects of the American Revolution, emphasizing the radical transformation that it produced.

ENDURING QUESTIONS

1. Why not display religious symbols on government property?
2. What does the court mean by "obscenity"?
3. Is all political advertising constitutional?

" **C** ivil liberties" is not simply an issue that people argue about before the courts. It is, instead, a defining characteristic of how we govern ourselves. This issue permeates every aspect of our political life.

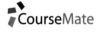
CourseMate

So What?

As we saw in the last chapter, we live under a Constitution that was, when written, only partially democratic. But today our politics is suffused with arguments about democracy. The Tea Party protest that erupted during the Obama administration, the lawsuits (some serious, some absurd) about our rights that preoccupy the courts, the arguments about whether newspapers should be free to discuss military secrets—all these and more define how we think about government. Compared to almost any other democratic nation, American politics is defined by the people's and the government's preoccupation with rights.

Americans do not merely expect or ask for, or even demand, their Social Security benefits or welfare checks; they say they have the *right* to them. When we discuss abortion, we do not just talk about whether abortion on demand would have good or bad results; we argue about whether the fetus has a *right* to life or whether the mother has a *right* to control her own body. We frequently argue over whether industry and government are doing all they should to keep our air clean and our water pure; to a degree that would astonish Europeans, we carry on these arguments by claiming that we have a *right* to a certain quality of air and water. Some high school students complain that their rights are being violated when the principal searches their lockers or tries to control the student newspaper. Some people say that every American has a *right* to a job and a decent standard of living.

None of these rights is mentioned in the Constitution. What is mentioned is a list of certain rights and liberties that can be grouped under three broad headings—freedom of expression, citizenship rights, and criminal and civil law—as shown in the box on page 39. Freedom of expression and freedom from arbitrary arrest and prosecution are usually called **civil liberties**; citizenship rights, including the right to vote and to be free from unjust discrimination, are usually called **civil rights**. In this chapter we will discuss civil liberties; in the next, civil rights.

The Constitution guarantees these rights against infringement by the government (in general, there are no constitutional protections against actions by private individuals). When the Constitution was first presented to the states for ratification, it contained only a few guaranteed rights—those mentioned in Article I, sections 9 and 10. When people in various states complained that the Constitution, as drafted, would leave citizens inadequately protected against unreasonable government actions, the Framers promised to amend it after it was ratified by the states. The First Congress proposed twelve amendments. Ten were ratified by the necessary number of states, and these amendments became known as the **Bill of Rights**.

Civil liberties
Rights—chiefly, rights to be free of government interference—accorded to an individual by the Constitution: free speech, free press, and so on.

Civil rights *The rights of citizens to vote, to receive equal treatment before the law, and to share equally with other citizens the benefits of public facilities (such as schools).*

Bill of Rights *The first ten amendments to the U.S. Constitution, containing a list of individual rights and liberties, such as freedom of speech, religion, and the press.*

Making Constitutional Rights Apply to the States

For many years after the Constitution was signed, the rights protected by it and the Bill of Rights affected only the national government. The Supreme Court made this clear in a case (*Barron* v. *Baltimore*) decided in 1833.[1] Except for Article I, which, among other things, banned *ex post facto* laws and guaranteed the right of habeas corpus,* the Constitution was silent on how states could treat their residents.

This began to change after the Civil War, when new amendments were added to the Constitution in order to ban slavery and protect newly freed slaves. The Fourteenth Amendment, ratified in 1868, was the most important. It said that no state shall "deprive any person of life, liberty, or property, without due process of law" (known as the **due-process clause**) and that no state shall "deny to any person within its jurisdiction the equal protection of the laws" (known as the **equal protection clause**).

Slowly the Supreme Court began to apply these two phrases to the states. In 1925, it held that constitutional guarantees of free speech and free press also applied to state governments.[2] In 1937, it went much further and said in *Palko* v. *Connecticut* that some rights ought to be applied to the states because, in the Court's words, they "represented the very essence of a scheme of ordered liberty" and were "principles of justice so rooted in the traditions and conscience of our people as to be ranked fundamental."[3]

In these cases, the Supreme Court set in motion the process of **incorporation,** whereby some but not all federal rights also governed the states. But which rights are so fundamental that they ought to apply to the states? There is no entirely clear answer to this question, but in general all of the Bill of Rights now apply to the states except for the right not to have soldiers forcibly quartered in private homes (Third Amendment), and the right to be indicted by a grand jury before being tried for a serious crime (Fifth Amendment). In 2010, the right to bear arms (Second Amendment) was largely incorporated in *McDonald* v. *City of Chicago*, a five-to-four decision that declared the right to keep a handgun for self-protection in the home to be a "fundamental" right.

Due-process clause *Protection against arbitrary deprivation of life, liberty, or property as guaranteed in the Fifth and Fourteenth Amendments.*

Equal protection clause *The provision in the Fourteenth Amendment to the Constitution guaranteeing that no state shall "deny to any person" the "equal protection of the laws."*

Incorporation *A doctrine whereby the Supreme Court incorporates—that is, includes—many parts of the Bill of Rights into restrictions on state government actions.*

Why Are Americans So Preoccupied with Rights?

The specific protections afforded by the Constitution are one reason that we are so preoccupied with rights, but there are other reasons as well. The Revolutionary War was fought out of a desire to assert the rights of colonists against the British government. When the new Constitution was written, the major argument over it concerned whether it had enough limitations against the new government to protect these hard-won rights. The Civil War was in

*These are defined in the box on page 39.

part a struggle over the question of what rights, if any, slaves were to have. Later on, many immigrants fled here because they suffered from religious or political persecution abroad, and they arrived keenly sensitive to their rights. Finally, the existence of an independent judiciary has provided an arena wherein citizens can sue the government in order to protect their rights, even to the extent of getting judges to declare acts of Congress unconstitutional (see Chapter 12).

The results of these legal, cultural, and historical forces are evident to all: Americans go into court to sue one another more often than the citizens of virtually any other nation. We are always complaining about myriad lawsuits ongoing on all about us. There is a cost to that, but there is a benefit as well: It is a measure of how committed (some would say overcommitted) we are to the assertion of rights.

That we always seem to be suing one another contains another important lesson: rights are in conflict. Few, if any, rights are absolute. Someone may assert his right to publish what he wishes, but you will counter with your right to protect your children from his obscene books. Or if someone distributes classified documents, the government will counter with its right to protect vital secrets from the enemy. Or a high school student may think his or her locker is private, but the school principal will assert his or her right to search that locker if it seems necessary to preserve order or prevent the distribution of drugs. Even freedom of religion is not absolute: You may worship however you please, but you cannot use your religious beliefs to justify carrying out a ritual murder or preventing your child from receiving essential medical care. Because rights are in conflict, the current definition of our rights represents an uneasy and changing balance between competing claims.

Freedom of Expression

Over the past two centuries, the courts have more or less steadily broadened the area of free expression. In 1798, it was illegal to publish "any false, scandalous, and malicious writing" against the president or Congress. Today it is hard to imagine what anyone might write about any politician that could get its writer in trouble with the law. In 1918, it was illegal to utter or print any disloyal, profane, or scurrilous language intended to promote the cause of the nation's enemies. Today condemning the United States in the most abusive manner or praising a foreign enemy in the most extravagant manner would not be grounds for a lawful arrest. As recently as the 1950s, local authorities regularly censored movies and banned books that contained four-letter words or any explicit discussion of sex. For example, in 1957, New York State banned a rather tame film, *Lady Chatterley's Lover*, on the grounds that its theme encouraged adultery. Today it is hard to find a large city that does not have many "adult" (that is, pornographic) bookstores and movie theaters. Indeed the Supreme Court has held that nude dancing and burning the American flag are forms of "speech" deserving of protection.[4]

Liberties in the Constitution

Freedom of Expression	Amendment
Freedom of speech, press, assembly, and petition	First
Free exercise of religion	First
No "establishment of religion"	First

Criminal and Civil Law	
No bill of attainder[a]	Article I, sec. 9 and sec. 10
No ex post facto law[b]	Article I, sec. 9 and sec. 10
Right to habeas corpus[c]	Article I, sec. 9
Ban on "unreasonable" searches and seizures	Fourth
Right to due process of law	Fifth and Fourteenth
Ban on double jeopardy[d]	Fifth
Right to just compensation if property is taken for public use	Fifth
Ban on being forced to testify against oneself	Fifth
Right to a trial that is speedy, public, impartial, and fair (right to know the charges, confront one's accuser, call witnesses, have help of a lawyer)	Sixth
Trial by jury	Seventh
No excessive bail or fines and no "cruel and unusual punishment"	Eighth

[a]Bill of attainder: a law that declares a person, without a trial, guilty of a crime.

[b]Ex post facto law: a law that makes criminal an act that was legal when it was committed, or that increases the penalty for a crime after it was committed, or that changes the rules of evidence to make conviction easier; a retroactive criminal law.

[c]Habeas corpus: a court order directing police officers, sheriffs, or wardens to bring a person in their custody before a judge and show that they have legal grounds for detaining that person.

[d]Double jeopardy: being tried twice for the same crime unless the first trial led to no conclusion (a mistrial or a hung jury).

Certain court-devised doctrines expanding the scope of permissible expression clearly place the burden on the government to prove that its restriction on speaking or publishing can be justified. These rules of thumb include the following:

1. *Preferred position:* The right of free expression, though not absolute, occupies a higher or more "preferred" position than any other constitutional rights, such as property rights.[5]
2. *No* **prior restraint:** With scarcely any exceptions, the courts will not allow the government to restrain or censor in advance any speaking or writing,

LANDMARK CASES

Free Speech

- *Gitlow* **v.** *New York* **(1925):** First Amendment applies to states.
- *Palko* **v.** *Connecticut* **(1937):** States must observe all "fundamental liberties."
- *Schenck* **v.** *United States* **(1919):** Speech may be punished if it creates a "clear and present danger" of violence.
- *Chaplinsky* **v.** *New Hampshire* **(1942):** First Amendment does not protect "fighting words."
- *New York Times* **v.** *Sullivan* **(1964):** To libel a public official, there must be "actual malice."
- *Miller* **v.** *California* **(1973):** An obscene text appeals to the prurient interests of an

average person and lacks literary, artistic, political, or scientific value.
- *Collin* **v.** *Smith* **(1978):** The Nazi Party may march through a largely Jewish neighborhood.
- *Texas* **v.** *Johnson* **(1989):** It is unconstitutional to ban flag burning.
- *McConnell* **v.** *Federal Election Commission* **(2003):** Campaign finance reform law does not violate First Amendment.
- *Citizens United* **v.** *Federal Election Commission* **(2010):** Corporations and unions may spend their money supporting or criticizing political candidates.

Prior restraint *The traditional view of the press's free speech rights as expressed by William Blackstone, the great English jurist. According to this view, the press is guaranteed freedom from censorship— that is, rules telling it in advance what it can publish. After publication, however, the government can punish the press for material that is judged libelous or obscene.*

even when they will allow punishment after the fact for publishing libels or obscenity.[6]

3. *Imminent danger:* You may utter inflammatory statements or urge people to consider committing dangerous actions, but unless there is an "imminent danger" that the utterances will actually lead to an illegal act, they are constitutionally protected.[7]

4. *Neutrality:* If the government requires a license for a parade, it must be neutral— that is, not favor one group more than another.[8]

5. *Clarity:* If the law forbids some form of expression, such as obscenity, it must contain a clear definition of it.[9]

6. *Least means:* If it is necessary to restrict the rights of one person to speak or publish in order to protect the rights of another, the restriction should involve the least intrusive means to achieve its end. For instance, restricting press coverage of a trial in order to ensure a fair trial should involve the least intrusive means (for example, transferring the case to another town rather than issuing a "gag order" against the press).[10]

Despite the stringency of these rules, not all forms of expression are protected by the Constitution. There are these exceptions:

Libel *Injurious written statements about another person.*

First, **libel** is not protected speech. If you harm another person by writing or publishing statements that defame his or her character, you can be sued by the injured party and cannot claim in defense that your freedom to speak and write is constitutionally guaranteed. However, the Court has made it very difficult for public

A Ku Klux Klan member uses his constitutional right to free speech to utter "white power" chants.

officials (and even "public figures" or celebrities) to protect themselves against false and defamatory statements provided they were not uttered with "actual malice"— that is, uttered with reckless disregard of their accuracy or while knowing them to be false.[11]

Second, you cannot ordinarily claim that illegal *action* should go unpunished because that action is meant to convey a political or social message. For example, if you burn your draft card to protest the foreign policy of the United States, you can be punished for the illegal act (burning the draft card) even if your intent was to communicate your political beliefs. The Court felt that if **symbolic speech** were given the same constitutional protection as actual speech or writing, then virtually any action—murder, arson, rioting—could be excused on the grounds that its perpetrator meant to send a message.[12] But when Texas authorities arrested a man for burning an American flag in order to send a message, the Court held that the statute that made flag burning illegal was an unconstitutional infringement of free speech. What, then, is the difference between burning a draft card and burning a flag? The Court argued that since the government has the right to run a military draft, it can protect the draft cards that are a necessary part of this process. But the only motive that government has in banning flag burning is to restrict a form of speech, and that is impermissible under the Constitution. Similarly, when a Des Moines high school punished some students for wearing black armbands to class, the Court ruled that the armbands were a protected form of speech.[13]

Third, you cannot freely use words that incite others to commit illegal acts or that directly and immediately provoke another person to violent behavior. As we have already seen, the Court has steadily expanded the protection afforded those who advocate illegal actions as long as that incitement to action is not immediate and direct. But the Court has sustained state laws that make it illegal to insult a person to his or her face in a way that provokes a fight; it has insisted, however,

Symbolic speech *An act that conveys a political message, such as burning a draft card to protest the draft.*

that laws prohibiting "fighting words" be carefully drawn and narrowly applied.[14] The provocation would probably have to be severe and person-to-person before the Court would allow it to be punished. When a group of American Nazis in 1977 wanted to parade through Skokie, Illinois, a community with a large Jewish population, lower courts (acting after Supreme Court prodding) held that, as noxious and provocative as their anti-Semitic slogans might be, the Nazis had a constitutional right to speak and parade peacefully.[15]

Fourth, *obscenity* is not protected by the First Amendment. The Court has always held that obscene materials, because they have no redeeming social value or are calculated chiefly to appeal to one's sexual rather than political or literary interests, can be regulated by the state. The problem, of course, arises with the meaning of "obscene." In one eleven-year period, 1957 to 1968, the Court decided thirteen major cases involving the definition of obscenity, which resulted in fifty-five separate opinions.[16] Some justices, such as Hugo Black, believed that the First Amendment protected all publications, even wholly obscene ones. Others believed that obscenity deserved no protection and struggled to define the term. Still others shared the view of former Justice Potter Stewart, who objected to "hard-core pornography" but admitted that the best definition he could offer was "I know it when I see it."[17]

It is unnecessary to review in detail the many attempts by the Court at defining obscenity. The justices have made it clear that nudity and sex are not, by definition, obscene and that they will provide First Amendment protection to anything that has any arguable political, literary, or artistic merit, allowing the government to punish only the distribution of "hard-core pornography." Their most recent (1973) definition of this is as follows: To be obscene, the work, taken as a whole, must be judged by "the average person applying contemporary community standards" to appeal to the "prurient interest" or to depict "in a patently offensive way, sexual conduct specifically defined by applicable state law" and to lack "serious literary, artistic, political, or scientific value."[18] In 1997, the Supreme Court expanded its protection of free speech to the Internet, unanimously ruling the Communications Decency Act of 1996 to be unconstitutional because it tried to ban "indecent" material from electronic communications. *Indecent* is too vague a term to be a standard for determining what can be sent or read. Congress reacted to that decision by passing the Child Online Protection Act, which would punish people for putting on the Internet material that was "harmful to minors." But the Supreme Court did not like that either. It blocked any use of that law and ordered a lower federal court to see if it could discover some technical means of protecting minors (for example, by installing a software filter on computers).[19]

Though the Court has taken a hard look at efforts to prohibit the distribution of pornography, it has been willing to let cities decide where in a city that distribution can occur. When one city adopted a zoning ordinance prohibiting an "adult" movie theater from being located within 1,000 feet of any church, school, park, or residential area, the Court upheld it. The purpose of the law, it said, was to regulate not speech or press but the use of land. Because the "adult" theater still had 5 percent of the city's land area in which to find a location, it was not being barred from operating.[20]

The American people clearly have fairly broad rights of expression. But who are "the people"? Do they include associations? Corporations? High-school students? Or just adult individuals? The Court has not said that corporations have all the rights of individuals, but they do enjoy a large number of them. A state cannot prevent a bank from spending money to influence votes in a local election, nor can an electric utility be required to enclose in its monthly bills statements written by groups attacking the utility. Liquor stores have a right to publicize their prices. Lobbying organizations enjoy First Amendment rights, as do their members.[21]

One big exception to the free press rights of organizations emerged in 2003 when the Supreme Court upheld the new campaign finance reform law (discussed in Chapter 8). One of the provisions of that law was to ban, for sixty days before a general election for federal offices, "electioneering communications" paid for by funds from corporations or labor unions. An electioneering communication is any statement made on radio or television that "refers" to a federal candidate, even if the statement does not endorse that person for election. This means that a company or a union could not run an ad that criticized or supported a bill proposed by Congressman Smith or Congresswoman Jones, even though the ad does not back or oppose that member's election campaign.

In 2010, the Supreme Court backed away from this view. A nonprofit organization produced a television film designed to criticize Hillary Clinton, then running for the Democratic presidential nomination. By a five-to-four vote, the Court held that this ad, and any ad by a corporation, labor union, or nonprofit organization that backed or opposed a candidate, could be run at any time. The Court held that the First Amendment denied to the government the power to "restrict political speech based on the speaker's corporate identity."[22]

High-school students do not have exactly the same rights as adults. In 1988, the Supreme Court held that the principal of a high school could censor the school's student newspaper by forbidding it to print stories about student pregnancies and parental divorces. It was important to the decision in this case that the paper was published using school money and was edited as part of a school journalism class. The Court held that while students cannot be punished for expressing their personal views on campus, what they do in class or as participants in school-sponsored activities can be controlled.[23]

Though the Constitution provides the legal basis for freedom of expression, that freedom would be—and in the past, has been—weak if public opinion did not provide reasonable support for it. The overwhelming majority of Americans have always supported freedom of expression in the abstract, but when we get down to concrete cases they have not always been so tolerant. Liberals tend to be intolerant of the rights of the ultraconservatives, and conservatives tend to be intolerant of the rights of ultraliberals. In general, however, the average American is willing to allow even rather unpopular groups, such as communists and atheists, to speak out, and the proportion willing to tolerate such acts has increased.

Church and State

Everybody knows that the plain language of the First Amendment protects freedom of speech and the press, though most people are not aware of how complex the law applying these terms has become. But many people also believe, wrongly, that the language of the First Amendment clearly requires the "separation of church and state." It does not.

What that amendment actually says is quite different and maddeningly unclear. It has two parts: The first, often referred to as the **free-exercise clause**, states that Congress shall make no law prohibiting the "free exercise" of religion. The second, called the **establishment clause**, states that Congress shall make no law "respecting an establishment of religion."

Free-exercise clause *A clause in the First Amendment to the Constitution stating that Congress shall make no law prohibiting the "free exercise" of religion.*

Establishment clause *A clause in the First Amendment to the Constitution stating that Congress shall make no law "respecting an establishment of religion."*

The Free-Exercise Clause

The free-exercise clause is the clearer of the two, though by no means free of ambiguities. It obviously means that Congress cannot, for example, pass a law prohibiting Catholics from celebrating Mass. Because the First Amendment has been applied to the states via the due-process clause of the Fourteenth Amendment, it means that state governments cannot pass such a law either. In general the courts have treated religion like speech: You can pretty much do what you want, as long as it does not cause some serious harm to others.

Even some laws that do not initially appear to apply to churches may be unconstitutional if their enforcement imposes particular burdens on churches or greater burdens on some churches than others. For example, a state cannot require a door-to-door solicitor to pay a license fee when the solicitor is a Jehovah's Witness selling religious tracts.[24]

Having the right to exercise your religion freely does not, however, exempt you from laws binding other citizens, even when the law goes against your religious beliefs. A man cannot have more than one wife, even if (as once was the case with Mormons) polygamy is thought desirable on religious grounds.[25] For religious reasons, you may oppose vaccinations or blood transfusions, but if the state passes a compulsory vaccination law or orders that a blood transfusion be given a sick child, the courts will not, on grounds of religious liberty, prevent such actions from being carried out.[26] And in an issue that remains bitterly controversial to this day, the courts have allowed local authorities to close down schools operated by fundamentalist religious groups if the schools were not accredited by the state.[27]

Conflicts between religious belief and public policy are always difficult to settle. What if you believe on religious grounds that war is immoral? The draft laws have always exempted a conscientious objector from military duty. The Court has upheld such exemptions, and gone even further, declaring that people cannot be drafted even if they do not believe in a Supreme Being or belong to any religious tradition, as long as their "consciences, spurred by deeply held moral, ethical, or religious beliefs, would give them no rest or peace if they allowed themselves to become part of an instrument of war."[28] Do exemptions on such grounds create an opportunity for some people to evade the draft because of their political preferences? Or the opportunity to create a "religion" for the sole purpose of staying out of the army? In trying to answer such questions, the courts have had to try to define a religion—no easy task.

Even when there is no question about your membership in a bona-fide religion, the circumstances under which you may claim exemption from laws that apply to everybody else are not really clear. What if you, a member of the Seventh-Day Adventists, are fired by your employer for refusing on religious grounds to work on Saturday, and then it turns out you can't collect unemployment insurance because you refuse to take an available job—one that also requires you to work on Saturday? Or what if you are a member of the Amish sect, which refuses, contrary to state law, to send its children to public schools past the eighth grade? The Court has ruled that the state must pay you unemployment compensation and cannot require you to send your children to public schools beyond the eighth grade.[29]

The Establishment Clause

What did the members of the First Congress mean when they wrote into the First Amendment language prohibiting Congress from making a law "respecting" an "establishment" of religion? The Supreme Court has more or less consistently interpreted this vague phrase to mean that the Constitution erects a "wall of separation" between church and state.

That phrase, so often quoted, is in neither the Bill of Rights nor the debates in the First Congress that drafted the Bill of Rights; it comes from the pen of Thomas Jefferson, who was opposed to having the Church of England as the established church of his native Virginia. (At the time of the Revolutionary War, there were established—that is, official, state-supported—churches in at least eight of the thirteen former colonies.) But it is not clear that Jefferson's view was the majority view.

During much of the debate in Congress, the wording of this part of the First Amendment was quite different and much plainer than what finally emerged. Up to the last minute, the clause was intended to read "no religion shall be established

How We Compare

Church and State

The American government cannot pay for or endorse any church. The national governments in England, Greece, Germany, Norway, and Scotland can. Moreover, until recently, there were state-supported churches in France, Italy, and Spain (among many other countries). Despite the absence of any governmental support for churches in this country, attendance here in churches, synagogues, and mosques is very high—by some estimates, as much as 40 percent of our population attend on a weekly basis. But in countries that have or recently had state-supported churches, attendance at religious events is very small. Only 4 percent of the English and 5 percent of the French attend church at least once a week.

How would you explain high church attendance in a country where churches lack government backing and low attendance where they have that backing?

High school students gather around their school's flagpole for a weekly morning prayer session since school-sponsored prayer is not allowed later in the day.

Wall of separation *A Supreme Court interpretation of the establishment clause in the First Amendment that prevents government involvement with religion, even on a nonpreferential basis.*

by law" or "no national religion shall be established." The meaning of those words seems quite clear: Whatever the states may do, the federal government cannot create an official, national religion or give support to one religion in preference to another.[30]

Congress instead adopted an ambiguous phrase, leaving the Supreme Court to decide what it meant. The Court subsequently declared that these words do not simply mean "no national religion" but mean as well no governmental involvement with religion at all, even on a nonpreferential basis. They mean, in short, erecting a **wall of separation** between church and state.[31] Though the proper interpretation of the establishment clause remains a topic of great controversy among judges and scholars, the Court has more or less consistently adopted the wall of separation interpretation.

Its first statement of this interpretation was a 1947 case involving a New Jersey town that reimbursed parents for the costs of transporting their children to school, including parochial (in this case, Catholic) schools. The Court decided that this reimbursement was constitutional, but it clearly stated that the establishment clause of the First Amendment applied (via the Fourteenth Amendment) to the states and that it meant, among other things, that the government cannot require a person to profess a belief or disbelief in any religion; it cannot aid one religion, some religions, or all religions; and it cannot spend any tax money, however small, in support of any religious activities or institutions.[32] The reader may wonder, in view of the Court's reasoning, why it allowed the town to pay for busing children to Catholic schools. Its answer was that busing is a religiously neutral activity, akin to providing fire and police protection to Catholic schools. Busing, available to public- and private-school children alike, does not breach the wall of separation.

LANDMARK CASES

Religious Freedom

- *Everson* v. *Board of Education* (1947): "Wall-of-separation" principle is announced.
- *Zorauch* v. *Clauson* (1952): Students may be released from public schools for religious instruction elsewhere.
- *Engel* v. *Vitale* (1962): No praying is allowed in public schools.
- *Lemon* v. *Kurtzman* (1971): Three tests proposed for deciding whether government can support a religious activity.
- *Lee* v. *Wiseman* (1992): Public schools may not hold prayers at graduation ceremonies.
- *Zelman* v. *Simmons-Harris* (2000): Voucher plan to pay school bills is upheld.

Since 1947, the Court has applied the wall of separation theory to strike down as unconstitutional every effort to have any form of prayer in public schools, even if it is nonsectarian,[33] voluntary,[34] or limited to reading a passage from the Bible.[35] Moreover, the Court has held that laws prohibiting teaching the theory of evolution or requiring giving equal time to "creationism" are religiously inspired and thus unconstitutional.[36] A public school may not allow its pupils to take time out from their regular classes for religious instruction if this occurs within the schools, though "released-time" instruction is all right if it is done outside the public-school buildings.[37] The school prayer decisions in particular have provoked a storm of controversy, but efforts to get Congress to propose to the states a constitutional amendment authorizing such prayers have failed.

Court-imposed restrictions on public aid to parochial schools have been almost as controversial, though here the wall of separation principle has not been used to forbid any and all forms of aid. For example, it is permissible for the federal government to provide aid for constructing buildings on denominational (as well as nondenominational) college campuses[38] and for state governments to loan free textbooks to parochial school pupils,[39] grant tax-exempt status to parochial schools,[40] and allow parents of parochial school children to deduct their tuition payments on their state income tax returns.[41] But the government cannot reimburse parents for the cost of parochial school tuition,[42] supply parochial schools with services such as counseling,[43] or give money to parochial schools to purchase instructional materials.[44] In 1997, the Court changed its position on whether public school systems could send teachers into parochial schools in order to teach, as required by federal law, remedial courses for needy children. In 1985, it said states could not do this; in 1997, it said they could. "We no longer presume," the Court wrote, "that public employees will inculcate religion simply because they happen to be in a sectarian environment."[45]

The Court has also ruled that the Constitution does not prevent a state government from paying for vouchers that enable a school child to attend a religious school. The case began in Cleveland, Ohio, where the state offered money to any family (especially poor ones) whose children attend a public school that has done so poorly that it is under a federal court order that requires the school to be run by the state superintendent of schools. The money—a voucher—could be used to send the child to any other public or a private school, including a private school run by a religious group. The Court held that this plan did not violate the establishment clause of the First Amendment because the aid went not to the school but to the families, who were then free to choose a school.[46]

If you find the twists and turns of Court policy in this area confusing, you are not alone. The wall of separation principle has not been easy to apply, and the Supreme Court has begun to alter its position on church-state matters. The Court has tried to sort out the confusion by developing a three-part test to decide under what circumstances government involvement in religious activities is improper.[47] That involvement is constitutional if it meets these tests:

1. It has a secular purpose.
2. Its primary effect neither advances nor inhibits religion.
3. It does not foster an excessive government entanglement with religion.

But no sooner had the test been developed than the Court decided that it was all right for the government of Pawtucket, Rhode Island, to erect a Nativity scene as part of the Christmas display in a local park. However, not every Christmas display will win the Court's approval. In 1989, Pittsburgh put up both a crèche (a Christian Nativity scene) and a menorah (the nine-branched candelabra used to celebrate the Jewish holiday of Chanukah) in front of the county courthouse.

Religious Groups on Campus

What rights do religious groups have in schools and colleges? For publicly supported schools, the Supreme Court has made these rulings:

*   It does not violate the establishment clause of the First Amendment for a public university to grant access to its facilities on an evenhanded basis to religious as well as nonreligious groups.[a]
*   If a school allows its property to be used to present all views on an issue except a religious one, then it has violated the Constitution.[b]
*   If a school or university subsidizes student publications or organizations, then it cannot deny that subsidy to a religious newspaper or organization[c]

In short, the state must be neutral toward religion. It cannot evade that obligation to be neutral by claiming that any involvement with religion violates the establishment clause of the First Amendment.

[a]*Widmar* v. *Vincent*, 454 U.S. 263 (1981).
[b]*Lamb's Chapel* v. *Center Moriches Union Free School District*, 113 S. Ct. 2141 (1993).
[c]*Rosenberger* v. *University of Virginia*, 115 S. Ct. 2510 (1995).

The Court said that the crèche had to go (because it was too close to the court-house and thus implied a government endorsement), but the menorah could stay (because it was next to a Christmas tree and would not lead people to think that Pittsburgh was endorsing Judaism).[48] If there is a principle that rationalizes these bewildering distinctions, it is not obvious.

Tradition seems to count for as much as doctrine in reaching these decisions. Though the Court has struck down prayer in schools, it has upheld prayer in Congress. Since the First Congress in 1789, the House and the Senate have hired chaplains to open each session with a prayer. Therefore when somebody complained that it was unconstitutional for the Nebraska legislature to do this, the Court disagreed.[49]

When state governments display the Ten Commandments on government grounds, a sharply divided Supreme Court has allowed it when (as in Texas) the Commandments were part of a display of over thirty historical markers around the state capitol, but struck it down when (as in Kentucky) two counties displayed the Commandments inside their courthouses.[50] Apparently a display of the Commandments is all right if it has been around for a long time and is part of many other historical markers, but not all right if it has been put up recently and is not part of a group of nonreligious symbols.

The Court has been clear about one issue that involves the establishment clause. Public schools may not be required by law to teach "creationism" as an alternative to the theory of evolution. Evolution means that all living creatures are the product of slow changes from one generation to the next. These changes can modify organisms by making their inherited traits useful in helping those organisms survive. Creationism, by contrast, means that living creatures, especially human beings, were created by God at one moment in time. Virtually all scientists believe in evolution; some religious leaders believe in creationism. When Louisiana passed a law saying that public schools had to teach creationism, the Supreme Court struck it down as a violation of the establishment clause of the First Amendment. A few years later, a school board in Pennsylvania required teachers to read a statement to all pupils about "intelligent design" (a renamed version of creationism) being an alternative to evolution. A federal district judge held this was unconstitutional.[51]

Crime and Due Process

Whereas the central problem in interpreting the religion clauses of the First Amendment has been to decide what they mean, the central problems in interpreting those parts of the Bill of Rights that affect people accused of a crime have been to decide not only what they mean but how to put them into effect. It is not obvious what constitutes an "unreasonable search," but even if we settle that question, we still must decide how best to protect people against such searches in ways that do not unduly hinder criminal investigations.

There are at least two ways to provide that protection. One is to let the police introduce in court evidence relevant to the guilt or innocence of a person, no matter how it was obtained, and then, after the case is settled, punish the police officers (or their superiors) if the evidence was gathered improperly (for example, by an unreasonable search). The other way is to exclude improperly gathered evidence from the trial in the first place, even if it is relevant to determining the guilt or innocence of the accused.

Most democratic nations, including Great Britain, use the first method; the United States uses the second. Because of this, many landmark cases decided by the Supreme Court have been bitterly controversial. Opponents of these decisions have argued that a guilty person should not go free just because the police officer blundered, especially if the mistake was minor. Supporters rejoin that there is no way to punish errant police officers effectively other than by excluding tainted evidence; moreover, nobody should be convicted of a crime except by evidence that is above reproach.[†]

The Exclusionary Rule

Exclusionary rule *A rule that holds that evidence gathered in violation of the Constitution cannot be used in a trial. The rule has been used to implement two provisions of the Bill of Rights—the right to be free from unreasonable searches or seizures (Fourth Amendment) and the right not to be compelled to give evidence against oneself (Fifth Amendment).*

The American method relies on the **exclusionary rule**, which holds that evidence gathered in violation of the Constitution cannot be used in a trial. The rule has been used to implement two provisions of the Bill of Rights: the right to be free from unreasonable searches or seizures (Fourth Amendment) and the right not to be compelled to give evidence against oneself (Fifth Amendment).

Not until 1949 did the Supreme Court consider whether to apply the exclusionary rule to the states. In a case decided that year, the Court made it clear that the Fourth Amendment prohibited the police from carrying out unreasonable searches and obtaining improper confessions but held that it was not necessary to use the exclusionary rule to enforce those prohibitions. It noted that other nations did not exclude improperly gathered evidence from a criminal trial. The Court said that the local police should not gather and use evidence improperly, but if they did, the remedy was to sue the police department or punish the officer.[52]

But in 1961, the Supreme Court changed its position on the use of the exclusionary rule. It began when the Cleveland police broke into the home of Dollree Mapp in search of drugs and, finding none, arrested her for possessing some obscene pictures they found there. The Court held that this was an unreasonable search and seizure because the police had not obtained a search warrant, though they had ample time to do so. Furthermore, such illegally gathered evidence could not be used in the trial of Mapp.[53] Beginning with this case—*Mapp* v. *Ohio*—the Supreme Court used the exclusionary rule as a way of enforcing a variety of constitutional guarantees.

There were two reasons for adopting the exclusionary rule. The first was deterrence: If the police could not use illegally obtained evidence in court, they would be deterred from using illegal means to gather evidence. The second was justice: Nobody should be convicted of a crime on the basis of tainted evidence. Since the

---

[†]We shall consider here only two constitutional limits: those bearing on searches and confessions. Thus we will omit many other important constitutional provisions affecting criminal cases, such as rules governing wiretapping, prisoner rights, the right to bail and to a jury trial, the bar on ex post facto laws, the right to be represented by a lawyer in court, the ban on "cruel and unusual" punishment, and the rule against double jeopardy.

rule was first adopted, scholars have argued about both reasons, but mostly over the first. Some claim that the rule has only made crimes harder to solve without improving police conduct; others claim that the rule has not impeded investigations and has made the police more law abiding.

Search and Seizure

After the Court decided to exclude improperly gathered evidence, the next problem was to decide what evidence was improper. Dollree Mapp's was an easy case. Hardly anybody argued that it was reasonable for the police without a warrant to break into someone's home, ransack one's belongings, and take whatever they could find that might be incriminating. Still, that left a lot of hard choices yet to be made.

Just when is a police search reasonable? Under two circumstances: when the officers have a search warrant and when they make a lawful arrest. A **search warrant** is an order from a judge authorizing the search of a place; the order must describe what is to be searched and seized, and the judge can issue it only if persuaded by the police that they have good reason (**probable cause**) to believe that a crime has been committed and the evidence bearing on that crime will be found at a certain location. (The police can also search a building if the occupant gives permission.)

You can also be searched when you are being lawfully arrested. When can you be arrested? If a judge has issued an arrest warrant for you, if you commit a crime in the presence of a police officer, or if the officer has probable cause to believe that you have committed a serious crime (usually a felony). If you are arrested and no search warrant has been issued, the police, and not a judge, decide what they can search. What rules should they follow?

In trying to answer that question, the courts have elaborated a set of rules that are complex, subject to frequent change, and quite controversial. In general the police, after arresting you, can search

1. you
2. things in plain view
3. things or places under your immediate control

As a practical matter, "things in plain view" or "under your immediate control" mean the room in which you are arrested but not other rooms in the house.[54] If the police want to search the rest of your house or a car parked in your driveway, they first have to go to a judge to obtain a search warrant. But if the police arrest a college student on campus for drinking under age and then accompany him back to his dormitory room so he can get proof that he was old enough to drink, the police can seize drugs that are in plain view in that room.[55] And if marijuana is growing in plain view in an open field, the police can enter and search that field even though it is fenced off with a locked gate and a "No Trespassing" sign, but they cannot use thermal imaging to find marijuana growing inside your home.[56]

What if you are arrested while driving your car? How much of it can the police search? The answer has changed almost yearly. In 1979, the Court ruled that the police could not search a suitcase taken from a car of an arrested person and, in

Search warrant *An order from a judge authorizing the search of a place; the order must describe what is to be searched and seized, and the judge can issue it only if he or she is persuaded by the police that good reason (probable cause) exists that a crime has been committed and that the evidence bearing on the crime will be found at a certain location.*

Probable cause *See Search warrant.*

1981, extended this protection to any "closed, opaque container" found in the car.[57] But the following year the Court decided that all parts of a car, closed or open, could be searched if the officers had probable cause to believe it contained contraband (that is, goods illegally possessed).[58]

The law may be confusing, but the purpose is clear: to find ways of protecting those places in which a person has a "reasonable expectation of privacy." Your body is one such place, and so the Court has held that the police cannot force you to undergo surgery to remove a bullet that might provide evidence of your guilt.[59] But the police can require you to take a Breathalyzer test to find out whether you have been drinking while driving (driving is a privilege, not a right).[60] Your house is another place where you have an expectation of privacy, but the barn next to your house is not, nor is your backyard viewed from an airplane, nor is your house if it is a motor home that can be easily driven away. The police therefore need no warrant to search there.[61]

If you work for the government, you may have an expectation that your desk and files are private; nonetheless, your supervisor may search them without a warrant provided that he or she is looking for something related to your work.[62]

Paul Conklin/Photo Edit

A police officer reads the Miranda warning to a man he has arrested.

You may think your brother's high-school locker is private, but school officials can search it without a warrant if they have a "reasonable suspicion" that he is hiding marijuana or other contraband in it.[63]

Since the Bill of Rights protects people against *government* action, a private employer has much more freedom to search your desk, files, or locker. Because of this, the Constitution does not restrict the power of corporations to require employees to undergo drug tests (state or federal law may, however, impose some restrictions).

Government testing for drugs and for AIDS (acquired immune deficiency syndrome) has opened up a new dimension for civil-liberties issues. In 1987, President Reagan called for AIDS tests for immigrants, federal prisoners, and certain other categories of persons. In 1986, he signed an executive order requiring drug testing for many federal employees. Are such tests, in the absence of any reasonable suspicion that an immigrant, prisoner, or an employee has contracted AIDS or is using drugs, an unreasonable search that the Constitution prohibits? Not all the answers are in, but in 1989 the Supreme Court upheld federal rules requiring drug tests of train crews involved in accidents and of customs officers who carry firearms or are involved in enforcing

The Miranda Rules

The Supreme Court has interpreted the due-process clause to require that local police departments issue warnings of the sort shown below to people they are arresting.

PHILADELPHIA POLICE DEPARTMENT

STANDARD POLICE INTERROGATION CARD

WARNINGS TO BE GIVEN ACCUSED

We are questioning you concerning the crime of (state specific crime).

We have a duty to explain to you and to warn you that you have the following legal rights:

A. You have a right to remain silent and do not have to say anything at all.

B. Anything you say can and will be used against you in Court.

C. You have a right to talk to a lawyer of your own choice before we ask you any questions, and also to have a lawyer here with you while we ask questions.

D. If you cannot afford to hire a lawyer, and you want one, we will see that you have one provided to you free of charge before we ask you any questions.

E. If you are willing to give us a statement, you have a right to stop any time you wish.

75-Misc.-3   (Over)

(6-24-70)

---

drug laws.[64] The Court also clearly ruled that a private employer who requires his or her workers to take drug tests is not violating the federal Constitution (it may, however, be violating its state's constitution.)

Confessions and Self-Incrimination

The constitutional ban on being forced to give evidence against oneself was originally intended to prevent the use of torture or "third-degree" police tactics to extract confessions. It has since been extended to cover many kinds of statements uttered not out of fear of torture but from lack of awareness of one's rights, especially the right to remain silent, whether in the courtroom or the police station.

For many decades, the Supreme Court had held that involuntary confessions could not be used in federal criminal trials but had not ruled that they were barred

LANDMARK CASES

Criminal Justice

- ***Mapp v. Ohio* (1961):** Evidence illegally gathered by police may not be used in a criminal trial.
- ***Gideon v. Wainwright* (1964):** Persons charged with a crime have a right to an attorney even if they cannot afford one.
- ***Miranda v. Arizona* (1966):** Prescribes warning police must give to arrested persons.

- ***United States v. Leon* (1984):** Illegally obtained evidence may be used in a criminal trial if it was gathered "in good faith."
- ***Rasul v. Bush and Hamdi v. Rumsfeld* (2004):** Terrorist detainees must have access to a neutral court to decide if they are legally held.

from state trials. In the early 1960s, this changed in two landmark cases: *Escobedo* and *Miranda*.[65] The story of the latter and the controversy it provoked is worth telling.

Ernesto A. Miranda was convicted in Arizona of the rape-kidnapping of a young woman. The conviction was based on a written confession that Miranda signed after two hours of police questioning. (The victim also identified him.) Two years earlier the Court had decided that the rule against self-incrimination applied to state courts.[66] The question now arose, what constitutes an "involuntary" confession? The Court decided that a confession would be presumed involuntary unless the person in custody had been fully and clearly informed of his or her right to be silent, to have an attorney present during any questioning, and to have an attorney provided free of charge if he or she could not afford one. The accused may waive these rights and offer to talk, but the waiver must be truly voluntary. Because Miranda did not have a lawyer present when he was questioned and had not knowingly waived his right to a lawyer, the confession was excluded from evidence in the trial and his conviction was overturned.[67]

Miranda was tried and convicted again, this time on the basis of evidence supplied by his girlfriend, who testified that he had admitted to her that he was guilty. Nine years later he was released from prison; four years after that he was killed in a barroom fight. When the Phoenix police arrested the prime suspect, they read him his rights from a "Miranda card."

Everyone who watches cops-and-robbers shows on television probably knows the "Miranda warning" by heart because the police now read it routinely to people they arrest, both on and off television. It is not clear whether it has much impact on who does or does not confess or what effect, if any, it may have on the crime rate.

In time the Miranda rule was extended to mean that you have a right to a lawyer when you appear in a postindictment police lineup[68] and when you are questioned by a psychiatrist to determine if you are competent to stand trial.[69] Some police departments tried to get around the need for a Miranda warning by training officers to question suspects before giving them a Miranda warning and then, if the suspect confessed, giving the warning and asking the same questions over again. The Supreme Court put an end to this in 2004.[70]

Relaxing the Exclusionary Rule

Such highly controversial cases as *Miranda* led to an effort in Congress during the 1960s to modify or overrule the decisions by statute—without much success. But as the rules governing police conduct became increasingly complex, pressure mounted to find an alternative. Some thought any evidence should be admissible, with the question of police conduct left to lawsuits or other ways of punishing official misbehavior. Others felt that the exclusionary rule served a useful purpose but had simply become too technical to effectively deter police misconduct (the police could not obey rules they could not understand). And still others felt the exclusionary rule was a vital safeguard to essential liberties and should be kept intact. Bills to enact the first and second positions were introduced in Congress during the 1980s.

The courts themselves began to adopt the second position, deciding a number of cases in ways that retained the exclusionary rule but modified it by limiting its coverage (police were given greater freedom to question juveniles[71]) and by incorporating what was called a **good-faith exception**. For example, if the police obtain a search warrant that they believe is valid, the evidence they gather will not be excluded if it later turns out that the warrant was defective for a minor reason (such as the judge having used the wrong form).[72] Further, the Court decided that "overriding considerations of public safety" may justify questioning a person without first reading him his rights.[73] Moreover, the Court changed its decision about the killer who had led the police to his victim's body. After the man was convicted a second time and again appealed, the Court in 1984 held that the body would have been discovered anyway; evidence will not be excluded if it can be shown that it would "inevitably" have been found.[74]

Good-faith exception
Admission at a trial of evidence that is gathered in violation of the Constitution if the violation results from a technical or minor error.

Terrorism and Civil Liberties

The attacks of September 11, 2001, raised important questions about how far the government can go in investigating and prosecuting individuals.

Not much more than a month after the attacks, Congress passed and the president signed the U.S.A. Patriot law to increase federal powers to investigate terrorists. Its main provisions were these:

- Telephone taps: The government may tap, if it has a court order, any

A cell in Guantanamo prison for enemy combatants.

Joe Skipper/Reuters/Corbis

telephone a suspect uses instead of having to get a separate order for each telephone.

- Internet taps: The government may tap, if it has a court order, Internet communications.
- Voice mail: The government, if it has a court order, may seize voice mail.
- Grand jury information: Investigators can now share with other government officials information learned in secret grand jury hearings.
- Immigration: The attorney general may hold any noncitizen who is thought to be a national security risk for up to seven days. If not charged with a crime or deported within that time, the person may still be detained if he or she is certified to be a security risk.
- Money laundering: The government was given new powers to track the movement of money across U.S. borders and among banks.
- Crime: The new law eliminates the statute of limitation on terrorist crimes and increases the penalties.

About a month later, President Bush, by executive order, proclaimed a national emergency under which any noncitizen believed to be a terrorist or to have harbored a terrorist will be tried by a military rather than a civilian court.

A military trial is carried on before a commission of military officers, not a civilian jury. The tribunal can operate in secret if classified information is used in evidence. Two-thirds of the commission must agree before the suspect can be convicted and sentenced. If convicted, the suspect can appeal to the secretary of defense and the president but not to a civilian court.

These measures were criticized by civil-liberties organizations and in time may be challenged in court. However, given their popular support and the fact that federal courts have usually given the federal government broad powers in wartime, the rules, or something like them, are likely to last at least as long as does the war on terrorism.

During the Second World War, a military tribunal tried several Nazi spies who landed in New York. Most were executed. The Supreme Court unanimously upheld the use of that tribunal, arguing that enemy combatants who, without wearing uniforms, come secretly during wartime for the purpose of committing hostile acts, are neither citizens nor prisoners of war but are "unlawful combatants."[75]

The biggest legal issue created by this country's war on terrorism is whether "enemy combatants" can be detained by our government without access to a court. An enemy combatant is someone at war with this country. Like German prisoners seized by the United States during World War II, they are held in prison camps so that they cannot rejoin their army and fight us again. During that war they could not appeal to any American court the fact that they were detained.

In two important decisions, the Supreme Court in 2004 decided that enemy combatants today have a right to appeal. One case involved a United States citizen captured by U.S. troops in Afghanistan, the other a group of foreigners who were also seized there. In the first case, the citizen could appeal in order to try to prove he was not an enemy combatant. In the second case, several hundred foreigners held at the American naval base in Guantanamo, Cuba, were given the right to ask for a hearing before some kind of American court—possibly a military tribunal.

WHAT WOULD YOU DO?

MEMORANDUM

To: Rebecca Saikia, Supreme Court justice

From: David Wilson, law clerk

Subject: Patriot Act and libraries

The Patriot Act allows the FBI to seek the records of possible terrorists from banks, businesses, and libraries. Many libraries claim this will harm the constitutional rights of Americans. You support these rights, but are also aware of the need to protect national security.

Arguments supporting the Patriot Act:

1. The Patriot Act does not target individuals who have not violated a criminal law and who do not threaten human life.

2. For the FBI to collect information about borrowers, it must first obtain permission from a federal judge.

3. Terrorists may use libraries to study and plan activities that threaten national security.

Arguments against the Patriot Act:

1. Freedom of speech and expression are fundamental constitutional guarantees that should not be infringed.

Friday,

High Court Hears From Libraries About War on Terror

April 22
WASHINGTON, D.C.

Two public libraries have asked the Supreme Court to strike down provisions of the Patriot Act that allow the Federal Bureau of Investigation to see the borrowing records of persons who are under investigation. . . .

2. The law might harm groups engaged in peaceful protests.

3. The law allows the government to delay notifying people that their borrowing habits are being investigated.

Your Decision:

Uphold this provision _____   Overturn this provision _____

At first no one knew what kind of courts would hear these appeals, what rules they would apply, or how many enemy combatants would appeal. In theory these decisions may make capturing enemy prisoners a complex and time-consuming legal problem, and so far it is unclear how it will work out.[76]

To try these enemy combatants, a law passed in 2006 authorized military commissions composed of at least five military officers to try foreign fighters who are not in uniform, such as members of most terrorist groups. The accused are given certain rights (such as to see evidence and to testify). If they are convicted, they may appeal to a court of military review and from there to a federal appeals court and to the Supreme Court.

The trials of terrorists need not be held in civilian courts. In 2009, the attorney general decided to try several Guantanamo inmates in a civilian court in New York City, but that met with local resistance. In the meantime, President Obama had promised to close the Guantanamo prison camp but was unable to do so because he could not find a place to put many of the inmates.

SUMMARY

Civil liberties are limitations placed by the Constitution on the government's powers over people. The due-process and equal protection clauses of the Fourteenth Amendment have been used to apply to state governments' limits on federal power.

There are now very few constitutional restrictions on speech and press except for a recent ban on "electioneering communication" by unions and corporations sixty days before a general election. People can freely exercise their religious views unless they use religion to justify an otherwise illegal act. Government support of religion remains controversial.

The rights of people accused of a crime have been broadened, with the exception of those labeled as terrorists.

RECONSIDERING THE ENDURING QUESTIONS

1. Why not display religious symbols on government property?

The Supreme Court declares that doing this threatens to "establish" a religion. But it has not objected to printing "In God We Trust" on currency, opening sessions of Congress with a prayer, or assigning chaplains to military units. Confused? So are a lot of people.

2. What does the court mean by "obscenity"?

It means writing or pictures that the average person, applying the standards of his or her community, believes appeal to the prurient interest and lack literary, artistic, political, or scientific value.

3. Is all political advertising constitutional?

Since a Supreme Court decision in early 2010, corporations, unions, and non-profit organizations can spend money for or against a candidate at any time.

Online Resources: Civil Liberties

CourseMate

- Civil Rights Division of the Justice Department: www.usdoj.gov/crt/crt-home.html
- Court cases: www.law.cornell.edu

Suggested Readings

Abraham, Henry J., and Barbara A. Perry, *Freedom and the Court*, 7th ed. New York: Oxford University Press, 1998. A comprehensive review of how the Constitution and the courts define civil liberties and civil rights.

Amar, Akhil Reed. *The Constitution and Criminal Procedure*. New Haven, Conn: Yale University Press, 1997. Brilliant reinterpretation of the Constitution's position on criminal justice.

Berns, Walter. *The First Amendment and the Future of American Democracy*. New York: Basic Books, 1976. A fresh look at what the Framers mean by the First Amendment.

Clor, Harry M. *Obscenity and Public Morality*. Chicago: University of Chicago Press, 1969. Argues for the legitimacy of legal bans on obscenity.

Levy, Leonard W. *Legacy of Suppression: Freedom of Speech and Press in Early American History*. Cambridge, Mass: Harvard University Press, 1960. Careful study of what the Framers meant by freedom of speech and the press.

4   Civil Rights

ENDURING QUESTIONS

1. Do you think there is a "right to privacy" in the Constitution?

2. Should numerical goals be used to ensure that students and workers are drawn from every racial group?

3. What are the Constitutional limits to the right to have on abortion?

If the government passes a law that treats different groups of people differently, that law is not necessarily unconstitutional. After all, most laws put people into groups. The income tax laws, for example, impose different tax rates on people depending on how much they earn. For a law to violate people's civil rights, it must make an *unreasonable* classification or impose an *unreasonable* burden. The Supreme Court's opinion as to what is unreasonable has changed, as we can see by looking at how the law has treated people based on race and sex.

AP Photo/Ralph Fres

So What?

All right, people differ. But what kinds of differences can the government allow? The courts have worked hard on this question and come up with three answers. The first and easiest difference is ordinary or minimum scrutiny. The court will uphold a classification if it "reasonably" relates to a "legitimate" government interest. A good example is income. The government can tax people at different rates based on how much they earn. You might go to court to challenge this classification, but the court would assume it was all right and put the burden on you to explain what was wrong with it.

A tougher standard is intermediate or heightened scrutiny. Here the government must prove that its classification is "substantially" related to an "important" government interest. This is the test under which classifications based on gender are evaluated.

The toughest standard is strict scrutiny. Here the courts will not allow the classification unless it is "closely" related to a "compelling" government interest. This is the rule that governs decisions based on racial classifications. Under this test the courts will assume that the classification is wrong unless you convince them that it is vital to some important and defensible governmental objective. In doing this, you will have to show that the classification uses the "least restrictive" means to achieve.

By now you are puzzled. What is the difference between "reasonable," "substantial," and "closely"? What is the difference between a "legitimate," an "important," and a "compelling" interest? There are obviously no objective ways to answer these questions. The best way to understand them is to see how they developed. To do that, we shall start with racial classifications.

Race and "Strict Scrutiny"

Until 1954, classifying people on the basis of race for the purpose of assigning them to schools was accepted by the Supreme Court. In establishing the **separate-but-equal doctrine**, it held that as long as the schools that blacks and whites attended were substantially equal in quality, then having racially segregated schools was not unconstitutional. In 1954, in the famous case of *Brown v. Board of Education*, the Court held that "separate educational facilities are inherently unequal," thus denying to blacks the equal protection of the law.[1] The authors of the Fourteenth Amendment probably had not intended the equal-protection clause to bar segregated schools (the schools of Washington, D.C., were segregated at the time Congress was debating the amendment, and no one seemed to think that the amendment was going to change that). But by 1954, the Court believed public education had become so important and segregated schools had become so harmful to blacks that the continued existence of such schools was incompatible with the concept of equality under the law.

Separate-but-equal doctrine *The doctrine, established in* Plessy v. Ferguson *(1896), in which the Supreme Court ruled that a state could provide "separate but equal" facilities for blacks.*

The protest march from Selma to Montgomery, Alabama, in 1965 was a milestone in the campaign to strengthen federal civil-rights laws.

Suspect classifications *Classifications of people on the basis of their race and ethnicity. The courts have ruled that laws classifying people on these grounds will be subject to "strict scrutiny."*

Strict scrutiny *The standard by which the Supreme Court judges classifications based on race. To be accepted, such a classification must be closely related to a "compelling" public purpose.*

Beginning with the *Brown* case, virtually every form of racial segregation imposed by law has been struck down. Race has become a **suspect classification** such that any law making racial distinctions is now subject to **strict scrutiny**. This means that the classification must be related to a "compelling government interest," be "narrowly tailored" to achieve that interest, and use the "least restrictive means" available.

No law may require that blacks be segregated in any public facility (such as a voting booth, public school, or municipal swimming pool). But the equal-protection clause limits the action of state *governments* only; it is not a limitation on purely private behavior. To ban discrimination in *private* transactions, it was necessary for Congress to pass a series of civil-rights laws that, beginning in 1964, made it illegal to discriminate on the grounds of race, color, religion, or national origin in public accommodations, such as restaurants, theaters, sports stadiums, or hotels, or in employing workers (provided that the firm employs more than twenty-five workers or has a federal contract). Subsequent laws banned discrimination in the sale or rental of most housing (see the box on page 65).

That race is a suspect category does not mean that the government cannot treat the races differently. Public schools can be required to bus black pupils to white schools. State universities can take race into account in admitting students to colleges, law schools, and medical schools, provided that no strict numerical quota is used and that the special consideration given to race is designed to help rather than hurt blacks.[2]

In short, the Supreme Court has not held that the Constitution is "color-blind." The law may make racial distinctions if their purpose is intended to remedy the consequences of past discrimination. This interpretation of the Constitution is controversial. Many people believe that policies designed to make it easier for

LANDMARK CASES

Civil Rights

- *Plessy* **v.** *Ferguson* **(1896):** Upheld separate-but-equal facilities for whites and blacks on railroad cars.
- *Brown* **v.** *Board of Education* **(1954):** Racially separate public schools are inherently unequal and thus unconstitutional.
- *Green* **v.** *New Kent County* **(1968):** Banned a freedom-of-choice plan; blacks and whites must actually attend the same schools.
- *Swann* **v.** *Charlotte-Mecklenburg* **(1971):** Students may be bused to achieve racial balance in schools.

blacks to get into state universities or to get government contracts are merely **reverse discrimination** and that busing to achieve racial balance in the schools is undesirable. These individuals argue that what is necessary is **equality of opportunities**, and to this end the Constitution should be color-blind. But others believe that the harmful effects of centuries of slavery and segregation can be overcome only if the government is allowed to take race into account in making policy. This is especially the case, they hold, if informal social forces lead blacks and whites to live in separate neighborhoods, thereby minimizing the amount of contact they have with one another and reducing black access to certain jobs and schools. These people argue that what is necessary is equality of results, and that to this end the Constitution should permit compensatory or **affirmative action** programs.

The Supreme Court has wrestled with this issue many times, and the results are not easily summarized. In general it has allowed race to be taken into account in giving people access to jobs and schooling *if* there has been a past practice of discrimination. But there remains much confusion in the law. Here are some important Court decisions on this matter:

1. *Schools can be required to admit black students even after they have repealed laws and rules that once kept blacks out. Giving blacks "freedom of choice" is not enough.* Formerly all-white schools can actually be required to have black students in attendance and to use busing to bring in black children.[3]
2. *The courts will order busing only within a city, unless it can be shown that the suburban areas have in fact practiced segregation.* Busing limited to the central city has been approved in Charlotte, Boston, Detroit, Atlanta, Denver, Indianapolis, and Richmond, among other places; busing across city lines has been approved in Louisville and Wilmington.[4]
3. *A public college cannot give minority applicants an automatic boost when they apply for admission.* In 2003, the Supreme Court by a five-to-four vote overturned the admissions policy of the University of Michigan, which gave every African American, Hispanic, and Native American applicants 20 points out of the 100 points needed to guarantee admission to its undergraduate program.[5] In doing

Reverse discrimination *Using race or sex to give preferential treatment to certain people.*

Equality of opportunities *A view that it is wrong to use race or sex either to discriminate against or give preferential treatment to blacks or women.*

Affirmative action *The requirement, imposed by law or administrative regulation, that an organization (business firm, government agency, labor union, school, or college) take positive steps to increase the number or proportion of women, blacks, or other minorities in its membership.*

so, the Court confirmed its 1978 decision stating that Alan Bakke, a white, had been wrongly denied admission to the University of California at Davis medical school.[6] In both cases, the Court objected not to the use of race as one factor in making a decision, but to giving to race a "fixed quota" or an exact numerical advantage to the exclusion of "individual" considerations. To avoid being overturned because they violate the equal protection clause of the Fourteenth Amendment, racial advantages must be "narrowly tailored" to achieve diversity.

4. *Public law schools, and by implication all public universities, can use race in a "narrowly tailored" way to achieve the schools' "compelling interest" in achieving "diversity."* The Supreme Court decided this case on the same day in 2003 that it announced its decision on undergraduate admissions. It allowed the University of Michigan Law School to act in accordance with the rule stated in the *Bakke* decision twenty-five years earlier: Race may be a "plus" factor, but it cannot reflect a quota system.[7] Because the law school had no quota, there was no unconstitutional action even though using race as a "plus" increased by a factor of three the proportion of minority applicants who were admitted.

5. *If an industry or occupation has a past history of racial discrimination, quotas may be used by voluntary agreement or government requirement to remedy the effects of that discrimination.* If there was a history of discrimination, contractors can be required to set aside 10 percent of their contract funds to purchase services from minority-owned businesses, unions can be required to recruit black members, and state police departments and municipal fire departments can be required to hire blacks on the basis of a quota system. But if there is no clear showing of past discrimination, setting aside a percentage of city contracts for minority-owned businesses is unconstitutional. A factory or a union can voluntarily adopt a quota system for selecting black workers for a training program.[8]

6. *If there is no past history of discrimination, no mandatory hiring or promotional plan favoring blacks is permissible.* Black teachers cannot be given preferential promotions over whites when it has not been proven that the school system has discriminated. But even without a history of past discrimination, a voluntary affirmative-action plan can be used to hire women in preference to men.[9]

The strongest statement the Supreme Court has yet made about affirmative action came on June 12, 1995, when it decided the *Adarand* case. Adarand was a small construction firm that failed to get a government contract to build guardrails along a federal highway despite the fact that it was the low bidder. It lost because of a government policy that favors small businesses owned by "socially and economically disadvantaged individuals"—namely, racial and ethnic minorities. In a five-to-four vote decision, the Court agreed with Adarand.

The essence of its decision is that any racial classification must be subject to strict scrutiny even if its purpose is to help, not hurt, a racial minority. "The Fifth and Fourteenth Amendments protect persons, not groups," the Court wrote. Strict scrutiny means two things:

- Any racial classification must serve a "compelling government interest."
- The classification must be "narrowly tailored" to serve that interest.[10]

Key Provisions of Major Civil-Rights Laws

1957   Made it a federal crime to try to prevent a person from voting in a federal election. Created the Civil Rights Commission.

1960   Authorized the attorney general to appoint federal referees to gather evidence and present findings about allegations that blacks were being deprived of their right to vote. Made it a federal crime to use interstate commerce to threaten or carry out a bombing.

1964   *Voting:* Made it more difficult to use administrative devices or literacy tests to bar blacks from voting.

  Public accommodations: Barred discrimination on grounds of race, color, religion, or national origin in restaurants, hotels, lunch counters, gasoline stations, movie theaters, stadiums, arenas, and lodging houses with more than five rooms.

  Schools: Authorized the attorney general to bring suit to force the desegregation of public schools on behalf of citizens. Did not authorize issuing orders to achieve racial balance in schools by busing.

  Employment: Outlawed discrimination in hiring, firing, or paying employees on grounds of race, color, religion, national origin, or sex. Eventually covered all firms employing twenty-five or more workers.

  Federal funds: Barred discrimination in any activity receiving federal assistance. Authorized cutting off federal funds to activities in which discrimination was practiced.

1965   *Voting registration:* Authorized appointment by the Civil Service Commission of voting examiners who would require registration of all eligible voters in federal, state, and local elections, general or primary, in areas where discrimination was found to be practiced or where fewer than 50 percent of voting-age residents were registered to vote in the 1964 election.

  Literacy tests: Suspended use of literacy tests or other devices to prevent blacks from voting. Directed the attorney general to bring suit challenging the constitutionality of poll taxes.

1968   *Housing:* Banned, by stages, discrimination in sale or rental of most housing (excluding private owners who sell or rent their homes without the services of a real estate broker).

  Riots: Made it a federal crime to use interstate commerce to organize or incite a riot.

1972   *Education:* Prohibited sex discrimination in education programs that receive federal aid.

1988   *Discrimination:* If any part of an organization receives federal aid, no part may discriminate on the basis of race, sex, age, or physical handicap.

1991   *Civil rights:* Reversed Supreme Court decisions that had narrowed the interpretation of federal civil-rights laws as they affected disputes between employees and employers over racial or gender discrimination.

  Race norming: Made it illegal for the government to adjust, or "norm," test scores by race.

After the *Adarand* decision, the Court ruled in 2003 that the University of Michigan could not admit undergraduates by giving to black and Hispanic applicants a 20-point bonus (out of 100 needed to guarantee admission) but that the university's law school could use race as a "plus factor" and not as a numerical quota. These two decisions—*Gratz* v. *Bollinger* and *Grutter* v. *Bollinger*—left matters up in the air. What exactly is the difference between a "numerical quota" and a "plus factor"? Four years later the Court held that race could not be used in deciding whom to admit to elementary or high schools. But why are elementary and high schools treated differently from a public law school?

The debate over affirmative action led voters in California and Washington in the late 1990s, Michigan in 2007, and Nebraska in 2008 to approve measures that would ban the use of "race, sex, color, or ethnicity" to discriminate against or give benefits to any individual or group. That debate, though important, should not obscure the extent of the changes that have occurred in race relations since the 1960s. A growing proportion of whites express (and probably act on) tolerant views about race, and the number of blacks holding elective office has steadily increased (see Table 4 .1).

Sex and "Reasonable Classifications"

While race is a "suspect" classification, sex is not. One reason may be that laws putting women in a special category had a different history and a different justification than laws putting blacks in a special category. Segregationist laws were designed to separate blacks from whites and thereby subjugate them to white rule. Laws limiting the opportunities of women did not aim at segregating them from men and were supposedly intended to protect women. For example, in 1908, the Supreme Court upheld an Oregon law that limited female laundry workers to a

LANDMARK CASES

Affirmative Action

- *Regents of the University of California* **v.** *Bakke* **(1978):** A quota for admitting blacks was unconstitutional, but race could be used as a "plus factor."
- *United Steelworkers* **v.** *Weber* **(1979):** Race may be used in an employment agreement between a factory and its workers.
- *Richmond* **v.** *Croson* **(1989):** Affirmative action plans must be narrowly tailored to serve a compelling state interest.

- *Grutter* **v.** *Bollinger and Gratz* **v.** *Bollinger* **(2003):** Numerical benefits cannot be used to admit blacks into state universities, but race can be a "plus factor."
- *Parents* **v.** *Seattle School District* **(2007):** Race cannot be used to assign students because doing so was not "narrowly tailored" to achieve a "compelling" goal.

10-hour workday (men were allowed to work as long as they wished). The Court held that men and women differed in strength, functions, and self-reliance, and thus women required special protection.[11]

The feminist movement has, of course, challenged the claim that men and women differ in ways that require different legal treatment. In response, Congress and state legislatures have passed laws that eliminate many of the old gender-based distinctions. Today discrimination based on sex in employment and education is (in general) illegal: Men and women must receive equal pay for equal work, and male and female students must receive equal opportunities in colleges and universities receiving federal funds.

At the same time, the Supreme Court began altering the standards it applied to laws and practices that treated men and women differently. The traditional standard, as we saw in the 1908 case, reflected a kind of protective paternalism; under it, no state law was ever held unconstitutional because of sex discrimination. In 1971, however, the Court overturned an Idaho statute that gave men preference over women in the appointment of administrators of the estates of deceased children. A unanimous Court set down a new standard: To be constitutionally permissible, any law that classifies people on the basis of sex "must be reasonable, not arbitrary, and must rest on some ground of difference having a fair and substantial relation to the object of the legislation so that all persons similarly circumstanced shall be treated alike."[12] In other decisions the Court has developed an "intermediate scrutiny" test under which there is an "exceedingly persuasive" justification for a policy that "substantially" achieves an important government objective.

In short, the Court can choose among three tests for deciding whether treating people differently is constitutional: "rational basis," "intermediate scrutiny,"

AP Photo/Danny Moloshok

University of Michigan students disagree about whether the Supreme Court should uphold affirmative action.

Table 4.1 Increase in Number of Black Elected Officials		
Office	**1970**	**2002**
Congress and state legislatures	182	636
City and county offices	715	5,753
Judges and sheriffs	213	1,081
Boards of education	362	1,960
Total	1,472	9,430

Source: Statistical Abstract of the United States.

and "strict scrutiny." It is not always easy to tell which standard ought to apply. For example, in one case some justices wanted to abandon the standard of reasonableness applied to sex and replace it with the same standard governing laws involving race—that they are "inherently suspect." But there was no majority for this view.[13]

Under the *reasonableness or intermediate scrutiny standard*, the courts have overturned some distinctions based on sex and have permitted others. See the examples in the Landmark Cases box.

Decisions Barring Differences Based on Sex

- A state cannot set different ages at which men and women become legal adults.[14]
- A state cannot set different ages at which men and women are allowed to buy beer.[15]
- Women cannot be barred from jobs by arbitrary height and weight requirements.[16]
- Employers cannot require women to take mandatory pregnancy leaves.[17]
- Girls cannot be barred from Little League baseball teams.[18]
- The Junior Chamber of Commerce and the Rotary Club, though private associations, cannot exclude women from membership.[19]
- Though women as a group live longer than men, an employer must pay women monthly retirement benefits equal to those received by men.[20]
- High schools must pay coaches of girls' sports the same salary they pay coaches of boys' sports.[21]

Decisions Allowing Differences Based on Sex

- A law that punishes males but not females for statutory rape is permissible; men and women are not "similarly situated" with respect to sexual relations.[22]
- All-boy and all-girl public schools are permitted if enrollment is voluntary and quality is equal.[23]

LANDMARK CASES

Rights for Women

- ***Reed* v. *Reed* (1971):** Gender discrimination violates the equal protection clause of the Constitution.
- ***Craig* v. *Boren* (1976):** Gender discrimination can be justified only if it is "substantially related" to "important government objectives."
- ***Rostker* v. *Goldberg* (1981):** Congress may draft men without drafting women.
- ***United States* v. *Virginia* (1996):** A state may not finance an all-male military school.

- States can give widows a property-tax exemption not given to widowers.[24]
- The navy may allow women to remain officers longer than men without being promoted.[25]

In a case that came very close to making sex a suspect classification, the Supreme Court ordered in 1996 that women be admitted to the Virginia Military Institute (VMI), until then an all-male, state-supported college that had for many decades supplied what it called "adversative" training in order to instill physical toughness and mental

A female and male soldier work side-by-side on the Guantanamo Bay military base.

discipline in its students. The Court said that for the state to spend money on a single-sex school, it must supply an "exceedingly persuasive justification." When the state offered to create an all-female equivalent of VMI, the Court said this was not enough. This case raises important questions about what, if anything, will happen to all-female private schools that receive state aid.[26]

Sexual Harassment

When Paula Corbin Jones accused President Clinton of sexual harassment, the judge threw the case out of court on the grounds that she had not submitted enough evidence such that, even if the jury believed her, she would have made a compelling argument. At about the same time, the Supreme Court was clarifying what sexual harassment meant.

Drawing on rulings by the Equal Employment Opportunity Commission, the Court has held that harassment can take one of two forms. First, it is illegal for someone to request sexual favors as a condition for employment or advancement (the "quid pro quo" rule). If someone does this, the employer is strictly liable, meaning that the employer can be held liable even if he or she did not know that a subordinate was requesting sex in exchange for hiring or promotion. Second, it is illegal for the employee to experience a work environment that is made hostile or intimidating by a steady pattern of offensive sexual jokes, teasing, or obscenity. Employers are guilty of allowing this second failure only if they were negligent—that is, they knew about the hostility and failed to correct it.

In 1998, the Court decided three cases that make these rules either worse or better, depending on your point of view. In one case it held that a school system is not liable for the conduct of a teacher who seduced a female student if the student never reported the actions. In another it held that a city is responsible for the sexually hostile work environment confronted by a female lifeguard even though she did not report this, either. In the third case an employee who was the object of sexual harassment but was promoted despite having rejected her boss's advances may still recover financial damages from her former firm, but the firm can avoid this if it has put in place an "affirmative defense." The Court, however, did not say what constitutes such a helpful policy.[27]

Sexual harassment is clearly a serious matter, but because there is almost no congressional law governing this matter, what constitutes harassment, and how one can avoid it, must be inferred from regulatory decisions and court rulings.

Perhaps the most far-reaching cases defining the rights of women have involved the draft and abortion. In 1981, the Court held in *Rostker* v. *Goldberg* that Congress may draft men but not women without violating the due-process clause of the Fifth Amendment.[28] In the area of national defense, the Court will give greater deference to congressional policy (Congress had already decided to bar women from combat roles). The controversy over whether women should be treated the same as men in the military was a major issue in the debate over the Equal Rights Amendment. If the ERA had been ratified, it would have overturned *Rostker* v. *Goldberg*.

Police powers *The authority of a government to safeguard and promote public order, safety, and morals.*

Privacy and Sex

Regulating sexual matters has traditionally been left to the states' **police powers**. These powers include not only the authority to create police forces but also to promote public order and secure the safety and morals of their citizens. Some

The Constitutional Position of Abortion Laws

The majority opinion of the Court in the 1992 *Casey* decision:

1. "It is a constitutional liberty of the woman to have some freedom to terminate her pregnancy. . . . No state may prohibit a woman from terminating her pregnancy" before the fetus becomes "viable."
2. After the fetus has become viable, a state may "regulate, and even proscribe, abortion except where it is necessary . . . for the preservation of the life and the health of the mother."
   Note: The point at which a fetus becomes "viable"—that is, capable of living outside the mother's womb—may change with advances in medical science. The old distinction in *Roe* between the first, second, and third trimesters was discarded in the *Casey* decision.
3. States may put restrictions on the right to an abortion, but these restrictions must not place an "undue burden" on the exercise of a woman's rights. An "undue burden" is defined as a legal restriction that has the "purpose or effect" of placing a "substantial obstacle in the path of a woman seeking an abortion before the fetus attains viability." Parental notification and waiting periods were not judged to be undue burdens.

This is the core argument of the justices who dissented from the *Casey* decision: *Roe* was wrongly decided and should be overturned because nothing in the Constitution provides for a right to abortion. It should be left to the political process in the states to decide this issue.

LANDMARK CASES

Privacy and Abortion

- *Griswold* v. *Connecticut* (1965): Finds a "right to privacy" in the Constitution that would ban state laws against sale of contraceptives.
- *Roe* v. *Wade* (1973): State laws against abortion are unconstitutional.
- *Webster* v. *Reproductive Health Services* (1989): States may ban abortions in public hospitals.
- *Planned Parenthood* v. *Casey* (1992): Reaffirmed *Roe* v. *Wade* but upheld certain limits on its use.
- *Steber* v. *Carhart* (2000): States may not ban partial-birth abortions if they fail to allow an exemption to protect the health of the mother.

have argued that the Tenth Amendment to the Constitution, by reserving to the states all powers not delegated to the federal government, meant that states can do anything not explicitly prohibited by the Constitution. That changed when the Supreme Court began expanding the power of Congress over business and later when it started to view sexual matters under the newly articulated doctrine of privacy.

In 1965, the Supreme Court held that states could not prevent the sale of contraceptives because by so doing, they would invade a "zone of privacy." Privacy is nowhere mentioned in the Constitution, but the Court argued that it could be inferred from "penumbras" (literally, "shadows") cast off by various provisions of the Bill of Rights.[29]

Eight years later the Court, in its famous *Roe* v. *Wade* decision, held that the "right of privacy" is "broad enough to encompass a woman's decision whether or not to terminate a pregnancy."[30] This 1973 ruling gave constitutional protection to abortion, at least during the first six months of a woman's pregnancy. After that point, when the fetus could live outside her body, the state might allow abortion to protect the woman's life or health.

In time this decision deeply divided the nation into two camps: a "right to choose" group that ardently defended abortion and sought federal funds to help pay for them, and a "right to life" camp that opposed such funding and tried to get a constitutional amendment that would permit states to ban abortions.

Neither movement has succeeded. Congress has refused to adopt the constitutional amendment and has passed, with the Court's blessing, a series of laws (the best known is the "Hyde Amendment") barring the use of federal funds for abortions in all but a few special circumstances. The Supreme Court has upheld the constitutionality of such laws, as well as that of even more restrictive state legislation.[31]

For sixteen years the Court defended *Roe* v. *Wade* by, for example, striking down a state law that required an underage girl to gain her parents' consent before

LANDMARK CASES

Gay Rights

- *Romer* **v.** *Evans* **(1996):** Prevented Colorado from enforcing a law that would prevent gays and lesbians from benefiting from quotas or acquiring a protected status.
- *Boy Scouts of America* **v.** *Dale* **(2000):** A private organization may ban gays from its membership.

- *Lawrence* **v.** *Texas* **(2003):** State law may not ban consensual sexual relations between same-sex partners.

getting an abortion. But in 1989, under the influence of justices appointed by President Reagan, the Court began to uphold some state restrictions on abortions.[32]

When that happened, many people predicted that, in time, *Roe* v. *Wade* would be overturned, especially if President George H. W. Bush appointed more justices. Although he did appoint two (Souter and Thomas), *Roe* survived. Justices O'Connor, Souter, and Kennedy cast the key votes. In 1992, in its *Casey* decision, the Court in a five-to-four vote explicitly refused to overturn *Roe*. It upheld a variety of restrictions imposed by the state of Pennsylvania on women seeking abortions. These included a mandatory 24-hour waiting period between the request for and the performance of an abortion, the obligation of teenagers to obtain the consent of one parent (or, in special circumstances, of a judge), and a state requirement that a woman contemplating an abortion be given pamphlets about alternatives. Similar restrictions had been enacted in many other states, all of which looked to the Pennsylvania case for guidance as to whether they could be enforced. The Court, however, struck down a state law that would have required a married woman to obtain the consent of her husband. In allowing these restrictions, the Court overruled some of its earlier decisions. The key provisions of the *Casey* decision are summarized in the box on page 70.[33]

For a while the right to privacy suffered a setback when the Supreme Court held in 1986 that no such right could protect gay men from being prosecuted for engaging in consensual sodomy* performed in their own home. By a 5–4 vote, the Court said in *Bowers* v. *Hardwick* that privacy was a right designed to protect "family, marriage, or procreation," things that "bore no connection" to homosexual activity.[34]

---

*Under Georgia law, sodomy was defined as "any sexual contact involving the sex organs of one person and the mouth or anus of another." The law could have been applied to heterosexual as well as homosexual conduct, but the Court heard an appeal only from homosexuals.

This limitation on a right to privacy disappeared in 2003 when the Court overruled the *Bowers* case. In Texas, a man was arrested for homosexual conduct under a law that, unlike the one in Georgia, applied only to homosexuals. It banned "deviate sexual intercourse with another individual of the same sex." The Court repeated the blunt language used earlier in cases involving abortion. If "the right to privacy means anything, it is the right of the individual, married or single, to be free from unwarranted governmental intrusion" into sexual matters. Not only is there really a right of privacy, it exists in the most sweeping terms: "At the heart of liberty is the right to define one's own concept of existence, of meaning, of the universe, and of the mystery of human life." To strengthen its argument, the Court majority said that its view was supported by the decisions of other nations and by the European Court of Human Rights.[35]

The privacy decisions have had a benefit and a cost. The benefit has been to strike down certain laws, such as those in Georgia and Texas, that were rarely enforced and probably could not be passed if introduced today. The cost has been to make the police power of the states vulnerable to a general claim of privacy. Critics of the Texas decision worry that the Court will someday decide that a right to privacy means that gay and lesbian couples can get married. Various states have taken steps to reserve marriage for heterosexual couples, but those decisions may not withstand a fresh Court challenge. And some states, such as Vermont, have made civil unions between homosexuals legal.

In 2003, the Massachusetts Supreme Judicial Court required that marriage licenses be issued to gay as well as heterosexual couples. It based its decision on provisions of the state, not the federal, constitution.[36] The Massachusetts legislature passed a bill that would amend that state's constitution to ban gay marriage but permit civil unions. That amendment required another ratification vote, which took place in 2007, when it was defeated.

In the meantime, the mayor of San Francisco, in apparent defiance of a state law approved by the voters, began issuing marriage licenses to hundreds of gay couples. In August 2004, the California Supreme Court overturned the mayor's decisions. The next year, the state legislature voted to make same-sex marriages legal, but Governor Arnold Schwarzenegger vetoed the bill. In 2008, the voters

How We Compare

Same-Sex Marriages at Home and Abroad

Same-sex marriages are legal in seven European countries: Belgium, Iceland, Netherlands, Norway, Portugal, Spain, and Sweden.

In the United States, they are legal in the District of Columbia and five states: Connecticut, Iowa, Massachusetts, New Hampshire, and Vermont.

In Europe and America, northern nations and states are much more likely to legalize same-sex marriages than southern ones. What do you think may explain this?

WHAT WOULD YOU DO?

MEMORANDUM

To: Justice Robert Gilbert

From: Ella Fitzgerald, law clerk

Until school segregation ended, southern blacks could attend only all-black colleges. Now they are free to apply to previously all-white colleges, and these schools are integrated. But the traditional black colleges still exist, and very few whites apply to them. In 1992, the Supreme Court held that the state could not solve the problem by requiring a race-neutral admissions policy.* Now the Court must decide whether a predominantly black college can receive state support.

Arguments for all-black colleges:

1. These schools have a long tradition that ought to be preserved.

2. Many black students will learn better in an all-black environment.

3. African American organizations, in particular the United Negro College Fund, raise money for these schools.

+

Friday,

Court to Rule on Black Colleges

January 19
WASHINGTON, D.C.

The Supreme Court has announced that it will decide whether all-black colleges in the South can receive state support if there are too few whites attending them. The case began in Mississippi, where . . .

Arguments against all-black colleges:

1. If the state once required single-race schools, it now has an obligation to dismantle them.

2. Race is a suspect classification, and thus no state program that serves people chiefly of one race can be allowed.

Your Decision:

Allow all-black colleges _____

Ban all-black colleges _____

_____

*United States v. *Fordice,* 505 U.S. 717 (1992).

approved a ballot measure banning gay marriage, but in 2010 a federal district judge overturned that vote. A federal appeals court has put the matter on hold while waiting to see if the Supreme Court will decide the issue.

SUMMARY

The equal protection and due-process clauses of the Fourteenth Amendment restrict the power of states to treat different groups of people differently. If a different treatment is unreasonable, it is unconstitutional. In deciding what is unreasonable, the courts have applied the strict scrutiny test to racial but not to sexual classifications. A racial classification is always suspect; a sexual one is not necessarily suspect, but must be reasonable. The Court will allow, for example, women to be excluded from the draft.

The right to an abortion and to same-sex unions is based on a right to privacy that the Court has found in the Constitution. A few limitations on abortion rights have been permitted.

RECONSIDERING THE ENDURING QUESTIONS

1. What is the "right to privacy"?

A right, found by the Supreme Court in a 1965 case about contraception, in which the use of contraception (and later, abortion and gay sex) was protected by a "zone of privacy" that derived not from any explicit constitutional rule but from the "penumbras and emanations" of various parts of the Bill of Rights.

2. Should numerical goals be used to ensure that students and workers are drawn from every racial group?

Numerical goals, or quotas, cannot be used by public organizations, such as tax-supported universities, but race can be a "plus factor" in deciding whom to admit.

3. What limits can be placed on abortions?

The government may deny the use of federal funds to pay for abortions except when the life of the mother is at stake; it can impose a 24-hour waiting period; it can require that teenagers obtain the consent of a parent or of a judge; and it can allow the distribution of pamphlets that discuss alternatives to abortion.

Online Resources: Civil Rights

 CourseMate

- Civil Rights Division of the Department of Justice: www.usdoj.gov
- Court cases: www.law.cornell.edu

Suggested Readings

Abraham, Henry J., and Barbara A. Perry, *Freedom and the Court*, 7th ed. New York: Oxford University Press, 1998. A comprehensive review of how the Constitution and the Supreme Court define civil rights and civil liberties.

Flexner, Eleanor. *Century of Struggle: The Women's Rights Movement in the United States*, rev. ed. Cambridge, Mass.: Harvard University Press, 1975. A historical account of the feminist movement and its political strategies.

Kluger, Richard. *Simple Justice*. New York: Random House/Vintage, 1977. Detailed and absorbing account of the school desegregation issue, from the Fourteenth Amendment to the *Brown* case.

Kull, Andrew. *The Color-Blind Constitution*. Cambridge, Mass.: Harvard University Press, 1992. Argues that the Supreme Court was wrong when it failed to declare that the Constitution was color-blind.

Mansbridge, Jane J. *Why We Lost the ERA*. Chicago: University of Chicago Press, 1986. Analyzes the politics of the Equal Rights Amendment.

Federalism

ENDURING QUESTIONS

1. **What is "sovereignty," and where is it located in American government?**

2. **How does the Constitution divide power between the state and federal governments?**

3. **How has that division changed since the first days of the Republic?**

Since the adoption of the Constitution in 1787, the single most persistent source of political conflict has been the relations between the national and state governments. The political conflict over slavery, for example, was intensified because some state governments condoned or supported slavery, while others took action to discourage it. The proponents and opponents of slavery thus had territorial power centers from which to carry on the dispute. Other issues, such as the regulation of business and the provision of social welfare programs, were largely fought, for well over a century, in terms of "national interest" versus "states' rights." Even after these debates had ended—almost invariably with a decision favoring the national government—the administration and financing of the resulting programs usually involved a large role for the states. In short, federalism has long been a central feature of American politics. It continues to be so even today, when many Americans think of the government in Washington as vastly powerful and state governments as weak or unimportant.

From time to time, the president and the Supreme Court may try to return some powers to the states, but usually with little effect. Washington has become more powerful and the states less so, but that does not mean the states are meaningless. They employ over six times as many government workers and imprison nine times as many inmates as does the federal government. Washington has become stronger, but the states still control most of what happens in transportation, law enforcement, public education, land-use controls, and much of the newest efforts in health care.

Governmental Structure

Federalism *A political system in which ultimate authority is shared between a central government and state or regional governments.*

Federalism refers to a political system in which local (territorial, regional, provincial, state, or municipal) units of government—whose existence is specifically protected—as well as a national government, make final decisions on at least some governmental activities.[1] Almost every nation in the world has local units of government of some kind, if for no other reason than to decentralize the administrative burdens of governing. But these governments are not federal unless the local units exist independently of the preferences of the national government and can make decisions on at least some matters without regard to those preferences (see Figure 5.1). The most important federal systems today are found in the United States, Canada, Australia, India, Germany, and Switzerland. In the United States, highways and some welfare programs are largely state functions (though they use federal money), while education, policing, and land-use controls are primarily local functions, controlled by cities, counties, or special districts.

The special protection that local governments enjoy in a federal system derives in part from the constitution of the country but also from the habits, preferences, and dispositions of the citizens and the actual distribution of political power in society. If the American Constitution were the only guarantee of the independence of the American states, the states would long ago have become mere administrative subunits of the government in Washington. Their independence depends in large measure on the commitment of Americans to the idea of local self-government and on the fact that Congress consists of people who are selected by and responsive to local constituencies.

Though the national government has come to possess vast powers, it exercises many of those powers through state governments. Many of us forget that "the government in Washington" spends much of its money and enforces most of its rules not on citizens directly, but on local units of government. A large part of the welfare system, all of the interstate highway system, virtually every aspect of programs to improve cities, the largest part of the effort to supply jobs to the unemployed, the entire program to clean up our water, and even much of our military power (in the form of the National Guard) are enterprises in which the

Figure 5.1   Lines of Power in Three Systems of Government

UNITARY SYSTEM

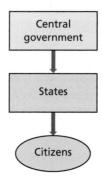

- Power centralized
- State or regional governments derive authority from central government
- Examples: Great Britain, France

FEDERAL SYSTEM

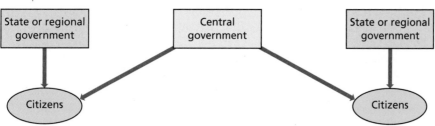

- Power divided between central and local, state, or regional governments
- Both the central government and the constituent governments act directly upon the citizens
- Both must agree to constitutional change
- Examples: Canada, United States since adoption of Constitution

CONFEDERAL SYSTEM (or CONFEDERATION)

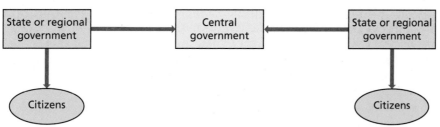

- Power held by independent states
- Central government is a creature of the constituent governments
- Examples: United States under the Articles of Confederation

national government does not govern so much as it seeks—by regulation, grant, plan, argument, and cajolery—to get the states to govern in accordance with nationally stated (though often vaguely defined) goals.

 So What?

Everybody knows that this country has states and cities. Why think about it? For two reasons. First, federalism affects the public policies we confront. To some critics, federalism means allowing states to block action, prevent progress, upset national plans, protect powerful local interests, and cater to the self-interest of hack politicians.[2] By contrast, others argue that the "virtue of the federal system lies in its ability to develop and maintain mechanisms vital to the perpetuation of the unique combination of governmental strength, political flexibility, and individual liberty, which has been the central concern of American politics."[3]

So diametrically opposed are these views that one wonders whether they refer to the same subject. They do, of course, but they are stressing different aspects of the same phenomenon. Whenever the opportunity to exercise political power is widely available (as among the fifty states, three thousand counties, and many thousands of municipalities), different people in different places will invariably use that power for different purposes. There is no question that allowing states and cities to make autonomous, binding political decisions will allow some people in some places to maintain racial segregation, protect vested interests, and facilitate corruption. It is equally true, however, that this arrangement also enables other people in other places to pass laws that attack segregation, regulate harmful economic practices, and purify politics—often long before these ideas gain national support or become national policy. Where you live affects what you get in schooling, drug laws, the death penalty, and the right to carry guns.

Second, federalism helps mobilize political activity. Unlike Don Quixote, most citizens do not tilt at windmills. They are more likely to become involved in organized political activity if they feel there is a reasonable chance of having a practical effect. The chances of that are greater when there are many elected officials and independent governmental bodies, each with a relatively small constituency, than when there are few elected officials, most of whom have the nation as a whole for a constituency. There are over 500,000 popularly elected state and local officials in this country. In short, a federal system, by virtue of the decentralization of authority, lowers the cost of organized political activity; a unitary system (such as in Great Britain or France), because of the centralization of authority, raises the cost of organizing protests and thus discourages local groups from challenging governmental decisions.

It is hard to say whether the Framers, when they wrote the Constitution, knew how it might affect either public policy or political participation. Many of the interesting questions had to be settled by over a century of protracted, often bitter, conflict.

How We Compare

American-Style Federalism

The United States has always had a federal form of government. By contrast, most of the nearly 200 nations in existence today have never had a federal form of government.

Depending on how stringent are the criteria used to delineate federal from unitary systems, the United States is one of a dozen to two dozen nations that now have federal forms of government: America, Australia, Belgium, Brazil, Canada, Ethiopia, Germany, India, Malaysia, Mexico, Nigeria, Pakistan, Russia, South Africa, Spain, and Switzerland are on nearly every expert's list of federal nations.

But some of these nations (for instance, Belgium, Spain, and South Africa) once had unitary systems, and many nations that have federal forms of government are multiparty parliamentary democracies. By contrast, American-style federalism has shaped and been shaped by the country's separation-of-powers system (see Chapter 2) and its two-party electoral system.

In some federal nations, public opinion favors the national government over subnational governments: People in these countries tend to trust their national governments as much or more than they trust other levels of government; however, Americans tend to trust their state and local governments more than they trust Washington.

Sources: "Trust in Government Remains Low," Gallup Organization, September 2008; Richard Cole and John Kincaid, "Public Opinion on U.S. Federal and Intergovernmental Issues," *Publiius* 36, Summer 2006, pp. 443-459; John Kincaid and G. Alan Tarr, eds., *Constitutional Origins, Structure, and Change in Federal Countries* (Montreal: McGill-Queens Press, 2005); Pradeep Chhibber and Ken Kollman, *The Formation of National Party Systems: Federalism and Party Competition in Canada, Great Britain, India, and the United States* (Princeton: Princeton University Press, 2004).

The Founding

The general intention of the Framers seems clear: Federalism was a device to protect personal liberty. They feared that placing final political authority in any set of hands—even those of persons popularly elected—would so concentrate power as to risk tyranny. They had seen what happened, however, when independent states tried to form a confederal system, as under the Articles of Confederation. The alliance among the states that existed from 1776 to 1787 was a **confederation**; that is, a system of government in which the people create state governments that in turn create and operate a national government. Because the national government in a confederation derives its powers from the states, it is dependent on their continued cooperation for its survival. By 1786, that cooperation was barely forthcoming. What the states had put together, they could—and did—take apart.

A Bold New Plan

A *federation*—or a "federal republic," as the Framers called it—derives its powers directly from the people, as do the state governments. As the Framers envisioned it, both levels of government, national and state, would have certain powers, but neither would have supreme authority over the other. It was an entirely new plan for

Confederation or **confederal system** *A political system in which states or regional governments retain ultimate authority except for those powers that they expressly delegate to a central government. The United States was a confederation from 1776 to 1787 under the Articles of Confederation.*

which no historical precedent existed. Nor did the Framers have a very clear idea of how it would work in practice, though they assumed from the outset that the national government would have only those powers granted by the Constitution. The Tenth Amendment was added to the Constitution only as an afterthought,[4] to allay fears that something else was intended. The amendment stipulates that "the powers not delegated to the United States by the Constitution, nor prohibited by it to the states, are reserved to the states respectively, or to the people."

Elastic Language

The need to reconcile the competing interests of large and small states and of northern and southern states, especially as they affected the organization of Congress, was sufficiently difficult without trying to spell out exactly the relationship that ought to exist between the national and the state systems. Though some clauses bearing on federal-state relations were reasonably clear, other clauses were quite vague. The Framers knew that they could not make an exact and exhaustive list of everything the federal government was empowered to do; circumstances would change and new exigencies would arise. Thus they added the following so-called elastic language to Article I: Congress shall have the power to "make all laws which shall be necessary and proper for carrying into execution the foregoing powers."

The Framers themselves carried away from Philadelphia different views of federalism. One view was championed by Alexander Hamilton. Because the people had created the national government, because the laws and treaties made pursuant to the Constitution were "the supreme law of the land" (Article VI), and because the most pressing needs were the development of a national economy and the conduct of foreign affairs, Hamilton thought that the national government was the superior and leading force in political affairs, and that its powers ought to be broadly defined and liberally construed.

The other view, championed by Thomas Jefferson (who had not attended the convention because he was serving abroad as minister to France), was that the federal government, though important, was the product of an agreement among the states. And though "the people" were the ultimate sovereigns, the principal threat to their liberties was likely to come from the national government. Thus Jefferson believed that the powers of the federal government should be narrowly construed and strictly limited. (James Madison, a strong supporter of national supremacy at the convention, later shifted his views and became a champion of states' rights.)

Hamilton argued for a strong federal government or *national supremacy*; Jefferson argued for *states' rights*. Though their differences were greater in theory than in practice, the differing interpretations they offered of the Constitution were to shape political debate in this country until well into the 1960s.

The History of Federalism

The Civil War settled one part of the argument over national supremacy versus states' rights. The war's outcome made it clear that the national government was supreme, its sovereignty derived directly from the people, and thus the states could not lawfully secede from the Union. But virtually every other aspect of the national supremacy issue was debated until the mid-twentieth century.

The Supreme Court Speaks

As arbiter of what the Constitution means, the Supreme Court became the focal point of that debate. In Chapter 12 we shall see how the Court made its decisions. For now it is enough to know that during the formative years of the new republic, the Supreme Court was led by a staunch and brilliant advocate of the Hamiltonian position, Chief Justice John Marshall. In a series of decisions, he and the Court vigorously defended the national supremacy view of the newly formed national government.

The most important decision came in 1819, in a case known as *McCulloch v. Maryland*, which arose when a branch of the Bank of the United States, created by Congress, refused to pay a state tax. The Supreme Court, in a unanimous decision, answered two questions in ways that expanded the powers of Congress and confirmed the supremacy of the federal government in the exercise of these powers.

The first question was whether Congress had the right to set up a bank, or any other corporation, because such a right is nowhere explicitly mentioned in the Constitution. Chief Justice Marshall ruled that because the Constitution empowers the national government to manage money—to lay and collect taxes, issue a currency, and borrow funds—Congress may reasonably decide that chartering a national bank is "necessary and proper" for carrying out these specified powers. Marshall's words were carefully chosen to endow the **necessary-and-proper clause** (sometimes called the "elastic clause") with the widest possible sweep:

> Let the end be legitimate, let it be within the scope of the Constitution, and all means which are appropriate, which are plainly adapted to that end, which are not prohibited, but consistent with the letter and spirit of the Constitution, are constitutional.[5]

The second question was whether a federal bank could lawfully be taxed by a state. To answer it, Marshall went back to first principles. The government of the United States was established not by the states, but by the people, and thus the federal government was supreme in the exercise of the powers conferred upon it. The federal government and its institutions must therefore be immune from destruction by the states. Because "the power to tax was the power to destroy," the states may not tax any federal instrument. Hence the Maryland law was unconstitutional.

Thus the federal government won the case. Half a century later, the Supreme Court decided that what was sauce for the goose was sauce for the gander—that the federal government, for its part, could not tax state instrumentalities. That meant that if you earned interest from a municipal bond, you did not have to pay federal income tax on it, just as you do not have to pay state income tax on interest from a United States bond. But, in 1988, the Supreme Court changed its mind. Now Congress is free to tax interest on municipal bonds, although so far it hasn't.[6]

Though the Supreme Court may decide a case, it does not always settle an issue. The battle over states' rights versus national supremacy continued to rage, ultimately leading to the Civil War. Ironically, the war had an effect opposite to

Necessary-and-proper clause or elastic clause *The final paragraph of Article 1, section 8, of the Constitution, which authorizes Congress to pass all laws "necessary and proper" to carry out the enumerated powers. Sometimes called the "elastic clause" because of the flexibility that it provides to Congress.*

what the southern states had hoped for. The necessities of war led to an expansion of the powers of the Union leaders, and their victory in turn brought about an enlargement of the powers of the federal government.

Nullification and War

Nullification *A theory first advanced by James Madison and Thomas Jefferson that the states had the right to "nullify" (that is, declare null and void) a federal law that, in the states' opinion, violated the Constitution. The theory was revived by John C. Calhoun of South Carolina in opposition to federal efforts to restrict slavery. The North's victory in the Civil War determined once and for all that the federal union is indissoluble and that states cannot declare acts of Congress unconstitutional, a view later confirmed by the Supreme Court.*

The struggle over states' rights took center stage with the doctrine of **nullification**. This word refers to the claimed ability of the states to declare a federal law null and void if, in their opinion, it violates the Constitution. The doctrine was first proposed by Jefferson and Madison as part of their opposition to a 1798 federal law that allowed newspaper editors to be punished if they published stories critical of the federal government. John C. Calhoun of South Carolina developed a more radical version of the doctrine as a way of blocking a federal tariff and, later, federal efforts to restrict slavery. Calhoun argued that if Washington attempted to ban slavery, the states had the right to nullify such a law.

The issue was finally settled by the Civil War. The northern victory meant that the Union could not be dissolved and that states could not declare acts of Congress unconstitutional, a conclusion later affirmed by the Supreme Court.[7]

Dual Federalism

Dual federalism *A constitutional theory that the national government and the state governments each have defined areas of authority, especially over commerce.*

After the Civil War, the debate about the meaning of federalism focused on the interpretation of the commerce clause (Article I, section 8) of the Constitution. From this debate emerged the doctrine of **dual federalism**, which held that though the national government was supreme in its sphere, the states were equally supreme in theirs, and that these two spheres of action could and should be kept separate.

Applied to commerce, the concept of dual federalism implied that there was such a thing as *inter*state commerce, which Congress could regulate, and *intra*state commerce, which only the states could regulate, and that the Supreme Court could define each. For a long period, the Court tried to define interstate commerce by the kind of business that was being conducted. But such product-based decisions were difficult to sustain. For example, was the sale of life insurance interstate or intrastate commerce? In 1869, the Court decided it was the latter, even though life insurance companies were becoming huge national businesses. In time, the effort to find clear principles that distinguished interstate from intrastate commerce was pretty much abandoned. Commerce was like a stream flowing through the country, drawing to itself contributions from thousands of scattered enterprises and depositing its products in millions of individual homes. The Supreme Court began to permit the federal government to regulate almost anything that affected this stream, so that by the 1940s not only had farming and manufacturing been redefined as part of interstate commerce,[8] but even the janitors and window washers in buildings that housed companies engaged in interstate commerce were considered to be part of that stream.[9]

The current Court interpretation of various laws pertaining to commerce is immensely complex, difficult to summarize, and impossible to explain. It would be only a mild overstatement, however, to say that the doctrine of dual federalism is almost extinct.

The States Reclaim Some Authority

In recent years, the Supreme Court, in a series of five-to-four decisions, has begun to breathe life back into the idea that the states have constitutional authority that Congress cannot set aside. In 1992, it struck down a federal law that dictated how states regulate radioactive waste within their borders; in 1995, it said that the power of Congress to regulate interstate commerce did not give it the right to ban handguns from being carried within one thousand feet of a school; in 1997, it refused to let Congress require local enforcement officers to run background checks on people buying handguns; and in 2000, it denied to Congress the authority to allow women who had been the victims of rape or domestic violence to sue their abusers in federal court.[10]

The Court was developing (or reviving) two general rules about how much authority Congress can exert over the states. The first is that "the Constitution requires a distinction between what is truly national and what is truly local." Among the things that are "truly local" is local law enforcement. The second is that the power of Congress to regulate local activities depends on their being part of interstate commerce, by which the Court means economic activities that cross state lines. A gun carried near a school, a background check on a local gun buyer, or a lawsuit brought by a woman against an attacker are not economic activities that warrant congressional action. (By contrast, the Supreme Court refused to overturn a law that made it a federal crime to cross a state line for the purpose of engaging in violence against women. When someone crosses a state boundary, he engages in interstate commerce; when he acts only locally, he does not.)

It is too early to tell whether these court cases, all decided by narrow majorities, will restore to authority the Tenth Amendment to the Constitution that for a century or more has become relatively meaningless. It reserves to the states and the people powers "not delegated to the United States." It has, until recently, become irrelevant because the Court almost always held that Congress's power to regulate interstate commerce gave to Washington all the authority it needs. Now the Court is not so sure.

The Division of Powers: Federal and State

What keeps the police, the schools, and land-use controls essentially in state and local hands? Two things: popular beliefs and a localistic Congress. The people have made it very clear that they want local control over the police and schools (and to a lesser extent over the use of land); by contrast, they have been quite willing to allow the federal government to regulate local business activity. These popular desires become powerful because members of Congress act in accordance with them. Any proposal for federal regulation of local police forces would immediately be met by objections in Congress that this would create a "national police force" and reduce the degree of local self-government. Any effort to pass federal regulations regarding the content of local school curricula would confront equally strong congressional resistance.

In fact, the police, schools, and land-use authorities have been affected by federal regulations. This has happened in two ways despite the overwhelming preference for local control. First, federal courts, by their interpretations of the Constitution, have profoundly shaped these local institutions. School desegregation was ordered by the courts; in some cases, such as Boston, the implementation of these orders led federal judges to supervise countless details of local school policies—what supplies to buy, where to build schools, what teachers to hire, and the like. Police and fire departments have been ordered to alter their hiring and training policies in order to ensure that women and minorities are given access to jobs in these agencies. Judges are not elected, so they can ignore local preferences when, in their opinion, certain constitutional rights are at stake.

The other way in which federal regulations have reduced local control over local governmental services has been by the development of federal grants-in-aid. This is often called *fiscal federalism.*

Fiscal Federalism

The first federal grants to the states began even before the Constitution was adopted, in the form of land grants made by the national government to the states in order to finance education. (State universities all over the country were built with the proceeds from the sale of these land grants; hence the phrase *land-grant colleges.*) Land grants were also made to support the building of wagon roads, canals, railroads, and flood-control projects.

Grants-in-aid *Federal funds provided to states and localities. Grants-in-aid are typically provided for airports, highways, education, and major welfare services.*

Cash **grants-in-aid** began almost as early. Grants-in-aid programs remained few in number and small in cost until the twentieth century. The great growth began in the 1960s: between 1960 and 1966, federal grants to the states doubled; from 1966 to 1970, they doubled again; between 1970 and 1975, they doubled yet again. By 2009, they amounted to more than $560 billion a year and were disbursed through more than four hundred separate programs. The five largest programs accounted for more than half the money spent and indicated the new priorities that federal policy had come to serve: housing assistance for low-income families, Medicaid, highway construction, services to the unemployed, and welfare programs for mothers with dependent children and for the disabled.

The grants-in-aid system, once under way, grew rapidly because it helped state and local officials resolve a dilemma. On the one hand, they wanted access to the superior taxing power of the federal government. On the other hand, prevailing constitutional interpretation, at least until the late 1930s, held that the federal government could not spend money for purposes not authorized by the Constitution. The solution was, obviously, to have federal money put into state hands: Washington would pay the bills; the states would run the programs.

Federal money seemed to state officials to be "free money." If Alabama could get Washington to put up the money for improving navigation on the Tombigbee River, then the citizens of the entire nation, not just Alabama, would pay for it. Of course, if Alabama gets money for such a purpose, every state will want it (and will get it). Even so, it was still an attractive political proposition: the governor of Alabama did not have to propose, collect, or take responsibility for federal taxes. Indeed, he could denounce the federal government for being profligate in its use of the people's money. Meanwhile, he would cut the ribbon in opening the new dam on the Tombigbee.

The States and the Constitution

The Framers made some attempt to define the relations between the states and the federal government and how states were to relate to one another. The following points were made in the original Constitution—before the Bill of Rights was added.

Restrictions on Powers of the States

States may not make treaties with foreign nations, coin money, issue paper currency, grant titles of nobility, pass a bill of attainder or an ex post facto law,[a] or, without the consent of Congress, levy any taxes on imports or exports, keep troops and ships in time of peace, or enter into an agreement with another state or with a foreign power. [Art. I, sec. 10]

Guarantees by the Federal Government to the States

The national government guarantees to every state a "republican form of government" and protection against foreign invasion and (provided the states request it) protection against domestic insurrection. [Art. IV, sec. 4]

An existing state will not be broken up into two or more states or merged with all or part of another state without the state's consent. [Art. IV, sec. 3]

Congress may admit new states into the Union. [Art. IV, sec. 3]

Taxes levied by Congress must be uniform throughout the United States; they may not be levied on some states but not others. [Art. I, sec. 8]

The Constitution may not be amended to give states unequal representation in the Senate. [Art. V]

Rules Governing How States Deal with Each Other

"Full faith and credit" shall be given by each state to the laws, records, and court decisions of other states. (For example, a civil case settled in the courts of one state cannot be retried in the courts of another.) [Art. IV, sec. 1]

The citizens of each state shall have the "privileges and immunities" of the citizens of every other state. (No one is quite sure what this is supposed to mean.) [Art. IV, sec. 2]

If a person charged with a crime by one state flees to another, he or she is subject to extradition— that is, the governor of the state that finds the fugitive is supposed to return the person to the governor of the state that has charged him or her. [Art. IV, sec. 2]

---

[a]For the definition of bill of attainder and ex post facto law, see the box on page 25.

Because every state had an incentive to ask for federal money to pay for local programs, it would be very difficult for one state to get money without every state getting some. The senator from Alabama who votes for the project to improve navigation on the Tombigbee will have to vote in favor of projects improving navigation on every other river in the country if he expects his Senate colleagues to support his request. Federalism as practiced in the United States means that when

Security personnel demonstrate a new backscatter imaging device, purchased with funding from the American Recovery and Reinvestment Act, at O'Hare International Airport in Chicago on March 15, 2010.

Washington wants to send money to one state or congressional district, it must send money to many states and districts.

Rise of Federal Activism

Until the 1960s, most federal grants-in-aid were conceived by or in cooperation with the states and were designed to serve essentially state purposes. Large blocs of voters and a variety of organized interests would press for grants to help farmers, build highways, or support vocational education. During the 1960s, however, an important change occurred: The federal government began devising grant programs based less on what states were demanding and more on what federal officials perceived to be important *national* needs (see Figure 5.2). Federal officials, not state and local ones, were the principal proponents of grant programs to aid the urban poor, combat crime, reduce pollution, and deal with drug abuse. Some of these programs even attempted to bypass the states, providing money directly to cities or even to local citizen groups. These were worrisome developments for governors who were accustomed to being the conduit for money on its way from Washington to local communities.

The Intergovernmental Lobby

State and local officials, both elected and appointed, began to form an important new lobby—the intergovernmental lobby—made up of mayors, governors, superintendents of schools, state directors of public health, county highway commissioners, local police chiefs, and others who had come to count on federal funds.[11] In 2009, lobbyists representing state and local employees and public officials spent over $80 million to influence legislation. The purpose of this intergovernmental lobby was the same as that of any private lobby: to get more money with fewer strings attached.

> ### Figure 5.2   The Changing Purposes of Federal Grants to State and Local Governments

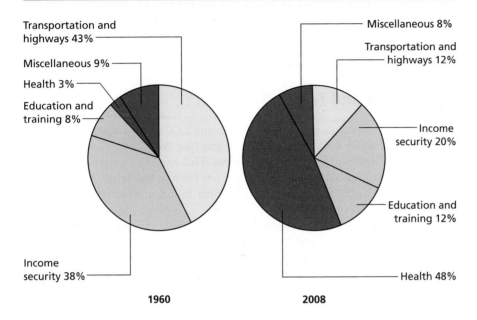

Transportation and highways 43%

Miscellaneous 9%

Health 3%

Education and training 8%

Income security 38%

1960

Miscellaneous 8%

Transportation and highways 12%

Income security 20%

Education and training 12%

Health 48%

2008

Note: Totals may not add up to 100 percent because of rounding.

Source: Harold H. Stanley and Richard G. Niemi, *Vital Statistics on American Politics 2007–2008* (Washington, D.C.: CQ Press, 2008), 335.

Categorical Grants Versus Block Grants

The effort to loosen the strings took the form of shifting, as much as possible, the federal aid from categorical grants to block grants or to revenue sharing. A **categorical grant** is one for a specific purpose defined by federal law: to build an airport or a college dormitory, for example, or to make welfare payments to low-income mothers. Such grants usually require that the state or locality put up money to "match" some part of the federal grant, though the amount of matching funds can be quite small. Governors and mayors complained about these categorical grants because their purposes were often so narrow that it was impossible for a state to adapt federal grants to local needs.

One response to this problem was to consolidate several categorical or project grant programs into a single **block grant** devoted to some general purpose and with fewer restrictions on its use. For example, several specific programs to improve cities were brought together into Community Development Block Grants. Block grants (sometimes called "special revenue sharing" or "broad-based aid") began in the mid-1960s. By 2004, block grants accounted for approximately 15 percent of all federal aid programs.[12]

Categorical grant *A federal grant for a specific purpose defined by federal law: to build an airport, for example, or to make welfare payments to low-income mothers. Such grants usually require that the state or locality put up money to "match" some part of the federal grant, though the amount of matching funds can be quite small.*

Block grant *Grant of money from the federal government to states for programs in certain general areas rather than for specific kinds of programs.*

In theory, block grants were supposed to give states and cities considerable freedom in deciding how to spend the money while helping to relieve their tax burdens. To some extent, they did. However, neither the goal of "no strings" nor the one of tax relief was really attained. First, the amount of money available from federal grants did not grow as fast as the states had hoped. Second, the federal government steadily increased the number of strings attached to the spending of this supposedly "no strings" money.

Federal Aid and Federal Control

Federal aid has become so important for state and local governments that mayors and governors, along with others, began to fear that Washington was well on its way to controlling local levels of government. This would jeopardize the constitutional protection of state government (as put forth in the Tenth Amendment) as a result of strings being attached to the grants-in-aid on which the states were increasingly dependent.

Mandates *Rules imposed by the federal government on the states as requirements that the states pay the costs of certain nationally defined programs.*

Conditions of aid *Federal rules attached to the grants that states receive. States must agree to abide by these rules in order to receive the grants.*

There are two kinds of federal controls on state government activities: **mandates** and **conditions of aid** (see the box on page 91). The states and the federal government, not surprisingly, disagree about the costs and benefits of such controls. Members of Congress and federal officials feel they have an obligation to develop uniform national policies with respect to important matters and to prevent states and cities from misspending federal tax dollars. State officials, on the other hand, feel that these national rules fail to take into account diverse local conditions, require the states to do things that the states must then pay for, and create serious inefficiencies. For example, in 1973 Congress passed—with little debate—a law forbidding discrimination against disabled people in any program receiving federal aid. Under pressure from organizations representing people who are disabled, federal agencies interpreted this law broadly, issuing regulations that required city transit systems receiving federal aid to equip their buses and subway cars with devices to lift wheelchairs on board. Although people who are disabled were pleased, state and local officials took a different view. The mayor of New York at that time, Edward Koch, argued that rebuilding existing buses and subways and buying new ones would make each trip by a wheelchair rider cost $38. It would be cheaper, he said, for the city to give every disabled person free taxicab rides, but the federal regulations would not permit that.[13] (In 1981, the Reagan administration relaxed the requirement that buses be able to lift wheelchairs aboard.)

In short, local officials discovered that "free" federal money was not quite free after all. In the 1960s, federal aid seemed entirely beneficial; what mayor or governor would not want such money? But just as local officials found it attractive to do things that another level of government then paid for, in time federal officials learned the same thing. Passing laws to meet the concerns of national constituencies—and leaving the cities and states to pay the bills and manage the problems—began to seem attractive to members of Congress.

Congress finally decided to draw the line on mandates. In 1995, it passed and President Clinton signed the Unfunded Mandates Reform Act, which instructs the Congressional Budget Office (CBO) to decide whether any federal mandate

Federal Controls on State Activities

Mandates

Federal laws or court rulings *requiring* states and cities to take certain actions whether or not they receive federal aid.

- Most mandates concern civil rights and environmental protection.
- States must comply with federal standards regarding clean air, pure drinking water, and sewage treatment.

Conditions of Aid

Voluntary federal restrictions on state action: "If you don't want the strings, don't take the money."

- In practice these are hard to refuse because the typical state depends on federal grants for a quarter or more of its budget.
- Over the last few decades, the number of conditions attached to federal aid has increased dramatically.[a]

---

[a]*Statistical Abstracts of the United States, 1995*, p. 157.

requires the states to spend money beyond what they get from Washington. If the mandate would cost states and cities more than $50 million, the CBO must tell Congress how much. Then a member of Congress can object by raising a *procedural point of order.* It is not often that raising such a point will get Congress to change its mind, but the existence of the opportunity has induced Congress to make some modifications in bills it was considering. To prevent a point of order, congressional committees will revise their bills to reduce unfunded mandates. But this law has not yet had much effect on how regulatory agencies behave. Blocking Washington's effort to pass unfunded mandates has had modest success, but it has not really altered the tendency for the federal government to decide what is best for the states.

Rivalry Among the States

The more important federal money becomes to the states, the more likely they are to compete among themselves for the largest share of it. For a century or better, the growth of the United States—in population, business, and income—was concentrated in the Northeast. In recent decades, however, that growth—at least in population and employment, if not in income—has shifted to the South, Southwest, and Far West. This change has precipitated an intense debate over whether the federal government, by the way it distributes its funds and awards its contracts, is unfairly helping some regions and states at the expense of others. Journalists and politicians have dubbed the struggle as one between "Snowbelt" and "Sunbelt" states.

Whether in fact there is anything worth arguing about is far from clear. The federal government has had great difficulty in figuring out where it ultimately spends what funds and for what purposes. For example, a $1 billion defense contract may go to a company in California, but much of the money may actually be spent in Connecticut or New York because the prime contractor in California buys from subcontractors in other states. Whether federal funds actually affect the growth rate of the regions is even less clear. The uncertainty about the facts has not prevented a debate about the issue, however. That debate focuses on the *distributional formulas* written into federal laws by which block grants and other federal funds are allocated. These formulas take into account such factors as a county's or city's population, personal income in the area, and housing quality. A slight change in a formula can shift millions of dollars in grants in ways that favor either the older, declining cities of the Northeast or the newer, still-growing cities of the Southwest.

With the advent of grants based on distributional formulas (as opposed to grants for a specific project), the results of the census, taken every ten years, assume monumental proportions. A city or state shown to be losing population may as a result forfeit millions of dollars in federal aid. There are more than one hundred programs (out of some five hundred federal grant programs in all) that distribute money on the basis of population. When the director of the census in 1960 announced figures showing that many big cities decreased in population, he was generally ignored. When he made the same announcement in 1980, 1990, and 2000, after the explosion in federal grants, he was roundly denounced by several big-city mayors.

Senators and representatives now have access to computers that can calculate instantly the effect on their states and districts of even minor changes in a formula by which federal aid is distributed. These formulas rely on objective measures, but the exact measure is selected with an eye to its political consequences. There is nothing wrong with this in principle because any political system must provide some benefit for everyone if it is to adhere. Given the competition among states in a federal system, however, the struggle over allocation formulas becomes especially acute. The results of these struggles are sometimes plausible, as when Congress decides to distribute money intended to help disadvantaged local school systems based largely on the proportion of poor children in each school district. But sometimes the results are a bit strange, as when the formula for determining federal aid for mass transit gives New York, a city utterly dependent on mass transit, a federal subsidy of 2 cents per transit passenger but gives Grand Rapids, a city that relies chiefly on the automobile, a subsidy of 45 cents per passenger.[14]

Evaluating Federalism

The tensions in the federal system do not arise from one level of government or another being callous or incompetent but from the kinds of political demands with which each must cope. Because of these competing demands, federal and state officials find themselves in a bargaining situation in which each side is trying to get some benefit (solving a problem, satisfying a pressure group) while passing on to the other side most of the costs (taxes, administrative problems).

The bargains struck in this process used to favor local officials because members of Congress were essentially servants of local interests—they were elected by local political parties, they were part of local political organizations, and they supported local autonomy. Beginning in the 1960s, however, changes in American politics shifted the orientation of many members of Congress toward favoring Washington's needs over local needs.

Even when presidents say they believe in state authority, they rarely do much to improve it. President Eisenhower, though he believed in the states, created the interstate highway system, with nine out of every ten dollars that it cost coming from Washington. President Nixon suggested that many federal grants be given to the states with no strings attached, but many state officials objected because the strings increased their local power. President Reagan tried to divide government powers between the federal and state levels, but nobody could agree on what that division should be. President George W. Bush led an effort to weaken local control of schools by helping pass the No Child Left Behind Act, which threatens state-run schools with sanctions if they fail

Part of the interstate highway system built largely with federal funds.

to reduce gaps in academic achievement. And after the terrorist attacks on 9/11, Congress passed and President Bush signed a law, the Real ID Act, that in effect creates a national identity card.

The one significant reversal in federal policy came when the welfare reform act was passed in 1996 by a Republican Congress and signed by President Clinton. This bill (officially, the Personal Responsibility and Work Opportunity Reconciliation Act) turned over to the states the authority to run the federal welfare program. The old policy, Aid to Families with Dependent Children (AFDC), created in 1935, was largely run under federal rules. Beginning in 1996, Washington kept paying the bills, but the states made the rules, urging applicants to look for work before applying for benefits, and—in part because of the law—the welfare rolls dropped sharply.

However, in other policy areas, the conflict between the states and Washington is taking new turns. For example, after the Health Care and Education Reconciliation Act passed in 2010, a group of state attorneys general issued legal challenges; they claimed that the new federal law was unconstitutional because it requires people to purchase a particular product, namely health insurance.

A federal system may be untidy, but in politics some things are more important than neatness. Federalism is a way of accommodating the differences in wants and beliefs of a diverse people without imposing an iron will on them. Americans agree on some issues and disagree on others. Federalism helps us stay together despite our ethnic, religious, and regional differences. The violent breakup of some former nations, such as Yugoslavia, shows what can happen when the central government attempts to rule without adjusting its policies to local preferences.

WHAT WOULD YOU DO?

MEMORANDUM

To: Representative Sue Kettl

From: Grace Viola, chief of staff

Subject: Faith-based preemption bill

As requested, I have researched state-funding policies. The main finding is that the state laws do hobble getting federal dollars to the religious groups that have been doing most of the actual recovery work. The immediate question before you is whether to sign on as a co-sponsor to the bill.

Arguments for:

1. Congress has already passed at least four laws that permit federal agencies to fund faith-based groups that deliver social services, subject to prohibitions against using public funds for proselytizing or such.

2. The faith-based organizations functioned as first responders when the hurricanes hit, and have since supplied billions of dollars worth of manpower and materials.

3. Some legal experts say that the existing laws already preempt the contrary state ones; besides, it polls great (75 percent in favor nationally, even higher in your district).

Arguments against:

1. You have traditionally argued in favor of states' rights and the separation of church and state.

2. Praiseworthy though their civic good works have been, some of the religious groups involved in the cleanup and recovery have beliefs and tenets

+

Friday,

Congress Debates Requiring States to Follow Feds' Lead on "Faith-Based" Hurricane Recovery Act

January 29
WASHINGTON, D.C.

Today the House begins debate on legislation requiring state governments to comply with federal laws on public funding for religious nonprofit organizations that deliver social services. In cities devastated by hurricanes, so-called faith-based organizations continue to play a major role in disaster recovery and rebuilding efforts. Federal laws already permit these groups to receive federal aid, but a recent audit found that contrary state laws were impeding their implementation. . . .

that seem discriminatory (a few even refuse to hire people of other faiths).

3. Expressly preempting more state laws could come back to bite us when it comes to state laws that we favor over contrary federal ones.

Your Decision:

Support bill _____   Oppose bill _____

SUMMARY

States participate actively both in determining national policy and in administering national programs. Moreover, they reserve to themselves or the localities within them important powers over public services, such as schooling and law enforcement, and important public decisions, such as land-use control, that in a unitary system are dominated by the national government.

How one evaluates federalism depends largely on how one evaluates the competing criteria of the equal treatment of citizens and local participation in government. Federalism means that citizens living in different parts of the country will be treated differently, not only in spending programs, such as welfare, but in legal systems that assign varying penalties for similar offenses or that differentially enforce civil-rights laws. But federalism also means that there are more opportunities for participation in making decisions—in influencing what is taught in the schools and in deciding where to build highways and government projects. Indeed, differences in public policy—that is, unequal treatment—are in large part the result of participation in decision making. It is difficult, perhaps impossible, to have more of one of these values without having less of the other.

Politics and public policy have become decidedly more nationalized of late, with the federal government, and especially the federal courts, imposing increasingly uniform standards on the states in the form of mandates and conditions of aid. Efforts to reverse this trend by shifting to block grants have only partially succeeded.

RECONSIDERING THE ENDURING QUESTIONS

1. What is "sovereignty," and where is it located in American government?

Sovereignty means supreme or ultimate political authority; a sovereign government is legally and politically independent of any other government. But sovereignty, thus defined, is nowhere to be found in the United States. The federal government is dependent on the states for its senators and representatives and must defer to state authority on some matters, such as commerce within a single state. The states are dependent on the federal government for power over foreign and military relations and commerce among the states and with foreign nations.

2. How does the Constitution divide authority between the state and federal governments?

It does not. The Constitution, with a few exceptions, is silent on what powers the states should have other than a general statement that the powers "not delegated to the United States" are "reserved to the states" (Tenth Amendment). The Supreme Court has decided what this means in practice. Most of the time, it has expanded federal authority, but of late it has protected some state claims.

3. How has that division of powers changed since the first days of the Republic?

Washington has gained power, and the states have lost power. Even so, the states remain important. They choose senators and representatives, ask for and spend a lot of money from federal taxes, run programs dealing with highways and education (as well as many other areas), and oversee local government. But they do these things subject to many federal mandates and controls.

Online Resources: Federalism

 CourseMate

- State and local government: www.stateline.org
- Supreme Court decisions: www.findlaw.com/casecode/supreme.html
- Information on state governments: www.csg.org
- National Governors' Association: www.nga.org

Suggested Readings

Beer, Samuel H. *To Make a Nation: The Rediscovery of American Federalism.* Cambridge, Mass.: Harvard University Press, 1988. A profound account of the philosophical origins of American federalism.

Conlan, Timothy. *From New Federalism to Devolution.* Washington, D.C.: Brookings Institution, 1998. A masterful overview of the politics of federalism from Richard Nixon to Bill Clinton.

Diamond, Martin. *As Far As Republican Principles Will Admit: Essays by Martin Diamond.* Washington, D.C.: American Enterprise Institute, 1992. In Chapters 6 through 9, Diamond offers a brilliant analysis of what the Founders meant by federalism.

Greve, Michael. *Real Federalism.* Washington, D.C.: American Enterprise Institute, 1999. A thoughtful defense of the opportunity federalism offers for increasing citizen choice and state competition.

Grodzins, Morton. *The American System.* Chicago: Rand McNally, 1966. Argues that American federalism has always involved extensive sharing of functions between national and state governments.

Peterson, Paul E. *The Price of Federalism.* Washington, D.C.: Brookings Institution, 1995. A careful review of how modern federalism works.

Peterson, Paul E., Barry G. Rabe, and Kenneth K. Wong. *When Federalism Works.* Washington, D.C.: Brookings Institution, 1986. An analysis of how federal grants-in-aid programs actually work.

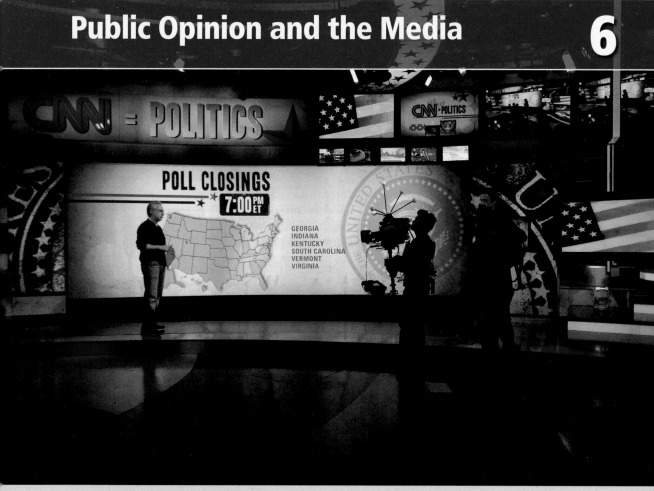

Public Opinion and the Media

6

ENDURING QUESTIONS

1. **Under the U.S. Constitution, how big a role should public opinion play in making policy?**

2. **What are the biggest sources of the political views of Americans?**

3. **What is meant by "liberal" and "conservative"?**

4. **Why is television news different from that in newspapers?**

5. **Are reporters biased in how they cover politics?**

I n the Gettysburg Address, Abraham Lincoln stated that the United States had a government "of the people, by the people, and for the people," which suggests that the government should do what the people want. If this is the case, it is puzzling that:

CourseMate

- The federal government often has a large budget deficit, but the people want a balanced budget.
- Courts order the busing of children to balance the schools racially, but the people oppose busing.

Jennifer S. Altman/WpN/UPPA/
Photoshot

97

- The Equal Rights Amendment to the Constitution was not ratified, but polls showed that most people supported it.
- The House of Representatives voted to impeach President Clinton even though most Americans opposed this.

Some people, reflecting on the many gaps between what the government does and what the people want, may become cynical and think our system is democratic in name only. That would be a mistake. There are very good reasons that government policy often appears to be at odds with public opinion.

First, the Framers of the Constitution did not try to create a government that would do from day to day "what the people want." They created a government for the purpose of achieving certain substantive goals. The Preamble to the Constitution lists six of these: "to form a more perfect union, establish justice, ensure domestic tranquility, provide for the common defense, promote the general welfare, and secure the blessings of liberty."

One means to achieve these goals was popular rule, as provided by the right of the people to vote for members of the House of Representatives (and later for senators and presidential electors). But other means were provided as well: representative government, federalism, the separation of powers, a Bill of Rights, and an independent judiciary. These were all intended to be *checks* on public opinion. In addition, the Framers knew that in a nation as large and diverse as the United States, there would rarely be any such thing as "public opinion"; rather, there would be many "publics" (that is, factions) holding many opinions. The Framers hoped that the struggle among these many publics would protect liberty (no one "public" would dominate) while at the same time permitting the adoption of reasonable policies that commanded the support of many factions.

Second, it is more difficult than one might suppose to know what the public thinks. We are so inundated these days with public-opinion polls that perhaps we assume that they reflect public opinion. That may be true on a few rather simple, clear-cut, and widely discussed issues, but it is not true for most matters on which government must act. The best pollsters know the limits of their methods, and citizens should know them as well.

Third, the more people are active in and knowledgeable about politics, the more weight their opinions carry in governmental affairs. For most of us, politics ranks way down on the list of things to think about, well below families, jobs, health, sweethearts, entertainment, and sports. Some people, however, are political activists who come to know as much about politics as the rest of us know about batting averages, soap operas, and car repair. Not only do these activists, or political elites, *know more* about politics than the rest of us, they *think differently* about it—they have different views and beliefs. The government attends more to the elite views than to the popular views, at least on many matters.

One important elite is the mass-communication media. The media—especially the national television networks, the news magazines, and the New York and Washington, D.C., newspapers—are shaped in part by the attitudes of the people who have been attracted into leading positions in journalism. The growth of the Internet and blogs has brought many more people into the ranks of political elites. Thousands of persons who most people never knew existed have acquired political influence by devoting their time to compiling facts and making arguments on the Web, there to be read by people who (mostly) agree with them. This has probably intensified the split between liberals and conservatives because each side now has so many more ways to acquire and strengthen their policy views. There has always been an adversarial relationship between those who govern and those who write, but events of recent decades have, as we shall see, made that conflict especially keen.

In the United States the media are accorded a degree of freedom greater than that found in almost any other nation, including other democracies. In England, for example, the laws governing libel are so strict that public figures frequently sue newspapers for defaming or ridiculing them—and they collect. But the law of libel in the United States is loose enough to permit intense and even inaccurate criticism of anybody who is in the public eye. The Freedom of Information Act (1966), together with a long tradition of leaking inside stories and writing memoirs about one's public service, virtually guarantee that in the United States very little can be kept very secret for very long. In sharp contrast, any past or present British government official can be punished for divulging to the press private government business.[1]

In America, radio and television stations are privately owned, and although the federal government licenses them, it does not have the power to censor or dictate the contents of routine stories. Until recently, the French government could censor or dictate to the broadcasting agencies, many of which are state owned.[2] We shall see, however, that the federal government's power to license broadcasters has been used, on occasion, to harass station owners who are out of favor with the White House.

Why Do We Distrust the Federal Government?

One aspect of public opinion worries many people. Since the early 1960s, there has been a more or less steady decline in the proportion of Americans who say they trust the government in Washington to do the right thing. In the past, polls showed that about three-quarters of us said we trusted Washington most of the time or just about always, but by 1980 that had declined sharply to about one-quarter (see Figure 6.1). The level of trust briefly rose during the Reagan administration but sank back down about the time he left office. Another measure pollsters use shows pretty much the same thing. In 1952, about one-third of us said we did not think public officials care much about what we think, but by 2008 that had risen to 60 percent.

Before we get too upset about this, we should remember that people are talking about government officials, not the system of government. Americans are much more supportive of the country and its institutions than Europeans are of theirs.

Even so, the decline in confidence in officials is striking. There are all sorts of explanations for why it happened. In the 1960s, there was our unhappy war in Vietnam; in the 1970s, President Nixon had to resign because of his involvement in the Watergate scandal; in the 1990s, President Clinton went through sexual scandals that led to his being impeached by the House of Representatives (but

So What?

You may think that there such a thing as "public opinion" and that this book will tell you what it is. Not quite. Let us begin with a story.

A few years ago some researchers at the University of Cincinnati asked twelve hundred local residents whether they favored passage of the Monetary Control Bill. About 21 percent said that they favored the bill, 25 percent said that they opposed it, and the rest said that they hadn't thought much about the matter or didn't know.

The members of Congress from Cincinnati would have been surprised to learn of this expression of "public opinion" from their constituents, for there was no such thing as the Monetary Control Bill. The researchers had made it up. Nor is there anything unusual about people in Cincinnati. A few years earlier, about 26 percent of the people questioned in a national survey also expressed opinions on the same piece of "legislation."

Ignorance (or an inclination to pretend that one is informed) is not limited to arcane bits of legislation. In any public opinion survey, only a small minority of voters will be able to tell you the name of the secretary of defense, the chief justice of the Supreme Court, or several prominent presidential candidates. Given this low level of name recognition, how much confidence should we place in the polls that presumably tell us what "the American people" think about our defense policy, the decisions of the Supreme Court, or the policies of presidential candidates?

There is not one big "public" that has one clear "opinion." We cannot talk about what "the public wants" or "the public demands." There are many publics—people who are men or women, whites or blacks, young or old, religious or nonreligious—who have views about what the government should do. And the views of these many publics, and of many categories within each public, vary enormously in accuracy, clarity, and consistency.

Even if people have heard of the matter, how we word the question can dramatically affect the answer we get. Suppose we want to know whether the public believes that the federal government should provide housing for people. One poll asked that question in three different ways. In the first example people were asked whether they agreed or disagreed with a one-sided statement ("The federal government should see to it that all people have adequate housing"). A majority agreed. In the second example people were given a choice between two statements, one favoring a federal housing policy (mentioned first) and the other favoring individual responsibility ("Each person should provide for his own housing"). Given this choice, a majority now opposed federal housing programs. In the third example the question was repeated, but this time with the individual-responsibility option mentioned first. Now more than 70 percent of the respondents opposed federal housing programs. Obviously just altering the *order* in which people are presented with options affects which option they choose and thus what "public opinion" is on housing programs.

Moreover, opinions on public issues may not be stable—that is, firmly held. In January and again in June of the same year, the same people were asked the same questions. The first had to do with how tough we should be in dealing with the Soviet Union, the second with whether spending should be cut on things like health and education programs. Many people gave one opinion in January and then a different one in June. Of those who said in January that we should cooperate more with the Soviet Union, one-quarter said in June that we should get tougher with the Soviets. Of those who said in January that the government should cut the services it provides, more than one-quarter said in June that they wanted to keep those services at the same level or expressed a middle-of-the-road position.

In sum, public opinion on many matters suffers from ignorance, instability, and sensitivity to the way the question is worded. This does not mean that the American people are ignorant, unstable, or gullible, only that most Americans do not find it worth their while to spend the amount of time thinking about politics that they spend on their jobs, families, and friends. Moreover, just because people do not think much about politics does not mean that democracy is impossible, only that it can work best when people are given relatively simple, clear-cut choices—like between Democrats and Republicans, or between one presidential candidate and another.

not convicted of that charge by the Senate); and, after 2003, President Bush's approval ratings declined as public distrust relating to his handling of the Iraq War became widespread.

But there is another way of looking at the matter. Maybe in the 1950s we had an abnormally *high* level of confidence in government, one that could never be expected to last no matter what any president did. After all, when President Eisenhower took office in 1952, we had won a war against fascism, overcome the Depression of the 1930s, possessed a near monopoly of the atom bomb, had a currency that was the envy of the world, and dominated international trade. Moreover, in those days not much was expected out of Washington. Hardly anybody thought that there should be important federal laws about civil rights, crime, illegal drugs, the environment, the role of women, highway safety, or almost anything else one now finds on the national agenda. Because nobody expected much out of Washington, nobody was upset that we did not get much out of it.

The 1960s and 1970s changed all of that. Domestic turmoil, urban riots, a civil-rights revolution, the war in Vietnam, economic inflation, and a new concern for the environment dramatically increased what we expected Washington to do. And because these problems are very difficult ones to solve, many people became convinced that our politicians could not do much.

All that changed on September 11, 2001, when hijacked airliners were crashed by terrorists into the World Trade Center in New York City and the Pentagon in Washington. There was an extraordinary outburst of patriotic fervor:

Figure 6.1 Trust in Government Index 1958–2008

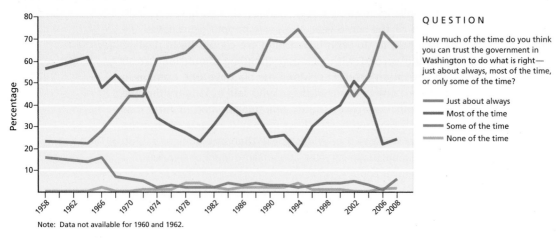

QUESTION

How much of the time do you think you can trust the government in Washington to do what is right—just about always, most of the time, or only some of the time?

— Just about always
— Most of the time
— Some of the time
— None of the time

Note: Data not available for 1960 and 1962.

Source: The National Election Studies, 1958–2008.

flags were displayed everywhere; fire and police heroes were widely celebrated; and there was strong national support for our going to war in Afghanistan to find the key terrorist, Osama bin Laden, and destroy the tyrannical Taliban regime that he supported. By November of that year, about half of all Americans of both political parties said they trusted Washington officials to do what is right most of the time—the highest level in many years. Well over 80 percent of the public approved of the job President George W. Bush was doing. This new level of support did not last, but the change does suggest that beneath our routine complaining about ordinary politics there still exists a strong passion for the country. Repeatedly, Americans used the same phrase to explain that passion: America stands for freedom.

The Origins of Political Attitudes

People take pride in having their own opinions—about politics as well as about music and movies. "Nobody tells me what to think," they say. But these same people lament the power of television and advertising: "The media manipulate the public," they argue, or "Television sells candidates the same way it sells soap." These views are a bit contradictory: If we all believe that we decide for ourselves what to think, then we can't all be the puppets of Madison Avenue.

The facts are a bit different from these popular conceptions. Our beliefs about politics are not entirely the result of independent thought and study; they reflect a variety of forces, some of which we may not even be aware. But neither is it the case that television seduces us into voting for a politician the way it might lure us into buying a bar of soap. To understand how we see the political world, we must look at what has been learned about the origin of political attitudes. Scholars call the process by which young people acquire such attitudes *political socialization.*

How We Compare

Opinions on Americans

It is not surprising that most Americans have a favorable view of Americans; but what opinion on Americans is held by people in other countries?

By the same token, a majority of Americans typically expresses confidence in the U.S. president; but do majorities in other nations share that confidence?

For several years now, the Pew Global Attitudes Project has conducted sophisticated, in-depth opinion polls in dozens of nations. Below are two sets of selected results from its 2009 survey.

Percent with "*a favorable view of the American people,*" 2009

Top Five		Bottom Five	
1. United States	90%	1. Turkey	14%
2. Kenya	87%	2. Pakistan	20%
		2. Palestinian Territory	20%

3. South Korea	83%	3. Argentina	38%
4. Nigeria	76%	4. Jordan	39%
5. France	75%	5. Egypt	40%

Percent with "*confidence in the U.S. President,*" 2009

Top Five & U.S.		Bottom Five	
1. Kenya	94%	1. Pakistan	13%
2. Germany	93%	2. Palestinian Territory	23%
4. Canada	88%	3. Jordan	31%
4. Nigeria	88%	4. Turkey	33%
5. Britain	86%	5. Russia	37%
11. United States	74%		

Source: Data from Pew Charitable Trusts.

The Role of the Family

The best-studied (though not necessarily the most important) case of opinion formation is that of party identification. Young people whose parents were Democrats tend to become Democrats; those whose parents were Republicans tend to become Republicans.[3] But the political views of young people do not merely reflect what they are taught by their parents. Recent evidence suggests that genetics strongly shape these views. We inherit as well as learn our political opinions. When we compare how identical twins (who are genetically the same) feel about politics with how fraternal twins (who share only half of their genes) think about politics, we discover that identical twins are much more likely to have similar views even if they were raised apart. About one-third of our political views come from genes and only about one-tenth from family influences.[4]

The ability of the family to inculcate a strong sense of party identification has declined in recent years. The proportion of citizens who say they consider themselves to be Democrats or Republicans has steadily declined since the early 1950s. This drop has been greatest among those who strongly identify with one party or

Poll *A survey of public opinion.*

Random sample *A sample selected in such a way that any member of the population being surveyed (e.g., all adults or voters) has an equal chance of being interviewed.*

another. In 1960, about three-quarters of the electorate identified with either the Republican or Democratic parties; by 2008, only about 60 percent claimed to be Democrats or Republicans. Accompanying this decline in partisanship has been a rise in the proportion of citizens describing themselves as independents. They were less than one-quarter of the 1960 electorate and nearly 40 percent of it in 2008.

Part of the decline in party identification results from the fact that young voters have always had a weaker sense of partisanship than older ones, and today there are, proportionally, a larger number of young voters than thirty or forty years ago. But the youthfulness of the population cannot explain all of the changes, for the decline in partisanship has occurred at all age levels. Moreover, those who reached voting age in the 1960s were less likely than those who came of age in the 1950s to acquire or maintain the party identification of their parents.[5] The decline in partisanship is real.

The Art of Public-Opinion Polling

A survey of public opinion—popularly called a **poll**—can provide us with a reasonably accurate measure of how people think, provided certain conditions are met. First, *the persons interviewed must be a* **random sample** of the entire population. (*Random* means that any given person, or any given voter or adult, must have an equal chance of being interviewed.) Most national surveys draw a sample of between a thousand and fifteen hundred persons by a process called stratified or multistage area sampling. The pollster makes a list of all geographic units in the country (say, all counties) and groups (or "stratifies") them by the sizes of their populations. The pollster then randomly selects units from each group or stratum in proportion to their total population. For example, if one stratum contains counties whose total population is 10 percent of the national population, then in the sample, 10 percent of the counties will be drawn from this stratum. Within each selected county, smaller and smaller geographical units (cities, towns, census tracts, blocks) are chosen and then, within the smallest unit, individuals are selected at random (by, for example, choosing the occupant of every fifth house). The key is to stick to the sample and not let people volunteer to be interviewed—volunteers often have views different from those who do not volunteer.

Second, *the questions must be comprehensible,* asking people about subjects of which they have some knowledge and some basis on which to form an opinion. Most people know, at least at election time, whom they would prefer as president; most people also have views about what constitute the most important national problems. But relatively few voters will have any opinion about our policy toward Bosnia (if indeed they have even heard of it) or about the investment tax credit. If everybody refused to answer questions about which they are poorly informed, no problem would arise, but unfortunately many of us like to pretend we know things that in fact we don't, or to be helpful to interviewers by inventing opinions on the spur of the moment.

Third, *the questions must be asked fairly*—in clear language, without the use of "loaded" or "emotional" words. They must give no indication of what the "right" answer is, but offer a reasonable explanation, where necessary, of the consequences of each possible answer. For example, in 1971, the Gallup poll asked people whether they favored a proposal "to bring home all U.S. troops [from Vietnam] before the end of the year." Two-thirds of the public agreed with that. Then the question was asked in a different way: Do you agree or disagree with a proposal to withdraw all U.S. troops by the end of the year "regardless of what happens there [in Vietnam] after U.S. troops leave"? In this form substantially less than half the public agreed.

Fourth, *the answer categories offered to a person must be carefully considered.* This is no problem when there are only two candidates for office—say, Barack Obama and John McCain—and you want only to know which one the voters prefer. But it can be a big problem when you want more complex information. For example, if you ask people (as does the Gallup Organization) whether they "approve" or "disapprove" of how the president is handling his job, you will get one kind of answer—let us say that 55 percent approve and 45 percent disapprove. On the other hand, if you ask them (as does the Harris Poll) how they rate the job the president is doing, "excellent, pretty good, only fair, or poor," you will get very different results. It is quite possible that only 46 percent will pick such positive answers as "excellent" or "pretty good," and the rest will pick the negative answers, "only fair" and "poor." If you are president, you can choose to believe Gallup (and feel pleased) or Harris (and be worried). The differences in the two polls do not arise from the competence of the two pollsters, but entirely from the choice of answers that they include with their questions.

Finally, remember that not every difference in answers is a significant difference. A survey is based on a sample of people. Select another sample, by equally randomized methods, and you might get slightly different results. This difference is called a **sampling error**, and its likely size can be computed mathematically. In general, the bigger the sample and the bigger the difference between the percentage of people giving one answer and the percentage giving another, the smaller the sampling error. If a poll of one thousand voters reveals that 47 percent favor we can be 95 percent certain that the *actual* proportion of *all* voters favoring a given candidate is within three percentage points of this figure—that is, it lies somewhere between 44 and 50 percent. In a close race an error of this size could be quite important. It could be reduced by using a bigger sample, but the cost of interviewing a sample big enough to make the error much smaller is huge.

As a result of sampling error and for other reasons, it is very hard for pollsters to predict the winner in a close election. From 1952 to 1998, every major national poll has in fact picked the winner of the presidential election, but there may have been some luck involved in such close races as the 1960 Kennedy-Nixon and the 1976 Carter-Ford contests. In 1980, the polls greatly underestimated the Reagan vote, partly because many voters made up their minds at the last minute and partly because a bigger percentage of Carter supporters decided not to vote at all. In 2000, the polls decided it was a dead heat.

Children are more independent of their parents in their policy preferences than in party identification. One reason for this is that our political ideology (that is, our core beliefs about what government should do) reflect our genes more than parental teaching. Whether we are liberal or conservative is in large part inherited. Sometimes that means we agree with our parents but other times (because of the way genes shape our views) that means we disagree with them.[6] The party label we embrace, on the other hand, seems to be largely learned from our parents. Like our parents we may be Democrats or Republicans, but unlike them we may be conservative Democrats or liberal Republicans.

Party identification is often influenced by a person's parents.

Sampling error *The difference between the results of two surveys or samples. For example, if one random sample shows that 60 percent of all Americans like cats and another random sample taken at the same time shows that 65 percent do, the sampling error is 5 percent.*

Effects of Religion

How the family forms and transmits political attitudes is not well understood, but one important factor seems to be its religious traditions. In general, Catholic families are somewhat more liberal, especially on economic issues, than white Protestant families, while Jewish families are decidedly more liberal on both economic and noneconomic issues than either.[7] Among northern whites, Protestants are likely to be Republican, Catholics are likely to be Democratic, and Jews are overwhelmingly Democratic.[8] This may strike some readers as strange, because in most elections and political debates no explicitly religious questions are at stake. But religion in the United States, and probably elsewhere, conveys to its adherents not simply a set of beliefs about God and morality but also a way of looking at human nature and human affairs. A religious tradition that emphasizes salvation through faith alone and the need to avoid personal dissipation and worldly sin is likely to imbue a different way of looking at politics than one that has an optimistic view of human nature, stresses the obligation to do good works, and is concerned as much about social justice as personal rectitude.

Because religious involvement is essentially a moral commitment, it is not surprising that born-again or evangelical Christians are likely to differ from other voters. If they think that the Bible should be taken literally as the word of God, they are more likely than those without this belief to oppose abortion, less likely to think that men and women should have equal roles, more likely to favor the ban on gays in the military, and less likely to self-identify as Democrats. But on a variety of issues—cuts in government spending and congressional term limits—there is very little difference between fundamentalist Christians and other voters.[9] Still, opinion surveys show that, since 1960, evangelical Christians have become more attached to Republican presidential candidates (except in 1976, when Jimmy Carter ran), while Jews and those without a religious orientation have been consistently supportive of the Democratic party.

Education

It is hard to think of a more powerful effect on public opinion than education, especially college and postgraduate schooling. Studies going back more than half a century show that attending college affects political attitudes, usually in a liberal direction, and that these changes persist after graduation.[10] Students entering college tend to have the same views as their parents, but four or five years later, their views have shifted.

One reason may be the influence of professors. Academics tend to be more liberal than members of other occupations; at the most prestigious schools, they are more liberal than at less celebrated ones; and in social studies, they are more

© Jim West/Alamy

liberal than in engineering or business.[11] Of course, students do not just soak up whatever professors say; moreover, many professors, both liberal and conservative, try to keep partisan politics out of their classes.

There are other factors at work as well. Students teach each other through campus organizations, political movements, and social contact. And much of college learning, even when taught in a politically neutral way, explains what might be wrong with the world as it is, offers models or ideals by which the world might be improved, and encourages critical thinking.

At one time, the liberalizing effect of college schooling had only a small impact because so few people went to college. In 1900, only 6 percent of Americans age seventeen had even graduated from high school, and less than 1 percent were college graduates. By 2008, over 86 percent of citizens over age 25 had graduated from high school, and nearly 30 percent were college graduates.[12] College has become as important as family and religion in shaping public opinion.

This fact is especially important when we try to understand the views of political elites. **Elite** does not mean people who are "better" than others; rather, they are people who have a large share of some valuable social resource such as money, prestige, or political power. Every society, capitalist or socialist, has political elites because in every one, a small number of people have more money, prestige, or power than do others.

American political elites have always been divided between liberals and conservatives, terms that we shall define in a moment. But that elite division tends to be a bit more extreme than the divisions among ordinary people. Elite liberals are often more liberal and elite conservatives are often more conservative than are the rank-and-file. Many women are feminists, but not many are as liberal as the feminist leaders of the National Organization for Women; many men are hunters, but not many are as conservative as the leaders of the National Rifle Association.

Elite (political) *An identifiable group of persons who possess a disproportionate share of some valued resource— such as money or political power.*

Table 6.1 Religion and Politics Among White Voters			
Which of these statements describes your view of the Bible? *The Bible is the actual word of God and is to be taken literally.* *The Bible is the word of God, but not everything should be taken literally.* *The Bible was written by men and is not the word of God.*			
	The Bible Is Literally True (36%)	The Bible Need Not Be Taken Literally (46%)	The Bible Was Written by Men (17%)
I am a Democrat	37%	44%	18%
No abortions	68	28	3
Equal roles for women	33	48	18
Homosexuals should not be allowed to serve in the armed forces	57	35	9
Source: The 2008 National Election Study.			

New class *That part of the middle class that has college and postgraduate degrees and works in occupations that involve using symbols (such as writers and teachers). It tends to have liberal views.*

Today, the many people with college and postgraduate degrees have come to be called a **new class**, one that differs from the **traditional middle class**. Members of the first group often live in big cities, have jobs that involve manipulating symbols (writers, actors, reporters, teachers), rarely attend religious services, have liberal views, and vote Democratic. Those in the other group often live in small towns or suburbs, have jobs in business or farming, often attend religious services, have conservative views, and vote Republican.

What is important is that these two groups differ even though they often have roughly the same income. In California, for example, people living in many cities in Orange County have roughly the same income as those who live in cities in Marin County, north of San Francisco, but the voting patterns of these two groups could not be more different: In most Orange County cities, they are Republicans; in most Marin County ones, they are Democrats.

Traditional middle class *That part of the middle class that has jobs in business or farming and tends to have conservative views.*

The two major political parties and many interest groups are led by people of similar incomes but very different views. The clash between these two sides—between the new class and the traditional middle class—is sometimes so intense that people refer to it as a *culture war*. The liberal side favors abortion on demand and quotas in admitting students and hiring workers, believes that society is largely responsible for crime and poverty, and is tolerant of social experimentation and nonmarital sex. The conservative side opposes abortion on demand and affirmative action, thinks that personal irresponsibility explains crime and poverty, and is committed to what it calls "traditional family values."

When the economy is sound and thus does not affect election outcomes, this culture war may dominate political campaigns, as it did in 1972, 1984, 1988, and 1994. In bad economic times, the economy may push the culture war into the background, as it did in 1980, 1992, and 2008.

The Gender Gap

Gender gap *Differences in the political views and voting behavior of men and women.*

In recent elections, much has been made of the **gender gap**—that is, the differences in political views between women and men. In fact, such differences have existed for as long as we have records, though they have not always been prominent enough to make much difference in elections. What has changed about the gender gap is the party it benefits.

During the 1950s, women were more likely than men to be Republicans; since the late 1960s, they have been more likely to be Democrats. The reason for the shift is that the political parties have changed their positions on the kinds of issues to which women respond differently from men—particularly certain social questions (such as prohibition and gun control) and foreign policy (especially the threat of war). For example, in the 1930s and 1940s, more women than men wanted to ban the sale of liquor and keep the country out of war; this helped Republicans, who were then more sympathetic to such policies than were Democrats. In 1980, the aversion women felt to any policy that might increase the risk of war hurt the Republicans, whom they saw being led by a president (Reagan) ready to send troops into combat.[13] In 1996, women supported Bill Clinton more strongly than did men, despite Clinton's involvement in extramarital sex. Apparently they liked his position on certain social issues.

The gender gap tends to disappear when gender-sensitive policies (such as war, gun control, or pornography) are not in the limelight and to reemerge when these topics become hotly partisan. Today the biggest male-female differences are over the use of force, and confidence in the future.[14] Notably, there are no great differences between men and women in their attitudes toward abortion (see Table 6.2).

Cleavages in Public Opinion

The opinions formed by heredity, family, religion, schooling, and sex are hardly the whole story. There are many splits among people even with similar families, religious backgrounds, and schooling. These cleavages in public opinion—based on (among other things) race, ethnicity, region, and occupation—complicate the study of Americans attitudes. Studying public opinion is especially difficult because a survey that would permit you to look at every relevant source and cleavage in attitudes would require huge and prohibitively expensive samples.

Some writers argue that matters are much simpler than this. A single factor, they argue, explains opinion, and that factor is social class, usually defined by income. That view certainly contains some truth, but it does not explain how people with similar incomes differ so much. Plumbers and professors may have identical incomes, but their views are likely to be very different.

In some other democracies, a single factor such as class may explain more of the differences in political attitudes than it does in the more socially heterogeneous United States. Most American blue-collar workers think of themselves as being "middle class," whereas most such workers in Britain or France describe themselves as "working class."[15] In Britain, the working class prefers the Labour party by a margin of three to one, while in the United States workers prefer the Democratic party by less than two to one (and in 1984 they gave most of their votes to Republican Ronald Reagan).[16]

Occupation

Indeed, some evidence indicates that occupation is becoming less important as an explanation of political opinions in this country than it once was. In the 1950s, differences in opinion on current political issues tended to be closely associated

Table 6.2 **The Gender Gap: Differences in Political Views of Men and Women**		
Issue	**Men (%)**	**Women (%)**
Favor banning all abortions	15	16
Agree same-sex couples should be able to marry	35	40
Women miss out on jobs due to discrimination	67	73
I think of myself as a Democrat	37	47
It was worth the cost of going to war with Iraq	23	20
Source: The 2008 National Election Study.		

with occupations: Those holding managerial or professional jobs had distinctly more conservative views on social-welfare policy and more internationalist views on foreign policy than did manual workers. During the next decade this pattern changed greatly.[17] Although some differences remain, over a long period of time—the data go back to the 1930s—the correlation between occupation (and income) and policy preferences has steadily weakened. No one is quite certain why this has happened, but it is probably due in part to the changing effects of education on all levels of society—especially on people entering higher-status occupations.

Race

If occupation has become less important in explaining political attitudes, race has become more so (see Table 6.3). Whites and blacks differ profoundly over busing to achieve racially balanced schools and the right of individuals to discriminate in housing sales, as well as differing over such nonracial matters as the death penalty (whites tend to favor), increased spending for national defense (whites tend to favor), and national health insurance (blacks tend to favor). In the 1960s, blacks were more opposed than whites to the war in Vietnam. The races feel pretty much the same, however, about such issues as wanting the courts to deal more harshly with criminals.[18]

Blacks have become the single most consistently liberal group within the Democratic party.[19] A majority of blacks believe that as a group they are better off today than they were 10 years ago and that their children's opportunities will be better yet.[20] Curiously—and perhaps ominously—it is among *better-off* blacks that one finds the greatest skepticism about American society. Blacks holding professional jobs are much more likely than black manual laborers to believe that whites get unfair advantages and to say that they have experienced discrimination.[21] Continued economic progress by blacks is no guarantee that black attitudes toward American society will change.

Table 6.3 White versus Black Opinions		
Issue	**Whites**	**Blacks**
Similar views		
Poor people are too dependent on government assistance	71%	66%
Women should return to their traditional roles	23	29
The country should do whatever is needed to protect the environment	77	76
Different views		
Support affirmative action programs	24	55
Homosexuality should be discouraged by society	42	55
Americans can always find ways to solve our problems	61	47

Source: From "The Black and White of Public Opinion," October 31, 2005, Pew Research Center for the People and the Press, a project of the Pew Research Center. Used by permission.

Region

Everybody believes that northerners and southerners disagree about politics. That is true—for some people and some issues. Because the racial mix and religious preferences of regions differ, one must look at people of the same race and religion to understand the effect of living in a certain region. If, for example, you look only at white Protestants, you will find that those living in the South are not very different in their political outlook from those living in the North or West on economic issues but are a good deal more conservative on social issues (such as abortion or homosexual rights).

This helps explain why the South was so long a part of the Democratic party coalition: On national economic and social welfare policies (and on foreign policy), southerners express views not very different from northerners. That coalition has been threatened, however, by the divisiveness produced by social issues involving race and liberty. In recent years, many white southerners have shifted from the Democratic to the Republican party.

Anyone who has lived in both regions knows that the southern lifestyle differs from that of the Northeast. The South has, on the whole, been more accommodating to business enterprise and less accommodating to organized labor than the Northeast. It gave greater support to the third-party candidacy of George Wallace in 1968, which was a protest against big government and the growth of national power as well as against the extension of civil rights. Moreover, there is some evidence that, by the 1970s, white southerners became more conservative than they had been in the 1950s—at least when compared to white northerners.[22] Finally, white southerners have become less attached to the Democratic party: whereas more than three-fourths described themselves as Democrats in 1952, only one-third did in 1986.[23] From 1980 through 2008, the South voted for the Republican presidential candidate by a large margin. These southern views are important. From 1940 to 1976, no Democrat except Lyndon Johnson in 1964 was able to win the presidency unless he carried the South.[24] In 1992 and again in 1996, Bill Clinton carried only four southern states but still won the presidency. In 2008, Barack Obama carried only three southern states but still won the presidency. The Democratic party, once based in the South, is now based in the North; much of the South has become Republican.

Political Ideology

Up to now we have used the words *liberal* and *conservative* as if everyone agrees on what they mean. But people do not agree on these matters even though the descriptions are very useful.

In a moment we shall take a closer look at these terms, but for now let us define them this way: A **liberal** is a person who wishes the government to do more to help improve lives, and a **conservative** is one who thinks that personal action rather than government programs improves lives.

Nevertheless, many people are neither liberal nor conservative. Liberalism and conservatism are **political ideologies**—a coherent and consistent set of beliefs about who ought to rule and what policies they should support. An ideology is

Liberal *In general, a person who favors a more active federal government for regulating business, supporting social welfare, and protecting minority rights, but who prefers less regulation of private social conduct.*

Conservative *In general, a person who favors more limited and local government, less government regulation of markets, more social conformity to traditional norms and values, and tougher policies toward criminals.*

Political ideology *A coherent and consistent set of attitudes about who should rule and what policies should be adopted.*

different from narrow self-interest. Somebody might like to get a higher wage because he or she wants more money; that is self-interest. But somebody else may think the government should make all employers pay higher wages even if the person believing this would not get any of the money; that is ideology.

Most studies of public opinion suggest that the great majority of citizens display relatively little ideology in their thinking, however that term is defined or measured. According to a leading study, people do not usually employ words like *liberal* or *conservative* in explaining or justifying their preferences for candidates or policies, not many more than half can define these terms, and there are relatively low correlations among the opinions people have on various political issues. From this, many scholars have concluded that the great majority of Americans do not think about politics in an ideological, or even very coherent, manner and make little use of such concepts—so dear to political commentators and professors—as liberal or conservative.[25]

Consistent Attitudes

This does not settle the question of ideology entirely, however. Critics who view Americans as ideological have argued that people can have general, and strongly felt, political dispositions even though they fail to use such terms as *liberal* correctly. Moreover, public-opinion polls must, of necessity, ask rather simple questions, and so the apparent inconsistency in the answers people give at different times may mean only that the nature of the problem or the wording of the question has changed in ways not obvious to people analyzing the surveys.[26]

Consistency is very much in the mind of the observer. A voter might well believe that he or she is being quite consistent by, for example, favoring both strong government efforts on behalf of various social programs and the use of military force to combat terrorism in the Middle East—yet to others, such a mixture of "liberal" and "conservative" views would be considered ideologically "inconsistent."

Finally, some scholars argue that the dramatic events of the 1960s—the civil-rights revolution, the war in Vietnam, and the riots and protest demonstrations—increased the extent to which voters followed coherent ideological lines. The signal increase in ideological thinking apparently occurred in 1964, when the election for president offered about as clear a choice as one could imagine between a defender of a large, activist federal government (Lyndon Johnson) and a staunch critic of such a government (Barry Goldwater).[27]

Other scholars disagree with this interpretation, arguing that changes in the way the questions were worded on opinion polls taken during the 1950s and 1960s make any comparison invalid.[28] Still others point out that voters may think more ideologically when one or both presidential candidates take sharply ideological positions (as happened in 1964, 1972, and 1980) and think less ideologically when both campaign as centrists (as in 1960, 1976, 1992, 1996, 2000, and 2008).

Activists

Political activists, however, are much more likely than the average citizen to think in ideological terms and to take "consistent" positions on various issues.[29] In part, this may simply be the result of better information: Activists spend all or most of their time on political affairs, and they may see relationships among issues that others do not. It may also reflect the kinds of people with whom activists associate. Politics does not ordinarily make strange bedfellows; rather, it brings like-minded people together. And activists have more structured opinions because, in part, the motives that lead them to engage in politics arise in many cases out of strong convictions about how the country ought to be run—that is to say, out of a political ideology to begin with.

Various Categories of Opinion

It is useful to divide into three broad categories the opinions to which different people subscribe. The first involves questions about government policy toward the *economy*. We will describe as liberal those people who favor government efforts to ensure that everyone has a job, to spend more money on educational and social programs, and to increase rates of taxation for well-to-do persons.

The second category involves questions about *civil rights* and race relations. Here, liberals favor strong federal action to increase hiring opportunities for minorities, to provide compensatory programs for minorities, and to enforce civil-rights laws strictly.

The third involves questions about *personal conduct*. Liberals are tolerant of protest demonstrations, favor decriminalizing marijuana use and other "victimless crimes," emphasize protecting the rights of the accused over punishing criminals, and see the solution to crime in eliminating its causes rather than in getting tough with offenders.

Analyzing Consistency

Obviously a person can take a liberal position on one of these issues and a conservative position on another without feeling the slightest degree "inconsistent"; several studies suggest that this is exactly what most people do.[30] Some people, though, have fairly consistent views. To simplify a complex picture, consider four ideological groups:

1. **Liberals:** Pure liberals are liberal on both economic and social issues. They want the government to reduce economic inequality, regulate business, tax the rich heavily, deal with crime by addressing its (allegedly) economic causes, protect the rights of accused criminals, allow abortion on demand, and guarantee the broadest possible freedoms of speech and press.
2. **Conservatives:** Pure conservatives are conservative on both economic and social issues. They want less government regulation of business, lower taxes, and a greater reliance on markets, and they advocate getting tough on criminals, punishing pornographers, and cutting back on welfare payments.
3. **Libertarians:** Libertarians are advocates of free markets, low taxes, and small government (which makes them economic conservatives), but they also support the greatest amount of personal freedom in social matters, such as speech, drug use, and abortion (which makes them social liberals).
4. **Populists:** Populists are liberal on economic matters, desiring government regulation of business and heavy federal spending on public programs, but conservative on social matters, opposing abortion on demand and favoring a

crackdown on crime, drug use, and pornography. Many also favor legalizing prayers in school.

Many individuals do not fit into any of these categories. Moreover, the classification scheme would become even more complicated if additional issues were added—foreign policy, for example. Nevertheless, the complicated nature in which these categories of opinion are packaged together can help us understand the diversity of political opinion in the United States and the difficulty of putting together—and keeping united—a winning coalition of groups.

Though the average citizen cannot be described as being purely liberal or purely conservative, bear in mind that political activists often do display a great deal of attitude consistency. In other words, if they are liberal on one set of issues, they are likely to be liberal on all others. This applies to both congressional candidates and voters who have the highest levels of education and the most information about politics and government.[31] Because such informed, educated people are more likely to vote and otherwise participate in politics than uninformed, uneducated people, the activists' ideology is more important than their numbers might indicate. Candidates, activists, and knowledgeable followers of politics may thus impart to political decision making a greater degree of ideological consistency than the average voter cares to see. This is one reason (though surely not the only one) that some policies preferred by the voters get filtered out by the process of political representation. Table 6.4 illustrates how politically engaged Democrats and Republicans differed on eight policy issues. ("Politically engaged" voters are those who tell pollsters that they are interested in an election campaign, have a good level of knowledge about it, and do more in the campaign than just vote.) There can be little doubt that activist Democrats and Republicans differ strongly.

The Impact of the Media

Ten years ago, an essay about the media and politics would have been about how newspapers and television influence events. No more. In 2008, half of all Americans used the Internet to get political news. They read not only candidate blogs

Table 6.4 **Policy Liberalism Among Politically Engaged Voters (2004)**		
Issue	**Democrats**	**Republicans**
Favor abortion	67	25
Oppose death penalty	52	10
Prefer diplomacy to force	74	15
Prefer environment to jobs	74	27
Favor gay marriage	69	18
Support health insurance	66	16

Source: Data from Alan Abramowitz and American National Election Study used to create table.

but look them up on Facebook and YouTube, and answer statements to them on the Internet and through Twitter. Candidates for office raise millions of dollars, mostly in small donations, from appeals sent out on the Internet. Newspapers, magazines, and television are still important, but most of them are losing readers and listeners while the Internet is growing rapidly.

The mass media have changed, and American politics has changed with them. In the 1930s, the newspapers rarely, if ever, showed a picture of President Roosevelt in a wheelchair or reported on his extramarital affair. In the 1960s, neither television nor the newspapers reported on President Kennedy's extramarital sexual flings in and out of the White House. In the 1990s, the media reported in detail on President Clinton's sexual harassment charge by Paula Jones and Monica Lewinsky and on the extramarital sexual conduct of several high military officers.

What happened? In part it was because members of the press have become adversaries of the government, a change brought about by their experience during the Vietnam War and the Watergate scandal. But in part it is also because the economics of the press have changed. In the 1930s, there were only a few newspapers that covered national affairs in much detail; in the 1960s, there were only a handful of television news programs. But by the 1980s and 1990s, there were vastly more reporters and editors struggling to find stories at a time when most newspapers, magazines, and television stations were losing readers and listeners.

In the 1970s, four out of every five Americans who watched television news watched one of the three networks—ABC, CBS, or NBC. In the 2000s, these viewers had the same three networks, *plus* three cable news networks, ten weekly TV news magazines, three cable business networks, two sports networks, a vast number of radio talk shows, and the Internet. As a result, by 2005, only one-fourth of TV viewers watched ABC, CBS, or NBC. Media competition has become what one veteran broadcaster called a "brutal, relentless pressure forcing normally careful reporters and producers to yield to temptations of wildness and recklessness."[32] And if they succeed, they earn top dollar—for TV anchors, $7 to $10 million a year.

Politicians are increasingly turning to social media sites to campaign, raise funds, and communicate with their constituents. Here we see Sarah Palin's Facebook page and Barack Obama's Twitter page.

What we see is influenced by what the media think we want to see. The Monica Lewinsky scandal, during its first month, consumed more than one-third of all network newscast time—more than all the time devoted to the winter Olympics, the pope's visit to Cuba, and a military showdown with Iraq combined. Americans like to say they are disgusted with what the media portrays. But they portray it only because we—or at least a large number of us—want to see it.

The Structure of the Media

The relationship between journalism and politics is a two-way street: though politicians take advantage, as best they can, of the media available to them, these media, in turn, attempt to use politics and politicians as a way of both entertaining and informing their audiences. The mass media, whatever they may say to the contrary, are not simply a mirror held up to reality. There is inevitably a process of selection, editing, and emphasis; this process reflects, to some degree, the way in which the media are organized, the kinds of audiences they hope to attract, and the preferences and opinions of the members of the media.

Degree of Competition

There has been a decline in the number of cities that have competing daily newspapers. Many of the largest cities—New York, Chicago, Los Angeles—have at least two central-city newspapers, but most smaller cities have only one. This is partially offset by the fact that many metropolitan areas have two or more neighboring cities that each have a newspaper with overlapping readership.

Radio and television, by contrast, are intensely competitive and becoming more so. Almost every American home has a radio and a television set. Though there are only a few national television networks, there are more than seven hundred television stations, each of which has its own news program. Local stations affiliated with a network are free to accept or reject network programs. There are also scores of cable television systems serving more than 64 million people, and more than nine thousand radio stations, some of which broadcast nothing but news, whereas others develop a specialized following among blacks, Hispanics, or other minorities. Magazines exist for every conceivable interest. The Internet now gives people access to countless reliable and unreliable news sources. The amount of news available to an American is vast.

In most other democratic nations (Great Britain, France, Sweden, Japan, and elsewhere), the media are owned and operated with a national audience in mind. But to a degree that would astonish most foreigners, the American press—radio, television, and newspapers—is made up of locally owned and managed enterprises and is primarily oriented to its local market and local audience. The result has been the development of a decentralized broadcasting industry that offers more local than national news.

The National Media

The local orientation of much of the American communications media is partially offset by the emergence of certain publications and broadcast services that constitute a kind of national press. The wire services—the Associated Press (AP) and United Press International (UPI)—supply most of the national news that local papers publish. Certain news magazines—*Time, Newsweek, U.S. News & World Report*—have a national readership. The news broadcasts produced by ABC, CNN, CBS, FOX, and NBC are carried by cable and television stations. The Web, linking millions of Internet users, is a check on the national media, it tests the accuracy of media stories, as it did with the (misleading) CBS account about President Bush's service in the Air National Guard. There are two large national newspapers, the *Wall Street Journal* and *USA Today,* but *The New York Times* and *The Washington Post* have national influence because they are read by every important Washington official and provide story leads to TV networks and local papers.[33]

The existence of a national press is important for two reasons. First, government officials in Washington pay great attention to what these media say about them—and much less, if any, attention to what local papers and broadcasters say. Second, reporters and editors for the national press tend to differ from local journalists: they are usually better paid, often graduates of more prestigious universities, and generally more liberal.[34] Above all, they seek—and frequently obtain—the opportunity to write "background," "investigative," or interpretive stories about issues and policies.[35]

The national press plays the roles of gatekeeper, scorekeeper, and watchdog for the federal government. As *gatekeeper* it can influence what subjects become national political issues, and for how long. Automobile safety, water pollution, and the quality of prescription drugs were not major political issues before the national press began giving substantial attention to them. Elite opinion about the war in Vietnam also changed significantly as the attitude toward the war expressed by the national media changed.

As *scorekeeper* the national media help make political reputations, note who is being "mentioned" as a presidential candidate, and help decide who wins and who loses in Washington politics. The media's attention can be very useful in launching a presidential campaign. As a virtually unknown former Georgia governor planning his presidential campaign in 1975, Jimmy Carter successfully cultivated the national press and, before the primary elections, was getting as much national news coverage as his better-known rivals. In 1992, a largely unknown Arkansas governor, Bill Clinton, did the same.

Finally, the media has a *watchdog* role. For example, Clinton's sex life and record were closely examined only after some early political victories, when the press decided he was the "man to beat." This close scrutiny is perfectly natural. The media have an instinctive—and profitable—desire to expose scandals and investigate personalities, to be tolerant of underdogs and tough on frontrunners.

Newspapers and television stations play these three roles in somewhat different ways. A newspaper can cover more stories in greater depth than a television station and faces less competition from other papers. A television station faces brutal competition, must select its programs in part for their visual impact, and has to keep its stories short and punchy. As a result, newspaper reporters have more freedom but earn less money than television news broadcasters, who have little freedom (the fear of losing audiences is keen) but can make a lot of money if they are attractive personalities who photograph well. Because of these organizational differences, it is newspapers and magazines, much more than television, that perform the gatekeeper, scorekeeper, and watchdog functions.

The Internet and the Web

Today there is a powerful new challenge to the national media: blogs that appear on the Web via the Internet. These blogs are daily statements about politics and the media written by a variety of people, both liberal and conservative. They go well beyond just stating opinions. They immediately react to newspaper and television reports about current events.

When Dan Rather, anchor of the *CBS Evening News*, broadcast a story in 2004 that claimed that George W. Bush had performed poorly during his service in the Air National Guard, various blogs reported within hours that he had the facts wrong. Within a few weeks, CBS began an investigation of the story, and Rather announced that he would retire.

Liberal blogs include the Daily Kos; conservative blogs include Powerline; libertarian blogs include Instapundit and the Volokh Conspiracy. Many people refer to these blogs as the New Media and compare it, often favorably, to the Mainstream Media. Blogs, of course, are run by individuals, are entirely unregulated, and can circulate their own mistakes. But being numerous and highly competitive, they check media stories rapidly and often.

Rules Governing the Media

Ironically, the most competitive branch of the media—radio and television broadcasting—must have a governmental license to operate and must conform to a variety of government regulations, whereas the least competitive branch—big-city newspapers—is almost entirely free from government regulation. The Internet is largely free of any government control.

Freedom of the Press

Newspapers and magazines need no license to publish. The First Amendment to the Constitution has been interpreted to mean that no federal or state government can place "prior restraints" (that is, censorship) on the press except in very narrowly defined circumstances. (For example, the Supreme Court refused to allow the federal government to stop *The New York* Times from publishing the Pentagon Papers, a set of secret documents that had been stolen by an antiwar activist.[36]) And once something is published—including attacks on public figures or private persons—the courts have so narrowly defined "libelous," "obscene," and "incitement to commit an illegal act" as to make it more difficult in the United States than in any other nation for the press to be found guilty of misconduct.[37]

Reporters believe they should have the right to keep confidential the sources of their stories. Although some states have passed laws to that effect, most states and the federal government have not. Thus, the courts must decide, in each case, whether a journalist's need to protect confidentiality outweighs the government's need to gather evidence in a criminal investigation or an accused person's need to be informed of the evidence against him.[38]

A columnist disclosed that Valerie Plame, a CIA officer, had helped send her husband to Africa, after which he wrote an op-ed critical of the Bush administration. (The op-ed was later proved to be largely false.) A special prosecutor was appointed to find out who leaked the fact that Plame worked for the agency in a secret position. Several reporters were asked to testify about this leak. Judith Miller of the *New York Times* refused and, in 2005, went to jail for eighty-five days for contempt of court. She was released when her source, Lewis "Scooter" Libby (an aide to Vice President Cheney) authorized her to describe their conversation. The Plame and Miller stories led some members of Congress to propose federal legislation that would allow reporters to keep their sources confidential, but by mid-2010 the bill had not passed.

Regulation and Deregulation

No one may operate a radio or television station without a license from the Federal Communications Commission (FCC), renewable every seven years for radio and every five for television. An application for renewal is rarely refused, but in order to get a renewal, the FCC until recently required the broadcaster to provide detailed information about its programming and how it planned to serve "community needs." Thereby the FCC could influence the station, for example, to reduce the amount of violence or to alter the way it portrayed ethnic groups. But of late, a movement has arisen to deregulate broadcasting on the grounds that competition should be allowed to determine how each station defines and serves a community's needs. Since the 1980s, licenses are automatically renewed unless some community group formally objects, in which case the FCC holds a hearing. As a result, some of the old rules—for instance, that each hour on TV could contain only sixteen minutes of commercials—are no longer strictly enforced.

Government and the News

Every government agency, and every public official, spends a great deal of time trying to shape public opinion. In a government of separated powers, any government agency that fails to cultivate public opinion will sooner or later find itself weak, without allies, and in trouble.

Prominence of the President

Theodore Roosevelt was the first president to raise to an art form the systematic cultivation of the press; Teddy's nephew, Franklin Roosevelt, institutionalized the relationship between reporters and the president by making his press secretary a major instrument for cultivating and managing, as well as informing, the press.

Today, the press secretary heads a large staff that meets with reporters, briefs the president on questions the president is likely to be asked, attempts to control the flow of news from cabinet departments to the press, and arranges briefings for out-of-town editors. All this effort is directed toward influencing (or bypassing) the White House press corps, a group of journalists who have a lounge within the White House. No other nation in the world has brought the press into such close physical proximity to the head of its government: The

On Background

When politicians talk to the press, they set certain ground rules that the press (usually) observes. These rules specify who, if anyone, is quoted as the source of the story.

On the Record

The official is quoted by name. For example: "I say that water runs downhill, and you can quote me on that."

Off the Record

What the official says cannot be printed. For example: "Off the record, the head of my party is a complete wacko."

On Background

What the official says can be printed, but it may not be attributed to him or her by name. For example: "A well-placed source said today that the sun will continue to rise in the east."

On Deep Background

What the official says can be printed, but it cannot be attributed to anybody. The reporter must say it on his or her own authority. For example: "In my opinion this administration secretly believes that two plus two equals five."

2011 © Cengage Learning

press is on hand if the president goes jogging, has any sort of medical problem, greets a Boy Scout, or takes a trip to his country retreat at Camp David.

Coverage of Congress

Congress has watched all this with irritation and envy, resenting the attention given the president but uncertain how it can compete. The 435 members of the House are so numerous and play such specialized roles that they do not get much individualized press coverage. And until the 1974 Nixon impeachment hearings, House committees generally refused to permit electronic coverage. In 1979, cable television began carrying House sessions gavel-to-gavel, though not many people watch.[39]

The Senate has used television much more fully, heightening the already substantial advantage senators have over representatives in getting into the public eye. Although televised debates on the Senate floor were not permitted until 1978, Senate committee hearings have been frequently televised ever since Senator Estes Kefauver, in his hearings about crime, demonstrated the power of the medium in 1950. In June 1986, regular television coverage of Senate floor debates began. Now you can see every meeting of the House and Senate, unedited and without commercials, on C-SPAN.

Its use of television has helped turn the Senate into the incubator of presidential candidates, for Washington is a city full of cameras, and an investigation, a scandal, a major political conflict, or an articulate and telegenic personality can usually get a senator on the air.

Interpreting Political News

Most Americans get their news from television, but increasingly they distrust what they see there. There is compelling evidence that journalists have political views very different from those of most Americans.[40] They are much more likely to be liberal and to vote for Democrats. However, there are other factors besides bias at work here. One is the intense, relentless competition among television networks for an audience. In the 1970s, there were three network news programs each day; today there are, in addition to those networks, three cable news networks that broadcast around the clock, ten weekly news magazine shows, and many news outlets on the Web. This competition has driven broadcasters to search desperately for something to say to fill up the hours, often in the guise of scandals, accusations, unconfirmed reports, and endless punditry. It should also be noted that young people are steadily becoming less interested in reading newspapers: between 1970 and 2008, the percentage of newspaper readers ages 18 to 34 fell from about 75 percent to 31 percent (6.2).

Before the terrorist attacks on the United States on September 11, 2001, the big news stories of the preceding years were the sexual conduct of President Clinton and the connection between California Representative Gary Condit and a missing young woman. After September 11, the press focused on a more important matter—defeating terrorism.

Figure 6.2   Percentage of Newspaper Readers Ages 18–34

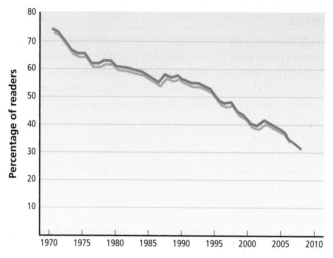

Note: 18–34 readership represents the average of 18–24 readership and 25–34 readership.

Source: The Wall Street Journal (February 15, 2007). Copyright ©2007 Dow Jones & Company, Inc. Reprinted with the permission of Dow Jones & Company, Inc., via Copyright Clearance Center; and Scarborough Research Center survey data in *The State of the News Media, Pew Project for Excellence in Journalism*, 2010. <http://www.stateofthemedia.org/2010/newspapers_audience.php>

Are News Stories Slanted?

One should not assume that the political opinions of journalists automatically lead them to slant their stories in certain ways. Other factors influence how these stories are written, including the need to meet an urgent deadline, the desire to attract an audience, a professional obligation to be fair and tell the truth, and the need to develop sources among people holding different views. For example, whatever their views, the national media gave, according to a careful study, quite evenhanded treatment to the opposing candidates during the 1980 presidential campaign.[41] In the 1984 campaign, on the other hand, Walter Mondale received more favorable coverage than Reagan; in the 1988 primaries, both leading Democratic candidates, Michael Dukakis and Jesse Jackson, got kinder treatment than George H.W. Bush, the Republican nominee; and, in 1992 and 1996, Clinton got nicer coverage than the elder Bush or Dole.

Still, it would be astonishing if strongly held beliefs had *no* effect on what is written or broadcast. To understand the circumstances under which a reporter's or editor's opinion can affect a story, and thus to interpret intelligently what we read and hear, we must distinguish among three *kinds* of stories:

1. **Routine Stories:** These are public events, routinely covered by reporters, involving relatively simple, easily described acts or statements.
2. **Feature Stories:** These are public events knowable to any reporter who cares to inquire, but involving acts and statements not routinely covered by a group

of reporters, such as an obscure agency issuing a controversial ruling, an unknown member of Congress conducting an investigation, or an interest group working for the passage of a bill.

3. **Insider Stories:** Events not usually made public become public because someone with inside knowledge about them tells a reporter. The reporter may have worked hard to learn these facts, in which case we say it is "investigative reporting"; or some official may have wanted a story to get out, in which case we call it a "leak."

Routine stories are covered in virtually the same way by almost all the media, differing only in their length, their headlines, and the position the story occupies in print or on the evening news broadcast. The wire services—AP and UPI—supply routine stories immediately to practically every daily newspaper in America. (Headlines and placement, however, can make a big difference in how the same story is perceived.) The political opinions of journalists have the least effect on these stories, especially if several competing journalists are covering the same story over a protracted period of time. That is why coverage of a presidential campaign tends to be evenhanded.

Even a routine news story can be incorrectly reported, however, if something dramatic or unique occurs. An important example was the reporting of the Tet Offensive toward the end of the Vietnam War—an all-out North Vietnamese attack on cities held by the South Vietnamese and their American allies. The attack failed—repulsed with heavy North Vietnamese casualties—but the news stories reported exactly the opposite: that the North Vietnamese could move and fight at will and that the Americans were helpless to oppose them. A painstaking analysis of the offensive later revealed the errors and omissions that led to the misleading versions published. Although the reporters' political views were not the whole explanation of these mistakes—it is always difficult for reporters, however fair, to grasp quickly and accurately a major military struggle—the antiwar views of most reporters probably did reinforce their interpretations of Tet.[42]

The grounds on which feature and insider stories are selected include the intrinsic interest of a story as well as the reporter's or editor's beliefs about what *ought* to be interesting. Among these beliefs are the political ideologies of the journalists. A liberal paper may choose to cover stories about white-collar crime, consumerism, the problems of minorities, and the arms race; a conservative paper might instead select stories about street crime, the decline of the central business district, and the problems of drug abuse and welfare fraud.

Nor are feature stories rare. In order to compete with television, newspapers increasingly print them, thereby becoming more like a magazine with something for everybody. As a result, a newspaper consists largely of precisely the kind of stories most likely to be influenced by the attitudes of reporters.

Every reader should examine such stories by asking: What beliefs or ideas led the editors to print this story rather than a quite different one? Sometimes the answer is simple: human interest or a desire to attract certain readers. At other times the answer is more complex: a belief in the virtue or threat of some cause or special interest.

There have been many studies of the *extent* to which large newspapers reveal a bias in their reporting of political news—there is no question that they do. One study compared how the ten largest newspapers covered economic news when either a Democrat or a Republican was the president. The economic news was standard material about sales, unemployment, and growth. When a Democrat was in the White House, the news got a positive spin; when a Republican was there, a negative one. Another study asked how the *New York Times* and the *Washington Post* described the most liberal and conservative senators. Conservatives were three times more likely to be called "conservatives" than liberals were to be called "liberals." Readers may attach more significance (or dislike) to stories about senators with a label than to those without one.[43]

News Leaks

Insider stories raise the most difficult questions of all: those of motive. When somebody in government with private or confidential information gives a story to a reporter, that somebody must have a reason for doing so. But the motives of those who leak information are almost never reported. Sometimes the reporter does not know the motives. More often, one suspects, the reporter is dependent on "highly placed sources" and is reluctant to compromise them.

American government is the leakiest in the world. The bureaucracy, members of Congress, and the White House staff regularly leak stories favorable to their interests. Of late, the leaks have become geysers, gushing forth torrents of insider stories. Many people in and out of government find it distressing that our government seems unable to keep anything secret for long. Others think that the public has a right to know even more information and that there are still too many secrets.

However you evaluate leaks, you should understand why we have so many. The answer can be found in the Constitution of the United States. Because we have separate institutions sharing power, each branch of government competes with the other branches to acquire it. One way to compete is to try to use the press to advance your pet projects and to make someone else look bad. There are far fewer leaks in other democratic nations, mainly because power is centralized in the hands of a prime minister who does not need to leak information in order to get the upper hand over the legislature and because the legislature has too little information to be a good source of leaks. In addition, we have no Official Secrets Act of the kind that exists in England; except for a few matters, it is not against the law for the press to receive and print government secrets.

The Influence of Media Opinions on Opinion and Politics

For the opinions of journalists to influence the opinions of the public, two things must happen. First, the views of journalists must affect what they write or televise. Second, what they write or televise must change what citizens think.

We have seen that the beliefs of journalists probably have the least effect on routine stories and the greatest effect on feature and insider stories. But even if we assume that the selection of these nonroutine stories is affected by the media's political beliefs, what effect do such stories have on readers and viewers? We cannot be certain, but in general the evidence seems to be this: If the citizenry has personal

*"Those are the headlines, and we'll be back in a moment
to blow them out of proportion."*

knowledge of the facts, the media are not likely to have much influence at all. Thus it makes little difference whether the media give much or little coverage to crime, interest rates, gasoline prices, or the quality of the public schools. Most people already have some knowledge and strong beliefs about these matters. Similarly the media are not likely to affect the outcome of important elections—say, presidential races—because people have lots of sources of information about presidential candidates: friends, neighbors, magazines, business and labor union associates, and the like.

The media are likely to have the greatest effect on how people think about matters on which they are not well informed. The American-led invasion of Iraq in 2003 brought journalists to that country, a place about which most Americans knew very little. During the major battles, journalists were *embedded* (that is, were sent out with) front-line troops. They produced graphic stories about the battles. But when the major battles were over and U.S. troops were coping with terrorists who attacked them and Iraqi civilians, the press tended to report only these conflicts and not the big gains the Americans were helping Iraqis make in rebuilding their country.

The press is interested in blood and blunders. During the war, there was a lot of blood on which to report and not much else. After the major battles were over, the press wanted to report on the real and alleged blunders of the Americans. The result for Americans at home was clear. At first they heard about big military victories; later, they heard only about peacetime problems. This seems to be inevitable. Reporting on war captured the public's attention and generated considerable support, but reporting on the creation of a new interim Iraqi government has generated less attention, especially because attacks on Americans and Iraqis by dissident groups continued. American views of Iraq were no doubt affected by what the press chose to cover.

The most important effect television has had on politics has been its ability to give candidates and officeholders access to tens of millions of people—provided these politicians supply stories that are profitable to produce. These are some of the qualities that appeal to television news broadcasters:

1. *Scandals:* Attacking your opponent has been part of American politics since the time of John Adams and Thomas Jefferson, but a juicy scandal or personal criticism gets more attention more quickly today than ever before. People may lament "negative advertising" and "attack journalism," but the blunt and sad truth is, they work.
2. *Visuals:* Rather than being interested in long speeches or policy papers, television wants to show action. Politicians therefore spend a lot of time finding opportunities to pose in front of dramatic backdrops (such as the scene of a hurricane) or with people who symbolize some message (such as police officers, factory workers, or senior citizens).
3. *Sound bites:* Radio and television do not want to broadcast an entire speech, or even one paragraph from a speech; nor do they want to dissect a complex argument. They prefer a ten-second phrase, called a sound bite, that they air, leading people to think that the bite conveys the whole message.
4. *Prettiness:* Television favors attractive faces and, among men, deep voices. It flatters youthfulness and penalizes old age; it makes chubby people look obese and causes high-pitched voices to sound shrill.

Politicians know this, and they play to it. Young, attractive candidates who pose in interesting settings have an advantage over those who are old and ugly or who spend their time in an office. Officials who can make their point in a dramatic ten-second phrase—especially one that attacks their rivals—have an advantage over those who think that clarifying an issue requires five or ten minutes and who feel that discussing a problem should not involve personalities.

The most important political debates in American history occurred between two candidates for the Senate who were campaigning in Illinois. At the time (1858), every word they said was reported and widely discussed. If television had been around, these debates wouldn't have been covered. Here was a tall, skinny man with a high-pitched voice, followed by a short, fat man, each talking for an hour or so while standing motionless on a platform. Moreover, a Senate race in one state was hardly as important as other events with more visual appeal that happened in 1858, such as a new stagecoach line completing its first trip to San Francisco. And so we would not have been aware of the debate between Abraham Lincoln and Stephen A. Douglas over the morality of slavery, the meaning of popular sovereignty, and the future of the republic. But we would have seen some great shots of that stagecoach pulling into San Francisco.

The Influence of Politicians on the Media

The media may, within limits, shape opinion and politics, but politicians can shape the media. They cannot regulate or control it, but they can influence it. Among the most effective techniques are these:

1. *Press officers:* Every agency and high-ranking official has at least one and sometimes scores of press officers who not only release information but try to shape the news so that it gets the most favorable attention.

WHAT WOULD YOU DO?

MEMORANDUM

To: Matthew Wilson, senator

From: Margaret Drinker, legislative assistant

Subject: Protecting Journalists

The Supreme Court has held that forcing a reporter to testify does not violate the First Amendment to the Constitution. But Congress could pass a law, similar to that in many states, banning such testimony if it reveals a confidential source.

Arguments for:

1. Thirty-four states now have shield laws similar to the one proposed by Congress.

2. Effective journalism requires protecting sources from being identified; without protection, many important stories would not be written.

Arguments against:

1. Every person accused in a criminal trial has a right to know all of the evidence against him or her and to confront witnesses. A shield law would deprive people of this right.

2. A shield law would allow any government official to leak secret information with no fear of being detected.

Friday,

Journalist

October 5
WASHINGTON, D.C.

Congress today began deliberating over whether it should pass a law that would ban federal prosecutors from asking a reporter to reveal his or her confidential sources in a criminal trial. It has been a hot issue since reporter Judith Miller went to jail because she refused to reveal who had told her that Valerie Plame was a CIA officer. . . .

Your Decision:

Support bill _____   Oppose bill _____

2. *Targeting the 6 P.M. news:* The White House especially, but many other government institutions as well, organize their daily business and speechmaking with one thought in mind: How will this look on the 6 P.M. news?

3. *Spin control:* When a political event occurs, presidents and presidential candidates rally key aides to contact reporters and appear on talk shows to shape, as best they can, the way the event is interpreted. This is called spin control, and people who are good at it are called spin doctors.

4. *Leaks, flattery, and ideology:* Politicians can win the goodwill of reporters, up to a point, by (a) giving them off-the-record information and insider stories that will enable the reporter to publish or broadcast an attention-getting story; (b) flattering reporters and editors by asking their advice or appearing to take them seriously; and (c) expressing the same ideological or political convictions that the journalists hold.

5. *Rewards and penalties:* The ultimate weapon a president has in his love-hate relationship with the press is to give special access to favored reporters and deny it to those who are disliked. Presidents Kennedy and Johnson regularly gave brutal but private tongue-lashings to journalists they did not like and exclusive interviews to those they did. President Nixon made the mistake of making his complaints public, thus earning him enduring hostility from the press.

These techniques have their limitations. The most important one is that running a good story, especially if it involves a scandal, will almost always be more important to a reporter or editor than maintaining good relations with political sources. Lyndon Johnson knew and practiced every trick in the book to win journalistic support, but after the Vietnam War became unpopular, it was all for naught. Richard Nixon was brought down by press exposés of Watergate. Jimmy Carter was never popular with most journalists while in office (he became more popular as an ex-president). Bill Clinton was attacked by the press during his first term but admired by it in his second. The press and the president need but do not trust one another; theirs is inevitably a stormy relationship.

SUMMARY

Political opinions are shaped by heredity, gender, family, religious, and ethnic traditions, occupational experiences, and higher education. Though still important, economic and occupational sources of opinion have become less significant with the increase in the number of people attending college and holding high-paying but nonbusiness jobs (the new class).

Many Americans do not have highly ideological (that is, systematic and "consistent") political views, but a substantial proportion of those active in political life—the political elite—can be described as liberals or conservatives. Among citizens at large, many people are likely to have mixed ideologies—for example, to be liberal on economic issues but conservative on social ones, or vice versa. A sense of party identification remains important, even though it has been growing weaker among many voters. Though parental influence is strong in shaping one's party identification, it is not decisive.

Changes in the nature of American politics have been accompanied by and influenced by changes in the nature of the mass media. The recent weakening of political parties has been accelerated by the ability of candidates to speak directly to their constituents by radio and television.

The role of journalists in a democratic society poses an inevitable dilemma: If they are to serve well in their functions as information gatherer, gatekeeper, score-keeper, and watchdog, they must be free of government control. But to the extent that they are free of such controls, they are also free to act in their own interests, whether political or economic. In the United States a competitive press largely free of government controls (except in the area of broadcast licenses) has produced a substantial diversity of opinion and a general (though not unanimous) commitment to the goal of fairness in news reporting. The national media are in general more liberal than the local media, but the extent to which a reporter's opinion affects a story varies greatly with the kind of story—routine, selected, or insider.

RECONSIDERING THE ENDURING QUESTIONS

1. Under the U.S. Constitution, how big a role should public opinion play in making policy?

The people elect representatives, but the representatives are not supposed to do simply what the people want in part because "public opinion" is often vague, changeable, and inconsistent. The federal government is expected to discuss and refine, and not simply respond to, public views.

2. What are the biggest sources of the political views of Americans?

Family, religion, education, and race probably make the most difference. Sex, region, social class, and occupation have some effect, but not as large a one as the first four. America is also distinctive in taking religion much more seriously than do most European democracies.

3. What is meant by "liberal" and "conservative"?

Loosely speaking, a modern liberal wants government to be more active in economic affairs, and a modern conservative wants it to be less active. But these views are complicated by social and foreign policy issues, resulting in at least four kinds of political ideology: pure liberals, pure conservatives, libertarians, and populists.

4. Why is television news different from that in newspapers?

Television must grab and hold an audience that readily changes channels, so TV news tends to be dramatic, focused on blood and blunders, delivered in short bursts, and with an emphasis on local community matters. Newspapers can put in much more news, rarely have major newspaper competitors for the readers' time, and can report stories in greater depth.

5. Are reporters biased in how they cover politics?

Up to a point, they are biased. Much depends on the kind of story they are covering. Routine news (for example, a major presidential speech) will be covered in a similar manner by most reporters, but feature and insider stories often reflect the political views of the reporters and editors. Most reporters are liberal, although the rise of Fox News has provided a conservative view.

Online Resources: Public Opinion and the Media

Opinion polls
- Gallup: www.gallup.com
- Rassmussen: www.rasmussenreports.com
- Zogby: www.zogby.com

Media
- CNN political news: www.cnn.com/politics
- Fox News: www.foxnews.com
- The Drudge Report: www.drudgereport.com
- To search many newspapers: www.ipl.org
- Daily local newspaper front pages: www.newseum.org/todaysfrontpages/
- National newspapers:
  - New York Times: www.nytimes.com
  - Washington Post: www.washingtonpost.com
  - Wall Street Journal: www.wsj.com
  - USA Today: www.usatoday.com

Suggested Readings

Asher, Herbert. *Polling and the Public,* 7th ed. Washington, D.C.: Congressional Quarterly Press, 2007. Good review of how polls are conducted.

Crouse, Timothy. *The Boys on the Bus.* New York: Random House, 1973. A lively, irreverent account by a reporter of how reporters cover a presidential campaign.

Epstein, Edward J. *Between Fact and Fiction: The Problem of Journalism.* New York: Random House, 1975. Essays by a perceptive student of the press on media coverage of Watergate, the Pentagon Papers, the deaths of Black Panthers, and other major stories.

———. *News from Nowhere.* New York: Random House, 1973. Analysis of how television network news programs are produced and shaped.

Erikson, Robert S., and Kent L. Tedin. *American Public Opinion,* 7th ed. New York: Longman, 2007. Careful and systematic review of how Americans think about politics.

Garment, Suzanne. *Scandal: The Culture of Mistrust in American Government.* New York: Random House, 1991. A penetrating analysis of our growing fascination with political scandal and the journalistic and governmental forces that pander to this obsession.

Goldberg, Bernard. *Bias.* Washington, D.C.: Regnery Publishing, 2002. A veteran CBS reporter tells his story of liberal bias at CBS.

Graber, Doris A. *Mass Media and American Politics,* 7th ed. Washington, D.C.: Congressional Quarterly Press, 2006. A good summary of what we know about the press and politics.

Iyengar, Shanto, and Donald R. Kinder. *News That Matters.* Chicago: University of Chicago Press, 1987. Reports on experiments that test the effect of television news on how we think about politics.

Lichter, S. Robert, Stanley Rothman, and Linda S. Lichter. *The Media Elite.* Bethesda, Md.: Adler & Adler, 1986. A study of the political beliefs of "elite" journalists and how those beliefs influence what we read and hear.

Nye, Joseph S., Philip D. Zelikow, and David C. King, eds. *Why People Don't Trust Government.* Cambridge, Mass.: Harvard University Press, 1997. A thoughtful collection of essays on popular suspicion of government.

Zaller, John R. *The Nature and Origins of Mass Opinion.* Cambridge: Cambridge University Press, 1992. Profound study of how people acquire political opinions.

ENDURING QUESTIONS

1. Why are political parties weaker today than in the past?

2. Why does America have just two major political parties?

3. Why does America have so many interest groups?

Matthew Staver/Bloomberg via Getty Images

The political parties of the United States are the oldest in the world; among democratic nations, they may also be the weakest. It is not their age that has enfeebled them, however; when they were a hundred years old, they were still vigorous and played a dominant role in national politics. Rather, they have declined in significance as a result of changes in the legal rules under which they operate and in the attitudes of the citizens whom they seek to organize. All of this has occurred—and is still occurring—in a constitutional system that has caused the parties, even in their heyday, to be decentralized and fragmented.

CourseMate

So What?

Studying parties and interest groups may strike you as not very interesting. As do many Americans, you might think of parties as two labels managed by extremist organizations, and interest groups as self-seeking lobbies that somebody ought to abolish.

But as every leader from Thomas Jefferson to the present has learned, you cannot run a democracy without some way of bringing people together so that they can decide who should hold office. And when you look at other countries, you will probably discover that having just two parties is much better than having six or seven.

As political parties get weaker, government does not necessarily become better. Instead, its policies are more influenced by interest groups. Interest groups have always been part of American political life. They existed before parties, and the Framers hoped that the constitutional machinery they were designing, as well as the federal republic's size and diversity, would keep interest groups (or **factions**, as they were then called) so divided among themselves that none would dominate. Some scholars believe that the decline of political parties has made it easier for interest groups to exercise influence—the lobbyists have rushed in to fill the vacuum created by the absence of strong party leaders.

But do not sneer at interest groups until you face up to the fact that you and your parents probably belong to one or more. If you or a family member is a lawyer, doctor, teacher, realtor, construction worker, police officer, or firefighter, they are almost surely a member of a lobby—even if it is called a trade union or a professional association.

Faction *According to James Madison, a group of people who seek to influence public policy in ways contrary to the public good.*

Parties—Here and Abroad

Political party *A group that seeks to elect candidates to public office by supplying them with a label—a "party identification"—by which they are known to the electorate.*

A political party is a group that seeks to elect candidates to public office by supplying them with a label—a party identification—by which they are known to the electorate.[1] This broad definition suggests the three political arenas within which parties operate. A party exists as a *label* in the minds of the voters, as an *organization* that recruits and campaigns for candidates, and as a *set of leaders* who try to organize and control the legislative and executive branches of government.

In the United States the labels of the two major parties have always had sufficient appeal for the voters so that third parties and independent candidates have rarely had much success at the national or even the state level. Even the party label, however, has of late begun to lose its hold on the voters' minds. There has never been a strong national party organization in this country, though there have been long periods in which certain state, city, or county components of the Democratic or Republican parties have been organizationally powerful. And only occasionally have the political parties been able to dominate Congress, though parties have always been able to influence the choice of congressional leaders and the votes of many members of Congress on at least certain matters.

Parties are very different in Europe, where party leaders select candidates. Parties—not candidates—run election campaigns; elected officials are expected to vote a party line; and the principal criterion by which voters choose among candidates is their party identification or label. (This has been changing somewhat of late: European parties, like American ones, have not been able to rely as heavily as in the past on voters' party loyalty.)

Decentralization

Several factors explain the striking differences between American and European political parties. The American federal system decentralizes political authority and thus decentralizes party organizations. Even the recent trend toward governmental centralization in the United States has not made the parties more centralized. If anything, parties have grown weaker and more decentralized—in part because American parties are closely regulated by federal and state laws that have had the effect of weakening them substantially. Perhaps the most important regulations are those that prescribe how a party's candidates are chosen.

In almost all states, candidates are selected not by party leaders but by the voters in primary elections, which are unknown in Europe. Furthermore, if an American political party wins control of Congress, it does not also win the right to select the chief executive of government—as happens in European countries. Elected independently of Congress, the president chooses his principal subordinates from outside Congress (if he chooses a member of Congress, that person must resign from Congress). All this weakens the significance and power of the party as a means of organizing and running the government.

Political Culture

The attitudes and traditions of American voters reinforce the institutional and legal factors that make American parties relatively weak. Unlike Europeans—who formally join political parties, pay dues, attend meetings, and often participate in the many party-organized social activities—Americans do not usually "join" parties except by voting for their candidates, and they tend to keep their social, business, working, and cultural lives almost entirely nonpartisan. Thus American parties play a limited, rather than comprehensive, role in citizens' lives, and even this role diminishes as more and more Americans proclaim themselves to be independents.

The Rise and Decline of American Political Parties

Our nation began without parties; today parties, though far from extinct, are about as weak as at any time in our history. In between the Founding and the present, however, parties arose and became powerful. We can see this process in four broad periods of party history (see Figure 7.1).

The Founders feared parties, thinking of them as "factions" motivated by ambition and self-interest. Their concerns were understandable, for the legitimacy and

Figure 7.1   Cleavages and Continuity in the Two-Party System

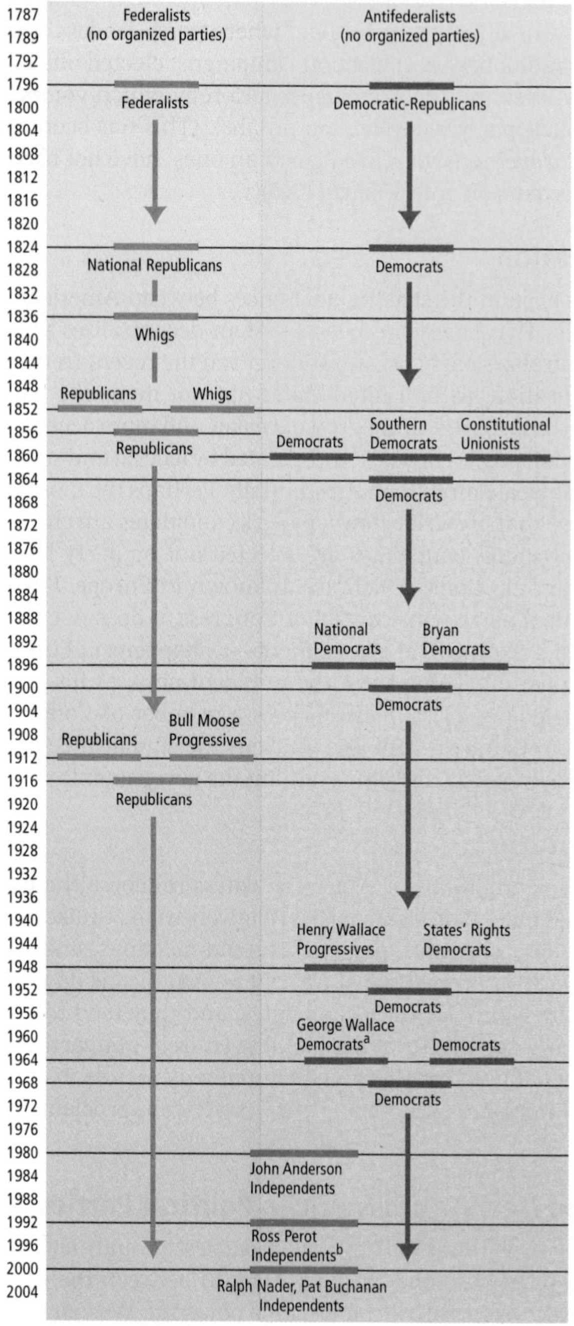

1787	Federalists	Antifederalists
1789	(no organized parties)	(no organized parties)
1792		
1796		
1800	Federalists	Democratic-Republicans
1804		
1808		
1812		
1816		
1820		
1824		
1828	National Republicans	Democrats
1832		
1836		
1840	Whigs	
1844		
1848	Republicans Whigs	
1852		
1856	Republicans	Democrats Southern Constitutional
1860		Democrats Unionists
1864		
1868		Democrats
1872		
1876		
1880		
1884		
1888		National Bryan
1892		Democrats Democrats
1896		
1900		Democrats
1904	Bull Moose	
1908	Republicans Progressives	
1912		
1916		
1920	Republicans	
1924		
1928		
1932		
1936		
1940		Henry Wallace States' Rights
1944		Progressives Democrats
1948		
1952		Democrats
1956		George Wallace
1960		Democrats[a] Democrats
1964		
1968		Democrats
1972		
1976		
1980	John Anderson	
1984	Independents	
1988		
1992		
1996	Ross Perot	
2000	Independents[b]	
2004	Ralph Nader, Pat Buchanan	
	Independents	

[a]American Independent party.

[b]United We Stand America or Reform Party.

stability of the newly created federal government were still very much in doubt. When Thomas Jefferson organized his followers, called the Democratic-Republicans, to oppose Alexander Hamilton's policies, Hamilton and *his* followers (who kept the name of Federalists) thought the Jeffersonians were out to subvert the government, and vice versa. This "first" party system was weak *because* it was the first: There was no ancestral party loyalty to defend, and the early parties were essentially small groups of local notables.

What is often called the "second party system" emerged around 1824 with Andrew Jackson's first run for the presidency and lasted until the eve of the Civil War. Its distinctive feature was that political participation became a mass phenomenon, with an enormous increase in the number of men eligible to vote and (by 1832) with presidential electors selected by popular vote in almost every state. The Jacksonian party system was built from the bottom up rather than, as in the period of the Founding, from the top down. It was during this period that the political convention emerged as a way of allowing for some measure of local control over the nominating process.

Though the Jacksonian party system was the first truly national system, with the Democrats (followers of Jackson) and Whigs (opponents of Jackson) fairly evenly balanced in most regions, it could not withstand the deep split in opinion created by the agitation over slavery. Because the issues of slavery and sectionalism could not be straddled, both parties split and new ones emerged. The modern Republican party began as a third party, but as a result of the Civil War, it became a major party that dominated national politics with only occasional interruptions until the 1930s. The fact that the post–Civil War Republicans solidly controlled the northern states and the Democrats the southern ones profoundly affected the organization of political parties, for it meant that most states were now one-party states. Because competition for office had to take place *within* a single dominant party, both parties were split into two factions: those in power and those wanting to be in power.

In the late nineteenth century, one group of outsiders, known as the Progressives, was generally losing its struggle against machine politics. If they were to have any power, they would have to attack the very concept of partisanship itself. Thus they began to espouse measures to curtail or even abolish political parties: primary elections to replace boss-manipulated nominating conventions, nonpartisan local elections, strict voter registration requirements (which, in fact, kept many ordinary citizens from voting), and civil-service reform to eliminate patronage. They were most successful in California and Wisconsin.

Progressive reforms substantially reduced the worst forms of political corruption and ultimately made boss rule difficult, if not impossible, but they also made political parties, no matter who led them, weaker, less able to make officeholders accountable, and less able to assemble the power necessary for governing the fragmented political institutions created by the Constitution. Above all, the Progressives failed to solve the problem of how to select candidates. Political candidacies, like people, are not products of virgin births. They must be arranged, if not by a party, then by another type of interest group, the mass media, or the candidates' families and personal supporters. These alternatives are best examined by looking at the forms of party structure now operating.

The National Party Structure Today

National convention *A meeting of party delegates—elected in state primaries, caucuses, or conventions—that is held every four years. Its primary purpose is to nominate presidential and vice-presidential candidates and to ratify a campaign platform.*

National committee *A committee of delegates from each state and territory that runs party affairs between national conventions.*

Congressional campaign committee *A party committee in Congress that provides funds to members who are running for reelection or to would-be members running for an open seat or challenging a candidate from the opposition party.*

National chairman *A paid, full-time manager of a party's day-to-day work who is elected by the national committee.*

Federal money *Money raised to support the campaign of a candidate for federal office. Amounts are regulated by federal law.*

Because political parties exist at the national, state, and local level, you might suppose that they are arranged like a big corporation, with a national board of directors giving orders to state managers, who in turn direct the activities of rank-and-file workers at the county and city level.

Nothing could be further from the truth. At each level a separate and almost entirely independent organization exists that does pretty much what it wants, and in many counties and cities there is virtually no organization at all.

On paper the national Democratic and Republican parties look quite similar. In both parties ultimate authority is in the hands of the **national convention** that meets every four years to nominate a presidential candidate. Between these conventions party affairs are managed by a **national committee** made up of delegates from each state and territory. In the Congress each party has a **congressional campaign committee** that helps members who are running for reelection or would-be members running for an open seat or challenging a candidate from the opposition party. The day-to-day work of the party is managed by a full-time, paid **national chairman**, who is elected by the committee.

For a long time, the two national parties were alike in behavior as well as description. The national chairman, if his party held the White House, would help decide who among the party faithful would get federal jobs. Otherwise the parties did very little.

But beginning in the late 1960s and early 1970s, the Republicans began to convert their national party into a well-financed, highly staffed organization devoted to finding and electing Republican candidates, especially to Congress. At about the same time, the Democrats began changing the rules governing how presidential candidates are nominated in ways that profoundly altered the distribution of power within the party. As a consequence the Republicans became a bureaucratized party, and the Democrats became a factionalized one. After the Republicans won five out of six presidential elections from 1968 to 1988 and briefly took control of the Senate, the Democrats began to suspect that maybe an efficient bureaucracy was better than a collection of warring factions, and so they made an effort to emulate the Republicans.

The national committees of the two parties have now become, in effect, national political consulting firms. The money they raise is used to recruit candidates, conduct polls, give legal and accounting advice, study issues and analyze voting trends, and finance party candidates. The national parties are no longer smoke-filled rooms; they are computer-filled rooms.

Each party raises money through its national committee, its House and Senate campaign committees, and its affiliated state and local party organizations. For the 2004 election, the Democrats spent about $656 million, the Republicans about $753 million.

Much of this money is regulated by the Federal Election Commission in ways that will be described in the next chapter. Federal rules limit how much anyone can contribute and how the money may be spent. But besides this so-called **federal money**, each party also raised a lot of nonfederal, or **soft money**. Soft money, which was not regulated by the government, consisted of funds used to pay for get-out-the-vote drives, party advertising that is not linked to the name of a particular candidate, and advertising on behalf of party issues. In practice, of course, soft money could easily be used to help candidates. In the 1996 campaign, the two parties spent more soft money—over $271 million—than regulated money. This gave rise to a demand for tougher campaign finance rules that would limit soft money, but as we shall see, that is not easily done. In the next chapter, we will see how the newest campaign finance law has affected the flow of election money.

Soft money *Money raised by political parties for activities other than directly supporting a federal candidate.*

National Conventions

The national committee selects the time and place of the national convention, sets the number of delegates from each state and territory, and indicates the rules under which delegates must be chosen. The number of delegates, and the manner of their selection, can significantly influence the chances for various presidential candidates, and considerable attention is thus devoted to working out extremely complex delegate-allocation formulas. In recent years, voting strength in the Democratic convention has shifted away from the conservative South and toward the North and West; in the Republican convention, it has shifted away from the more liberal East and toward the South and Southwest. This is but one sign—others will be mentioned later in this chapter—of the tendency of the two parties' conventions to move in opposite directions, the Democrats to the left and the Republicans to the right.

The exact formula for apportioning delegates to the conventions is complex. The Democrats, beginning in 1972, have developed an elaborate set of rules designed to weaken the control of local party leaders over delegates and to increase the proportion of women, young people, and minorities attending the convention. These rules were first drafted by a party commission headed by Senator George McGovern (who was later to make skillful use of them in

A liberal blog (left) and a conservative blog (right) that appear daily on the Web.

his successful bid for the presidential nomination) and have been revised every few years thereafter. The general thrust of these rules commissions during the 1970s was to broaden the antiparty changes begun by the Progressives at the beginning of this century. But whereas the earlier reformers had sought to minimize the role of parties in the election process, those of the 1970s sought to weaken the influence of leaders within the party—to create *intra*party democracy as well as *inter*party democracy. In 1981, however, yet another party commission changed some of these rules in order to increase the influence of elected officials and to make the convention more of a deliberative body; in 1986, the Democrats increased the role of senators and representatives still further.

Rules have consequences. New ones adopted for 1992 abolished winner-take-all primaries. Delegates to the Democratic convention were assigned to candidates in proportion to their primary or caucus vote, provided the candidate won at least 15 percent of those votes. This change hurt Hillary Clinton in 2008.

But the "reform" of the parties, especially of the Democrats, has had far more profound consequences than merely helping one candidate or another. Before 1968, the Republican party represented essentially white-collar voters, and the Democratic party represented blue-collar ones. After a decade of reform, the Republican and Democratic parties each represented two ideologically different sets of white-collar voters.[2] Democratic delegates are usually very liberal, Republican delegates very conservative.

Moreover, the reforms have changed the nature of national political conventions. Before 1972, the Democratic convention was where party leaders met to bargain over the selection of their presidential candidate; after 1972, it became a place where delegates met to ratify decisions made by voters in primary elections and local caucuses. Party leaders gathering in a smoke-filled room were replaced by ideologically motivated activists assembling before television cameras.

Most Americans dislike bosses, deals, and manipulation and prefer democracy, reform, and openness. However, we might make the mistake of assuming that anything carried out in the name of reform is a good idea. Rules must be judged by their practical results as well as by their conformity to some principle of fairness. Rules affect the distribution of power: They help some candidates win and others lose. Later in this chapter we shall try to assess delegate selection rules by looking more closely at how they affect who attends conventions and which presidential candidates are chosen.

State and Local Parties

To the extent that there is anything like regular, ongoing party organizations, they are found at the city, county, and state levels. In their day-to-day affairs, they are autonomous, independent units, affiliated with—but not controlled by—the national Democratic or Republican parties.

Formally these party units are organized under state law. Occasionally, the power structure follows the formal structure: a hierarchy of committees from the state level down to the county, sometimes city or town, and sometimes even precinct level. But more often the party can be understood only in terms of the informal processes whereby workers are recruited and leaders selected. There is no single kind of local party organization but rather five kinds, each of which operates within a party structure defined by law: Legally they are all precinct, city, or county organizations.

The Machine

The **political machine** is a party organization that recruits its members by the use of tangible incentives—political jobs, an opportunity to get favors from government—and that is characterized by a high degree of leadership control over member activity. At one time, many local party organizations were machines. Chicago still has one, though it is far less powerful than when it was led by Richard Daley a generation ago. In the nineteenth century, well before the arrival of vast numbers of immigrants, old-stock Americans had perfected the machine, run up the cost of government, and systematized vote fraud and corruption. When the

Political machine *A party organization that recruits its members by dispensing patronage—tangible incentives such as money, political jobs, an opportunity to get favors from government and that is characterized by a high degree of leadership control over member activity.*

Bettmann/Corbis

When New York's Tammany Hall was the Democratic party's headquarters, political parties were powerful institutions in many big cities.

immigrants began flooding the eastern cities, the machines provided them with all manner of services—akin to an informal welfare system—in exchange for their support at the polls.

The abuses of the machine gradually diminished through stricter voter registration, civil-service reform, competitive bidding laws, and the Hatch Act of 1939, which took federal employees out of machine politics. But far more important than the various progressive reforms that weakened the machines were changes among voters. As voters grew in education, income, and sophistication, they depended less on the advice and leadership of local party officials. And as the federal government created a bureaucratic welfare state, the party's welfare system declined in value.

In its heyday, the machine was both a self-serving organization and an informal social-welfare system—but above all, it was a frank recognition that politics requires organization. Even allowing for vote fraud, these organizations turned out huge votes: More people participated in politics when mobilized by a machine than when appealed to by television or "good government" associations.[3] And because the machines were interested in winning, they were willing to support the presidential candidate with the best chance of winning, regardless of his policy views (provided, of course, that he was not determined to wreck the machine once in office). Republican machines helped elect Abraham Lincoln as well as Warren G. Harding; Democratic machines were crucial in electing Franklin D. Roosevelt and John F. Kennedy. The old-style machine is almost extinct, though important examples can still be found in the Democratic organization in Cook County (Chicago) and the Republican organization in Nassau County (New York).

Ideological Parties

Ideological party *A party that values principled stands on issues above all else, including winning. It claims to have a comprehensive view of American society and government radically different from that of the established parties.*

At the opposite extreme from the machine is the **ideological party**. Where the machine values winning above all else, the ideological party values principle above all else. Where the former depends on monetary incentives, the latter spurns them. Whereas the former is strongly hierarchical and disciplined, the latter is usually contentious and riddled by factions.

The typical ideological party is a "third party," such as the Socialist, Socialist Workers, Prohibition, and Libertarian parties. But even within the mainstream Democratic and Republican parties, local units can be found that are, if not rigidly ideological, then certainly more devoted to issues and principles than to party loyalty.

Important examples of issue-oriented groups within the two main parties are the "reform" or "amateur" clubs that sprang up in the late 1950s and early 1960s in such cities as New York, Los Angeles, and San Francisco and in many parts of Wisconsin and Minnesota. The New York clubs successfully challenged the Democratic machine and became a dominant force in Manhattan. In California, where there was no machine to attack, the clubs moved to fill a vacuum created by the absence of any other kind of organization. From time to time they have been the major locus of power in the state.[4] Similarly, in California, the Republican Assembly—a collection of conservative clubs—was for a long time more important than the formal party machinery in promoting candidates.

Members of these clubs became active in politics because of their strong interest in issues, and they expected that decisions within the party would be as participatory and democratic as possible. Thus such clubs were subject to intense internal conflict, and, unlike the machines, their leaders had much less room to maneuver without being accused of "selling out." Because politics, especially in a two-party system, requires that coalitions be built among groups and people who do not always agree on issues, this constraint on the ability of a club leader to make useful alliances can be a weakness.

Democratic club members tend to be much more liberal than the average Democratic voter, and Republican members, much more conservative than the typical Republican voter.[5] Recently, two new groups of issue-oriented activists— conservative Christians and anti-spending backers of the Tea Party movement— have become important forces in some local parties. They have won control of many city and county Republican party organizations.

Solidary Groups

The most common types of party organizations are not machines or issue-oriented clubs, but groups of people who participate in politics because they enjoy the game, or because it is a way of meeting and being with people. These groups are called "sociability" or **solidary** associations.

Solidary *An incentive that relies on friendship or sociability.*

Some of these associations were once machines that have lost their patronage but whose members—especially the older ones—continue to serve in the organization out of a desire for camaraderie. In other cases, precinct, ward, and district committees are built up in the same way as bowling leagues and bridge clubs—on the basis of friendship networks.[6]

The advantage of such groups is that they are neither corrupt nor inflexible; the disadvantage is that they often do not work very hard. Knocking on doors on rainy November evenings to talk people into voting for your candidate is not especially appealing if you joined the party primarily because you like to attend meetings or drink coffee with your friends.[7]

Sponsored Parties

Sometimes a relatively strong party organization can be created among volunteers without heavy reliance on money or ideology and without depending entirely on people finding the work fun. This occurs when another organization exists in the community that can create, or at least sponsor, a local party structure. The clearest example of this is the Democratic party in and around Detroit, which has been developed, led, and to some extent financed by the political arm of the United Auto Workers (UAW) union. The UAW has had a long tradition of rank-and-file activism, and because Detroit is virtually a one-industry town, it was not hard to transfer some of this activism from union organizing to voter organizing.[8]

Few locations have organizations that can bolster, sponsor, or even take over the weak formal party structure as effectively or as dominantly as the UAW. Thus sponsored local parties are not common in the United States.

Personal Followings

Because in most areas candidates can no longer count on the backing of a machine, because issue-oriented clubs are limited to upper-middle-class members

Personal following *The political support provided to a candidate on the basis of personal popularity and networks.*

and sponsored parties to a few unionized areas, and because solidary groups are not always very productive, a person wanting to win an election will usually try to form a **personal following**, a group that will work for him or her without pay during a specific election campaign and then disband until the next election rolls around.

For this approach to succeed, a candidate must have an appealing personality, many friends, or a big bank account. The Kennedy family has had all three, and the electoral successes of John F. and Edward M. Kennedy in Massachusetts and of Robert Kennedy in New York became legendary. Other powerful politicians who have relied on personal followings have included Mayor James Michael Curley of Boston (often erroneously described as a "boss") and such southerners as Eugene and Herman Talmadge in Georgia; Huey, Earl, and Russell Long in Louisiana; and Harry F. Byrd Sr. and Jr. in Virginia. George H. W. Bush also established such a following. After he was president, one son (Jeb) became governor of Florida and another one (George W.) became governor of Texas and then president. The name "Bush" began to have a direct appeal to the voters.

Before radio and television, many politicians wishing to build a personal following had to content themselves with running in small constituencies where they could easily become known. Radio and television changed all that, permitting a candidate to speak directly to large numbers of voters, without editing, and thus to build statewide and even national followings completely outside the party structure.

Some readers may take it for granted that a personal following is a good thing because it makes it easier to vote for the person rather than the party and to keep party "bosses" from interfering with the popular will. But there is another side to the story. With so many offices to be filled and so many personalities offering to fill them, the average voter will be lucky to form a reasonable judgment about even two or three of the candidates in the course of a year.

Though all these kinds of local parties are important, political activists on the national scene increasingly do not work their way up from the local parties but enter the national party directly via various interest groups, such as those concerned with abortion, civil rights, or union affairs. At one Democratic national convention, for example, a large number of delegates were members of three organizations: the AFL-CIO, the National Education Association, and the National Organization for Women.[9] At Republican conventions, many delegates are Christian fundamentalists. Increasingly, political elites come not from the parties, but from social movements concerned with abortion, feminism, civil rights, or evangelical religions.

The Two-Party System

With so many different varieties of local party organizations (or nonorganizations) and with such a great range of opinion found within each party, it is remarkable that we have had only two major political parties for most of our history. In the world at large, a two-party system is a rarity; most European democracies are multiparty systems.[10] Not only do we have but two parties with any chance of winning nationally; these parties have been, over time, rather evenly balanced. And whenever one party has achieved a temporary ascendancy and the other has been pronounced dead, the "dead" party has displayed remarkable powers of recuperation, coming back with important victories.

At the state or congressional district level, however, the parties are not evenly balanced. Though all regions are now more competitive than they once were—the South is no longer exclusively Democratic, and much of New England is no longer unshakably Republican—one party or the other tends to enjoy a substantial advantage in at least half the states and in perhaps two-thirds of the congressional districts.

Scholars do not entirely agree as to why the two-party system should be so permanent a feature of American political life, but two kinds of explanations are of major importance: electoral laws and public opinion.

The Two-Party System and Electoral Laws

In several ways the laws governing elections make it hard for a third-party candidate to win. First, members of the House of Representatives are elected from **single-member districts**. Because the candidate of only one party can win a seat in a given district, only two parties are likely to put up candidates. Third and fourth parties would have no chance to win. By contrast, in France and Israel the members of the national legislature are chosen by **proportional representation**, which means that several members are elected from each district and are divided among the parties in proportion to the number of votes each party receives. For example, if a party wins 37 percent of the votes, it gets 37 percent of the seats; if it gets 5 percent of the votes, it gets 5 percent of the seats. Thus even the smallest parties have a chance to win and so, many third parties form and run candidates.

Second, the winner in a race for the Senate or the House of Representatives is determined by a candidate's ability to win a **plurality** of votes cast. (Winning a plurality means simply getting more votes than any other candidate, even if the winner does not get a majority—more than half—of all the votes cast.) In most states there are no runoff elections between the two candidates with the most votes. If there were runoff elections, many parties might enter the first election hoping to do well enough to get into the runoff, at which time they would form alliances with the other minor parties in an effort to win a majority. Just this sort of thing happens in some European nations, and in a few American states in their primary elections to choose party candidates.

The most dramatic example of the plurality system is the American electoral college. The presidential candidate who carries a state—even with a minority of the popular vote—gets all that state's electoral votes (except in Maine and Nebraska). Minor parties cannot compete under this system. Voters know this and are often reluctant to "waste" their votes on a minor-party candidate who cannot win. Because the presidency is the greatest prize of American politics, parties that hope to win must be as broadly based as possible. As a practical matter, there will thus be only two parties—one made up of the supporters of the party in power and the other encompassing everyone else. In 1992, Ross Perot learned

Single-member districts *Legislative districts from which one representative is chosen.*

Proportional representation *A voting system in which representatives in a legislature are chosen by the proportion of all votes each candidate (or each candidate's party) gets.*

Plurality system *An electoral system, used in almost all American elections, in which the winner is the candidate who gets the most votes, even if he or she does not receive a majority of the votes.*

that lesson: Though he received 19 percent of the popular vote, he got no electoral votes. Some states have voted to cast their electoral votes for whomever wins the most popular votes nationally, but for that to happen the Constitution would have to be amended.

The Two-Party System and Public Opinion

The other explanation for the persistence of the two-party system is found in the opinions of the voters. Though there have been periods of bitter dissent, most citizens have agreed often enough to permit them to come together into two broad coalitions. In some European countries, such major issues as the nature of the economic system, the prerogatives of the monarchy, and the role of the church in government have been so divisive that they have helped prevent the formation of broad coalition parties.

Americans have had other deep divisions—between black and white or between North and South—and yet the two-party system has endured. This suggests that electoral procedures are of great importance, making it impossible to form an all-white or all-black party except as an act of momentary defiance or as a ploy (perhaps attempted by George Wallace in 1968) to take enough votes away from the two major parties to force the presidential election into the House of Representatives. Both Democratic and Republican parties have changed their procedures and policies enough to keep most would-be dissidents inside the major parties and away from third parties.

The minor (or "third") parties that have had the greatest influence on public policy were those formed as factional offshoots of the major parties—the Liberal Republicans of the post–Civil War era; Theodore Roosevelt's Bull Moose Progressives of 1912; Robert La Follette's Progressives of 1924; and the Dixiecrat, Wallace, and Ross Perot's Reform Party movements of more recent times (see Figure 7.1). The formation of all these groups probably encouraged the major parties to pay more attention to the issues the groups raised: civil-service reform, business regulation, desegregation, and the budget deficit. The threat of a factional split is a risk both major parties must face. In their efforts to avoid such splits, each party tends to accommodate the views of minority factions in ways that usually keep these factions from forming third parties.

Nominating a President

As we have seen, the major parties are pulled by two contrary pressures. One, generated by a desire to win the presidency, pushes them in the direction of nominating a candidate who can appeal to the majority of voters and who will thus have essentially middle-of-the-road views. The other, produced by the need to keep dissident elements in the party from bolting and forming a third party, leads them to compromise with dissidents or extremists in ways that may damage the party's standing with the voters.

The Democrats and Republicans have always faced such conflicting pressures, but of late the strains have become especially acute. Conventions are no longer

Types of Minor Parties

1. Ideological Parties

Parties professing a comprehensive view of American society and government radically different from that of the established parties. Most have been Marxist in outlook, but some are quite the opposite, such as the Libertarian party.

EXAMPLES

Socialist party (1901 to 1960s)
Socialist Labor party (1888 to present)
Socialist Workers party (1938 to present)
Communist party (1920s to present)
Libertarian party (1972 to present)
Green party (1984 to present)

2. One-Issue Parties

Parties seeking a single policy, usually revealed by their names, and avoiding other issues.

EXAMPLES

Free Soil party—to prevent spread of slavery (1848–1852)
American or "Know-Nothing" party—to oppose immigration and Catholics (1856)
Prohibition party—to ban the sale of liquor (1869 to present)
Women's party—to obtain the right to vote for women (1913–1920)

3. Economic-Protest Parties

Parties, usually based in a particular region, especially involving farmers, that protest against depressed economic conditions. These tend to disappear as conditions improve.

EXAMPLES

Greenback party (1876–1884)
Populist party (1892–1908)

4. Factional Parties

Parties that are created by a split in a major party, usually over the identity and philosophy of the major party's presidential candidate.

EXAMPLES

Split off from the Republican party:
"Bull Moose" Progressive party (1912)
La Follette Progressive party (1924)
Split off from the Democratic party:
States' Rights ("Dixiecrat") party (1948)
Henry Wallace Progressive party (1948)
American Independent (George Wallace) party (1968)
Split off from both parties:
Reform party (1992–present)

AP Photo/Reed Saxon

Ross Perot founded the independent Reform party in 1996.

dominated by party leaders and elected officials who, in order to win, usually ignore dissident factions. Today, with most delegates selected in primary elections and with the power of party leaders greatly diminished, a larger proportion of the delegates are likely to be more actively interested in issues and less amenable to compromise.[11]

Are the Delegates Representative of the Voters?

There would be no conflict between the party's desire to win and its desire to uphold principles if the delegates to nominating conventions had the same policy views as most voters, or at least as most party supporters. But they do not. In recent years, the difference between the views of party activists and the rank-and-file has become very great.

At every Democratic National Convention since 1972, the delegates had views on a variety of important issues—welfare, military policy, school desegregation, crime, and abortion—that were vastly different from those of rank-and-file Democrats. Likewise, the delegates to most recent Republican conventions were ideologically different from the voters at large. The Democratic delegates have been more liberal, the Republicans more conservative.[12] A rare exception to this pattern occurred in 2008, when Democratic voters self-identified as liberal (48 percent) at a higher rate than did Democratic delegates (see Table 7.1).

Still, the post-1972 disparity in both parties between delegate opinion and rank-and-file voter attitude (and often delegate candidate preferences) remains significant and difficult to explain. Some have attributed the discrepancy to the revised rules (described earlier in this chapter) by which delegates are chosen, especially those rules that require increased representation for women, minorities, and the young. But this does not explain why the Republicans nominated Barry Goldwater in 1964 and almost nominated Ronald Reagan instead of Gerald Ford in 1976. Moreover, women, minorities, and youth have among them all

Table 7.1   Party Delegates and Party Voters by Ideology, 2004 and 2008

	Democrats		Republicans	
Ideology	Delegates 2004/2008	Voters 2004/2008	Delegates 2004/2008	Voters 2004/2008
Liberal	41%/43%	34%/48%	1%/0%	8%/5%
Conservative	3/3	19/16	63/72	61/63

Source: *New York Times*/CBS News Poll, Aug. 3–23, 2004 and Jul. 16–Aug 17, 2008; Jul. 23–Aug. 26, 2008

shades of opinion. Why are only *certain* elements in these groups heavily represented at the conventions?

Who Votes in Primaries and Caucuses?

A second explanation is the growth in the number and importance of primaries and caucuses. Between 1952 and 1968, fewer than half of each party's delegates were selected in primaries, and some presidential nominees—Adlai Stevenson in 1952, Hubert Humphrey in 1968—won the nomination without even *entering* a primary. But beginning in 1972, the number of primaries increased, and from then on, no candidate could win the presidential nomination without first winning the largest share of primary votes.[13] Today, three-fourths of the states have primaries that choose the great majority of convention delegates. Primaries are no longer, as Harry Truman once called them, "eyewash."

Primaries affect the kind of delegates chosen to attend the convention because people who vote in such primary elections tend to differ from those who vote in the general elections. Only about half as many people vote in a primary as in general elections, and those who do tend to be more affluent and better educated than the average voter.[14] Because upper-status voters are more likely to have a consistent ideology, it stands to reason that Democratic primary voters will support more liberal candidates, and Republicans more conservative ones, than would the average voter.

Caucuses overrepresent activist opinion even more than do primaries, because going to a **caucus**—an alternative to a state primary in which party members attend a meeting, often lasting for hours and held in the dead of winter in a schoolhouse miles from home—is far more arduous than voting in a primary. Hence only the most dedicated partisans attend. For the Democrats, these have tended to be the most liberal Democrats. In 1988, Jesse Jackson, the most liberal Democratic candidate, made his best showing among white voters in those states that held caucuses—he beat Michael Dukakis, the more moderate candidate, in Alaska, Delaware, Michigan, and Vermont, all caucus states. By contrast, Dukakis beat Jackson among white voters in those states that held primaries. On the Republican side, Pat Robertson, the conservative television evangelist, could not win a single primary, but he won the caucuses in Alaska, Hawaii, and Washington.

Caucus (congressional)
An association of members of Congress created to advocate a political ideology or a regional, ethnic, or economic interest.

How We Compare

How Many Political Parties?

The United States has two political parties in Congress.

Other countries have fewer or more parties in their legislatures:

China	1
Canada	4
United Kingdom	5
Germany	6
Mexico	9

Russia	9
Israel	11
France	17
Brazil	19
India	52 (more or less)

Source: Arthur S. Banks, et al., *Political Handbook of the World: 2007* (Washington, D.C.: CQ Press, 2007).

Who Are the New Delegates?

A third explanation is that no matter how delegates are chosen, they are a different breed today than they once were. Far more Republican and Democratic delegates are now issue-oriented activists with a "purist" attitude toward politics than was formerly the case when conventions were dominated by professional politicians. And the activists have generally favored the more ideological candidate. Moreover, it is no longer clear that voters are drifting away from their loyalty to political parties. In his study of voter loyalty, Larry Bartels has shown that partisan loyalties have rebounded among voters in both presidential and congressional elections. The proportion of voters who strongly identify with one of the two major parties has increased while the share of those who are independent has shrunk. As a result, since the 1980s, partisan voting has become more common. This is true outside as well as inside the South and among both young and old and well-schooled and poorly schooled voters.[15] The 2000 election was a good illustration of this. The great majority of Democrats voted for Gore, and Republicans for Bush. The election was decided by a small group of independent voters.

In sum, presidential nominating conventions are now heavily influenced by ideologically motivated activists. The Democratic convention has a heavy representation from organized feminists, unionized school teachers, and abortion-rights activists; the Republican convention has large numbers of anti-abortion activists, Christian conservatives, and small-government libertarians. As a result the presidential nominating system is now fundamentally different from what it was as late as the mid-1960s. The advantage of the new system is that it increases the opportunity for those with strong policy preferences to play a role in the party and thus reduces the chance that they will form a factional minor party. The disadvantage is that it increases the chances that one or both parties may nominate presidential candidates who do not appeal to the average voter or even to a party's rank and file.

Do the Parties Differ?

Many people think that there are no real differences between the Democratic and the Republican parties. They may agree with George Wallace (Alabama governor and third-party candidate for president in 1968), who liked to say that there was not "a dime's worth of difference" between the two parties.

It is true that the need to win elections pulls each party to the political center as it tries to attract the uncommitted voter. But there is still a significant difference in the general policy attitudes of the two parties, especially among leaders and activists. And some differences in preference are evident between rank-and-file voters who identify with one party or another (see Table 7.2). For example, voters who identified with the Democratic party were slightly more liberal on a number of policy questions—in favor of federal spending on day care, paying more attention to the needs of blacks, and reducing military spending—than were voters who identified with the Republican party.[16] But if these were the only differences between the parties, one might be justified in concluding that they are but two slightly different versions of the same political creed.

Among party activists, leaders, and officeholders, however, the differences between the two parties are major. The delegates to the Democratic and Republican presidential nominating conventions usually have almost totally opposed views on such broad and basic questions as welfare, busing, crime, and the military. Studies of party activists from 1972 to the present confirm this.[17] And among people elected to office, the same partisan differences are apparent.

Table 7.2	**Policy Preferences of Democratic and Republican Voters, 2008**	
	Preferences of	
Issue	**Democratic Voters**	**Republican Voters**
Allow people to invest part of Social Security taxes on their own	27%	47%
By law, a woman should always be able to obtain an abortion	47	26
The federal government should make it more difficult to obtain a gun	61	36
Favour the death penalty	54	84
Same-sex couples should be allowed to marry	41	20
Protect environment, even if it costs jobs and standard of living	41	24

Source: The 2008 National Elections Study.

It seems that the differences between the two parties grew in the 1960s and 1970s. As we saw in Chapter 6, there is some evidence that more people consider themselves liberals or conservatives today than formerly. This change has especially affected activists in the Democratic party. In 1968 and again in 1972, the proportion of Democratic activists who had distinctly liberal views was more than twice that in 1956 or 1960.[18]

These facts suggest the central problem faced by a political party today. In most elections, voters cluster in the middle of the political spectrum. But the activists, leaders, convention delegates, and officeholders within each party tend to be closer to the political extremes than to the middle. Thus a person seeking to obtain power in a party, to become a convention delegate, or to win a party's nomination for office must often move closer to the extremes than to the center. This creates a potential dilemma: the stance one takes to obtain the support of party activists is often quite different from the stance one must take to win a general election. In Chapter 8 we shall look closely at how politicians try to cope with that dilemma.

Interest Groups

Almost every tourist arriving in Washington will visit the White House and the Capitol. Many will stop by the Supreme Court building. But hardly any will walk down K Street, where much of the political life of the country occurs. In these ordinary-looking office buildings, and in similar ones lining nearby streets, are the offices of the nearly seven thousand organizations that are represented in Washington and that participate in politics. These are **interest groups**—organizations that seek to influence the decisions of government. They are often called lobbies.

Interest group *An organization of people, or a "letterhead" organization, sharing a common interest or goal that seeks to influence the making of public policy.*

The Proliferation of Interest Groups

There are several reasons that these organizations play so important a role in American politics. First, the more cleavages in a society, the greater the variety of interests that will exist. In addition to divisions along lines of income and occupation found in any society, America is a nation of countless immigrants and many races. As James Madison stated in *Federalist* No. 10, "The latent causes of factions are thus sown in the nature of man." Second, the decentralized American constitutional system contributes to the number of interest groups by multiplying the points at which groups can gain access to the government; the more chances there are to influence policy, the more interest groups there will be that seek to influence policy.

Third, the weakness of political parties in this country may help explain the number and strength of interest groups. Where parties are strong, interest groups work through the parties; where parties are weak, interests operate directly on the government. Thus in Chicago, where the Democratic party has been very strong, labor unions, business associations, and citizens' groups have had to work with the party and on its terms. But in Boston or Los Angeles, where the parties are very weak, interest groups proliferate and play a large role in making policy.[19] The difference is even more striking when one contrasts the United States with Europe.[20] In Europe, parties are still very strong; interest groups are much less powerful.

WHAT WOULD YOU DO?

MEMORANDUM

To: Elizabeth Bunting, All for Life president

From: Ralph Marx, political consultant

Subject: Upcoming presidential election

Without regard to your organization's cause or issue, I have been hired to brief you on the pros and cons of backing or fielding a third-party candidate in the presidential election.

Arguments for:

1. Independent and third-party candidates can garner votes for president or tip an election result. In 1992, Ross Perot won nearly a fifth of the votes. In 2000, Green party candidate Ralph Nader got only 3 percent, but that included 100,000 votes in Florida where Republican Bush was credited with only 600 votes more than Democrat Gore.

2. Third-party candidates (Eugene Debs, Robert La Follette, George Wallace) can make a mark on American politics. Third parties have advocated policies later championed by the two main parties: abolishing slavery (Free-Soil party), women's right to vote (Woman's party), direct election of U.S. senators (Progressive party), and many others.

Friday,

Big Anti-Abortion Group Might Leave GOP, Back a Pro-Life Party

June 6
NEW YORK.

The head of one of the largest pro-life groups in the United States announced yesterday that her organization will not endorse the Republican presidential candidate unless the party's platform includes a detailed plan for outlawing all abortions. "The days when Republicans could take us for granted are over," said Elizabeth Bunting. "If the platform is not satisfactory, we might just get behind a third party," she threatened.

Arguments against:

1. It is virtually impossible to win, thanks to the winner-take-all system of elections. Since the 1850s, over one hundred third parties have come and gone. There will be a brief media frenzy when you bolt; but, after that, you might be ignored. Better to grumble but be heard inside a major party than to shout but not be heard inside a minor party.

2. Splitting off from a major party could weaken support for your issue and lead one or the other major party to "resolve" it in a watered-down way. In the 1930s, the Democrats plucked Social Security from the Socialist party's far-reaching plan. In the 1980s, the Republicans' position on taxes only faintly echoed the Libertarian party's.

Your Decision:

Back or begin a third party _____

Stay with the major party _____

The Birth of Interest Groups

American interest groups are not only numerous but have proliferated rapidly in the last two decades. Roughly 70 percent of all groups now represented in Washington located there after 1960, and nearly half opened their doors just since 1970.[21] These have included numerous environmental, consumer, and political-reform organizations, such as those sponsored by Ralph Nader.

There have been other periods in our history when political associations were created in especially large numbers: in the 1770s, groups agitated for American independence; in the 1830s and 1840s, religious associations and antislavery groups organized; in the 1860s, craft-based trade unions, the Grange (a farmers' group), and various fraternal organizations emerged; in the 1880s and 1890s, business associations proliferated. The great era of organization building, however, was in the first two decades of the twentieth century, which saw the formation of such groups as the Chamber of Commerce, the National Association of Manufacturers, the American Medical Association, the NAACP, the Urban League, the American Farm Bureau, the Farmers' Union, the National Catholic Welfare Conference, the American Jewish Committee, and the Anti-Defamation League.

The fact that associations in general, and political interest groups in particular, are created more rapidly in some periods than in others suggests that these groups do not arise inevitably out of natural social processes. At least four factors help explain the episodic rise of interest groups.

First, broad economic developments create new interests and redefine old ones. Farmers began organizing when market forces changed; large mass-membership labor unions did not exist until there arose mass-production industry operated by large corporations.

Second, government policy itself helped create interest groups. Wars create veterans, who in turn demand pensions and other benefits from the government. The first large veterans' organization, made up of Union soldiers, formed after the Civil War. The federal government indirectly encouraged the formation of the American Farm Bureau Federation. The Chamber of Commerce was launched at a conference attended by President William Howard Taft. Medical and legal societies became important in part because state governments gave such groups the power to decide who was qualified to become a doctor or lawyer. And unions, especially those in mass-production industries, began to flourish in the 1930s after Congress outlawed many unfair labor practices.[22]

Third, political organizations do not emerge automatically even when economic conditions and government policy seem to encourage them: somebody must exercise leadership, often at substantial personal cost. At certain times leaders—frequently young people caught up in social change—appear in greater numbers. In the 1830s and 1840s, young people, affected by a great religious revival, created antislavery and other moral-reform organizations. Between 1890 and 1920, the rapidly growing college-educated middle class established numerous reform and professional organizations. And in the 1960s, when college enrollments more than doubled, many new organizations appealed to young people powerfully influenced by the civil-rights and anti–Vietnam War movements.

Finally, the expansion of government into a given area stimulates the expansion of groups and lobbies interested in that area. Most Washington offices representing corporations, labor unions, and trade and professional associations were established before 1960, in a period when government began to make policies important to business and labor. The great majority of environmental and consumer-protection lobbies, social welfare associations, and groups concerned with civil rights, the elderly, and the disabled came to Washington after 1960, when policies of interest to these causes were being adopted.[23]

Kinds of Organizations

When we think of an organization, we often think of the Boy Scouts or the League of Women Voters—a group consisting of individual members. In Washington, however, many organizations do not have individual members at all, but are offices operated by a staff or "letterhead" organizations that get most of their money from foundations or from the government. It is a bit misleading to call such organizations "interest groups" because that name implies a group (or association) of interested members. But the term *interest group* has become too common to abandon it now. So instead we shall speak of two kinds of interest groups—*institutional interests* and *membership interests*.[24]

Institutional Interests

Institutional interests are individuals or organizations representing other organizations—business firms, local governments, foundations, and universities. More than five hundred firms have representatives in Washington, most of whom have opened their offices since 1970. Business firms that do not want to maintain a full-time representative in Washington can hire a Washington lawyer or public-relations expert on a part-time basis (often at $400 or more an hour). Between 1970 and 1980, the number of lawyers in Washington more than tripled; the Washington, D.C. Bar Association in 1996 had over 43,000 members—more than Los Angeles, a city three times its size.[25] Another kind of institutional interest is the trade or governmental association, such as the National Independent Retail Jewelers or the National Association of Counties.

Institutions that represent other organizations tend to be interested in bread-and-butter issues of vital concern to their clients; their leaders often earn a lot, and they are expected to deliver a lot. Just what they are expected to deliver, however, varies with the diversity of the groups making up the organization. Those that represent a limited number of firms with a similar outlook can formulate and carry out clear policies squarely based on their business interests. By contrast, the United States Chamber of Commerce represents thousands of different businesses in hundreds of different communities. Its membership is so large and diverse that it can take clear positions on only certain issues (like lower taxes), while ignoring others (like tariffs) over which business leaders are divided.

Membership Interests

Although Americans claim to be a nation of joiners, they are distinctive only for their readiness to join religious and civic or political associations.[26] This proclivity to get together with other citizens to engage in civic or political action reflects, apparently, a greater sense of **political efficacy** (a citizen's sense that he or she can understand and influence politics) and civic duty in this country. Asked in a survey what they would do to protest an unjust local regulation, 56 percent of the Americans—but only 34 percent of the British and 13 percent of the Germans—said they would try to organize their neighbors to write letters, sign petitions, or otherwise act together.[27] In the same spirit, Americans are also more likely than Europeans to think that organized activity is an effective way to influence the national government, remote as that institution may seem. And this American willingness to form civic or political groups is not only a product of higher levels of education; at every level of schooling, Americans are political joiners.[28]

We take for granted that Americans join many organizations, but when you think about it, it is a puzzle. No matter how dutiful a citizen may be, no matter how much that citizen understands and worries about an issue, why should that person pay dues to an organization when those dues—maybe $15 or $25 a year—will have little effect on the power of the organization? Why should that person attend a meeting when, chances are, his or her presence will scarcely be noticed? Why do *anything* for an organization if you can't make a difference and you benefit anyway from whatever success the organization has in influencing policy?

To get people to join large membership organizations like the Sierra Club, the NAACP, or the National Rifle Association, organizations must offer would-be members some kind of incentive. There are three kinds.

Solidary incentives encompass the sense of pleasure, status, or companionship that arises out of meeting together in small groups. Because such rewards require face-to-face contact, national interest groups offering them often organize themselves as coalitions of small, local units—something more easily done in the United States than in Europe because of the great importance of local government in our federal system. Examples include the League of Women Voters, the Parent-Teacher Association, the NAACP, the Rotary Club, and the American Legion; all have local chapters that keep busy with local affairs while the national staff pursues larger goals.

Material incentives are offered by some groups to make it financially attractive to join. Farm organizations offer members supplies at discount prices, marketing through cooperatives, and low-cost insurance; AARP (an organization for people over 50) has recruited more than 30 million members by supplying them with everything from low-cost life insurance to group travel plans. Although such organizations get most of their money from members who join for their own material benefit, they claim to represent these members and lobby accordingly.

The third—and most difficult—kind of reward is the **purposive incentive**. Many associations rely chiefly on the appeal of their stated goals to recruit members, who obviously must feel passionately about the goal, have a strong sense of

---

Political efficacy *A citizen's sense that he or she can understand and influence politics.*

Solidary incentives *The social rewards that lead people to join local or state political organizations. People who find politics fun and want to meet others who share their interests are said to respond to solidary incentives.*

Material incentives *Benefits that have monetary value, including money, gifts, services, or discounts received as a result of one's membership in an organization.*

Purposive incentive *The benefit that comes from serving a cause or principle from which one does not personally benefit.*

duty, or be unable to say no to a friend. Organizations that rely wholly on a sense of purpose tend to be small. The American Civil Liberties Union relies chiefly on purpose as incentive.

When the purpose of the organization, if attained, will principally benefit non-members, it is customary to call the group a **public-interest lobby**. (Whether the public at large will benefit is, of course, a matter of opinion, but at least the group members think they are working selflessly for the common good.) Many such organizations are highly controversial, and it is precisely the controversy that attracts members--or at least those members who support one side of the issue. Most of these groups are either markedly liberal or markedly conservative in outlook.

Perhaps the best known of the liberal public-interest groups are those founded by or associated with Ralph Nader, who first won fame in the mid-1960s as a critic of unsafe automobiles. Nader created various organizations dealing with matters of interest to consumers and turned over to them the money he had made from an out-of-court settlement with General Motors (which had clumsily attempted to discredit him), from the sale of his books, and from lecture fees. He also founded Public Citizen, which raised money by direct-mail solicitation from thousands of small contributors and sought foundation grants. Finally, he helped create Public Interest Research Groups (PIRGs) in a number of states, supported by fees from college students and concerned with organizing student activists to work on local projects.

Membership organizations relying on their stated purpose as incentive, especially deeply controversial purposes, tend to be shaped by the mood of the times. To stay in the public eye, the issues they espouse must be hot. Thus they devote a lot of attention to getting publicity, especially by developing good contacts with the media. And they often do best at getting members and attention when the national administration is hostile, not sympathetic, to their views. That is because it is easier to raise money from small donors by calling their attention to the powerful "enemies" the organization faces.

Public-interest lobby *A political organization, the stated goals of which will principally benefit nonmembers.*

The Influence of the Staff

When all members have a clear and similar stake in an issue, an interest group simply exerts influence politically on behalf of its members. But if the members have joined mainly to obtain solidary or material benefits, they may not care very much about many of the issues in which the organization gets involved. Thus what the interest group does may reflect more what the staff wants than what the members believe. A good example is the aggressive lobbying that a large labor union did on behalf of tougher civil-rights laws, even though most of the union's members did not think they were needed.[29] Likewise the National Council of the Churches of Christ, an organization of various Protestant denominations with several million members, has taken a strongly liberal position on many political issues, almost certainly unrepresentative of the conservative views of most white Protestants, especially southern ones.[30] These organizations can do this because people generally join unions or churches for reasons other than how staff members in New York or Washington think.

Funds for Interest Groups

All interest groups have some trouble raising money, but membership organizations have more trouble than most, and membership organizations relying on appeals to purpose have the most difficulty.

To raise more money than members supply in dues, lobbying organizations have turned to three sources that have become important in recent years: foundation grants, government grants, and direct-mail solicitation.

Foundation Grants

One study of eighty-three (primarily liberal) public-interest lobbying groups found that one-third of them received half or more of their funds from foundation grants; one-tenth received more than 90 percent from such sources.[31] In one ten-year period, the Ford Foundation alone contributed about $21 million to liberal public-interest groups.[32] Conservative foundations do the same for like-minded interest groups.

Federal Grants and Contracts

The expansion of federal grants during the 1960s and 1970s benefited interest groups as well as cities and states; the cutbacks in those grants during the early 1980s hurt those groups even more than it hurt local governments.[33] Of course the federal government usually does not give the money directly to support lobbying itself; instead funds are given to support some project the organization has undertaken. But money for a project helps support the organization as a whole and thus enables it to press Congress for more money and for favorable policies. Beneficiaries of such grants have ranged from the National Alliance of Business for summer youth job projects to the Reverend Jesse Jackson for his community-development organization, PUSH.

Because most public-interest groups pursue liberal policies, the Reagan administration was not only interested in saving federal money by reducing grants to interest groups but particularly wanted to cut back on money spent to lobby for liberal causes. But complaints by conservative activists as late as the 1990s that federal money was still "funding the left" show how difficult it is to make sweeping changes in anything the federal government does.

Direct Mail

If one technique is unique to the modern membership group, it is the sophistication with which computerized mailings are used to both raise money and mobilize supporters. Mailing lists themselves are frequently sold to other groups with similar views, and letters can be tailor-made to target the most likely contributors. But raising money by mail is expensive. To bring in more money than it spends, an organization must write a letter that will galvanize at least 2 or 3 percent of the names on the list to send in a check. Some organizations that use direct mail spend 80 or 90 cents out of every dollar received to pay for fundraising and administrative costs.

The Problem of Bias

The interest groups active in Washington certainly reflect an upper-class bias: well-off people are more likely than poor people to join and be active in interest groups, and interest groups representing business and the professions are much more numerous and better financed than those representing minorities, consumers, or the disadvantaged.[34] More than half of the nearly seven thousand groups represented in Washington are corporations, and another third are professional and trade associations. Only 4 percent are public-interest groups; fewer than 2 percent are civil-rights or minority groups.[35]

But these facts alone say nothing about who wins and who loses on particular issues. Moreover, business-oriented interest groups are often divided among themselves. This divisiveness is even more characteristic of agricultural organizations, representing many different commodities and regions. Thus, although farmers still have great influence in *blocking* a bill they oppose, they encounter increasing difficulty in getting Congress to *pass* a bill they want.[36]

Whenever American politics is described as having an "upper-class bias," it is important to ask exactly what this bias is. Most major conflicts in American politics—over foreign policy, economic affairs, environmental protection, or equal rights for women—are conflicts *within* the upper-middle classes; they are conflicts, that is, among politically active elites. As we saw in Chapter 6, there are profound cleavages of opinion among these elites. Interest-group activity reflects these cleavages.

At one time, scholars liked to describe the American political system as **pluralist**, representing the free, complete, and effective competition of interest groups. But when these accounts were written in the 1950s, they were probably wrong, or at least incomplete. Blacks, women, consumers, and environmentalists were largely unorganized and thus underrepresented in the world of pressure politics. Today all these groups are represented by a variety of organizations that win a significant number of political victories, so that American politics is now more pluralistic than it used to be despite the fact that interest-group leaders tend to be upper middle class.

Pluralist theory (politics) *A theory that competition among all affected interests shapes public policy.*

The Activities of Interest Groups

The size and wealth of an interest group are no longer accurate measures of its influence—if, indeed, they ever were. Depending on the issue, the key to political influence may be the ability to generate a dramatic newspaper headline, mobilize a big letter-writing campaign, stage a protest demonstration, file suit in a federal court to block (or compel) some government action, or supply information quietly to key legislators. All these actions require organization, but only some require big or expensive organizations.

Information

Of all these tactics open to interest groups, the single most important one is the ability to supply credible information to the right person. To busy members of

Congress and bureaucrats, information is in short supply. Legislators in particular must take positions on a staggering number of issues about which they cannot possibly be fully informed. And the kind of detailed, up-to-the-minute information that politicians need is ordinarily unavailable in encyclopedias and other standard reference sources; it can be gathered only by a group that has a strong interest in some issue. Most lobbyists are not flamboyant arm-twisters, but specialists who collect information (favorable to their client, naturally) and present it in as organized, persuasive, and factual manner as possible. Information provided by lobbyists is often most valuable when it concerns a fairly narrow, technical issue rather than broad and highly visible national policy. But lobbyists must maintain the trust of those with whom they deal; misrepresenting an issue or giving bad advice can seriously damage their long-term credibility with legislators.

Cue (political) *A signal telling a congressional representative what values (e.g., liberal or conservative) are at stake in a vote—who is for, who against a proposal—and how that issue fits into his or her own set of political beliefs or party agenda.*

Public officials want not only technical information but also political cues. A **cue** is a signal telling the official what values are at stake in an issue—who is for and who against a proposal—and how that issue fits into the official's own political beliefs. Often all a legislator needs to know is how the AFL-CIO, the NAACP, the Americans for Democratic Action, the Farmers' Union, and various Naderite organizations—or corresponding conservative groups—stand on an issue. (A legislator will worry and try to look more closely, however, if such organizations are split.) As a result of this process, lobbyists often work together in informal coalitions based on general political ideology.

Both political information and political cues now arrive in the offices of politicians at a faster rate than ever before, thanks to the advent of the fax machine. Many interest groups and political activists have banks of computer-operated fax machines that can get a short, snappy document into the hands of every legislator within minutes. William Kristol, a Republican activist, used this technique to good effect in 1993 when he bombarded Republican members of Congress with arguments as to why they should oppose President Clinton's health-care plan. Many credit him with having played a major role in the defeat of that plan. Today, e-mail adds to the information flow.

Public Support: The Rise of the New Politics

Once upon a time, when the government was small, Congress less individualistic, and television nonexistent, lobbyists used mainly an *insider strategy:* They worked closely with a few key members of Congress, meeting them privately to exchange information and (sometimes) favors. Matters of mutual interest could be discussed at a leisurely pace, over dinner, or while playing golf. Public opinion was important on some highly visible issues, but there were not many of these.[37]

The insider strategy is still a valuable approach, but increasingly interest groups have turned to an *outsider strategy.* The individualistic nature of the new Congress (see Chapter 9) has made it useful; modern technology has made it possible. Radio, fax machines, and the Internet disseminate news almost immediately. Satellite television can link interested citizens meeting in various locations across the country. Publicized toll-free telephone numbers enable voters to call the offices of their members of Congress without charge. Public-opinion polls, conducted by telephone, measure and help generate support for or opposition to proposed legislation virtually overnight. Computerized databases can create mailing lists of people already known to have an interest in a given matter.

This is *grassroots lobbying*—campaigns to mobilize citizens to contact the government about an issue. It is central to the outsider strategy. The "public" that generates this pressure is not every voter, or even most voters; it is that part of the public (sometimes called an *issue public*) that is directly affected by or deeply concerned with a government policy. Modern technology has made possible the overnight mobilization of specific issue publics.

Not every issue lends itself to an outsider strategy. It is hard to get many people excited about, for example, complex tax legislation affecting only a few firms. But as the government does more and more, its policies affect more and more people, and so more and more will join in grassroots lobbying efforts over such matters as abortion, Medicare, Social Security, environmental protection, and affirmative action.

Interest Groups at Work: Two Stories

Jack Abramoff, a member of a respectable lobbying organization, decided to represent Indian tribes that wanted to open gambling casinos. He charged them huge fees for his services, perhaps $85 million in all. To induce some tribes to pay, Abramoff would organize lobbying campaigns *against* the tribes in order to make his services seem more desirable. The money he raised was used to bribe some government officials. When investigators uncovered the fraud, Abramoff was in 2006 sentenced to prison for five years. Other officials, including a member of Congress, a former White House executive, and various congressional staffers were sent to prison.

Not only were bribes paid but the tribal leaders who put up the money, though motivated by greed, got nothing in return. And the corruption did not stop with gambling casinos. The Guam Superior Court used Abramoff's services to lobby against a bill it disliked, an action that led to two men being indicted. And he used fake documents to prove he had made a down payment on the purchase of a casino. It was corrupt lobbying at its worst.

But most lobbying is not like that. When Tufts University wanted to build a new veterinary school, its president hired a Washington lobbyist who discovered that Washington State University also wanted to put up such a school. The lobbyist decided he would get members in Congress from Massachusetts to support the Washington plan if members from Washington would support the Tufts plan. But then the University of Pennsylvania, which already had a veterinary school, argued that it did not want competition from Tufts. To deal with that, the lobbyist suggested that Congress give an extra $10 million to Penn.

It worked. Tufts, Penn, and Washington State all got federal money. Today, we call such an arrangement an "earmark," and many people worry about it. But even though a lobbyist and not the president of the United States put the deal together, condemning it as an earmark is an inadequate complaint. The nation got two new and one expanded veterinary schools. (Of course, my view may be biased by the fact that my son graduated from Tufts.)

Citizens protesting government policies at a Tea Party rally in Arizona.

In short, sorting out what is good and what is bad lobbying is not as easy as criticizing (rightly) the Abramoff deal.

Money and PACs

Interest groups have always given money to politicians, usually for campaigns, sometimes as favors, occasionally as bribes. But the scope of giving reached gargantuan proportions only after laws were passed to regulate how the money may be given. The effect of trying to reform the process of making campaign contributions, as we shall see in Chapter 8, unleashed a torrent of fresh cash by means of legally regulated *political action committees* (PACs).

Between 1975 and 1982, the number of PACs more than quadrupled—to a total of around three thousand. Today there are well over four thousand. In the 1982 elections, these organizations gave more than $83 million to federal candidates;[38] in the 2008 elections, they gave nearly $413 million to them.

Almost any kind of organization can form a PAC. More than half of all PACs are sponsored by corporations, about a tenth by labor unions, and the rest by a variety of groups, including ideological ones. Contrary to popular impression, the biggest PACs are not run by corporations. Of the top ten givers in 2007-2008, most were labor unions or professional associations (see Table 7.3).

The most remarkable development in interest-group activity in recent years has been the rise of ideological PACs. They have increased in number faster than business or labor PACs, and in the 1980 and 1982 elections they raised more money than either business or labor. In the 1996 election, there were more than one thousand ideological PACs; about one-third were liberal, about two-thirds conservative.[39]

Table 7.3 **Ten Largest PAC Contributors, 2007–2008**			
PAC affiliation	**Amount**	**%Dems**	**% Reps**
National Assn of Realtors	$4,020,900	58%	42%
Intnl Brotherhood of Electrical Workers	$3,344,650	98	2
AT&T Inc.	$3,108,200	47	52
Amer Bankers Assn	$2,918,143	43	57
Natl Beer Wholesalers	$2,869,000	53	47
Natl Auto Dealers	$2,860,000	34	66
Intnl Fire Fighters	$2,734,900	77	22
Operating Engineers	$2,704,067	87	13
Amer Assn for Justice	$2,700,500	95	4

Source: Federal Election Commission, July 13, 2009. The names are those of the sponsoring organizations, not the PACs.

Though the ideological PACs raised more money than business or labor PACs, they spent less on campaigns and gave less to candidates. This is because even a well-run ideological PAC must usually spend 50 cents on expensive direct-mail solicitation for every dollar it takes in. (Many spend even more.) By contrast, a typical business or labor PAC can inexpensively solicit money from the members of a single corporation or union.[40]

The popular image of rich PACs pumping huge sums into political campaigns and thereby buying the attention, and possibly the favors, of the grateful candidates is a bit overdrawn. For one thing, the typical PAC contribution is rather small. The typical corporate PAC donation to a House candidate is about $500. (The average labor PAC donation is more than twice that, but still small.) Most PACs distribute small sums to many candidates, and by law none can give more than $5,000 to any candidate.[41] Despite their great growth in numbers and expenditures, PACs still account for only about one-third of all the money spent by candidates for the House.[42]

Most money from PACs goes to incumbents. Because most House incumbents in 1994 were Democrats, even PACs sponsored by corporations and trade associations (traditionally Republican-friendly) gave more money to Democratic than to Republican candidates for House seats. Likewise, because most Senate incumbents were Republicans, most business PACs (traditionally Democrat-friendly) gave their money to Republican Senate candidates. In 2004, with both the House and the Senate controlled by the Republicans, Republicans got most of the PAC money (except from unions—they give almost exclusively to Democrats, regardless of incumbency). (See Table 7.4.)

No systematic evidence has been found that PAC contributions affect how members of Congress vote. On most issues, how legislators vote can be explained primarily by their general ideological outlook and the characteristics of their constituents; how much PAC money they have received turns out to be a trivial factor. There is, however, a slight correlation between PAC contributions and votes on issues in which most constituents have no interest and ideology provides little guidance. Even here, the correlation may be misleading, for the same groups that

---

Table 7.4 Spending by Political Action Committees (PACs), 2004

During the 2004 campaign more than four thousand PACs divided up their contributions as follows:

Corporations	$25.5	$56.3	$75.2	$2.0	$4.6	$11.4	$20.9	$24.2	$1.3	$6.7
Associations	23.4	41.4	59.1	2.4	5.4	6.9	11.1	12.8	1.1	4.0
Labor unions	37.8	5.6	33.7	5.3	4.6	7.3	1.0	5.1	0.9	2.3
"Nonconnected" (i.e., ideological) groups	11.6	24.3	22.2	6.1	7.6	6.7	9.1	8.1	2.2	5.4

Note: Dem. 5 Democrat; Rep. 5 Republican; In. 5 Incumbent; Ch. 5 Challenger.
Source: Harold W. Stanley and Richard G. Niemi, *Vital Statistics on American Politics 2005–2006* (Washington, DC: CQ Press 2006), 111. Reprinted by permission of CQ Press, a division of Congressional Quarterly Inc.

give money also wage intensive lobbying campaigns. These studies may therefore be measuring the effect of arguments, not money.[43]

Money probably affects legislative behavior in ways that will never appear in studies of roll-call votes in Congress. A representative or senator will be more willing to set aside time for a group that has given money than for a group that has not: The money has opened the door. Or contributions might influence how a member of Congress behaves on the committees to which he or she has been assigned. No one knows because the research has not been done.

The "Revolving Door"

Interest groups can also affect policy not by giving government officials things of value while they are in office but by holding out the prospect of lucrative jobs in private industry after they leave government.[44] For example, after Michael Deaver left the Reagan White House in 1985, he began representing, for a fat fee, various interests seeking to influence national politics. He had gone through the revolving door, but he went too far—he was convicted of perjury in a case arising out of charges that he had illegally used his political connections to line his own pocket.

It is hard to draw a clear line between making proper use of an ex-official's political expertise and improperly exploiting that expertise for unfair gain. The few studies done on the revolving door have focused on government agencies that regulate business. These studies have found some conspicuous abuses of power in return for business favors, but there seems to be no systematic pattern of abuse in the relationship of business employment to bureaucratic behavior.[45]

Demonstrations

Public displays and disruptive tactics—protest marches, sit-ins, picketing, and violence—have always been a part of American politics, dating back to the struggle for independence in 1776.

Both ends of the political spectrum have used display, disruption, and violence. On the left, feminists, antislavery agitators, coal miners, auto workers, welfare mothers, blacks, antinuclear power groups, public housing tenants, the American Indian Movement, Students for a Democratic Society, and the Weather Underground have created trouble ranging from peaceful sit-ins at segregated lunch counters to bombings and shootings. On the right, the Ku Klux Klan has used terror, intimidation, and murder; parents opposed to forced busing of schoolchildren have demonstrated; business firms once used strong-arm squads against workers; and an endless array of "anti-" groups have taken their disruptive turns on stage. Morally a sit-in demonstration is quite different from (for example) a lynching, but politically all these activities constitute a similar problem for a government official.

To understand interest-group politics, it is important to remember that holding demonstrations and causing disruptions have become quite conventional political resources and are no longer the last resort of extremist groups. Making trouble is now an accepted political tactic of ordinary middle-class citizens as well as of the disadvantaged or the disreputable.

There is, of course, a long history of "proper" people using disruptive methods, dating back to early-twentieth-century British and American feminists who, campaigning for women's right to vote, would chain themselves to lampposts or

Wendy Maeda/The Boston Globe/Landov Media

Lawsuits, such as this one arguing that Massachusetts allow marriage among gay and lesbian couples, are often more effective than protest demonstrations in changing policies.

engage in what we would now call sit-ins. Then, as now, the object was to disrupt the workings of some institution and force it to negotiate or, failing that, to gain the sympathy of third parties (including the media and other interest groups) who would call for negotiations—or, at the very least, to goad the police into making martyrs.

The civil-rights and anti–Vietnam War movements of the 1960s gave experience in these methods to thousands of young people and persuaded others of the effectiveness of such methods under certain conditions. Though these earlier movements have abated or disappeared, their veterans and emulators have used such tactics in, for example, anti-abortion and disabled-rights demonstrations.

Government officials dread this kind of trouble. They usually find themselves in a no-win situation—accused of arrogance if they ignore it, encouraging more demonstrations if they give in, and risking bad publicity and lawsuits if they call in the police and violence ensues.

Regulating Interest Groups

Interest-group activity is a form of political speech protected by the First Amendment to the Constitution; it cannot lawfully be abolished or even much curtailed. In 1946, Congress passed the Federal Regulation of Lobbying Act, which required groups and individuals seeking to influence legislation to register with the secretary of the Senate and the clerk of the House and to file quarterly financial reports. The Supreme Court upheld the law but restricted its application to lobbying efforts involving direct contacts with members of Congress.[46] The act had little practical effect. Not all lobbyists took the trouble to register, nor was there any guarantee that the financial statements filed were accurate or complete because no staff in the Senate or House was in charge of enforcing the law or investigating violations of it.[47] And more general grassroots interest-group activity was not restricted at all by the government.

After years of growing popular dissatisfaction with Congress, prompted in large measure by the (exaggerated) view that legislators were the pawns of powerful special interests, Congress in late 1995 unanimously passed a bill that tightened up the registration and disclosure requirements. Signed by the president, the law restates the obligation of lobbyists to register with the House and Senate but broadens the definition of a lobbyist to:

- People who spend at least 20 percent of their time lobbying
- People who are paid at least $5,000 in any six-month period to lobby
- Corporations and other groups that spend more than $20,000 in any six-month period on their own lobbying staffs

The law covers people and groups who lobby the executive branch and congressional staffers as well as elected members of Congress and includes law firms that represent clients before the government. Twice a year, all registered lobbyists must report these facts and figures:

- The names of their clients
- Their income and expenditures
- The issues on which they worked

The registration and reporting requirements do not, however, extend to grassroots organizations. Nor was any new enforcement organization created, although congressional officials may refer violations to the Justice Department for investigation. Fines for breaking the law could amount to $50,000. In addition, the law bars tax-exempt, nonprofit advocacy groups that lobby from getting federal grants, a provision aimed at such organizations as AARP.

Even before this last provision was added, federal laws already restricted what tax-exempt organizations could do. To get and retain a tax-exempt status, and therefore to make it possible for people to donate tax-deductible money to it, an organization must not only be not-for-profit, it may not devote a "substantial part" of its activities to "attempting to influence legislation."[48] Exactly what constitutes a "substantial" portion of its activities is not clear, but some groups have crossed the line. In 1968, for example, the Internal Revenue Service revoked the tax-exempt status of the Sierra Club because it lobbied so extensively.

Some voluntary associations deal with this problem by setting up separate organizations to collect tax-exempt money—for example, the NAACP, which lobbies, must pay taxes, but the NAACP Legal Defense and Educational Fund, which does not lobby, is tax exempt.[49]

Finally, the campaign-finance laws (described in detail in Chapter 8) limit to $5,000 the amount any PAC can spend on a given candidate in a given election. These laws have sharply curtailed the extent to which any single group can give money, though they may well have increased the total amount different groups in the same sector of society (labor, business, dairy farmers, lawyers) are providing.

Beyond making bribery or other manifestly corrupt forms of behavior illegal and restricting the sums that campaign contributors can donate, there is probably no system for controlling interest groups that would both make a useful difference and leave important constitutional rights unimpaired. Ultimately the only remedy for imbalances in interest-group representation is to devise a political system that gives all affected parties a reasonable chance to be heard on matters of public policy. Rightly or wrongly, that is exactly what the Founders thought they were doing.

SUMMARY

A political party exists in three arenas: among the voters who psychologically identify with it, as a grassroots organization staffed and led by activists, and as a group of elected officials who follow its lead in lawmaking. In this chapter we have looked at the party primarily as an organization and seen the various forms it takes at the local level—the machine, the ideological party, the solidary group, the sponsored party, and the personal following.

Nationally the parties are weak, decentralized coalitions of these local forms. As organizations that influence the political systems, parties are getting weaker. Voters no longer strongly identify with one of the major parties as they once did. The spread of the direct primary has made it harder for parties to control who is nominated for elective office, thus making it harder for the parties to influence the behavior of these people once elected. Delegate-selection rules, especially in the Democratic party, have helped shift the center of power in the national nominating conventions. Because of the changes in rules, power has moved away from officeholders and party regulars and toward the more ideological wings of the parties.

The two-party system is maintained, and minor parties are discouraged, by an election system (winner-take-all, plurality elections) that makes voters reluctant to waste a vote on a minor party and by the ability of potential minor parties to wield influence within a major party by means of the primary system.

The decay of parties in recent decades has been paralleled by a vast proliferation of organized interest groups, or lobbies. Such groups in the United States are more numerous and fragmented than those in nations, such as Great Britain, where the political system is more centralized and political parties are stronger.

The goals and tactics of interest groups reflect not only the interests of their members but also the size of the groups, the incentives with which they attract supporters, and the role of the professional staffs. Because of the difficulty of organizing large numbers of people, a group purporting to speak for mass constituencies will often have to provide material benefits to members or acquire an affluent sponsor (such as a foundation). The chief source of interest-group influence is information; public support, money, and the ability to create trouble are also important. The right to lobby is protected by the Constitution, but tax and campaign-finance laws impose significant restrictions on how money donated to such groups may be used.

RECONSIDERING THE ENDURING QUESTIONS

1. Why are political parties today weaker than in the past?

The parties have become weaker because voters, candidate selection methods, and campaign-finance laws have changed. Voters now get a lot of information from the media and are more likely to think of themselves as independents; caucuses and primary elections have largely replaced a party choice of nominees; and campaign-finance reform laws have hurt the ability of parties to raise money.

2. Why does America have just two major political parties?

One major reason is that we select congressional representatives by giving the candidate with the most votes the victory, even if he or she had less than a majority. This forces opposition groups to coalesce. And we choose presidents by a system (the electoral college) that gives all of most states' votes to whomever gets the most votes, even if the challenger also receives a lot of votes. This also forces parties to form two big blocs.

3. Why does America have so many interest groups?

There are so many opportunities to influence policy making here that it provides opportunities for many interests. Even small groups can influence state and local governments, appeal to congressional committees and subcommittees, and bring suits in court to change laws. Fewer interest groups would mean a more centralized, less open political system.

Online Resources: Political Parties and Interest Groups

CourseMate

Some political parties:
- Democratic National Committee: www.democrats.org
- Republican National Committee: www.rnc.org
- Green party: www.greens.org
- Libertarian party: www.lp.org
- Reform party: www.reformparty.org

Some interest groups:
- Two overviews: www.lib.umich.edu/govdocs/psusp.html
                            www.vote-smart.org
- A few specific interest groups:

Conservative:
- American Conservative Union: www.conservative.org

Liberal:
- American Civil Liberties Union: www.aclu.org
- Americans for Democratic Action: www.adaction.org

Civil rights:
- NAACP: www.naacp.org
- Center for Equal Opportunity: www.ceousa.org

Feminists:
- National Organization for Women: www.now.org
- Independent Women's Forum: www.iwf.org

Suggested Readings

Aldrich, John H. *Why Parties? The Origin and Transformation of Political Parties in America.* Chicago: University of Chicago Press, 1995. Explains why parties form and are essential to democracy.

Berry, Jeffrey M. *Lobbying for the People.* Princeton, NJ: Princeton University Press, 1977. Discusses the general characteristics of more than eighty "public interest" lobbies, with a detailed discussion of two.

Cigler, Allan J., and Burdett A. Loomis, eds. *Interest Group Politics,* 7th ed. Washington, D. C.: CQ Press, 2007. A good collection of essays on interest groups.

Goldwin, Robert A., ed. *Political Parties in the Eighties.* Washington, D. C.: American Enterprise Institute, 1980. Essays evaluating parties and efforts to reform them.

Heinz, John P., et al. *The Hollow Core.* Cambridge, Mass.: Harvard University Press, 1993. A close study of how interest groups affect national politics in agriculture, energy, health, and labor.

Key, V. O., Jr. *Southern Politics.* New York: Knopf, 1949. A classic account of how politics once operated in the one-party South.

Lowi, Theodore J. *The End of Liberalism.* New York: Norton, 1969. A critique of the role of interest groups in American government.

Olson, Mancur. *The Logic of Collective Action.* Cambridge, Mass.: Harvard University Press, 1965. A theory of interest-group formation from an economic perspective.

Ranney, Austin. *Curing the Mischiefs of Faction: Party Reform in America.* Berkeley: University of California Press, 1975. History and analysis of party "reforms" with special attention on the 1972 changes in the Democratic party rules.

Riordan, William L. *Plunkitt of Tammany Hall.* New York: Knopf, 1948 (first published in 1905). Amusing and insightful account of how an old-style party boss operated in New York City.

Schattschneider, E. E. *Party Government.* New York: Holt, Rinehart and Winston, 1942. An argument for a more disciplined and centralized two-party system.

Wilson, James Q. *Political Organizations,* rev. ed. Princeton: Princeton University Press, 1995. A theory of interest groups and political parties that emphasizes the incentives they use to attract members.

ENDURING QUESTIONS

1. **What is the best way to calculate the rate at which Americans vote?**
2. **What factors chiefly influence who wins a presidential election?**
3. **Can federal laws keep big money out of political campaigns?**

CourseMate

There are more elections to fill more offices in the United States than in perhaps any other major democracy. Public participation in American elections, however, is lower than in elections elsewhere. Moreover, political parties, as both organizations and labels, play a smaller role in American elections and campaigns than in other countries.

These three facts—the large number of offices filled by election, the low participation in those elections, and the weak condition of political parties—have important implications for a theory of democracy. As matters now stand, many offices (particularly the less important ones) are filled by people elected by less than a majority vote and with no political party accountable for their actions. If we were to get rid of many lesser elective offices in order to focus public attention—and participation—on a single elective office, we might get large turnouts and majority rule, but that majority would control only a small segment of the governmental structure.

Such is the case in Great Britain and other parliamentary democracies. Voters elect only one or two officials—their parliamentary representatives—who assemble in the parliament and form the government, which in turn appoints all the rest of the country's officials. In most parliamentary democracies, voter participation is very high. Sometimes, as in Italy and Australia, compulsory voting yields turnouts well over 90 percent. But even where voting is voluntary, as in France and Great Britain, turnout regularly exceeds 70 or 80 percent of the eligible population.

In America, voter turnout in 2008 was 57 percent of the voting age population (that is, people age 18 and older) and 62 percent of the voting eligible population (that is, people 18 and older who are citizens and not convicted felons). Measured either way, turnout was higher in 2008 than in any election since 1964.[1]

Political Participation

People of different social and especially educational backgrounds not only have different political opinions but also participate in politics in different ways. Ordinarily we think of such participation in terms of voting, but there are many other—and probably more important—ways to participate: A citizen can join political organizations, contribute money to candidates, write to members of Congress, or simply talk politics with friends and neighbors.

Forms of Participation

The fact that Americans are involved in politics in many more ways than just voting may help explain why the turnout in American elections is so much lower than in most other democratic countries. Here Americans who care about issues can get involved in ways that people in other countries are less likely to use.

Americans can participate in politics in at least six ways. At one extreme are the complete **activists**—individuals, often outside government, who actively promote their political party or issue by voting, donating money to candidates, working in political campaigns, and joining interest-group organizations. These people tend to be highly educated and have high incomes. At the other extreme are inactive people—they do not vote, give money, or join groups. They tend to be people with little schooling and low incomes. In between are some people who only vote and some other people who vote but limit their organizational energies to community activities of a nonpartisan nature.[2]

It is striking that more than 40 percent of Americans either do not participate in politics at all or limit that participation strictly to voting. People avoid politics for a number of reasons, but one deserves special mention: For most people, politics offers few rewards. Even voting imposes a number of burdens (registering to vote, waiting in line, missing work, making sense of a long ballot), and hardly anybody ever casts a vote that affects the outcome of an election. The wonder is that the proportion of people who do vote is not smaller than it is.

Activist *An individual, usually outside government, who actively promotes a political party, philosophy, or issue he or she cares about.*

Why People Participate

One reason that people vote is that many Americans have a strong sense of civic duty that tells them that they ought to vote, and afterward they feel good about having voted. The sense of civic obligation is stronger in the United States than in many other democratic nations. But if more Americans than Britons (for example) say they *ought* to vote, are they hypocrites because fewer of them *actually* vote? Not really. As we shall see, Americans face greater difficulties in registering to vote than citizens of almost any other country. American political parties are less effective than their European counterparts in luring voters to the polls. And most important, Americans find being active in the community a more rewarding form of participation than merely voting.[3]

Who Participates?

Whatever the form of participation, those who are the most active tend to have more education (and, to a lesser degree, higher incomes) than those who are the least active. Indeed, educational differences explain more of the variations in political participation in the United States than in any other country in which comparable studies have been done. Older people are more active than younger ones, and men are more active than women.[4]

Overall, blacks participate in politics less frequently than whites, but among people of roughly the same income and level of education, blacks tend to participate *more* than whites.[5] This is particularly true for blacks who are financially better off or who are especially sensitive to racial issues. But the forms of participation among blacks are somewhat different from those of whites. Blacks, compared with whites, are less likely to contact public officials about their problems and are slightly less likely to vote, but are much more likely to join civic organizations or become active in political campaigns.[6]

The rate at which people have been participating in politics in ways other than voting has shifted somewhat over the last several decades. For example, since 1964, the percentage of people who attended political meetings during presidential election years hit a low of 5.1 percent in 2000 and a high of 9.3 percent in 2008; the percentage who worked for a candidate or a party averaged 4 percent from 1964 through 1988 and 3.1 percent from 1992 through 2008; and the percentage who contributed money to a campaign has increased in each of the last five presidential elections, rising from 6.6 percent in 1992 to 12.9 percent (a post-1960 high) in 2008.[7]

Government officials tend to be better informed about and more in agreement with the opinions of people most active in politics than with the views of the rank-and-file citizenry.[8] There is nothing particularly sinister about this; people who try to have influence on government are going to have more influence than people who do not try. Thus we should be especially interested in the political opinions of political activists. To sum up, activists tend to have more extreme views—whether liberal or conservative—than the citizens for whom they supposedly speak. Republican activists are often more consistently conservative than the average Republican; Democratic activists are more consistently liberal than the average Democrat.

How We Compare

Laws on Voting

Ratified in 1971, the Twenty-Sixth Amendment to the U.S. Constitution forbids states to deny "on account of age" the right to vote of citizens who are age eighteen or older. But most states deny voting rights to voting-age citizens who have been convicted of felony crimes. Relevant state laws vary; for instance, Kentucky and Virginia have largely maintained laws that disenfranchise felons for life, while Maine and Vermont have permitted certain presently incarcerated felons to vote.

The legal voting age in almost all other nations is also eighteen. In about a dozen other countries, however, the legal voting age has been sixteen (as in Brazil) or seventeen (as in Indonesia); and in about twenty other nations the legal voting age is nineteen (as in South Korea), twenty (as in Japan), or twenty-one (as in Lebanon).

Some democracies (for example, the United Kingdom) deny prisoners the right to vote, but it is far more common for democracies to permit all prisoners (save, in some nations, persons convicted of electoral fraud or related crimes) to vote. America is almost alone among democracies in the extent to which laws deny ex-prisoners the right to vote.

America is also in the international minority with respect to laws on voter registration. In most other nations it is legally compulsory for voters to register; a central, regional, or local government, or, most commonly, a specialized "Electoral Management Body," is expressly responsible for registering voters in national elections.

In America, voter registration is not legally required, and under a diverse array of state laws, individual voting-age citizens remain responsible for registering to vote.

Source: ACE Electoral Knowledge Network and United Nations Development Program, data on Voter Registration and Voting Age, http://aceproject.org, accessed May 2010; "Felony Disenfranchisement in the United States," The Sentencing Project, September 2008.

Historical Voting Patterns

It is ironic that relatively few citizens vote in American elections because it was in this country that the mass of people first became eligible to vote.

The Rise of the American Electorate

At the time the Constitution was ratified, the vote was limited to taxpayers or property owners (who, however, constituted a rather large proportion of the white male population). By the administration of Andrew Jackson (1829–1837), it had broadened to include virtually all white males, except in a few southern states.

The most important changes in elections have been those that extended the suffrage to women, blacks, and eighteen-year-olds and made mandatory the direct popular election of United States senators. After the Civil War, the Fifteenth Amendment (1870) was ratified, stipulating that "the right of citizens of the United States to vote shall not be denied . . . on account of race, color, or previous condition of servitude." Nevertheless, throughout the South, blacks were systematically barred from the polls by all manner of state stratagems after the end of Reconstruction. Between 1915 and 1944, the Supreme Court overturned some of these discriminatory rules, but still only a small proportion of voting-age southern blacks were able to register and vote. A dramatic change did not take place until the passage of the Voting Rights Act in 1965. This law suspended the use of literacy tests (which had been used in a blatantly discriminatory fashion) and authorized the appointment of federal examiners who could order the registration of blacks in states and counties (mostly in the South) where fewer than 50 percent of the voting-age population were registered or had voted in the previous presidential election. The law also provided criminal penalties for interfering with the right to vote.

Though implementation in some places was slow, the number of blacks who voted rose sharply throughout the South. In Mississippi, for example, the proportion of voting-age blacks who registered increased from 5 percent to more than 70 percent in just ten years.[9] In 1984, the campaign by a black, Jesse Jackson, for the Democratic presidential nomination helped increase black registration everywhere—but especially in the South, where nearly 700,000 more blacks were registered in 1984 than in 1980. These changes had a profound effect on the behavior of many white southern politicians. For example, George Wallace stopped making prosegregation speeches and began courting the black vote.

AP Photo

When these blacks registered to vote in 1965 in Americus, Georgia, it was in the aftermath of days of racial violence. Beginning in that year, federal law empowered the national government to protect voting rights at the local level.

Though women could vote in some state elections, it was not until the Nineteenth Amendment was ratified in 1920 that women's suffrage was extended throughout the nation. At one stroke, the size of the eligible voting population almost doubled—but no dramatic change occurred in the conduct of elections, the identity of the winners, or the substance of public policy. Initially, at least, women voted more or less in the same manner as men, though not quite as frequently. From time to time, however, issues arose that created the gender gap described in Chapter 6.

The Twenty-sixth Amendment, ratified in 1971, gave the vote to eighteen-year-olds, but the political impact of the youth vote was also less than expected. In the 1972 presidential election, the turnout of the voters between the ages of eighteen and twenty-one was lower than for the population as a whole. And those who did vote generally supported Richard Nixon rather than George McGovern. McGovern had counted on attracting a large youth vote but received only the support of college students.[10] Today young voters are somewhat more likely to be Republican than are older voters.

Voter Turnout

Given all the legal safeguards that now bring almost every aspect of voter eligibility under national standards, one might expect that participation in elections would have risen sharply. In fact, the proportion of the voting-age population that has gone to the polls in presidential elections for the past thirty years or so has remained about the same—between 49 percent and 60 percent of those eligible—and today appears to be much smaller than it was in the latter part of the nineteenth century.

Scholars have vigorously debated the meaning of these figures. One view is that even allowing for the shaky data on which the estimates are based, this decline in turnout has been real and the result of a decline in popular interest in elections and a weakening of the extent to which the two major parties are competitive. During the nineteenth century, according to this theory, the parties fought hard, got voters to the polls, made politics a participatory activity, kept registration procedures easy, and looked forward to close, exciting elections. But after 1896, when the South became a one-party Democratic region and the North heavily Republican, both parties became more conservative, national elections usually resulted in lopsided Republican victories, and citizens began losing interest.[11]

Another view, however, argues that the decline in voter turnout has been more apparent than real. Though nineteenth-century elections were certainly more of a popular sport than they are today, the parties were no more democratic in those days than now, and the voters then may have been more easily manipulated. Until the early twentieth century, vote frauds—including ballot-box stuffing—were common.[12] If votes had been legally cast and honestly counted, the statistics of nineteenth-century election turnouts might well have been much lower than the inflated figures we now have, so that the current decline in voter participation may not be as great as some have suggested.

To answer this puzzle, we have to calculate voter turnout accurately. *Turnout* means the percentage of the voting-age population that votes; an accurate measure of turnout means having an accurate count of both how many people voted and how many people could have voted. In fact we do not have very good measures of either number.

Before the beginning of the twentieth century, people often voted publicly, not privately, on ballots given them by political parties, and they did not have to register in advance. No one can be certain that these vote counts were very accurate. Things got better after the country adopted the so-called **Australian ballot**. Advocated by Progressives, this ballot was printed and distributed by the government and secretly cast in a private election booth by each voter. Moreover, local officials began to get tougher about registering voters. But, well into the twentieth century, many cities and towns grew lax about registration and indifferent to (or fraudulent about) accurate vote counts. So the big drop in turnout that is supposed to have happened between 1900 and 1948 may or may not have been real; we cannot know because we cannot know whether the vote counts were accurate.

Today, votes are probably counted more accurately, but as we learned from the recounts in Florida during the 2000 presidential election, there is still not exact accuracy. However, we still cannot be certain how many people are eligible to vote. Eligible voters are derived from census reports that count the **voting-age population (VAP)** is—that is, the number of people who are age twenty-one and over (or, after younger people were allowed to vote, the number age eighteen and over). But within the VAP are many people who cannot vote, such as prisoners and aliens; the **voting-eligible population (VEP)** omits these groups.

When scholars adjust the VAP to take into account these differences, it turns out that voting participation has not fallen since the early 1970s as much as previously though.[13] VAP has measured an average of about 4 percent less than VEP since 1980.

Explaining—and Improving—Turnout

Take a look at Table 8.1. Column A compares democratic nations in terms of the average percentage of their voting-age population that went to the polls in dozens of post-1945 national legislative (congressional or parliamentary) elections. The United States ranks dead last with 47.7 percent voter turnout.

Now look at Column B. It compares these same nations in terms of the percentage of **registered voters** (those eligible voters who have completed a registration form by a set date) that went to the polls in these same legislative elections. The United States still ranks very low but looks somewhat better, with 66.5 percent registered voter turnout.

By the same token, post-1968 U.S. presidential elections have drawn between 49 and 57 percent of the voting-age population, but over 70 percent of all registered voters, to the polls.

Still, there is yet a turnout gap between the United States and many other democracies, and it is related in part to differences in registration practices.

In most European nations, every adult citizen is automatically registered by the government to vote. In Australia and some other countries, voting is compulsory; nonvoters are subject to a small fine.

By contrast, in America nonvoting is perfectly legal and the burden of registering remains entirely on the citizens. They have to learn how and when to register, take the trouble of getting a registration form, fill it out, and, depending on their

Australian ballot *A government-printed ballot of uniform size and shape to be cast in secret that was adopted by many states around 1890 in order to reduce the voting fraud associated with party-printed ballots cast in public.*

Voting-age population (VAP) *Citizens who are eligible to vote after reaching a minimum age requirement. In the United States, a citizen must be at least eighteen years old in order to vote.*

Voting-eligible population (VEP) *The VAP minus aliens and felons.*

Registered voters *People who are registered to vote. While almost all adult American citizens are theoretically eligible to vote, only those who have completed a registration form by the required date may do so.*

Table 8.1 Two Ways of Calculating Voting Turnout, Here and Abroad

A Turnout as Percentage of Voting-Age Population		B Turnout as Percentage of Registered Voters	
Italy	92.0%	Australia	94.5%
New Zealand	86.0	Belgium	92.5
Belgium	84.8	Austria	83.1
Austria	84.4	New Zealand	90.8
Australia	84.2	Italy	89.8
Sweden	84.1	Netherlands	87.5
Netherlands	83.8	Sweden	87.1
Denmark	83.6	Denmark	85.9
Canada	82.6	Germany	85.4
Germany	80.2	Norway	80.4
Norway	79.2	United Kingdom	75.2
United Kingdom	73.8	Canada	73.9
France	67.3	France	73.8
Switzerland	51.9	**United States**	**66.5**
United States	**47.7**	Switzerland	56.5

Source: Rafael Lopez Pintor, Maria Gratschew, and Kate Sullivan, "Voter Turnout Rates from a Comparative Perspective" in *Voter Turnout Since 1945: A Global Report* (Stockholm, Sweden: International Institute for Democracy and Electoral Assistance, 2002).

state's rules, deliver or mail it to a local registrar. If they move to a new county or state, they must register all over again.

Over the last several decades, the United States has simplified its registration procedures and lightened the burdens associated with registering. In 1993, the U.S. Congress passed a **"motor-voter" law** that allows people in all fifty states to register to vote when applying for a driver's license or at other state offices, and to vote by mail. By 2004, all states gave voters the option to vote prior to election day via absentee ballot; over half had "no-fault" absentee voting (meaning that absentee voters need not demonstrate that they reside outside their home state or give any other reason) and many had same-day registration (permitting people to register on the same day and at the same time they vote). Finally, Election Day isn't quite what it used to be. In 2008, one-third of the voters cast their ballots before Election Day using absentee or early voting laws. They had to be reached early in the campaign.

On the other hand, the impact of increased registration on voter turnout has been far less dramatic than had been widely predicted. In the 2006 congressional elections and again in the 2008 presidential election, some 80 million voting-age

Motor-voter law *A law passed by Congress in 1993 to make it easier for Americans to register to vote. The law, which went into effect in 1995, requires states to allow voter registration by mail, when one applies for a driver's license, and at state offices that serve the disabled or poor.*

citizens did not vote: About 40 million of these nonvoters were not registered to vote, and another 40 million or so were registered but still did not vote.

When registered nonvoters were surveyed regarding why they did not vote, their number one answer was scheduling conflicts (school or work, mostly).[14] Would making Election Day a national holiday or holding national elections on weekends get most registered nonvoters to vote? Nobody really knows.

What about various get-out-the-vote (GOTV) tactics? Based on over a hundred field experiments with various GOTV tactics, the authors of a 2008 study concluded that, while campaign leaflets, direct mail, radio or television ads and election-day festivals had only ambiguous or nonexistent effects on voter turnout, door-to-door canvassing and phone calls each had statistically significant results in boosting voter turnout; but even most prospective voters touched by these tactics did not vote.[15] In a separate 2008 study, the same analysts found that "social pressure" exerted through mailings increased turnout; yet 62 percent of those pressured still did not vote.[16]

For all the voter registration and GOTV efforts, one reason why turnout is still lower here than abroad could be that politics is not as important to Americans as it is to Swedes or Belgians. That is the case in part because government plays a smaller role in the lives of Americans than it does in the lives of Swedes or Belgians. A second reason is that political parties do not mobilize voters and get them to the polls with the same efficiency as do many European parties. Again, that is because parties do not play as large a role in our lives as they do in the lives of many Europeans.

Whether the goal is to narrow the present-day turnout gap between America and other democracies, to bring turnout levels here nearer to their historical highs, or merely to increase turnout rates from one recent national election to the next, the voters must be mobilized through political campaigns.

Political Campaigns

Political campaigns, once mounted by party organizations, are today largely run by the personal followers of the candidate. The candidate creates a staff and an organization to work directly for him or her, but it is a temporary organization that ceases to exist the day after the election. Furthermore, campaigns for national offices are usually organized on behalf of an individual candidate, not a slate of candidates of the same party.

Jemal Countess/Getty Images

Rap mogul Sean "Diddy" Combs visits a New York polling station at Coalition High School as part of his get out the vote program on February 5, 2008.

Several features of our political system have contributed to the rise of personal rather than party-run campaigns. Primary elections, as we have seen, have weakened or eliminated a major source of party power in many states—the ability of party leaders to select the party's nominee. Especially if a candidate wins the primary over the opposition of the party leadership, the party may feel little obligation to work hard for that person's victory in the general election.

Political funds and political jobs are increasingly under the control of candidates and officeholders, not party leaders. And as we shall see, the public financing of presidential campaigns means that most of the money used to help elect a candidate goes to the candidate or his or her personal organization, and is not funneled through the party. The ability to reward followers with patronage jobs is, in many places, in the hands of an elected official rather than a party boss.

The increased reliance on the mass media for campaigning means that candidates purchase advertising and give interviews largely to bolster their own chances of victory. With the high cost of radio and television advertising, it hardly makes sense for one candidate to give others a free ride by including them on a slate. Furthermore, electronic advertising is usually devoted to building a candidate's image—that is, to emphasizing his or her *personal* qualities—which cannot easily be done for a slate or a party ticket.

Finally, the decline in party identification has made any appeal to party loyalty a weaker basis for building a winning coalition than was once the case. Except in heavily Democratic or Republican areas, candidates today omit references to their party identification lest they alienate voters who might like them as individuals.

Strategy

A campaign for president is affected by how the states hold primary elections and how the candidates mobilize their resources. Over recent years many states rushed to hold their caucuses and primaries as early as possible so that they would become important places for candidates to campaign. California, for example, held its 1988 primary on June 5. To achieve more influence, it moved the election for 2000 back to March 7. Then it moved the date for the 2008 primary back to February 2. Its primary was now four months earlier than it had been, but it gained little influence because in that year twenty-four states held their elections on February 5, including such large ones as Illinois and New York.

As big states front-loaded their caucuses and primaries, the smaller ones, notably Iowa and New Hampshire, moved theirs even earlier. The Iowa caucuses met on January 3, and the New Hampshire primary was held on January 8. (Twenty years earlier, it had been held in March.)

Front-loaded primaries compel candidates to start running for president as much as two years before the general election. Plans have been suggested to change this endless struggle for being first, but none has been adopted.

To run campaigns for so long a period, the candidates must raise a lot of money. In 2008, the leading contenders refused federal money (because it was not enough) and sought cash from supporters. They need not only money but also unimaginable endurance. How does one compete in twenty-four primaries held on one day, especially after having waded through the snow in Iowa and New Hampshire for several months?

Kinds of Elections

There are two kinds of elections in the United States: general and primary. A **general election** is used to fill an elective office. A **primary election** is intended to select a party's candidates for an elective office, though in fact those who vote in a primary election may or may not consider themselves party members. Some primaries are **closed**: You must declare in advance, sometimes by as much as several weeks, that you are a registered member of the political party in whose primary you wish to vote. About forty states have closed primaries.

Other primaries are **open**—that is, you can decide when you enter the voting booth on primary election day in which party's primary you wish to participate. You are given every party's primary ballot, but you may vote on only one. Idaho, Michigan, Minnesota, Montana, North Dakota, Utah, Vermont, and Wisconsin have open primaries. A variant of the open primary is the **blanket** (or "free love") **primary**—in the voting booth you mark a ballot that lists all the candidates for nomination from all the parties, and thus you can select the Democratic candidate for one office and the Republican candidate for another. Alaska and Washington have blanket primaries.

The differences among these kinds of primaries should not be exaggerated, for even the closed primary does not create any great barrier for a voter who wishes to vote in the Democratic primary in one election and the Republican primary in another. Some states also have a **runoff primary**: If no candidate gets a majority of the votes, there is a runoff between the two candidates with the most votes. Runoff primaries are common in the South.

A special kind of primary is used to pick delegates to the presidential nominating conventions of the major parties; these **presidential primaries** come in a bewildering variety. A simplified list of the kinds of presidential primaries looks like this:

1. *Delegate selection only:* Only the names of prospective delegates to the convention appear on the ballot. They may or may not indicate their presidential preference.
2. *Delegate selection with advisory presidential preference:* Voters pick delegates and indicate their preferences among presidential candidates. The delegates are not legally bound to observe these preferences.
3. *Binding presidential preference:* Voters indicate their preferred presidential candidate. Delegates must observe these preferences, at least for a certain number of convention ballots. The delegates may be chosen in the primary or by a party convention.

In 1981, the Supreme Court decided that each political party, and not the state legislatures, has the right to decide how delegates to national conventions are selected. In particular, Wisconsin could not retain an open primary if the national Democratic party objected (*Democratic Party* v. *La Follette*, 450 U.S. 107, 1981). Henceforth, the parties can insist that only voters who declare themselves Democrats or Republicans can vote in presidential primaries. The Supreme Court's ruling may have relatively little practical effect, however, because the "declaration" might occur only an hour or a day before the election.

Regardless of the schedule, presidential candidates face a strategic problem: They must say things during the primary campaigns that will arouse their most die-hard supporters but then find ways of backing away from those statements in November when they must appeal to more centrist voters. To mobilize enthusiasts, one can say, "I will take our troops out of Iraq now!" or "We must back the surge in Iraq," but in the general election, where voters are not so clearly divided, it will become important to say "I will pull the troops out . . . in time" or "We must back the surge . . . up to a point."

Events will often upset the best-laid plans, but at the beginning, at least, the candidate and his or her staff try to make some basic choices. Should they run a positive (build me up) or a negative (attack the opponent) campaign? What theme—a simple idea of broad appeal—should be developed? Should the campaign make a major effort early, or start slowly and build to a peak? What kinds of voters can be swayed by what kinds of appeals? Where should the most money be spent—on television, direct mail, or campaign trips?

Sometimes one has little choice in these matters. For example, an incumbent has to run on his or her record. For most voters an election is a retrospective judgment on the performance of whoever has been in office. The most important focus of that judgment is the economy. If times are good, incumbent presidents do well at the polls—as Ronald Reagan did in 1984 and Bill Clinton did in 1996. If times are bad, as they were for Jimmy Carter in 1980 and George H. W. Bush in 1992, the incumbent is likely to lose (see Figure 8.1). In 2008, for the first time since 1952, neither party had an incumbent president or vice president running for election.

General election *An election used to fill an elective office.*

Primary election *An election prior to the general election in which voters select the candidates who will run on each party's ticket.*

Closed primary *A primary election limited to registered party members. Prevents members of other parties from crossing over to influence the nomination of an opposing party's candidate.*

Open primary *A primary election that permits voters to choose on election day the party primary in which they wish to vote. They may vote for candidates of only one party.*

Blanket primary *A primary election that permits all voters, regardless of party, to choose candidates. A Democratic voter, for example, can vote in a blanket primary for both Democratic and Republican candidates for nomination.*

Runoff primary *A second primary election held in some states when no candidate receives a majority of the votes in the first primary; the runoff is between the two candidates with the most votes. Runoff primaries are common in the South.*

Figure 8.1 Economic Performance and Vote for the Incumbent President's Party

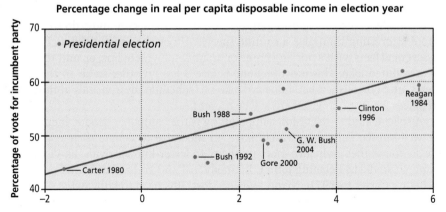

Note: Each dot represents a presidential election showing the popular vote received by the incumbent president's party. 1992 data do not include votes for independent candidate H. Ross Perot.

Source: Robert S. Erikson and Kent L. Tedin, "Economic Performance and Vote for the Incumbent President's Party," *American Public Opinion*, 5th ed., p. 271, fig. 9.5. Copyright © 1995 by Addison-Wesley Educational Publishers, Inc. Reprinted by permission of Pearson Education, Inc.

Presidential primary *A special kind of primary used to pick delegates to the presidential nominating conventions of the major parties.*

At one time almost all campaigning was aimed at making personal contact with as many voters as possible through rallies, "whistle-stop" train or bus tours, and handshaking outside factory gates. This still occurs, but more and more candidates for statewide and national office devote their energies to getting on television. Television reaches more people than all other campaign methods combined, and voters say in polls that they get more of their political information from television than from any other single source, including newspapers.

Using Television

Though laws guarantee that candidates can buy time at favorable rates on television, not all candidates take advantage of this, for television is not always an efficient means of reaching voters. A television message is literally "broadcast"—spread out to a mass audience without regard to election districts. Presidential candidates, of course, always use television because their constituency is the nation as a whole. Candidates for senator or representative, however, may or may not use it depending on whether the boundaries of their state or district conform well to the boundaries of a television market.

Spots (campaign) *Short television advertisements used to promote a candidate for government office.*

Visual (campaign) *A campaign activity that appears on a television news broadcast.*

There are two ways to use television—by running paid advertisements (**spots**) and by getting on the nightly news broadcasts (**visuals**). Much has been written—mostly by advertising executives, who are not known for underestimating their abilities—about packaging the candidate through the preparation of spots. No doubt spots can have an important effect in some cases, and occasionally a little-known candidate (like Jimmy Carter) can win a primary campaign through the clever use of spots.

But visuals—a brief filmed episode showing the candidate doing something—are at least as important. They cost the candidate nothing and, being "news," are likely to have greater credibility with the viewer.[17] To get on the air, visuals must seem newsworthy to television editors. Thus the candidate must do something more interesting than give a routine speech: He or she must make a charge or assert new facts, visit a nursing home or an unemployment line, or sniff the water of a polluted lake. This must be done before 3 P.M. in order to be on the 6 P.M. news, and obviously great pains are taken to schedule these visuals at times and in places where photographers will be present.

A special kind of television campaigning is the campaign debate. Incumbents or well-known candidates rarely have an incentive to debate their opponents. By so doing, they only give more publicity to lesser-known rivals, as Vice President Nixon did by debating John F. Kennedy in 1960 and as President Ford did by debating Carter in 1976. Nixon and Ford lost. It is hard to know what effect television debates have on election outcomes, but poll data suggest that voters who watched the debates in 1980 were reassured by Reagan's performance; after the second debate with Carter he took a lead in the polls that he never relinquished. In 1984, most people believed Reagan lost the first debate against Mondale but held his own in the second. There is no evidence to suggest that debates in 1984, 1988, 1992, 1996, 2000, or 2004 changed enough minds to make any difference in the election.

The Internet, blogs, and social networking (such as Facebook, Twitter, and YouTube) have become important new forces in campaigning. They have many of the advantages of direct mail (that is, a candidate can target his or her campaign to particular kinds of voters) but social networking and the Internet are much cheaper and much faster than mail. This means that voters who use the Internet (and at least half of them do) can be urged to attend particular meetings or contribute money very quickly, right in step with changes in political news.

Some digital lobbying firms specialize in using digital information to reach and mobilize people. As described by Phillip N. Howard, they have amassed an enormous amount of information about Americans and can use it to "narrowcast" (rather than broadcast, as radio and television do) messages to people carefully selected for their personal traits. One company has basic information on 150 million registered voters and more detailed records on four out of every ten adults in the country.[18] The firm gives people a little box they attach to their television sets. This gives them free access to the Internet. In return, the users tell the company their personal characteristics and respond to a periodic survey that tests potential TV ads. The company can quickly learn which ad works the best for what kind of voter.

The other firm practices what politicians call "astroturfing." Astroturf is artificial grass; thus, astroturfing is a substitute for a grassroots movement. Here is how it works. To get letters written to four members of Congress whose votes you want to change, the company will run 3 million ads on the Web aimed at people in these four districts. This will lead 30,000 people to learn that there is an issue that interests them; of these, 2,700 will agree to join a campaign. Of these, 270 will send telegrams to the four members of Congress. These telegrams often change key congressional votes.[19]

The Effects of Campaigns

It is hard to know whether campaigns make a difference and, if so, which aspects influence which voters. This causes great uncertainty for candidates and great frustration for their managers. In a general election, perhaps two-thirds of the voters vote on the basis of their traditional party loyalties. In most congressional races, that is enough to ensure that the candidate of the locally dominant party will win. Presidential races, however, are usually much closer.

A key campaign task is to get people to vote. Of late we have learned more about how this can be done. Careful experiments done in several cities and states have told scholars what works and what does not. Here are things that do *not* increase the turnout of voters:

- Reminding people to vote.
- Telling them where to vote.
- Mailing partisan appeals to voters.

Here are some things that do increase turnout:

- Telling people how often they have voted in the past.
- Telling people how often their neighbors have voted.

In short, people respond to social pressures. Showing one hundred voters their past participation rate produces five more votes; telling them both their own and their neighbors' participation rate produces eight more votes.[20] These gains may not look large, but many elections are settled by small margins.

Many campaigns rely on negative ads—that is, ads that attack a candidate's opponent. Some scholars warn that such ads either have no effect on election results or reduce turnout. But the latest research confirms what many campaign managers have long believed: Negative ads are an effective way of generating votes.[21] You may not like negative ads (you may not like advertising at all), but they make a difference—which is why you see so many of them.

Until recently, more people identified with the Democratic than with the Republican party. Why then don't the Democrats always win? There are three reasons. First, people who consider themselves Democrats are less firmly wedded to their party than are Republicans. Since 1952, at least 84 percent of Republican voters have supported the Republican candidate (omitting the unusual 1964 election when Goldwater ran). There has been a much higher rate of defection among Democratic voters.[22] In most races since 1952, Republicans have won more votes from independents, who tend to be young whites (see Table 8.2). Finally, a higher percentage of Republicans than of Democrats vote in elections.

Most voters usually decide whom they will support for president soon after the nominating conventions end. The campaign thus is aimed at the minority of voters who have not yet made up their minds. Just who these people are and what they want is the concern of the growing number of professional polling organizations hired by candidates. Scarcely any serious politician running for major office would dream of proceeding without a series of polls. These private polls are meant not to predict who will win but to find out how the voters perceive the candidates and what kinds of appeals will reach undecided voters.

Sometimes these polls can help the candidate: in 1952, Eisenhower learned from a poll that the public wanted an honorable end to the Korean War and went on television to announce that he would "go to Korea." The promise captured the public mood and helped elect Eisenhower. Usually, however, the private polls will not suggest any masterstroke that can have a dramatic effect on the election. They will supply only general guidance about what campaign themes or tactics should be used—or avoided. Thus his private polls in 1980 told Reagan he should be reassuring, emphasizing such themes as competence, experience, leadership, and moderation—advice he followed skillfully, drawing votes from middle-of-the-roaders and former Carter supporters.[23] Bill Clinton ordered endless polls, sometimes weekly, to help him decide what positions to adopt.

No one is sure what effect campaigns have on general elections, especially for president. Because the voter receives stimuli from so many sources, perhaps we shall never know which, if any, stimuli are of decisive importance. Probably a good rule of thumb is this: The fewer the other sources of voter information, the more the campaign will make a difference. Campaigns are more likely to be important (1) for low-visibility offices; (2) in primary campaigns where the voter is confronted with many candidates, all of whom have the same party label; and

Table 8.2   Percentage of Popular Vote by Groups in Presidential Elections, 1956–2008

		Total	Republicans	Democrats	Independents
1956	Stevenson	42%	4%	85%	30%
	Eisenhower	58	96	15	70
1960	Kennedy	50	5	84	43
	Nixon	50	95	16	57
1964	Johnson	61	20	87	56
	Goldwater	39	80	13	44
1968	Humphrey	43	9	74	31
	Nixon	43	86	12	44
	Wallace	14	5	14	25
1972	McGovern	38	5	67	31
	Nixon	62	95	33	69
1976	Carter	51	11	80	48
	Ford	49	89	20	52
1980[a]	Carter	41	11	66	30
	Reagan	51	84	26	54
	Anderson	7	4	6	12
1984	Mondale	41	7	73	35
	Reagan	59	92	26	63
1988	Dukakis	46	8	82	43
	Bush	54	91	17	55
1992	Clinton	43	10	77	38
	Bush	38	73	10	32
	Perot	19	17	13	30
1996	Clinton	49	13	84	43
	Dole	40	80	10	35
	Perot	9	6	5	17
2000	Bush	48	91	11	45
	Gore	49	8	86	47
2004	Bush	51	95	7	48
	Kerry	48	5	93	52
2008	Obama	52	9	89	52
	McCain	46	89	10	44

[a]The 1980 figures fail to add up to 100 percent because of missing data.

Source: Updated from Gallup poll data compiled by Robert D. Cantor, *Voting Behavior and Presidential Elections* (Itasca, IL: Peacock, 1975), p. 35; Gerald M. Pomper, *The Election of 1976* (New York: David McKay, 1977), p. 61; Gerald M. Pomper, *The Election of 1980* (Chatham, NJ: Chatham House, 1981), p. 71; and news stories in 1988, 1992, 1996, 2000, and 2004.

2010 Election

The political party of almost every president loses congressional seats in off-year elections. In eighteen such races from 1938 through 2006, the presidential party lost House seats in sixteen elections and Senate seats in thirteen. But in 2010, the Democratic party lost approximately 61 House and 6 Senate seats, one of the largest losses in modern history. Control of the House shifted from Democrats to Republicans, and in the Senate the Democratic majority, once sixty seats, was cut to 53. What happened?

Three things. First, the country was in the grip of a recession that began in 2008 and was still underway late in 2010. Voters hold the party in office responsible for high levels of unemployment and bad economic news. No party would have been able to withstand all of this bad news.

Second, President Obama and Democratic leaders in Congress sought to expand the role and cost of government by enacting a major new health care plan, trying to pass legislation (called "cap and trade") that would have raised the cost of energy, and passed a bill increasing government regulation of financial and investments firms. The health care plan was unpopular with voters, cap-and-trade legislation seemed to threaten them with higher gasoline and fuel oil prices, and more intense regulation of business upset small (and many not so small) businesses. It is possible that in ordinary and prosperous times these bills might have won popular support, but in the midst of a recession they struck citizens as a risky diversion from what should have been the main goal: getting people back to work, inducing business firms to expand operations, and helping banks extend credit to people trying to finance home purchases.

Third, the combined effect of a bad economy and unpopular policies nationalized the election. Instead of the congressional elections turning on local issues that would protect most incumbents, it was a referendum on a president who, though very popular when first elected, steadily lost support in the polls.

A spontaneous popular movement, called the Tea Party, galvanized this opposition with countless rallies all over the country composed mostly of middle-aged and middle-class whites. There is no central leadership or policy for this group, but its members, based on their signs and speeches, called for an end to deficit spending, repeal of the health care bill, lower taxes, and a balanced budget. In primary elections they have helped win Republican Senate nominations for Sharon Angle in Nevada, Christine O'Donnell in Delaware, Ron Johnson in Wisconsin, Joe Miller in Alaska, and Marco Rubio in Florida, while at the same time contributing to the end of the careers of Republicans Bob Bennett in Utah and Mike Castle in Delaware. It is hard to know whether Tea Party support or opposition made a difference, though 41 percent of the voters said they supported it. Johnson, Paul, and Rubio won while Angle and O'Donnell lost in the general election. Miller (as of early November 2010) may or may not win when all of the votes are counted.

Though the House is under Republican control and the Democratic strength in the Senate is much reduced, Barack Obama remains in the White House, and so it is unlikely that new policy directions from Republicans will make a difference. But some modest changes are possible.

(3) in elections not extensively covered by the media. The less the voter can learn from other sources and the more confusing the choices he or she faces, the more helpful may be campaign literature, door-to-door canvassing, coffee parties, and speeches.

Single-Issue Groups

According to some observers, with the decline in the power of political parties has come a rise in the influence of single-issue, ideological groups that urge their followers to vote for or against a candidate solely on the basis of some cause. In the 1990s, one of the best known such groups was the Christian Coalition, a group of conservative fundamentalists. On the liberal side was the National Organization for Women.

There is nothing new about such groups. In the nineteenth century, the Anti-Slavery Society and the National Woman Suffrage Association demanded that politicians take sides on emancipation for blacks and voting rights for women. During the early twentieth century, the Women's Christian Temperance Union made life miserable for candidates who tried to duck the question of prohibition. And during all this time, the parties were relatively strong, at least by today's standards.

Although they have become more powerful of late, it is not clear whether single-issue ideological groups have a large effect on general elections. In the 1980 election, for example, the National Conservative Political Action Committee (NCPAC) spent more than $7 million, mostly to defeat five liberal Democratic senators; four of them lost. But all four came from traditionally Republican states. Was NCPAC's effect on the campaign decisive? There is as yet little evidence that such ideological groups make a significant difference in a general election, at least for senator or president.

However, they may make a difference in *primary* elections, which, as we have seen, can often be won by people who mobilize a small, dedicated following, especially if many candidates are running. The recent rise in the importance of primaries may give greater influence to single-issue or ideological groups, but there is no evidence with which to test this speculation.

Campaigns do have one indisputable effect: They provide for the passage of time between the nomination and the election. During that time—in a national election, roughly the beginning of September to the first week in November—several things happen. Traditional party loyalties start to reassert themselves. (Right after a presidential convention, the person just nominated tends to have a big lead in the polls. Usually this lead quickly dwindles as time goes on.) The candidates have a chance to make mistakes. Generalized perceptions of the candidates' personalities begin to take hold in the voters' minds. Finally, events happen—strikes, riots, disasters, economic changes—and voters can watch how the candidates respond to these challenges.[24]

 So What?

You may think you know how elections are won. The victor spends more money than his or her rivals and puts on the air more convincing television ads. In a presidential race, the winner chooses as the vice presidential nominee a person who can deliver the votes of his or her state and performs better in presidential debates.

Well, not exactly. Some of these things may make a small difference, but a few make no difference and taken together they do not explain much. Scholars cannot say exactly what decides an election, but most agree that three things count the most:

1. Political party affiliation
2. The state of the economy
3. The character of the candidates

For over a century, there has rarely been an election in which either the Democrats or the Republicans got fewer than 40 percent of the vote (see Figure 8.2). For all the talk about voting for "the person, not the party," in fact 80 percent of the vote will go to the candidates of the two main parties, no matter whom they nominate. This means that the election will be decided by the 20 percent of the voters who cannot be counted on to vote either Democratic or Republican. The campaign will be an effort to reach those 20 percent.

The biggest factor affecting how those 20 percent will vote is the state of the economy. In good times, the party holding the White House does well; in poor times, it does badly (see Figure 8.1). This is called the "pocketbook vote." But it is not clear that it is the state of *your* pocketbook that determines how you will vote. Many people who are doing well financially will vote against the party in power if the country as a whole is not doing well. There are several reasons for this. A person who is doing well may have friends or family members who are doing poorly; this person may vote so as to help those individuals change politicians. Or the well-off voter may think that if the country is doing poorly, he or she will soon feel that pinch by losing a job or losing customers; as a result, that voter will vote for the challenger to help protect his or her own future.

Figure 8.2 Partisan Division of the Presidential Vote in the Nation, 1824–2008

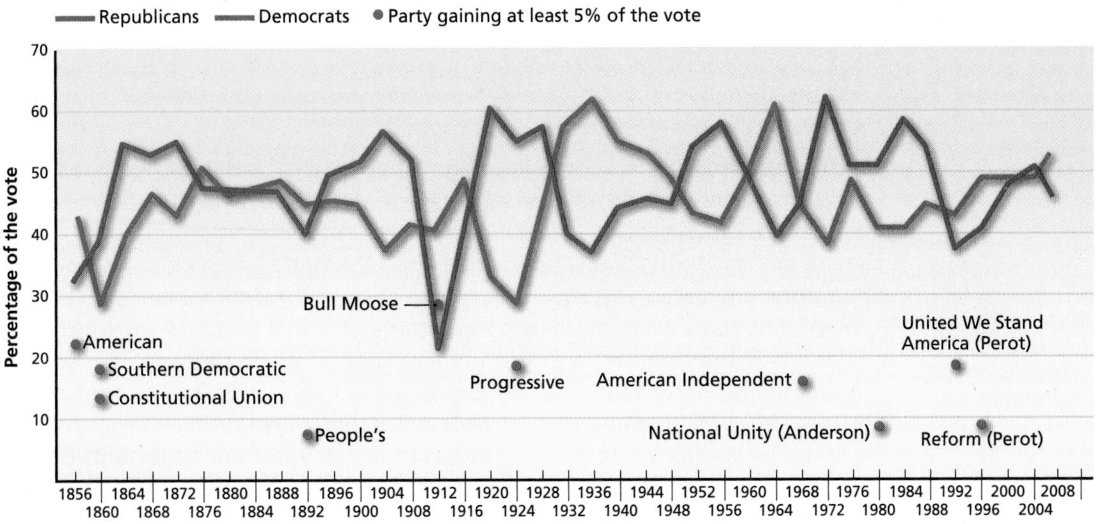

Source: Information for 1856–1988, updated from Historical Data archive, Inter-University Consortium for Political Research, as reported in William H. Flanigan and Nancy H. Zingate, *Political Behavior of the American Electorate*, 3rd ed., 32. For 1992: *World Almanac and Book of Facts 1994*, 73.

Voters also care about presidential character. Character means several things: Is the candidate honest and reliable? Does the candidate think as the voter thinks about important social issues, such as crime, abortion, gun control, or school prayer? Does the candidate act "presidential"? Acting presidential seems to mean being an effective speaker, displaying dignity and compassion, and sounding like one will "take charge" and get things done.

Lest you think that this list includes everything that could affect an election, notice what has *not* been listed:

• The vice-presidential nominee (there has rarely been an election when that made any difference)

• The role of the mass media (they may make a difference in some outcomes, but they rarely decide presidential elections)

• The issues the candidate proposes (assuming the candidate has not violated some political taboo, he or she can forget about developing detailed positions on most issues)

• Religion (once, being a Catholic was a bar to winning, but since the 1960 victory of Kennedy, a Catholic, that probably isn't an issue anymore)

Of course, there are some things that may or may not make a difference, but we do not know because the trait has not been tested in a presidential race. For example, only in 2008 did we discover that a black candidate could prevail.

You may still think that issues matter in elections. They do, but in ways that are not obvious. First, one of the reasons four out of five voters support one party or another is not because they are blind loyalists but because they may think the parties represent their positions on issues. Liberals vote Democratic; conservatives vote Republican. Not all voters are liberals or conservatives, but those who are support parties that seem to have similar positions. When V. O. Key, Jr., looked at voters who had switched parties between elections, he discovered that they usually changed in a way that was consistent with their political interests and preferences.[25] Voters are no fools.

Second, some issues are more important than others, and issues generally are more important in some elections than in others. For many decades, the federal government had a huge deficit. Most Americans thought it should be eliminated, yet few voters knew which party had the better idea for doing so—and thus not many voters cast their vote on the basis of the deficit issue. By contrast, when crime rates were growing, people made an effort to figure out which candidate took the tougher line on crime and supported that person. It is an odd situation: Presidents can influence the deficit but cannot do much about crime, but voters let crime influence their vote more than they let the deficit influence it. In some elections, the issues that do influence votes are important. During the late 1960s and early 1970s, crime, civil rights, and the war in Vietnam were hot topics, and so in the campaigns that occurred then these issues made a difference.[26] In 1996 and 1998, by contrast, there were not many issues of the sort that influence votes, and so there was not much issue voting.

Retrospective voters *Those who vote for or against the candidate or party in office because they like or dislike how things have gone in the recent past. (Retrospective means "backward-looking.")*

Third, many people do try to judge issues, but do so in different ways. Most voters are **retrospective voters**. That is, they look back at how the party that controls the White House has performed and support it if the nation is in good shape, especially economically. But some people are **prospective voters**. That is, they look ahead and try to figure out how a candidate will behave in the future. They worry about how the economy will look next year or two years from now, not how it looked yesterday. They are less interested in past performance than in future prospects.[27] Studies of public opinion suggest that the average voter is retrospective, while political activists and people with strong political ideologies are prospective.[28]

Prospective voters *Those who vote for a candidate because they favor his or her ideas for addressing issues after the election. (Prospective means "forward-looking.")*

Congressional elections are a bit different from presidential elections for two reasons. First, in many districts, one party or another has a huge advantage. No predominantly African American district will elect a Republican, and few affluent white suburbs will elect a Democrat. The same party always wins. Second, a congressional district is small enough that its member in Congress can get to know the voters, attend countless civic, business, and labor meetings, perform services for voters who need help, and send letters to selected voters. As a result, the advantages of being an incumbent are great no matter what is happening to the nation in a whole.

But in districts where one party does not have a big advantage, the same things that determine presidential elections determine congressional ones. Incumbents will benefit from a good national economy and will be hurt if they are shown to have a bad character. And if the district changes its social composition—if it changes from white to black, or from Caucasian to Asian—that will lead to a change in representation.

Election Outcomes

To the candidates and perhaps to the voter, the only interesting outcome of an election is who wins. To a political scientist, the interesting outcomes are the broad trends in winning and losing and what they imply about the attitudes of voters, the operation of the electoral system, and the fate of political parties.

Figure 8.2 shows the trend in the popular vote for president since the rise of the party system. Before 1896, the two parties were hotly competitive. Beginning in 1896, the Republicans became the dominant party and, except for 1912 and 1916, when Democrat Woodrow Wilson won (owing to a split in the Republican party), the Republicans carried every presidential election until 1932. In that year of the Depression, Franklin D. Roosevelt put together what has since become known as the New Deal coalition, and the Democrats became the dominant party. They won every election until 1952, when Eisenhower, a Republican and a popular military hero, was elected for two terms.

Party Realignments

To help explain the alternations of dominance between the two parties, scholars have developed the notion of **critical**, or **realigning**, **periods**. During such periods a sharp, lasting shift occurs in the popular coalition supporting one or both parties. The issues that separate the two parties change, and so the kinds of voters supporting each party change. This shift may occur at the time of the election or just after, as the new administration draws new supporters.[29] There seem to have been five realignments so far, during or just after these elections: 1800 (when the Jeffersonian Republicans defeated the Federalists); 1828 (when the Jacksonian Democrats came to power); 1860 (when the Whig party collapsed and the Republicans under Lincoln came to power); 1896 (when the Republicans defeated William Jennings Bryan); and 1932 (when the Democrats under Roosevelt came into office). Some observers are struck by the fact that these realignments have occurred with marked regularity every twenty-eight to thirty-six years and have speculated on whether they are the result of inevitable cycles in American political life.

Critical, or **realigning**, **periods** *Periods during which a sharp, lasting shift occurs in the popular coalition supporting one or both parties. The issues that separate the two parties change, and so do the kinds of voters supporting each party.*

Such speculations need not concern us, for it is more important to understand why a realignment occurs at all. There are at least two kinds of realignments. In one, a major party is so badly defeated that it disappears and a new party takes its place. This happened to the Federalists in 1800 and to the Whigs between 1856 and 1860. In the other, the two existing parties continue, but voters shift their support from one to the other; this happened in 1896 and 1932. The three clearest cases of a critical election followed by a realignment seem to be 1860, 1896, and 1932.

In 1860, the central issue was slavery. The Democrats split between a southern group that defended slavery and a northern group that waffled on the issue. The remnants of the old Whig party tried to unite the nation by ignoring the issue. And a new Republican party had formed four years earlier (in 1856) in clear-cut opposition to slavery. The Republicans won, eliminating the Whigs, who had straddled the fence on slavery. The Civil War ensued, fixing new party loyalties deeply in the popular mind. Thus, the structure of party competition was set for nearly forty years.

In 1896, economics and religion were at issue. A series of depressions hurt midwestern and southern farmers badly, and so they were prepared to turn against urban economic interests. At the same time, the cities were rapidly filling up with immigrant Catholics whose lifestyle offended many Protestant farmers. William Jennings Bryan captured the Democratic nomination and saw to it that the party adopted a platform responding to both the economic and cultural grievances of farmers. Anti-Bryan urban Democrats deserted the party in droves and helped elect Republican William McKinley. The old split between North and South was partially replaced by an East versus West, urban versus rural cleavage. This alignment persisted until 1932.[30]

In 1932, the realignment was precipitated by a nationwide economic depression. The **New Deal coalition** that emerged brought together in the Democratic party urban workers, southern whites, northern blacks, and Jewish voters, making the Democrats the majority party. These disparate groups made for a strange coalition, but the federal government under Roosevelt supplied enough benefits to keep each of them loyal and to provide a new basis for party identification.

In short, an electoral realignment occurs when a new issue of utmost importance to voters cuts across existing party divisions and replaces old issues that were formerly the basis of party identification. Some observers have speculated that we have experienced a sixth party realignment now, as tensions within the New Deal coalition become more evident and memories of Roosevelt and the Great Depression fade.

Did the Republican victories in 1980, 1984, and 1988 mark another realignment? Although most voters approved of some of Reagan's stands against big government and high taxes, poll data indicate that voters continue to support federal spending on most domestic programs, such as health, education, the environment, and social security. Reagan won in 1980 because voters were dissatisfied with the performance of his predecessor, Jimmy Carter.[31] He won again in 1984 because they were satisfied with the condition of the economy. The elder Bush won in 1988 because economic conditions continued to be good in most parts of the country and because his rival, Dukakis, seemed too liberal on many social issues. When the economy turned sour in 1992, the voters rejected Bush.

But there is much evidence that a realignment has occurred, though it did not come after a single, dramatic election. It occurred chiefly among white voters in the South. Well into the 1960s, these voters were overwhelmingly Democratic in their political preferences. Since the 1970s, they have moved steadily into the Republican camp—first at the presidential level, and now at the congressional level as well. This change has been so great that a region that was once solidly Democratic has now become almost as solidly Republican, at least as long as Democratic candidates are perceived as liberal and Republican candidates as conservative. When the Democrats nominated Arkansas governor Bill Clinton in 1992, they revived their hopes of carrying at least part of the South, but ended up with only four of the eleven states. In 1996, Clinton did no better, and in 2000 and 2004, Democratic candidates did not carry a single southern state.

The result of this new party alignment is best known by the famous split between "Blue States" (where Democrats usually win) and "Red States" (where Republicans usually win). In fact, however, many Blue or Red states are deeply divided, so it is better to talk about Blue Counties (for example, the coastal counties

New Deal coalition *The different, sometimes opposed voters— southern whites, urban blacks, union workers, and intellectuals— whom Franklin D. Roosevelt made part of the Democratic party in the 1930s and 1940s.*

Split-tickets *Voting for candidates of different parties for various offices in the same election. For example, voting for a Republican for senator and a Democrat for president.*

of California) and Red Counties (for example, the inland counties of California). These are displayed in the map on this page.

Party Decline

Parties are decaying as well as realigning. The number of people identifying with one or another party declined between 1960 and 2000. Many people (about one-fifth in recent elections) vote **split tickets** by supporting one party for president and the other party for House or Senate seats.

Ticket splitting was almost unheard of in the nineteenth century and for a very good reason: Either the voter was given a ballot by the party of his choice, which he then dropped intact into the ballot box (thereby voting for everybody on the ticket), or he was given a government-printed ballot that listed all the candidates of each party in columns, at the top of which he could mark an X to vote for all the party's candidates (a **party-column ballot**). Around 1900, the Progressive party began to persuade states to adopt the **office-bloc ballot**, listing candidates by the office they were running for, not by party, and thus making **straight-ticket voting** more difficult. Not surprisingly, states using office-bloc ballots (or voting machines) show more ticket splitting than those that do not.[32]

A Winning Coalition

If the strength of each party's hold on the loyalty of its voters is declining, then we would expect the composition of each party's voting coalition to vary from

Party-column ballot *A ballot listing all candidates of a given party together under the name of that party; also called an "Indiana" ballot.*

Office-bloc ballot *A ballot listing all candidates for a given office under the name of that office; also called a "Massachusetts" ballot.*

Straight-ticket voting *Voting for candidates who are all of the same party. For example, voting for Republican candidates for senator, representative, and president.*

Figure 8.3 Election by County, 2008

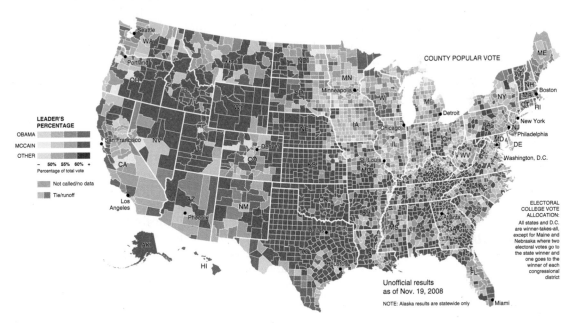

Source: AP Election Research; USGS; Census Bureau; AP Photo.

election to election. This happens, though the persistence of party loyalty and policy preferences among various groups provides some continuity in the votes that each party receives.

There are two ways to examine a party's voting coalition. One is to ask what percentage of various identifiable groups in the population supported the Democratic or Republican candidate for president. The other is to ask what proportion of a party's total vote came from each of these groups. The answer to the first question tells us how *loyal* farmers, blacks, union members, and others are to the party or its candidate; the answer to the second tells us how *important* each group is to the party. These figures describe both the continuity and the changes within the coalitions supporting each party.

Blacks are the most loyal Democratic voters—85 to 90 percent vote Democratic (see Table 8.3). Jewish voters are the next most loyal—about two-thirds support the Democrats. Most Hispanics have been Democrats, though the label "Hispanic" conceals differences among Cuban Americans (who often vote Republican) and Mexican Americans and Puerto Ricans (who are strongly Democratic). The Democrats have lost their once-strong hold on Catholics, southerners, and white blue-collar workers; these groups have become swing voters.

The Republican coalition is often described as the party of business and professional people. The loyalty of these groups to the Republican party is strong; only in 1964 did they desert the party to support Democrat Lyndon Johnson. Farmers have usually been Republican, but they are a volatile group, highly sensitive to the level of farm prices—and thus quick to change parties. They abandoned the Republicans in 1948 and 1964. Contrary to popular wisdom, the Republican party usually wins the votes of the poor. Only in 1964 did most poor people support the Democratic candidate. This can be explained by the fact that the poor include quite different elements—low-income blacks (who are Democrats) and many elderly retired people (usually Republicans).

In sum, the loyalty of most identifiable groups to either party is not overwhelming. Only blacks, businesspeople, and Jews usually give two-thirds or more of their votes to one party or the other; other groups display tendencies, but none that cannot be changed.

The contribution each of these groups makes to the party coalitions is a different matter. Though blacks are overwhelmingly and persistently Democratic, they make up so small a portion of the total electorate that only in recent years have they accounted for as much as one-fifth of the total Democratic vote. The groups that make up the largest part of the Democratic vote—Catholics, union members, southerners—are also the least dependable components of that coalition.[33]

When representatives of various segments of society make demands on party leaders and presidential candidates, they usually stress either their

ELECTORS OF PRESIDENT AND VICE PRESIDENT

Vote for ONE

BALDWIN and CASTLE · · · · · · · · · · · Constitution ◯

BARR and ROOT · · · · · · · · · · · · · · · Libertarian ◯

McCAIN and PALIN · · · · · · · · · · · · · Republican ◯

McKINNEY and CLEMENTE · · · · · · Green-Rainbow ◯

NADER and GONZALEZ · · · · · · · · · · · Independent ◯

OBAMA and BIDEN · · · · · · · · · · · · · · Democratic ◯

DO NOT VOTE IN THIS SPACE. USE BLANK LINE BELOW FOR WRITE-IN.

WRITE-IN SPACE ONLY ◯

William Francis Galvin/Secretary of the State of Massachusetts

| Table 8.3 | | Percentage of Various Groups Saying They Voted for the Democratic Presidential Candidate, 1964–2008 | | | | | | | | | | | |

		1964	1968[a]	1972	1976	1980[b]	1984	1988	1992[c]	1996	2000	2004	2008
Sex	Men	60	41	37	53	37	37	41	41	43	42	45	49
	Women	62	45	38	48	45	42	49	46	54	54	52	56
Race	White	59	38	32	46	36	34	40	39	44	45	42	43
	Black	94	85	87	85	82	90	86	82	84	90	89	95
Education	College	52	37	37	42	35	40	43	44	44	45	47	49
	Grade school	66	52	49	58	43	49	56	55	59	52	51	63
Occupation	Professional and business	54	34	31	42	33	37	40	na	na	na	na	na
	Blue collar	71	50	43	58	46	46	50	na	na	na	na	na
Age	Under 30	64	47	48	53	43	41	47	44	53	48	54	66
	50 and over	59	41	36	52	41[d]	39	49	50	48	48	46	48
Religion	Protestant	55	35	30	46	na	na	33[e]	38	41	42	41	45
	Catholic	76	59	48	57	40	44	47	42	53	50	48	54
	Jewish[f]	89	85	66	68	45	66	64	68	78	79	76	78
Southerners		52	31	29	54	47	36	41	42	na	na	41	na

[a] 1968 election had three major candidates (Humphrey, Nixon, and Wallace).

[b] 1980 election had three major candidates (Carter, Reagan, and Anderson).

[c] 1992 election had three major candidates (Clinton, George H. W. Bush, and Perot).

[d] For 1980–1992 and 2004, refers to age 60 and over.

[e] For 1988, white Protestants only.

[f] Jewish vote estimated from various sources; because the number of Jewish persons interviewed is often less than 100, the error in this figure, as well as that for nonwhites, may be large.

na = not available.

Source: Gallup poll data as tabulated in Jeane J. Kirkpatrick, "Changing Patterns of Electoral Competition," in Anthony King, ed., *The New American Political System* (Washington, D.C.: American Enterprise Institute, 1978), pp. 264–265. Copyright © 1978 by the American Enterprise Institute. Reprinted by permission. 1980, 1984, 1988, 1992, 1996, 2000, and 2004 data from CBS News/*New York Times* survey and CNN poll.

numbers or their loyalty, but rarely both. Black leaders, for example, sometimes describe the black vote as of decisive importance to Democrats and thus deserving of special attention from a Democratic president. But blacks are so loyal that a Democratic candidate can almost take their votes for granted, and in any event, they are not as numerous as other groups. Union leaders, by contrast, will emphasize how many union voters exist, but they cannot "deliver" the rank-and-file vote—much of which may well go Republican, whatever the union leaders say. Thus, for any president and for either party, a winning coalition must be assembled anew in every election. Few voters can either be taken for granted or written off as a lost cause.

Modern Technology and Political Campaigns

In 1950, Estes Kefauver was a little-known senator from Tennessee. Then he chaired a special Senate investigating committee that brought before it various figures in organized crime. When these dramatic hearings were televised to audiences numbering in the millions, Kefauver became a household name and subsequently emerged in 1952 as a leading contender for the Democratic nomination for president. He was a strong vote getter in the primaries and actually led on the first ballot at the convention, only to lose to Adlai Stevenson. The lesson was not lost on other politicians. From that time on, developing a recognized name and a national constituency through the media became important to many candidates.

Today everyone believes the media have a profound effect, for better or for worse, on politics. Unfortunately, very little scholarly evidence can prove or measure that effect, probably because scholars have chiefly tried to measure the effect of the media on election outcomes.[34] But as we have seen, elections—especially general elections for important, highly visible offices—are occasions when the voter is bombarded with all manner of cues from friends, family, interest groups, candidates, radio, television, newspapers, memories, and loyalties. It would be very surprising if the effect of the media would be very strong, or at least very apparent, under these circumstances.

Television, Radio, and Newspapers

Selective attention *Paying attention only to those parts of a newspaper or broadcast story with which one agrees. Studies suggest that this is how people view political ads on television.*

Efforts to see whether voters who watch a lot of television, or who see candidates on television frequently, vote differently from those who do not watch television at all, or who watch only nonpolitical programming, have generally proved unavailing.[35] This is quite consistent with studies of political propaganda generally. At least in the short run, television and radio suffer from processes called **selective attention** (the citizen sees and hears only what he or she wants) and *mental tune-out* (the citizen simply ignores or gets irritated by messages that do not accord with existing beliefs). Radio and television may tend to reinforce existing beliefs, but it is not clear that they change them.[36] Besides, both sides use commercially prepared television spots; if they are well done, they are likely to cancel each other out.

Despite what most people think, commercial spots probably give viewers more information than visuals (and television newscasts generally). The best research we have suggests that news programs covering elections tend to convey very little information (they often show scenes of crowds cheering or candidates shouting slogans) and make little or no impression on viewers. Spots, on the other hand, especially the shorter ones, often contain a good deal of information that is seen, remembered, and evaluated by a public quite capable of distinguishing between fact and humbug.[37]

Except in 1964, local newspapers have generally endorsed Republican presidential candidates throughout this century. Since the Democrats won eight of the twelve presidential elections between 1932 and 1976, newspaper endorsements might seem worthless. They may have some value, however, under some circumstances. A careful study of the 1964 campaign found that, at least in the North, a newspaper endorsement may have added about five percentage points to what the Democrat, Lyndon Johnson, would otherwise have obtained.[38] Today, fewer newspapers make presidential endorsements.

Computers and Direct Mail

Less visible than television, but perhaps just as important in campaigns, is the computer, which makes possible sophisticated direct-mail advertising and fundraising. This in turn allows a candidate to address specific appeals to particular voters and to solicit people for campaign contributions.

Whereas television is directed to everybody—and thus encourages candidates to avoid offending anyone—direct mail is aimed at particular groups to whom specific views can be expressed with much less risk of offending someone. So important are the lists of names of potential contributors to whom the computer sends appeals that a prize resource of any candidate, guarded as if it were a military secret, is "The List." Novices in politics must slowly develop their own lists or beg sympathetic incumbents for a peek at theirs.

In 2004, the Internet played a big role in the primary elections held to choose presidential candidates as well as in the subsequent general election. The Internet, Facebook, and Twitter have become the latest ways whereby politicians can send specific message and request campaign donations from their followers.

Are Today's Voters "Manipulated"?

Citizens are not idiots: though they may try a deodorant because an ad catches their fancy, they know that the stakes are low and that they can change brands if they are dissatisfied. They can also tell a Democrat from a deodorant, know that government is more serious than smelling nice, and realize that they will be stuck with an elected official for years. Hence they evaluate political commercials more carefully. In short, it is not yet clear that a "gullible" public is being sold a bill of goods by slick Madison Avenue advertisers, whether the goods are automobiles or politicians.

The major effect of the media probably has less to do with how people vote in an election and much more to do with how politics is conducted, how candidates are selected, and how policies are formulated. To get elected, candidates must look attractive on television. Even hitherto unknown persons can become candidates by the skillful use of the media. And the media can put issues on the national agenda if they involve matters—such as foreign affairs—with which people are not familiar.[39] But people are much less likely to take their cues from the media on matters that affect them personally. Everyone who is unemployed, the victim of crime, or worried about high food prices will identify these matters as issues whether or not the media emphasize them.[40] In short, the media help set the political agenda on matters with which citizens have little personal experience but have much less influence on how people react to—and vote on—issues that touch their lives directly.

The chief consequence of the new style of campaigning, with its extensive reliance on sophisticated technology, is not, as some think, that it is more "manipulative" than old-style campaigning (picnics with free beer and $5 bills handed to voters can be just as manipulative as television ads). Rather, the chief consequence is that running the campaign has become divorced from the process of governing. Formerly, party leaders who ran the campaign would take an active part in the government once it was elected, and, since they were *party* leaders, they had to worry about getting their candidate *re*elected. Modern political consultants take no responsibility for governing, and by the time the next election rolls around, they may be off working for somebody else.

Elections and Money

"Money is the mother's milk of politics," a powerful California politician once observed, and few candidates who have struggled to raise a campaign chest would disagree. Indeed, raising money has become even more important to the candidate as party organizations have declined. If no machine can supply battalions of precinct workers paid for with patronage jobs, then such workers must either be dispensed with, hired on a temporary basis, or recruited from the sometimes undependable ranks of volunteers. Even more important, increased reliance on television and radio advertising and on direct-mail campaigning has dramatically raised the cost of running for office. A one-minute commercial on national television in prime time, for example, can cost $150,000 or more. And expenditures on the broadcast media can account for about half of the campaign budget of a presidential candidate. As Will Rogers said, "You have to be loaded just to get beat."

Impact of Money

In the twenty-nine presidential elections between 1860 and 1972, the winner outspent the loser twenty-one times. This does not, however, mean that victory was the result of spending more money. People often donate money to candidates whom they think will win in order to get into their good graces. Often these candidates would have won even if they spent less. From 1972 through 2004, the major-party presidential candidates have *officially* spent the same amount of money in general elections because the federal government has paid the bills. But if you add in the unregulated issue ads run by party supporters, one candidate may still outspend the other.

The most careful effort to calculate the effect of spending on elections has been done for congressional races. There are no legal limits on what congressional candidates can spend, but since 1972, they have had to disclose their campaign finances. Gary C. Jacobson used complex statistical techniques to calculate whether, other things being equal (such as the candidates' parties and whether they are challengers or incumbents), spending more money produces more votes. In the elections of 1972, 1974, 1976, and 1978, how much an *incumbent* spent was apparently of little importance, but the *challengers* who spent more did better than those who spent less.[41] The money purchased such things as advertising that could be used to overcome the incumbents' natural advantages of name recognition and access to media.

If spending more money gives no edge to an incumbent but provides a significant edge for a challenger, then it is in the interest of incumbents to find some way—for example, by passing campaign-finance laws—to restrict the ability of candidates to raise money. As we shall see, this is exactly what they have done.

Where Does the Money Come From?

Many people think that well-heeled donors—fat cats—provide most of the money for political campaigns in hopes of getting something for themselves out of government. For a long time that may have been the case. During a brief period in 1972, for example, President Nixon's reelection campaign raised nearly $20 million, mostly from wealthy contributors who preferred to remain anonymous. About forty gave more than $100,000 apiece, and a few contributed in excess of $1 million each. Some of these people just liked Nixon, but some wanted favors, ranging from special treatment in policy making to an appointment as ambassador to some pleasant country. Nixon's rival, George McGovern, also got big individual contributions. Some of Nixon's money was received in cash and was used to pay the men hired to break into the headquarters of the Democratic National Committee, located in the Watergate Hotel.

When the break-in was discovered, the Watergate scandal unfolded. It had two political results: President Nixon was forced to resign, and a new campaign-finance law was passed. This law limited how much money an individual could give to federal candidates, authorized federal tax money to be spent on part of every major candidate's primary election campaign, paid with tax money for almost all of the cost of the presidential general election, and allowed organizations to create **political action committees (PACs)** to raise money for federal candidates.

What happened was that the amount of money spent on elections went up, not down, and PACs became an important source of that cash. This result led to demands for a new campaign finance law that would, in effect, reform the old reform law. In 2002, after a long debate, Congress passed and President Bush signed the Bipartisan Campaign Reform Act, or BCRA, that was sponsored by Senators John McCain and Russell Feingold.

The first reform law limited individual contributions to federal candidates to $1,000 per election and PAC contributions to $5,000 per election. Since most candidates have to run in both primaries and a general election, the effective limits for an election year were $2,000 for each individual and $10,000 for every PAC. A PAC had to have at least fifty members and give money to at least five federal candidates. By 2000, there were about four thousand PACs that gave nearly $260 million to congressional candidates.

But most money candidates spent came from individual donors, and very few PACs ever gave anything like their maximum donations. The problems with the original law, in the eyes of its critics, were not PACs or individual limits, but two other activities that had not been regulated.

The first of these were **independent expenditures**. A PAC, corporation, or labor union could spend whatever it wanted on advertising supporting or opposing a candidate as long as this spending was "independent," that is, not coordinated with or made at the direction of a candidate.

The second problem was **soft money**. Under the law, individuals, corporations, and labor unions could give unlimited amounts of money to political parties provided that the parties did not use these funds to back candidates by name.[42] But these dollars could be used to help candidates indirectly by financing voter registration and get-out-the-vote drives. In 1999–2000, nearly half a billion dollars in

Political action committee (PAC) *A committee set up by and representing a corporation, labor union, or special-interest group that raises and spends campaign contributions on behalf of one or more candidates or causes.*

Independent expenditures *Political money raised and spent by an organization on behalf of a candidate done without direction of or coordination with the candidate.*

Soft money *Money raised by political parties for activities other than directly supporting a federal candidate.*

Former President Jimmy Carter, left, and former Secretary of State James Baker, cochair the Commission on Federal Election Reform, examining the state of America's federal elections and recommending improvements.

soft money (sometimes called "nonfederal money") was spent by the Democratic and Republican parties. The 2002 law banned soft money.

The new BCRA law left essentially unchanged the original law's plan for financing presidential elections. Under this system, people running in a primary election for their party's presidential nomination can receive **matching funds**. To do so, the candidate must raise at least $5,000 in contributions of $250 or less from people living in each of twenty states. Once eligible, the candidate gets federal matching funds, dollar for dollar, to match whatever he or she has raised in contributions of $250 or less.

After winning a major party's nomination, each candidate can receive a grant from the federal government to pay for the entire cost of the campaign up to a limit set by federal law. In 2000, each major candidate was entitled to get a little over $67 million. Candidates of a minor party, like Pat Buchanan (Reform party) and Ralph Nader (Green party), would get partial support from the federal government provided that in the previous election, the party's nominee won at least 5 percent of the vote. A candidate who gets federal money to pay for the campaign must agree to raise no private money and to limit expenditures to what money Washington sends him or her.

Candidates can choose not to take federal money and thus be free to raise and spend as much as they want and free to ignore the many regulations that come with federal funding. George W. Bush did this in 2000 and he, John Kerry, and Howard Dean did it in 2004. In 2008, Obama did the same.

The BCRA made three important changes in 2002. First, it banned soft money contributions to national political parties. After the federal election in 2002, no national party or committee can accept soft, or nonfederal, money. All money donated to it by individuals and PACs is limited by the law.

Matching funds *In presidential elections, money given by the national government to match, under certain conditions, money raised by each candidate.*

Major Federal Campaign-Finance Rules

General

- All federal election contributions and expenditures are reported to a Federal Election Commission.
- All contributions over $100 must be disclosed, with name, address, and occupation of contributor.
- No cash contributions over $100 and no foreign contributions.
- No ceiling on how much candidates may spend out of their own money (unless they accept federal funding for a presidential race).

Individual Contributions

- An individual may not give more than $2,000 to any candidate in any election.
- An individual may not make federal political gifts exceeding $95,000 every two years, of which only $37,500 may go to candidates.

Political Action Committees (PACs)

- Each corporation, union, or association may establish one.

- A PAC must register six months in advance, have at least fifty contributors, and give to at least five candidates.
- PAC contributions may not exceed $5,000 per candidate per election or $15,000 to a national political party.

Ban on Soft Money

- No corporation or union may give money from its own treasury to any national political party after November 2002.

Presidential Primaries

- Federal matching funds can be given to match individual contributions of $250 or less.
- To be eligible, a candidate must raise $5,000 in each of twenty states in contributions of $250 or less.

Presidential Election

- The federal government can pay all campaign costs (up to a legal limit) of major-party candidates and part of the cost of minor-party candidates (those winning between 5 and 25 percent of the vote).

Second, independent expenditures by corporations, labor unions, trade associations, and some nonprofit groups are sharply restricted. Now none of these organizations can use their money to run advertisements that "refer" to a federal candidate during the sixty days preceding a general election and thirty days preceding a primary contest. In 2010, however, the Supreme Court struck down this provision of the BCRA, ruling that such a ban violated free speech rights of corporations, labor unions, and nonprofit organizations.

Third, the limit on individual contributions to federal candidates was raised from $1,000 per candidate in each election to $2,000, and that amount was indexed so that it will rise with inflation.

Newspapers, magazines, and radio and television stations are not affected by the law, so they can say whatever they want for or against a candidate. One way of evaluating the law is to observe that it shifts influence away from businesses and unions and toward the media.

The law further weakens political parties by making it even harder for them to raise and spend money. Their ability to run ads, register voters, and mount get-out-the-vote drives has been sharply reduced. But that does not mean that no money will be spent on these matters. Quite the contrary: Under the law, certain kinds of organizations can raise and spend as much as they want to influence elections. Many exist to support either Democrats or Republicans, and some have been backed by well-known figures, such as financier George Soros. They have no connection to national political parties, they are not PACs, and some, such as the Republican Governors' Association and the Democratic Governors' Association, openly use partisan names. Many of these groups are organized under obscure provisions of the federal tax code; some are called " **527s**" (after section 527 of the Internal Revenue Service's rules), others "501(c) 4s" (after another provision). It is not entirely clear how the BCRA will affect these groups, but if it raises problems, other ways will no doubt be found to raise and spend political money.

527s *Organizations that raise money for political campaigns that are not (yet) regulated by campaign-finance laws.*

There is no way to keep money out of politics. New groups that face few regulations will arise to do what heavily regulated political parties used to do. Rich people and interest groups, both liberal and conservative, will spend money on radio and television ads supporting their causes.

In December 2003, the Supreme Court, in a five-to-four decision, upheld almost all parts of the BCRA.[43] It found (albeit not on the basis of much scientific evidence) that prohibiting soft money would reduce the "actual and apparent corruption of federal candidates," and it decided that restrictions on electioneering ads on radio and television did not violate constitutional rights of free speech and press. Considering that the Supreme Court has in the past forbidden congressional restrictions on virtual pornography, tobacco advertising, and sexually explicit cable programming, it is remarkable that it looked with favor on restrictions on political advertising—at least for radio and television. Newspapers and magazines were unaffected.

Since 2003, however, the Supreme Court has issued several decisions that undercut (some say gut) the BCRA and related restrictions on political advertising. In 2007, the Court struck down BCRA's limitations on airing issue advertisements before primary and general elections. In 2008, the Court struck down BCRA's

New Ways of Raising Political Money

Because political parties can no longer raise soft or nonfederal money, new organizations have sprung up to do the job for them. These are organized under certain provisions of the Internal Revenue Code. Most can engage in political advocacy, provided it is not their primary activity.[a] Some claim to be able to engage in unlimited activity on behalf of issues, as long as they do not lobby for a candidate.[b]

[a]Organizations formed under sections 501(c)(3) and 501(c)(4) of the tax code.

[b]Section 527 of the tax code.

"Millionaire's Amendment" that raised contribution limits for candidates facing opponents who were self-funding their campaigns. And in 2010, the Court struck down the ban on corporate and union spending on advertisements for and against political candidates, overturning a 1990 precedent and a portion of BCRA.

One way to bypass many of the federal rules on campaign finance is to solicit money over the Internet. By intensively using the Internet, one can build up a list of tens of thousands of donors who, though they give less than $100 a person, produce a flood of cash and help identify volunteers to work on a campaign.

The Effects of Elections on Policy

Cynics complain that elections are meaningless. No matter who wins, crooks, incompetents, or self-serving politicians still hold office. People of a more charitable disposition may concede that elected officials are decent enough people but argue that public policy remains more or less the same no matter which official or which party is in office.

There is no brief and simple response to this view. One reason it is so hard to generalize about the policy effects of elections is that the offices to be filled are so numerous—and the ability of the political parties to unite behind a common policy is so weak—that any policy proposal must run a gauntlet of potential opponents. Though we have but two major parties, and though only one party can win the presidency, each party is a weak coalition of diverse elements that reflect the many divisions in public opinion. The proponents of a new law must put together a majority coalition almost from scratch, and a winning coalition on one issue tends to be different—quite often dramatically different—from a winning coalition on another issue.

Despite the weakness of parties and the strength of interest groups, American politics often produces big changes. After 1860, the nation ended slavery; after 1932, the New Deal produced Social Security; after 1964, we acquired Medicare, federal aid to education, and new civil rights and environmental laws; after 1980, there were major tax cuts.

In view of all this, it is hard to argue that the pace of change in our government is always slow and that elections never make a difference. Studies confirm that elections are often significant, despite the difficulty of getting laws passed. One analysis of roughly 1,400 promises made between 1944 and 1964 in the platforms of the two major parties revealed that 72 percent were carried out.[44]

Why then do we so often think that elections make little difference? It is because public opinion and the political parties enter a phase of consolidation and continuity between periods of rapid change. During this phase the changes are, so to speak, digested, and party leaders adjust to the new popular consensus that may (or may not) evolve around the merits of these changes. Historically these periods of consolidation have followed the great realigning elections of 1860, 1896, and 1932.

Elections have another, more complex effect on policy making. The kinds of campaigns people must run in order to win affect the kinds of people who are willing to run. A century ago, presidential candidates did not even campaign. Television advertising did not become important until the 1960s. During the 1970s,

WHAT WOULD YOU DO?

MEMORANDUM

To: Arjun Bruno, National Party Chairman

From: Arlene Marcus, State Party Chairwoman

Subject: Supporting a National Primary

In the past few election cycles, our state's role in the party nomination for president virtually has disappeared with a May primary date. Several states have leap-frogged ahead of us, and party leaders have indicated that they do not want any more states to move up their primary date. The national party needs to find a way to ensure that all states, large and small, have a real voice in nominating a presidential candidate.

Arguments for:

1. A single national primary permits equal participation by all states and presents a fair compromise with the increased number of delegates that larger states send to the national conventions, much like the compromises during the original constitutional debates.

2. The nominating process needs to be less costly, particularly when presidential candidates realistically need to raise $100 million a year before the general election to be competitive for the nomination. Holding all primaries and caucuses on a single day will reduce overall election expenses significantly.

3. If the American electorate knows presidential nominations will be decided by each party on one day, then they will be more likely to vote—a significant factor for elections in which, historically, fewer than 20 percent of eligible voters typically participate.

Arguments against:

1. Each state decides in conjunction with the national party when its primary or caucus will take place, and the federal system of government designed by the Framers did not guarantee that all states would be treated equally at all times.

2. A national primary would favor candidates with high name recognition and funding to further that recognition and would severely disadvantage lesser-known candidates within the party.

Friday,

State Party Organizations Support a National Presidential Primary

January 8
LITTLE ROCK, AK.

Party leaders in several states are urging their elected officials to support a one-day national primary for presidential candidates. As more states move toward early primary dates in February, states with later nominating processes argue that their elections are little more than symbolic. They argue that to give all states an equal say in nominating presidential candidates, a single election is both fair and cost efficient. Critics question, however, whether one nationwide primary would favor the best-known candidate with the most funds in each party, severely limiting the prospects for "dark-horse" candidates to prevail . . .

3. Even though the general election takes place on one day, voter turnout in the United States still is lower than in other advanced industrialized democracies, which suggests that other factors influence who participates.

Your Decision:

Support National Primary _____

Oppose National Primary _____

political outsiders determined that they could run for president if they worked nonstop for three or four years. In the 1980s, campaign managers perfected the technique of learning how voters react to different messages and then spreading those messages in ads and speeches.

People who can run successfully in campaigns organized this way may not have the ability to govern effectively once they are elected. Today's candidates, rather than being picked by knowledgeable peers in the party or in Congress, are self-selected. In any other democratic country in the world, people would be amazed to find candidates for the highest office running without having any experience in elective office (for example, Pat Buchanan, Jesse Jackson, and Ross Perot), or experience in state politics but not national politics (for example, Jimmy Carter, Bill Clinton, Michael Dukakis, Ronald Reagan, and George W. Bush), or experience in Congress but not in any executive position (for example, Al Gore, Bob Dole, John Edwards, Richard Gephardt, George McGovern, Gary Hart, John Kerry, Barack Obama, and John McCain). Some of these men might have made (or did make) good presidents, but there is no way to predict this from the experience they brought to the job.

Our election system rewards people who can mobilize small but strongly motivated constituencies, who can portray themselves as outsiders to the system they plan to run, who have the talent to utter newsworthy sound bites, and who are willing and able to spend three or four years campaigning.

SUMMARY

The United States has more elective offices and more elections than any other major nation. The decision of who is eligible to vote in those elections—originally made almost entirely by the states—is now largely under federal control. Though the franchise has gradually been extended to include all people eighteen years of age and over, we have seen an accompanying decline in voter participation in elections. This change may not be as significant as it appears because miscounting and vote frauds artificially inflated turnouts in the nineteenth century. But some decline has indisputably occurred, perhaps because politics is less interesting to citizens than it once was, perhaps also because the political parties have become weaker and less able to mobilize voters.

Political campaigns have increasingly become personalized, with little or no connection to formal party organizations, as a result of the decay of parties, the rise of the direct primary and the electronic media, and the institution of campaign-finance laws. Candidates face the problem of creating a temporary organization that can raise money from large numbers of small donors, mobilize enthusiastic supporters, and win a primary nomination in a way that will not harm their ability to appeal to a more diverse constituency in the general election. Campaigning has an uncertain effect on election outcomes, but election outcomes can have important effects on public policy, especially in those times—during *critical* or *realigning* elections—when new voters are coming into the electorate in large numbers, old party loyalties are weakening, or a major issue is splitting the majority party.

RECONSIDERING THE ENDURING QUESTIONS

1. What is the best way to calculate how many Americans vote?

It is not by calculating what fraction of the voting-age population has voted. Many people who are age eighteen and over cannot vote because they are not citizens, are prisoners, or are released felons. When these groups are subtracted from the voting-age population, a higher percentage of Americans vote. And if only registered voters are considered, an even higher percentage vote. Still, voting is less common in the United States than in many other nations.

2. What factors chiefly influence who wins a presidential election?

The political party with which voters identify makes a very big difference, though many people claim that party does not count. It does: People who identify as Democrats or Republicans tend to vote that way. The election is really about changing the views of perhaps one-fifth of all voters. The easiest way to do that is for the party in power to benefit from a strong economy; usually that ensures victory. (It did not in 2000, but it did in 1984, 1988, and 2004.)

3. Can federal laws keep big money out of political campaigns?

No. Money is the "mother's milk of politics," and ways will always be found to spend it in politically helpful ways. Campaign-finance reform laws often create as many problems as they solve. The 2002 BCRA weakened political parties, strengthened private interest groups, and called into question our commitment to a free press.

Online Resources: Campaigns and Elections

 CourseMate

- Federal Election Commission: www.fec.gov
- Project Vote Smart: www.vote-smart.org
- Campaign finance: www.opensecrets.org
- Electoral college: www.avagara.com/e_c
- History of presidential elections: www.multied.com/elections

Suggested Readings

Brady, David W., John F. Logan, and Morris P. Fiorina, *Continuity and Change in House Elections.* Stanford: Stanford University Press, 2000. Excellent collection of analyses about getting elected to the House.

Burnham, Walter Dean. *Critical Elections and the Mainsprings of American Politics.* New York: Norton, 1970. An argument about the decline in voting participation and the significance of the realigning election of 1896.

Ehrenhalt, Alan. *The United States of Ambition.* New York: Random House, 1991. A brilliant analysis of the kinds of people willing and able to practice modern politics.

Erikson, Robert S., and Kent L. Tedin. *American Public Opinion,* 7th ed. New York: Longman, 2007. A careful analysis of how polling is done, what Americans think about political issues, and how elections affect policies.

Fiorina, Morris P. *Retrospective Voting in American National Elections.* New Haven, Conn.: Yale University Press, 1981. A careful analysis of how voters judge politicians retrospectively—and rationally.

Green, Donald P., and Alan S. Gerber. *Get Out the Vote: How to Increase Voter Turnout.* 2d ed. Washington, D.C.: Brookings Institution, 2008. Careful study of what does and does not increase political participation.

Jacobson, Gary C. *The Politics of Congressional Elections,* 5th ed. Boston: Little, Brown, 2001. How people are elected to Congress, with close attention paid to the role of money.

Kenski, Kate., et al. *How Media, Money, and Message Shaped the 2008 Election.* New York: Oxford University Press, 2010. Deep analysis of spending patterns and early voting affected the outcome.

Key, V. O., Jr. *The Responsible Electorate.* Cambridge, Mass.: Harvard University Press, 1966. An argument, with evidence, that American voters are not fools.

Sundquist, James L. *Dynamics of the Party System: Alignment and Realignment of Political Parties in the United States,* rev. ed. Washington, D.C.: Brookings Institution, 1983. Historical analysis of realigning elections from 1860 to the nonrealignment of 1980.

9 Congress

ENDURING QUESTIONS

1. **Are the members of Congress representative of the American people?**
2. **Does Congress prefer strong leadership, or does it allow its members a lot of freedom?**
3. **How important are political parties in Congress?**
4. **Why does it take so long for Congress to act?**

Every democratic nation has a legislature that passes laws. Does this mean they are all pretty much alike? Not at all. As the late Senator Daniel Patrick Moynihan once remarked, the United States is the only major democratic nation with a real legislature. He meant that only in this country does the lawmaking body have great powers that it can exercise independently of the executive branch.

The Evolution of Congress

The Framers chose to place legislative powers in the hands of a congress rather than a parliament for philosophical and practical reasons. They did not want to have all powers concentrated in a single government institution, even one that

So What?

To see why our legislature is more powerful than those in many other countries, we must understand the difference between a congress and a parliament.

The United States, and most Latin American nations, have congresses; Great Britain and most Western European nations have parliaments. A **congress** is an assemblage of elected representatives empowered to make laws but not to select the chief executive of the nation; that individual is elected by the people. A **parliament** is an assemblage of elected representatives who both pass laws and select the nation's chief executive (usually called a prime minister).

Ordinarily a person becomes a member of a parliament (such as the British House of Commons) by being nominated by party leaders; voters generally choose between parties, not personalities; and thus parliaments tend to be made up of people loyal to the national party leadership who meet to debate and vote on party issues. By contrast, a person becomes a member of the United States Congress by winning both a primary and a general election, elections in which personalities—not party identity—are usually most important to voters. Thus a congress tends to be made up of people who think of themselves as independent representatives of their districts or states and who, while willing to support their party on many matters, expect to vote as their (or their constituents') beliefs and interests require.

Members of a parliament can usually make only one important decision—whether to support the government (the government consisting of the prime minister and various cabinet officers selected from the party that has won the most seats in the last election). If members of a party in power in parliament vote against their leaders, a new government must be formed. Thus the party leaders insist that all party members vote together on most issues under threat of not being renominated.

In the United States, voters—not members of Congress—select the head of the executive branch of government, the president. This, however, makes members of Congress more, not less, powerful, for they can vote on proposed laws without worrying that their votes will cause the government to collapse and without fearing that a failure to support their party will lead to their removal from the ballot in the next election. Because Congress is constitutionally independent of the president and because its members are not tightly disciplined by party leaders, members are free to express their views, to vote as they wish, and to become involved in the minute details of creating laws, establishing budgets, and supervising agencies. They do this through an elaborate and growing set of committees and subcommittees.

Because members of a parliament have little independent power, they receive poor pay, few perquisites, little or no office space, and virtually no staff. But even the most junior member of the United States House of Representatives has power and is rewarded accordingly. A representative earns a substantial salary ($169,300 in 2008), receives generous retirement benefits, has at least a three-room suite of offices, is supplied with a staff of at least eighteen, can make thirty-three free trips to the home district each year, and can mail newsletters and certain other documents free under the **franking privilege**. Representatives with more seniority and senators receive even more benefits.

Congress *A national legislature composed of elected representatives who do not choose the chief executive (typically, a president).*

Parliament *A national legislature composed of elected representatives who choose the chief executive (typically, the prime minister).*

Franking privilege *The ability of members of Congress to mail letters to their constituents free of charge by substituting their facsimile signature (frank) for postage.*

The Powers of Congress

The powers of Congress are found in Article I, section 8, of the Constitution:

- To lay and collect taxes, duties, imposts, and excises.
- To borrow money.
- To regulate commerce with foreign nations and among the states.
- To establish rules for naturalization (becoming a citizen) and bankruptcy.
- To coin money, set its value, and punish counterfeiting.
- To fix the standard of weights and measures.
- To establish a post office and post roads.
- To issue patents and copyrights to inventors and authors.
- To create courts inferior to (below) the Supreme Court.
- To define and punish piracies, felonies on the high seas, and crimes against the law of nations.
- To declare war.
- To raise and support an army and navy and make rules for their governance.
- To provide for a militia (reserving to the states the right to appoint militia officers and to train the militia under congressional rules).
- To exercise exclusive legislative powers over the seat of government (the District of Columbia) and over places purchased to be federal facilities (forts, arsenals, dockyards, and "other needful buildings").
- To "make all laws which shall be necessary and proper for carrying into execution the foregoing powers, and all other powers vested by this Constitution in the government of the United States." (*Note:* This "necessary and proper" or "elastic" clause has been broadly interpreted by the Supreme Court, as is explained in Chapter 12.)

Bicameral legislature *A lawmaking body made up of two chambers or parts. The U.S. Congress is a bicameral legislature composed of a Senate and a House of Representatives.*

was popularly elected, because they feared that such a concentration could lead to rule by an oppressive or impassioned majority. At the same time, they knew that the states would never consent to a national constitution that did not protect their interests. Hence they created a **bicameral** (two-chamber) **legislature**, with a House of Representatives elected directly by the people and a Senate, consisting of two members from each state, chosen (originally) by the legislatures of each state. Though "all legislative powers" were to be vested in the Congress, those powers would be shared with a president (who could veto acts of Congress), limited to those explicitly conferred on the federal government, and, as it turned out, subject to the power of the Supreme Court to declare acts of Congress unconstitutional.

Although they designed these checks and balances to prevent legislative tyranny, the Framers nevertheless expected that Congress would be the dominant institution in the national government. And for at least a century and a half, it was, except for a few brief periods when activist presidents (such as Andrew Jackson, Abraham Lincoln, and Theodore Roosevelt) were able to challenge congressional supremacy. During the twentieth century, the major struggles for national political power did not occur between Congress and the president but rather *within* Congress—generally over matters of great national significance. At issue has been a disagreement over the distribution of power within Congress itself. Should Congress have a strong central leadership? Or should the power of individual members (and the constituencies they represent) be enhanced, a situation that could result in weak leadership, rules allowing for delay and extended discussion, and many opportunities for committee and subcommittee activity?

During more than two hundred years of growth and experimentation, the House has usually embraced the view that the power of individual members should be protected at the expense of opportunities for leadership. It flirted with strong party leadership in the late nineteenth and early twentieth centuries, but the members revolted and weakened central party control, allowing it to be replaced by strong committee chairmen. But of late, party leadership has begun to reassert itself. When the Republicans gained control of the House in 1994, Speaker Newt Gingrich became more powerful than his Democratic predecessor. That power was later challenged when some Republican members tried to have him replaced. And when the Republicans lost House seats in the 1998 election, Gingrich announced he would resign as Speaker and as a representative.

Despite the ups and downs of party *leadership,* the power of party *loyalty* has grown in the House. In 1993, every single Republican in both the House and the Senate voted against the Clinton budget plan. And in 1998, virtually every House Republican voted to impeach the president, while almost all Democrats voted against it. Though party loyalty has become weaker among voters, it has become stronger among members of Congress.

The Senate never even flirted with tight organization. Because they are so few in number, senators have always insisted on the right to unlimited debate and have always resisted the emergence of leaders with strong formal powers. A major change in the politics of the Senate occurred when the Constitution was amended in 1913 to require that senators be directly elected by the people instead of—as was originally the case—by state legislatures. The Seventeenth Amendment reflected in part popular revulsion against the appearance that the Senate had become a "millionaires' club," but its practical effect was small. Having a lot of money still helps (though it is not essential) if you wish to become a senator.

Who Is in Congress?

Because Congress has such great power and because its internal structure, especially in recent years, has been so decentralized, the behavior of Congress is importantly affected by the kinds of people who are in it and how they get there. The barebones facts are these:

The Congress of the United States consists of two chambers, the House of Representatives and the Senate. The size of the House is fixed by law at 435 members, apportioned among the states roughly in accordance with their population. Each state must have at least one representative; how many more it has depends on its population. Every ten years, following the count of the nation's population by the Bureau of the Census, the House reapportions its seats among the states on the basis of a mathematical formula worked out many years ago. Because of population movements within the country, many of the northeastern states have been losing seats in the House in recent decades while many of the states in the South and Southwest have been gaining seats. A Supreme Court ruling requires that within each state, the districts from which representatives are elected be approximately equal in population.[1] Representatives serve two-year terms.

The Senate consists of two senators from each state, each serving for a six-year term. Whereas federal law determines how many representatives each state has, the Constitution (Article I) requires that each state have two senators and prohibits the Constitution from being amended to change this allocation. The two senators from a given state serve staggered terms so that the two do not stand for reelection during the same year.

This constitutional and legal system has brought to both houses of Congress a total of 535 members who, *on the average*, are middle-aged white males. The growth in the number of blacks, Hispanics, and women in Congress is shown in Table 9.1.

The importance of the personal characteristics (age, sex, or race) of members of Congress varies with the issues. On some matters, such as civil rights, they can be very important. Black members of the House will be far more solidly supportive of new civil-rights laws than will white members. But even civil-rights laws get

Table 9.1   Blacks, Hispanics, and Women in Congress, 1971–2010

	House			Senate		
Congress	Blacks	Hispanics	Women	Blacks	Hispanics	Women
111th	42	25	77	1	3	17
110th	38	23	74	1	3	16
109th	37	23	59	1	0	14
108th	39	23	62	0	0	13
107th	36	19	59	0	0	13
106th	39	19	58	0	0	9
105th	37	17	51	1	0	9
104th	39	18	49	1	0	8
103rd	38	17	48	1	0	6
102nd	25	10	29	0	0	2
101st	23	11	25	0	0	2
100th	22	11	23	0	0	2
99th	19	11	22	0	0	2
98th	20	10	21	0	0	2
97th	16	6	19	0	0	2
96th	16	6	16	0	0	1
95th	16	5	18	1	0	0
94th	16	5	18	1	1	0

Source: Updated from NES data as reported in Harold W. Stanley and Richard G. Niemi, *Vital Statistics on American Politics, 2005–2006* (Washington, D.C.: Congressional Quarterly Press, 2006), p. 207. Reprinted by permission of CQ Press, a division of Congressional Quarterly Inc.

How We Compare

Number of Legislators

Writing in Federalist Paper No. 55, James Madison insists that in any legislative body the number of legislators "ought at most to be kept within a certain limit, in order to avoid the confusion and intemperance of a multitude."

America has heeded Madison's advice. With 435 members of the House and 100 members of the Senate, the Congress has a total of 535 members representing over 300 million citizens, or roughly one national legislator for every 561,000 citizens.

In most democracies, the ratio of national legislators to citizens is far higher than it is in the United States. For example, with a population of just over 60 million, the British Parliament's two houses total over 1,300 members, or roughly one national legislator for every 46,000 citizens; and, with a population of about 10 million, Sweden's legislature has nearly 350 members, or roughly one national legislator for every 28,600 citizens.

At the same time, however, America has more numerous and more powerful subnational legislators (over 7,300 in all) than most other nations do, including, in Madison's home state of Virginia, 140 state lawmakers representing about 8 million citizens, or roughly one state lawmaker for every 57,000 citizens.

Also, the U.S. Constitution would permit the U.S. House to expand enough to approximate the representation ratios of nations like Britain and Sweden and states like Virginia: Article 1, Section 2 states that "the Number of Representatives shall not exceed one for every thirty Thousand."

Thus, given 300 million citizens, the Constitution would allow there to be as many as 10,000 members of the U.S. House (300 million divided by 30,000). But the mere thought heralds Madison's warning, harkening back to ancient Greece's large legislatures, that even if "every Athenian citizen had been a Socrates, every Athenian assembly would have been a mob."

---

a lot of support from white members. And in 1972, a male-dominated Congress proposed the Equal Rights Amendment to the Constitution. Likewise, support for aid to Israel wins consistent support from many non-Jewish members of Congress. Today, as in the past, some of the most affluent senators take the leadership in pressing for spending programs aimed at helping the poor.

Age, sex, and race are not nearly as important as seniority, partisanship, ideology, and constituency preferences in explaining how members of Congress vote.

Years of Service

The most important change in the composition of Congress occurred so gradually that most people did not notice it. In the nineteenth century, a majority of members often served only one term. Being in Congress was not regarded as a career, partly because the federal government's actions were not very important; partly because Washington was a distant, expensive, and unpleasant place to live; and partly because members of Congress were not well paid.

By the 1950s, serving in Congress had become a career. Between 1863 and 1969, the proportion of first-termers in the House fell from 58 percent to 8 percent.[2] As the public took note of this shift, people began to complain about "professional politicians" being "out of touch with the people." A movement to impose term limits was started. In 1995, the House reported out a constitutional amendment to do just that, but it died in the Senate. Then the Supreme Court struck down an effort by Arkansas to impose term limits on its own members of Congress.

As it turned out, natural political forces were already doing what the term-limits amendment was supposed to do. The 1992 and 1994 elections brought scores of new members to the House, with the result that by 1995, the proportion of members who were serving their first or second term had risen sharply. Three factors were responsible for this change. First, when congressional district lines were redrawn after the 1990 census, many incumbents found themselves running in new districts that they could not carry. Second, voter disgust at a variety of Washington political scandals made them receptive to appeals from candidates who could describe themselves as "outsiders." Third, the Republican congressional victory in 1994—made possible in part by the conversion of the South from a Democratic bastion to a Republican stronghold—brought a lot of new faces to the Capitol.

This influx of freshman members should not obscure the fact that incumbents still enjoy enormous advantages in congressional elections.[3] In 2000, almost 98 percent of all House incumbents and over 79 percent of Senate incumbents were reelected.

Scholars do not agree on why incumbents win so frequently. If it is the result of television and other ways of reaching the voters through the media, then why don't challengers also benefit? Another possibility is that voters are more likely to vote for the person rather than the party, and thus to vote for the person they have heard of—the incumbent representative who can deluge the voters with free mailings, travel frequently (at public expense) to meet the voters, and get free publicity by sponsoring bills or conducting investigations. Challengers have much more difficulty gaining recognition. Finally, incumbents can use their powers to get programs passed (or to block unpopular ones) or to fund projects that benefit their districts—for example, by building highways, taking credit for federal grants, or making certain that a particular industry or union is protected by tariffs.[4]

Party

The tendency of voters to return incumbents to office means that, in ordinary times, no one should expect dramatic changes in the composition of Congress. Because the advantages of incumbency began to take effect after the Democrats were in control of Congress, these advantages help explain why the Democrats dominated Congress for half a century. But by the 1990s, the advantages of incumbency had turned into disadvantages. Voters increasingly came to dislike "professional politicians" who they claimed were responsible for "the mess in Washington." Just what "the mess" was varied according to which voter you asked, but it included chronic budget deficits, a congressional habit of exempting itself from laws that affected everybody else, constant bickering between Congress and the White House, and various congressional scandals. During the 1980s, about forty members of Congress were charged with misconduct, ranging from having sex with minors to accepting illegal gifts. When it was disclosed that the House had its own bank that would cash checks even for members who (temporarily) had no funds in their accounts, public indignation exploded, even though almost no taxpayer money was lost. Public respect for Congress, as measured by the polls, plummeted.

The Democrats had the misfortune of being the majority party in Congress when all this happened. The anti-incumbent mood, coupled with the effects of redistricting after the 1990 and 2000 censuses and the shift of the South to the Republican party, brought the Republicans into power in the House and Senate in the 1994 elections, power they held until 2000, lost briefly in 2001–2002, regained in 2002, and lost again in 2006.

Getting Elected to Congress

To get elected to the House or Senate in most states, you need only win more votes than the other candidates running from your district or state in a given congressional election. You need not win a majority of the votes cast, only a plurality. In fact most representatives and senators actually do receive a majority of the votes cast because most races involve no more than two candidates. Because voters almost always vote only for a Democrat or a Republican, you must have "Democrat" or "Republican" designated after your name on the general election ballot if you hope to win.

To acquire that party label, you must usually win a primary election (as described in Chapter 8). Ordinarily you enter a primary by collecting enough signatures on a petition to get your name listed on the primary ballot. In a hotly contested race, five or six names might be entered in the primary. In most states, plurality rule decides those primaries. This means that, in theory, you could win the primary with only 21 percent of the vote (if there are five candidates). Each candidate running in the general election could, in theory, be preferred by only a small minority of the Democratic and Republican voters (which may explain why, in some races, the average voter isn't attracted to either candidate). To deal with this, some states, notably in the South, have a second or **runoff primary** in which the two top vote getters (if neither has won a majority of the votes) run against each other so that the final nominee will have a majority of the votes cast by his or her party's members.

Runoff primary *A second primary election held in some states when no candidate receives a majority of the votes in the first primary; the runoff is between the two candidates with the most votes. Runoff primaries are common in the South.*

Because of the primary system and because in most states party organizations cannot control who enters or wins the primary election, congressional campaigns have become highly personalized. This means that candidates try to develop among their constituents a good opinion of themselves as candidates and not of the party, of their party in Congress, or even of Congress itself. To the extent that they succeed in building trust in themselves, they can enjoy great freedom in how they vote on particular issues and have less need to explain away votes that displease their constituents. (Downplaying a record may be more difficult if a strong-minded, single-issue group concerned with gun control, abortion, or the like, is active in their district.) Furthermore, many members of Congress cater to their constituents' heightened distrust of Congress and the federal government by promising to help "clean things up." Thus, paradoxically, opinion polls show that many Americans have a low opinion of Congress but a high opinion of their own member of Congress.[5]

The Organization of Congress: Parties and Interests

Congress is not a single organization; it is a vast and complex collection of organizations by which the business of Congress is carried on and through which members of Congress form alliances. Unlike the British Parliament, in which the political parties are the only important kind of organization, parties are only one of many important units in Congress. In fact, other organizations have grown in number as party influence has declined.

Party Organizations

The Democrats and Republicans in the House and the Senate are organized by party leaders, who in turn are elected by the full party membership within the House and Senate.

■ **The Senate**   The majority party chooses one of its members—usually the person with the greatest seniority—to be president pro tempore of the Senate. This is usually an honorific position, required by the Constitution so that the Senate will have a presiding officer when the vice president of the United States (according to the Constitution, the president of the Senate) is absent. In fact, both the president pro tem and the vice president usually assign the tedious chore of presiding to a junior senator.

The real leadership is in the hands of the majority and minority leaders. The principal task of the **majority leader** is to schedule the business of the Senate, usually in consultation with the **minority leader**. A majority leader who has a strong personality and is skilled at political bargaining (such as Lyndon Johnson, the Democrats' leader in the 1950s) may also acquire much influence over the substance of Senate business.

A **whip**, chosen by each party, helps party leaders stay informed about what the party members are thinking, rounds up members when important votes are taken, and attempts to keep a nose count of how voting on a controversial issue is likely to go. Several senators assist each party whip.

Each party also chooses a *Policy Committee* composed of a dozen or so senators who help the party leader schedule Senate business, choosing what bills will be given major attention and in what order.

For individual senators, however, the key party organization is the group that assigns senators to the Senate's standing committees: for the Democrats, a twenty-two-member Steering Committee; for the Republicans, an eighteen-member Committee on Committees. For newly elected senators, their political careers, opportunities for favorable publicity, and chances for helping their states and constituents depend in great part on the committees to which they are assigned.

Achieving ideological and regional balance is a crucial—and delicate—aspect of selecting party leaders, making up important committees, and assigning freshmen senators to committees. Liberals and conservatives in each party fight over the choice of majority and minority leaders.

■ **The House of Representatives**   The party structure is essentially the same in the House as in the Senate, though the titles of various posts are different. But leadership carries more power in the House than in the Senate because of the

Majority leader (floor leader) *The legislative leader elected by party members holding the majority of seats in the House of Representatives or the Senate.*

Minority leader *The legislative leader elected by party members holding a minority of seats in the House of Representatives or the Senate.*

Whip *A senator or representative who helps the party leader stay informed about what party members are thinking, rounds up members when important votes are to be taken, and attempts to keep a nose count on how the voting on controversial issues is likely to go.*

Key Facts About Congress

Qualifications

REPRESENTATIVE

- Must be twenty-five years of age (when seated, not when elected).
- Must have been a citizen of the United States for seven years.
- Must be an inhabitant of the state from which elected. (*Note:* Custom, but *not* the Constitution, requires that a representative live in the district he or she represents.)

SENATOR

- Must be thirty years of age (when seated, not when elected).
- Must have been a citizen of the United States for nine years.
- Must be an inhabitant of the state from which elected.

Judging Qualifications

Each house is the judge of the "elections, returns, and qualifications" of its members. Thus, Congress alone decides disputed congressional elections. On occasion it has excluded a person from taking a seat on the grounds that the election was improper.

Privileges

Members of Congress have certain privileges, the most important of which, conferred by the Constitution, is that "for any speech or debate in either house they shall not be questioned in any other place." This doctrine of "privileged speech" has been interpreted by the Supreme Court to mean that members of Congress cannot be sued or prosecuted for anything they say or write in connection with their legislative duties.

When Senator Mike Gravel read the Pentagon Papers—some then-secret government documents about the Vietnam War—into the *Congressional Record* in defiance of a court order restraining their publication, the Court held this was "privileged speech" and beyond challenge [*Gravel v. United States,* 408 U.S. 606 (1972)]. But when Senator William Proxmire issued a press release critical of a scientist doing research on monkeys, the Court decided the scientist could sue him for libel because a press release was not part of the legislative process [*Hutchinson v. Proxmire,* 443 U.S. 111 (1979)].

The Size of Congress

Congress decides the size of the House of Representatives. The House began with 65 members in 1790 and has had 435 members since 1912. Each state must have at least one representative. Regardless of its population, each state has two senators. Equal suffrage for states in the Senate is enshrined in Article I of the Constitution, the only provision that cannot be amended (see Article V).

House rules. Being so large (435 members), the House must restrict debate and schedule its business with great care; thus leaders who manage scheduling and determine how the rules shall be applied usually have substantial influence.

The **Speaker**, who presides over the House, is the most important person in that body and is elected by whichever party has a majority. Unlike the president pro tem of the Senate, this position is anything but honorific, for the Speaker is also the principal leader of the majority party. Though Speakers as presiders are expected to be fair, Speakers as party leaders are expected to use their powers to help pass legislation favored by their party.

Speaker *The presiding officer of the House of Representatives and the leader of his or her party in the House.*

In helping his or her party, the Speaker has some important formal powers. He or she decides who shall be recognized to speak on the floor of the House; rules whether a motion is relevant and germane to the business at hand; and decides (subject to certain rules) the committees to which new bills shall be assigned. He or she influences what bills are brought up for a vote and appoints the members of special and select committees. Since 1975, the Speaker has been able to select the majority-party members of the Rules Committee, which plays an important role in the consideration of bills.

The Speaker also has some informal powers: He or she controls some patronage jobs in the Capitol building and the assignment of extra office space. Even though the Speaker now is far less powerful than some of his predecessors, he or she is still an important person to have on one's side.

In the House, as in the Senate, the majority party elects a floor leader, called the majority leader. The other party chooses the minority leader. Traditionally, the majority leader becomes Speaker when the person in that position dies or retires—provided, of course, that his party is still in the majority. Each party also has a whip, with several assistant whips in charge of rounding up votes. For the Democrats, committee assignments are made and the scheduling of legislation is discussed in a Steering and Policy Committee chaired by the Speaker. The Republicans have divided responsibility for committee assignments and policy discussion between two committees. Each party also has a congressional campaign committee to provide funds and other assistance to party members running for election or reelection to the House.

Party Voting

Party vote *There are two measures of such voting. By the stricter measure, a party vote occurs when 90 percent or more of the Democrats in either house of Congress vote together against 90 percent or more of the Republicans. A looser measure counts as a party vote any case where at least 50 percent of the Democrats vote together against at least 50 percent of the Republicans.*

The effect of this elaborate party machinery can be crudely measured by the extent to which party members vote together in the House and the Senate. A **party vote** can be defined in various ways; naturally, the more stringent the definition, the less party voting we will observe. Figure 9.1 shows two measures of party voting in the House of Representatives during the last century. By the strictest measure, a party vote occurs when 90 percent or more of the Democrats vote together against 90 percent or more of the Republicans. A looser measure counts as a party vote one in which at least 50 percent of the Democrats vote together against 50 percent of the Republicans. By the 90 percent measure, the extent of party voting is low and has declined since the turn of the century. By the 50 percent measure, it is as high today as it was in 1920 and has risen sharply since 1970.

Given that political parties as organizations do not tightly control a legislator's ability to get elected, what is surprising is not that strict party votes are relatively rare, but that they occur at all. There are several reasons that congressional members of one party sometimes do vote together against a majority of the other party. First, members of Congress do not randomly decide to be Democrats or Republicans; at least for most members, these choices reflect some broad policy agreements. By tabulating the ratings that several interest groups give members of Congress for voting on important issues, it is possible to rank each member of Congress from most to least liberal in three policy areas: economic affairs, social questions, and foreign and military affairs. Democrats in the House and Senate are much more liberal than Republicans, and this has been true for many years.

Figure 9.1   Party Votes in the House, 1877–2008

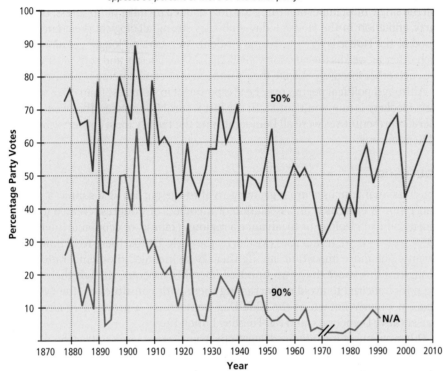

——— Percentage of votes in which 50 percent or more of one party opposes 50 percent or more of the other party.

——— Percentage of votes in which 90 percent or more of one party opposes 90 percent or more of the other party.

Note: A party vote occurs when the specified percentage (or more) of one party votes against the specified percentage (or more) of the other party.

Source: Updated from NES data as reported in *2001–2002*, Harold W. Stanley and Richard G. Niemi, *Vital Statistics on American Politics*, CQ Press, 2001, p. 211. Reprinted by permission of Congressional Quarterly, Inc.

The ideological differences between the parties are so pronounced that even the average southern Democrat in the House is more liberal than the average northern Republican.

In addition to their personal views, members of Congress have other reasons for supporting their party's position at least some of the time. On many matters that come up for vote, members of Congress often have little information and no opinions. It is only natural that they look to fellow party members for advice. Furthermore, supporting the party position can work to the long-term advantage of a member interested in gaining status and influence in Congress. Though party leaders are weaker today than in the past, they are hardly powerless. Sam Rayburn reputedly told freshman members of Congress that "if you want to get along, go along." That is less true today, but still good advice.

In short, party *does* make a difference—not as much as it did eighty years ago and not nearly as much as it does in a parliamentary system—but party affiliation is still the single most important thing to know about a member of Congress. Because party affiliation in the House today embodies strong ideological preferences, the mood of the House is often testy and strident. Members no longer get along with each other as well as they did forty years ago. Many liberals and conservatives dislike each other intensely, despite their routine use of complimentary phrases.

Although political parties may be less powerful in Congress than once was the case, ideology is more influential. In the last several Congresses, the twenty most liberal representatives were all Democrats and the twenty most conservative were all Republicans.

Caucuses

Congressional caucuses are a growing rival to the parties as a source of policy leadership. A **caucus** is an association of members of Congress created to advocate a political ideology or to advance a regional, ethnic, or economic interest. In 1959, only four such caucuses existed; by the early 1980s, there were more than seventy. The more important among them have included the Democratic Study Group (uniting more than two hundred liberal Democrats, though their names are not publicized to avoid embarrassing them with constituents), the Coalition (more popularly known as the Blue Dog Democrats), a group of moderate-to-conservative Democrats, and the Tuesday Lunch Bunch.

Other caucuses include the delegations from certain large states who meet on matters of common interest, as well as the countless groups dedicated to racial, ethnic, regional, and policy interests. The Congressional Black Caucus in the House is one of the best known of these and is probably typical of many in its operations. It meets regularly and employs a staff. As with most other caucuses, some members are very active, others only marginally so. On some issues it simply registers an opinion; on others it attempts to negotiate with leaders of other blocs so that votes can be traded in a mutually advantageous way. It keeps its members informed and on occasion presses to put a member on a regular congressional committee that has no blacks. In 1995, the House Republican majority decided to eliminate government funding of caucuses, forcing some to shrivel and others to seek outside support.

The Organization of Congress: Committees

The most important organizational feature of Congress is the set of legislative committees of the House and Senate. In the chairmanship of these committees, and their subcommittees, most of the power of Congress is found. The number and jurisdiction of these committees are of the greatest interest to members of Congress because decisions on these subjects determine what groups of legislators

Caucus (congressional) *An association of members of Congress created to advocate a political ideology or a regional, ethnic, or economic interest.*

Standing committees *Permanently established legislative committees that consider and are responsible for legislation within certain subject areas. Examples are the House Ways and Means Committee and the Senate Judiciary Committee.*

with what political views will pass on legislative proposals, oversee the workings of agencies in the executive branch, and conduct investigations.

A typical Congress has, in each house, about two dozen committees and well over one hundred subcommittees. Periodically, efforts have been made to cut the number of committees to give each a broader jurisdiction and to reduce conflict between committees over a single bill. But as the number of committees declined, the number of subcommittees rose, leaving matters much as they had been.

There are three kinds of committees: **standing committees** (more or less permanent bodies with specific legislative responsibilities), **select committees** (groups appointed for a limited purpose, which do not introduce legislation and which exist for only a few years), and **joint committees** (on which both representatives and senators serve). An especially important kind of joint committee is the **conference committee**, made up of representatives and senators appointed to resolve differences in the Senate and House versions of a bill before final passage.

Though members of the majority party could in theory occupy all the seats on all the committees, in practice they take the majority of the seats, name the chairman, and allow the minority party to have the remainder of the seats. The number of seats varies from about six to more than fifty. Usually the ratio of Democrats to Republicans on a committee roughly corresponds to their ratio in the House or Senate.

Standing committees are more important because, with a few exceptions, they are the only committees that can propose legislation by reporting a bill out to the full House or Senate. Each member of the House usually serves on two standing committees (but members of the Appropriations, Rules, or Ways and Means committees are limited to one committee). Each senator may serve on two major committees and one minor committee (see the boxes on pages 219 and 221), but this rule is not strictly enforced.

Select committees
Congressional committees appointed for a limited time and purpose.

Joint committees
Committees on which both representatives and senators serve. An especially important kind of joint committee is the conference committee made up of representatives and senators appointed to resolve differences in the Senate and House versions of the same legislation before final passage.

Conference committees
See joint committees.

Standing Committees of the Senate

Major Committees

No senator is supposed to serve on more than two.*

Agriculture, Nutrition, and Forestry
Appropriations
Armed Services
Banking, Housing, and Urban Affairs
Budget
Commerce, Science, and Transportation
Energy and Natural Resources
Environment and Public Works
Finance
Foreign Relations
Homeland Security and Governmental Affairs
Health, Education, Labor, and Pensions
Judiciary

Minor Committees

No senator is supposed to serve on more than one.

Rules and Administration
Small Business and Entrepreneurship
Veterans' Affairs

Select Committees

Aging
Ethics
Indian Affairs
Intelligence

*Despite the rules, some senators serve on more than two major committees.

In the past, when party leaders were stronger, committee chairmen were picked on the basis of loyalty to the leader. When this leadership weakened, seniority on the committee came to govern the selection of chairmen. Of late, however, seniority has been under attack. In 1971, House Democrats decided in their caucus to elect committee chairmen by secret ballot; four years later, they used that procedure to remove three committee chairmen who held their positions by seniority. Between 1971 and 1992, the Democrats replaced a total of seven senior Democrats with more junior ones as committee chairmen. When Republicans took control of the House in 1995, Speaker Newt Gingrich ignored seniority in selecting several committee chairmen, picking instead members who he felt would do a better job. In this and other ways, Gingrich enhanced the Speaker's power to a degree not seen since 1910.

Throughout most of the twentieth century, committee chairmen dominated the work of Congress. In the early 1970s, their power came under attack, mostly from liberal Democrats upset at the opposition by conservative southern Democratic chairmen to civil-rights legislation. The liberals succeeded in getting the House to adopt rules that weakened the chairmen and empowered individual members. Among the changes were these:

- Committee chairmen must be elected by the majority party, voting by secret ballot.
- The ability of committee chairmen to block legislation by refusing to refer it to a subcommittee for a hearing was banned.
- All committees and subcommittees must hold public meetings unless the committee voted to close them.
- Subcommittee chairmen must be elected by committee members.
- Subcommittee chairmen can hire their own staffs, independent of the committee chairman.

The effect of these and other changes was to give individual members more power and committee chairmen less. When the Republicans took control of the House in 1995, they made more changes, including the following:

- They reduced the number of committees and subcommittees.
- They authorized committee chairmen to hire subcommittee staffs.
- They imposed term limits on committee and subcommittee chairmen of three consecutive terms (or six years) and on the Speaker of four consecutive terms (or eight years).
- They prohibited chairmen from casting an absent committee member's vote by proxy.

The House Republican rules gave back some power to chairmen (for example, by letting them pick all staff members) but further reduced it in other ways (for example, by imposing term limits and banning proxy voting). The commitment to public meetings remained.

In the Senate there have been fewer changes, in part because individual members of the Senate have always had more power than their counterparts in the House. There were, however, three important changes made by the Republicans in 1995:

- A six-year term limit was set on all committee chairmen (but not on the term of majority leader).

Standing Committees of the House

Exclusive Committees

Member may not serve on any other committee, except Budget.

Appropriations
Rules
Ways and Means

Major Committees

Member may serve on only one major committee.

Agriculture
Armed Services
Education and Labor
Energy and Commerce
Financial Services
Foreign Affairs
Homeland Security
Judiciary
Transportation and Infrastructure

Nonmajor Committees

Member may serve on one major and one non-major or two nonmajor committees.

Budget
Oversight and Government Reform
House Administration
Natural Resources
Science and Technology
Small Business
Standards of Official Conduct
Veterans Affairs

Select Committee

Energy Independence and Global Harming
Intelligence

Note: In 1995, the House Republican majority abolished three committees—District of Columbia, Post Office and Civil Service, and Merchant Marine and Fisheries—and gave their duties to other standing committees.

- Committee members were required to select their chairmen by secret ballot.
- Beginning in 1997, the chairmen of Senate committees were limited to one six-year term.

Despite these new rules, the committees remain the place where the real work of Congress is done. These committees tend to attract different kinds of members. Some, such as the committees that draft tax legislation (the Senate Finance Committee and the House Ways and Means Committee) or that oversee foreign affairs (the Senate and House Foreign Relations Committees), have been attractive to members who want to shape public policy, become expert on important issues, and have influence with their colleagues. Others, such as the House and Senate committees dealing with public lands, small business, and veterans' affairs, are attractive to members who want to serve particular constituency groups.[6]

The Organization of Congress: Staffs and Specialized Offices

In 1900, representatives had no personal staff, and senators averaged fewer than one staff member each. By 1979, the average representative had sixteen assistants and the average senator had thirty-six. From 1976 to today, the numbers have remained about the same. To the more than ten thousand people on the

AP Photo/Haraz N. Ghanbari

Rep. Steve Scalise, R-La., holds a photo of an oil covered pelican as he questions BP CEO Tony Hayward on Capitol Hill in Washington, June 17, 2010, during the House Oversight and Investigations subcommittee hearing on the role of BP in the Deepwater Horizon explosion and oil spill.

personal staffs of members of Congress must be added another three thousand who work for congressional committees and yet another three thousand employed by various congressional research agencies. Congress has produced the most rapidly growing bureaucracy in Washington: The personal staffs of legislators have increased more than fivefold since 1947.[7] Though many staffers perform routine chores, many others help draft legislation, handle constituents, and otherwise shape policy and politics.

Tasks of Staff Members

A major function of a legislator's staff is to help constituents solve problems and thereby help that member of Congress get reelected. Indeed, over the last two decades, a growing portion of congressional staffs have worked in the local (district or state) offices of the legislator rather than in Washington. Almost all members of Congress have at least one such home office, and most have two or more. Some scholars believe that this growth in constituency-serving staff helps explain why it is so difficult to defeat an incumbent.[8]

The legislative function of congressional staff members is also important. With each senator serving on an average of more than two committees and seven subcommittees, it is virtually impossible for members of Congress to become familiar with the details of all the proposals that come before them or to write all the bills that they feel ought to be introduced.[9] The role of staff members has expanded in proportion to the tremendous growth in Congress's workload.

The orientation of committee staff members differs. Some think of themselves as—and to a substantial degree they are—politically neutral professionals whose job it is to assist members of a committee, whether Democrats or Republicans, in holding hearings or revising bills. Others see themselves as partisan advocates, interested in promoting Democratic or Republican causes, depending on who hired them.

Those who work for individual members of Congress, as opposed to committees, see themselves entirely as advocates for their bosses. They often assume an entrepreneurial function, taking the initiative in finding and selling a policy to their boss—a representative or senator—who can take credit for it. Lobbyists and reporters understand this completely and therefore spend a lot of time cultivating congressional staffers.

The increased reliance on staff has changed Congress, mainly because the staff has altered the environment within which Congress does its work. In addition to their role as entrepreneurs promoting new policies, staffers act as negotiators: Members of Congress today are more likely to deal with one another through staff intermediaries than through personal contact. Congress has thereby become less collegial, more individualistic, and less of a deliberative body.[10]

Staff Agencies

In addition to increasing the number of staff members, Congress has also created a set of staff agencies that work for Congress as a whole. These have come into being in large part to give Congress specialized knowledge equivalent to what the president has by virtue of his position as chief of the executive branch. One of these, the *Congressional Research Service (CRS)*, is part of the Library of Congress and employs almost nine hundred people; it is politically neutral, responding to requests by members of Congress for information and giving both sides of arguments. The *General Accounting Office (GAO)*, once merely an auditing agency, now has about five thousand employees and investigates policies and makes recommendations on almost every aspect of government; its head, though appointed by the president for a fifteen-year term, is very much the servant of Congress rather than the president. The *Congressional Budget Office (CBO)*, created in 1974, advises Congress on the likely impact of different spending programs and attempts to estimate future economic trends.

How a Bill Becomes Law

Some bills zip through Congress; others make their way painfully and slowly, sometimes emerging in a form very different from their original one. Congress is like a crowd, moving either sluggishly or, when excited, with great speed.

In the following account of how a bill becomes law (see Figure 9.2), keep in mind that the complexity of congressional procedures ordinarily gives powerful advantages to the opponents of any new policy. There are many points at which action can be blocked. This does not mean that nothing gets done, but that to get something done, a member of Congress must *either* slowly and painstakingly assemble a majority coalition or take advantage of enthusiasm for some new cause that sweeps away the normal obstacles to change.

Introducing a Bill

Any member of Congress may introduce a bill—in the House by handing it to a clerk or dropping it in a box; in the Senate by being recognized by the presiding

Figure 9.2   How a Bill Becomes Law

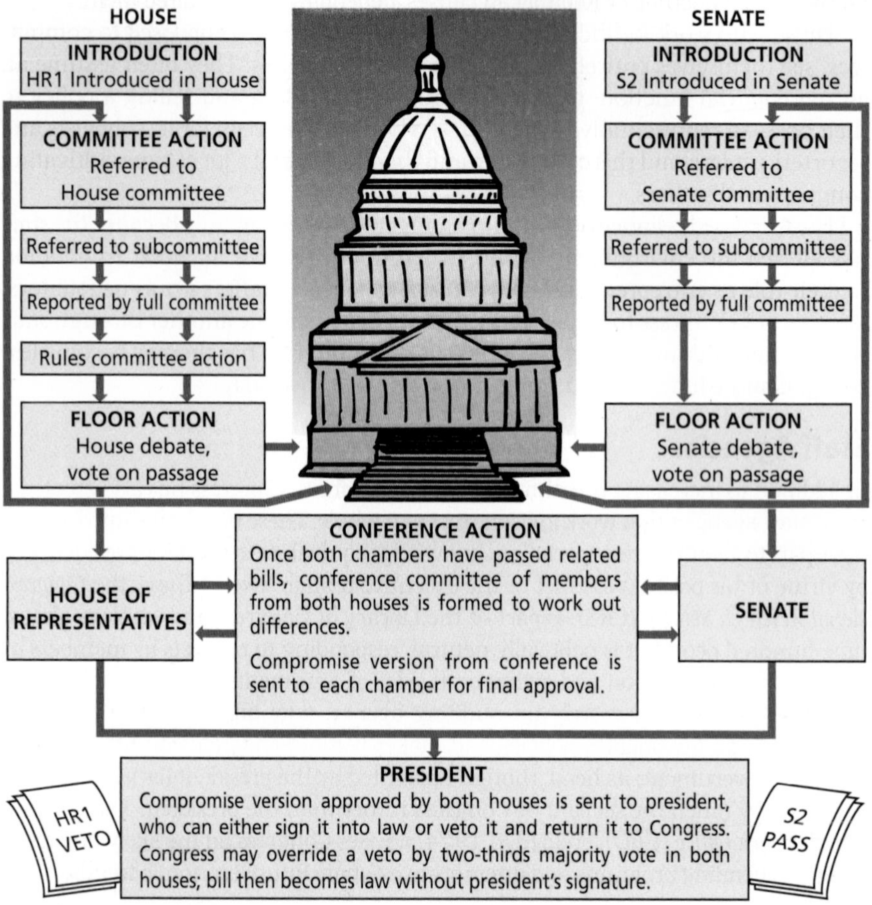

HOUSE

INTRODUCTION
HR1 Introduced in House

COMMITTEE ACTION
Referred to
House committee

Referred to subcommittee

Reported by full committee

Rules committee action

FLOOR ACTION
House debate,
vote on passage

SENATE

INTRODUCTION
S2 Introduced in Senate

COMMITTEE ACTION
Referred to
Senate committee

Referred to subcommittee

Reported by full committee

FLOOR ACTION
Senate debate,
vote on passage

HOUSE OF REPRESENTATIVES

CONFERENCE ACTION
Once both chambers have passed related bills, conference committee of members from both houses is formed to work out differences.

Compromise version from conference is sent to each chamber for final approval.

SENATE

PRESIDENT
Compromise version approved by both houses is sent to president, who can either sign it into law or veto it and return it to Congress. Congress may override a veto by two-thirds majority vote in both houses; bill then becomes law without president's signature.

HR1 VETO

S2 PASS

Simple resolution
An expression of opinion either in the House of Representatives or the Senate to settle housekeeping or procedural matters in either body. Such expressions are not signed by the president and do not have the force of law.

Concurrent resolution
An expression of congressional opinion without the force of law that requires the approval of both the House and Senate but not of the president. Used to settle housekeeping and procedural matters that affect both houses.

officer and announcing the bill's introduction. Bills are then numbered and printed. If a bill is not passed within one session of Congress, it is dead and must be reintroduced during the next Congress.

We often hear that legislation is initiated by the president and enacted by Congress. The reality is more complicated. Congress often initiates legislation (for example, most consumer and environmental laws passed since 1966 originated in Congress), and even laws formally proposed by the president have often been incubated in Congress. Even when he is the principal author of a bill, a president usually submits it (if he is prudent) only after careful consultation with key congressional leaders. In any case, he cannot himself introduce legislation; he must get a member of Congress to do it for him.

In addition to bills, Congress can also pass resolutions. Either house can use **simple resolutions** for such matters as establishing operating rules. **Concurrent resolutions** settle housekeeping and procedural matters that affect both houses.

Simple and concurrent resolutions are not signed by the president and do not have the force of law. A **joint resolution** requires approval by both houses and presidential signature; it is essentially the same as a law. A joint resolution is also used to propose a constitutional amendment; in this case it must be approved by a two-thirds vote in each house, but it does not require the signature of the president.

Study by Committees

A bill is referred to a committee for consideration by either the Speaker of the House or the Senate's presiding officer. If a chairperson or committee is known to be hostile to a bill, assignment can be a crucial matter. Rules govern which committee will get which bill, but sometimes a choice is possible. In the House, the Speaker's right to make such a choice (subject to appeal to the full House) is an important source of his power.

The Constitution requires that "all bills for raising revenue shall originate in the House of Representatives." The Senate can and does amend such bills, but only after the House has acted first. Bills that are not for raising revenue—that is, that do not alter tax laws—can originate in either chamber. In practice, the House also originates *appropriations bills* (bills that direct the spending of money). Because of the House's special position on revenue legislation, the committee that handles tax bills—the Ways and Means Committee—is particularly powerful.

Most bills die in committee. They are often introduced only to get publicity for various members of Congress or to enable them to say to a constituent or pressure group that they "did something" on some matter. Bills of general interest—many of them drafted in the executive branch though introduced by members of Congress—are assigned to a subcommittee for a hearing where witnesses appear, evidence is taken, and questions are asked. These hearings are used to inform members of Congress, to permit interest groups to speak out (whether or not they have anything helpful to say), and to build public support for a measure favored by the majority on the committee.

Though committee hearings are necessary and valuable, they also fragment the process of considering bills dealing with complex matters. Both power and information are dispersed in Congress, and thus it is difficult to take a comprehensive view of matters cutting across committee boundaries. This has made it harder to pass complex legislation. For example, President Carter's energy proposals were dissected into small sections for the consideration of the various committees that had jurisdiction; after a year and a half, five laws emerged. But strong White House leadership and supportive public opinion can push controversial measures through both houses without great delay, as in the case of the Reagan budget cuts of 1981. It remains to be seen whether the slow energy package or the speedy budget cut is the wave of the future.

After the hearings, the committee or subcommittee makes revisions and additions (sometimes extensive) to the bill, but these changes do not become part of the bill unless they are approved by the entire house. If a majority of the committee votes to report a bill favorably to the House or Senate, it goes forward, accompanied by an explanation of why the committee favors it and why it wishes to see its amendments, if any, added; committee members who oppose the bill may include their dissenting opinions.

Joint resolution
A formal expression of congressional opinion that must be approved by both houses of Congress and by the president. Joint resolutions proposing a constitutional amendment need not be signed by the president.

Discharge petition *A device by which any member of the House, after a committee has had a bill for thirty days, may petition to have it brought to the floor. If a majority of the members agree, the bill is discharged from the committee. The discharge petition was designed to prevent a committee from killing a bill by holding it for too long.*

Restrictive rule *An order from the House Rules Committee in the House of Representatives that permits certain kinds of amendments but not others to be made to a bill on the legislative floor.*

If the committee does not report the bill out to the house favorably, that ordinarily kills it, though there are complex procedures whereby the full House can get a bill that is stalled in committee out and onto the floor. It involves getting a majority of all House members to sign a **discharge petition**. If 218 members sign, then the petition can be voted on; if it passes, then the stalled bill goes directly to the floor for a vote. These procedures are rarely attempted and even more rarely succeed.

For a bill to come before either house, it must first be placed on a calendar. There are five of these in the House and two in the Senate. Though the bill goes onto a calendar, it is not necessarily considered in chronological order or even considered at all. In the House, the powerful Rules Committee—an arm of the party leadership, especially of the Speaker—reviews most bills and sets the *rule*— that is, the procedures—under which they will be considered by the House. A **restrictive** or **closed rule** sets strict limits on debate and confines amendments to those proposed by the committee; an **open rule** permits amendments from the floor. The Rules Committee is no longer as mighty as it once was, but it can still block any House consideration of a measure and can bargain with the legislative committee by offering a helpful rule in exchange for alterations in the substance of a bill. In the 1980s, closed rules became more common.

The House needs the Rules Committee to serve as a traffic cop; without some limitations on debate and amendment, nothing would ever get done. The House can bypass the Rules Committee in a number of ways, but it rarely does so unless the committee departs too far from the sentiments of the House.

House-Senate Differences: A Summary

House

435 members serving two-year terms

House members have only one major committee assignment, and thus tend to be policy specialists
Speaker referral of bills to committee is hard to challenge
Committees almost always consider legislation first
Scheduling and rules controlled by majority party
Rules Committee powerful; controls time of debate, admissibility of amendments
Debate usually limited to one hour nongermane amendments may not be introduced from floor

Senate

100 members serving six-year terms

Senators have two or more major committee assignments, tend to be policy generalists
Referral decisions easy to challenge
Committee consideration easily bypassed
Scheduling and rules generally agreed to by majority and minority leaders
Rules Committee weak; few limits on debate or amendments
Unlimited debate unless shortened by unanimous consent or by invoking cloture
Nongermane amendments may be introduced

No such barriers to floor consideration exist in the Senate, where bills may be considered in any order at any time whenever a majority of the Senate chooses. In practice, bills are scheduled by the majority leader in consultation with the minority leader.

Floor Debate

Once on the floor, the bills are debated. In the House all revenue and most other bills are discussed by the *Committee of the Whole*—that is, whoever happens to be on the floor at the time, so long as at least one hundred members are present. The Committee of the Whole can debate, amend, and generally decide the final shape of a bill but technically cannot pass it—that must be done by the House itself, for which the quorum is half the membership (218 representatives). The sponsoring committee guides the discussion, and normally its version of the bill is the version that the full House passes.

Procedures are a good deal more casual in the Senate. Measures that have already passed the House can be placed on the Senate calendar without a committee hearing. There is no Committee of the Whole and no rule (as in the House) limiting debate, so that **filibusters** (lengthy speeches given to prevent votes from being taken) and irrelevant amendments, called **riders**, are possible. Filibusters can be broken if three-fifths of all senators agree to a **cloture resolution**. This is

Closed rule *An order from the House Rules Committee in the House of Representatives that sets a time limit on debate and forbids a particular bill from being amended on the legislative floor.*

Open rule *An order from the House Rules Committee in the House of Representatives that permits a bill to be amended on the legislative floor.*

Filibuster *An attempt to defeat a bill in the Senate by talking indefinitely, thus preventing the Senate from taking action on it. From the Spanish filibustero, which means a "freebooter," a military adventurer.*

Riders *Amendments on matters unrelated to a bill that are added to an important bill so that they will "ride" to passage through the Congress. When a bill has many riders, it is called a Christmas-tree bill.*

Cloture resolution *A rule used by the Senate to end or limit debate. Designed to prevent "talking a bill to death" by filibuster. To pass in the Senate, three-fifths of the entire Senate membership (or sixty senators) must vote for it.*

Keith Jewell/U.S. House of Representatives

The electronic voting system in the House of Representatives displays each member's name on the wall of the chamber. By inserting a plastic card in a box fastened to the chairs, a member can vote "Yea," "Nay," or "Present," and the result is shown opposite his or her name.

Double tracking *Setting aside a bill against which one or more senators are filibustering so that other legislation can be voted on.*

a difficult and rarely used procedure. (Both conservatives and liberals have found the filibuster useful, and therefore its abolition is unlikely.) The sharp increase in Senate filibusters has been made easier by a new process called **double tracking**. When a senator filibusters against a bill, it is temporarily put aside so the Senate can move on to other business. Because of double tracking, senators no longer have to speak around the clock to block a bill. Once they talk long enough, the bill is shelved. So common has this become that, for all practical purposes, any controversial bill can pass the Senate only if it gets enough votes—sixty—to end a filibuster.

The Senate has made an effort to end filibusters aimed at blocking the nomination of federal judges. In 2005, seven Democrats and seven Republicans agreed not to filibuster a nomination except in "exceptional circumstances." A few nominees whose appointment had been blocked managed to get confirmed by this arrangement. Whether it holds for the future depends on how senators define "exceptional circumstances."

One rule was once common to both houses: Courtesy, often of the most exquisite nature, was required. Members always refer to each other as "distinguished" even if they are mortal political enemies. Personal or ad hominem criticism was frowned upon, but of late it has become more common. In recent years, members of Congress—especially of the House—have become more personal in their criticisms of one another, and human relationships have deteriorated.

Voice vote *A congressional voting procedure in which members shout "aye" in approval or "no" in disapproval; allows members to vote quickly or anonymously on bills.*

Division vote *A congressional voting procedure in which members stand and are counted.*

Roll-call *A congressional voting procedure that consists of members answering "yea" or "nay" to their names. When roll calls were handled orally, it was a time-consuming process in the House. Since 1973, an electronic voting system permits each House member to record his or her vote and learn the total automatically.*

Methods of Voting

There are several methods of voting in Congress, which can be applied to amendments to a bill as well as to the question of final passage. Some observers of Congress make the mistake of deciding who was for and who against a bill by the final vote. This can be misleading. Often, a member of Congress will vote for final passage of a bill after having supported amendments that, if they had passed, would have made the bill totally different. To keep track of someone's voting record, therefore, it is often more important to know how that person voted on key amendments than how he or she voted on the bill itself.

Finding that out is not always easy, though it has become simpler in recent years. The House has three procedures for voting. A **voice vote** consists of the members shouting "aye" or "no"; a **division** (or standing) **vote** involves the members standing and being counted. In neither case are the names recorded of who voted which way. This is done only with a **roll-call vote**. Since 1973, an electronic voting system has been in use that greatly speeds up roll-call votes, and the number of recorded votes has thus increased sharply. To ensure a roll-call vote, one-fifth of house members present must request it. Voting in the Senate is simpler: It votes by voice or by roll call; there are no teller votes or electronic counters.

If a bill passes the House and Senate in different forms, the differences must be reconciled if the bill is to become law. If they are minor, the last house to act may simply refer the bill back to the other house, which then accepts the alterations. Major differences must be ironed out in a conference committee, though only a minority of bills require a conference. Each house must vote to form such a committee. The members are picked by the chairmen of the standing committees that have been handling the legislation; the minority as well as the majority party is represented. No decision can be made unless approved by a majority of *each* delegation. Bargaining is long and hard; in the past it was also secret, but some sessions are now public. Often—as with Carter's energy bill—the legislation is substantially rewritten in conference. Theoretically nothing already agreed to by both the House and Senate is to be changed, but in the inevitable give-and-take, even those matters already approved may be modified.

Conference reports on spending bills usually split the difference between the House and Senate versions. Overall, the Senate tends to do slightly better than the House.[11] But whoever wins, conferees report their agreement back to their respective houses, which usually consider the report immediately. The report can be accepted or rejected; it cannot be amended. In the great majority of cases, it is accepted—the alternative is to have no bill at all, at least for that Congress. The bill, now in final form, goes to the president for signature or **veto**. A vetoed bill returns to the house of origin, where an effort can be made to override the veto. Two-thirds of those present (provided there is a quorum) must vote, by roll call, to override. If both houses override, the bill becomes law without the president's approval.

Veto *Literally, "I forbid": It refers to the power of a president to disapprove a bill; it may be overridden by a two-thirds vote of each house of Congress.*

How Members of Congress Vote

Voting on bills is not the only thing a member of Congress does, but it is among the more important and probably the most visible. Because leaders in Congress are not nearly so powerful as those in a typical parliament, with political parties declining in influence, and because Congress has gone to great lengths to protect the independence and power of the individual member, it is by no means obvious what factors will lead a representative or senator to vote for or against a bill or amendment.

There are at least three kinds of explanations: representational, organizational, and attitudinal. A *representational* explanation is based on the reasonable assumption that members want to get reelected, and therefore they vote to please their constituents. The *organizational* explanation is based on the equally reasonable assumption that because most constituents do not know how their legislator has voted it is not essential to please them. However, it *is* important to please fellow members of Congress whose goodwill is valuable in getting things done and in acquiring status and power in Congress. The *attitudinal* explanation is based on the assumption that there are so many conflicting pressures on members of Congress that they cancel one another out, leaving them virtually free to vote on the basis of their own beliefs.

For decades, political scientists have studied, tested, and argued about these (and other) explanations of voting in Congress, and never has a consensus emerged. Some facts have been established, however.

Representational View

The representational view has some merit under certain circumstances—namely, when constituents have a clear view on some issue and a legislator's vote on that issue is likely to attract their attention. Such is often the case on civil-rights laws: representatives with significant numbers of black voters in their districts are not likely to oppose civil-rights bills.

One study of congressional roll-call votes and constituency opinion showed that the correlation between the two was quite strong on civil-rights bills. There was also a positive (though not as strong) correlation between roll-call votes and constituency opinion on social-welfare measures. Scarcely any correlation, however, was found between congressional votes and hometown opinion on foreign-policy measures.[12] Foreign policy is generally remote from the daily interests of most Americans, and public opinion about such matters can change rapidly. It is not surprising therefore that congressional votes and constituent opinion should be different on such questions.

In general the problem with the representational explanation is that public opinion is not strong and clear on most measures on which Congress must vote. Many representatives and senators face constituencies that are divided on key issues. Some constituents go to special pains to make their views known. But as we indicated, the power of interest groups to affect congressional votes depends on, among other things, whether a legislator sees them as united and powerful in his or her district or as divided and unrepresentative.

This does not mean that constituents rarely have a direct influence on voting. The influence they have probably comes from the fact that legislators risk defeat should they steadfastly vote in ways that can be held against them by a rival in the next election. Even though most congressional votes are not known to most citizens, blunders (real or alleged) quickly become known when an electoral opponent exploits them.

Still, any member of Congress can choose the positions he or she takes on most roll-call votes (and on all voice or standing votes where names are not recorded). Furthermore, even a series of recorded votes that are against constituency opinion need not be fatal: a member of Congress can win votes in other ways—for example, by doing services for constituents or by appealing to the party loyalty of the voters.

Organizational View

When voting on matters on which constituency interests or opinions are not vitally at stake, members of Congress respond primarily to cues provided by their colleagues. This is the organizational explanation of their votes. The principal cue is party; as already noted, the party a member of Congress belongs to explains more of his or her voting record than any other single factor. Additional organizational cues come from the opinions of colleagues with whom the member of Congress feels a close ideological affinity. For liberals in the House, it is the Democratic Study Group; for conservatives, it has often been the Republican Study Committee or the Wednesday Club. But party and other organizations do not have clear positions on all matters. For the scores of votes that do not involve the "big questions," a representative or senator is especially likely to be influenced by the members of his or her party on the sponsoring committee.

It is easy to understand why. Suppose you are a Democratic representative from Michigan who is summoned to the floor of the House to vote on a bill to authorize a new weapons system. You haven't the faintest idea what issues might be at stake. There is no obvious liberal or conservative position on this matter. How do you vote? Simple. You take your cue from several Democrats on the House Arms Services Committee that handled the bill. Some are liberal; others are conservative. If both liberals and conservatives support the bill, you vote for it unhesitatingly. If liberals and conservatives disagree, you vote with whichever Democrat is generally closest to your own political ideology. If the matter is one that affects your state, you can take your cue from members of your state's delegation to Congress.

Attitudinal View

Finally, there is evidence that a member of Congress's ideology affects how he or she votes. We have seen that Democratic and Republican legislators differ sharply on a liberal-versus-conservative scale. On both domestic and foreign-policy issues, many tend to be consistently liberal or conservative.

This consistency isn't surprising; as we saw in Chapter 6, political elites think more ideologically than the public generally.

On some issues the average member of the House has opinions close to those of the average voter. Senators, by contrast, are often less in tune with public opinion. Two senators from the same state often mobilize quite different bases of support. The result is that many states, such as California, Delaware, and New York, have been represented by senators with almost diametrically opposed views.

A Polarized Congress in an Unpolarized Nation

The sharp increase in party votes among members of Congress since 1970 is remarkable because it is not obvious that the Americans who vote for these members are as deeply divided by party. When social scientists describe a trait among people—say, their height—they usually note that there are a few very short ones and a few very tall ones, but that most people are in the middle. They call this distribution "unimodal." But when you describe voting in Congress, except on matters of national urgency, the votes are "bimodal"—that is, almost all of the Democrats vote one way and almost all of the Republicans vote a different way.

For example, when President Clinton was impeached, 98 percent of the House Republicans voted for at least one of the four impeachment articles and 98 percent of the House Democrats voted against all four, and this happened despite the fact that most Americans did not want the president impeached. In fact, the Republican vote did not even match how people felt who lived in districts represented by Republicans. On abortion, most Americans favor it, but with some important limitations. In Congress, however, Democrats almost always support it with no restrictions, and Republicans usually want to enact lots of restrictions. Votes on less emotional matters, like the tax bills, often show the same pattern of Democrats and Republicans at loggerheads.

How Congress Responds to the Misconduct of Members

Under Article I, section 5, of the Constitution, Congress may "punish its members for disorderly behavior." There are two basic ways that Congress disciplines its members; neither is used frequently.

Censure

- May include condemnation, loss of seniority, and fines
- Some memorable cases:

Senate motion to "condemn" Senator Joseph McCarthy of Wisconsin in 1954 for overzealous attacks on innocent citizens and officials accused of being communists or communist sympathizers

House vote to fine ($25,000) and exclude Representative Adam Clayton Powell, Jr., for the abuse of his official authority and congressional privileges

Censure of members who accepted bribes in the "Abscam" affair of the early 1980s

Expulsion

- Each chamber can expel a member by a two-thirds vote
- Of twenty cases (five in the House, fifteen in the Senate), seventeen occurred in the Civil War era

How could these things happen in a democratic nation? If the American people are usually in the center on political issues, why are congressional Democrats almost always liberal and congressional Republicans almost always conservative?

There is no simple or agreed-upon answer to this question. Some scholars have showed that in the last thirty years or so, voters have in fact become more partisan, meaning that they see important differences between the two parties, they identify themselves as either conservatives or liberals, and they favor parties that share their ideological preferences.[13] We know the change cannot simply be the result of gerrymandering because Senate seats do not change their boundaries.

A third reason is that voters are becoming more partisan as a result of Congress having become more partisan. When House Democrats vote liberal and House Republicans vote conservative, many voters follow this cue and take positions based on a similar ideology.[14] People who do not see the world this way have either become less numerous or vote less often.

And a final reason is the role of seniority. The chairmen of committees are (typically) the members who have been on that committee the longest, and they will, of course, be from the safest districts. Because the chairmen have considerable influence over how bills are written, their views—which have been shaped by a lifetime dedication to Democratic or Republican causes—will be very important. When the Democrats won control of the House in 2006, the chairmanship of several committees changed from very conservative Republicans to very liberal Democrats. Harry Waxman replaced Dan Burton in Government Reform, John Conyers replaced Henry Hyde on Judiciary, and Charles Rangel replaced Bill Archer on Ways and Means.

Ethics and Congress

The Framers hoped that members of Congress would be virtuous citizens, but they feared some would not. They designed the system of checks and balances in part to minimize the chance that anybody, by gaining corrupt influence over one part of the government, would be able to impose his or her will on the other parts. But perhaps this very separation of powers made corruption more likely than it would be in a centralized nation. When power is allocated among many hands, there are many opportunities to exercise influence, and many officials have something to sell at a price many favor seekers can afford.

In all likelihood, the cruder forms of influence wielding are less common today than in the nineteenth and early twentieth centuries. Citizens are better educated and have higher standards of proper official conduct, party bosses have lost power, and the mass media have a strong incentive to find and expose improper influence and corruption.

But scandals continue to occur. From 1941 to 1981, nearly fifty members of Congress faced criminal charges; most were convicted. A dramatic scandal—the Abscam affair—unfolded during the 96th Congress, when six representatives and one senator were indicted and eventually convicted for having accepted large bribes from undercover FBI agents posing as Arabs seeking political favors. All either resigned or were defeated for reelection. In 2005, the FBI videotaped Congressman William Jefferson, a Democrat from Louisiana, apparently receiving cash bribes from an FBI informant; the following year, the Bureau raided Jefferson's home and found in his freezer a large amount of cash (the serial numbers matched those on the bills paid to him by the informant). He was indicted by a federal grand jury, convicted, and sentenced to thirteen years in prison. Jack Abramoff, a Republican lobbyist, pled guilty in 2006 to charges of fraud. Guilty as well were a Republican congressman and several other officials.

When the criminal law is broken, the moral issues are clear. It is, after all, hard to maintain one's innocence when one is shown on videotape taking envelopes stuffed with money. Far harder to judge are cases in which members of Congress take advantage of their position in ways that are not clearly illegal but may be questionable. For example, what other sources of employment or income should members of Congress have? What kinds of campaign contributions should they accept? When does a legislator's attempt to influence a regulatory agency on behalf of a constituent become improper?

Over the years the House and Senate have steadily tightened their ethics rules to the point that today members can rarely accept anything from anybody, except for regulated campaign contributions as described in Chapter 8. As of 1996, every member must file an annual financial disclosure report that is made public. No representative or senator may

- accept a fee or honorarium for giving a speech
- accept any gift worth $50 or more from anyone except a relative or close personal friend
- accept gifts worth more than $250 from personal friends without getting approval from the ethics committee

- accept gifts including anything of monetary value, such as meals and tickets to sporting or theatrical events
- lobby Congress within one year after leaving Congress

The ethics code was based on the assumption that improper influence is associated with financial transactions, yet obviously that is not always the case. Many members of Congress who in the past earned substantial incomes from speaking and writing did not have their votes corrupted by such activities; other members who rarely take such fees may be heavily influenced, perhaps unduly so, by personal friendships and political alliances that have no direct monetary value at all. And no ethics code can address the bargaining among members of Congress, or between members of Congress and the president, involving the exchange of favors and votes. The ethics code was put to a major test in 1989 when former Speaker Jim Wright was charged by the House Committee on Standards of Official Conduct with having improperly accepted funds from constituents interested in legislation. Wright resigned.

The Framers' objective was to create, not a simon-pure Congress, but one that was powerful, that would be composed of representatives who (at least in the lower house) would be closely checked by the voters, and that would offer manifold opportunities for competing interests and opinions to check one another. Their goal was liberty more than morality, though they knew that in the long run the latter was essential to the former.

The Power of Congress

Almost all members of Congress and many scholars believe that, since the 1930s and especially during the 1960s, Congress lost power to the president. The president came to dominate the making of foreign policy; sent troops into combat without congressional approval; initiated most proposals for new domestic policies; refused to spend money Congress had appropriated; and sometimes denied to Congress, in the name of executive privilege, information and documents it sought.

This claim that Congress became weak as the president became strong is a bit overdrawn. As we shall see in Chapter 10, the view from the White House is different. Recent presidents have complained of their inability to get Congress even to act on, much less to approve, many of their key proposals and have resented what they regard as congressional interference in the management of executive-branch agencies and the conduct of foreign affairs.

To any visitor from abroad, Congress seems extraordinarily powerful, probably the most powerful legislative body in the world. But Congress has always been jealous of its constitutional independence and authority. Certain events—the increasingly unpopular war in Vietnam, which Congress supported with growing reluctance and despair, and the Watergate scandals, which revealed a White House meddling illegally in the electoral process—led Congress to reassert what it felt were its diminished powers.

In 1973, Congress passed, over a presidential veto, the *War Powers Act*, giving itself greater voice in the use of American forces abroad. The following year it

AP Photo/JSteven Senne

Nancy Pelosi, Democrat from California, became the first female Speaker of the House following her party's victory in the 2006 election.

passed the *Congressional Budget and Impoundment Control Act*, which denied the president the right to not spend money appropriated by Congress and improved Congress's capacity to play a major role in the budget process. It passed laws containing a legislative veto over proposed presidential actions, especially with respect to the sale of arms abroad. Not all these steps withstood the tests of time or Supreme Court review, but together they symbolized the resurgence of congressional authority and helped set the stage for sharper conflicts between Congress and the presidency.

But conflict and stalemate are not inevitable. Even with the presidency and Congress in different partisan hands, much legislation is adopted because both parties sense that the voters, or influential interest groups, want it. Sometimes Congress even surrenders a bit of its power. In 1976, Congress passed a law that prevented President Ford from giving aid to a pro-Western faction fighting against a Marxist regime in Angola. A decade later, Congress allowed that law to lapse, and President Reagan, freed of this restriction, moved quickly to supply aid (the civil war was still going on).

One of the reasons Congress is willing to follow the lead of even a president with whom it disagrees is that members of Congress are aware that no large legislative body can exercise leadership except in a few unusual cases. If a budget is to be prepared at all, the president must do it; if foreign affairs are to be conducted at all, the president must be the leader. Congress can come up with ideas and propose new legislation (Congress, not the president, wrote much of the environmental

Congress Obeys the Law

Before 1995, Congress had routinely passed laws that applied to everybody except Congress. Among these were the Civil Rights Act, the Equal Pay Act, the Age Discrimination Act, the Freedom of Information Act, the Privacy Act, the National Labor Relations Act, the Occupational Safety and Health Act, and the Family and Medical Leave Act.

On assuming power in Congress, the Republicans made it their first order of business to change this. A bill applying eleven labor laws to Congress was quickly passed with bipartisan support and signed by President Clinton.

The Congressional Accountability Act of 1995 had to solve a key problem: Under the constitutional doctrine of separated powers, it would have been unwise and perhaps unconstitutional for the executive branch to enforce on Congress compliance with executive branch regulations. So Congress created an independent Office of Compliance and an employee grievance procedure to deal with implementation.

and consumer-protection legislation of the 1970s and the welfare reform legislation of 1996), but it cannot administer the executive branch or deal with foreign powers.

Perhaps most important, Congress is reluctant to challenge a popular president. It may delay, modify, or amend major presidential initiatives, but if the president is determined and persistent and effective, Congress cannot ignore those initiatives. How the president manages his resources—his executive powers and popular standing—to deal with a staunchly independent Congress is a major theme of the next chapter.

 ## So What?

Congress is a powerful but complicated institution with many rules and obscure procedures. But its constitutional position and internal arrangements produce some power effects. Congress

1. Has a localistic viewpoint
2. Is highly decentralized
3. Consists of individualists with highly partisan views
4. Does not often engage in careful deliberation

When senators and representatives must get themselves nominated by running in primaries and then get themselves elected without much help from the parties, they are going to spend a lot of time providing services, speeches, and mail to their local constituents. This *localistic* viewpoint is inevitable. As former Speaker Tip O'Neill liked to put it, "In Congress all politics is local politics."

Members who forget that may suddenly find that they are no longer members. What is surprising, given the role that they must play, is that members sometimes vote contrary to their constituents' views. They did this when they deregulated the airlines in 1978, reformed the tax code in 1986, refused to support congressional term limits or a balanced budget amendment in 1995, voted to impeach President Clinton in 1998, and considered President Obama's health care plan in 2010.

Because the real business of Congress is done in committees and subcommittees, the process of making policy is highly *decentralized.* More than 125 members of the House chair a committee or subcommittee; nearly half of all senators do the same. Each chairperson has a stake in shaping legislation, conducting hearings, and protecting his or her committee's jurisdiction (or turf) from that of rival committees. When complex legislation must be considered, it is often referred to several committees. If it passes the House and Senate, the conference committee convened to reconcile any differences may number more than a hundred people.

Men and women loyal to localities operating in a decentralized committee system are *individualists.* That is, rather than blindly following party leaders (as they do in England) in deciding how to vote, they try to get publicity for themselves. Though Democrats usually vote with other Democrats, and Republicans with other Republicans, this is not because anyone has cracked a whip; it is because of the ideological agreement within the parties. Being individualists, members will look for issues that they can claim as their own and bills that they can introduce for which, if passed, they can take credit.

These three factors have operated more or less continually since the early decades of the nineteenth century. What has changed is the greatly increased size of the federal government, the vastly expanded scope of federal policies, and consequently the hugely increased workload of the members. There is *relatively little deliberation.* People often ridicule members for voting on bills they have not read (and sometimes that have not even been printed in final form), but that is not a measure of the personal indifference or weaknesses of members; it is how we all would behave if we had to spend sixteen hours a day meeting visitors, going to hearings, speaking to the press, and traveling back and forth from our home districts to Washington.

Of late, however, the polarization that exists that makes almost every Democrat a liberal and every Republican a conservative has meant that Congress is more likely to act in ways that many people have trouble understanding. In the midst of the deep recession of 2009, when most voters were worrying about unemployment and business failures and when you would think Congress would single-mindedly be pursuing stimulus programs, Congress enacted a stimulus bill but then went on to consider new programs, such as a bold health care policy, that if passed would raise taxes for many people and force up the cost of health care. It seemed as if many members of Congress believed that doing this was worth the electoral losses they were likely to suffer in the 2010 elections.

WHAT WOULD YOU DO?

MEMORANDUM

To: Representative Peter Skerry

From: Martha Bayles, Legislative Aide

Subject: The Size of the House of Representatives

The House can decide how big it wishes to be. When it was created, there was one representative for every 30,000 people. Now there is one for every 600,000. In most other democracies, each member of parliament represents far fewer than 600,000 people. Doubling the size of the House may be a way of avoiding term limits.

Arguments for:

1. Doubling the size of the House would reduce the huge demand for constituent services each member now faces.

2. A bigger House would represent more shades of opinion more fairly.

3. Each member could raise less campaign money because his or her campaign would be smaller.

Arguments against:

1. A bigger House would be twice as hard to manage, and it would take even longer to pass legislation.

Friday,

Should We Have a Bigger Congress?

November 15
WASHINGTON, D.C.

A powerful citizens' organization has demanded that the House of Representatives be made larger so that voters can feel closer to their members. Each representative now speaks for about 600,000 people—far too many, the group argues, to make it possible for all points of view to be heard. In its petition...

2. Campaigns in districts of 300,000 people would cost as much as ones in districts with 600,000 people.

3. Interest groups do a better job of representing public opinion than would a House with more members.

Your Decision:

Increase size of House: _____   Do not increase size of House: _____

SUMMARY

A congress differs from a parliament in that it does not choose the nation's chief executive and is composed of members who attach greater importance to representing local constituencies than to supporting a national party leadership. Power in the American Congress is fragmented, specialized, and decentralized. Most important decisions are made in committees and subcommittees. Though there have been periods—such as the late nineteenth century—when party leaders in Congress were powerful, the general tendency, particularly in the last forty years, has been to enhance the independence and influence of individual members of Congress.

The great majority of representatives are secure in their seats—a security that has been acquired chiefly by serving local constituency interests and by developing a personal following. The ability of political parties to determine who shall become a candidate for Congress has declined. As a result, votes in Congress are less likely to follow strict party lines than votes in most European parliaments. Nonetheless, party affiliation remains the most important influence on the behavior of members of Congress. In part this is because party loyalties in Congress correspond, to a degree, to the personal ideologies of members of Congress. Senators and representatives are more ideological than the public at large. Congressional Democrats are much more liberal than congressional Republicans.

The organization and procedures of the House are tightly structured to facilitate action and orderly debate. The committees therefore tend to dominate decisions made on the House floor. Senate procedures, on the other hand, permit lengthy debate and many floor amendments, with the result that individual senators have as much or more influence than Senate committees.

Congress does not simply respond to presidential needs for action; it initiates some proposals on its own and influences the kinds of proposals a president will offer. In shaping the policies of Congress, congressional staffs have become important. Though most of their time is spent on serving the constituency interests of members of Congress, the multiple committee assignments and heavy workload of senators and representatives mean that staffers often acquire substantial influence.

When Republicans assumed control of the House in 1995, they set about restoring some of the lost power of the Speaker and of party leaders in order to create greater unity among their members and thereby facilitate the passage of their conservative agenda. Speaker Gingrich became the most powerful person to hold that post since 1910; under his leadership, party unity increased. But unlike in past eras of strong party leaders, this era was to have an end—both the Speaker and committee chairmen were given fixed terms in power.

RECONSIDERING THE ENDURING QUESTIONS

1. Are the members of Congress representative of the American people?

They tend to be older and are more likely to be white and male and to be more ideological than the average voter. Nevertheless, they pay a lot of attention to what the people back home want.

2. Does Congress prefer strong leadership, or does it allow its members a lot of freedom?

The Senate has always valued freedom over leadership. The House experimented with strong leadership toward the end of the nineteenth century and again toward the end of the twentieth, but it always moved back to giving members freedom, or at least as much freedom as is possible when there are 435 members. The House, unlike the Senate, strictly limits the length of debate and amendments that can be introduced, and it has in the Speaker a more powerful leader.

3. How important are political parties in Congress?

Very important. Party loyalty explains most of the difference in votes, but this loyalty is not coerced. It reflects the belief of most Democratic members that they are liberals and the belief of most Republicans that they are conservatives.

4. Why does it take so long for Congress to act?

Congress is designed to make legislation proceed slowly. In each house, subcommittees and then committees discuss every important bill. The ideological divisions in Congress are very sharp, and so compromises must be worked out. And when the House and Senate disagree, as they often do, the two bodies must negotiate an agreement. But when there is a national crisis, as there was on September 11, 2001, Congress can act very quickly.

Online Resources: Congress

 CourseMate

- House of Representatives: www.house.gov
- Senate: www.senate.gov
- Library of Congress website on Congress: thomas.loc.gov

For news about Congress:
- *Roll Call* magazine: www.rollcall.com
- C-SPAN programs about Congress: www.c-span.org
- How Congress works: congress.indiana.edu

Suggested Readings

Arnold, R. Douglas. *The Logic of Congressional Action.* New Haven, Conn.: Yale University Press, 1990. Explains why Congress enacts the policies it does, especially those that serve general as opposed to special interests.

Davidson, Roger H., and Walter J. Oleszek, *Congress and Its Members*, 9th ed. Washington, D.C.: Congressional Quarterly Press, 2004. Good nonpartisan summary of how people get to Congress and how they behave while there.

Dodd, Lawrence C., and Bruce I. Oppenheimer, eds. *Congress Reconsidered*, 8th ed. Washington, D.C.: Congressional Quarterly Press, 2005. Recent studies of congressional politics.

Fenno, Richard F., Jr. *Congressmen in Committees.* Boston: Little, Brown, 1973. Study of the styles of twelve standing committees.

Maass, Arthur. *Congress and the Common Good.* New York: Basic Books, 1984. Insightful account of congressional operations, especially those involving legislative-executive relations.

Mayhew, David R. *Congress: The Electoral Connection.* New Haven, Conn.: Yale University Press, 1974. Argues that a member of Congress's desire to win reelection shapes his or her legislative behavior.

Oleszek, Walter J. *Congressional Procedures and the Policy Process,* 7th ed. Washington, D.C.: Congressional Quarterly Press, 2007. Clear, factual summary of how Congress operates.

Poole, Keith T., and Howard Rosenthal, *Congress: A Political-Economic History of Roll Call Voting.* New York: Oxford University Press, 1997. For 200 years, ideology, more than any other factor, explains how members of Congress vote.

Smith, Steven S., et al. *The American Congress,* 6th ed. New York: Cambridge University Press, 2009). Excellent summary of what we know about how our Congress operates.

ENDURING QUESTIONS

1. **Did the Founding Fathers want the president to be stronger or weaker than Congress?**

2. **Does character influence how the president does his job?**

3. **Should we abolish the electoral college?**

CourseMate

Professor Jones speaks to his political science class: "The president of the United States occupies one of the most powerful offices in the world. Presidents Kennedy and Johnson sent American troops to Vietnam, President Reagan sent them to Grenada and Lebanon, the first President Bush sent them to the Persian Gulf, and President Clinton sent them to Haiti, all without war being declared by Congress. President Nixon imposed wage and price controls on the country. Presidents Carter and Reagan between them selected most of the federal judges now on the bench; thus the political philosophies of these two men were imposed on the courts. President George W. Bush created military tribunals to try captured terrorists. No wonder people talk about our having an 'imperial presidency.'"

A few doors down the hall, Professor Smith speaks to her class: "The president, compared to the prime ministers of other democratic nations, is one of the

AP Photo/J. Scott Applewhite

weakest chief executives anywhere. President Carter signed an arms limitation treaty with the Soviets, but the Senate wouldn't ratify it. President Reagan was not allowed even to test antisatellite weapons, and in 1986 Congress rejected his budget before the ink was dry. Subordinates who were supposedly loyal to Reagan regularly leaked his views to the press and undercut his programs before Congress. The first President Bush couldn't get his nominee for secretary of defense confirmed by the Senate. President Clinton's health-care plan was rejected by Congress, and the House voted to impeach him. President George W. Bush had difficulty getting the Senate to confirm his judges. No wonder people talk about the president being a 'pitiful, helpless giant.'"

Can Professors Jones and Smith be talking about the same office? Who is right? In fact, they are both right. The American presidency is a unique office, with elements of both great strength and profound weakness built into it by its constitutional origins.

The popularly elected president is an American invention. Of the roughly five dozen countries in which there is some degree of party competition and thus, presumably, some measure of free choice for the voters, only sixteen have a directly elected president, and thirteen of these are nations of North and South America. The democratic alternative is for the chief executive to be a prime minister, chosen by and responsible to the parliament. This system prevails in most West European countries as well as in Israel and Japan. Few purely presidential political systems exist in Europe; France combines a directly elected president with a prime minister and parliament.[1]

One obvious result of the different ways presidents and prime ministers are chosen is that, whereas the prime minister's party (or coalition of parties) always has a majority in the parliament (if it did not, somebody else would be prime minister), the president's party often does not have a majority in Congress. Since Franklin D. Roosevelt was president, eight had to deal with an opposition party that controlled one or both houses of Congress: Truman, Eisenhower, Nixon, Ford, Reagan, George H. W. Bush, Clinton, and George W. Bush.

Other differences are less obvious but just as important. An American presidential candidate is nominated through primaries and conventions, whereas potential prime ministers are generally chosen by a caucus of veteran political leaders, with an eye to who can best hold the party together in parliament. Presidential candidates often have no experience in Congress, but potential prime ministers have always served in parliament. Once in office, a prime minister chooses cabinet officers primarily or exclusively from among members of his or her party in parliament and must appear regularly in parliament to defend the government's policies. The president of the United States, on the other hand, selects his cabinet officers and advisers not to control Congress but to reward personal followers, recognize important constituencies, and mobilize nongovernmental expertise; and he never has to answer hostile questions before Congress.

The results of these differences are clear. Prime ministers in two-party nations (such as Great Britain) have very great power because they can dominate the cabinet and the legislature. (In countries with multiparty systems, such as Italy or Israel, prime ministers are much weaker because the cabinet is usually an unstable coalition.) Although the president of the United States is elected by the

How We Compare

Presidential Systems

Most modern democracies feature one of three systems:

- *Parliamentary systems* (like the United Kingdom) in which prime ministers are selected by a legislative majority and can be removed by a legislative majority at virtually any time;
- *Presidential systems* (like the United States) in which the president and the legislators are separately elected and serve fixed terms, with the president subject to removal by the legislature only under extreme circumstances (for example, in the United States, impeachment by the House and removal from office by the Senate); and
- *Semipresidential systems* (like France) in which there is a prime minister selected and subject to removal by a parliamentary majority, as well as a president who is separately elected.

Using a multidimensional definition of "democratic," in 1950, about 60 percent of democratic nations had parliamentary systems, 30 percent had semipresidential systems, and 10 percent had presidential systems.

Today, however, about two-thirds of all democratic nations have either semipresidential (about 36 percent) or presidential (about 30 percent) systems.

Are elected officials and party leaders in presidential systems like that in the U.S. more or less likely to deliver on campaign promises than are their counterparts in the other two systems?

The most in-depth studies to date say "less likely": The rate at which a party in power pursues the policies it offered to voters in its platform is generally lower in presidential systems; and the incidence of "policy-switching" (pursuing policies directly contrary to those promised during the campaign) is more than four times as common in presidential systems as it is in parliamentary systems, with semipresidential systems in the middle.

Source: David Samuels and Matthew Shugart, *Presidents, Parties, and Prime Ministers: How the Separation of Powers Affects Party Organization and Behavior* (Cambridge University Press, 2010); "Presidents, Prime Ministers, and Mandate Representation: A Global Test," paper prepared for presentation at the 2006 Annual Meeting of the American Political Science Association, Philadelphia, Pennsylvania.

---

people at large and occupies an office with powers derived from the Constitution, he may have great difficulty in exercising any legislative leadership at all owing to his inability to control Congress—even if, as in the case of John F. Kennedy, his own party has the majority in Congress.

The Powers of the President

The president's formal powers are few and vaguely defined; they are set forth in Article II of the Constitution:

Powers of the President Alone

- Serve as commander in chief of the armed forces
- Commission officers of the armed forces

- Grant reprieves and pardons for federal offenses (except impeachment)
- Convene Congress in special sessions
- Receive ambassadors
- Take care that the laws be faithfully executed
- Wield the "executive power"
- Appoint officials to lesser offices

Powers of the President Shared with the Senate

- Make treaties
- Appoint ambassadors, judges, and high officials

Powers of the President Shared with Congress as a Whole

- Approve legislation

Interpreted narrowly, this list of powers is not very impressive. Obviously the president's authority as commander in chief is important, but most of the other constitutional grants amount to making the president a kind of chief clerk of the country. That is exactly how the office appeared a hundred years ago, even to as astute an observer as Woodrow Wilson in his 1885 book *Congressional Government*.[2] But Wilson was overlooking some examples of enormously powerful presidents, such as Lincoln, and was not sufficiently attentive to the potential for presidential power found in the more ambiguous clauses of the Constitution as well as in the political realities of American life. For example, the president's duty to "take care that the laws be faithfully

Brown Brothers

Every successful modern president has worked hard at cultivating the press. Theodore Roosevelt was perhaps the first president to begin this courtship in earnest.

executed," interpreted broadly, enabled Grover Cleveland to break a labor strike in the 1890s and Dwight Eisenhower to send troops to integrate a public school in Little Rock, Arkansas, in 1956. And the president's authority as commander in chief has grown—especially, but not only, in wartime—to encompass not simply the direction of the military forces but the management of the economy and the direction of foreign policy as well. A quietly dramatic reminder of the awesome implications of the president's military power occurs at the precise instant a new president assumes office, when a military officer carrying a locked briefcase (insiders call it the "football") moves from the side of the outgoing president to the side of the new one. In the briefcase are the secret codes and orders that permit the president to authorize the launching of American nuclear weapons.

The greatest source of presidential power, however, is found not in the Constitution at all but in politics and public opinion. Increasingly since the 1930s, Congress has passed laws that confer on the executive branch grants of authority to achieve some general goals, leaving it up to the president and his deputies to define the regulations and programs that will actually be put into effect. Moreover, the American people look to the president—always in time of crisis, but increasingly as an everyday matter—for leadership and hold him responsible for a large and growing portion of our national affairs.

The Evolution of the Presidency

In 1787, few issues inspired as much debate or concern among the Framers of the Constitution as the problem of defining the powers of the chief executive. Fearing anarchy and monarchy in about equal measure, the delegates considered a number of proposals for an executive authority before finally deciding on a single president with significant powers. Most were reassured by the assumption that George Washington would be the first president, though some still feared that the presidency would become "the fetus of monarchy." The electoral college and the provision for the House settling inconclusive elections, for example, were designed to minimize the possibility of future presidents' attempts to hold office for life through bribery, intrigue, or force.

In retrospect, these concerns seem misplaced. The real sources of the expansion of the president's power—his role in foreign affairs, his ability to shape and lead public opinion, his position at the head of the executive branch—were hardly predictable in 1787. The pattern of relationships between the president and Congress that we see today is the result of a process of evolution extending over two centuries.

Establishing the Legitimacy of the Presidency

The first problem for the Framers was to establish the legitimacy of the presidency itself, that is, to ensure, if possible, public acceptance of the office, its incumbent, and its powers, and to establish an orderly transfer of power from one incumbent to the next. Although we take this for granted, in much of the world today such peaceful transfers of power are still relatively unusual.

The Electoral College

Until November 2000, it was almost impossible to get a student interested in the electoral college. But in the 2000 presidential election, Florida's electoral vote hung in the balance for weeks, with George W. Bush (though he had fewer popular votes than Al Gore) finally winning it and the presidency.

Here are the essential facts. Each state gets electoral votes equal to the number of its senators and representatives (the District of Columbia also gets three, even though it has no representatives in Congress). There are 538 electoral votes. To win, a candidate must receive at least half, or 270.

In all but two states, the candidate who wins the most popular votes wins all of the state's electoral votes. Maine and Nebraska have a different system. They allow electoral votes to be split by awarding some votes on the basis of a candidate's statewide total and some on the basis of how the candidate did in each congressional district.

The "winner-take-all" system in effect in forty-eight states makes it possible for a candidate to win at least 270 electoral votes without winning a majority of the popular votes. This happened in 2000, 1888, and 1876, and almost happened in 1960 and 1884. Today a candidate need only win the eleven largest states to achieve a presidential victory.

This means that the candidates have a strong incentive to campaign hard in big states they have a chance of winning. In 2004, John Kerry worked hard in California, New York, and Pennsylvania but pretty much ignored Texas, where Bush was a shoo-in. Bush campaigned hard in Florida, Illinois, and Ohio but not so much in New York, where Kerry was an easy winner.

If no candidate wins 270 electoral votes, the House of Representatives chooses the president from among the three leading candidates, with each state casting one vote. By House rule, each state's vote is given to the candidate preferred by a majority of the state's House delegation. If there is a tie within a state, its vote is not counted.

Most Americans would like to abolish the electoral college. But doing away with it entirely

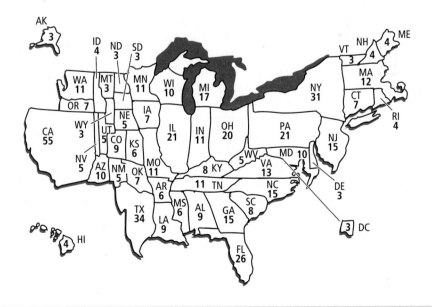

would have some unforeseen effects. If we relied solely on the popular vote, there would have to be a runoff election between the two leading candidates if neither got a majority because of third-party candidates siphoning away votes. This would encourage the formation of third parties. (Imagine, for example, a Jesse Jackson party, a Pat Buchanan party, a Pat Robertson party, or a Ralph Nader party.) Each third party would then be in a position to negotiate with one of the two major parties between the first election and the runoff for favors it wanted in return for its support. American presidential politics might come to look like the multiparty systems in France and Italy.

The electoral college also serves a larger purpose: It makes candidates worry about carrying states as well as popular votes and so heightens the influence of states in national politics.

The first presidents were among the most prominent men in the new nation, and they tended to distrust the emerging political parties as "factions." (As it turned out, this hostility to party was unrealistic: Parties are as natural to democracy as churches to religion.) The national government had relatively little to do, and the first presidents kept the office modest. Appointees to federal offices were men with standing in their communities. Presidents cast vetoes sparingly, and then only when they thought a proposed law was not only unwise but also unconstitutional. Washington established the precedent of a two-term presidency, and his immediate successors honored it. By treading cautiously, the first presidents did much to make their office legitimate to the citizenry.

The Jacksonians and the Reemergence of Congress

At a time roughly corresponding to the presidency of Andrew Jackson (1829–1837), broad changes began to occur in American politics. Mass political participation and modern political parties emerged. Together with the personality of Jackson himself, these changes altered the relations between president and Congress and the nature of presidential leadership. Seemingly old and frail, Jackson nevertheless used the powers of his office as no one before him had. He vetoed more bills than all his predecessors put together, on policy as well as on constitutional grounds, seeing himself—as the only official elected by the entire voting citizenry—as the "Tribune of the People." Not shrinking from conflict with Congress, Jackson showed what a popular president could do. His view of a strong and independent presidency was ultimately to triumph, for better or worse.

With the end of Jackson's second term, however, Congress—and particularly the Senate—quickly reasserted itself, and for almost a century the presidency became the subordinate branch of the national government. This was an intensely partisan era, with public opinion sharply divided and most presidential elections very close. Only Lincoln broke new ground for presidential power. In response to the Civil War, he made unprecedented use of the vague gift of powers found in the Constitution, especially those he felt were implied or were inherent in the phrase "take care that the laws be faithfully executed," and in the express authorization for him to act as commander in chief.

After Lincoln, Congress reasserted its power; until the 1930s, Congress generally formulated legislative programs, and the president was at best a negative force—a source of opposition to, not leadership for, Congress. But Lincoln had made it abundantly clear that a national emergency could equip the president with great powers, and Theodore Roosevelt (1901–1909) and Woodrow Wilson (1913–1921) showed that a popular and strong-willed president could expand his powers even without an emergency. Wilson, for example, was the first president since John Adams to deliver personally the State of the Union address, and one of the first to develop and argue for a presidential legislative program.

The Modern Presidency

The popular conception of the president as the central figure of national government, devising a legislative program and commanding a large staff of advisers, is very much a product of the modern era and of the enlarged role of government. Only since the 1930s, has the presidency been powerful no matter who occupied the office and whether or not there was a crisis.

Every modern president is the titular head of the huge federal administrative system (whether he is the real boss is another matter). Whereas once Grover Cleveland personally answered the White House telephone and Abraham Lincoln often answered his own mail, presidents today are surrounded by hundreds of assistants and by the trappings of power—helicopters, guards, and limousines. The resources at the president's disposal are awesome—in fact, he now confronts an army of assistants so large that it constitutes a bureaucracy he has difficulty controlling. Normally presidential assistants are influential in accordance with the Rule of Propinquity: Power is wielded by persons who are in the room when a decision is made. Presidential appointments can thus be classified in terms of their proximity, physically and politically, to the president.

Circular structure *A method of organizing a president's staff in which several presidential assistants report directly to the president.*

Pyramid structure *A method of organizing a president's staff in which most presidential assistants report through a hierarchy to the president's chief of staff.*

Cluster structure *A system for organizing the White House in which a group of subordinates and committees all report to the president directly.*

The White House Office

The White House Office consists of aides who are the president's personal staff; their appointments do not have to be confirmed by the Senate—he can hire and fire them at will. These are the men and women who have offices in the White House, usually in the West Wing of that building. Their titles often do not reveal the functions they actually perform; in general they oversee the political and policy interests of the president.

A president can organize his staff as a circle, a pyramid, or a cluster. In a **circular structure**, a few key assistants report to him. Jimmy Carter did this. In a **pyramid structure**, most report through one chief of staff. Eisenhower, Nixon, Reagan (after 1985), and the elder Bush did this.[3] In a **cluster structure**, ad hoc task forces and key advisers have access to the president with no clear chain of command. Franklin Roosevelt did this; Clinton did it for a while and then began to make greater use of a chief of staff.

Circles and clusters are favored by presidents who want to get personally involved in the details of policy; they provide a lot of information, but at the price of confusion and conflict. Pyramids are favored by presidents who like order and clear lines of authority, even at the risk of reduced information.

Typically, senior White House staff members are drawn from the ranks of the president's campaign staff—longtime associates in whom he has confidence. A few members, however, will be experts brought in after the campaign—for example, Nixon's assistant for national security affairs, Henry Kissinger. These men and women have to work in small, cramped offices, but they willingly put up with any discomfort in return for the privilege (and the power) of being *in* the White House. The arrangement of offices (especially their proximity to the president's Oval Office) is a good measure of the relative influence of the people in them.

To an outsider, the amount of jockeying among the top staff for access to the president may seem comical or even perverse. But more than power plays and ego trips are involved. Who sees the president and who sees and "signs off" on memoranda going to him affect in important ways who influences policy and thus whose goals and beliefs become embedded in policy.

Executive Office of the President

The agencies that make up the executive office of the president include the Office of Management and Budget (OMB), the Council of Economic Advisers, the Office of the U.S. Trade Representative, the Council on Environmental Quality, and the Office of Science and Technology Policy. These agencies report directly to the president and perform staff services for him but are not located in the White House. Their individual members may or may not enjoy intimate contact with him; some of these agencies are rather large bureaucracies. The president appoints the heads of these organizations, but unlike White House staff positions, the Senate must confirm most of them.

In terms of the president's need for assistance in running the federal government, probably the most important of these agencies is the OMB. Besides assembling and analyzing the figures for the yearly national budget that the president submits to Congress, it also studies the operations of the executive branch, devises reorganization plans, improves the flow of information about government programs, and reviews the cabinet department's budgetary proposals. Its staff of several hundred is highly professional and traditionally nonpartisan, although in recent administrations the agency has played a major role in advocating rather than merely analyzing policies.

The Cabinet

At one time, the heads of the federal departments (such as State and Treasury) met regularly to discuss matters with the president, and some people (particularly those critical of strong presidents) would like to see this kind of cabinet decision making reestablished. But, in fact, the cabinet is largely a fiction. It is not even mentioned in the Constitution, and presidents from George Washington on have found that it does not work as a presidential committee. Dwight Eisenhower is one of the only modern presidents who came close to making the cabinet a truly deliberative body; even under him, it neither had influence over presidential decisions nor helped him obtain more power over the government.

The President: Qualifications and Benefits

Qualifications

- A natural-born citizen (can be born abroad of parents who are American citizens).
- At least thirty-five years of age.
- A resident of the United States for at least fourteen years (but not necessarily the fourteen years just preceding the election).

Benefits

- A nice house
- A salary of $400,000 per year (taxable)
- Expense account of $50,000 per year (taxable)
- Travel expenses of $100,000 per year (tax free)
- Pension, on retirement, equal to that of a cabinet member (taxable)
- Staff support and Secret Service protection on leaving the presidency
- A White House staff of 400–500 persons
- A place in the country: Camp David
- A personal airplane: *Air Force One*
- A fine chef

Cabinet officers are the heads of the fifteen administrative departments that, by custom or law, are considered part of the **cabinet** (see Table 10.1). Though the president, with the consent of the Senate, appoints the heads of these cabinet departments, his power over them is sharply limited. In only the large departments (such as the State Department) can the president appoint more than 1 percent of the employees, and many of these are ambassadors; the vast majority are civil-service personnel who cannot easily be fired. But the main reason for the cabinet's weakness is that its members are heads of vast organizations that they seek to defend, explain, and enlarge—often in sharp competition with one another. Thus cabinet officers can seldom give the president effective collective advice.

Cabinet *By custom, the cabinet includes the heads of the fifteen major executive departments.*

The Department of Homeland Security, authorized in 2002, is one of the largest federal agencies, with a budget of around $36 billion. It brings together in one place bureaus that previously were scattered throughout the government, including the Customs Service and Secret Service (formerly in the Treasury Department), much of the Immigration and Naturalization Service (formerly in the Justice Department), the Coast Guard and the Transportation Security Administration (formerly in the Transportation Department), and the Federal Emergency Management Agency (formerly an independent bureau).

It is best known for issuing security alerts with an associated color based on whether terrorist threats to the country are low (green), guarded (blue), elevated (yellow), high (orange), or severe (red). These threat advisories are meant to tell other agencies what security measures they should implement, what facilities should be under special surveillance, and how intensively agency activity should be coordinated. Beyond this, it is concerned with protecting airlines and ports, sharing intelligence, developing antiterrorist technologies, and controlling the borders.

Independent Agencies, Commissions, and Judgeships

The president also appoints people to four dozen or so agencies and commissions that are not considered part of the cabinet and that by law often have a

Table 10.1 The Cabinet Departments

Department	Created	Approximate Civilian Employment (2009)
State	1789	36,000
Treasury	1789	111,000
Defense[a]	1947	682,000
Justice	1789	108,000
Interior	1849	71,000
Agriculture[b]	1889	99,000
Commerce	1913	41,000
Labor	1913	16,000
Health and Human Services[c]	1953	62,000
Housing and Urban Development	1965	10,000
Transportation	1966	55,000
Energy	1977	15,000
Education	1979	4,000
Veterans Affairs	1989	265,000
Homeland Security	2002	166,000

[a]Formerly the War Department, created in 1789. Figures are for civilians only.
[b]Agriculture Department created in 1862, made part of cabinet in 1889.
[c]Originally Health, Education, and Welfare; reorganized in 1979.

Source: Created from data from Statistical Abstract of the U.S. and the Department of Homeland Security.

quasi-independent status. Many of these are regulatory commissions (such as the Federal Trade Commission and the Federal Communications Commission) whose members serve for fixed terms and can be removed only for cause. Other agencies, such as the Environmental Protection Agency, are headed by people who can be removed by the president at any time.

The president also appoints federal judges, subject to the consent of the Senate; they serve during "good behavior" (which usually means until they choose to retire). They can be removed only by impeachment and conviction. This tenure is required by the Constitution and is necessary to preserve the independence of the judiciary.

Who Gets Appointed

Because so many departments employ permanent civil-service personnel, a president can make relatively few appointments; furthermore, he rarely knows more than a few of the people he does appoint. He is fortunate if most cabinet officers turn out to agree with him on major policy questions.

Usually cabinet officers and their immediate subordinates have had some prior federal experience, and many are "in and outers" who alternate between jobs in the federal government and jobs in the private sector, especially in law firms and universities. At one time, the cabinet included many people with strong political followings of their own, such as former senators and governors and powerful local party leaders. Of late, however, presidents have tended to place in their cabinet individuals known for their expertise or their administrative experience rather than for their political following. This has come about in part because political parties are now so weak that party leaders can no longer demand a place in the cabinet and in part because presidents want (or think they want) "experts."

A president's desire to appoint experts who do not have independent political power is modified—but not supplanted—by his need to recognize various politically important groups, regions, and organizations. It would be quite costly for a president *not* to appoint a woman and a black to every cabinet. The secretary of labor must be acceptable to the AFL-CIO, the secretary of agriculture to at least some organized farmers, and so on.

Because political considerations must be taken into account in making cabinet and agency appointments, and because any head of a large organization will tend to adopt the perspective of that organization, an inevitable tension—even a rivalry—develops between the White House staff and the department heads. Staff members, many of them young and lacking in executive experience, see themselves as extensions of the president's personality and policies. Department heads

Bettmann/Corbis

President Franklin D. Roosevelt broadcasting a radio address.

see themselves as repositories of expert knowledge (often of knowledge of why the president's plans won't work); they get irritated when White House staffers tell them what to do and deny them access to the president.

Popularity and Influence

Every president strives for personal popularity because it is the key to congressional support (and improved chances for reelection). It is not obvious, of course, why Congress should care about a president's popularity. After all, most members of Congress are secure in their seats, and the president cannot ordinarily provide credible electoral rewards (or penalties) for them. Not even Franklin Roosevelt could purge members of Congress who opposed his program, and seldom does presidential support make a difference in a congressional race (see Table 10.2).

Table 10.2	Partisan Gains or Losses in Congress in Presidential Election Years			
			Gains or Losses of President's Party in:	
Year	President	Party	House	Senate
1932	Roosevelt	Dem.	+90	+9
1936	Roosevelt	Dem.	+12	+7
1940	Roosevelt	Dem.	+7	−3
1944	Roosevelt	Dem.	+24	−2
1948	Truman	Dem.	+75	+9
1952	Eisenhower	Rep.	+22	+1
1956	Eisenhower	Rep.	−3	−1
1960	Kennedy	Dem.	−20	+1
1964	Johnson	Dem.	+37	+1
1968	Nixon	Rep.	+5	−2
1972	Nixon	Rep.	+12	−2
1976	Carter	Dem.	+1	+1
1980	Reagan	Rep.	+33	+12
1984	Reagan	Rep.	+16	−2
1988	Bush	Rep.	−3	−1
1992	Clinton	Dem.	−9	+1
1996	Clinton	Dem.	+9	−2
2000	Bush	Rep.	−3	−4
2004	Bush	Rep.	+4	+4
2008	Obama	Dem.	+21	+9

Source: Updated from N. J. Ornstein, T. E. Mann, and M. J. Malbin. *Vital Statistics on Congress, 1997–1998* (Washington, D.C.: Congressional Quarterly Press, 1998), p. 54. Copyright © 1998. Reprinted with the permission of the American Enterprise Institute for Public Policy Research, Washington, DC. The 2008 numbers did not include six House and three Senate races that were undecided on November 10, 2008.

Figure 10.1 Presidential Popularity

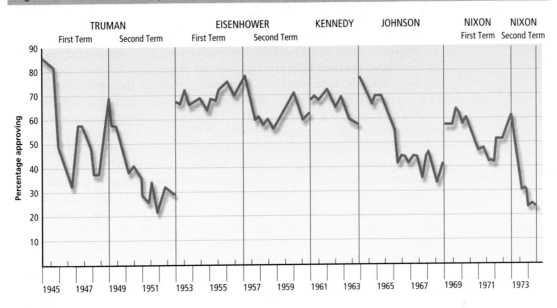

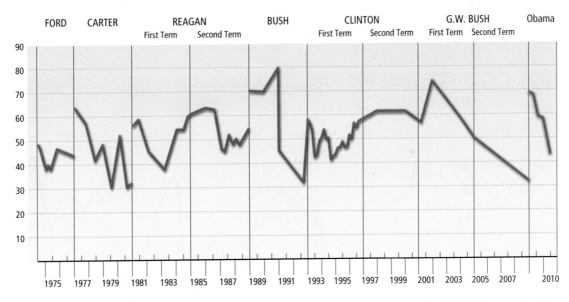

Note: Popularity was measured by asking every few months, "Do you approve of the way ——— is handling his job as president?"

Source: Thomas E. Cronin, *The State of the Presidency.* Copyright ©1975 by Thomas E. Cronin. Reprinted by permission of the author. Updated with Gallup poll data, 1976–2010.

Careful studies of voter attitudes and of how presidential and congressional candidates fare in the same districts suggest that whatever influence the presidential coattails once had, their effect is quite small today. The weakening of party loyalty and of party organizations, combined with the enhanced ability of members of Congress to build secure relations with their constituents, has tended to insulate congressional elections from presidential ones. When voters support members of Congress from the same party as an incoming president, they probably do so out of a desire for a general change and as an adverse judgment about the outgoing party's performance as a whole, and not because they want to support the new president with legislators favorable to him.[4] The unusual increase in Republican representatives and senators that accompanied the election of Ronald Reagan in 1980 was probably as much a result of the unpopularity of the outgoing president and the circumstances of various local races as it was of Reagan's coattails.

Nonetheless, a president's personal popularity may have a significant effect on how much of his program Congress passes. Though members of Congress may not fear a president who threatens to campaign against them, they do have a sense that it is risky to oppose too adamantly the policies of a popular president. It can be shown statistically that a president's popularity, as measured by the Gallup poll (see Figure 10.1), is associated with the proportion of a president's legislative proposals that are approved by Congress (see Figure 10.2). Other things being equal, the more popular the president, the higher the proportion of his bills Congress will pass.[5]

Figure 10.2   Percentage of Roll-Call Votes in Congress in Which the Side Publicly Favored by the President Won

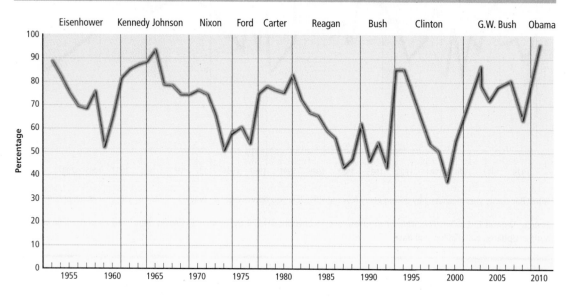

Source: Congressional Quarterly Weekly Report, various years.

The Decline in Popularity

Though presidential popularity is an asset, its value tends inexorably to decline. As Figure 10.1 shows, every president except Eisenhower, Reagan, and Clinton lost popular support between his inauguration and the time he left office, except when his reelection gave him a brief burst of renewed popularity.

Because a president's popularity tends to be highest right after an election, political commentators like to speak of a "honeymoon," during which the president's love affair with the people and possibly with Congress can be consummated. Certainly Franklin Roosevelt, in his legendary "hundred days" after taking office in 1933, enjoyed a honeymoon during which he obtained from a willing Congress a vast array of new laws that created new agencies and authorized new policies. But those were the extraordinary times of the Great Depression, with millions out of work, banks closed, farmers impoverished, and the stock market ruined. It would have been political suicide for Congress to have blocked, or even delayed, action on measures that appeared designed to help the nation out of the crisis.

Table 10.3	**Partisan Gains or Losses in Congress in Off-Year Elections**			
			Gains or Losses of President's Party in	
Year	**President**	**Party**	**House**	**Senate**
1934	Roosevelt	Dem.	+9	+9
1938	Roosevelt	Dem.	−70	−7
1942	Roosevelt	Dem.	−50	−8
1946	Truman	Dem.	−54	−11
1950	Truman	Dem.	−29	−5
1954	Eisenhower	Rep.	−18	−1
1958	Eisenhower	Rep.	−47	−13
1962	Kennedy	Dem.	−5	+2
1966	Johnson	Dem.	−48	−4
1970	Nixon	Rep.	−12	+1
1974	Ford	Rep.	−48	−5
1978	Carter	Dem.	−12	−3
1982	Reagan	Rep.	−26	0
1986	Reagan	Rep.	−5	−8
1990	Bush	Rep.	−9	−1
1994	Clinton	Dem.	−52	−9
1998	Clinton	Dem.	+5	0
2002	Bush	Rep.	+8	+2
2006	Bush	Rep.	−32	−6
2010	Obama	Dem.	−61	−6

Source: Harold W. Stanley and Richard G. Niemi, *Vital Statistics on American Politics,* 2009–2010. (Washington, D.C.: Congressional Quarterly Press, 2010), p. 30. Reprinted by permission of CQ Press, a division of Congressional Quarterly, Inc. The 2010 data may change when recounts are completed.

Other presidents, serving in more normal times, have not enjoyed such a honeymoon, though some have won a few victories. Reagan, in his first year in office, persuaded Congress to enact major cuts in taxes and spending on domestic programs, and George W. Bush received great support after the terrorist attacks of September 11, 2001.

The decay in the reputation of the president and his party in midterm is evident from the pattern of off-year elections. Except for 1998, the president's party has lost seats in either the House or the Senate in every off-year election held since 1934. But in 2002, the Republicans gained seats in both the House and Senate owing to President Bush's popularity and the public's worries about terrorism (see Table 10.3).

Presidential Character

Every president brings to the White House a distinctive personality; the way the White House is organized and run reflects that personality. Moreover, the public judges the president not only in terms of what he has accomplished but also in terms of its perception of his character. Thus personality plays a more important role in explaining the presidency than it does in explaining Congress.

Dwight Eisenhower brought an orderly, military style to the White House. He was accustomed to delegating authority and to having careful and complete staff work done for him by trained specialists. Though critics often accused him of having a bumbling, incoherent manner of speaking, in fact much of that was a public disguise—a strategy to avoid being pinned down in public on matters where he wished to retain freedom of action. His private papers reveal a very different Eisenhower—sharp, precise, deliberate.

John Kennedy brought a very different style to the presidency. He projected the image of a bold, articulate, and amusing leader who liked to surround himself with talented amateurs. Instead of clear, hierarchical lines of authority, there was a pattern of personal rule and an atmosphere of improvisation. Kennedy did not hesitate to call very junior subordinates directly and tell them what to do, bypassing the chain of command.

Lyndon Johnson was a master legislative strategist who had become majority leader of the Senate on the strength of his ability to persuade other politicians in face-to-face encounters. He was a consummate dealmaker who, having been in Washington for thirty years before becoming president, knew everybody and everything. As a result he tried to make every decision himself. But the style that served him well in political negotiations did not serve him well in speaking to the country at large, especially when trying to retain public support for the war in Vietnam.

Richard Nixon was a highly intelligent man with a deep knowledge of and interest in foreign policy coupled with a great suspicion of the media, his political rivals, and the federal bureaucracy. In contrast to Johnson, he disliked personal confrontations and tended to shield himself behind an elaborate staff system. Distrustful of the cabinet agencies, he tried first to centralize power in the White House and then to put into key cabinet posts former White House aides loyal to him. As with Johnson, his personality made it difficult for him to mobilize popular support. Eventually he was forced to resign under the threat of impeachment arising out of his role in the Watergate scandal.

Gerald Ford, before being appointed vice president, had spent his political life in Congress and was at home with the give-and-take, discussion-oriented procedures of that body. He was also a genial man who liked talking to people. Thus he preferred the circular to the pyramid system of White House organization. But this meant that many decisions were made in a disorganized fashion in which key people—and sometimes key problems—were not taken into account.

Jimmy Carter was an outsider in Washington and boasted of it. A former Georgia governor, he was determined not to be "captured" by Washington insiders. He also was a voracious reader with a wide range of interests and an appetite for detail. These dispositions led him to try to do many things and to do them personally. Like Ford, he began with a circular structure; unlike Ford, he based his decisions on reading countless memos and asking detailed questions. His advisers finally decided that he was trying to do too much in too great detail, and toward the end of his term he shifted to a pyramid structure.

Ronald Reagan was also an outsider, a former governor of California. But unlike Carter, he wanted to set the broad directions of his administration and leave the details to others. He gave wide latitude to subordinates and to cabinet officers, within the framework of an emphasis on lower taxes, less domestic spending, a military buildup, and a tough line with the Soviet Union. In the Iran-contra crisis, some of his subordinates let him down by doing a poor job of thinking through the secret exchange of arms for American hostages in the Middle East and by concealing from him the diversion of the profits from the arms sale to aid the civil war being waged by the contras in Nicaragua. A report on the affair by a presidential commission concluded that Reagan's management style had been too lax and remote. At the same time, he was a superb leader of public opinion, earning the nickname "The Great Communicator."

George H. W. Bush was, on paper, the best-prepared president since Richard Nixon. He had been a member of Congress, ambassador to China, director of the Central Intelligence Agency, and vice president of the United States. He was a close personal friend of many foreign leaders. These contacts and experiences were put to good use when he mobilized a coalition of nations to participate in Operation Desert Storm, the military operation that, with United Nations backing, ousted Iraqi troops from Kuwait. Despite his skill at one-on-one foreign diplomacy, he was unable to persuade Americans faced with an economic recession that he had a plan to get the nation moving again.

Bill Clinton ran for president as a centrist "new" Democrat, but once elected, he began governing as a liberal "old" Democrat. His first major initiative was a complex, expensive health-care plan that Congress largely ignored. When the Republicans gained control of Congress in 1994, Clinton returned to being a centrist, endorsing welfare reform, supporting uniforms for schoolchildren, and being photographed with the military and police officers. An extraordinary campaigner, he won reelection easily in 1996, but then his sexual affair with Monica Lewinsky (and possibly with several other women) was revealed. The grand jury investigating the matter believed he lied under oath and tampered with witnesses

President Barack Obama meets with Afghan President Hamid Karzai at the presidential palace in Kabul, Afghanistan, March 2010.

in an attempt to conceal his relationship with Lewinsky, a White House intern. This led to his being impeached by the House of Representatives, but the Senate did not convict him.

George W. Bush ran as a candidate interested in domestic issues and with little background in foreign affairs. His domestic argument was to favor "compassionate conservatism" that would help the poor without excessive regulation; in this respect, his view was different from Reagan's argument that "government was the problem." The attacks of September 11, 2001, changed his presidency to one preoccupied with fighting terrorism. He threw the Taliban out of Afghanistan and conquered Iraq and began the effort to install democratic governments in both places.

Barack Obama succeeded Bush in 2009. He was the first African American to win a major party's presidential nomination and only the third person elected to the presidency while a sitting U.S. Senator. After Harvard, he taught constitutional law part time at the University of Chicago. After entering politics and winning an Illinois State Senate seat, he was elected to the U.S. Senate in 2004. His electrifying speech at the 2004 Democratic National Convention catapulted him to national attention. He criticized Democratic presidential candidates who had supported military action against Iraq, and he campaigned in 2008 as the candidate of change and hope ("Yes we can!" was his most popular mantra). He came to office in January 2009 amid a global economic crisis that included devastating losses in America's real estate sector and financial markets. By mid-2010, he had proposed the largest budget in U.S. history and enacted plans for comprehensive health insurance.

The Power to Say No

Presidential character and skills are important, but a president also has a special bargaining chip: the power to say no. The Constitution gives the president the power to veto legislation. In addition, most presidents have asserted **executive privilege**—the right to withhold information Congress may want to obtain from him or his subordinates—and some presidents have tried to impound funds appropriated by Congress. These efforts by the president to say no are not only a way of blocking action but also a way of forcing Congress to bargain with him over the substance of policies.

Executive privilege *A presidential claim that he may withhold certain information from Congress.*

Veto

If a president disapproves of a bill passed by both houses of Congress, he may veto it in one of two ways. One is by sending a **veto message** to Congress within ten days explaining his objections; the other is by exercising a **pocket veto**, that is, by refusing to sign it within a ten-day period, during which time Congress adjourns. The Supreme Court ruled that a pocket veto can be used only just before Congress is about to adjourn at the end of its second session; it cannot be used if Congress merely recesses to take summer vacation or to permit its members to campaign during an off-year election.

A bill that is neither signed nor vetoed within ten days while Congress is still in session becomes a law automatically, without the president's approval. A bill that has been returned to Congress with a veto message can be passed over the president's objections if at least two-thirds of each house vote to override the veto. A bill that has been pocket-vetoed obviously must be reintroduced in the next session if Congress wants to press the matter.

The president must accept or reject the entire bill; unlike most governors, he cannot exercise a **line-item veto**, which rejects some provisions and accepts others. In 1996, Congress and the president agreed on a bill authorizing a line-item veto. Under it the president was able to veto certain provisions, except for those affecting entitlement spending and other politically sacrosanct items. Congress could overturn each such veto by a two-thirds vote. But in 1998, the Supreme Court declared the legislative effort to create a line-item veto to be unconstitutional.[6]

The veto power is a substantial one because Congress rarely has the votes to override. From George Washington through Bill Clinton, less than 4 percent of presidential vetoes have been overridden. (During at least the first five years of his presidency, George W. Bush never vetoed a single bill.) Often the vetoed legislation is revised by Congress and passed in a form suitable to the president. There is no tally of how often this happens, but it is frequent enough that both branches of government recognize that the veto, or even the threat of it, is part of an elaborate process of political negotiation in which the president has substantial powers.

Veto message *One of two ways for a president to disapprove a bill sent to him by Congress. The veto message must be sent to Congress within ten days after the president receives the bill.*

Pocket veto *One of two ways for a president to disapprove a bill sent to him by Congress. If the president does not sign the bill within ten days of his receiving it and Congress has adjourned within that time, the bill does not become law.*

Line-item veto *The power of an executive to veto some provisions in an appropriations bill while approving others. The president does not have the right to exercise a line-item veto and must approve or reject an entire appropriations bill.*

Executive Privilege

The Constitution says nothing about whether the president is obliged to divulge private communications between himself and his principal advisers, but presidents have acted as if they did have that privilege of confidentiality. The presidential claim is based (1) on the doctrine of the separation of powers, interpreted to mean that one branch of government does not have the right to inquire into the internal operations of another, and (2) on the principle that the president should be able to obtain confidential and candid information from subordinates, free of public scrutiny.

For almost two hundred years there was no challenge to the claim of presidential confidentiality, though Congress was never happy with it. But in 1973, during the Watergate scandal, the Supreme Court for the first time confronted the issue. The question was whether President Nixon could, by invoking executive privilege, deny a special prosecutor access to tape recordings of presidential conversations with his advisers. The Court ruled (8–0) that, although there might be a sound basis for the claim, especially where sensitive military or diplomatic matters are involved, there is no "absolute unqualified Presidential privilege of immunity from judicial process under all circumstances."[7] To admit otherwise would be to block the constitutionally defined function of the federal courts to decide criminal cases. Thus Nixon had to surrender the disputed tapes. During the investigation of President Clinton by Kenneth Starr, the independent counsel, the president's lawyers attempted to claim executive privilege for the Secret Service officers and government-paid lawyers advising the president, but the courts rejected these arguments.

Impoundment of Funds

Legislative veto
The rejection of a presidential or administrative-agency action by a vote of one or both houses of Congress without the consent of the president. In 1983, the Supreme Court declared the legislative veto to be unconstitutional.

From time to time, presidents have refused to spend money appropriated by Congress. The precedent for impounding funds goes back at least to Thomas Jefferson. But what has precedent is not thereby constitutional. The Constitution is silent on whether the president *must* spend the money Congress appropriates. The major test of the question came when President Nixon, hoping to reduce federal spending, impounded funds already appropriated by Congress. Congress responded by passing the Budget Reform Act of 1974 that, among other things, requires the president to spend all appropriated funds unless he first tells Congress what funds he wishes not to spend, and Congress, within forty-five days, agrees to delete the items. It is not clear, however, that this will settle the matter, especially because the Supreme Court has subsequently declared the **legislative veto**—on which the Budget Reform Act depends—unconstitutional.[8] Congress may have to rely instead on political pressure to get the money spent.

Signing Statements

Signing Statements
Written comments by the president about a bill he has just signed. Those that raise constitutional questions are controversial.

Since at least the times of James Monroe, the president has issued statements about bills he has just signed into law. These are called **signing statements** and have one or more of three purposes: to define vague terms in the bill, to rally people to support its implementation, or to challenge the constitutionality of it. It is only this third purpose that is controversial. Members of Congress are upset by what appears to be a presidential effort to block the enforcement of some part of the law. Bills have been introduced to block this practice, but none has passed. The Supreme Court has yet to speak on the issue.

But signing statements are not a recent invention, If we just count the number of those statements that raise constitutional issues that have been used since 1980, we find the following:

Ronald Reagan signed 86

George H. W. Bush signed 107

Bill Clinton signed 70

George W. Bush signed 118

Barack Obama, while running for president, said that he opposed the issuance of signing statements, but from the time he became president through 2009, he signed five that raised constitutional objections to laws he had just approved.

The President's Program

Imagine that you have just spent three or four years running for president, essentially giving the same speech over and over again. You have had no time to study the issues in any depth. To reach a large television audience, you have couched your ideas in rather simple—if not simple-minded—slogans. Your principal advisers are political aides, not legislative specialists.

You win. Now you must *be* president instead of just talking about it. Foreign governments and the stock market hang on your every word; soon you must make the State of the Union address and send an enormously complex budget to Congress. What will you do?

The Constitution merely directs you to recommend "such measures" as you judge "necessary and expedient" and to "take care that the laws be faithfully executed." And at one time an incoming president was not expected to do very much. Today, he must have something to say (and offer) to everybody.

Putting Together a Program

There are essentially two ways for a president to develop a program. Like President Carter, he can have a policy on almost everything, working endless hours trying to learn something about—and then state his position on—a large number of policies. Or, like President Reagan, he can concentrate on a few major initiatives or themes, leaving everything else to subordinates.

But even when a president has a governing philosophy, as did Reagan, he cannot risk plunging ahead on his own. Before he fully commits himself, he must judge public and congressional reactions to the program, often by leaking part of it to the press. Reagan, for example, floated as a **trial balloon** his ideas on Social Security and tax reform to test the popular reaction; so did his opponents in the bureaucracy. President Clinton, to his regret, kept the details of his health-care plan secret until it was published.

In addition to the risks of adverse reaction, the president faces three constraints on his ability to plan a program. First is the sheer limit on his time and attention span. Typically he must put in a ninety-hour week; even so he has great difficulty

Trial balloon *Information provided to the media by an anonymous public official as a way of testing the public reaction to a possible policy or appointment.*

keeping up with all the proposed legislation he is supposed to know and make decisions about, including four hundred to six hundred bills that Congress passes each year. Second is the unexpected crisis: All modern presidents have had to respond to major domestic or foreign crises, usually when they least expect them. And third is the fact that the federal government and most federal programs, as well as the federal budget, can be changed only marginally, except in special circumstances. The vast bulk of federal expenditures are beyond the president's control in any given year—the money must be spent whether he likes it or not. Many federal programs have sufficiently strong congressional or public support that they must be left intact or modified only slightly. This means that most federal employees can count on being secure in their jobs, whatever a president's views on the size of the bureaucracy.

The result of these constraints is that the president, at least in ordinary times, must be selective about what he wants. If he wants to get the most return on his limited stock of influence and prestige, he must invest it carefully in enterprises that promise substantial gains—in public benefits and political support—at reasonable cost. Each newly elected president tends to speak in terms of changing everything at once. But beneath the rhetoric (of a "New Frontier," a "Great Society," or a "New Covenant"), he must identify a few specific proposals on which he wishes to bet his resources, remembering to keep a substantial stock in reserve to handle the inevitable crises. In recent decades, events have required every president to devote a substantial part of his time and resources to two key issues: the state of the economy and foreign affairs. What he manages to do in addition to this depends on his personal views and his sense of what the nation, as well as his reelection, requires.

Measuring Success

There are two ways of measuring presidential success: by the proportion of bills the president submits to Congress that it approves, and by the proportion of the votes taken in Congress on which his position prevails. By the first method, the president usually wins less than half the time. By the second method (the line in Figure 10.2 on page 256), he does better—he is on the winning side perhaps three-fourths of the time. This latter measure is misleadingly high, however, because it ignores bills the president favors that do not even come up for a vote and because it counts those that he may only reluctantly support (with congressional amendments) after originally proposing them. (By contrast, in Great Britain, more than 90 percent of the prime minister's bills are passed by Parliament.) The most successful recent president was Lyndon Johnson; the least successful, Nixon.

Presidential Transitions

No president except Franklin Roosevelt has served more than two full terms and, since the ratification of the Twenty-second Amendment to the Constitution in 1951, no president will do so again. But more than tradition or the Constitution escorts the president from office. Only a minority of all the presidents since George Washington have been elected to a second term. Four died in office during their first term. But the remainder either did not seek or more often could not obtain reelection. Of the eight presidents who died in office, four were assassinated (Lincoln, Garfield, McKinley, and Kennedy). At least six other presidents were the objects of unsuccessful assassination attempts.

The presidents who served two or more terms fall into certain periods, such as the Founding (Washington, Jefferson, Madison, Monroe) or wartime (Lincoln, Wilson, Franklin Roosevelt, Lyndon Johnson), or happened to hold office in especially tranquil times (Monroe, McKinley, Eisenhower, and Clinton). When the country was deeply divided, as during the years before and after the Civil War, it was a rare president who was reelected. Reagan was the first president since Eisenhower to serve two full terms in the White House.

The Vice President

Eight times a vice president has become president because of the death of a predecessor. It happened first to John Tyler, who became president in 1841 when William Henry Harrison died peacefully after only one month in office. Tyler and the country faced a substantial question: Was he simply the acting president and thus a kind of caretaker until a new president was elected, or was he *president* in every sense of the word? Despite criticism and what might perhaps have been the Framers' contrary intention, Tyler decided on the latter course and was confirmed in that decision by an act of Congress. Since then the vice president has automatically become president, in title and powers, on the death or resignation of the occupant of the White House.

But if vice presidents frequently acquire the presidency because of death, they rarely acquire it by election. Except for John Adams and Thomas Jefferson,[9] only three vice presidents have become president by election without their predecessor dying in office: Martin Van Buren (Jackson's vice president) in 1836, Richard Nixon (Eisenhower's vice president) in 1968, and George H. W. Bush (Reagan's vice president) in 1988. No one who wishes to become president should assume that the vice presidency is the best way to get there.

The office is just what so many of its occupants have said it is: a rather empty job. The vice president's only official task is to preside over the Senate and to vote in case of a tie; his leadership powers in the Senate are weak. From time to time, presidents have found relatively minor tasks for their vice presidents, but essentially the vice president can do little more than endorse whatever the president does, and wait. But Vice Presidents Al Gore (in the Clinton administration) and Dick Cheney (in the Bush administration) have played large roles in directing the government.

Problems of Succession

Since the time of John Tyler, it has been clear that if the president dies in office, the vice president is sworn in as president. But two questions remain: What if the president falls seriously ill but does not die? And if the vice president steps up, who then becomes the new vice president?

The first question has arisen on a number of occasions. After President Garfield was shot in 1881, he lingered through the summer before dying. Woodrow

Wilson collapsed from a stroke and was a virtual recluse for seven months in 1919 and an invalid for the rest of his term. Eisenhower had three serious illnesses while in office; Reagan was shot and seriously wounded.

The second question has arisen on eight occasions when the vice president became president owing to the death of the incumbent. In these cases no elected person was available to succeed the new president should he die in office.

The Twenty-fifth Amendment, ratified in 1967, addressed both problems. First, it allows the vice president to serve as acting president in the case of presidential disability. *Disability* can be declared by either the president himself or the vice president and a majority of the cabinet; the latter case is subject to a two-thirds vote of Congress. Second, it requires a vice president who has succeeded to the presidency to name a new vice president, subject to confirmation by a majority in Congress. Whenever there is no vice president, an earlier 1947 law still applies: Next in line for the presidency are the Speaker of the House, the president pro tempore of the Senate, and then the fifteen cabinet officers, beginning with the secretary of state.

The disability problem has not arisen as a major issue since the adoption of the amendment, but the succession problem has. In 1973, Vice President Spiro Agnew resigned, having pleaded no contest to criminal charges. President Nixon nominated Gerald Ford as vice president, who, after extensive hearings, was confirmed and sworn in. Then, on August 9, 1974, Nixon resigned the presidency—the first man to do so—and Ford became president. Ford nominated as his vice president Nelson Rockefeller, who was confirmed by both houses of Congress—again, after extensive hearings—and was sworn in on December 19, 1974. For the first time in history, the nation had as its two principal executive officers men elected to neither the presidency nor the vice presidency. It is a measure of the legitimacy of the Constitution that this arrangement caused no crisis in public opinion.

Impeachment

There is one other way—besides death, disability, or resignation—by which a president can leave office before his term expires, and that is by impeachment. Not only the president and vice president but also all "civil officers of the United States" can be removed from office by being impeached and convicted. As a practical matter, civil officers—cabinet officers, bureau chiefs, and the like—are never impeached because the president can remove them at any time and usually will if their behavior makes them a serious political liability. Federal judges, who serve during good behavior and are constitutionally independent of the president and Congress, have been subject to impeachment more frequently than anyone else.

An **impeachment** is like an indictment in a criminal trial. It is a set of charges against somebody voted by (in this case) a majority in the House of Representatives. To be removed from office, the impeached officer must be *convicted* by a two-thirds vote of the Senate, which sits as a court, hears the evidence, and makes its decision under whatever rules it wishes to adopt. Article II, Section 4, of the Constitution specifies "treason, bribery, or other high crimes and misdemeanors" as impeachable offenses. But no clear definition exists of what acts do (or do not) qualify as high crimes and misdemeanors, leaving Congress to decide as it wishes.

Impeachment *An accusation against a high federal official charging him or her with "treason, bribery, or other high crimes and misdemeanors." An impeachment requires a majority vote in the House of Representatives. To be removed from office, the impeached official must be tried before the Senate and convicted by a vote of two-thirds of the members present.*

Most scholars, however, agree that the charge must involve something illegal or unconstitutional, not just unpopular. Thirteen persons have been impeached by the House, and four have been convicted by the Senate. The last conviction was in 1986, when a federal judge was removed from office for lack of integrity.

Only two presidents have been impeached—Andrew Johnson in 1868 and Bill Clinton in 1998—but Richard Nixon would surely have been impeached had he not resigned in 1974. The Senate did not convict either Johnson or Clinton by the necessary two-thirds vote. The case against Johnson was entirely political—radical Republicans, who wished to punish the South after the Civil War, were angry at Johnson's soft policy toward the South and found a flimsy legal excuse to justify impeachment.

The case against Clinton was more serious. The House Judiciary Committee, relying on the report of independent counsel Kenneth Starr, charged Clinton with perjury (lying under oath about his sexual affair with Monica Lewinsky), obstruction of justice (trying to block the Starr investigation), and abuse of power (making false written statements to the House committee). The vote in the committee was strictly along party lines and that in the House nearly so. Half of the Senate voted to convict Clinton, but that vote—mostly along party lines—fell well short of the necessary two-thirds.

The problem of a president dying or becoming disabled while in office is not remote—succession has occurred nine times and disability at least twice. The first and fundamental problem is to make the office legitimate. That was the great task George Washington set himself, and that was the substantial accomplishment of his successors. Despite bitter and sometimes violent partisan and sectional strife, beginning almost immediately after Washington stepped down, presidential succession has always occurred peacefully, without a military coup or a political plot. For centuries, in the bygone times of kings as well as in the present times of dictators and juntas, peaceful succession has been a rare phenomenon among the nations of the world. Many critics of the Constitution believed in 1787 that peaceful succession would not happen in the United States either; somehow, the president would connive to hold office for life or to handpick his successor. Their predictions were wrong, though their fears were understandable.

The President and Public Policy

The President Versus Congress

The president and Congress are rivals, even when the same political party controls both offices. The rivalry arises from two sources. First, the Constitution requires the two branches to share powers; in the effort to achieve that sharing, each branch will try to serve its own needs. The president wants to control the bureaucracy, but Congress wants to control it as well. The president wants to create a budget, but Congress insists on changing it to suit its needs. The president wants to appoint judges who match his ideological interests, but the Senate wants to confirm judges whom its members like.

Second, the president and Congress serve two different political constituencies. The chief executive is elected by electors chosen by all of the people, especially those in the largest states; Congress is elected by local constituencies (in the House) and individual states (in the Senate). The president and senators from large states feel pressure from national interest groups, but House members feel the demands of small local groups. The president views a nation that is one-eighth black and seven-eighths white, but many House members come from districts that are almost all black or all white.

How these tensions are managed can be seen in foreign and domestic affairs.

The President and Foreign Affairs

Most of the examples of the exercise of great presidential power given at the beginning of this chapter came from the area of foreign affairs. Because the president is commander in chief of the armed forces, because he appoints and receives ambassadors, and because Congress recognizes that it cannot negotiate with other nations, the president tends to be stronger in foreign than in domestic policy.

Until well into this century, and with only a few exceptions, foreign policy was often made and usually carried out by the secretary of state. As America became a permanent world power beginning with World War II, the president personally has become more deeply involved in managing our foreign relations. Franklin Roosevelt, John Kennedy, Lyndon Johnson, and Richard Nixon all played major roles in foreign policy, and accordingly, the power and stature of the secretary of state waned during their administrations. To ensure their control over foreign policy, Kennedy, Johnson, and Nixon brought into the White House a national security adviser who was often far more influential than the secretary of state. For example, when Nixon was getting ready to reopen diplomatic relations with the People's Republic of China (after decades during which we did not recognize that country), he gave the job to his national security adviser, Henry Kissinger, who did not even tell the secretary of state, William Rogers, what was going on until shortly before the public announcement. Later on, Kissinger replaced Rogers as secretary of state while still retaining his White House job as national security adviser, thereby making certain that no new White House staffer would challenge his power.

Four major agencies support the president's conduct of foreign affairs. The Department of State is the oldest. Located in an area of the capital known as "Foggy Bottom," it is organized by geographic areas and staffed with career foreign-service officers. In Washington it has the reputation for representing the interests of foreign nations to this country as much as it represents American interests to *other* countries.

A major rival to the State Department is the Defense Department. Historically the military did not play much of a role in making foreign policy. But today we have military alliances with and provide military aid to many nations, and hundreds of thousands of military personnel are stationed abroad. As a result, the Department of Defense (often referred to as DOD) has become a major influence in making foreign policy, especially if the secretary of defense is personally close to the president. The DOD, located in the Pentagon building across the Potomac River from downtown Washington, has its own miniature state department built into its organization. Headed by the assistant secretary of defense for international security affairs, this unit provides advice on foreign policy to the secretary of defense, who often becomes a major rival of the secretary of state for influence with the president.

The Central Intelligence Agency (CIA), based in Langley, Virginia, has intelligence officers serving abroad in scores of countries as well as intelligence analysts at work at headquarters. The director of the CIA has the job of keeping the president informed on the actions, intentions, and capabilities of foreign powers. But giving information is not easily kept separate from giving advice, and so a strong DCI (such as William Casey, DCI for President Reagan) can be a major influence on foreign policy. Moreover, the CIA often carries out operations abroad that are referred to as "covert," though many of them—such as providing aid to the rebels fighting against the Sandinista government in Nicaragua and against the Soviet army in Afghanistan—have hardly been secret. Planning and implementing these operations deeply involve the CIA in the making of foreign policy.

When the 9/11 Commission (officially, the National Commission on Terrorist Attacks Upon the United States) issued its report, it recommended that a new post, the Director of National Intelligence (DNI) be created that would oversee the DCI and the heads of all other intelligence agencies. In late 2004, Congress approved and President Bush signed this proposal into law. It is still unclear just how much influence the DNI will have over the CIA, the FBI, and Defense Department intelligence agencies.

David Furst/AFP/Getty Images

U.S. Army soldiers patrol the mountains along the Afghanistan-Pakistan border in an effort to disrupt Taliban safe havens in the region.

The fourth organization, though the smallest, is perhaps the most influential. The National Security Council (NSC) is a committee, created by law and chaired by the president, on which sit (by law) the vice president and the secretaries of state and defense. The Director of National Intelligence (DNI) and the chairman of the Joint Chiefs of Staff are regular advisers to the NSC. Assisting the council is a staff headed by the national security adviser. Major foreign-policy issues are discussed by the NSC. The staff summarizes these discussions, carries out tasks assigned to it by the president, filters and manages the foreign-policy paperwork flowing to the president, and drafts decision memoranda for the president to sign. Though few in number, these staff people occupy a key position in the foreign-policy system because they chiefly decide what the president will read and write on many foreign-policy issues.

Because the American people look to the president for leadership in foreign affairs and tend to support him in most foreign-policy crises, they may think he is more powerful than he actually is. Not only is he checked by disagreements among his principal advisers, but Congress plays an important role in setting the limits of presidential action. The Senate must confirm all ambassadorial appointments and ratify all treaties; Congress must approve all military spending; and only Congress can declare war. In the original draft of the Constitution, Congress was given the power to "make war," but this was changed, presumably to allow the president to repel a sudden attack without waiting for Congress to assemble.

Since the early 1970s, Congress has tried to claim additional powers over foreign policy. Congress in 1973 passed (over President Nixon's veto) the War Powers Act. This law, which every president from Nixon to George W. Bush has claimed to be unconstitutional, places the following restrictions on the president's ability to use military force:

- He must report in writing to Congress within forty-eight hours after he introduces U.S. troops into areas where hostilities have occurred or are imminent.
- Within sixty days after troops are sent into hostile situations, Congress must, by declaration of war or other specific statutory authorization, provide for the continuation of hostile action by U.S. troops.
- If Congress fails to provide such authorization, the president must withdraw the troops (unless Congress has been prevented from meeting as a result of an armed attack).
- If Congress passes a concurrent resolution (which the president may not veto) directing the removal of U.S. troops, the president must comply.

Sometimes the president has complied with the notification procedure; other times he has not. President Reagan sent marines into Lebanon and the army into Grenada but did not officially report this action as required by the War Powers Act; Congress itself authorized the marine deployment but took no action on the Grenada case. Many commentators believe that the act as written is politically unenforceable: If the president takes a popular action, the people will rally around him and Congress will have little voice in the matter. In practice, almost every use of force by an American president has, in the short run, acquired popular support, even when the effort failed (as with President Carter's efforts to rescue American hostages in Iran).

Congress created two committees, one in the House and one in the Senate, to oversee the CIA. By law the president must keep each committee "fully and currently informed" on all intelligence activities, including covert operations. The committees do not have the power to disapprove of these activities, but they are still an important check on presidential authority because they pass on the CIA budget and can make public any activities they feel are questionable.

Ultimately, however, the decisive check on presidential authority is public opinion. In general, the public will support the president in most foreign-policy actions, even those that backfire. The American people tend to "rally 'round the flag" when the president takes a bold foreign-policy step. When President Carter sent troops to rescue American hostages held captive in Iran, his standing in public opinion went up even though the mission was unsuccessful. When President Reagan sent troops into Grenada, his stock also rose, and some of the few congressional leaders who had criticized the move soon recanted so as not to appear to oppose a popular presidential move. When George H. W. Bush sent U.S. troops (along with many from our allies) to oust the Iraqi army from Kuwait, his popularity soared. When President George W. Bush sent troops to Afghanistan and Iraq, there was overwhelming public support, at least initially.

When the party identification of the president changes, we get a chance to see how powerfully foreign realities affect the incumbent. During the election, Barack Obama, a Democrat, promised that he would close the prison camp at Guantanamo, amend the Patriot Act that gives federal agencies new authority to investigate terrorists, change the Foreign Intelligence Surveillance Act (FISA) that sets the policy on government eavesdropping, start bringing American troops home from Iraq by March 2008, and withdraw all combat troops out by August 2010.

After he took office, President Obama found out that he could not close Guantanamo as soon as he wanted because it was hard to find places where many prisoners there could be sent. He allowed the Patriot Act and FISA to be renewed without any important changes. Despite his announced opposition to the surge, he kept American forces in Iraq well into 2010. He also authorized sending more troops to Afghanistan. Foreign and military policies, as all presidents discover, have a compelling quality that makes quick changes difficult.

The President and Economic Policy

If the American people are supportive and forbearing with respect to the president's conduct of foreign policy, they are critical and quick-tempered regarding his conduct of economic policy. Voters, having no way to judge for themselves, will pretty much take the president's word when he describes U.S. interests abroad. But these same voters, having firsthand knowledge of unemployment, inflation, farm prices, and foreign competition for jobs, will hold the president strictly accountable for the condition of the economy. Elections are only occasionally won or lost over foreign-policy questions, but they are frequently won or lost over economic ones. George H. W. Bush knows this all too well: The stalled economy cost him his reelection in 1992.

This makes life difficult for the president because he has far less control over economic policy than he does over foreign policy. For one thing, nobody really knows what makes the economy tick. Professional economists disagree over what policy we should follow and are not very good at predicting economic conditions even six months in advance.

For another, authority over economic policy is more widely dispersed in the government than is authority over foreign policy. The president gets economic advice from three key subordinates, but none of these has much direct influence over how the economy performs. The director of the Office of Management and Budget (OMB) tells the president how much the government is spending and taking in from taxes and helps him cut or increase the amounts some executive branch agencies are spending. But OMB and the president have little influence over most government spending because nearly three-fourths of it is politically (and perhaps legally) uncontrollable: payments to retired and disabled people under Social Security, payments of benefits to veterans and others, payments to military contractors for equipment and supplies they have agreed to furnish—all these and more are virtually impossible to change from one year to the next. This means that a president who wishes to cut spending must find his cuts in the one-fourth of the budget that is controllable. And every item in this part of the budget is fiercely defended by agencies, interest groups, and congressional subcommittees.

The president also gets advice from the Council of Economic Advisers (CEA), and especially from its chairman. This group carries out important economic studies, mostly of high quality, but the limits of economic knowledge are such that a president can ignore such advice, or find economists who give him the advice he wants to hear, without too much difficulty. President Reagan's first CEA

Ben Bernanke, chairman of the Federal Reserve Board.

chairman, Harvard economist Martin Feldstein, regularly warned of what he felt were the dangers of a large federal deficit (that is, of the government spending more than it took in from taxes), but his warnings were largely ignored and in time he resigned.

The secretary of the treasury also gives advice that usually reflects the concerns of bankers here and abroad who worry about interest rates and the value of the dollar relative to that of other currencies (the euro, the British pound, or the Japanese yen). Unlike the director of OMB or the chairman of the CEA, the secretary of the treasury has some important powers, such as the ability to buy and sell foreign currencies in an effort to influence the value of the dollar.

Perhaps the most important agency affecting economic policy is the Federal Reserve Board, but unlike the first three, it is not directly under presidential control. "The Fed," as it is known, consists of seven persons who are appointed by the president and confirmed by the Senate and who serve for fourteen-year terms. One member is designated chairman for a term of four years. In theory, and to a large degree in practice, the Fed is independent of both the president and Congress. Its powers are very great, so great that many people regard the chairman of the Fed as the second most influential person in Washington.

The Federal Reserve Board influences both the supply of money and the price of money (interest rates) in three ways. First, it buys and sells government securities (notes and bonds issued by the Treasury Department in order to borrow money). When it buys securities, the Fed writes a check to the Treasury Department, which cashes the check and uses the money to pay government bills. But unlike the situation when you and I write checks, the Fed does not have any money in its bank account. When it writes a check, it is actually *creating* money. (Conversely, when the Fed sells Treasury securities, it is taking money out of circulation.) Second, the Fed regulates the amount of money that member banks of the Federal Reserve System must keep on hand as a reserve to back up its customers' deposits. The higher the reserve requirement, the less money the bank can lend out. Third, the Fed sets the interest rate it charges banks that wish to borrow money from it. The higher this rate, the more costly it is for banks to get additional funds and thus the higher the interest rates they charge their customers.

All of these agencies, together with Congress, come together in the annual fight over the federal budget. Under the current procedure, this is what is supposed to happen:

- *First Monday in February:* The president submits his budget request to Congress. (For months before this, OMB has been compiling and adjusting budget requests from the separate departments and agencies.)
- *February and March:* House and Senate budget committees discuss the president's proposed budget.
- *April 15:* Congress is supposed to pass a **budget resolution** that states the total amount of allowable spending. Within the overall budget amount, there are supposed to be *caps* on total spending in four areas: defense, foreign aid, entitlements (such as Medicare), and discretionary spending (most domestic programs).

Budget resolution
A proposal submitted by the House and Senate budget committees to their respective chambers recommending a total budget ceiling and a ceiling for each of several spending areas (such as health or defense) for the current fiscal year. These budget resolutions are intended to guide the work of each legislative committee as it decides what to spend in its area.

Any spending above these caps must be paid for by an equal reduction in spending in some other program in the same cap area.

- *May and June:* Congress is supposed to act on thirteen appropriations bills that provide money to the departments and agencies. The total amount of money these bills provide is not supposed to exceed the amount in the budget resolution.
- *Summer:* President signs or vetoes these appropriations bills.
- *October 1:* The new fiscal year starts.

Continuing resolution *A congressional enactment that provides funds to continue government operations in the absence of an agreed-upon budget.*

Budget deficit *A situation in which the government spends more money than it takes in from taxes and fees.*

Budget surplus *A situation in which the government takes in more money than it spends.*

Having read the word *supposed* several times, you probably have guessed that things don't always work this way. And they don't. Congress may, and often does, miss these deadlines. The president and Congress may disagree over how much should be spent, as was often the case during the Reagan, Clinton, and both Bush administrations. The result of such a disagreement is that the government has no budget on October 1. (When that occurs, Congress passes a set of **continuing resolutions** that allows the government to stay in business and pay its bills on the basis of how much it had to spend in the previous year.)

Haunting this entire process is the specter of the budget deficit. The **budget deficit** is the shortfall between what the government takes in from taxes and fees and what it spends. The total *national debt* is the accumulation since 1789 of all of the annual deficits, less whatever may have been paid back as a result of running a **budget surplus** in some years. The government covers its debt by borrowing money, which it does by selling Treasury bonds that pay interest.

Politicians say they don't like deficits, but for decades they did little to curb them. The reason is simple—those who want to cut the deficit are divided between those who want to raise taxes and those who want to cut spending. The tax raisers and spending cutters rarely agree. After President George W. Bush took office in 2001, there was a sharp debate in Congress over whether tax rates should be reduced, as he proposed, or kept at their present levels. Bush argued that because the budget had a surplus, giving unneeded money back to the people was the right thing to do; Democrats, by contrast, argued that the extra money would be needed in the years ahead to prevent a new deficit from occurring. The tax cuts were passed, but were made temporary, expiring around 2010.

President Obama has promised to end them for people making over $250,000 a year, but as of mid-2010 no law on this matter had been passed.

The entire federal system for making economic policy was put to the test with the deep recession that began toward the end of President Bush's term and continued into President Obama's term. It was thought to be the worst since the Great Depression of 1929. Both presidents were preoccupied by it, but it was never obvious what policy changes would restore the economy to good health. The recession was the result of a perfect storm:

- Banks gave mortgages to people who could not afford them
- Government enterprises recklessly insured the loans
- Securities were sold that combined good and bad mortgages
- Lots of people went into debt buying houses they could not afford
- When people did not make payments on their mortgages, many banks faced bankruptcy

So What?

In view of the president's important role in foreign and economic policy, nobody needs to know why he is important. If you wonder why you are studying the presidency in this textbook, you haven't being paying attention to current affairs. Indeed, the presidency is so important that most Americans revere the office even when they do not like who occupies it.

- The federal government tried everything to end the recession, but no one was sure which of these things worked;
- February 2008: Checks were sent out to taxpayers to stimulate demand, but most people did not spend the money.
- October 2008: A program (TARP) was created to invest government money supporting troubled financial institutions and two auto makers (GM and Chrysler).
- February 2009: The American Recovery and Reinvestment Act (ARRA) was passed to funnel $787 billion into helping the unemployed and paying for long-term investments.
- The Federal Reserve Board cut interest rates until they were close to zero and found ways of adding money to the economy.

No one knows by how much any of these programs helped matters. No doubt ARRA money sent to unemployed workers helped them, but the long-term investments it authorized may not have any effect for years. The Fed kept many businesses alive but created so much money that there is a risk of inflation in our future.

SUMMARY

A president, though chosen directly by the people, has less power than a British prime minister, even though the latter depends on the support of his or her party in Parliament. The separation of powers in the American system means that a president, however personally popular he may be, must deal with a political competitor—Congress—in setting policy and managing the executive branch.

The constitutional basis of presidential power is modest; the great growth in that power since the 1930s has resulted from the growth in the size and scope of the federal government, the increased importance of foreign affairs, and the president's enhanced ability to communicate directly with the people through radio and television.

Every president can depend on some support from his party's members in Congress, but not enough to guarantee success—even when his party is in the majority in both houses (a rare event in the last thirty or so years). To increase his power, the president depends on personal popularity and on the bargaining power he has by virtue of his ability to veto bills.

In foreign affairs the president has substantial power and, in a crisis, popular support. But Congress has reasserted some of its powers by bringing the CIA under congressional scrutiny and by passing the War Powers Act.

In economic policy the president has less power, but the public expects more from him. Elections often turn on economic issues, yet the president rarely has the knowledge, advice, or power to shape the economy to his liking. Congress is an especially important rival in this area because it controls the power of the purse.

RECONSIDERING THE ENDURING QUESTIONS

1. Did the Founding Fathers want the president to be stronger or weaker than Congress?

While the Founders desired "energy in the executive," they expected Congress to be the first branch of government because of its ability to approve expenditures, confirm high appointments, and pass laws over the president's veto. For well over a century, Congress *was* the leading branch except in periods of crisis, but starting in the 1930s, the presidency became a somewhat more powerful branch.

2. Does character influence how the president does his job?

Of course, but it is only one of several factors at work. Equally important is how popular the president is with the public and the size of his party's majority (if he has one) in Congress. Presidents Reagan and Clinton were very popular, but in their second terms they did not get much done in Congress. Congress and the White House are often enemies, and though presidential character makes a difference, it is usually not decisive.

3. Should we abolish the electoral college?

Most Americans think we should, but most probably do not know the consequences of such a change. The system strengthens federalism, and hence the power of the states, and helps maintain a two-party system. With direct elections, we would have more, and more powerful, third parties and possibly the kind of weak coalition politics one sees in Italy and Israel.

Online Resources: The Presidency

 CourseMate

- White House: www.whitehouse.gov
  www.lib.umich.edu/govdocs/fedprs
- Presidential biographies, speeches, agencies: http://govinfo.ucsd.edu/pres.html

Suggested Readings

General

Barber, James David. *The Presidential Character,* 3d ed. Englewood Cliffs, N.J.: Prentice-Hall, 1985. Analyzes how a president's personality evolves and shapes his conduct in office.

Corwin, Edward S. *The President: Office and Powers,* 5th ed. New York: New York University Press, 1984. Historical, constitutional, and legal development of the office.

Jones, Charles O. *Passage to the Presidency.* Washington, D.C.: Brookings Institution, 1998. Insightful account of how four presidents—Nixon, Carter, Reagan, and Clinton—moved from the campaign to the presidency.

King, Gary, and Lyn Ragsdale. *The Elusive Executive.* Washington, D.C.: Congressional Quarterly Press, 1988. Compilation of and commentary about statistics on the presidency.

Neustadt, Richard E. *Presidential Power: The Politics of Leadership,* rev. ed. New York: Wiley, 1976. How presidents try to acquire and hold political power in the competitive world of official Washington, by a man who has been both a scholar and an insider.

On Particular Modern Presidents

FRANKLIN D. ROOSEVELT

Burns, James MacGregor. *Roosevelt: The Lion and the Fox.* New York: Harcourt Brace, 1956.

Leuchtenberg, William E. *Franklin D. Roosevelt and the New Deal, 1932–1940.* New York: Harper & Row, 1963.

HARRY S. TRUMAN

McCullough, David. *Truman.* New York: Simon & Schuster, 1992.

DWIGHT D. EISENHOWER

Greenstein, Fred I. *The Hidden-Hand Presidency: Eisenhower as Leader.* New York: Basic Books, 1982.

JOHN F. KENNEDY

Paper, Lewis J. *The Promise and the Performance: The Leadership of John F. Kennedy.* New York: Crown, 1975.

Sorenson, Theodore M. *Kennedy.* New York: Harper & Row, 1965.

LYNDON B. JOHNSON

Evans, Rowland, and Robert Novak. *Lyndon B. Johnson: The Exercise of Power.* New York: New American Library, 1968.

Kearns, Doris. *Lyndon Johnson and the American Dream.* New York: Harper & Row, 1976.

RICHARD M. NIXON

Ambrose, Stephen E. *Nixon—The Education of a Politician, 1913–1962.* New York: Simon and Schuster, 1987.

JIMMY CARTER

Bourne, Peter G. *Jimmy Carter.* New York: Scribner, 1997.

RONALD REAGAN

Cannon, Lou. *President Reagan.* New York: Simon & Schuster, 1991.

GEORGE H. W. BUSH

Parmet, Herbert C. *George Bush.* New York: Scribner, 1997.

BILL CLINTON

Klein, Joe. *The Natural: The Misunderstood Presidency of Bill Clinton.* New York: Doubleday, 2002.

11 The Bureaucracy

ENDURING QUESTIONS

1. Why did the bureaucracy become known as the "fourth branch" of American government?

2. How many people work for the federal government?

3. What can be done to improve bureaucratic performance?

Bureaucracy *A large, complex organization composed of appointed officials. The departments and agencies of the U.S. government make up the federal bureaucracy.*

There is probably not a man or woman in the United States who has not, at some time or other, complained about "the bureaucracy." Your letter was slow in getting to Aunt Minnie? The Internal Revenue Service took months to send you your tax refund? The Defense Department paid $435 for a hammer? The Occupational Safety and Health Administration told you that you installed the wrong kind of portable toilets for your farm workers? The "bureaucracy" is to blame.

For most people and politicians, *bureaucracy* is a pejorative implying waste, confusion, red tape, and rigidity. But for scholars—and even for bureaucrats—*bureaucracy* is a word with a neutral, technical meaning. A **bureaucracy** is a large, complex organization composed of appointed officials. By *complex* we mean

278

Ed Kashi/Corbis

that authority is divided among several managers; no one person is able to make all the decisions. A large corporation is a bureaucracy; so are a big university and a government agency. With its sizable staff, even Congress has become, to some degree, a bureaucracy.

Distinctiveness of the American Bureaucracy

Bureaucratic government has become an obvious feature of all modern societies, democratic and nondemocratic. In the United States, however, four aspects of our constitutional system and political traditions give to the bureaucracy and its operations a distinctive character. First, political authority over the bureaucracy is shared between the presidency and Congress—with its many committees and subcommittees—so that every senior appointed official has at least two masters. This divided authority encourages bureaucrats to play one branch of government against the other and to make heavy use of the media. All this is unknown in nations with parliamentary governments, like Great Britain, where the prime minister and cabinet control the bureaucracy.

Second, most federal agencies share their functions with related agencies in state and local government. Though some federal agencies deal directly with the people (for example, the Internal Revenue Service, the Federal Bureau of Investigation, and the Postal Service), many concerned with such matters as education, health, housing, and employment work with other organizations at state levels of government. In France, by contrast, such programs are centrally run with little or no control exercised by local governments.

Third, the institutions and traditions of American life, especially since the 1960s, have led to an expansion of personal rights. The defense of rights and claims, through lawsuits as well as political action, is now given central importance. A government agency in this country operates under closer public scrutiny and with a greater prospect of court challenges than in almost any other nation.

Fourth, the scope as well as the style of bureaucratic government differs. In most Western European nations, the government owns and operates large sectors of the economy. Publicly operated enterprises account for about 12 percent of all employment in parts of Europe but less than 3 percent in the United States.[1] The U.S. government, however, regulates privately owned enterprises to a degree not found in many other countries.

The Growth of the Bureaucracy

The Constitution did not mention departments and bureaus, and it made scarcely any provision for an administrative system other than to give the president the power, subject to the Senate's advice and consent, to appoint officials.

A crucial issue was decided in the First Congress of 1789. While considering a bill to create the Department of State, both houses debated long and heatedly over whether appointed officials could be removed by the president alone. At stake was the locus of power in what was to become the bureaucracy. Opponents wanted officials to be removable only with the Senate's consent. James Madison, who spoke for the Washington administration, argued that without the unfettered right of removal, the president would not be able to control his subordinates and thus would be unable to discharge his constitutional obligation to "take care that the laws be faithfully executed." By very narrow margins, Madison's view won (in the Senate, a tie vote had to be broken, in favor of the president, by Vice President Adams). The Department of State, and all cabinet departments subsequently created, would be run by people removable by the president.

That did not resolve the question of who would really control the bureaucracy, however. Congress retained the right to appropriate money, to investigate the administration, and to shape the laws that would be executed by the administration—more than ample power to challenge any president who claimed to have sole authority over his subordinates. And many members of Congress expected that the cabinet departments, even though headed by people removable by the president, would report to Congress.

Bureaucracy Before the New Deal Era

The national government in Washington was at first minuscule. The State Department started with only nine employees; the War Department did not have eighty civilian employees until 1801. Only the Treasury Department, concerned with collecting taxes and finding ways to pay the public debt, had much power, and only the Post Office Department provided any significant service.

Small as the bureaucracy was, men struggled, often bitterly, over who would be appointed to it. From Washington's day to modern times, presidents have found making appointments one of their most important and difficult tasks. Bureaucratic appointments affected how the laws were interpreted, how effectively the public business would be discharged, and how strong the political party in power would be. And as John Adams remarked, every appointment creates one ingrate and ten enemies.

Congress was the dominant branch of government during most of this period, and so congressional preferences often controlled the appointment of officials. This meant that appointments were generally made with an eye to rewarding the local supporters of members of Congress or building up local party organizations—in a word, on the basis of political patronage. After the Civil War the patronage system became a major issue, galvanizing various reform movements that aimed to purify politics and raise the competence of the public service. These demands became reality in 1881 after Charles Giteau assassinated President James Garfield, who had denied Giteau a diplomatic post. This murder created public demand for reform, and in 1883 the Pendleton Act was passed, establishing a Civil Service Commission, and open, nonpartisan tests to select bureaucrats began.

Many of the abuses that reformers complained about were real, but patronage served some useful purposes. The president could expect that his subordinates would be reasonably supportive of his policies, and he could use patronage as leverage on members of Congress. It also enabled party organizations to be built up to perform the necessary functions of nominating candidates and mobilizing voters.

Meanwhile there were more and more jobs to fight over. From 1816 to 1861, the number of federal employees increased eightfold, largely through the expansion of the Post Office.[2] The great watershed in bureaucratic development, however, was the Civil War, when many new officials were hired. The war revealed the federal government's administrative weakness and spurred reformers' demands for a better civil service. Finally, the war was followed by rapid industrialization and the emergence of a national economy. The effects of these developments could no longer be managed by state governments acting alone.

More than 200,000 new federal employees were added from 1861 to 1901, many of them in new agencies created to deal with the new national economy, such as the Pension Office; the Departments of Agriculture, Labor, and Commerce; and the National Bureau of Standards. These agencies had one thing in common: Their role was to serve—to do research, gather statistics, pass out benefits—but not to regulate. Not until the Interstate Commerce Commission (ICC) was created in 1887 did the federal government begin to regulate the economy (other than by managing the currency).

Late-nineteenth-century federal officials tended to avoid seeing themselves as regulators for several reasons. Belief in limited government and states' rights, and fear of concentrated discretionary power—the values that had shaped the Constitution—were still strong. And under the prevailing interpretation of the Constitution, only Congress had the power to regulate commerce among the states; any agency (such as the ICC) to which Congress might delegate its regulatory authority could function only if Congress first set down clear standards that would govern the agency's decisions. As late as 1935, the Supreme Court held that a regulatory agency could only apply the standards enacted by Congress. The Court's view was that the legislature may delegate its powers to neither the president nor an administrative agency.[3]

These restrictions on what administrators could do were set aside during wartime: World War I, for example, saw an enormous expansion of government regulation of the economy.[4] Extraordinary grants of power generally ended with the war, but some changes in the bureaucracy did not. From the Civil War to the Vietnam War, each major conflict brought a sharp increase in the number of the government's civilian (as well as military) employees. And though there was some reduction in personnel afterward, each war left a larger number of federal employees than before.[5]

A Change in Role

The bureaucracy as we know it is largely a product of two events: the Depression of the 1930s (and the concomitant New Deal programs of President Roosevelt) and World War II. Though many agencies have been added since, the basic features of the bureaucracy were set mainly as a result of changes in public attitudes and constitutional interpretation that occurred during these periods. The government was now expected to play an active role in dealing with economic and social problems. Reversing its earlier decisions, the Supreme Court began to uphold as constitutional those laws that permitted Congress merely to authorize agencies to make whatever decisions seemed necessary to solve a problem or to serve "the public interest."[6]

World War II was the first occasion during which the government made heavy use of federal income taxes—on individuals and corporations—to finance its activities. Income taxes had been small between 1913 (when they were first

Figure 11.1   The Growth of the Bureaucracy

The federal bureaucracy has not grown in total size—there are about the same number of civilian employees today as there were in 1970—but there has been an explosive growth in the number of political appointees at the top who try to run it. Between 1960 and 1992, the number of top political appointees rose from 451 to 2,393, an increase of 430 percent.

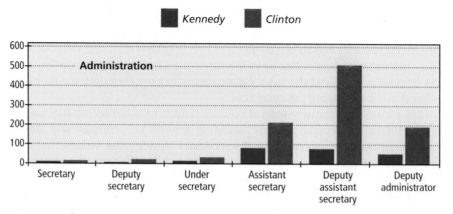

Source: Paul C. Light, *Thickening Government* (Washington, D.C.: Brookings Institution, 1995). Copyright © 1995. Reprinted by permission of the Brookings Institution.

authorized by the Sixteenth Amendment) and 1940 (when the average American paid only $7 in federal taxes). But between 1940 and 1945, total federal tax collections increased from about $5 billion to nearly $44 billion, and the end of the war brought no substantial tax reduction. World War II thus created the first great financial boom for the government, permitting the sustained expansion of a great variety of programs that in turn supported a large number of administrators.[7] Today, the federal bureaucracy is large and the number of people in top jobs has increased enormously (see Figure 11.1).

The federal bureaucracy has grown for several reasons. The country is larger than it once was, so now there are more administrators to manage the traditional tasks the government has always performed. And the public now expects the government to do many new things, including some (such as environmental regulation or civil rights) that once were thought to be entirely private matters and others (such as crime and drug abuse control) that were thought to belong to local governments.

The bureaucracy has also grown for reasons internal to the government. To satisfy the demand of Congress and the courts that certain procedures be followed, the bureaucracy has become, in Paul Light's words, "thicker," by which he means that the bureaucracy has added many more middle-level managers, such as assistant secretaries and inspectors general, all designed to cope with internal government rules. These rules had to do with following orders, responding to complaints, managing conflict, and conforming to new laws about hiring and contracting.[8]

Consider the Department of Agriculture. Between 1960 and 1992, the number of top jobs in that department increased from 80 to 242 even though, during the same period, the number of farms, the number of farm employees, and the amount of land that farms occupy declined.[9]

Finally, government organizations, though not quite immortal, endure far longer than private firms. One scholar traced 175 federal government organizations from 1923 to 1973 and found that 85 percent of those that existed in 1923 still existed fifty years later. During the same half-century, 246 new governmental agencies were created.[10] By contrast, for every two private businesses started in a typical year, about one fails.[11]

The tendency of government agencies to endure and add even more high-level administrators was first given prominent notice by C. Northcote Parkinson, a British writer who observed that the number of ships, officers, and men in the British Navy declined between 1914 and 1928, while the number of Admiralty workers, clerks, and officials based ashore rose. From this he deduced Parkinson's Law: "Work expands so as to fill the time available for its completion." From this law he deduced two corollaries: "An official wants to multiply subordinates, not rivals," and "Officials make work for each other."[12]

The Federal Bureaucracy Today

The federal bureaucracy is huge, with its members performing an extraordinary variety of tasks. Though all bureaucrats are subordinate to the president, many have a good deal of freedom. Table 11.1 lists some of these agencies. Except for a few in the White House, such as the personal staffs of the president and vice president and certain other offices, the heads of all bureaucratic agencies must be confirmed by the Senate. However, the president can fire any of these people except for the members of the independent commissions, who are appointed for fixed terms to protect their independence.

Presidents like to claim that the number of civilians working for the federal government has not increased significantly in recent years and is about the same today (three million persons) as it was in 1970, and less than it was during World War II.[13] But this ignores the fact that as many as four persons earn their living *indirectly* from the federal government for every one person earning it directly. While federal employment has remained more or less stable, employment among federal contractors and consultants and in state and local governments has mushroomed.

The power of the bureaucracy should be measured not by the number of employees, but rather by the extent to which appointed officials have **discretionary authority**—that is, their ability to choose courses of action and to make policies that are not spelled out in advance by law. In Figure 11.2 we see that the volume of regulations issued and the amount of money spent have risen much faster than the number of employees who write the regulations and spend the money.

By this test, the power of the federal bureaucracy has grown enormously. Congress has delegated substantial authority to administrative agencies in three areas: (1) paying subsidies to particular groups and organizations in society (farmers, veterans, retired people, scientists, schools, universities, hospitals); (2)

Discretionary authority *The extent to which appointed bureaucrats can choose courses of action and make policies that are not spelled out in advance by laws.*

Table 11.1	The Executive Branch	
President		
Vice President		

White House Office	**The Cabinet**
Council of Economic Advisers	Agriculture
Director of National Intelligence	Commerce
Domestic Policy Council	Defense
Drug Control Office	Education
Environmental Quality	Energy
Faith-Based and Community Initiatives	Health and Human Services
National Security Council	Homeland Security
Office of Management and Budget	Housing and Urban Development
Trade Representative	Interior
Independent Commissions	Justice
Many, including:	Labor
Consumer Products Safety Commission	State
Federal Communications Commission	Transportation
Federal Election Commission	Treasury
Federal Reserve System	Veterans Affairs
Federal Trade Commission	**Independent Agencies**
General Services Administration	*Many, including:*
National Labor Relations Board	Central Intelligence Agency
Securities and Exchange Commission	Environmental Protection Agency
Tennessee Valley Authority	National Aeronautics and Space Administration
U.S. Postal Service	Occupational Safety and Health Commission
Federal Advisory Committees	Office of Personnel Management
About 1,000 of them	Small Business Administration

transferring money from the federal government to state and local governments (the grants-in-aid program described in Chapter 5); and (3) devising and enforcing regulations (such as the pure food and drug laws). Congress closely monitors some of these administrative functions, such as grants-in-aid to the states; others, such as the regulatory programs, often operate with a large degree of independence. These delegations of authority, especially in the areas of paying subsidies and regulating the economy, did not become commonplace until the 1930s, and then only after the Supreme Court decided that such delegations were constitutional.

Delegated authority now permits appointed officials to decide, within rather broad limits, who may own a television station, what safety features automobiles

Figure 11.2 **The Growth of the Federal Government in Money, People, and Rules, 1940–2010**

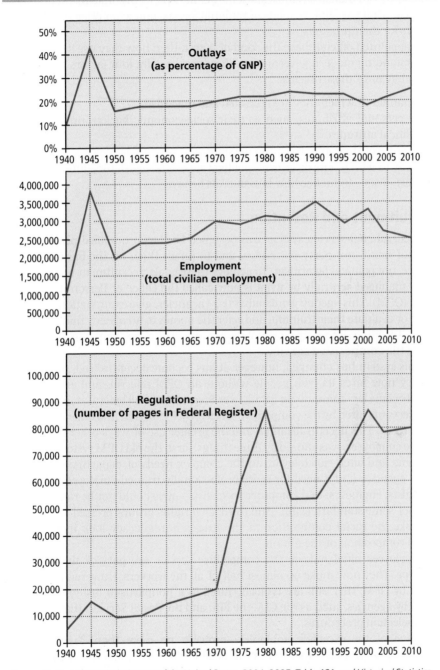

Source: Outlays: *Statistical Abstract of the United States, 2004–2005, Table 461, and Historical Statistics of the United States*, Series F-32 and Y-340. Civilian employment and pages in the *Federal Register*: Harold W. Stanley and Richard G. Niemi, *Vital Statistics on American Politics* (Washington, D.C.: Congressional Quarterly Press, 2010), 255.

must have, what kinds of scientific research shall be especially encouraged, what drugs shall appear on the market, which dissident groups shall be investigated, what fumes an industrial smokestack may emit, which corporate mergers shall be allowed, what use shall be made of national forests, and what price farmers shall receive for their products.

If appointed officials have this kind of power, then how they use it is crucial to understanding modern government. There are, broadly, four factors that explain the behavior of these officials:

The manner in which they are recruited and rewarded.

Their personal attributes, such as their socioeconomic backgrounds and their political attitudes.

The nature of their jobs: roles and missions.

The way in which outside forces—political superiors, legislators, interest groups, journalists—influence how bureaucrats behave.

Recruitment and Retention

The federal civil-service system was designed to recruit qualified people on the basis of merit, not party patronage, and to retain them on the basis of performance, not political favoritism. To achieve these goals, recruitment was for many years managed centrally by what is now called the Office of Personnel Management (OPM). This agency would advertise vacancies, give examinations to candidates or evaluate their training, and refer the names to an agency that might hire them. Traditionally, an agency had to pick one of the top three names. This was called the **competitive service**.

Competitive service *The government offices to which people are appointed on grounds of merit as ascertained by a written examination or by having met certain selection criteria (such as training, educational attainments, or prior experience).*

This system has changed, however. It has become decentralized, so that each agency now hires its own people without an OPM referral, and examinations have become less common. In 1952, over 86 percent of all federal employees were civil servants hired by the competitive service; by 1996, that had fallen to less than 54 percent. This decentralization, and the greater use of ways other than exams to hire employees, was caused by three things. First, the old OPM system was cumbersome and often not relevant to the complex needs of departments. Second, these agencies had a need for more professionally trained employees—lawyers, biologists, engineers, and computer specialists—who could not be ranked on the basis of some standard exam. And third, civil rights groups pressed Washington to make the racial composition of the federal bureaucracy look more like the racial composition of the nation.

Excepted service *Provision for appointing federal offices without going through the competitive service.*

Employees hired outside the competitive service are part of the **excepted service**. They now make up almost half of all the workers. However, though not hired by OPM, they still are typically hired in a nonpartisan fashion. Some are hired by agencies, such as the CIA, the FBI, and the Postal Service, that have their own selection procedures.

Some of the excepted employees—probably no more than 3 percent—are appointed on grounds other than or in addition to merit, narrowly defined. These legal exceptions exist to permit the president to select, for policy-making and politically sensitive posts, people who are in agreement with his policy views. Whereas in the nineteenth century practically every federal job was a patronage job, political

Pedro Ramirez Jr./NCTC Image Library/U.S. Fish and Wildlife Service

Federal employees aren't just paper shufflers; many, such as this biologist, perform skilled professional tasks.

appointments today constitute only a tiny fraction of all federal jobs. Such appointments are generally of three kinds:

1. *Presidential appointments* authorized by statute (cabinet and subcabinet officers, judges, U.S. marshals and U.S. attorneys, ambassadors, and members of various boards and commissions).
2. *Schedule C jobs* described as having a "confidential or policy-determining character" below the level of cabinet or subcabinet posts (including executive assistants, special aides, and confidential secretaries).
3. *Noncareer Executive Assignments* (NEA jobs) given to high-ranking members of the regular competitive civil service or to people brought into the civil service at these high levels as advocates of presidential programs or as participants in policy-making.

■ **The Buddy System** The actual recruitment of civil servants, especially in the middle- and upper-level jobs, is somewhat more complicated, and slightly more political, than the laws and rules might suggest. Though many people

Name-request job *A job to be filled by a person whom a government agency has identified by name.*

enter the federal bureaucracy by learning of a job opening, filling out an application, perhaps taking a test, and being hired, many also enter on a name-request basis. A **name-request job** is filled by a person whom an agency has already identified. In this respect, the federal government is not so different from private business: The head of a bureau decides in advance whom to hire. The agency must still send a form describing the job to the OPM, but it also names the person it wishes to hire. Occasionally this name-request job is offered to a person at the insistence of a member of Congress who wants to repay a political supporter; more often it is made available because the bureaucracy itself has identified the individual it wishes to hire and wants to circumvent an elaborate search. This is sometimes called the "buddy system."

The buddy system does not necessarily produce poor employees. Indeed, it is often a way of hiring able people who are known quantities with specific skills. But it also opens up the possibility of hiring people whose policy views are congenial to those already in office. Bureaucrats in consumer-protection agencies, for example, recruit new staff from private groups with an interest in consumer protection, such as the various organizations associated with Ralph Nader, or from academics of a proconsumer orientation.

■ **Senior Executive Service** With the passage of the Civil Service Reform Act of 1978, Congress recognized that many high-level positions in the civil service have important policy-making responsibilities and that the president and his cabinet officers ought to have more flexibility in recruiting such people. Accordingly the law created a Senior Executive Service (SES) of about eight thousand top federal managers who could be hired, fired, and transferred more easily than ordinary civil servants. Moreover, members of the SES would be eligible for substantial cash bonuses if they were judged to have performed their duties well. (To protect the rights of SES members, anyone who is removed from the SES is guaranteed a job elsewhere in the government.)

Things did not work out quite as the sponsors of the SES had hoped. Only a modest proportion of higher-ranking positions in agencies were filled by transfers from other agencies; the cash bonuses did not prove to be an important incentive; and hardly any members of the SES were actually fired.

The great majority of civil-service bureaucrats who do not hold presidential appointments have jobs that are, for all practical purposes, beyond reach. Realistically, no one is fired unless his or her superior is prepared to invest a great deal of time and effort in the attempt. Only a tiny fraction of all civil-service employees are fired for misconduct or poor performance. Such a state of affairs would be inconceivable in any private organization. To cope, political executives devise various stratagems for bypassing or forcing out civil servants with whom they cannot work effectively.

■ **Agency Point of View** When one realizes that most agencies are staffed with people recruited by that agency, sometimes on a name-request basis, and who are virtually immune to dismissal, it becomes clear that the recruitment and retention policies of the civil service ensure that most bureaucrats will share the agency's point of view. Even with the encouragement for transfers created by the SES, in 1980 only 10 percent of the people appointed to the three top civil-service grades in a given agency came from other agencies.[14]

The Senior Executive Service is not likely to change this pattern. Most government agencies are dominated by people who have grown up in that agency, have not served in any other agency, and have been in government service most of their lives. This situation has some advantages. Most bureaucrats are expert in the procedures and policies of their agencies, and a substantial continuity in agency policy will be maintained, no matter which political party is in power. But it has costs as well. Political executives entering an agency and responsible for shaping its direction will discover that they must carefully win the support of their career subordinates. A subordinate has an infinite capacity for discreet sabotage and can make life miserable for a political superior by delaying action, withholding information, following the rulebook with literal exactness, or appealing to those senators or representatives sympathetic to the bureaucrat's point of view.

Personal Attributes

Another factor that shapes the way bureaucrats behave is their personal attributes: social class, education, and personal political beliefs. The federal civil service looks very much like a cross-section of American society in the education, sex, race, and social origins of its members. But at the higher-ranking levels, where the most power is found, the typical civil servant is very different from the typical American. In the great majority of cases, the individual is a middle-aged white male with a college degree whose upbringing was somewhat more advantaged than the average (see Table 11.2).

Because the higher civil service is not representative of the average American, some people speculate that people holding these top jobs think and act in ways very different from most Americans. Depending on their politics, these critics have concluded that the bureaucracy is either more conservative or more liberal than the country it helps govern.[15]

A survey of the attitudes of some two hundred top-level, nonpolitical federal bureaucrats suggests that they are, in fact, slightly more liberal than the average American voter, but considerably less liberal than key members of the media. About 56 percent of those interviewed in 1982 described themselves as liberals

Table 11.2 Minority Employment in the Federal Bureaucracy, by Rank, 2005		
Rank	**Percentage Black**	**Percentage Hispanic**
GS 1–4	27	8
GS 5–8	26	9
GS 9–12	16	8
GS 13–15	12	5
SES	7	3

Note: "GS" stands for General Service. The higher the number, the higher the rank.

Source: Office of Personnel Management, 2006.

and said they had voted for the Democratic candidate for president in 1968, 1972, 1976, and 1980. (By contrast, a much smaller proportion of voters think of themselves as liberals, and most voted for Republican presidential candidates in 1968, 1972, and 1980.) But on most specific policy questions, bureaucrats do not have extreme positions. However, the kind of agency for which a bureaucrat works makes a difference. Those employed in "activist" agencies, such as the Federal Trade Commission, Environmental Protection Agency, and Food and Drug Administration, have much more liberal views than those who work for more traditional agencies, such as the Departments of Agriculture, Commerce, and Defense.[16] (See Table 11.3.)

This association between attitudes and the kind of agency has been confirmed by other studies. Even when the bureaucrats come from roughly the same social backgrounds, their policy views seem to reflect the kind of government work they do. For example, those holding foreign-service jobs in the State Department are usually more liberal than those coming from similar family backgrounds who perform similar tasks in the Defense Department.[17] It is not clear whether the jobs produce these differences in attitudes or whether certain jobs attract people with certain beliefs. Probably both forces are at work.

Table 11.3 **Political Attitudes of High-Level Federal Bureaucrats**			
	Percentage Agreeing		
Attitude	**All Bureaucrats**	**"Traditional" Agencies**	**"Activist" Agencies**
I am a liberal.	56	48	63
I voted for:			
Humphrey (1968)	72	67	76
McGovern (1972)	57	47	65
Carter (1976)	71	65	76
Carter (1980)	45	34	55
Less regulation of business is good for the United States.	61	66	57
U.S. military should be the strongest in the world, regardless of cost.	25	31	19
Women should get preference in hiring.	34	28	40
Blacks should get preference in hiring.	44	35	53
Homosexuality is wrong.	47	54	40
Nuclear plants are safe.	52	58	46

Source: Stanley Rothman and S. Robert Lichter, "How Liberal Are Bureaucrats?" *Regulation* (November–December 1983), pp. 17–18.

We have only fragmentary evidence of the extent to which these differences in attitudes affect bureaucratic behavior. It may seem obvious that individuals will act in accordance with their beliefs, but that common-sense observation is true only when the nature of the job allows people to make decisions based on their beliefs. Sociologists use the term *roles* to describe the different things people do in their lives, and they distinguish between roles that are loosely structured (such as being a voter) and those that are highly structured (such as being an air traffic controller). Personal attitudes greatly affect loosely structured roles and only slightly affect highly structured ones. Applied to the federal bureaucracy, this suggests that civil servants performing tasks that are routinized (such as filling out forms), tasks that are closely defined by laws and rules (such as issuing welfare checks), or tasks that are closely monitored by others (such as supervisors, special-interest groups, or the media) probably perform them in ways that are not much affected by their personal attitudes. But civil servants performing complex, loosely defined tasks that are not closely monitored may carry out their work in ways powerfully influenced by their attitudes.

One personal attribute has a clear effect on bureaucratic behavior: the *professional values* of a civil servant. An increasing number of bureaucrats are lawyers, economists, engineers, and physicians. The values and ways of thinking that these professionals learned in training for their profession tend to weigh heavily when they make important policy decisions. For example, lawyers and economists in the Federal Trade Commission may differ over what kinds of antitrust cases to prosecute: The lawyers prefer to take on smaller cases they believe can be won, and the economists favor big cases that represent the greatest potential savings to consumers.

Roles and Mission

The tasks people are given often explain more of their behavior than the attitudes they have or the way in which they are hired or fired. We have already seen how a highly structured role often powerfully affects behavior, notwithstanding personal attitudes. But even a loosely structured role is shaped by forces inside the bureaucracy that civil servants cannot easily ignore—especially those doctrines and attitudes that the agency instills in them and expects them to recall when they exercise discretionary authority.

When an organization has a clear view of its purpose and methods, a view that is widely shared by its members, we say it has a sense of *mission.* Some federal agencies have a sense of mission, some do not. The Forest Service, the Federal Bureau of Investigation, and the Public Health Service are examples of agencies that have, or have had, a powerful sense of mission.[18] This leads to easier management, higher morale, and tighter controls on behavior. But it also makes such organizations hard to change and sometimes resistant to political direction. This dilemma—whether to indoctrinate organization members with a sense of the mission of the agency or to keep them accountable to the public—is one of the central problems of bureaucratic government.

In addition to a consciously developed sense of mission, constraints are imposed on bureaucrats by government rules and laws. Civil-service regulations on hiring and firing staff, already discussed, are one example of these. There are many others:

- The Freedom of Information Act gives citizens the right to inspect most of the files and records of agencies.
- Various laws require careful accounting of all money spent.
- Laws and orders oblige agencies to provide equal opportunities to minorities and women when hiring employees.
- Environmental impact statements must be compiled before certain construction projects may be undertaken.
- The Administrative Procedure Act requires that interested people be notified of, and given a chance to comment on, proposed new rules, and that they be afforded an opportunity to introduce evidence at hearings that must be held before certain rules can be enforced.

Perhaps the most important constraint on bureaucratic power is that agencies are complicated organizations, the component parts of which do not always see things the same way. Before action can be taken, one part of an agency must consult with another part and get its agreement, and sometimes that agency must then consult with other agencies. This process of *concurrences* reflects the fragmentation of power in our government. Action requires persuading—rather than ordering—other people to go along. These constraints do not mean that the bureaucracy is feeble, but they do mean that it is often easier to block an action than to implement one. Decisive action is likely only on those matters where just a few people need agree or where the action has little public visibility. In Washington, there are almost no such matters.

These limits on bureaucratic power are not obvious to people who object to how that power is used. But they are all too obvious to those who enter the government eager to take power and use it for what they regard as good ends.

Outside Forces

Bureaucrats do not operate in a vacuum. They exist in a constellation of political forces in and out of government that affect agency behavior. There are at least seven external forces with which a government bureau must cope: executive branch superiors (such as cabinet officers), the White House (especially the president's staff), congressional committees, interest groups, the media, the courts, and rival government agencies.

Not every agency is equally exposed to these external sources of influence. Much depends on the task the agency performs, the degree of public or political interest in the agency, and the extent to which those affected by its actions are organized, knowledgeable, and effective.

At the most general level, one can distinguish between those agencies that are more oriented toward presidential control and those that are more sensitive to congressional control. All these agencies are nominally subordinate to the president; the difference in orientation is the result of political forces. Presidential agencies include those that carry out policies that do not distribute benefits among significant groups, regions, or localities within the United States. Thus they do not (usually) affect important congressional constituencies—or at least do not affect them differently in different places. They include the State, Treasury, and Justice Departments; the Central Intelligence Agency; the Office of the Secretary of Defense; and the Arms Control and Disarmament Agency.

Congressional agencies are those whose actions have a more pronounced distributional effect within the country; among them are the Departments of Agriculture, Interior, Homeland Security, Housing and Urban Development, and Veterans Affairs; the Army Corps of Engineers; and the Small Business Administration. Many other agencies have neither a presidential nor a congressional orientation and can act somewhat independently of both.

■ **Desire for Autonomy** Government bureaucrats, like people generally, prefer to be left alone so they can do their work as they wish. When they are left more or less alone, free of conflict with bureaucratic rivals and without close political supervision, we say an agency has autonomy. All agencies would like more autonomy than they have, and some have managed to get a great deal. The FBI, by skillful publicity and by some striking investigative successes, developed such strong public support during its first forty-five years that it was virtually immune to criticism—and thus to serious presidential or congressional supervision. It had acquired autonomy to an enviable degree. When the National Aeronautics and Space Administration (NASA) succeeded in landing a man on the moon, it was at the crest of a wave of popular support that conferred upon it substantial autonomy. But autonomy, like beauty, invariably fades. In the 1970s, when the FBI was publicly shown to have exceeded its powers, it lost much of its autonomy and came under a most searching congressional inspection and supervision. After the space shuttle *Challenger* exploded in 1986, NASA was subject to scathing criticism.

■ **Agency Allies** Because many federal agencies were created explicitly to promote some sector of society—agriculture, business, labor, environmentalism, minorities—it is hardly surprising that organizations representing those sectors should have substantial influence over the agencies designed to serve them. Such relations exist between the American Legion (and other veterans' groups) and the Department of Veterans Affairs, the AFL-CIO and the Department of Labor, the NAACP and the Equal Employment Opportunity Commission, and the Environmental Defense Fund and the Environmental Protection Agency. These interest groups lobby to ensure that their favored agencies have adequate funds and legal powers—and protest when the agency acts contrary to their wishes.

Given the conflict-ridden political environment that most government agencies face, these bureaucracies have a powerful incentive to develop strong allies in the private sector. They must often pay a price for that alliance, however, by deferring to the policy preferences of their ally.

Some scholars view these agency–interest group relations as so close that they speak of the agency as having been *captured* by the interest group and thus the interest group as having become the agency's client. This, indeed, happens. For example, it is inconceivable that the Department of Labor would ever recommend to Congress a decrease in the minimum wage even though many economists believe that a high minimum wage increases unemployment. The AFL-CIO would not tolerate such a position.

Iron triangle *A close relationship among an agency, a congressional committee, and an interest group that often becomes a mutually advantageous alliance.*

Iron triangle is another phrase often used to describe how external forces sometimes heavily influence agency decisions. Supposedly the three points on the triangle are these:

1. An agency.
2. An interest group.
3. A congressional committee that ensures that the agency takes the views of the interest group seriously.

An example of an iron triangle is the Department of Veterans Affairs, organized veterans (such as the American Legion), and the House and Senate Veterans Affairs committees.

Iron triangle is a vivid journalistic phrase, and perhaps it was once accurate, but today it is quite misleading. Almost all agencies are now part not of an iron triangle but of an **issue network**. These are made up of a large number of interest groups, think tanks, policy experts, news reporters, and congressional committees that watch over the agencies and try to get them to do what each partner of the issue network prefers. The Environmental Protection Agency, for example, will be alert to pressure not just from one interest group (say, the Sierra Club) but from many such groups (farmers, corporations, oil companies, consumer activists) and not just from one congressional committee (say, the House Energy and Commerce Committee) but from several (at least three House committees and three in the Senate) and will also have to worry about what both liberal and conservative think tanks and their media allies have to say. Even the Department of Agriculture, an old-line agency dealing mostly with farmers, has to worry about *which* farmers to satisfy—those that produce crops, or cattle, or pigs, or dairy cows—and which farm organizations—there are three national ones—to consult.[19]

Issue network *A loose collection of leaders, interest groups, bureaucratic agencies, and congressional committees interested in some public policy.*

Congressional Oversight

Some interest groups are important to agencies mainly because they are important to Congress. Not every interest group in the country has substantial access to Congress, but those that do and that are taken seriously by the relevant committees or subcommittees must also be taken seriously by the agency. Furthermore, even apart from interest groups, members of Congress have constitutional powers over agencies and policy interests in how agencies function.

Congressional supervision of the bureaucracy takes several forms. First, no agency may exist (except for a few presidential offices and commissions) without congressional approval. Congress influences—and sometimes determines precisely—agency behavior by the statutes it enacts. In the past, Congress passed statutes that gave broad discretion to regulatory agencies, such as the Federal Communications Commission, but since the 1960s Congress has tended to sharply restrict agency discretion.

Authorization legislation

Legislative permission to begin or continue a government program or agency. An authorization bill may grant permission to spend a certain sum of money, but that money does not ordinarily become available unless it is also appropriated. Authorizations may be annual, multiyear, or permanent.

Second, no money may be spent unless it has first been authorized and appropriated by Congress. **Authorization legislation** originates in a legislative committee (such as Agriculture, Energy and Commerce, or Natural Resources) and states the maximum amount of money an agency may spend on a given program.

So What?

By this point, your eyes may be glazed over. Thinking about a government bureaucracy is less fun than an ingrown toenail. But almost everybody works for a bureaucracy: accountants, sales people, factory workers, flight attendants, and clerks at McDonald's or Burger King. Even professors. The key question is this: Why is a government bureaucracy different from a business one? After all, both have a lot of rules and procedures and both can equip you with a lot of dull duties.

But the public and private sector have important differences. Here are some:

1. Private bureaucracies must compete for customers; government agencies are usually monopolies that will exist whether people like them or not.

2. Successful private bureaucracies can pay a lot of money to their top executives; government bureaucracies can pay a lot to lower-ranking workers but not very much to the top people.

3. Private bureaucracies usually have a clear goal (make a profit); government bureaucracies usually have an unclear one (educate students, represent this country before the United Nations).

4. Private bureaucracies, when given a choice, can say "yes" or "no"; government bureaucracies, when given a choice, tend to say "maybe" or "it depends."

5. Private bureaucracies can keep the money they earn and invest it next year; government bureaucracies must return any money remaining at the end of the year to the Treasury Department.

6. Private bureaucracies can decide to open a new office, build a new plant, or change the products it makes; government bureaucracies cannot do any of these unless Congress agrees.

7. Private bureaucracies can hire, promote, demote, and fire their employees; government bureaucracies must follow rules about whom they can hire. They find it difficult to demote people and next to impossible to fire anyone.

None of this means that government agencies are useless. Quite the contrary; many are essential. Nor does it mean that all are badly managed. But all these points do mean that government agencies are hard to run and sometimes persist long after the reason for their creation has disappeared.

The message to readers of this book is this: Think twice before creating a new government agency, because it is hard to be sure it will do what you want. Look for chances to pay private firms to do what once a government agency did. (For example, think about whether private schools can do a better job than public ones or private contractors can do many of the jobs soldiers and sailors once did). These are not easy choices to make but they are much more important than many legislators suppose. And do not forget that there are many government agencies that offer unparalleled chances for serving the country.

How We Compare

Outsourcing Government

In the United States, government by proxy is the norm. Bureaucrats in Washington pay state and local governments and private groups to staff and administer most federal programs.

For instance, Medicaid, the main federal health program for low-income citizens, is administered mainly by state agencies. The federal government has co-funded nonprofit groups to lead recovery efforts in the hurricane-ravaged Gulf Coast. At points during the second Gulf War, there were nearly as many for-profit workers as U.S. soldiers in Iraq.

The Canadian and Indian central governments each administer many policies via provincial or territorial governments; and every European government uses private contractors for at least some functions.

But most other democracies restrict and regulate outsourcing more than the U.S. does; for example, German law directs that all persons involved in administering national policies must be directly supervised by a government official.

And no other nation follows the American practice whereby government bureaucracies give tax-exempt organizations, including local faith-based groups, grants to administer myriad health and human services programs.

Many experts argue that outsourcing and proxy government have gone too far in this country; but none is sure whether or how it can be reined in, and most admit that public administration in other democracies is also far from perfect.

Sources: Donald F. Kettl, *The Next Government of the United States: Why Our Institutions Fail Us and How to Fix Them* (New York: W. W. Norton); Paul R. Verkuil, *Outsourcing Sovereignty: Why Privatization of Government Functions Threatens Democracy and What We Can Do About It* (Cambridge: Cambridge University Press, 2007); John J. Dilulio, Jr., "Government by Proxy: A Faithful Overview," *Harvard Law Review*, March 2003, pp. 1271–1284.

This authorization may be permanent, it may be for a fixed number of years, or it may be annual (that is, it must be renewed each year or the program or agency goes out of business). Today most federal spending is done on the basis of permanent authorizations, especially the funds used to pay Social Security benefits and hire military personnel. Increasingly, however, there has been a trend toward annual authorizations to enable Congress to strengthen its control over certain executive agencies. Foreign aid, the State Department, NASA, and the procurement of military equipment by the Defense Department are now subject to annual authorizations.

Appropriation
Legislative grant of money to finance a government program.

Third, even funds that have been authorized by Congress cannot be spent unless (in most cases) they are also *appropriated*. **Appropriations** are usually made annually, and they originate not with the legislative committees but with the House Appropriations Committee and its various (and influential) subcommittees. An appropriation may be, and often is, for less than the amount authorized. The Appropriations Committee's action thus tends to have a budget-cutting effect. Some funds can be spent without an appropriation, but in virtually every part of the bureaucracy each agency is keenly sensitive to congressional concerns at the time that the annual appropriations process is underway.

The Appropriations Committee and Legislative Committees

Because an agency budget must be both authorized and appropriated, each agency serves not one congressional master but several, and these masters may be in conflict. The real power over an agency's budget is exercised by the Appropriations Committee; the legislative committees are especially important when a substantive law is passed, when the agency is created, or when an agency is subject to annual authorization.

The power of the Appropriations Committee in the past was rarely challenged: from 1947 through 1962, 90 percent of its recommendations on expenditures were approved by the full House without change.[20] Furthermore, the Appropriations Committee tends to recommend less money than an agency requests (except for some especially favored agencies, such as the FBI, the Soil Conservation Service, and the Forest Service). Finally, the process of *marking up* (revising, amending, and approving) an agency's budget requests gives the Appropriations Committee, or one of its subcommittees, substantial influence over the policies the agency follows.

The legislative and budget committees have begun to reclaim some of the power over agencies exercised by the Appropriations Committee by getting laws passed that entitle people to certain benefits (for example, Social Security or retirement payments) and creating **trust funds** to pay for them. These funds are not subject to annual appropriations. Legislative committees have gained influence by making their annual authorizations more detailed.[21] The Budget Committee may direct the Appropriations Committee to spend less.

There are informal ways by which Congress can control the bureaucracy. An individual member of Congress can call an agency head on behalf of a constituent—generally only to obtain information but sometimes to attempt to secure special privileges. Congressional committees may also obtain the right to pass on certain agency decisions. This is called **committee clearance**, and though it is usually not legally binding on the agency, few agency heads will ignore the express wish of a committee chairperson that he or she be consulted before certain actions are taken.

Congressional Investigations

Perhaps the most visible and dramatic form of congressional supervision of an agency is the investigation. Since 1792, congressional investigations of the bureaucracy have been a regular feature—sometimes constructive, sometimes debasing—of legislative-executive relations. The investigative power is not mentioned in the Constitution but has been inferred from the power to legislate. The Supreme Court has consistently upheld this interpretation, though it has also said that such investigations should not be held solely to expose the purely personal affairs of private individuals and must not operate to deprive citizens of their basic rights.[22] Congress can compel a person to attend an investigation by issuing a subpoena. Anyone who ignores the subpoena may be punished for contempt: Congress can vote to send the person to jail or refer the matter to a court for further action. As explained in Chapter 10, the president and his principal subordinates have refused to answer certain congressional inquiries on grounds of executive privilege.

Trust funds *Funds for government programs that are collected and spent outside the regular government budget; the amounts are determined by preexisting law rather than by annual appropriations. The Social Security trust fund is the largest of these.*

Committee clearance *The ability of a congressional committee to review and approve certain agency decisions in advance and without passing a law. Such approval is not legally binding on the agency, but few agency heads will ignore the expressed wishes of committees.*

Although many methods of congressional oversight—budgetary review, personnel controls, investigations—are designed to control the exercise of bureaucratic discretion, other provisions are intended to ensure the freedom of certain agencies from effective control, especially by the president. In dozens of cases Congress has authorized department heads and bureau chiefs to operate independently of presidential preferences. Congress has resisted, for example, presidential efforts to ensure that policies to regulate pollution do not impose excessive costs on the economy, and interest groups have brought suit to prevent presidential coordination of various regulatory agencies. If the bureaucracy sometimes works at cross-purposes, it is usually because Congress—or competing committees in Congress—wants it that way.

Bureaucratic "Pathologies"

Everyone complains about bureaucracy in general (though rarely about bureaucratic agencies that one believes are desirable). This chapter should persuade you that it is difficult to say anything about bureaucracy "in general"; there are too many different kinds of agencies, kinds of bureaucrats, and kinds of programs to label the entire process with a single adjective. Nevertheless, many people who recognize the enormous variety among government agencies still believe that they all have some general features in common and suffer from certain shared problems or "pathologies."

This is true enough, but the reasons for it—and the solutions, if any—are often not understood. There are five major problems with bureaucracies: red tape, conflict, duplication, imperialism, and waste. **Red tape** refers to the complex rules and procedures that must be followed to get something done. Conflict exists because some agencies seem to be working at cross-purposes with other agencies. Duplication occurs when two government agencies seem to be doing the same thing. Imperialism refers to the tendency of agencies to grow without regard to the benefits their programs confer or the costs they entail. Waste means spending more than what is necessary to buy some product or service.

These problems exist, but not necessarily because bureaucrats are incompetent or power hungry. Most exist because of the very nature of government. Take red tape: It is also found in business and is in part the consequence of bigness. A great amount of governmental red tape also results from the need to satisfy legal and political requirements for fairness, accountability, and citizen access. Or take conflict and duplication. They do not occur because bureaucrats enjoy them—quite the contrary! They exist because Congress, in setting up agencies and programs, often wants to achieve a number of different, partially inconsistent, goals.

Imperialism results largely from government agencies that seek goals so vague and so difficult to measure that it is hard to tell when they have been attained. When Congress is unclear as to exactly what an agency is supposed to do, the agency will often convert that vagueness into bureaucratic imperialism by taking the largest possible view of its powers—sometimes on its own, but more often because interest groups and judges rush to fill the vacuum left by Congress. Thus the Department of Transportation, under pressure from organized groups of

Red tape *Complex bureaucratic rules and procedures that must be followed to get something done.*

handicapped people, converted a vague antidiscrimination provision in the 1973 Rehabilitation Act into a requirement that virtually every big-city bus have a device installed to lift wheelchairs on board—a prohibitively expensive solution to the problem. (The rule was later repealed.)

Waste is probably the biggest criticism that people have of the bureaucracy. Everybody has heard stories of the Pentagon paying $91 for screws that cost three cents in the hardware store. President Reagan's "Private Sector Survey on Cost Control,"—generally known as the Grace Commission, after its chairman, J. Peter Grace—publicized these and other tales in a 1984 report.

No doubt there is waste in government. After all, unlike a business worried about maximizing profits, a government agency has only weak incentives to keep costs down. If a business employee cuts costs, he or she often receives a bonus or a raise, and the firm gets to add the savings to its profits. If a government official cuts costs, he or she receives no reward, and the agency cannot keep the savings—they go back to the Treasury.

But many of the horror stories are either exaggerations or unusual occurrences.[23] Most of the screws, hammers, and light bulbs purchased by the government are obtained at low cost by means of competitive bidding among several suppliers. When the government does pay outlandish amounts, the reason typically is that it is purchasing a new or one-of-a-kind item not available at your neighborhood hardware store—for example, a new bomber or missile.

Even when the government is not overcharged, it still may spend more money than a private firm in buying what it needs. The reason is more red tape—rules and procedures designed to ensure that when the government buys something, it will do so in a way that serves the interests of many groups. For example, it must often buy from American rather than foreign suppliers even if the latter charge a lower price; it must make use of contractors that employ minorities; it must hire only union laborers and pay them the "prevailing" (that is, the highest) wage; it must allow public inspection of its records; it frequently is required to choose contractors favored by influential members of Congress; and so on. Private firms do not have to comply with all these rules and thus can buy for less.

Bureaucratic problems are hard to solve in large part because Congress is reluctant to make hard choices. Sometimes it may make matters worse by trying to solve a social problem by creating new layers of bureaucracy. After the terrorist attacks on September 11, 2001, the Department of Homeland Security (DHS) was established to coordinate governmental responses to disasters. Four years later, it still had not produced a plan to manage a disaster. Indeed, for some problems things became worse. When, in 2005, Hurricane Katrina devastated New Orleans and much of the Gulf Coast, the Federal Emergency Management Agency (FEMA) did not respond well. One of the reasons was that FEMA, once an independent agency, had become part of DHS, where it lost status. It underwent budget cuts and was led by a not-very-competent political appointee. Congress investigated why the government performed so poorly, but you can be sure that in that investigation it did not ask why Congress had unwisely merged FEMA into DHS.

For all of these reasons, it is a mistake to think of the bureaucracy as some reckless, out-of-control monster. The main problem with executive agencies is not that they have too few controls, but that they have too many; not that they are

AP Photo/Lenny Ignelzi

These long lines of cars at the border between the United States and Mexico may be a symbol of "bureaucratic red tape" to some travelers, but they are a sign of "effective law enforcement" to people who want to cut off the flow of drugs and illegal immigrants.

independent of political authority, but that they are dependent on many rival authorities; not that they are wantonly wasteful or inefficient, but that the system provides them with no incentives to save money and many incentives to spend every dollar they are allocated. In short, the problem of bureaucracy is inseparable from the problem of government in general.

Reinventing Government

Given these problems, one wonders whether anything at all can be done to make a government agency more responsive to its citizens. A major effort to answer that question was undertaken by the Clinton administration with its National Performance Review, popularly called "reinventing government," or REGO. Led by Vice President Al Gore, REGO consisted of an extensive survey of government agencies to find out which ones were especially efficient and responsive, and why.

Unlike previous efforts to streamline the government, this one did not focus on strengthening the powers of the president or consolidating independent agencies into a few big departments. Instead, it emphasized "cutting red tape," "putting customers first," and "empowering employees." It borrowed this emphasis from the recent efforts of business firms to become more flexible, innovative, and customer-friendly. The goal was to create a government that "works better and costs less."

The Office of Personnel Management has scrapped its 10,000-page *Federal Personnel Manual* in order to simplify the way in which bureaucrats are hired and promoted. The Defense Department is trying to buy fewer "designer" goods and more things off the shelf. The laws governing federal purchasing procedures have been streamlined. Government agencies can now buy items costing as much as $100,000 without following any complex regulations. Many agencies have created customer-service standards (for example, the Social Security Administration says it will mail out Social Security cards within five days, and the Postal Service promises to deliver local first-class mail within one day).

Not all these promises will be kept all the time, as anyone knows who has waited for a letter to make its way across town. Certainly, however, these efforts are laudable. What no one yet knows is how big a change they can make in a government agency that, unlike a business firm, cannot fire bad employees, has no profits that management can try to maximize, and must observe all the laws and rules that Congress chooses to write.

WHAT WOULD YOU DO?

MEMORANDUM

To: Dr. Robert Smith, president of Cybersystems

Engineering

From: James Logan, secretary of defense

Subject: Becoming an assistant secretary of defense

As both secretary and a dear old college buddy of yours, I write again to express my hope that you will accept the president's call to service. We all desperately want you aboard. Yes, conflict-of-interest laws will require you to sell your stock in your present company and drop out of its generous pension plan. No, the government won't even pay moving costs. And once you leave office, you will be barred for life from lobbying the executive branch on matters in which you were directly involved while in office, and you will be barred for two years from lobbying on matters that were under your general official authority. Your other concerns have teeth, too, but let me help you weigh your options.

Arguments for:

1. I hate to preach, but it is one's duty to serve one's country when called. Your sacrifice would honor your family and benefit your fellow Americans for years to come.

2. As an accomplished professional and the head of a company that has done business with the government, you could help the president succeed in reforming the department so that it works better and costs less.

3. Despite the restrictions, you could resume your career once your public service was complete.

Arguments against:

1. Since you will have to be confirmed by the Senate, your life will be put under a microscope, and everything (even some of our old college mischief together) will be fair game for congressional staffers and reporters.

2. You will face hundreds of rules telling you what you can't do and scores of congressmen telling you what you should do. Old friends will get mad at you for not doing them favors. The president will demand loyalty.

Friday,

New Administration Struggling to Fill Top Posts Cabinet Secretaries Say "The President Needs Help!"

May 20
WASHINGTON, D.C.

Four months into the new administration, hundreds of assistant secretary and deputy assistant secretary positions remain unfilled. In 1960, the total number of presidential political appointees was just 450. Today the total is over 2,400, but sheer growth is not the whole story. Rather, say experts on federal bureaucracy, plum public service posts go unfilled because the jobs have become so unrewarding, even punishing...

The press will pounce on your every mistake, real or imagined.

3. Given the federal limits on whom in the government you can deal with after you leave office, your job at Cybersystems may well suffer.

Your Decision:

Accept position _____   Reject position _____

SUMMARY

Bureaucracy is characteristic of almost all aspects of modern life, not simply the government. Government bureaucracies, however, pose special problems because they are subject to competing sources of political authority, must function in a constitutional system of divided powers and of federalism, and often have vague goals. The power of bureaucracy should be measured by its discretionary authority, not by the number of its employees or the size of its budget.

War and depression have been the principal sources of bureaucratic growth, aided by important changes in constitutional interpretation in the 1930s that permitted Congress to delegate broad grants of authority to administrative agencies. Congress has sought to check or recover those grants by controlling budgets, personnel, and policy decisions and by the exercise of legislative vetoes—with only partial success. The uses to which bureaucrats put their authority can be explained in part by their recruitment and job security (they have an agency orientation), their personal political views, and the nature of the tasks they are performing.

Bureaucratic pathologies—red tape, duplication, conflict, and agency imperialism—are to a degree inherent in any government that serves competing goals and is supervised by rival elective officials. Efforts to "reinvent" government may help matters, but they can't solve the problem.

RECONSIDERING THE ENDURING QUESTIONS

1. Why did the bureaucracy become known as the "fourth branch" of American government?

The Constitution makes no provision for an administrative system except by allowing the president to appoint, with senatorial consent, senior officials. But the growth in government and its countless new duties (mostly in response to public demands), its own internal need to manage complex relations among the political branches, and the tendency of agencies to live almost forever have created a large administrative state.

2. How many people work for the federal government?

We do not really know. We do know how many people work for civilian or military agencies (about 3.8 million), but not how many work for the CIA or the National Security Agency. We have only a rough guess as to how many work for it indirectly as private contractors (for example, the defense industry) or consultants, or how many state and local officials or private agencies have their salaries paid by Washington.

3. What can be done to improve bureaucratic performance?

Many things have been tried, but a lot depends on what *improve* means. If it means "more effective," so that the president can more easily control it, the

White House's powers will increase. But if it means "more responsive," the power of the White House falls and that of courts and Congress increases. And if it means "more efficient," it can work more like a business. The last effort was embodied in the National Performance Review (NPR) begun by the Clinton administration, with some limited success.

Online Resources: The Bureaucracy

 CourseMate

For addresses and reports of various cabinet departments:
• Documents and bulletin boards: www.fedworld.gov

A few specific Web sites of federal agencies:
• Department of Defense: www.defenselink.mil
• Department of Education: www.ed.gov
• Department of Health and Human Services: www.dhhs.gov
• Department of State: www.state.gov
• FBI: www.fbi.gov
• IRS: www.irs.gov

Suggested Readings

Garvey, Gerald. *Facing the Bureaucracy.* San Francisco: Jossey-Bass, 1993. What life is really like inside a government agency (the Federal Energy Regulatory Commission).

Johnson, Ronald L., and Gary D. Libecap. *The Federal Civil Service System and the Problem of Bureaucracy* (Chicago: University of Chicago Press, 1994). Two economists analyze how federal bureaucrats acquire protected positions and salaries.

Moore, Mark H. *Creating Public Value: Strategic Management in Government.* Cambridge: Harvard University Press, 1995. Thoughtful account of how wise bureaucrats can make government work better.

Parkinson, C. Northcote. *Parkinson's Law.* Boston: Houghton Mifflin, 1957. Half-serious, half-joking explanation of why government agencies tend to grow.

Wilson, James Q. *Bureaucracy.* New York: Basic Books, 1989. How and why government agencies behave as they do.

Wolf, Charles. *Markets or Governments,* 2nd ed. Cambridge, Mass.: MIT Press, 1993. A superb analysis of the strengths and weaknesses of using market arrangements or government agencies to achieve goals.

ENDURING QUESTIONS

1. Should judges be limited to interpreting the Constitution and federal laws?

2. Why should federal courts be able to declare an act of Congress unconstitutional?

3. Why is the Supreme Court so deeply divided on so many questions?

E very nation has courts, but in most places the question of who serves on them is not a very important political matter. Here it is. The Senate must confirm the president's nomination of federal judges, and that confirmation process can often by very contentious. By contrast, in many other nations and some American states, the legislature plays no role in picking judges. In several European countries, judges are recruited by having them pass a test, as if they were civil servants. In Canada and England, and elsewhere, a high-level advisory commission chooses people to be nominated for a judgeship, with the final choice from this slate left to the prime minister or other executive branch figure.

© Tom Brakefield/Getty Images

So What?

The selection of Supreme Court justices has become bitterly partisan. In 1987, the Senate refused to confirm Robert Bork. Four years later, it confirmed by a narrow margin Clarence Thomas to be a justice. In 2005–2006, there were angry arguments over the nomination of John Roberts to be chief justice and Samuel Alito to be a justice; both were confirmed, but most Democrats opposed the choices.

Things were different in the past. The Senate almost always confirmed the president's choice. In 1986, Antonio Scalia, though very conservative, won easily in the Senate even though it was under Democratic control.

The main reason for the change is that judges now play so large a role in making or interpreting public policy that many senators believe that the judges' identity is crucial to their party's ideology. This has been especially true of Senate Democrats who led the fight against the confirmation of Bork, Thomas, Roberts, and Alito.

The central issue in this ideological struggle was abortion. Supporters of the Supreme Court's 1973 decision creating a constitutional right to abortion feared that Republican presidents might appoint justices who would overturn it. From 1987 on, this led to Democratic hostility toward Republican nominees. Democrats defend their stance by claiming it is crucial to pay attention to ideology; Republicans criticize it by saying that legal skills and a commitment to judicial restraint are more important.

In those American states where the top judges are elected by the people rather than be appointed by the governor, the public, not the legislature, makes the final choice. In other states the governor makes the selection. In California, for example, the governor chooses the supreme court justices, with a small commission (of two senior judges and the attorney general) having to confirm his choice. The legislature plays no role.

Judicial Review

The argument over ideology versus restraint flows from the fact of **judicial review**—the authority of the federal courts to declare laws of Congress and acts of the executive branch to be void if they are in conflict with the Constitution. From 1789 to 2002, the Supreme Court has declared 158 federal laws unconstitutional. In Britain, by contrast, Parliament is supreme, and no court may strike down a law that it passes. As the second Earl of Pembroke is supposed to have said, "A parliament can do anything but make a man a woman and a woman a man." All that prevents Parliament from acting contrary to the (unwritten) constitution of Britain are the consciences of its members and the opinion of the citizens. About sixty nations do have something resembling judicial review, but in only a few cases does this power mean much in practice.[1]

Judicial review *The power of the courts to declare acts of the legislature and the executive to be unconstitutional and, hence, null and void.*

Elena Kagan (left) answers questions from members of the Senate Judiciary Committee during her confirmation hearings in 2010. Samuel Alito (right) was confirmed after a bitter fight.

Strict constructionist approach (judicial) *The view that judges should decide cases on the basis of the language of the Constitution.*

Activist approach (judicial) *The view that judges should discern the general principles underlying the Constitution and its often vague language and assess how best to apply them in contemporary circumstances, in some cases with the guidance of moral or economic philosophy.*

Judicial review is the federal courts' chief weapon in the system of checks and balances on which the American government is based. Today few people would deny the courts the right to decide that a legislative or executive act is unconstitutional—though once that right was controversial. What remains controversial is the method by which such review should be conducted.

There are two competing views, each ardently pressed during the Bork fight. The first holds that judges should only judge—that is, they should confine themselves to applying those rules that are stated in or clearly implied by the language of the Constitution. This is often called the **strict constructionist approach**. The other view argues that judges should discover the general principles underlying the Constitution and its often vague language, amplify those principles on the basis of some moral or economic philosophy, and apply them to the case. This is sometimes called the **activist approach**.

The difference between strict constructionist and activist judges is not necessarily the same as the difference between liberals and conservatives. Fifty years ago, judicial activists tended to be conservatives and strict constructionists tended to be liberals; today, the opposite is usually the case.

Here is an example of the tension between the activist and the strict constructionist approach. In 1954, the Supreme Court declared that the government could not require that black and white children attend separate, racially distinct schools. It based its judgment on that part of the Fourteenth Amendment that said that states could not deprive any person of "the equal protection of the laws."

For strict constructionists this decision created a problem. When the Fourteenth Amendment was approved by Congress and ratified by the states, the legislators who voted for it did not think it applied to education. The original intent of its framers was, as far as we can tell from the historical record, that the equal protection clause did not govern schools. But this is unsatisfactory: the decision was obviously the right one. It made the Constitution colorblind, as almost everyone agrees it should be.

But the activists also had a problem. On what grounds can we say that the Constitution is colorblind? To try to answer that question, the Court's opinion cited sociological studies of the effects of segregation on young children. But that means activists will make constitutional decisions on the basis of academic studies (many of which have since be reversed by new scholarship).

There is no easy answer to the problem of constitutional interpretation. Strict constructionists will be led to ignore compelling moral arguments, and activists will be led to embrace anything they think is a moral argument as long as they can find an academic study they like.

The Development of the Federal Courts

Most Founders probably expected the Supreme Court to have the power of judicial review (though they did not say that in so many words in the Constitution), but they did not expect federal courts to play so large a role in making public policy. The traditional view of civil courts was that they judged disputes between people who had direct dealings with each other—they had entered into a contract, for example, or one had dropped a load of bricks on the other's toe—and decided which of the two parties was right. The court then supplied relief to the wronged party, usually by requiring the other party to pay damages.

This traditional understanding was based on the belief that judges would find and apply existing law. The purpose of a court case was not to learn what the judge believes but what the law requires. The rise of judicial activism occurred when judges questioned this view and argued instead that judges do not merely find the law, they make the law.

The view that judges interpret the law and do not make policy made it easy for the Founders to justify the power of judicial review and led them to predict—as Hamilton did in *Federalist* No. 78—that the courts would play a relatively neutral, even passive, role in public affairs. Obviously things have changed since Hamilton's time. The evolution of the federal courts, especially the Supreme Court, toward the present level of activism and influence has been shaped by the political, economic, and ideological forces of three historical eras. From 1787 to 1865, the great issues were nation building, the legitimacy of the federal government, and slavery; from 1865 to 1937, the dominant issue was the relationship between government and the economy; from 1938 to the present, the major issues confronting the Court have involved personal liberty and social equality

John Marshall, chief justice of the United States, 1801–
1835, developed the principles of constitutional interpretation, established the right of the Court to declare acts of
Congress unconstitutional, and expanded the powers of the
federal government.

Ankers Photography/The Supreme Court Historical Society

and the potential conflict between the two. In the first period, the Court asserted the supremacy of the federal government; in the second, it placed important restrictions on the powers of that government; and in the third, it enlarged the scope of personal freedom and narrowed that of economic freedom.

National Supremacy and Slavery

Under the leadership of Chief Justice John Marshall, the Supreme Court answered what has been called "that greatest of all the questions left unresolved by the Founders—the nation-state relationship."[2] The Court declared that the national law was in all instances the supreme law, with conflicting state law having to give way, and that the Supreme Court had the power to decide what the Constitution meant. In *Marbury* v. *Madison* in 1803, the Court, speaking through Marshall, held that the Supreme Court could declare an act of Congress unconstitutional (see the box on page 309).

In *McCulloch* v. *Maryland*, decided in 1819, the Court, again speaking through Marshall, held that the power granted to the federal government flows from the people and should be generously construed so that any laws "necessary and proper" to the attainment of constitutional ends would be permissible, and that federal law is supreme over state law even to the point that the state may not tax an enterprise (such as a bank) created by the federal government.[3] In other decisions, the Marshall Court asserted broad powers to review any state court decision if that decision seemed to violate federal law or the federal Constitution, and it upheld the supremacy of federal law in regulating interstate commerce.[4]

All of this may sound rather obvious today, when the supremacy of the federal government is largely unquestioned. In the early nineteenth century, however, these were almost revolutionary decisions. The Jeffersonian Republicans were in power and had become increasingly devoted to states' rights. They were aghast at the Marshall decisions. President Andrew Jackson reportedly said of a later Court ruling he did not like, "John Marshall has made his decision—now let him enforce it!"[5]

In 1836, Roger B. Taney succeeded Marshall as chief justice, deliberately chosen by Andrew Jackson because he was an advocate of states' rights. Taney began to chip away at federal supremacy. But by this time another conflict had arisen that was even more divisive than any previous ones: slavery. In 1857, Taney wrote perhaps the most disastrous judicial opinion ever issued. In the *Dred Scott*

Marbury v. *Madison*

The story of *Marbury* v. *Madison* is often told but deserves another telling because it illustrates so many features of the role of the Supreme Court: how apparently small cases can have large results, how the power of the Court depends not simply on its constitutional authority but on its acting in ways that avoid a clear confrontation with other branches of government, and how the climate of opinion affects how the Court goes about its task.

When President John Adams lost his 1800 bid for reelection to Thomas Jefferson, he—and all members of his party, the Federalists—feared that Jefferson and the Republicans would weaken the federal government and turn its powers to what the Federalists believed were wrong ends (states' rights, an alliance with the French, hostility to business). Feverishly, as his hours in office came to an end, Adams worked to pack the judiciary with fifty-nine loyal Federalists by giving them so-called midnight appointments before Jefferson took office.

John Marshall, as Adams's secretary of state, had the task of certifying and delivering these new judicial commissions. In the press of business he delivered all but seventeen; these he left on his desk for the incoming secretary of state, James Madison, to send out. Jefferson and Madison, however, were furious at Adams's behavior and refused to deliver the seventeen. William Marbury and three other Federalists who had been promised these commissions hired a lawyer and brought suit against Madison to force him to produce the documents. The suit requested the Supreme Court to issue a writ of mandamus (from the Latin, "we command") ordering Madison to do his duty. The right to issue such writs had been given to the Supreme Court by the Judiciary Act of 1789.

Marshall, the man who had failed to deliver the commissions to Marbury and his friends in the first place, had become the chief justice and was now in a position to decide the case. These days a justice who had been involved in an issue before it came to the Court would probably disqualify himself or herself, but Marshall had no intention of letting others decide this question. He faced, however, not simply a partisan dispute over jobs but what was nearly a constitutional crisis. If he ordered the commissions delivered, Madison might still refuse, and the Court had no way—if Madison was determined to resist— to compel him. The Court had no police force, whereas Madison had the support of the president of the United States. And if the order were given, whether or not Madison complied, the Jeffersonian Republicans in Congress would probably try to impeach Marshall. On the other hand, if Marshall allowed Madison to do as he wished, the power of the Supreme Court would be seriously reduced.

Marshall's solution was ingenious. Speaking for a unanimous Court, he announced that Madison was wrong to withhold the commissions, that courts could issue writs to compel public officials to do their prescribed duty—*but that the Supreme Court had no power to issue such writs in this case because the law (the Judiciary Act of 1789) giving it that power was unconstitutional. The law said that the Supreme Court could issue such writs as part of its "original jurisdiction"— that is, persons seeking such writs could go directly to the Supreme Court with their request (rather than to a lower federal court and then, if dissatisfied, appeal to the Supreme Court). Article III of the Constitution, Marshall pointed out, spelled out precisely the Supreme Court's original jurisdiction; it did not mention issuing writs of this sort and plainly indicated that on all matters not mentioned in the Constitution, the Court would have only appellate jurisdiction. Congress may not change the Constitution; hence the part of the Judiciary Act attempting to do this was null and void.

A showdown with the Jeffersonians was thus avoided—Madison was not ordered to deliver the commissions—but the power of the Supreme Court was unmistakably clarified and enlarged. As Marshall wrote, "It is emphatically the province and duty of the judicial department to say what the law is." Furthermore, "a law repugnant to the Constitution is void."

case, Taney held that blacks were not citizens of the United States and could not become so, and that the federal law prohibiting slavery in northern territories— the Missouri Compromise—was unconstitutional.[6] The public outcry against this view was enormous, and the Court and Taney were discredited, at least in northern opinion. A civil war was fought over what the Court mistakenly had assumed it could treat as a purely legal question.

Government and the Economy

The supremacy of the federal government may have been established by John Marshall and the Civil War, but the scope of the powers of that government, or even of the state governments, was still to be defined. During the period from the end of the Civil War to the early years of the New Deal, the dominant issue the Court faced was to decide under what circumstances the economy could be regulated by state or nation. The Court revealed a strong though not inflexible attachment to private property. In general it developed the view that the Fourteenth Amendment, adopted in 1868 primarily to protect black claims to citizenship from hostile state action, also protected private property and corporations from unreasonable state action. But the Court quickly found itself in a thicket: It began passing on the legality and constitutionality of so many efforts by government to regulate business or labor that its workload rose sharply, and its decisions were often inconsistent.

To characterize the Court during this period as "probusiness" or "antiregulation" is both simplistic and inexact. More accurately it was supportive of the rights of private property but unsure how to draw the lines that would distinguish reasonable from unreasonable regulation. The Court found itself trying to make detailed judgments it was not always competent to make and to invent legal rules where no clear legal rules were possible. In one area, however, the Court's judgments were clear: The Fourteenth and Fifteenth Amendments were construed so narrowly as to give blacks only the most limited benefits of their provisions. In a long series of decisions, the Court upheld segregation in schools and on railroad cars and permitted blacks to be excluded from voting in many states.

The Protection of Political Liberty and Economic Regulation

After 1936, the Supreme Court stopped imposing any serious restrictions on state or federal power to regulate the economy, leaving such matters in the hands of the legislatures. From 1937 to 1974, the Court did not overturn a single federal law designed to regulate business, but it did void thirty-six congressional enactments that violated personal political liberties.

This new direction began when one justice, Owen J. Roberts, changed his mind and began supporting Roosevelt's New Deal measures, which he had formerly opposed. This was the famous "switch in time that saved nine." Until then the justices had been striking down New Deal legislation by a five-to-four margin, prompting President Roosevelt to attempt to "pack" the Court. The attempt failed, but with Justice Roberts's change of mind, it was no longer necessary. He had yielded to public opinion in a way that Chief Justice Taney, a century before, had

Figure 12.1   Economics and Civil Liberties Laws Overturned by the U.S. Supreme Court, by Decade, 1900–2006

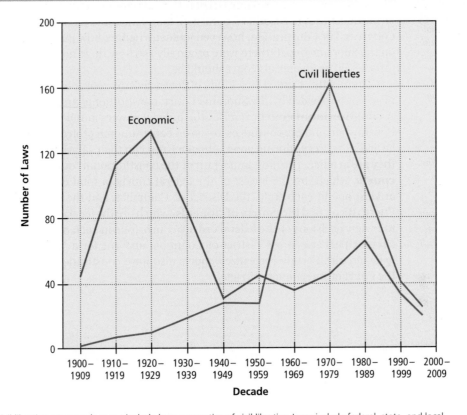

Note: Civil liberties category does not include laws supportive of civil liberties. Laws include federal, state, and local.

Source: Harold W. Stanley and Richard G. Niemi, *Vital Statistics on American Politics, 2007–2008,* 5th ed., p. 302 (Washington, D.C.: CQ Press, 2008). Reprinted by permission of CQ Press; a division of Congressional Quarterly, Inc.

not, thus forestalling an assault on the Court by the other branches of government. Shortly thereafter several justices stepped down, and Roosevelt was able to make his own appointments. From then on, the Court turned its attention to new issues: political liberties and, in time, civil rights (see Figure 12.1).

With the arrival in office of Chief Justice Earl Warren in 1953, the Court began its most activist period yet. The new activism involved the relationship between the citizen and the government and was especially concerned with protecting the rights and liberties of citizens from governmental trespass. In a large measure, the Court has always seen itself as protecting citizens from arbitrary government. Before 1937, that protection was of a sort that conservatives preferred; after 1937, it was of a kind that liberals preferred.

The Structure of the Federal Courts

Constitutional court *A federal court exercising the judicial powers found in Article III of the Constitution and whose judges are given constitutional protection: they may not be fired (they serve during "good behavior"), nor may their salaries be reduced while they are in office. The most important constitutional courts are the Supreme Court, the ninety-four district courts, and the courts of appeals (one in each of eleven regions plus one in the District of Columbia).*

District courts *The lowest federal courts where federal cases begin. They are the only federal courts where trials are held. There are a total of ninety-four district courts in the United States and its territories.*

Courts of appeals *The federal courts with authority to review decisions by federal district courts, regulatory commissions, and certain other federal courts. Such courts have no original jurisdiction; they can hear only appeals. There are a total of twelve courts of appeals in the United States and its territories, plus one for a nationwide circuit.*

The only federal court that must exist is the Supreme Court, required by Article III of the Constitution. All other federal courts and their jurisdictions are creations of Congress. The Constitution, however, indicates neither how many justices shall be on the Supreme Court (there were originally six, now there are nine) nor what its jurisdiction as an appeals court should be.

Congress has created two kinds of lower federal courts to handle cases that need not be decided by the Supreme Court: constitutional and legislative courts. A **constitutional court** exercises the judicial powers found in Article III of the Constitution and thus its judges are given constitutional protection: They may not be fired (they serve during good behavior), nor can their salaries be reduced while they are in office. The most important of the constitutional courts are the **district courts**, which are the lowest of the federal courts (a total of ninety-four, with at least one in each state, the District of Columbia, and the Commonwealth of Puerto Rico), and the **courts of appeals**, which are the federal courts authorized to review decisions of the federal district courts (one in each of eleven regions, or circuits, plus one in the District of Columbia and one for a "federal" or nationwide circuit). Certain specialized courts also have constitutional status, such as the Court of International Trade.

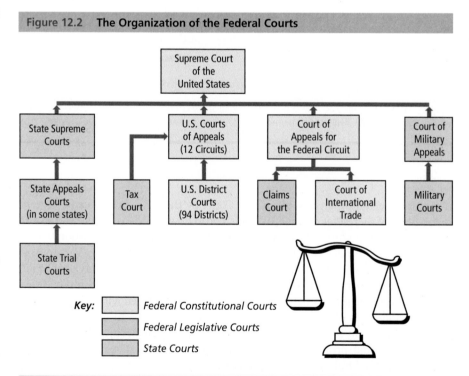

Figure 12.2   The Organization of the Federal Courts

A **legislative court** is set up by Congress for some specialized purpose and staffed with persons who have fixed terms of office and who can be removed or have their salaries reduced. Legislative courts include the Court of Military Appeals (see Figure 12.2).

Because the judges on the constitutional courts serve for life and because they are the chief interpreters of the Constitution, how they are selected and the attitudes they bring to the bench are obviously important. All are nominated by the president and confirmed by the Senate; almost invariably the president nominates a member of his own party. Though presidents do sometimes manage to tilt the Supreme Court in a liberal or conservative direction by the appointments they make, it is not clear that party background makes a great deal of difference or even that a president can predict how a judge will behave. Theodore Roosevelt, Franklin Roosevelt, and Richard Nixon all had reason to complain about the actions of some of their most important Supreme Court appointees—Oliver Wendell Holmes, Jr., Felix Frankfurter, and Warren Burger.[7] Ronald Reagan, an opponent of abortion, was probably disappointed when a justice he nominated, Sandra Day O'Connor, voted to uphold (with restrictions) the right to an abortion.

No president can exercise much control over the lower federal courts, though several have tried. For one thing, a district judgeship is heavily influenced by the preferences of the senators from the state in which the vacancy occurs. By the tradition of **senatorial courtesy**, the Senate will not confirm a judicial nominee if the senator from the candidate's state and of the president's party objects. Of late, many senators have created expert screening panels to advise them on candidates for appointment. But the process, of necessity, remains political: Nominees who fail to get past their senators have little hope of appointment.

Recently the controversy over who becomes a federal judge has become intense. Although the Senate confirmed most of President George W. Bush's nominees, it filibustered against at least six. Because it takes sixty Senate votes to end a filibuster, approving these appointments also takes sixty. Republicans complained that this is unconstitutional, and a simple majority should be enough to confirm. Democrats responded that they would not allow such a vote if they disliked the nominee's ideology, especially when it comes to abortion. President Bush responded by giving one of his nominees a recess appointment. (A recess appointment can be made when Congress is not in session, but it can last only during the next session.) The issue of filibustering court nominees may be before the Senate for some time.

Of the 145 Supreme Court nominees presented to it, the Senate has failed to confirm 29, though only 7 in the twentieth century.[8] (In 1991, the Senate came within a few votes of rejecting Clarence Thomas.) The reasons for rejecting a Supreme Court nominee are complex—each senator may have a different reason—but have involved such matters as a record of hostility to civil rights, questionable personal financial dealing, a poor record as a lower court judge, and (in the Bork case) Senate opposition to the nominee's legal philosophy. Nominations of district court judges are rarely defeated because, typically, no nomination is made unless the key senators approve in advance.

The judges who are confirmed in office are almost invariably of the same party as the president who nominated them. And they differ in more ways than their party label. In the box on page 316, we see the attitudes expressed by Democratic

Legislative court *A court that is created by Congress for some specialized purpose and staffed with judges who do not enjoy the protection of Article III of the Constitution. Legislative courts include the Court of Military Appeals and the territorial courts.*

Senatorial courtesy *A tradition that makes it impossible to confirm a presidential nominee for office if a senator files a personal objection.*

and Republican judges as of 1984. There were clear differences in ideology (Democrats were far more likely to be liberals than were the Republicans) and on a number of policy issues. These differences have some effect on certain issues the judges decide. But as we shall see, judging is a complex, technical process in which the facts of the case, the content of the law, and higher-court decisions all sharply restrict a judge's freedom to decide a matter in any way he or she pleases. In most cases ideological differences probably do not affect the outcomes.

When ideology does make a difference, much depends on the circuit in which the case is heard. There are more liberal judges in the Ninth Circuit (most of the far western states) and more conservative ones in the Eighth Circuit (the upper Midwest). The appeals judges in the Fifth Circuit (Texas, Louisiana, and Mississippi) once banned affirmative-action admissions programs in state law schools. Because the Supreme Court does not have the time to settle every disagreement, federal interpretations of the law may differ around the country (later the Supreme Court did overrule the Fifth Circuit's attack on affirmative action).

Since the mid-1970s, the number of blacks, Hispanics, and women serving on federal courts has increased (see Figure 12.3). The increases began with President Carter, continued (at a lower level) under Reagan and Bush, and accelerated under Clinton.

The Jurisdiction of the Federal Courts

Federal-question cases *Cases concerning the Constitution, federal law, or treaties over which the federal courts have jurisdiction as described in the Constitution.*

Diversity cases *Cases involving citizens of different states over which the federal courts have jurisdiction because at least $75,000 is at stake.*

We have a dual-court system—one state, one federal—and this complicates enormously the task of describing what kinds of cases federal courts may hear and how cases beginning in the state courts may end up in the Supreme Court. The Constitution lists the kinds of cases over which federal courts have jurisdiction (in Article III and the Eleventh Amendment); by implication, all other matters are left to state courts. Federal courts can hear all cases "arising under the Constitution, the laws of the United States, and treaties" (these are **federal-question** cases) and cases involving citizens of different states (**diversity cases**). In addition, certain cases can be heard in either federal or state courts. For instance, legal battles between citizens of different states when more than $75,000 is at stake may be heard in either federal or state courts. If a person robs a federally insured bank, he or she has broken both state and federal laws and hence can be prosecuted in either state or federal courts. Lawyers have become quite sophisticated in deciding whether, in a given civil case, their clients will get better treatment in state or federal court. Prosecutors often refer a person who has broken both federal and state law to whichever court system is likely to give the toughest penalty.

Furthermore, a matter that is exclusively in the province of a state court—for example, a criminal case in which the defendant is charged with violating only a state law—can be appealed to the Supreme Court of the United States under certain conditions (discussed later). Thus federal judges can supervise state court rulings even when they have no jurisdiction over the original matter. Under what circumstances this should occur is the subject of longstanding controversy between the state and federal systems.

Some matters, however, are exclusively under the jurisdiction of federal courts. When a federal criminal law—but not a state one—is broken, the case is heard in federal district court. If you wish to appeal the decision of a federal regulatory

Figure 12.3 Female and Minority Judicial Appointees

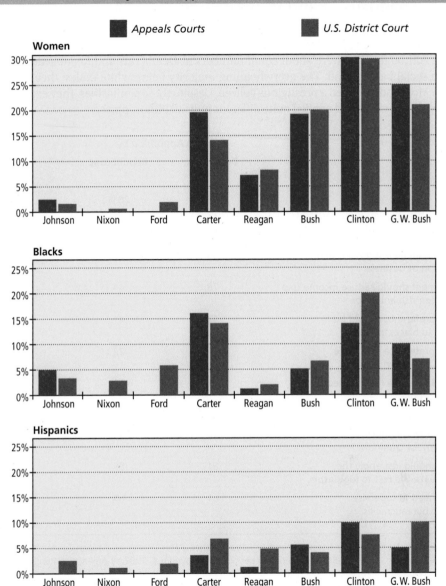

Source: Data from Harold W. Stanley and Richard G. Niemi, *Vital Statistics on American Politics 2009–2010* (Washington, D.C.: CQ Press, 2010), pp. 270–272.

agency, such as the Federal Communications Commission, you can do so only before a federal court of appeals. And if you wish to declare bankruptcy, you do so only in federal court. If there is a controversy between two state governments, the case can be heard only by the Supreme Court.

How Partisanship Affects Judicial Attitudes

In 1984, more than one hundred federal judges were interviewed about their background and attitudes. Although there were about equal numbers of Democrats and Republicans, they were similar in social background. The overwhelming majority being white males; their average age was sixty. Most had attended a prestigious college. Despite these similarities, they expressed quite different political views and applied quite different judicial philosophies.

Attitudes	Judges Appointed by	
	Democrats	Republicans
Political ideology		
Liberal	75%	28%
Conservative	11	37
Policy positions		
There should be less government regulation of business.	54	85
Government should reduce income gap between rich and poor.	78	44
Special preference should be given to blacks in hiring.	62	41
Special preference should be given to women in hiring.	47	22
A woman has the right to decide on abortion.	81	80
Judicial philosophy		
Courts show too much concern for criminals.	16	44
Judges should just apply the law, leave the rest to legislators.	51	69
Judges need to supervise public bureaucracies.	81	64

Source: Althea K. Nagai, Stanley Rothman, and S. Robert Lichter, "The Verdict on Federal Judges," *Public Opinion* (November–December 1987): 52–56, Reprinted with permission. Copyright © 1987 by American Enterprise Institute.

The vast majority of all cases heard by federal courts begin in the district courts. The volume of business there is huge. In 2005, the 670 or so district court judges received over 323,000 cases. Most of these involve rather straightforward applications of the law, and few lead to the making of new public policy. But those that do affect the interpretation of the law or the Constitution can begin with seemingly minor events. For example, a major broadening of the Bill of Rights—requiring for the first time that all accused persons in state as well as federal criminal trials be supplied with a lawyer, free if necessary—began when impoverished Clarence Earl Gideon, imprisoned in Florida, wrote an appeal in pencil on prison stationery and sent it to the Supreme Court.[9]

At one time, many matters could be appealed directly from district courts to the Supreme Court, but as the latter became overloaded with work, Congress passed laws giving the Court the power to control its workload by selecting, in most instances, the kinds of cases it wanted to hear.

The main route to the Supreme Court is by a **writ of certiorari**. *Certiorari*, a Latin term translating roughly to "made more certain," describes a procedure the Supreme Court can use whenever, in the opinion of at least four of its members, the decision of the highest state court involves a "substantial federal question" (the Supreme Court decides what that is). This procedure is also invoked when the decision of a federal court of appeals involves the interpretation of federal law or the Constitution. Either side in a case may ask the Supreme Court for certiorari, and the Court can decide whether to grant it without divulging its reasons.

In exercising its discretion in granting certiorari, the Supreme Court is on the horns of a dilemma. If it grants it frequently, it will be inundated with cases. As it is, the workload of the Court has risen from fewer than nine hundred cases in 1930 to over seven thousand in recent years. If, on the other hand, the Court grants certiorari only rarely, then the federal courts of appeal have the last word on the interpretation of the Constitution and federal laws—and, because there are twelve of these courts staffed by more than 160 judges, they may well be in disagreement. In fact this diversity of constitutional interpretation is evident: Because the Supreme Court reviews only about 1 percent of appeals court cases, applicable federal law may differ in different parts of the country.[10] One proposal to deal with this dilemma would be to devote the Supreme Court's time entirely to major questions of constitutional interpretation and to create a national court of appeals that would ensure that the twelve circuit courts of appeals are producing uniform decisions, but Congress has not found that idea attractive.

The Supreme Court's workload has also increased the influence of the law clerks hired by the justices. These clerks play a large role in deciding which cases should be heard under a writ of certiorari, and many of the opinions issued by the justices are in fact written by the clerks. The justices still decide cases, but the reasons for their decisions—reasons that in the long run may turn out to be more influential than the decisions—are often drafted by clerks who have only recently graduated from law school.[11]

Writ of certiorari *A Latin term meaning "made more certain." An order issued by a higher court to a lower court to send up the record of a case for review. Most cases reach the Supreme Court through the writ of certiorari, issued when at least four of the nine justices feel that the case should be reviewed.*

Getting to Court

In theory the courts are the great equalizer in the federal government. To use the courts to settle a question, or even to alter fundamentally the accepted interpretation of the Constitution, one need not be powerful or rich. Once the contending parties are before the court, they are legally equal.

It is too easy to believe this theory uncritically or to reject it cynically. In fact it is hard to get before the Supreme Court—it rejects about 95 percent of the applications for certiorari it receives. And the costs involved in getting to the Court can be high, though there are ways to lower them. If you are indigent (without funds) you can file and be heard as a pauper for no cost; about half the petitions arriving before the Supreme Court are **in forma pauperis**, such as that from Gideon cited earlier (page 317). If your case began as a criminal trial in the district courts and you are poor, the government supplies a lawyer at no charge. If the matter is not a criminal case and you cannot afford to hire a lawyer, interest groups representing a wide spectrum of opinion sometimes are willing, if the issue in the case seems sufficiently important, to take up the cause.

In forma pauperis *A procedure whereby a poor person can file and be heard in court as a pauper, free of charge.*

Fee Shifting

Unlike most of Europe, each party to a lawsuit in this country must pay its own way. This is called the *American rule.* But various laws have made it increasingly easy to get someone else to pay. **Fee shifting**, as it is called, enables the plaintiff (the party that initiates the suit) to collect its costs from the defendant if the defendant loses. Even more important to individuals, Section 1983 of the *United States Code* allows a citizen to sue anybody acting in some legal capacity—say, a police officer or a school superintendent—who deprives the citizen of some constitutional right or withholds some benefit to which the citizen is entitled. If the citizen wins, he or she can collect money damages and lawyers' fees from the government. There has been a flood of such Section 1983 suits in the courts. The Supreme Court has restricted fee shifting to cases authorized by statute,[12] but it is clear that the drift of policy has made it cheaper for citizens to go to court, at least for some cases. In addition, foundations and private associations called public-interest law firms will sometimes pay the costs of important cases.

Fee shifting *A law or rule that allows the plaintiff (the party that initiates the lawsuit) to collect its legal costs from the defendant if the defendant loses.*

Standing

There is an important nonfinancial restriction on getting into federal court. To sue, one must have standing. **Standing** is a legal concept that defines who is entitled to bring a case. It is especially important in determining who can challenge the laws or actions of the government. A complex and changing set of rules govern standing; some of the important ones are these:

Standing *A legal concept establishing who is entitled to bring a lawsuit to court. For example, an individual must ordinarily show personal harm in order to acquire standing and be heard in court.*

1. There must be an actual controversy between real adversaries, not a "friendly" suit that you hope to lose in order to prove a friend right, or a hypothetical or imaginary case in which you seek an advisory opinion.
2. You must show that you have been harmed by the law or practice about which you are complaining; it is not enough simply to dislike the government or a corporation or a labor union.
3. Merely being a taxpayer does not ordinarily entitle you to challenge the constitutionality of a federal government action. (You may not want your tax money spent in certain ways, but your remedy is to vote against the politicians doing the spending.)

Congress and the courts in recent years have made it easier to acquire standing. It has always been the rule that a citizen could ask the courts to order federal officials to carry out some act that they were under legal obligation to perform (such as issuing a welfare check) or to refrain from some action that was contrary

The Jurisdiction of the Federal Courts

Supreme Court of the United States

(1 court with 9 justices)

Original jurisdiction (cases begin in the Supreme Court) over controversies involving:

1. Two or more states.
2. The United States and a state.
3. Foreign ambassadors and other diplomats.
4. A state and a citizen of a different state (if begun by the state).

Appellate jurisdiction (cases begin in another, lower court): hears appeals, at its discretion, from:

1. Lower federal courts.
2. Highest state court.

United States Courts of Appeals

(1 in each of 11 circuits plus 1 in the District of Columbia and 1 federal circuit)

No original jurisdiction; hear only appeals from:

1. Federal district courts.
2. U.S. regulatory commissions.
3. Certain other federal courts.

United States District Courts

(1 in each of 94 districts)

Do not hear appeals; have only original jurisdiction over cases involving:

1. Federal crimes.
2. Civil suits under federal law.
3. Civil suits between citizens of different states when the amount exceeds $75,000.
4. Admiralty and maritime cases.
5. Bankruptcy cases.
6. Review of actions of certain federal administrative agencies.
7. Other matters assigned to them by Congress.

---

to law. A citizen can also sue a government official personally in order to collect damages if the official acted contrary to law.

However, you cannot sue the government itself without its consent. This is the doctrine of **sovereign immunity**. By statute, Congress has increasingly given its consent for the government to be sued in many cases involving a dispute over a contract or damage done as a result of negligence. Over the years these statutes have made it easier and easier to take the government into court as a defendant.

Even some of the oldest rules defining standing have been liberalized. The rule that merely being a taxpayer does not entitle you to challenge in court a government decision has been relaxed in cases in which the citizen claims that a right guaranteed under the First Amendment is being violated. The Supreme Court allowed a taxpayer to challenge a federal law that would have given financial aid to parochial (that is, church-related) schools on the grounds that this aid violated the constitutional separation between church and state. On the other hand, another taxpayer suit to force the CIA to make public its budget failed because the Court decided the taxpayer did not have standing in matters of this sort.[13]

Sovereign immunity *A doctrine that a citizen cannot sue the government without its consent. By statute Congress has given its consent for the government to be sued in many cases involving a dispute over a contract or damage done as a result of negligence.*

Class-Action Suits

Under certain circumstances individual citizens can benefit directly from a court decision even though they have not gone into court themselves. This can happen

Class-action suit *A case brought into court by a person on behalf of not only himself or herself but all other persons in the country under similar circumstances. For example, in* Brown v. Board of Education of Topeka, *the Court decided that not only Linda Brown but all others similarly situated had the right to attend a local public school of their choice without regard to race.*

by means of a **class-action suit**: a case brought into court by a person on behalf of not only himself or herself but all other people in similar circumstances. One of the most significant of such cases was the school desegregation decision of the Supreme Court in 1954. In *Brown v. Board of Education* it found that Linda Brown, a black girl attending the fifth grade in the Topeka, Kansas, public schools, was denied the equal protection of the laws (guaranteed under the Fourteenth Amendment) because the schools in Topeka were segregated. The Court did not limit its decision to Linda Brown's right to attend an unsegregated school but extended it—as Brown's lawyers from the NAACP had asked—to cover all "others similarly situated."[14] It was not easy to design a court order that would eliminate segregation for black schoolchildren, but the principle was clearly established in this class action.

Many other groups have been quick to take advantage of the opportunity created by class-action suits. By this means, the courts could be petitioned to give relief not simply to a particular person but to all those represented in the suit. Subsequent landmark class-action suits have involved malapportioned state legislatures,[15] civil-rights issues, the rights of prisoners, and antitrust actions against corporations. These suits became more common for three reasons: Congress was not addressing issues of concern to many people; it was often easier to make national policy through the courts than through the legislature; and lawyers often found it more profitable to bring a suit on behalf of thousands of people rather than on behalf of just one person.

When Linda Brown was refused admission to a white elementary school in Topeka, Kansas, the NAACP brought suit. The result was the 1954 landmark decision, Brown v. Board of Education. Today, children from diverse racial and ethnic backgrounds attend the same public schools.

The resulting flood of class-action suits greatly increased the Supreme Court's workload, and in 1974 it decided to tighten drastically the rules governing these suits. It held that it would no longer hear (except in certain cases defined by Congress, such as civil-rights matters) class-action suits seeking monetary damages unless each and every ascertainable member of the class was individually notified of the case. To do this is often prohibitively expensive, and so the number of such cases declined and the number of lawyers seeking them dropped somewhat.[16] There are still huge class-action suits, though, such as those that involve the alleged harm done by breathing asbestos or having a silicone breast implant.

Although federal courts have made it harder to bring class-action suits, many state courts make it very easy to bring them. In some states, a successful class-action suit will make the defendant change its practices in all fifty states— even in those where the defendant's existing policies are required by law. In 2005, Congress enacted a law that requires class actions involving people from two or more states and claims totaling more than $5 million to be heard in federal, not state, courts (unless two-thirds or more of the class members are from the same state).

In sum, getting into court depends on having standing and having resources. The rules governing standing are complex and changing but generally have been broadened to make it easier to enter the federal courts, especially for the purpose of challenging the actions of the government. Obtaining the resources is not easy but has become easier because laws in some instances now provide for fee shifting, because private interest groups are willing to finance some cases, and because it is sometimes possible to bring inexpensively a class-action suit that lawyers find lucrative.

The Supreme Court in Action

If your case should find its way to the Supreme Court—and the odds are that it will not—you will be able to participate in one of the more impressive, sometimes dramatic ceremonies of American public life. The Court is in session in its white marble building for thirty-six weeks out of each year, from early October until the end of June. The nine justices read briefs in their individual offices, hear oral arguments in the large, stately courtroom, and discuss their decisions with one another in a conference room where no outsiders are allowed.

Most cases, as we have seen, come to the Court on a writ of certiorari. The lawyers on each side may then submit their **briefs**—documents summarizing the lower-court decision, giving the arguments for their side, and discussing the other cases the Court has ruled on that bear on the issue. Then the lawyers are allowed to present their oral arguments in open court. These usually summarize the briefs or emphasize particular points in them, and are strictly limited in time—usually to no more than half an hour. The oral arguments give the justices a chance to question the lawyers, sometimes searchingly.

Because the federal government is a party—as either plaintiff or defendant—to about half the cases the Supreme Court hears, the government's top trial lawyer,

Brief *A legal document prepared by an attorney representing a party before a court. The document sets forth the facts of the case, summarizes the law, gives the arguments for its side, and discusses other relevant cases.*

the solicitor general of the United States, appears frequently before the Court. The solicitor general decides what cases the government will appeal from the lower courts and personally approves every case the government presents to the Supreme Court.

In addition to the arguments made by lawyers for both sides, written briefs and even oral arguments may also be offered by a "friend of the court," or **amicus curiae**. An amicus brief is from an interested party not directly involved in the suit. For example, when Allan Bakke complained that he had been the victim of reverse discrimination when he was denied admission to a University of California medical school, fifty-eight amicus briefs were filed supporting or opposing his position. Before such briefs can be filed, both parties must agree or the Court must grant permission. These documents are a kind of polite lobbying of the Court that, though they sometimes offer new arguments, generally are a declaration of each side's interests. The ACLU, the NAACP, the AFL-CIO, and the United States government itself have been among the leading sources of such briefs.

These briefs are not the only source of influence on the justices' views. Leading legal periodicals, such as the *Yale Law Journal* and the *Harvard Law Review*, are frequently consulted and cited in decisions, so that the outside world of lawyers and law professors can help shape, or at least supply arguments for, the justices' conclusions.

The justices retire to their conference room every Friday, where in complete secrecy they debate the cases they have heard. The chief justice speaks first, followed by the other justices in order of seniority. After the arguments they vote, traditionally in reverse order of seniority. In this process an able chief justice can exercise considerable influence—in guiding or limiting debate, in setting forth the issues, and in handling sometimes temperamental personalities. In deciding a case, a majority of the justices must be in agreement. If there is a tie, the lower-court decision is left standing (there can be a tie among the nine justices if one is ill or disqualifies himself or herself because of prior involvement in the case).

Though the vote is what counts, by tradition the Court usually issues a written decision, the **Opinion of the Court**. Sometimes this opinion is brief and unsigned (called a **per curiam opinion**); sometimes it is quite long and signed by the justices agreeing with it. If the chief justice is in the majority, he will either write the opinion or assign it to a justice who agrees with him. If he is in the minority, the senior justice on the winning side will decide who writes the Court's opinion. There are four kinds of signed opinions: *unanimous, majority* (the majority opinion of the Court when it is divided), **concurring** (an opinion by one or more justices who agree with the majority's conclusion but for different reasons that they wish to express), and **dissenting** (the opinion of one or more justices on the losing side).

The justices, like all other people in public life, tend to take consistent positions on issues based on their political philosophies. When issues arise that raise philosophical problems, the justices tend to form voting blocs. There are usually three: a *liberal/activist* bloc, a *conservative/strict constructionist* bloc, and a *swing* bloc.[17]

In early 2006, two new members (Chief Justice John Roberts and Justice Samuel Alito) joined the Court. There was on the Court a liberal/activist

---

Amicus curiae *A Latin term meaning "a friend of the court." Refers to interested groups or individuals, not directly involved in a suit, who may file legal briefs or make oral arguments in support of one side.*

Opinion of the Court *A Supreme Court opinion written by one or more justices in the majority to explain the decision in a case.*

Per curiam opinion *A brief, unsigned opinion issued by the Supreme Court to explain its ruling.*

Concurring opinion *A Supreme Court opinion by one or more justices who agree with the majority's conclusion, but for different reasons.*

Dissenting opinion *A Supreme Court opinion by one or more justices in the minority to explain the minority's disagreement with the Court's ruling.*

Members of the Supreme Court in Washington, D.C., October 2010. Seated from left to right are: Clarence Thomas, Antonin Scalia, Chief Justice John Roberts, Anthony M. Kennedy, and Ruth Bader Ginsburg. Standing from left to right are: Sonia Sotomayor, Stephen Breyer, Samuel Alito, Jr., and Elena Kagan.

bloc (Stephen Breyer, Ruth Bader Ginsburg, David Souter, and John Paul Stevens); a conservative/strict constructionist bloc (Antonin Scalia and Clarence Thomas), which Roberts and Alito joined; and a swing bloc (Anthony Kennedy). In 2009 Souter retired and in 2010 Stevens stepped down. They were replaced by Sonia Sotomayor and Elena Kagan, respectively. Their judicial views have not yet been revealed. But these labels, while useful, can be misleading. In the first forty-seven cases decided by the Court three-fourths of the decisions were either unanimous or decided by lopsided majorities (that is, with no more than two dissents). Only 10 percent were decided by a five-to-four (or four-to-four) vote. Only in a few high-profile cases do these "blocs" matter. Supreme Court cases are complex, difficult issues that require the justices to think through legal precedents and discuss the questions with their colleagues.

The Power of the Courts

The great majority of cases in federal courts have little to do with public policy: people accused of drug smuggling are tried, disputes over contracts are settled, and personal injury cases are heard. In most instances, the courts are simply applying a relatively settled body of law to a specific controversy.

The Power to Make Policy

The courts do make national policy whenever they interpret the law or the Constitution in a new way, extend the reach of existing laws to cover matters not

Stare decisis *A Latin term meaning "let the decision stand." The practice of basing judicial decisions on precedents established in similar cases decided in the past.*

previously thought to be covered, or design remedies for problems in ways that require the judges to act in administrative or legislative ways. By these tests the courts have become exceptionally powerful.

One measure of that power is that more than 150 federal laws have been declared unconstitutional, though since 1937 relatively few of these had broad national significance. On matters about which Congress feels strongly, it can often get its way by passing slightly revised versions of the voided law.

A second measure of judicial power is the frequency with which the Supreme Court changes its mind. An informal rule of judicial decision making has been **stare decisis**, meaning "let the decision stand." It is the principle of **precedent**— a court case today should be settled in accordance with prior decisions on similar cases. (What constitutes a similar case is not always clear.) There are two reasons that precedent is important. The practical reason should be obvious: If the meaning of the law continually changes, if the decisions of judges become wholly unpredictable, then human affairs affected by those laws and decisions become chaotic. The other reason is at least as important: If the principle of equal justice means anything, it means that similar cases should be decided in a similar manner. Of course times change and the Court can make mistakes; the Court will then change its mind. But however compelling the arguments for flexibility, the pace of change can become dizzying. By one count, since 1810 the Court has overruled its own previous decisions in more than 140 cases[18]—and in fact it may have done so more often (when it does not say it is abandoning a precedent but is merely distinguishing the present case from a previous one).

Precedent *A judicial rule that permits the court ruling settling an old case to settle a similar new one.*

The third measure of judicial power is the degree to which courts are willing to handle matters once left to the legislature. The Supreme Court once regarded the determination of congressional district boundaries, for example, as a **political question** that it would leave to another branch of government—in this case, Congress—to decide for itself. Then, in 1962, the Court decided that it was competent to deal with this question after all.[19]

Political question *An issue that the Supreme Court refuses to consider because it believes the Constitution has left it entirely to another branch to decide. Its view of such issues may change over time, however. For example, until the 1960s, the Court refused to hear cases about the size of congressional districts, no matter how unequal their populations. In 1962, however, it decided that it was authorized to review the constitutional implications of this issue.*

A fourth indicator can be found in the kinds of remedies the courts will impose. A **remedy** is a judicial order setting forth what must be done to correct what a judge believes is wrong. In ordinary cases the remedy is straightforward—for example, the loser pays the winner for some injury to the winner. Today, however, judges design remedies that go far beyond what is required to do justice to the parties who actually appear in court. The remedies now imposed often apply to large groups and affect the circumstances under which thousands or even millions work, study, or live; they affect, for example, inmates in a prison system that a judge orders revamped, or people previously ineligible who are declared eligible for welfare.[20]

The basis for these sweeping court orders can sometimes be found in the Constitution. Others are based on court interpretations of federal laws, as when the Court interpreted the 1964 Civil Rights Act as meaning that the San Francisco school system must teach English to Chinese students unable to speak it.[21] Local courts and legislatures elsewhere decided that same decision meant classes must be taught in Spanish for Hispanic children. What Congress meant exactly by the Civil Rights Act's prohibition of discrimination on grounds of "race, color, or national origin" was not clear; what is important is that it was the Court, not Congress, that decided what Congress meant.

Remedy *A judicial order preventing or redressing a wrong or enforcing a right.*

How the Supreme Court Helped Impeach Clinton

Impeachment is entirely a matter reserved to Congress. But the Clinton impeachment began when Paula Corbin Jones sued President Clinton, claiming that when he was governor of Arkansas, Clinton had sexually harassed her in a hotel room. The federal judge hearing the Jones cases ruled that she was entitled to know about any other women from whom Clinton had sought sexual favors. Clinton answered this request with one word, "None."

In January 1997, Clinton's lawyers asked the Supreme Court to rule that a sitting president could not be sued at least until after he had left office. In May the Court, by a unanimous vote, ruled against Clinton (520 U.S. 681 [1997]).

With the civil trial now restored, Clinton was asked about his relationship with former White House intern Monica Lewinsky. Under oath, he denied having a "sexual affair" with her. She filed a sworn statement agreeing that there had been no sex. But later independent counsel Kenneth Starr was able to negotiate an arrangement with Ms. Lewinsky under which, in exchange for immunity, she testified that she had had many sexual encounters with Clinton. This testimony, and evidence supporting it, became the chief basis for Starr reporting to the House of Representatives in September 1998 that Clinton might be impeached for having lied under oath.

The House agreed, voting to impeach the president on two counts and to send the matter to the Senate for trial. Clinton was not convicted.

If the Supreme Court had ruled that the president could not be sued while in office, the Lewinsky case might never have been investigated, and so impeachment might not have occurred.

Views of Judicial Activism

Judicial activism has, of course, been controversial. Supporters argue that the federal courts must correct injustices when the other branches of the federal government, or the states, refuse to do so. The courts are the last resort for those without the influence to obtain new laws, and especially for the poor and powerless. State legislatures and Congress, after all, tolerated segregated public schools for decades. If the Supreme Court had not declared segregation unconstitutional in 1954, it might still be the law today.

Critics of the activist courts rejoin that judges usually have no special expertise in matters of school administration, prison management, or environmental protection. However desirable court-declared rights and principles may be, implementing those principles means balancing the conflicting needs of various interest groups, raising and spending tax monies, and assessing the costs and benefits of complicated alternatives—all things that judges are not good at. Finally, judges are appointed, not elected, and thus are immune to popular control. As a result, if they depart from their traditional role of making careful and cautious interpretations of a law or the Constitution, and instead begin formulating wholly new policies, they become unelected legislators.

Supreme Court Justices in Order of Seniority

Name (Birthdate)	Home State	Prior Experience	Appointed by (Year)
John G. Roberts, Chief Justice (1955)	Maryland	Fed judge	G.W. Bush (2005)
Antonin Scalia (1936)	New York	Fed judge	Reagan (1986)
Anthony Kennedy (1936)	California	Fed judge	Reagan (1988)
Clarence Thomas (1948)	Georgia	Fed judge	G.H.W. Bush (1991)
Ruth Bader Ginsburg (1933)	New York	Fed judge	Clinton (1993)
Stephen B. Breyer (1938)	Massachusetts	Fed judge	Clinton (1994)
Samuel Alito (1950)	New Jersey	Fed judge	G.W. Bush (2006)
Sonia Sotomayor (1954)	New York	Fed judge	Obama (2009)
Elena Kagan (1960)	Washington, D.C.	Solicitor General	Obama (2010)

The Causes of Activism

Some people think that we have activist courts because we have so many lawyers. The more we take matters to courts for resolution, the more likely it is that the courts will become powerful. It is true that we have more lawyers in proportion to our population than most other nations. There is one lawyer for every three hundred Americans, but only one lawyer for every fifteen hundred French, and every seven thousand Japanese.[22] But this may well be a symptom, not a cause, of court activity. We have an adversarial culture based on an emphasis on individual rights and an implicit antagonism between people and government. Generally, lawyers do not create cases; contending interests do, thereby generating a demand for lawyers.

A more plausible reason has been the developments, discussed earlier in this chapter, that have made it easier for people to get into court, which in turn increases the number of cases being heard. Between 1961 and 1983, the increase in civil-rights, prisoner-rights, and Social Security cases was phenomenal: Civil-rights cases rose by 6,567 percent, Social Security cases by 3,683 percent, and prisoner petitions by 2,490 percent.[23] Such matters are the fastest-growing portion of the courts' civil workload.

An increase in cases will not by itself lead to sweeping remedies. For change to occur, the law must be sufficiently vague to permit judges wide latitude in interpreting it, and the judges must want to exercise that opportunity to the fullest. The Constitution is filled with words of seemingly ambiguous meaning—"due process of law," "equal protection of the laws," "privileges and immunities of citizens." Such phrases may have been clear to the Framers, but the Court today finds them equivocal. How the Court has chosen to interpret such phrases has changed greatly over the last two hundred years—and particularly in the last fifty—in ways that can be explained in part by the justices' political beliefs.

Congress has passed laws that also contain vague language, thereby adding immeasurably to the courts' opportunities for designing remedies. Various civil-rights acts outlaw discrimination but do not say how one is to know whether discrimination has occurred or what should be done to correct it if it does occur. Implementation is left to the courts and the bureaucracy. Various regulatory laws empower administrative agencies to do what the "public interest" requires but say little about how the public interest is to be defined. Laws intending to alleviate poverty or rebuild neighborhoods speak of "citizen participation" but fail to identify which citizens should participate, or how much power they should wield.

Even clear laws can induce litigation. Almost every agency that regulates business makes decisions that cause the agency to be challenged in court—by business firms if the regulations go too far and by consumer or labor organizations if they do not go far enough. One study found that federal courts of appeal heard 506 cases in which they had to review the decisions of a regulatory agency. In two-thirds of those cases the agency's position was supported; in the other third the agency was overruled.[24] Perhaps one-fifth of those cases arose out of agencies or programs that did not even exist in 1960. The federal government is more likely to be on the defensive in court today than it was forty years ago.

Finally, the judges' attitudes powerfully affect their decisions, especially when the law gives them wide latitude. There have been very few studies of the attitudes of federal judges, but their decisions and opinions have been extensively analyzed—well enough at least to know that different judges often decide the same case in different ways.[25] Many judges and law professors believe the courts *ought* to make policy, and this belief probably affects what courts actually do.

Checks on Judicial Power

No institution of government, including the courts, operates without restraint. The fact that judges are not elected does not make them immune to public opinion or to the views of the other branches of government. The importance of these restraints varies from case to case, but in the broad course of history they have been significant.

One restraint exists because of the very nature of courts. A judge has no police force or army; his or her decisions can sometimes be resisted or ignored if the resister is not highly visible and is willing to risk being caught and charged with contempt of court. For example, praying, Bible reading, and segregation continued in schools all over the country for years after the Supreme Court found them unconstitutional. But the courts' power is usually unchallenged when a failure to comply is easily detected and punished.

Congress and the Courts

Congress has a number of ways to check the power of the judiciary. It can gradually alter the composition of the judiciary by the kinds of appointments the Senate is willing to confirm, or it can impeach judges of whom it disapproves. In practice, however, impeachment proceedings are rarely be used to make much of an impact on the federal courts because simple policy disagreements are not generally regarded as adequate grounds for trying to impeach a judge, and most judicial appointments are not challenged.

But policy differences have become a major factor in confirmation hearings. The Senate rejected Robert Bork because it disagreed with his views and came close to rejecting Clarence Thomas because it disagreed with his. (In addition, Thomas had to face charges of sexual harassment brought by a former staff member.) To cope with these difficulties, conservative presidents began to nominate either candidates who had not clearly taken a position on controversial issues such as abortion (as George H.W. Bush did when he nominated David Souter) or ones whom the Senate would find it difficult to reject on other grounds (as the same president did when he nominated Thomas, a black). But policy differences are not the whole story; many senators have voted to confirm justices with whom they disagreed.

Congress can alter the number of judges, and by increasing the number sharply, it can give a president a chance to appoint judges to his liking. Franklin Roosevelt proposed to do this in his 1937 Court-packing plan in order to change the political persuasion of the Supreme Court. In 1979, Congress created 152 new federal district and appellate judges to help ease the workload. This bill, combined with normal judicial retirements and deaths, allowed President Carter to appoint more than 40 percent of the federal bench. During and after the Civil War, Congress tried to influence Supreme Court decisions by changing the size of the Court three times in six years.

On rare occasions Congress and the states can also undo a Supreme Court decision interpreting the Constitution by amending that document. The Eleventh Amendment was ratified to prevent a citizen from suing a state in federal court; the Thirteenth, Fourteenth, and Fifteenth, to undo the *Dred Scott* decision regarding slavery; the Sixteenth, to make it constitutional for Congress to pass an income tax; and the Twenty-sixth, to give the vote to eighteen-year-olds in state elections.

Sometimes Congress merely repasses a law that the Court has declared unconstitutional. That has occurred more than thirty times, as when a bill to aid farmers, voided in 1935, was accepted by the Court in a slightly revised form three years later.[26] (In the meantime, of course, the Court had changed its collective mind about the New Deal.)

One of the most powerful potential sources of control over the federal courts, however, is the authority of Congress to dictate the entire jurisdiction of the lower courts and the appellate jurisdiction of the Supreme Court shall be. In theory Congress could prevent a matter on which it did not want federal courts to act from ever coming before the courts. In 1868, under the exceptional circumstances of Reconstruction in the South, it did just that—and the Court conceded Congress's right to do so.[27]

Congress has threatened to do this on other occasions, and the mere existence of the threat may have influenced the nature of Court decisions. In the 1950s, for example, congressional opinion was hostile to Court decisions on civil liberties and civil rights, and proposed legislation that would have curtailed the Court's jurisdiction in these areas. It did not pass, but the Court may have allowed the threat to temper its decisions.[28] On the other hand, as congressional resistance to Roosevelt's Court-packing plan shows, the Supreme Court enjoys a good deal of prestige in the nation, even among people who disagree with some of its decisions. Passing laws that would directly attack it would not be easy, except perhaps in times of national crisis.

Furthermore, laws changing jurisdiction or restricting the kinds of remedies a court can impose are often blunt instruments that might not achieve their proponents' purposes. Consider, for example, the issue of school busing for racial balance. A law denying the Supreme Court appellate jurisdiction over school busing orders to achieve desegregation would leave lower federal and state courts free to go on ordering busing for this purpose. A law denying *all* federal courts the right to order busing as a remedy for racial imbalance would still leave them free to order busing for other reasons (such as to facilitate redistricting). And so on, to the ridiculous extreme of forbidding schoolchildren to enter a bus for any reason. Finally, the Supreme Court might well decide that if busing is essential to achieve a constitutional right, then any congressional law prohibiting such busing would be unconstitutional. Trying to think through how that dilemma would be resolved is like trying to visualize two kangaroos simultaneously jumping into each other's pouches.

Public Opinion and the Courts

Though not elected, judges read the same newspapers as members of Congress, and thus they too are aware of public opinion, especially elite opinion. While it may be going too far to say that the Supreme Court follows the election returns, it is nevertheless true that the Court is sensitive to certain bodies of opinion, especially of those elites—liberal or conservative—to which its members happen to be attuned. The justices will recall cases when, by defying opinion frontally, their predecessors very nearly destroyed the legitimacy of the Court itself. This was the case with the *Dred Scott* decision, which infuriated the North and was widely disobeyed. No such crisis exists today, but it is altogether possible that changing political moods will affect the kinds of remedies judges will think appropriate.

Opinion not only restrains the courts; it may also energize them. The most activist periods in Supreme Court history have coincided with times when the political system was undergoing profound and lasting changes. The assertion by the Supreme Court, under John Marshall's leadership, of the principles of national supremacy and judicial review occurred at the time when the Jeffersonian Republicans were coming to power and their opponents, the Federalists, were collapsing as an organized party. The proslavery decisions of the Taney Court came when the nation was so divided along sectional and ideological lines as to make almost any Court decision on this matter unpopular. Supreme Court review of economic regulation in the 1890s and 1900s occurred when the political parties were realigning and the Republicans were acquiring dominance that was to last for several decades. The Court decisions of the 1930s corresponded to another period of partisan realignment.

Until the 1950s, the Court rarely struck out in new directions or used its powers very actively as long as there was a broad public consensus as to the correct course of action. Beginning with *Brown* v. *Board of Education* and accelerating with the Court decisions restricting police powers, requiring busing to integrate schools, and upholding affirmative-action plans, the Court was responsible for an

How We Compare

JUDICIAL REVIEW IN CANADA AND EUROPE

Courts outside the United States can declare laws to be unconstitutional, but most do so in ways that are very different from those in America.

Canada: The highest court can declare a law unconstitutional, but not if the legislature has passed it with a provision that says the law will survive judicial scrutiny. Such laws must be renewed every five years.

Europe: The European Court of Human Rights in Strasbourg can decide human rights cases that begin in any nation that is part of the European Community.

France: The Constitutional Council can declare a law to be unconstitutional, but only if it is asked to do so by government officials and only before the law goes into effect.

Germany: The Federal Constitutional Court can declare, in an advisory opinion, before a case has emerged, that a law is unconstitutional. In America, the courts cannot issue advisory opinions.

extraordinary amount of policymaking, often in the teeth of public opposition. This opposition has led Congress to consider bills that would weaken the Court's powers or change its jurisdiction, but none passed.

Public opinion may strongly object to certain Court *decisions* but it seems unprepared to attack the Court as an *institution.* Polls reveal that the percentage of people saying they have "a great deal of confidence" in the Court fell sharply from 1966 to 1971, went up again around 1974, seesawed back and forth for a few years, then rose again after 1982. These trends seem to reflect the public's view not only of what the Court is doing but what the government generally is doing. From 1966 to 1971, the Court lost support, partly because of its controversial decisions but also because the government as a whole was losing support. In 1974, the Court gained strength because it was not tarnished by the Watergate scandal that afflicted the White House; after 1982, it gained support because the government as a whole was becoming (briefly) more popular.[29] In 2002, approximately one-third of all Americans said they had a "great deal" of confidence in the Court.

WHAT WOULD YOU DO?

MEMORANDUM

To: Senator Ann Gilbert

From: Amy Wilson, legislative assistant

The Supreme Court has held that the attorney general cannot use his authority over federally controlled drugs to block the implementation of the Oregon "Death With Dignity" law. Now some of your colleagues want to enact a federal equivalent of that law that would allow physicians to prescribe deadly drugs to patients who request them.

Arguments for:

1. The law respects the people's rights to choose the time and place of their own death.

2. It is already permissible to post "Do Not Resuscitate" orders on the charts of terminally ill patients.

3. Physicians can be held to high standards in implementing the law.

Arguments against:

1. The law will corrupt the role of doctors, as many think has happened in Holland, where a similar law has led some physicians to kill patients prematurely or without justification.

+

Friday,

Legalizing Assisted Suicide

February 24
WASHINGTON, D.C.

Congress is discussing a federal law that would allow physicians to administer drugs that will lead to the death of patients who request them. Oregon already has a "Death With Dignity" statute and now some legislators wish . . .

2. Such a law will lead some physicians to neglect or ignore the desires of the patient.

3. This law will undermine the more important goal of helping patients overcome pain and depression.

Your Decision:

Support the law _____   Oppose the law _____

SUMMARY

An independent judiciary with the power of judicial review—the right to decide the constitutionality of acts of Congress, of the executive branch, and of state governments—can be a potent political force in American life. That influence has been realized from the earliest days of the nation, when Marshall and Taney put the Supreme Court at the center of the most important issues of the time. From 1787 to 1865, the Supreme Court was preoccupied with the establishment of national supremacy. From 1865 to 1937, it struggled to define the scope of political power over the economy. In the present era, it has sought to expand personal liberties.

The scope of the courts' political influence has increasingly widened as various groups and interests have acquired access to the courts, as the judges serving on them have developed a more activist stance, and as Congress has passed more laws containing vague or equivocal language. Whereas in other political arenas (the electorate, Congress, the bureaucracy) the influence of contending groups is largely dependent on their size, intensity, prestige, and political resources, the influence of contending groups before the courts depends chiefly on their arguments and the attitudes of the judges.

Though the Supreme Court is the pinnacle of the federal judiciary, most decisions, including many important ones, are made by the twelve circuit courts of appeals and the ninety-four district courts. The Supreme Court can control its own workload by deciding when to grant certiorari. It has become easier for citizens and groups to gain access to the federal courts (through class-action suits, by amicus curiae briefs, by laws that require government agencies to pay fees, and because of the activities of private groups such as the NAACP and the ACLU).

At the same time, the courts have widened the reach of their decisions by issuing orders that cover whole classes of citizens or affect the management of major public and private institutions. However, the courts can overstep the bounds of their authority and bring upon themselves a counterattack from public opinion and from Congress. Congress has the right to control much of the courts' jurisdiction, but it rarely does so. As a result, the ability of judges to make laws is only infrequently challenged directly.

RECONSIDERING THE ENDURING QUESTIONS

1. **Should judges be limited to interpreting the Constitution and federal laws?**

   The problem with the strict constructionist view is that there many phrases in the Constitution (and in some federal laws) are ambiguous. Judges will differ as to what is meant by "due process of law" or the "equal protection of the laws." The problem with the activist approach is that judges have not been elected, and their political and philosophical views should not replace the Constitution or federal laws. There is no easy answer.

2. Why should federal courts be able to declare an act of Congress unconstitutional?

The Constitution does not give federal courts that power in so many words, but if the Constitution is to control political behavior, some agency must enforce it. Federal courts have taken on that task, and it is hard to think of any alternative.

3. Why is the Supreme Court so deeply divided on so many questions?

Justices are appointed by presidents with different views, and so the justices tend to reflect those views. Moreover, many Americans (and the groups that represent them) prefer a strict constructionist view, and many others prefer an activist one. Justices reflect that difference.

Online Resources: The Judiciary

CourseMate

- Federal Judicial Center: www.fjc.gov
- Federal courts: www.uscourts.gov
- Supreme Court decisions: www.law.cornell.edu
- Finding laws and reports: www.findlaw.com

Suggested Readings

Abraham, Henry J., and Barbara A. Perry. *Freedom of the Court*, 8th ed. Lawrence: University of Kansas Press, 2003. Careful review of civil-rights and civil-liberties cases.

Arkes, Hadley. *Constitutional Illusions & Anchoring Truths*. New York: Cambridge University Press, 2010. A subtle argument defending natural law as the proper basis for constitutional interpretation.

Bork, Robert H. *The Tempting of America*. New York: Free Press, 1990. A defense of judicial restraint and the doctrine of original intent.

Cardozo, Benjamin N. *The Nature of the Judicial Process*. New Haven, Conn.: Yale University Press, 1921. Important statement about how judges make decisions, by a former Supreme Court justice.

Carp, Robert A., Ronald Stidham, and Kenneth L. Manning. *Judicial Process in America*, 7th ed. Washington, D.C.: CQ Press, 2007. Useful overview of how federal and state courts operate.

Greenburg, Jan Crawford. *Supreme Conflict*. New York: Penguin, 2007. Fascinating account of how the modern Supreme Court works.

Hall, Kermit A. *The Oxford Companion to the Supreme Court*, 2d ed. New York: Oxford University Press, 2005. Everything you ever wanted to know about the Court, its justices, and its decisions.

McCloskey, Robert G., and Sanford Levinson. *The American Supreme Court*, 4th ed. Chicago: University of Chicago Press, 2005. Superb brief history of the Court.

Wolfe, Christopher. *The Rise of Modern Judicial Review*. New York: Basic Books, 1986. Excellent analysis of how the Court has used judicial review.

ENDURING QUESTIONS

1. Do interest groups have too much power?

2. Can the president make the country prosperous?

3. Why do we have a public debt?

CourseMate

Deficit *Money the government spends each year beyond what it receives in revenue.*

National debt *The total of all deficits that the government has acquired.*

Whatever the government wishes to do, it must pay for. Most of the money it needs it gets from collecting taxes, but when (as is usually the case) tax revenues are less than expenses, it borrows money by selling Treasury bonds. The amount it spends beyond what it has collected in taxes each year is called the **deficit**; the total of all debts it has accumulated over the years is the **national debt**. That debt is huge and growing rapidly. In 2009, it was $8.1 trillion, and by 2012, the Congressional Budget Office (CBO) estimates that it will be $10.5 trillion—an increase of 30 percent.[1] Much of that growth will result from the big expenses the government made in an effort to end the recession, but a lot of it will result from the federal government running out of money to pay for Medicare and other health programs.

Most Americans worry about this. They think the government should operate the way ordinary people do. If you want to buy a car or a house, you borrow money and have to pay it back by a certain date. If you run up so many charges on your credit card that it is maxed out, you won't be able to charge anything more, and if you keep this up, you will have to declare bankruptcy. Surely, they think, the federal government should operate the same way.

But it doesn't. With just a few exceptions, the government has spent more than it has taken in during almost every year since at least 1960. How does it get away with this?

There are three reasons: one economic, one substantive, and one political. The economic reason is that the national debt is important only if people who own Treasury bonds do not believe they will be paid back when they sell them. But almost everyone here and abroad who owns these bonds trusts the government to buy them back with stable and valuable cash. Though the national debt is very large, all the government has to pay each year is the interest on that debt. In 2010, it took about 9.5 percent of the federal budget to pay that interest. Federal interest payments require something over 2 percent of the **gross domestic product** (GDP), which is the total value of all goods and services the nation produces. But a big risk lies ahead. The rapidly growing cost of Social Security, Medicare, and Washington's new health care plan will require either much higher taxes or much heavier borrowing. The cost of these programs, unless something is done to fix them, will make our interest payments explode.

Gross domestic product *The total value of all goods and services the nation produces.*

When people borrow money, it is usually for something that has lasting value, such as a car or a house. This substantive argument is lost in Washington. If government borrowed *only* to buy things with lasting value—such as schools, roads, or aircraft carriers—politicians would be behaving like voters. But Washington borrows without regard to the substance of what it is buying.

The political argument is the most important one. Politicians do not like the deficit and will speak out against deficit financing, but they will offer two opposed ways of eliminating a deficit. One, advanced by conservatives, is to cut spending; the other, advanced by liberals, is to raise taxes. But as voters tend to like both spending on programs and lower taxes, they often support neither conservative nor liberal policies. Voters might think they could have both expensive programs and lower taxes if politicians just eliminated the waste in how tax money is spent, but they are wrong. Though there surely is waste, if it were all eliminated we would still be borrowing heavily to pay for federal programs.

But things may change. The nonpartisan Congressional Budget Office reported in June 2010 that our debt is bigger than 60 percent of everything the national produces and sells (its GDP), and if new cost-cutting policies are not adopted, that debt will equal 150% of GDP by 2035. By then, we won't be able to pay interest on the national debt without charging very high interest rates.

Politics and the Economy

"It's the economy, stupid." In that memorable phrase, James Carville, who ran Bill Clinton's 1992 presidential campaign, reminded us of what that election (and many others) was all about. Other issues affect an election, but when candidates have similar characteristics and there is no foreign crisis, the economy often makes the difference.

Up to a point, presidents endeavor to achieve a healthy economy, but neither they nor the entire federal government can guarantee one. Whether employment is growing or falling and whether business investment is rising or declining are matters largely controlled by individual workers, companies, and investors.

The United States has a largely free-market, capitalist economy, and that is both a blessing and a problem. It is a blessing because no other economy (socialist, communist, fascist, or otherwise government managed) can possibly produce as much wealth as a capitalist one. After World War II, a number of countries were divided into market-based and state-run areas (among them were West and East Germany, South and North Korea, and mainland China and Taiwan). In every case, the capitalist, market-based regions of these countries vastly outperformed the state-run areas. In the capitalist regions, the average person had a better job and earned much more money.

The problem is that there are real limits to what the government can do to make the economy run better. It cannot reasonably set wages and prices, direct investments, or hire more people to work on government projects. Although it has some economic policy tools, these are limited.

What Economic Numbers Hurt the President?

Unemployment hurts. According to an old story, we have a recession when your neighbor is unemployed and a depression when you are unemployed. But you do not have to be unemployed to worry about the economy. Political scientists have been able to show that rising unemployment or a decline in the gross domestic product makes even employed people less willing to support the incumbent party.[2] Though these voters have jobs, they worry that soon they might not, and that people they know are unemployed. Moreover, they worry about the economy and expect the president to do something about it.

Inflation also hurts. When prices rise, taxpayers grumble and are likely to vote against the incumbent White House party.[3] There is some evidence that when unemployment is up, people are more likely to vote for Democratic candidates, and when inflation is increasing, they are more likely to vote for Republicans, but much depends on the context.

How the Government Tries to Manage the Economy

As we saw in Chapter 10, the federal government has several agencies that try to make the economy work. The Council of Economic Advisers (CEA) consists of some talented economists who advise the president; the Congressional Budget Office (CBO) does the same for Congress. The Office of Management and Budget (OMB) prepares the president's budget and tries to ensure that government agencies follow the president's lead. The secretary of the Treasury, a person often drawn from Wall Street or the world of big business, represents this country abroad and tells the president what the financial community thinks ought to be done.

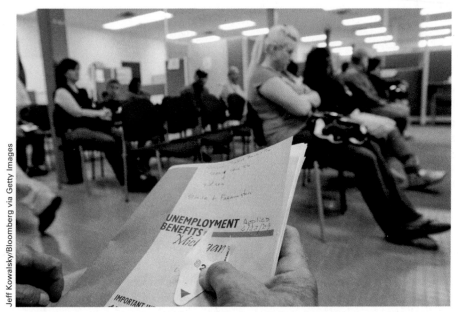

During the recession, people, including middle class workers, line up at the unemployment office.

All of these groups face two large problems. The first is that no one knows how to predict the economic future. The CEA and CBO, for example, cannot even predict very far in advance the size of the federal deficit. The second is that no one can be confident of knowing how to make the economy work well.

One independent agency plays probably the largest role in economic policy: the Federal Reserve Board (or Fed). Created in 1913, the Fed is made up of seven members appointed by the president with Senate approval for fourteen-year terms. One of these is designated by the president as the chair for a four-year term. The entire federal reserve system is composed of this board plus the heads of the twelve federal reserve banks scattered around the country. Interest rates are shaped by the decisions of the Federal Open Market Committee, which is composed of the seven board members plus the president of the Federal Reserve Bank of New York and, on a rotating basis, the presidents of four other Federal Reserve banks. The box on page 338 explains how the Fed manages monetary policy. For example, during the recession that lasted through much of 2001 and 2002, the Fed cut interest rates to the lowest point in decades in an effort to encourage consumption and production. After the economy recovered, the Fed raised interest rates in order to prevent inflation. When the economy was hurt in 2008 because banks had lent money carelessly to some home buyers who could not pay off their mortgages, the Fed lowered interest rates again. Manipulating interest rates and changing the supply of money in the economy are not, however, easy routes to prosperity. If the Fed cuts rates too much, people will take out foolish loans and prices may go up; if it raises rates too high, investments will slow down and new jobs will not be created.

The Federal Reserve Board

The Fed implements its monetary policy using these tools:

1. **Buying and selling federal government securities** (bonds, Treasury notes, and other instruments that constitute government IOUs). When the Fed buys securities, it in effect puts more money into circulation and takes securities out of circulation. With more money around, interest rates tend to drop, and more money is borrowed and spent. When the Fed sells government securities, it in effect takes money out of circulation, causing interest rates to rise and making borrowing more difficult.
2. **Regulating the amount of money that a member bank must keep in reserve** to back up its customers' deposits. A bank lends out most of the money deposited with it. If the Fed says that it must keep in reserve a larger fraction of its deposits, then the amount that it can lend drops, loans become harder to obtain, and interest rates rise.
3. **Changing the interest charged banks** that want to borrow money from the Federal Reserve System. Banks borrow from the Fed to cover short-term needs. The interest that the Fed charges for this is called the *discount* rate. The Fed can raise or lower that rate; this will have an effect, though usually rather small, on how much money the banks will lend.

Federal Reserve Board (Seven Members)

- Determines how many government securities will be bought or sold by regional and member banks.
- Determines interest rates to be charged by regional banks and amount of money member banks must keep in reserve in regional banks.

Regional Federal Reserve Banks (Twelve)

- Buy and sell government securities.
- Loan money to member banks.
- Keep percentage of holdings for member banks.

Member Banks (6,000)

- Buy and sell government securities.
- May borrow money from regional banks.
- Must keep percentage of holdings in regional banks.
- Interest rates paid to regional banks determine interest rates charged for business and personal loans and influence all bank interest rates.

Fiscal Policy

Fiscal policy
The taxing and spending decisions of the government.

The Fed cannot, even in theory, manage the government's efforts to solve economic problems. Government spending and tax law will have their own effect. Taxing and spending decisions are called **fiscal policy**. Some economists once believed that it would be easy to have a fiscal policy that helped the economy. If we are in a recession, increase government spending and lower taxes, which will give people better programs and more money. And if we experience not a recession but inflation, the government should reduce spending and raise taxes, which will take money out of circulation and reduce federal expenditures, thereby reducing inflation.

If it were only that simple. Politics makes it very hard to cut federal spending or raise (or even lower) taxes. Candidates rarely run for president by promising to do less for the voters or to raise their taxes. As we have seen, the public likes federal spending and dislikes higher taxes. Politicians will not attack inflation by spending fewer dollars; they will be inclined to spend (and spend more) on programs, whatever the condition of the economy. And liberal and conservative politicians will disagree about the effects of changing tax laws. Liberals tend to believe that lower taxes will increase the deficit, whereas conservatives are inclined to think that lower taxes will produce a stronger economy and hence more government revenue.

If someone suggests cutting taxes, liberals will denounce this as "helping the rich." If someone suggests increasing taxes, conservatives will denounce this as "hurting the producers." There is a little exaggeration in both arguments. Any tax cut will give more money to affluent voters. Couples earning over $250,000 a year make up only 2 percent of all people yet pay 44 percent of all federal income taxes collected.[4] President Obama has promised to raise taxes on this group, while Republican congressional leaders have argued this will hurt people whose investments can help end the recession.

Tax rates have changed dramatically over time. Figure 13.1 shows that during World War II and the Korean War, the highest individual income tax rates took in about 90 percent of the last dollar earned. By the 1980s and 1990s, however, the highest individual tax rates took in less than 40 percent of the last dollar earned.

The total tax bill that Americans pay is less than in many other democratic nations (Figure 13.2). The chief reasons for this are the constitutional system and the key role of state governments. Under the Constitution, it is hard to create a new program. There are too many places at which it can be blocked: in congressional subcommittees and committees, by a presidential veto, or by a Supreme Court ruling. The late Senator Russell Long put it this way: "Don't tax you, don't tax me, tax the fellow behind that tree." Of course, there aren't any people "behind that tree."

The fifty state governments also raise and spend a lot of money. But the states have to compete with one another to attract and hold people and businesses, so it is risky for one state to have a much higher tax rate than a neighboring one. Thus, limits on federal power and competition among states tend to keep tax rates lower than they are in, say, Sweden, France, or Germany.

Social Security and Medicare

The federal government spends money on many things, but the three largest are Social Security and Medicare, national defense, and interest on the national debt. Defense is discussed in the next chapter; interest payments were discussed earlier in this chapter. We turn here to two of the largest ways of paying money to citizens.

| Figure 13.1 | **Federal Highest Tax Rates, 1913–2004** |

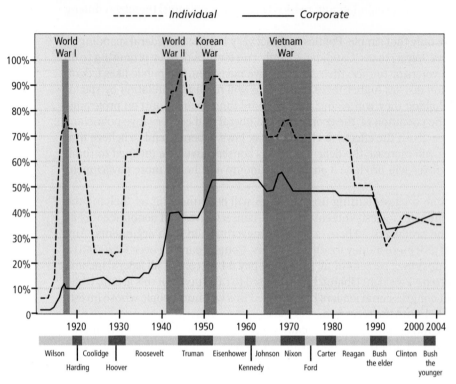

Source: Updated from *Congressional Quarterly Weekly Report*, September 18, 1993, p. 2488.

Social Security, the program that helps support retired persons, was created in 1935 during the Roosevelt administration and has proved to be extremely popular. Medicare, which helps pay hospital and doctor bills for retired people, was created in 1965 during the Johnson administration and it, too, has many ardent supporters. Workers are required to contribute money to each program. In 2003, Congress and President Bush added a new program to Medicare that, beginning in 2006, helps pay for prescription drugs.

The problem is that we do not contribute enough to keep either program solvent. Unless some changes are made, in a few years both programs will be hard to sustain.

Changing Social Security

When Social Security began in 1935, there were forty-two workers paying taxes for each beneficiary receiving a retirement check. Today there are only 3.4 workers per beneficiary. As a result we are spending money faster than we are taking it in.

The current Social Security tax is 12.4 percent of a person's earnings (half of this is paid by the employer). This money is used to make payments to current

Figure 13.2 Average Personal Income Tax Rates (2006) for Married Couple with Two Children

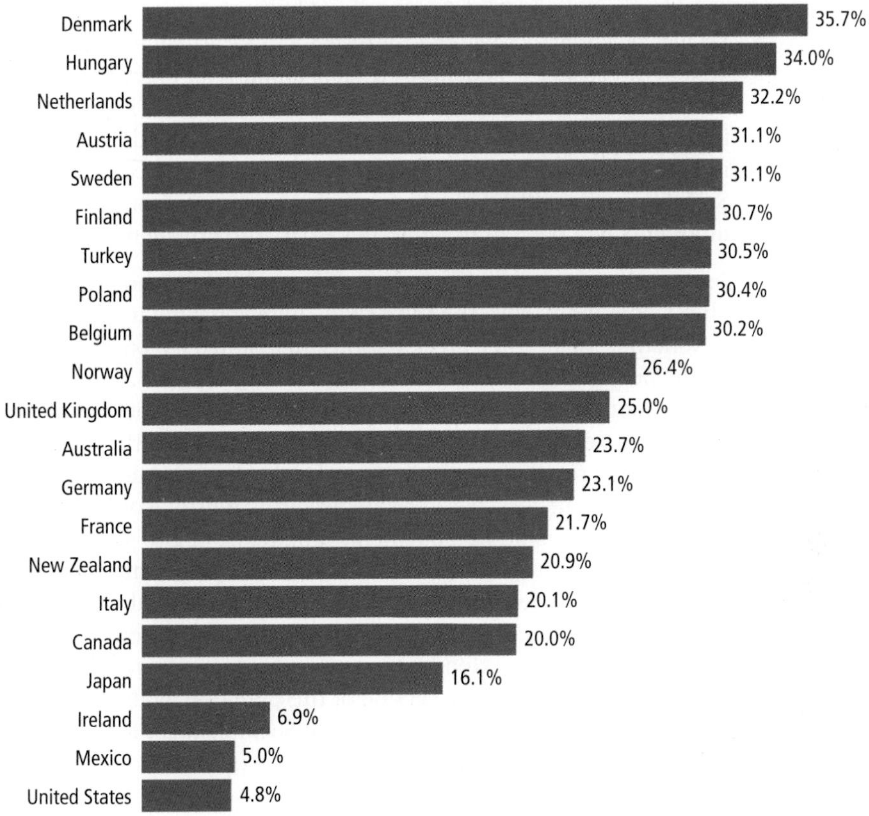

Denmark	35.7%
Hungary	34.0%
Netherlands	32.2%
Austria	31.1%
Sweden	31.1%
Finland	30.7%
Turkey	30.5%
Poland	30.4%
Belgium	30.2%
Norway	26.4%
United Kingdom	25.0%
Australia	23.7%
Germany	23.1%
France	21.7%
New Zealand	20.9%
Italy	20.1%
Canada	20.0%
Japan	16.1%
Ireland	6.9%
Mexico	5.0%
United States	4.8%

Source: Organization for Economic Co-Operation and Development (2006).

retirees, with the leftover funds invested in government bonds owned by the Treasury Department. These bonds help pay for the government's annual deficit, but by around 2016 the number of older persons eligible for retirement will have grown so large that the Social Security program will no longer be able to pay money to retirees out of what it takes in every year in taxes. Unless it makes other changes, paying for these bonds will require the government to raise taxes. Here are at least five things the government could do:

1. *Raise the retirement age:* If you could not collect Social Security until you became seventy years old, this would close the long-term funding gap by about 20 percent.
2. *Reduce benefits for high-earners:* People who retire after having earned a lot of money now receive about $2,120 per month. Cutting this by 10 percent would reduce the funding gap by about 25 percent.
3. *Raise taxes:* If we raised the Social Security tax from 12.4 percent to 13.4 percent, this would reduce the funding gap by about half.

4. *Increase the wage cap:* Today people pay Social Security taxes on only the first $97,500 of what they earn. If we increased this wage cap to $150,000, this would reduce the funding gap by about half.

5. *Let individuals invest some or all of their Social Security funds:* The Social Security system increases the benefits by a small amount for every year a worker makes tax payments. If all or part of these tax payments were invested by the worker into an approved, safe mutual fund, the worker would receive much more in benefits when he or she retired. Alternatively, one could keep the existing Social Security system but then require workers to contribute an additional amount (say, 2 percent of what they earn) into private mutual funds.

Because Social Security is so popular, any politician who proposes a change is touching what many call "the third rail," thereby risking instant political extinction. Nonetheless, in 2001 President Bush appointed a bipartisan commission to study the problem. It did, and filed a fascinating report . . . in December 2001, just a few months after the terrorist attacks on the World Trade Center and the Pentagon. With everyone's attention focused on terrorism, the report was ignored.

It suggested creating a voluntary personal retirement account to supplement Social Security benefits. These private accounts mostly would be paid for by the worker making an additional payment, ranging from 2 to 4 percent of his or her income, into safe mutual funds. Such accounts would in time pay out one-third to one-half more than does Social Security. Ironically, federal employees, including members of Congress, now have just such a program for themselves, but Congress has not been inclined to extend it to people who do not work for Washington.

President Bush suggested a version of this plan that would, unlike the commission report, set aside part of *existing* Social Security taxes for private investment, but his idea went nowhere.

Changing Medicare

When the Medicare law was passed in 1965, its sponsors said it would cost about $12 billion a year. But in 2010, we spent over $500 billion. The costs became much higher for several reasons: people are living longer and thus consuming more health care; new medical and surgical techniques are saving more lives—but at very high prices; Medicare encourages people to request medical care they may not really need; and there is a good deal of fraud perpetrated by some unscrupulous people.

Part A of Medicare pays for hospital care, Part B pays for doctors' fees, and Part D subsidizes the use of prescription drugs. Workers pay a Medicare tax of 2.4 percent (half paid by their employers). After they reach age sixty-five, they pay a fee of $93.50 a month (deducted from their Social Security check) to help pay for Part B coverage.

The management of Medicare leaves a lot to be desired. Up to a certain financial limit, and after having paid a deductible amount, visits to doctors or hospitals are (partially) covered by the program. Most of these visits are to deal with important problems, but some are for services the patient may not really need. A few doctors and hospitals overcharge for their services, and because the government decides how much a doctor or hospital will be paid for a visit, public officials can arbitrarily cut these payments whenever the government wants to "save money."

How We Compare

Social Security

Most European democracies began social security systems earlier than the United States did. Even for its time, the U.S. Social Security program that began in 1935 was a relatively modest insurance-based retirement program.

Today, over seven decades later, the U.S. Social Security program has grown dramatically and covers more than "old age, disability, and survivors." Still, European nations not only started sooner but have developed far more comprehensive—and expensive—social security systems than America has yet known.

In many European countries, social security programs extend well beyond retirement benefits or pensions to funding for work-related injuries, sickness, maternity leaves, and more; the retirement age for eligibility is lower than it is in the United States; and the benefits are, on average, greater.

For example, while the average American has received maybe half of his or her working-life income in benefits, a typical French or German worker has retired several years earlier and received as much as 70 percent of his or her working-life income in benefits. Social security benefits here are earnings-related, but many European nations (Ireland, Switzerland, and the United Kingdom, to name just three) provide a flat-rate pension independent of earnings.

Nothing is free: Europeans have paid two to three times as much as Americans in program-related taxes. And, unlike some European and other nations, the United States has avoided "dual Social Security taxation" via bilateral agreements and policies that do not require either foreign workers in America or Americans who work abroad to pay social security to both countries.

Sources: U.S. Social Security Administration, *Social Security Programs Throughout the World*, September 2008, and "U.S. International Social Security Agreements," 2009, accessed May 27, 2010 at www.ssa.gov/international/agreements_overview.html.

To deal with these problems, President Clinton in 1997 created a bipartisan commission to recommend solutions, but when it issued its report the president repudiated it. Changing Medicare, like changing Social Security, exposes leaders to a political third rail.

Many other countries manage health care by having the government pay for it all, as in Canada and Great Britain. This has enabled them to reduce the rate at which health care costs are rising below what is true in this country, but at a price: When the government runs all or most of the health industry, it can lengthen the time it takes for a patient to be admitted to a hospital, discourage the adoption of new technologies, and surround physicians with endless red tape.

The New Health Care Plan

In 2010, Congress passed a new health care plan. Its main provisions are these:

- Extends health care insurance to some 32 million uninsured Americans
- Provides federal subsidies to people who have trouble paying
- Penalizes people who do not buy health insurance
- Dependent children under age 26 would be covered by parent's insurance

- Adds more people to Medicaid
- Levies fees and taxes on medical devices, drugs, high-cost health insurance plans, health insurers

The bill was passed by the House and Senate without a single Republican vote. Thirty-four Democrats in the House and three in the Senate voted against it. When it passed, public opinion polls indicated the plan was not popular. Its defenders argued that as the law goes into effect it will win over most people, and that in time its cost will go down. Its critics claimed that it will stifle health care by heavy regulations and rapidly rising costs. In the November 2010 congressional elections, the law was not popular and may have contributed to large Republican gains in the House and Senate.

Making Policy Decisions

How are public policies proposed and then passed, rejected, or modified? Let us consider a simple way of classifying the politics of policy-making. We begin by observing that each policy has a **cost** and a **benefit**. A cost is the burden of a program, whether it is financial or social, that is placed on people. It includes taxes, unpleasant regulations, or social stigma. A benefit is the gain, whether financial or social, that flows to people. This includes payments, subsidies, tax reductions, government contracts, or heightened prestige.

It is important to bear in mind that these are *perceived* costs and benefits. For example, some people may think the nation benefits by massive military and other defense spending. Others disagree and believe the country is better served by social spending. By the same token, some people may think that a government regulation is a cost, while others may think it is a benefit. It is also important to understand that people differ in their beliefs about who gets a benefit and who pays a cost. Those beliefs are about the **legitimacy** of various groups. For example, some people may think that public assistance to the needy is legitimate. Others believe that it is not legitimate for the needy to receive such benefits.

Perceived costs and benefits can be widely distributed or narrowly concentrated. Figure 13.3 shows four simple possibilities:

- Widely distributed benefits and widely distributed costs, or **majoritarian politics**. This means that all or most people benefit and all or most people pay.
- Narrowly concentrated benefits and widely distributed costs, or **client politics**. A few people, or some particular community or organization benefits, but most people pay for what they get.
- Narrowly concentrated benefits and narrowly concentrated costs, or **interest-group politics**. A few people, communities, or organizations benefit, and a few people, communities, or organizations pay.
- Widely distributed benefits and narrowly concentrated costs or **entrepreneurial politics**. Almost everybody benefits, but only a few people, communities, or organizations pay the cost.

Cost *Any burden, monetary or nonmonetary, that some people must bear, or think they must bear, if a policy is adopted.*

Benefit *Any satisfaction, monetary or nonmonetary, that people believe they will enjoy if a policy is adopted.*

Legitimacy *Political authority conferred by law or public opinion.*

Majoritarian politics *A policy from which almost everybody benefits (or thinks they benefit), and for which almost everybody pays.*

Client politics *The policy under which some small group receives the benefits and the public at large endures the costs.*

Interest-group politics *A policy under which one small group bears the costs and another small group receives the benefits.*

Entrepreneurial politics *A policy under which society as a whole benefits while some small group pays the costs.*

Figure 13.3 **A Way of Classifying and Explaining the Politics of Different Policy Issues**

Perceived Costs

	Distributed	Concentrated
Perceived Benefits — Distributed	**Majoritarian Politics**	**Entrepreneurial Politics**
Perceived Benefits — Concentrated	**Client Politics**	**Interest-Group Politics**

Source: Organization for Economic Co-Operation and Development (2006).

Majoritarian Politics

Social Security and Medicare are good examples of majoritarian politics. Not everybody gets these benefits all at once, but almost everybody benefits from them at retirement. In the meantime, almost everybody pays for Social Security and Medicare. Other examples of majoritarian politics are national defense and crime control.

Majoritarian politics are not dominated by interest groups. Because everybody is going to get the benefit and pay the bill, few people have any incentive to join an organization in order to get it or to avoid paying for it. The policy may be, or may become, controversial, but only because people are worried about the size of the benefit or the magnitude of the cost. When we are on the verge of a possible war, interest groups are not important proponents or opponents; instead, popular attitudes and personal ideology matter most.

When Social Security began in 1935 and Medicare in 1965, many people benefited and the cost was small. In 1965, supporters of Medicare said it would not cost more than $8 billion a year. Today, Medicare costs at least thirty times that much each year, and every expert knows that it will cost dramatically more in the future. In the late 1930s, an old-age check for a retired person was paid for by taxes levied on 42 workers; today, only 3.4 workers pay for each retired person.

The federal government has struggled to solve these problems. In 2003, a new Medicare bill was passed, designed in part to change the system by allowing people to save, tax free, money for medical expenses. But whatever gains this may produce were probably outweighed by a huge new benefit to retired persons: payments for prescription drugs. In 2001, the bipartisan Commission to Strengthen Social Security suggested, and President Bush proposed, modifying Social Security by allowing people to invest a portion of their tax contributions into private mutual funds that generate higher returns than what the government can pay.* Congress did not agree. If they are to continue, both Social Security and Medicare would require major changes: an increase in the minimum retirement age or an increase in taxes.

Client Politics

Client politics helps prospective beneficiaries organize. If they are to get a benefit limited to them, it makes sense to work to make that happen. But if everybody else is going to pay for it, these payers have very little incentive to organize, especially if the cost is small.

Subsidies paid to farmers and dairies and regulations restricting the importation of sugar from abroad are classic examples of client politics. Consumers may pay more for a loaf of bread, a quart of milk, or a box of sugar, but they are not likely to know how much the extra amount costs. And even if they did, they would not have much incentive to do much about it because the money saved by winning the political fight would be minimal. And taxpayers probably do not know how much they pay in extra taxes for these subsidies and regulations; even if they did, it would be hard to find allies. A bill passed with bipartisan support and signed by President Bush in 2002 is paying farmers some $171 billion through 2012. Much of that will go to big agribusinesses that grow wheat, corn, rice, cotton, and soybeans. (Farmers who produce cattle, hogs, poultry, or fruit were left out.) But taxpayers have little incentive to block such a program. Most people know very little about it.

Many tax shelters are also examples of client politics. Few people other than the beneficiaries know what various clients get out of the tax laws, and so there is often little opposition to enacting and preserving shelters. In fact, getting a tax shelter is often much less controversial than getting a cash subsidy from the government. An agricultural subsidy gets voted up or down, but a shelter can often become an unnoticed part of a huge tax bill and generate almost no opposition.

Client politics seems like an irresistible force, but sometimes it gets changed. This can happen when people decide that either the product is undesirable or the recipients are illegitimate. For many years, tobacco farmers received big federal subsidies, heavily supported in that by members of Congress from key tobacco-growing states such as Kentucky and North Carolina. But the strength of that support began to change when the health risks of smoking became clear. Slowly, public indifference to tobacco subsidies began to evaporate, and the program was changed: Except for administrative costs, the subsidies are now paid for by tobacco farmers alone.

Welfare recipients have also been a client for federal payments. At one time, the program raised few objections because the recipients were thought to be the widows of soldiers and coal miners who, through no fault of their own, had been left to care for young children. But then the public began to feel that welfare was akin to a government handout that was perpetuating poverty. This public hostility

---

*The commission provided this example: If the average worker paid 1 percent of his or her income, matched by 1 percent contributed by the government, into a mutual fund that held both stocks and bonds, and he or she worked from age twenty-one to age sixty-five, that person at age sixty-five would have over $500,000, in addition to Social Security. If both husband and wife worked all of these years, they would have over $1 million.

led Congress to pass and President Clinton to sign the 1996 welfare reform act that led to TANF.

Even tax shelters can get changed if Congress, eager to have more money without raising taxes, decides to comb through the tax bill and eliminate some shelters that have only weak support. It is not easily or frequently done, but it can happen.

Even some very powerful clients can be defeated. Auto manufacturers opposed an auto safety bill in the 1960s and lost; many businesses opposed a cut in their tax shelters in the 1986 tax reform bill and lost.

Interest-Group Politics

When a small group gets many of the benefits and a small one pays much of the cost, both sides have a strong incentive to form interest groups. Interest-group politics has become much more common in American politics because the government, having undertaken so many tasks, has provided reasons for the beneficiaries of its aid to organize. Moreover, certain groups, such as women and racial minorities, who in the past had very little by way of organized interest groups, are now full participants in politics. And because funds are limited and rival groups want to change the benefits, these opponents also have a reason to organize.

Television broadcasters and cable companies fight intensely about the laws that will govern their access to an audience. After the telephone monopoly AT&T was broken up, its separate parts began fighting with each other and the remains of AT&T for access to homes. Cable companies fight against phone companies over which one will, and at what cost, feed home computers. For years banks could not sell insurance. When they sought to win that right, insurance companies fought back.

When labor unions in the 1930s wanted federal help to get organized, many business groups fought them. And after the unions won with the passage of the Wagner Act in 1935, the struggle continued before the National Labor Relations Board (NLRB) and in the courts and Congress. In the 1960s, labor unions demanded the passage of legislation to protect worker safety. Many manufacturing firms thought that its provisions were too radical and fought back, but in 1970 the Occupational Safety and Health Act (OSHA) was passed, giving labor most of what it had requested.

Members of Congress often dislike interest-group politics because it can force them to make some hard choices, especially if members of the opposed groups are active in their districts. To deal with this conflict, they often make statements about the issue that some may find meaningless or distasteful. But if you were in their shoes you would probably talk just the same way, unless you did not care about getting elected.

Entrepreneurial Politics

Often, laws are passed that benefit (sometimes quite modestly) society as a whole over the objection of an interest group that is responsible for paying most of the costs. For instance, laws set safety standards for automobiles at the expense (at least initially) of auto manufacturers and standards for air and water pollution that were passed over the objections of some business firms. These are examples of entrepreneurial politics.

In the past, railroads and trucking companies benefited from the rules laid down by the Interstate Commerce Commission (ICC) and airlines benefited from the decisions of the Civil Aeronautics Board (CAB). This form of economic regulation reduced competition and made it easier for the regulated firms to earn money. Now the ICC and the CAB no longer exist. They were abolished as Congress decided to let train, truck, and airline prices be set by the market.

Congress did not do this because businesses demanded it. Many key firms strongly opposed deregulation because market pressures would reduce profit margins. A government-guaranteed price was a much safer arrangement than a market-set price.

These sorts of changes are often the result of a dramatic crisis or compelling leadership. When the *Exxon Valdez* oil tanker ran aground along the Alaska coast in 1990, a strong demand arose for tougher rules on oil shipments. When an oil spill occurred near Santa Barbara, California, in 1970, there was a demand (re-enforced by the annual celebration of Earth Day) for tighter rules on water quality. When in 2010 a much greater oil spill occurred in the Gulf of Mexico by the failure of BP Oil, a national crisis took place.

Policy entrepreneur
A political leader who has the ability to mobilize an otherwise uninterested majority into supporting a policy opposed by a well-organized group.

Leaders who manage to galvanize public and congressional support for the change are **policy entrepreneurs**. Sometimes they are members of government. In the early 1970s, Senator Edmund Muskie led the fight for tougher air and water standards. Senator Estes Kefauver was able to tighten rules on pharmaceutical companies by holding well-publicized hearings in the 1960s.

Kari Goodnough/Bloomberg via Getty Images

A clean-up crew gathers oil from the BP Deepwater Horizon oil spill in the Gulf of Mexico near Orange Beach, Alabama.

More often, policy entrepreneurs are private persons with a talent for leadership. Ralph Nader is a well-known policy entrepreneur who has campaigned against some forms of business regulation and advocated tougher ones. When he started out, he wrote a book arguing for tougher regulations on car manufacturers. He might never have been noticed if General Motors had not hired a private detective to gather (or manufacture) gossip harmful to Nader. When that story broke, Nader became a champion of consumers. There also have been conservative entrepreneurs, such as the late Howard Jarvis, who led the fight to put a cap on property taxes in California by getting voters to approve Proposition 13 in 1978.

Policy entrepreneurs face two risks. One is that their need to dramatize an issue can lead them to exaggerate or misstate a problem. To them, publicity is as important as accuracy. A liberal entrepreneur can easily denounce "big business" or argue in favor of "eliminating products that cause cancer"; a conservative one can readily denounce "big-spending liberals" or attack "Muslim terrorists." Neither entrepreneur will necessarily be very careful about exactly what problem a big business, a liberal, or a given Muslim may represent, or be very precise about what products cause cancer.

The second risk is that an agency created to carry out an entrepreneurial policy will be captured by the very client firms it set out to regulate. This difficulty has been addressed in several ways. Agencies put in charge of entrepreneurial policies, such as the Environmental Protection Agency, the Occupational Safety and Health Administration, and the Consumer Product Safety Commission, are headed by a single administrator. In addition, they are responsible for a wide variety of firms instead of just one industry, they are often given precise legislative standards to enforce, and they have important allies in the mass media. In the past, regulatory agencies—such as the ICC, the CAB, and the Federal Communications Commission—were led by committees on which client industries could be represented, they regulated only a single industry instead of industry generally, and they had few media allies.

What These Political Differences Mean

Majorities can be produced in Congress by any one of these four types of politics. As a result, it is risky to generalize about politics by saying that "the rich," "big businesses," "labor unions," or "party bosses" actually rule. The rich have influence, but they have regularly seen their tax rates increase. Businesses have influence, but they have lost on many environmental and labor issues. Labor unions have influence, but the North America Free Trade Agreement was passed over their objections. Party bosses, to the extent they even exist anymore, cannot control majoritarian politics. *On any given issue*, one or another group may be powerful, but no group is powerful across all issues.

Policy in Action: Health Care

When Medicare was enacted in 1965, Democrats in the House and Senate voted for it by a large margin, but roughly half of the Republicans in each house also supported it. But the 2010 health care bill was passed without any Republican support and made its way through the House by a narrow seven-vote margin, with thirty-four Democrats opposing it. The Medicare bill went to President Johnson with bipartisan support, but the health care bill went to President Obama with narrow partisan backing.

Using the scheme shown earlier in this chapter, here is a summary of how the costs and benefits of the plan affected the political coalitions that formed around health care.

Majoritarian politics: The bill was opposed by a majority of the American people for a variety of reasons. Many thought it too expensive ($940 billion over ten years) or worried about the government regulations the law contained.

Client politics: Drug manufacturers looked forward to having many new customers as more people owned health insurance. To get this benefit, the pharmaceutical companies agreed to pay up to $85 billion in higher taxes. Many hospitals thought they would be helped by having more patients who could pay their bills with health care insurance.

Interest group politics: Labor unions wanted health care coverage, but business firms were upset by the higher taxes and fees they would have to pay. Poorer people liked it, but those earning over $200,000 a year would see their taxes escalate. Elderly people on Medicare and many doctors worried that the new law promised to cut payments to physicians, but the American Medical Association endorsed the law.

Policy entrepreneurs: The winners were President Obama and the Democratic leaders in the House who got a bill passed over popular and interest group opposition. In the elections of November 2010 we will learn whether the congressional Democratic party will pay a political price for this victory.

The Medicare and health care bills mobilized very different coalitions because, between 1965 and 2010, Congress became a more polarized institution and that deep partisan divide in Washington may reflect a deeper party split among many voters. Most major pieces of social legislation in the past reflect majoritarian politics, but the health care bill was based on a combination of client, interest group, and entrepreneurial politics.

Policy in Action: The Auto Bailout

When the Big Three American auto companies ran into trouble in 2008, they asked Washington for help. Americans were buying more Japanese cars more than America cars. The Japanese and German auto plants located in this country employ nonunion labor; the Big Three employ workers represented by the United Auto Workers (UAW). Among the benefits the UAW has obtained from Chrysler, Ford, and General Motors is a "Job Banks" program under which every worker laid off because a plant closes or technology has made their services no longer of value will receive 85 to 95 percent of their wages and benefits for the rest of their lives. For this and other reasons, the Big Three firms were heavily in debt.

There were two ways to handle this problem. The first was to have the Big Three enter bankruptcy and let a bankruptcy judge who would have the power to change union contracts, reduce manufacturing costs, direct that many dealerships be closed, and induce bondholders to forgive some of the firm's debt. The second is to have the federal government provide money to the firms to tide them

WHAT WOULD YOU DO?

MEMORANDUM

To: Elizabeth Gilbert, chairperson, Council of Economics

From: Edward Larson, White House speechwriter

Subject: Flat tax proposal

The President would like your advice on whether to endorse a flat tax. His likely opponent is pushing this issue.

Arguments for:

1. A flat tax is fair because it treats all income groups the same. We could leave the lowest income group with no taxes.

2. With a flat tax, we could eliminate almost all deductions and loopholes from the tax code.

3. Countries with a flat tax, such as Lithuania, have achieved great economic prosperity.

Arguments against:

1. A flat tax is unfair because it treats all income groups the same. The rich should be taxed more heavily.

2. Many tax deductions, such as the one for home mortgages, are desirable.

3. We could eliminate undesirable tax loopholes without creating a flat tax.

Friday,

Should We Have a Flat Tax?

January 31
BOSTON, MA

White House candidate David Wilson declared yesterday that he would seek a fundamental overhaul of the nation's tax system by creating a single rate for all taxpayers. The President is expected to respond to this in his State of the Union . . .

Your Decision:

Support _____   Oppose _____

over while their management was changed, executive bonuses were curtailed, and the firms would report to a government-appointed "car czar," In December 2008, President Bush ordered that some of the antirecession money in the TARP bill (see Chapter 10) be given to the automakers.

Soon Chrysler and GM declared bankruptcy, and Washington committed more money to them to help them manage this change. By the end of 2009, Chrysler and GM had received around $80 billion. In return, the federal government became the biggest stockholder in GM and one of the largest in Chrysler. Washington fired GM's chief executive officer, and directed that the company build more fuel-efficient cars. In July 2009, GM emerged from bankruptcy having agreed to close many plants and stop making several car brands. Chrysler emerged from bankruptcy under the ownership of Fiat, an Italian car maker, and the U.S. and Canadian governments.

The politics of this issue were complicated. The American people opposed the bailouts, so it was not a majoritarian issue. Instead, it was strongly supported by the auto companies and the UAW, and so it was a form of client politics. It became possible because both a Republican and a Democratic president supported the bailout.

But a deeper issue remains. There have been many bailouts in recent American history: of the Pennsylvania Railroad, the City of New York, and various bank and insurance companies. In each case, there was a major dilemma: If you bail out the firm, you are saving it and the jobs it provides—but at the same time you are telling businesses that they are "too big to fail" and thereby offering them an incentive to take imprudent risks. This is something scholars call a "moral hazard": encouraging people to take chances because they think someone will step in and save them if they make a mistake.

SUMMARY

Domestic policy issues must get onto the political agenda by means of a crisis, public demand, or leadership proposals. The major issues are usually the state of the economy, the level of taxes, the existence of deficits, spending to support favored programs, and regulations aimed at constraining the activities of individuals and organizations.

The state of the economy and the level of benefits paid to persons enrolled in contributory programs, such as Social Security, are politically the most powerful issues. A rise in unemployment or a decline in economic growth tend to be bad for the party occupying the White House. For a long time, any talk of cuts in Social Security constituted the "third rail" of politics, promising doom to the advocate.

By contrast, cuts in noncontributory programs have been easier to arrange because the recipients of welfare benefits often lack political power.

Regulation of business may either be economic or social. The former determines what firms can enter a market and what prices they can charge; the latter affects how firms manage employees, customers, and the environment. Economic regulations have become less common and social ones more common.

Government decisions about what policies to adopt are affected by the kinds of coalitions that support or oppose the proposal. Majoritarian decisions involve cases in which most people benefit and most pay the costs; client decisions are those where a few benefit and many pay the costs; interest-group politics involve cases where the benefits and costs are paid by two distinct groups; and entrepreneurial politics involve proposals to provide benefits to many at a heavy cost to a small group.

But practicing client politics may create a moral hazard by encouraging the client (and other groups who want to become clients of government policies) to act irrationally, thinking they will get a life preserver if they need it.

RECONSIDERING THE ENDURING QUESTIONS

1. Do interest groups have too much power?

They obviously have a great deal of power, but some kinds of politics (majoritarian and entrepreneurial) do not depend on interest groups. Moreover, interest groups today represent a much larger segment of public opinion than once was the case.

2. Can the president make the country prosperous?

There are real limits—in knowledge, authority, and executive capacity—to the president's ability. In general, a market economy works well most of the time. In a recession, there are things a president and Congress can do to make matters better; to avoid inflation, there are things the Fed can do.

3. Why do we have a public debt?

It is hard not to have a public debt because people tend to vote for politicians who promise to give them more things without raising their taxes.

Online Resources: Making Domestic Policy

 CourseMate

- Nonpartisan reviews of policy issues: www.policy.com
                                        www.publicagenda.com
- Taxes: www.taxpolicycenter.org
- Social welfare: www.ssa.gov
            www.acf.hhs.gov/programs/ofa/
            www.socialsecurityreform.org

Suggested Readings

Cogan, John F., R. Glenn Hubbard, and Daniel P. Kessler, *Healthy, Wealthy, and Wise*. Washington, D.C.: American Enterprise Institute, 2005. Brief survey of five ways to improve our health-care insurance system.

Cutler, David N. *Your Money or Your Life*. Oxford: Oxford University Press, 2004. A review of new health technologies that improve our lifespan.

Newhouse, Joseph P. *Free for All? Lessons from the RAND Health Insurance Experiment*. Cambridge: Harvard University Press, 1993. Careful measurement of the effects of different health-care insurance programs.

President's Commission. *Strengthening Social Security and Creating Personal Wealth for Americans*. Washington, D.C.: December 21, 2001. Comprehensive review of ways to improve Social Security.

ENDURING QUESTIONS

1. **How has terrorism changed U.S. foreign and military policy?**

2. **Does the United States know how to rebuild nations?**

3. **How important is the United Nations to America in taking military action abroad?**

CourseMate

Formulating a sensible foreign policy is probably the toughest task any government faces. If it makes a bad mistake, its international trade could be disrupted or it could lose a war. Or an aggressive enemy could gather its strength and attack it. When England and France failed to defeat Hitler after his aims became clear, the result was World War II. When the United States lost the war in Vietnam, it not only had to retreat in disgrace but left behind thousands of dead soldiers and a legacy of domestic political conflict.

Good foreign policy is not only hard to determine, it is difficult to settle. Statesmanship was required to decide whether the United States should help Hungary when the Soviets attacked it (we did not), Tibet when China occupied it (we did not), Rwanda when a civil war killed thousands (we did not), Kosovo and Bosnia in the Balkans when they erupted in chaos (we did), Haiti when a new president could not take office (we did), Iraq when it invaded Kuwait (we did), or Iraq when it refused to obey United Nations resolutions (we did).

Some writers think that foreign policy is especially difficult in a democracy. Alexis de Tocqueville, the great French writer who toured the United States early in the nineteenth century, wrote that a "democracy can only and with great difficulty regulate the details of an important undertaking, persevere in a fixed design, and work out its execution in spite of serious obstacles. It cannot combine its measures with secrecy or await their consequences with patience."[1] Other writers say that the strength of democracy is that though democratic nations rarely, if ever, wage an unjustified war on another country, its people, when mobilized by the president, support its overseas engagement even when many deaths occur.[2]

Kinds of Foreign Policy

Some foreign policy issues are questions of war and peace. These, as well as military spending and arms limitation agreements, are examples of majoritarian policies that confer both benefits and costs on almost everybody. Other policies involve interest-group politics in which some groups (say, labor and environmental groups) oppose free trade, and other groups (say, business firms and consumer representatives) favor it. There are also cases of client politics, as when corporations doing business overseas get favorable tax breaks. For a long while, U.S. policy toward Israel tended to reflect the political influence of Jews in the United States. Now, Muslim American groups have pressed a rival view. When foreign policy is chiefly majoritarian, the president usually plays the dominant role; when it has an interest-group flavor, Congress typically is dominant. But policies can undergo a change in their political structure. In 1986, President Reagan traded arms to Iran to help release U.S. hostages and then used some of this money to aid an anticommunist rebel group in Nicaragua. That would seem to be a majoritarian issue. But when all of this became known, Congress organized a major investigation.

The Constitutional Framework

The Constitution names the president commander-in-chief of the armed forces but requires that Congress appropriate all money for the military. The president appoints ambassadors, but the Senate must confirm them. The president can sign treaties, but they have no meaning unless the Senate, by a two-thirds vote, ratifies them. Congress must "declare" war, but the United States has often gone to war without any formal declaration. The reason is simple: America backs its fighting forces, and when they are put in harm's way, Congress pays their bills.

American troops have fought abroad over 125 times, but only five of the fourteen major wars it has fought followed a declaration of war.[3] As we saw in Chapter 10 on the presidency, Congress has tried to curb the president's war-making powers by passing, as it did in 1973, the War Powers Act and by authorizing two committees of Congress to oversee U.S. intelligence agencies. In fact, the War Powers

Act has had little effect, and congressional oversight of the CIA, the National Reconnaissance Office, and the Defense Intelligence Agency have rarely limited presidential authority.

The major agencies that help the president discharge that authority are the National Security Council, the State Department, and the Defense Department. In fact, there are even more than these, for in most large American embassies abroad, one can find not only State Department officials and CIA officers, but representatives of the FBI, the DEA, the Agency for International Development, the United States Information Agency, and representatives from the Departments of Agriculture, Commerce, and Labor.

The key limitation on the president is not this collection of bureaucratic helpers or the skeptical views of Congress but public opinion. Many decades ago, that opinion was strongly isolationist. It told the president to keep U.S. forces and money at home. But beginning with World War II, America has become more interested in the larger world. This does not mean that Americans are eager to charge off and fight abroad, but it does mean that they are usually willing to support the president when he sends our forces overseas. In Table 14.2 on page 361 we shall see some powerful evidence of this.

The New International World

September 11, 2001, was a date that changed America's foreign and military policy. Before the terrorist attacks on the World Trade Center and the Pentagon, President George W. Bush had expressed little interest in foreign policy and even

How We Compare

Opinion on Global Issues

Americans agree with people in other countries on some questions and disagree on others. Here and abroad there is support for putting limits on nuclear weapons and giving financial aid to other countries. And Americans, who before World War II were strongly isolationist, now are deeply internationalist, with 75 percent thinking that this country should "do its share to solve international problems with other countries."

But there are also big differences. Only a third of Americans think global warming is a very serious problem or that it is the result of human activity. Well over half of all Americans oppose paying higher prices to control the environment while over half of the British, French, and Germans support higher prices.

Americans are also more willing than Europeans to support the use of military force and are more skeptical about international financial bodies.

Sources: Council on Foreign Relations, "Public Opinion on Global Issues" (November 2009); Pew Research Center, "Global Warming Seen as a Major Problem Around the World" (December 2, 2009) and "Fewer Americans See Solid Evidence of Global Warming" (October 22, 2009).

less in rebuilding foreign nations. U.S. military forces were still chiefly organized around principles learned during the Cold War. Heavily armed divisions with many large tanks were ready to fight similar forces dispatched by a hostile nation. Though several national commissions had warned about terrorist attacks, little was done about their reports.

September 11—9/11, as it will always be known—brought home the reality of terrorist threats. Nearly 3,000 people were killed by hijackers who commandeered airline flights. Tragic as this was, the lasting problem has been to redirect U.S. foreign and military policy to cope not with a rival superpower but with terrorist groups around the world.

The United States sent troops to Afghanistan and, with the aid of local rebels, overthrew the Taliban regime that was in part supported by the Al Qaeda network run by Osama bin Laden. When Iraq refused to reveal what weapons of mass destruction it either had or once had and harassed United Nations inspectors, the United States invaded that country and in a few weeks destroyed the regime of its long-time ruler, Saddam Hussein.

Three Major Problems

The United States now faces three major problems. Can it help rebuild nations that (like Afghanistan) were in ruins or (like Iraq) were under siege from local terrorists? Can it develop a foreign policy that provides clear guidance as to how and when to use force? And can it reorganize the military so that it is able to move quickly and decisively against small groups of terrorists abroad?

Rebuilding Nations

The United States has had a lot of experience—some good and some bad—with rebuilding nations. It helped put Germany and Japan back on their feet after World War II. From 1992 to 1994, it tried to bring peace among warring factions to the east African country of Somalia. From 1994 to 1996, it worked to install a democratically elected president and rebuild the local police force in the Caribbean country of Haiti. Starting in 1995, it worked with European allies to restore order to Bosnia and Kosovo, located in what used to be Yugoslavia. In 2001, it began helping Afghans create a new government and economy and in 2003 started doing the same thing in Iraq.

The United States succeeded in Germany and Japan, failed in Haiti and Somalia, has made some progress in Bosnia and Kosovo, and remains in the middle of the struggle in Afghanistan and Iraq.[4]

American Special Forces, working with dissident Afghan groups, drove the radical Taliban regime out of power in Afghanistan. The United Nations created a military presence there staffed by both American and NATO forces that helped bring a new leader (Hamid Karzai) to power, but the country remains divided. Remaining Taliban terrorists still attack civilians and independent warlords, a few of whom are supported by the nation's production of heroin poppies and are not fully supportive of a civilian national government.

Our military victory in Iraq was a brief and stunning success, but rebuilding that nation has been a difficult problem. At first we abolished the Iraqi army, declared that supporters of the dictator Saddam Hussein could not hold office, and limited our military to striking back at the growing number of terrorist assaults. A democratically elected Iraqi government took power, but its strength was divided among many competing ethnic and religious groups.

As our efforts in Iraq became unpopular in America, the president changed course. He assigned a new military leader (General David Petraeus) to Iraq, sent several thousand more troops there, and supported Petraeus's new strategy of building alliances with local tribal leaders and keeping American forces in neighborhoods (instead of in remote military bases) to protect Iraqi civilians. These tactics were very successful; the number of terrorist assaults on Americans and civilians dropped sharply during the latter half of 2007 (Table 14.1).

In Iraq, America's initial success, later difficulties, and ultimate progress reveal how difficult nation building can be. And that story poses a problem for our military. Do you train and equip an army for the war you are already fighting, or do you do that only in part, saving much money and effort for a war that you have not yet fought? During the Cold War this country constructed a military designed to defeat the Soviet Union, but it was completely unprepared for the war in Vietnam. Though we (especially the Marines) made some helpful changes in Vietnam, after that struggle ended we went back to our Cold War mentality. That strategy enabled us easily to defeat Saddam Hussein, but left us unprepared for coping with the insurgents that began killing us after we had defeated the Iraqi army. The

A U.S. Army operation in the Khakeran valley of Afghanistan.

Table 14.1 Decline in Iraq Violence, 2006–2007		
Violence	Nov. 2006	Nov. 2007
Iraqi civilian deaths from violence	3,450	650
U.S. troop deaths	69	40
Daily attacks by insurgents	180	80
Multiple-fatality bombings	65	22
U.S. troops in Iraq	140,000	162,000
Iraqi security forces	323,000	430,000

Source: Jason H. Campbell and Michael E. O'Hanlon, "The State of Iraq: An Update," Brookings Institution (2007).

lessons General Petraeus taught us in Iraq have proved helpful in Afghanistan. But when that fighting ends, will the military prepare only for counterinsurgency, or will it recognize that traditional national military forces (possibly from China) may in the future attack us or an ally?

Foreign Policy and Terrorism

Foreign policy is made by the president working with the secretary of state and the national security adviser. Congress plays a role—at times a very important role. When the United States is about to send troops into battle, the president sometimes asks Congress for a resolution supporting him. Technically, this is required by the Constitution, which gives to Congress the sole power "to declare war," and by the 1973 War Powers Act, which declares that Congress must support any presidential military action within sixty days.

In practice, neither the Constitution nor the War Powers Act has made much difference. Only five of the fourteen major wars the United States has fought have followed a formal declaration of war by Congress.[5] No president has acknowledged that the War Powers Act is constitutional, and experience has suggested it is probably not effective. Americans almost always support a presidential decision to send troops abroad and want those troops to be successful. This is often called the "rally around the flag" effect. A president's popularity tends to rise dramatically during a military crisis (see Table 14.2). In the face of such public opinion, it would be foolhardy for Congress to tell the president to bring the troops home after sixty days.

Some presidents have asked for congressional approval of their proposed military actions. George H. W. Bush, the forty-first president, got congressional approval to send troops to oust Iraq from Kuwait in 1991. The measure passed the House by a vote of 250 to 183 and the Senate by the narrow vote of 52 to 47. George W. Bush, the forty-third president, got that approval when he sent troops to invade

Table 14.2	Percentage of Public Saying They Approve of How the President Is Handling His Job		
Foreign Policy Crisis		**Before**	**After**
1960	American U-2 spy plane shot down over Soviet Union	62%	68%
1961	Abortive landing at Bay of Pigs in Cuba	73	83
1962	Cuban missile crisis	61	74
1975	President Ford sends forces to rescue the American ship *USS Mayaguez*	40	51
1979	American embassy in Teheran seized by Iranians	32	61
1980	Failure of military effort to rescue hostages in Iran	39	43
1983	U.S. invasion of Grenada	43	53
1989	U.S. invasion of Panama	71	80
1990	U.S. troops to Persian Gulf	60	75
1995	U.S. troops to Bosnia	59	54
1999	U.S. troops to Kosovo	55	51
2001	U.S. combat in Afghanistan	51	86
2003	U.S. invasion of Iraq	58	71

Source: Updated from Theodore J. Lowi. *The End of Liberalism* (New York: Norton, 1969), 184. Poll data are from the Gallup Poll. The time lapse between "before" and "after" was in no case longer than one month.

Iraq in 2003. The resolution passed the House by a vote of 296 to 133 and the Senate by a vote of 77 to 23. By contrast, President Clinton never asked for congressional support for military action in Haiti, Bosnia, or Kosovo, nor did President George H. W. Bush for his intervention in Somalia. (After U.S. troops were killed in a way dramatized by the motion picture *Black Hawk Down*, Congress demanded that forces be withdrawn from Somalia, and President Clinton agreed.)

The big problem for any president is to enunciate the principles that govern his own decisions. When the Cold War was on, each president, operating through the National Security Council (composed, by law, of the president, vice president, and the secretaries of state and defense and, by custom, of the Director of National Intelligence and the chair of the Joint Chiefs of Staff), made it clear that his chief goal was to prevent the Soviet Union from overrunning Western Europe, bombing the United States, or invading other nations. But the Soviet Union has disappeared and no other nation has acquired its superpower status. During the Cold War, the world was made up of two superpowers—a **bipolar world**. Now the United States is the only superpower—a **unipolar world**. Although this superpower status means no other country can challenge the United States militarily, the nation remains vulnerable at home and abroad to terrorist attacks, as 9/11 amply confirms.

Bipolar world *A world that is militarily dominated by two superpowers, as was the case when the United States and the Soviet Union confronted each other.*

Unipolar world *A world that is militarily dominated by one superpower, as is the case with the United States today.*

To respond, President George W. Bush in September 2002 issued a document that emphasized new policies. Instead of waiting to be attacked, the president said that America "will act against such emerging threats before they are fully formed" because "[we] cannot defend America and our friends by hoping for the best." The United States will identify and destroy a terrorist threat "before it reaches our borders" and "will not hesitate to act alone."[6] In the case of Iraq, this meant a commitment to "regime change"—that is, getting rid of a hostile government, even without United Nations support. This has been called a doctrine of preemption: attacking a determined enemy before it can launch an attack against the United States or an ally. In fact, it is not really new. President Bill Clinton launched cruise missile strikes against training camps that followers of Osama bin Laden were using in the aftermath of their bombing of American embassies in Kenya and Tanzania in 1998. President Bush elevated the policy of preemption into a clearly stated national doctrine.

Supporters of this view hailed it as a positive step to defeat terrorists abroad before they could attack the United States at home. Critics attacked the argument as justifying preemptive and possibly unjust wars and abandoning the United Nations. This debate has divided Congress in a way that puts an end to the old adage that partisanship ends at the water's edge. That view emerged in 1942 when politicians who favored America's staying home and out of European or Asian wars decided, in view of the attack on Pearl Harbor on December 7, 1941, that the country had to be united against a common enemy.

Since the end of the Cold War, the United States has not had a common enemy that, in the opinion of critics of U.S. overseas efforts, should justify a nonpartisan view. Most liberal Democrats opposed the effort to get Iraq out of Kuwait in 1991, and they opposed the invasion of Iraq in 2003; most Republicans supported both efforts.[7] But when President Clinton launched attacks on hostile forces in Kosovo, he was supported by many liberal Democrats and opposed by many conservative Republicans.[8] Party differences and political ideology now make a big difference in foreign policy.

Sometimes the United States has sought and obtained United Nations support, as it did when going to war in Korea (1951) and in launching the effort to force Iraqi troops out of Kuwait (1991). It did not seek UN support in fighting against North Vietnam (in the 1960s), occupying Haiti (1994), or going to the assistance of friendly forces in Bosnia (1994) or Kosovo (1999). When the United States invaded Iraq in 2003, it asked for but did not get UN support; it went anyway, aided by a few allies, including Britain and Australia.

Changing the Military

Secretary of Defense Donald Rumsfeld was an ardent advocate of redesigning the military so that it can move more quickly, in smaller units, and with close cooperation among the armed services. In Afghanistan, he was able to rely on special forces, such as Army Rangers and Navy Seals, to work with Afghan rebels, and he made it possible for the air force to cooperate very closely with these units. In Iraq, that close cooperation persisted, aided by the use of battlefield computers, global positioning satellites, and speedy communications.

But fundamentally the army is still organized around ten large divisions and the marine corps around three large expeditionary forces. Each military force is headed by a chief of staff (or, in the case of the navy, a chief of naval operations). These top leaders meet as members of the Joint Chiefs of Staff (JCS), headed by a chair and a nonvoting vice chair. The JCS is an advisory group, and its members are appointed, with Senate confirmation, by the president. Not only that, but the chain of command is entirely civilian, headed by the president, who then gives orders to the secretary of defense, who then passes them on to individual military leaders. These orders may be transmitted through the JCS, but by law it does not have command authority.

The military, like all other government agencies, is composed of large bureaucracies with long traditions, conventional career paths, and a commitment to techniques learned in the past. Moreover, it uses its officers in ways that do not allow much room for effective changes. The typical officer will hold an assignment for no more than eighteen months before moving on to a new, and often quite different, job. Imagine how a business firm might operate if, after eighteen months, every key administrator had to change jobs, so that each warehouse manager then became an accountant and then a sales director and then a personnel director. By the time these persons had learned what their job entailed, they would have to move on to another one.

Congress has been asked to support, or at least not actively oppose, major changes in how the military operates. It must vote for the military budget and all of the major weapons the armed forces acquire. Because the armed forces have

Alex Wong/Getty Images News/Getty Images

General David Petraeus and Ambassador Ryan Crocker testify before Congress on the war in Iraq.

good relations with key congressional committees, the efforts of a secretary of defense to make a big difference can often founder on congressional hostility. Making big changes in the military requires civilian leaders to engage in careful and prolonged negotiations.

Much the same thing is true of our intelligence agencies. In November 2002 a law passed by Congress and signed by President Bush created the National Commission on Terrorist Attacks Against the United States, also known as the 9/11 Commission. Composed of equal numbers of Democrats and Republicans and co-chaired by a Democrat (former Congressman Lee Hamilton) and a Republican (former New Jersey Governor Thomas Kean), it held lengthy hearings that were often highly partisan. But when it issued its report in the summer of 2004, the Commission produced a careful, balanced document that gave the history of the 9/11 attacks and ended with many recommendations for changing U.S. intelligence agencies to reduce the chances that a future attack, like that of 9/11, would go undetected. A key recommendation was a call for the creation of a National Intelligence Director, who could coordinate the work of the CIA, the Defense Department, and the FBI. This was done, but so far with unclear results.

The Politics of Foreign and Military Policy

We can use the scheme presented in the last chapter to help us understand the politics of foreign and military policy. As with our domestic examples, this scheme is quite simplified and leaves out of account many subtle and complex differences.

Majoritarian politics *A policy from which almost everybody benefits (or thinks they benefit) and almost everybody pays for.*

Foreign policy decisions about going to war or not going to war are examples of **majoritarian politics**. The benefits go to almost everybody, as do the costs (in money). (Of course, the costs in terms of personal danger go directly to the military forces.) Like all other domestic examples of majoritarian politics, the war/no war decision does not involve interest groups or constituency pressures as much as it involves political ideology. Figure 14.1 shows how popular support for defense spending increased when Americans were held hostage by Iran in 1979 and when military struggles broke out in the old Yugoslavia in the 1990s.

When the United States is directly attacked, as it was on December 7 and on 9/11, politicians are almost unanimous in expressing their outrage. When it comes time to do something, divisions begin to appear. Recall that party differences affected congressional attitudes and votes on U.S. actions in Bosnia, Kosovo, and Iraq. These differences reflect difference in public and elite opinion.

About one-fifth of all Americans strongly opposed going to war in Iraq, about the same percentage as during the Korean and Vietnam crises. This opposition in the public is greatest among Democrats, African Americans, and persons with postgraduate university degrees.[9] These critical attitudes provided support for the campaign for the Democratic presidential nomination in 2004, especially as waged first by candidate Howard Dean and then by John Kerry.

Four times as many conservative Republicans as liberal Democrats endorse a preemptive war started by the United States. The gender gap between men and women, however, has disappeared on war issues. Such a gap existed before 9/11 but has gone away since then.[10] Men and women have the same views on the

Figure 14.1   Public Sentiment on Defense Spending

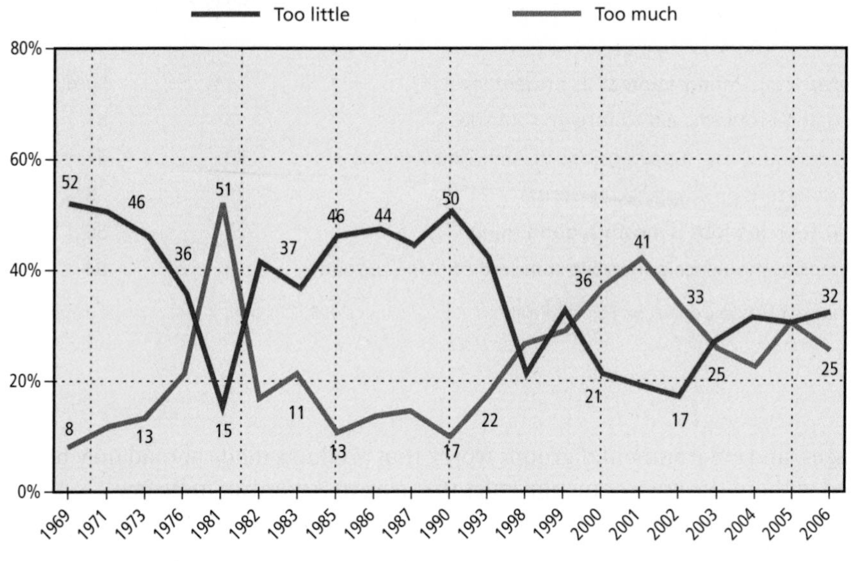

Source: Updated from *The Public Perspective* (August/September 1997), 19, and Gallup Poll.

importance of military strength as a means of ensuring peace. Over the long run, political attitudes have supported keeping the defense budget roughly the same in inflation-adjusted dollars.

Foreign policy elites also have different views on many issues than does the public at large. ("Elites" in this context means those who are actively involved in debating foreign policy issues because of their positions in government agencies, private organizations, and the mass media.) A poll taken in 2004 suggests that ordinary citizens are less likely than foreign policy elites to support high levels of immigration, expand economic aid to foreign countries, and help improve standards of living abroad but much more likely to support protecting the jobs of American workers and using torture on suspected terrorists (see Table 14.3).

But public views are easily changed by events, not because the public has fickle attitudes but because it supports the country when it is attacked and wants to punish those responsible. Elite views are less likely to be changed by events.

Many aspects of foreign affairs are shaped by **interest-group politics**. Perhaps the most obvious examples are the efforts to promote free trade, such as when the United States in 1993 adopted the North American Free-Trade Agreement, which created free trade among Canada, Mexico, and the United States. Industries that want to sell American products abroad support free trade because it abolishes tariffs and lowers the cost of selling goods to other nations. But many labor unions and environmental organizations oppose free trade because the unions fear jobs in the United States might be shifted to countries that pay lower

Interest-group politics *A policy under which one small group bears the costs and another small group receives the benefits.*

Table 14.3   How the Public and the Elites See Foreign Policy

	Percentage Agreeing	
	Public	**Elites**
Keep legal immigration at its present level	31%	50%
Expand economic aid to foreign countries	8	61
Very important to protect jobs of American workers	78	41
Use torture on suspected terrorists	29	8
Outsourcing jobs is mostly a good thing	22	56
America should help improve standard of living abroad	18	64

Source: Chicago Council on Foreign Relations, *Global Views 2004* (Chicago, 2004), various pages.

wages, and environmental groups worry that products made abroad may be created without the environmental rules that govern American industry.

In 1993, the free traders won, and NAFTA was approved. Since then, efforts to create broader free-trade agreements with the Caribbean, the rest of Latin America, and Africa have been intensely opposed, and new programs on these matters will be harder to achieve. There is no doubt that free trade does expand exports; after 1993, U.S. trade with NAFTA partners increased by about two-thirds, while trade with non-NAFTA countries increased by only one-tenth.[11]

American public opinion tends to be skeptical of free trade, and so labor and environmental groups have important allies. And presidents know this. Thus, President George W. Bush imposed higher tariffs on imported steel coming into the United States—in large measure, one assumes, because American steel companies that must compete (often not very effectively) with foreign steel are located in states, such as Ohio and Pennsylvania, that Bush wanted to carry in the 2004 election. But after European nations threatened to retaliate by increasing their tariffs on certain American products, he backed down and repealed the tariff increases.

Client politics *A policy under which some small group receives the benefits and the public at large endures the costs.*

One important aspect of U.S. military policy reflects **client politics**. The United States has hundreds of military bases, many created decades or even centuries ago. As the military has modernized and changed its focus, many of these bases have become useless. Secretaries of defense in both Democratic and Republican administrations have wanted to close many of them and sell the land to local governments or private organizations.

But each base has a client consisting of local governments and commercial enterprises near the base that benefit from the business and employment a base can generate. All congressional representatives will fight to keep bases in their home districts open. At the same time, most members of Congress will privately admit that the United States has too many bases. The problem is to find a way to close a base without creating political problems for Congress.

The solution began in 1988 with the creation of the Commission on Base Realignment and Closure. It consisted of private citizens, some with past political

WHAT WOULD YOU DO?

MEMORANDUM

To: The president

From: National security adviser

Subject: Hostages

The six Americans held hostage in the Middle East are beginning their second year of captivity. One, a CIA officer, is undergoing torture. It has been the policy of this administration not to negotiate with terrorists. Criticism of this refusal is being heard from hostage families and their sympathizers. The terrorist groups are demanding that we end our support of Israel. A government in the region has secretly indicated that, in exchange for military supplies, it may be able to help win the release of "some" hostages.

Friday,

American Hostages Begin Second Year of Captivity

Families Urge President to Negotiate Freedom

July 13

WASHINGTON, D.C.

The families of the six American hostages held captive in the Middle East today criticized the president for failing to win their release . . .

Your options:

1. Maintain the "no-negotiations" policy but use quiet diplomacy with friendly nations in the region to see whether they can intercede with the terrorist groups on behalf of the hostages.

    Advantages: (a) Our "no-negotiations" policy remains credible, and this will deter other terrorist groups from thinking that they can win concessions by capturing Americans. (b) This policy is consistent with our insistence that U.S. allies not negotiate with terrorists.

    Disadvantages: (a) There is no evidence that our traditional policy will get the hostages released. (b) Public sympathy for the hostages may increase, and this will lead to more criticism of this administration for failing to free captive Americans.

2. Secretly exchange arms for the release of Americans.

    Advantages: (a) Some or all hostages may be released. (b) We may earn the goodwill of more moderate elements in the area and thereby increase our influence there.

    Disadvantages: (a) We may deliver arms and no hostages will be released. (b) If secret arms deliveries become public, we will be heavily criticized for abandoning our "no-negotiations" policy.

3. Use military units to find and free the hostages.

    Advantage: The hostages may be freed without our having to make any concessions.

    Disadvantages: (a) The military is not optimistic that it can find and free the hostages, who are being kept in hidden, scattered sites. (b) The hostages may be killed during the rescue effort.

Your Decision:

Option 1 _____   Option 2 _____   Option 3 _____

experience, who would consider base-closing recommendations from the secretary of defense. It would then issue a report. Congress would have forty-five days to vote the report up or down without being able to change any of its details. In 1989, it voted the report up, and it did the same again with another commission report in 1991. When Congress was asked in 2001 to create a third such commission, it did so, and in 2005 Congress approved its recommendations.

Military contracts are also influenced, but not necessarily determined, by client politics. Total defense spending is set by a president and Congress that respond to the general public mood (after the country is attacked, as the U.S. Iranian embassy was in 1979 and on 9/11, that mood was very pro-spending). But Congress will insist that key military suppliers remain intact. This means that though Congress may sometimes cut the proposed military budget, it rarely, if ever, does so in ways that would harm a valued client—in this case, a weapons manufacturer located in a congressional district. Because every manufacturer is in some member's district, few ever get turned down.

Military modernization often reflects **entrepreneurial politics**. The entrepreneurs are sometimes dissident officers in the armed services who press for change and sometimes key civilian leaders, such as the secretary of defense. It is an uphill fight, but change does occur. President John F. Kennedy argued for the creation of special forces in the military, an idea opposed by key military leaders at the time. Other presidents have argued for the creation of intercontinental ballistic missiles, an idea that originally had little support from the air force. Secretary of Defense Rumsfeld argued for even broader changes—not just in creating new units or buying new weapons but in deciding how each military service would be organized and run.

Entrepreneurial politics *A policy under which society as a whole benefits while some small group pays the costs.*

SUMMARY

The great issues of national diplomacy and military policy are shaped by majoritarian politics. The president is the dominant figure, political ideology is important, and interest groups have small roles except in cases where material interests are directly affected, as with free trade and defense contracts.

Majority opinion tends to be weakly defined, with most people favoring the United States playing a modest role internationally but otherwise staying home and worrying about domestic issues. But when a war occurs, the public tends to support the president.

Elite opinion is very important in foreign policy, but that elite is deeply divided between people who want the United States to be active militarily and those who are skeptical of such interventions.

Terrorism has redefined our foreign and military policy by forcing the nation to react to disasters such as the attack on the World Trade Center and the Pentagon. Fighting terrorism has also led to proposals to reshape the military so that it is smaller and more mobile than the forces we used in Europe to deter Soviet aggression.

RECONSIDERING THE ENDURING QUESTIONS

1. How has terrorism changed U.S. foreign and military policy?

The 9/11 terrorist attacks and attacks abroad over the past two decades have led the United States to adopt a more aggressive military policy. It waged war in Afghanistan (where Al Qaeda was lurking) and in Iraq (which may or may not have supported terrorist groups).

2. Does the United States know how to rebuild nations?

The United States started its rebuilding efforts in Germany and Japan in 1945 and has continued elsewhere. It has done well in some places, such as Germany and Japan, and reasonably well in Bosnia and Kosovo, but it failed in Haiti and Somalia, and is still trying in Afghanistan and Iraq.

3. How important is the United Nations to America taking military action abroad?

It is not very important. The United States had organized UN support in Korea and Kuwait but not in Haiti, Somalia, Bosnia, Kosovo, or Afghanistan.

Online Resources: Making Foreign and Military Policy

- U.S. Army: www.army.mil
- U.S. Air Force: www.af.mil
- U.S. Navy: www.navy.mil
- Central Intelligence Agency: www.odci.gov
- State Department: www.state.gov

Suggested Readings

Allison, Graham T. *Essence of Decision: Explaining the Cuban Missile Crisis.* Boston: Little, Brown, 1971. Shows how an important foreign and military policy decision was shaped by organizational and bureaucratic factors.

Fisher, Louis. *Presidential War Power,* 2d ed. Lawrence: University Press of Kansas, 2004. Argues that the president has usurped military power from Congress in ways that violate the Constitution.

Holsti, Ole R. *Public Opinion and American Foreign Policy,* rev. ed. Ann Arbor: University of Michigan Press, 2004. Shows that American public opinion on foreign policy, though often uninformed, is stable and reasonable.

Kepel, Gilles. *Jihad: The Trail of Political Islam.* Cambridge, Mass.: Harvard University Press, 2002. An excellent, comprehensive survey of efforts by the radical fringe of Islam to bring a holy war (*jihad*) to the West and against moderate Islamic governments.

Mead, Walter Russell. *Special Providence.* New York: Knopf, 2001. Argues that American foreign policy, though often criticized, has been remarkably successful.

S uppose you were a student of American government sixty years ago. I was. You would not have studied civil rights laws, environmental regulations, the right to an abortion, deficit financing, Medicare, or a demand for government-supported health care. These laws, regulations, problems, and arguments did not exist. That is a puzzle. In a government whose leaders are chosen by a competitive struggle for the people's vote, candidates have a strong incentive to propose that, if elected, they will do more for the public. But for some reason, these programs were rarely proposed. Why not?

There were three reasons. First, the Constitution was interpreted in a way that sharply limited what policies the federal government could adopt. Until the middle of the twentieth century, the Supreme Court did not allow the federal government extensive powers to regulate business and said that the Bill of Rights limited only what Washington could do, not what states could do. For example, it was not until 1963 that states had an obligation to supply a lawyer to defend poor people in a criminal trial.

Second, public opinion did not demand many new programs. There was little interest in federal aid to education, federal efforts to reduce crime, or federal action to curtail segregation. The American Federation of Labor, led by Samuel Gompers, resisted federal involvement in labor-management disputes and did not make major demands for a social security program. Public opinion polls taken during the Great Depression indicated that as many as half the voters were opposed to a federal unemployment compensation program.

Third, there were few interest groups pressing for new programs. People who might have wanted to mobilize citizens behind efforts to end racial segregation, improve the environment, enlarge the status of women, or enhance consumer safety did not have the computerized mailing lists, foundation grants, radio talk shows, or public-interest law firms that would help their efforts. Some political scientists then said that American politics was pluralistic—that is, it reflected a broad range of interests—but it really wasn't.

In recent decades, these restraints on government growth have largely disappeared. The Supreme Court now gives the federal government broad authority to regulate business and has made clear that most of the amendments that make up the Bill of Rights affect state governments, as well as the national one. It has found in the Constitution phrases that justify ending school segregation and providing a right to an abortion.

Public opinion has changed so that much more is expected out of Washington. The Great Depression made it essential for national officials to manage the economy and provide benefits to people who were poor or elderly. Rising crime rates and the advent of drug abuse led voters to demand that Washington do something about these issues.

Political elites were well ahead of the public in making these demands, but now they had the resources to generate mass support and make effective political demands. The number and variety of interest groups has increased dramatically and their influence has been heightened by foundation grants, Web pages, computerized mass mailings, and radio talk shows. The public to which political elites appeal has changed greatly. In 1900, only 6 percent of all adults had graduated from high school; today, 16 percent of adults have graduated from college and another fifth have attended one. Education increases political knowledge, and more knowledge tends to mean more expectations.

So great have been the changes in American policy-making that we can refer, with only a little exaggeration, to an Old System having been replaced by a New System (see the box on page 372).

The Old System

The Old System had a small agenda. Though people apparently voted at a high rate and took part in torchlight parades and other mass political events, political leadership was professionalized in the sense that the leadership circle was small, access to it was difficult, and the activists in social movements were generally kept out. Only a few major issues were under discussion at any time. A member of Congress had a small staff (if any at all), dealt with his or her colleagues on a personal

How American Politics Has Changed

Old System		New System
	CONGRESS	
Chairs relatively strong		Chairs relatively weak
Small staff		Large staff
Few subcommittees		Many subcommittees
	INTEREST GROUPS	
A few large blocs (farmers, business, labor)		Many diverse interests that form ad hoc coalitions
Rely on "insider" lobbying		Mobilize grass roots
	PRESIDENCY	
Small staff		Large staff
Reaches public via press conferences		Reaches public via radio and television
	COURTS	
Allow government to exercise few economic powers		Allow government to exercise broad economic power
Take narrow view of individual freedoms		Take broad view of individual freedoms
	POLITICAL PARTIES	
Dominated by state and local party leaders meeting in conventions		Dominated by activists chosen in primaries and caucuses
	POLICY AGENDA	
Brief		Long
	KEY QUESTION	
Should the federal government enter a new policy area?		How can we fix or pay for an existing policy?
	KEY ISSUE	
Would a new federal program abridge states' rights?		Would a new federal program prove popular?

basis, deferred to the prestige of House and Senate leaders, and tended to become part of some stable coalition (the farm bloc, the labor bloc, the southern bloc) that persisted across many issues.

When someone proposed adding a new issue to the public agenda, a major debate often arose over whether it was legitimate for the federal government to take action at all on the matter. A dominant theme in this debate was the importance of "states' rights." Except in wartime, or during a very brief period when the nation expressed an interest in acquiring colonies, the focus of policy debate was on domestic affairs. Members of Congress saw these domestic issues largely in terms of their effect on local constituencies. The presidency was small and somewhat personal; there was only a rudimentary White House staff. The president would cultivate the press, but there was a clear understanding that what he said in a press conference was never to be quoted directly.

For the government to take bold action under this system, the nation usually had to be facing a crisis. War presented such a crisis, and so the federal government during the Civil War and World Wars I and II acquired extraordinary powers to conscript soldiers, control industrial production, regulate the flow of information to citizens, and restrict the scope of personal liberty. Each succeeding crisis left the government bureaucracy somewhat larger than it had been before, but when the crisis ended, the exercise of extraordinary powers ended. Once again, the agenda of political issues became small, and legislators argued about whether it was legitimate for the government to enter some new policy area, such as civil rights or industrial regulation.

The New System

The New System began in the 1930s but did not take its present form until the 1970s. It is characterized by a large policy agenda, the end of the debate over the legitimacy of government action (except in the area of First Amendment freedoms), the diffusion and decentralization of power in Congress, and the multiplication of interest groups. The government has grown so large that it has a policy on almost every conceivable subject, and so the debate in Washington is less often about whether it is right and prudent to take some bold new step and more often about how the government can best cope with the strains and problems that arise from implementing existing policies. As is commonly said, the federal government is now more concerned with managing than with ruling.

For example, in 1935, Congress debated whether the nation should have a Social Security retirement system at all; in the 1980s, it debated whether the system could best be kept solvent by raising taxes or by cutting benefits; in the early 2000s, it debated whether some part of each person's Social Security payments could be invested in the stock market. In the 1960s, Congress argued over whether there should be any federal civil-rights laws at all; by the 1980s and 1990s, it was arguing over whether those laws should be administered in a way that simply eliminated legal barriers to equal opportunity for racial minorities or in a way (by affirmative action) that made up for the disadvantages that burdened such minorities in the past. As late as the 1950s, the president and Congress argued over whether it was right to adopt a new program if it meant that the government had to borrow money to pay for it. As late as the 1960s, many members of Congress believed the federal government had no business paying for the health care of its citizens; today hardly anyone protests Medicare, but many worry about how best to control its rising costs.

The differences between the Old and New Systems should not be exaggerated. The Constitution still makes it easier for Congress to block the proposals of the president, or for some committee of Congress to defeat the preferences of the majority of Congress, than in almost any other democratic government. The system of checks and balances operates as before. The essential differences between the Old and the New Systems are these:

1. Under the Old System, the checks and balances made it difficult for the federal government to start a new program, and so the government remained relatively small. Under the New System, these checks and balances made it hard to change what the government is already doing, and so the government remains large.
2. Under the Old System, power was somewhat centralized in the hands of party and congressional leaders. There was still plenty of conflict, but the number of people who had to agree before something could be done was limited. Under the New System, power is much more decentralized, and so it is harder to resolve conflict because so many more people—party activists, interest-group leaders, individual members of Congress, heads of government agencies—must agree.

The transition from the Old to the New System occurred chiefly during two periods in American politics. The first was in the early 1930s, when a catastrophic depression led the government to explore new ways of helping the needy, regulating business, and preventing a recurrence of the disaster. Franklin Roosevelt's New Deal was the result. The huge majorities enjoyed by the Democrats in Congress, coupled with popular demand to solve the problem, led to a vast outpouring of new legislation and the creation of dozens of new government agencies. Though initially the Supreme Court struck down some of these measures as unconstitutional, the Court changed its mind; by the late 1930s, the Court had virtually ceased opposing any economic legislation.

The second period was in the mid-1960s, a time of prosperity. There was no crisis akin to the Great Depression or World War II, but two events helped change the face of American politics. One was an intellectual and popular ferment that we now refer to as the spirit of "the Sixties"—a militant civil-rights movement, student activism on college campuses aimed at resisting the Vietnam War, growing concern about threats to the environment, the popular appeal of Ralph Nader and his consumer-protection movement, and an optimism among many political and intellectual leaders that the government could solve whatever problems it was willing to address. The other was the 1964 election that returned Lyndon Johnson to the presidency with a larger share of the popular vote than any other president in modern times. Johnson swept into office bringing with him liberal Democratic majorities in both the House and Senate. The combination of organized demands for new policies, elite optimism about the likely success of those policies, and extraordinary majorities in Congress meant that President Johnson was able, for a few years, to get almost any program he wanted enacted into law.

These two periods—the early 1930s and the mid-1960s—changed the political landscape in America. Of the two, the latter was perhaps the more important, for not only did it witness the passage of so much unprecedented legislation, but also it saw major changes in the pattern of political leadership. It was during this time that the great majority of the members of the House of Representatives came to enjoy relatively secure seats, the primary elections came to supplant party conventions as the decisive means of selecting presidential candidates, interest groups increased greatly in number, and television began to play an important role in shaping the political agenda and perhaps influencing the kinds of candidates that are nominated.

President Lyndon Johnson (left) signs the Medicare Act in 1965 in the company of Vice President Hubert Humphrey (standing) and former president Harry S. Truman (seated).

WHAT WOULD YOU DO?

MEMORANDUM

To: President Daniel Gilbert

From: Fowler Brown, legislative liaison

Subject: Replacing Social Security

You face a difficult decision. Despite past reforms, the program can no longer be funded without large tax increases. Here are the arguments for and against allowing workers to invest their taxes in private mutual funds.

Arguments for:

1. Workers pay 15 percent of their salary to Social Security, with no guarantee that they will get their money back when they retire.

2. There are only two workers for every retired person (in the 1930s, there were 16 for every retiree). People must be encouraged to invest in their own retirement.

3. The federal government spends a quarter of its budget on Social Security, far more than it devotes to national defense.

Arguments against:

1. Workers have no guarantee that the mutual funds in which they put their tax money will earn enough.

2. We should raise taxes on all high-income workers to save Social Security.

3. Social Security is more important than national defense.

Your Decision:

Uphold this provision _____   Overturn this provision _____

+

Friday,

Policies for the Future

January 2021
WASHINGTON, D.C.

The President will make a major announcement about Social Security in his 2021 State of the Union message next week. The program, while popular, is running out of memory . . .

The New Politics Meets New Problems

When the Old Politics operated, the federal government, except for waging wars, did little that was important. Now it tries to do almost everything. During the Great Depression in the early 1930s, the federal government distributed money to citizens by creating the Works Progress Administration (WPA) and the Civilian Conservation Corps, which hired the unemployed. During the recession of 2008-2009, Washington had to use existing (and complicated) programs that tried to funnel money to people by means of unemployment insurance, Food Stamps, Medicaid payments, and state-run construction projects that took months (in some cases, years) to get started. The more Washington was already doing, the more complicated was its effort to cope with an economic downturn.

New challenges lie just ahead. Medicare, Medicaid, and Social Security will run out of money in the near future. We must find ways to keep them solvent. The health care bill that President Obama supported and Congress adopted in 2010 will bring millions of uninsured people into a health insurance plan; this will cost billions of dollars. The United States military must not only prevail in Afghanistan and Iraq, it must prepare for unknown new wars that will inevitably occur in the future. No one can know what future wars will be like or whether they will involve coping with traditional national armies or (more likely) armed bands of insurgents that terrorize distant foreign nations.

Even if we manage to solve these problems, many less dramatic ones still surround us. For example, can we find a way to make the tax code comprehensible to ordinary people, or will we leave in place its thousands of pages, which can only be understood by well-paid tax professionals? Is there a way to make Congress a more effective institution so that it searches for bipartisan agreements, thereby improving its miserably low standing in public opinion polls?

The new politics will make solving these problems harder, not easier, for one simple reason: the New Politics involves a much wider variety of people and interests. Pluralism is a political system in which many people and groups participate. We like it because it means that no small, shadowy elite is making decisions about how we should live. But with this benefit there is a cost; the wider the array of participants in a policy decision, the harder it is to make a decision.

Political scientists, myself included, are not very good at making predictions, and so you will finish reading this book aware that the future will bring new challenges but without much guidance as to how we will meet them and at what cost. Good luck.

THE DECLARATION OF INDEPENDENCE

In Congress, July 4, 1776

*The Unanimous Declaration of the
Thirteen United States of America*

When, in the course of human events, it becomes necessary for one people to dissolve the political bands which have connected them with another, and to assume, among the powers of the earth, the separate and equal station to which the laws of nature and of nature's God entitle them, a decent respect to the opinions of mankind requires that they should declare the causes which impel them to the separation.

We hold these truths to be self-evident: That all men are created equal; that they are endowed by their Creator with certain unalienable rights; that among these are life, liberty, and the pursuit of happiness; that, to secure these rights, governments are instituted among men, deriving their just powers from the consent of the governed; that whenever any form of government becomes destructive of these ends, it is the right of the people to alter or to abolish it, and to institute new government, laying its foundation on such principles, and organizing its powers in such form, as to them shall seem most likely to effect their safety and happiness. Prudence, indeed, will dictate that governments long established should not be changed for light and transient causes; and accordingly all experience hath shown that mankind are more disposed to suffer, while evils are sufferable, than to right themselves by abolishing the forms to which they are accustomed. But when a long train of abuses and usurpations, pursuing invariably the same object, evinces a design to reduce them under absolute despotism, it is their right, it is their duty, to throw off such government, and to provide new guards for their future security. Such has been the patient sufferance of these colonies; and such is now the necessity which constrains them to alter their former systems of government. The history of the present King of Great Britain is a history of repeated injuries and usurpations, all having in direct object the establishment of an absolute tyranny over these states. To prove this, let facts be submitted to a candid world.

He has refused to assent to laws, the most wholesome and necessary for the public good.

He has forbidden his governors to pass laws of immediate and pressing importance, unless suspended in their operation till his assent should be obtained; and, when so suspended, he has utterly neglected to attend to them.

He has refused to pass other laws for the accommodation of large districts of people, unless those people would relinquish the right of representation in the legislature, a right inestimable to them, and formidable to tyrants only.

He has called together legislative bodies at places unusual, uncomfortable, and distant from the depository of their public records, for the sole purpose of fatiguing them into compliance with his measures.

He has dissolved representative houses repeatedly, for opposing, with manly firmness, his invasions on the rights of the people.

He has refused for a long time, after such dissolutions, to cause others to be elected; whereby the legislative powers, incapable of annihilation, have returned to the people at large for their exercise; the state remaining, in the mean time, exposed to all dangers of invasions from without and convulsions within.

He has endeavored to prevent the population of these states; for that purpose obstructing the laws for naturalization of foreigners; refusing to pass others to encourage their migration hither, and raising the conditions of new appropriations of lands.

He has obstructed the administration of justice, by refusing his assent to laws for establishing judiciary powers.

He has made judges dependent on his will alone, for the tenure of their offices, and the amount and payment of their salaries.

He has erected a multitude of new offices, and sent hither swarms of officers to harass our people and eat out their substance.

He has kept among us, in times of peace, standing armies, without the consent of our legislatures.

He has affected to render the military independent of, and superior to, the civil power.

He has combined with others to subject us to a jurisdiction foreign to our constitution, and unacknowledged by our laws, giving his assent to their acts of pretended legislation:

For quartering large bodies of armed troops among us:

For protecting them, by a mock trial, from punishment for any murders which they should commit on the inhabitants of these states;

For cutting off our trade with all parts of the world;

For imposing taxes on us without our consent;

For depriving us, in many cases, of the benefits of trial by jury;

For transporting us beyond seas, to be tried for pretended offenses;

For abolishing the free system of English laws in a neighboring province, establishing therein an arbitrary government, and enlarging its boundaries, so as to render it at once an example and fit instrument for introducing the same absolute rule into these colonies;

For taking away our charters, abolishing our more valuable laws, and altering fundamentally the forms of our governments;

For suspending our own legislatures, and declaring themselves invested with power to legislate for us in all cases whatsoever.

He has abdicated government here, by declaring us out of his protection and waging war against us.

He has plundered our seas, ravaged our coasts, burned our towns, and destroyed the lives of our people.

He is at this time transporting large armies of foreign mercenaries to complete the works of death, desolation, and tyranny already begun with circumstances of cruelty and perfidy scarcely paralleled in the most barbarous ages, and totally unworthy the head of a civilized nation.

He has constrained our fellow-citizens, taken captive on the high seas, to bear arms against their country, to become the executioners of their friends and brethren, or to fall themselves by their hands.

He has excited domestic insurrections among us, and has endeavored to bring on the inhabitants of our frontiers the merciless Indian savages, whose known rule of warfare is an undistinguished destruction of all ages, sexes, and conditions.

In every stage of these oppressions we have petitioned for redress in the most humble terms; our repeated petitions have been answered only by repeated injury. A prince, whose character is thus marked by every act which may define a tyrant, is unfit to be the ruler of a free people.

Nor have we been wanting in our attentions to our British brethren. We have warned them, from time to time, of attempts by their legislature to extend an unwarrantable jurisdiction over us. We have reminded them of the circumstances of our emigration and settlement here. We have appealed to their native justice and magnanimity; and we have conjured them, by the ties of our common kindred, to disavow these usurpations, which would inevitably interrupt our connections and correspondence. They, too, have been deaf to the voice of justice and of consanguinity. We must, therefore, acquiesce in the necessity which denounces our separation, and hold them, as we hold the rest of mankind, enemies in war, in peace friends.

We, therefore, the representatives of the United States of America, in General Congress assembled, appealing to the Supreme Judge of the world for the rectitude of our intentions, do, in the name and by the authority of the good people of these colonies, solemnly publish and declare, that these United Colonies are, and of right ought to be, FREE AND INDEPENDENT STATES; that they are absolved from all allegiance to the British crown, and that all political connection between them and the state of Great Britain is, and ought to be, totally dissolved; and that, as free and independent states, they have full power to levy war, conclude peace, contract alliances, establish commerce, and do all other acts and things which independent states may of right do. And for the support of this declaration, with a firm reliance on the protection of Divine Providence, we mutually pledge to each other our lives, our fortunes, and our sacred honor.

JOHN HANCOCK [*President*]
[*and fifty-five others*]

THE CONSTITUTION OF THE UNITED STATES

We the People of the United States, in Order to form a more perfect Union, establish Justice, insure domestic Tranquility, provide for the common defence, promote the general Welfare, and secure the Blessings of Liberty to ourselves and our Posterity, do ordain and establish this Constitution for the United States of America.

ARTICLE I.

Section 1.   All legislative Powers herein granted shall be vested in a Congress of the United States, which shall consist of a Senate and House of Representatives.

Section 2.   The House of Representatives shall be composed of Members chosen every second Year by the People of the several States, and the Electors in each State shall have the Qualifications requisite for Electors of the most numerous Branch of the State Legislature.

No Person shall be a Representative who shall not have attained to the age of twenty five Years, and been seven Years a Citizen of the United States, and who shall not, when elected, be an Inhabitant of that State in which he shall be chosen.

Representatives and direct Taxes shall be apportioned among the several States which may be included within this Union, according to their respective Numbers, which shall be determined by adding to the whole Number of free Persons, including those bound to Service for a Term of Years, and excluding Indians not taxed, three fifths of all other Persons.[1] The actual Enumeration shall be made within three Years after the first Meeting of the Congress of the United States, and within every subsequent Term of ten Years, in such Manner as they shall by Law direct. The Number of Representatives shall not exceed one for every thirty Thousand, but each State shall have at Least one Representative; and until such enumeration shall be made, the State of New Hampshire shall be entitled to chuse three, Massachusetts eight, Rhode-Island and Providence Plantations one, Connecticut five, New-York six, New Jersey four, Pennsylvania eight, Delaware one, Maryland six, Virginia ten, North Carolina five, South Carolina five, and Georgia three.

When vacancies happen in the Representation from any State, the Executive Authority thereof shall issue Writs of Election to fill such Vacancies.

The House of Representatives shall chuse their Speaker and other Officers; and shall have the sole Power of Impeachment.

---

[1]Changed by the Fourteenth Amendment, Section 2.
Note: Excluding the Preamble and Closing, those portions set in italic type have been superseded or changed by later amendments.

Section 3. The Senate of the United States shall be composed of two Senators from each State, *chosen by the Legislature thereof,*[2] for six Years; and each Senator shall have one Vote.

Immediately after they shall be assembled in Consequence of the first Election, they shall be divided as equally as may be into three Classes. The Seats of the Senators of the first class shall be vacated at the Expiration of the second Year, of the second Class at the Expiration of the fourth Year, and of the third Class at the Expiration of the sixth Year, so that one third may be chosen every second Year; *and if Vacancies happen by Resignation, or otherwise, during the Recess of the Legislature of any State, the Executive thereof may make temporary Appointments until the next Meeting of the Legislature, which shall then fill such Vacancies.*[3]

No Person shall be a Senator who shall not have attained to the Age of thirty Years, and been nine Years a Citizen of the United States, and who shall not, when elected, be an Inhabitant of that State for which he shall be chosen.

The Vice President of the United States shall be President of the Senate, but shall have no Vote, unless they be equally divided.

The Senate shall chuse their other Officers, and also a President pro tempore, in the Absence of the Vice President, or when he shall exercise the Office of President of the United States.

The Senate shall have the sole Power to try all Impeachments. When sitting for that Purpose, they shall be on Oath or Affirmation. When the President of the United States is tried the Chief Justice shall preside: And no Person shall be convicted without the Concurrence of two thirds of the Members present.

Judgment in Cases of Impeachment shall not exceed further than to removal from Office, and disqualification to hold and enjoy any Office of honor, Trust or Profit under the United States: but the Party convicted shall nevertheless be liable and subject to Indictment, Trial, Judgment and Punishment, according to Law.

Section 4. The Times, Places and Manner of holding Elections for Senators and Representatives, shall be prescribed in each State by the Legislature thereof; but the Congress may at any time by Law make or alter such Regulations, except as to the Places of chusing Senators.

The Congress shall assemble at least once in every Year, and such Meeting shall be on the *first Monday in December, unless they shall by Law appoint a different Day.*[4]

Section 5. Each House shall be the Judge of the Elections, Returns and Qualifications of its own Members, and a Majority of each shall constitute a Quorum to do Business; but a smaller number may adjourn from day to day, and may be authorized to compel the Attendance of absent Members, in such Manner, and under such Penalties as each House may provide.

Each House may determine the Rules of its Proceedings, punish its Members for disorderly Behaviour, and, with the Concurrence of two thirds, expel a Member.

---

[2]Changed by the Seventeenth Amendment.
[3]Changed by the Seventeenth Amendment.
[4]Changed by the Twentieth Amendment, Section 2.

Each House shall keep a Journal of its Proceedings, and from time to time publish the same, excepting such Parts as may in their Judgment require Secrecy; and the Yeas and Nays of the Members of either House on any question shall, at the Desire of one fifth of those Present, be entered on the Journal.

Neither House, during the Session of Congress, shall, without the Consent of the other, adjourn for more than three days, nor to any other Place than that in which the two Houses shall be sitting.

Section 6.   The Senators and Representatives shall receive a Compensation for their Services, to be ascertained by Law, and paid out of the Treasury of the United States. They shall in all Cases, except Treason, Felony and Breach of the Peace, be privileged from Arrest during their Attendance at the Session of their respective Houses, and in going to and returning from the same; and for any Speech or Debate in either House, they shall not be questioned in any other Place.

No Senator or Representative shall, during the Time for which he was elected, be appointed to any civil Office under the Authority of the United States, which shall have been created, or the Emoluments whereof shall have been encreased during such time; and no Person holding any Office under the United States, shall be a Member of either House during his Continuance in Office.

Section 7.   All Bills for raising Revenue shall originate in the House of Representatives; but the Senate may propose or concur with Amendments as on other Bills.

Every Bill which shall have passed the House of Representatives and the Senate, shall, before it become a Law, be presented to the President of the United States; If he approve he shall assign it, but if not he shall return it, with his Objections to that House in which it shall have originated, who shall enter the Objections at large on their Journal, and proceed to reconsider it. If after such Reconsideration two thirds of that House shall agree to pass the Bill, it shall be sent, together with the Objections, to the other House, by which it shall likewise be reconsidered, and if approved by two thirds of that House, it shall become a Law. But in all such Cases the Votes of both Houses shall be determined by yeas and Nays, and the Names of the Persons voting for and against the Bill shall be entered on the Journal of each House respectively. If any Bill shall not be returned by the President within ten Days (Sundays excepted) after it shall have been presented to him, the Same shall be a Law, in like Manner, as if he had signed it, unless the Congress by their Adjournment prevent its Return, in which Case it shall not be a Law.

Every Order, Resolution, or Vote to which the Concurrence of the Senate and House of Representatives may be necessary (except on a question of Adjournment) shall be presented to the President of the United States; and before the Same shall take Effect, shall be approved by him, or being disapproved by him, shall be repassed by two thirds of the Senate and House of Representatives, according to the Rules and Limitations prescribed in the Case of a Bill.

Section 8.   The Congress shall have Power To lay and Collect Taxes, Duties, Imposts and Excises, to pay the Debts and provide for the common Defence and general Welfare of the United States; but all Duties, Imposts and Excises shall be uniform throughout the United States.

To borrow Money on the credit of the United States;

To regulate Commerce with foreign Nations, and among the several States, and with the Indian Tribes;

To establish an uniform Rule of Naturalization, and uniform Laws on the subject of Bankruptcies throughout the United States;

To coin Money, regulate the Value thereof, and of foreign Coin, and fix the Standard of Weights and Measures;

To provide for the Punishment of counterfeiting the Securities and current Coin of the United States;

To establish Post Offices and post Roads;

To promote the Progress of Science and useful Arts, by securing for limited Times to Authors and Inventors the exclusive Right to their respective Writings and Discoveries;

To constitute Tribunals inferior to the Supreme Court;

To define and punish Piracies and Felonies committed on the high Seas, and Offences against the Law of Nations;

To declare War, grant Letters of Marque and Reprisal, and make Rules concerning Captures on Land and Water;

To raise and support Armies, but no Appropriation of Money to that Use shall be for a longer Term than two Years;

To provide and maintain a Navy;

To make Rules for the Government and Regulation of the land and naval Forces;

To provide for calling forth the Militia to execute the Laws of the Union, suppress Insurrections and repel Invasions;

To provide for organizing, arming, and disciplining, the Militia, and for governing such Part of them as may be employed in the Service of the United States, reserving to the States respectively, the Appointment of the Officers, and the Authority of training the Militia according to the discipline prescribed by Congress;

To exercise exclusive Legislation in all Cases whatsoever, over such District (not exceeding ten Miles square) as may, by Cession of Particular States, and the Acceptance of Congress, become the Seat of the Government of the United States, and to exercise like Authority over all Places purchased by the Consent of the Legislature of the State in which the Same shall be, for the Erection of Forts, Magazines, Arsenals, dock-Yards and other needful Buildings;—And

To make all Laws which shall be necessary and proper for carrying into Execution the foregoing Powers, and all other Powers vested by this Constitution in the Government of the United States, or in any Department or Officer thereof.

Section 9.   The Migration or Importation of such Persons as any of the States now existing shall think proper to admit, shall not be prohibited by the Congress prior to the Year one thousand eight hundred and eight, but a Tax or duty may be imposed on such Importation, not exceeding ten dollars for each Person.

The Privilege of the Writ of Habeas Corpus shall not be suspended, unless when in Cases of Rebellion or Invasion the public Safety may require it.

No bill of Attainder or ex post facto Law shall be passed.

No Capitation, or other direct, Tax shall be laid, *unless in Proportion to the Census or Enumeration herein before directed to be taken.*[5]

No Tax or Duty shall be laid on Articles exported from any State.

No Preference shall be given by any Regulation of Commerce or Revenue to the Ports of one State over those of another; nor shall Vessels bound to, or from, one State, be obliged to enter, clear or pay Duties in another.

No Money shall be drawn from the Treasury, but in Consequence of Appropriations made by Law; and a regular Statement and Account of the Receipts and Expenditures of all public Money shall be published from time to time.

No Title of Nobility shall be granted by the United States: And no Person holding any Office of Profit or Trust under them, shall, without the Consent of the Congress, accept of any present, Emolument, Office, or Title, of any kind whatever, from any King, Prince, or foreign State.

Section 10. No State shall enter into any Treaty, Alliance, or Confederation; grant Letters of Marque and Reprisal; coin Money; emit Bills of Credit; make any Thing but gold and silver Coin a Tender in Payment of Debts; pass any Bill of Attainder, ex post facto Law, or Law impairing the Obligation of Contracts, or grant any Title of Nobility.

No State shall, without the Consent of the Congress, lay any Imposts or Duties on Imports or Exports, except what may be absolutely necessary for executing its inspection Laws; and the net Produce of all Duties and Imposts, laid by any State on Imports or Exports, shall be for the Use of the Treasury of the United States; and all such Laws shall be subject to the Revision and Controul of the Congress.

No State shall, without the Consent of Congress, lay any Duty of Tonnage, keep Troops, or Ships of War in time of Peace, enter into any Agreement or Compact with another State, or with a foreign Power, or engage in War, unless actually invaded, or in such imminent Danger as will not admit of delay.

ARTICLE II.

Section 1. The executive Power shall be vested in a President of the United States of America. He shall hold his Office during the term of four Years, and, together with the Vice President, chosen for the same Term, be elected, as follows

Each State shall appoint, in such Manner as the Legislature thereof may direct, a Number of Electors, equal to the whole Number of Senators and Representatives to which the State may be entitled in the Congress: but no Senator or Representative, or Person holding an Office of Trust or Profit under the United States, shall be appointed an Elector.

The Electors shall meet in their respective States, and vote by Ballot for two Persons, of whom one at least shall not be an Inhabitant of the same State with them-selves. And they shall make a List of all the Persons voted for, and of the Number of Votes for each; which List they shall sign and certify, and transmit sealed to the Seat of the Government of the United States, directed to the President of the Senate. The President of the Senate shall, in the Presence of the Senate and House of Representatives, open all the

---

[5]Changed by the Sixteenth Amendment.

Certificates, and the Votes shall then be counted. The Person having the greatest Number of Votes shall be the President, if such Number be a Majority of the whole Number of Electors appointed; and if there be more than one who have such Majority, and have an equal Number of Votes, then the House of Representatives shall immediately chuse by Ballot one of them for President; and if no Person have a Majority, then from the five highest on the List the said House shall in like Manner chuse the President. But in chusing the President, the Votes shall be taken by States, the Representation from each State having one Vote; a quorum for this Purpose shall consist of a Member or Members from two thirds of the States, and a Majority of all the States shall be necessary to a Choice. In every Case, after the Choice of the President, the Person having the greatest Number of Votes of the Electors shall be the Vice President. But if there should remain two or more who have equal Votes, the Senate shall chuse from them by Ballot the Vice President.[6]

The Congress may determine the Time of chusing the Electors, and the Day on which they shall give their Votes, which Day shall be the same throughout the United States.

No Person except a natural born Citizen, or a Citizen of the United States, at the time of the Adoption of this Constitution, shall be eligible to the Office of President; neither shall any person be eligible to that Office who shall not have attained to the Age of thirty five Years, and been fourteen Years a Resident within the United States.

In Case of the Removal of the President from Office, or of his Death, Resignation, or Inability to discharge the Powers and Duties of the said Office, the Same shall devolve on the Vice President, and the Congress may by Law provide for the Case of Removal, Death, Resignation or Inability, both of the President and Vice President, declaring what Officer shall then act as President, and such Officer shall act accordingly, until the Disability be removed, or a President shall be elected.[7]

The President shall, at stated Times, receive for his Services, a Compensation, which shall neither be encreased nor diminished during the Period for which he shall have been elected, and he shall not receive within that Period any other Emolument from the United States, or any of them.

Before he enter on the Execution of his Office, he shall take the following Oath or Affirmation:—"I do solemnly swear (or affirm) that I will faithfully execute the Office of President of the United States, and will to the best of my Ability, preserve, protect and defend the Constitution of the United States."

Section 2. The President shall be Commander in Chief of the Army and Navy of the United States, and of the Militia of the several States, when called into the actual Service of the United States; he may require the Opinion, in writing, of the principal Officer in each of the executive Departments, upon any Subject relating to the Duties of their respective Offices, and he shall have Power to grant Reprieves and Pardons for Offences against the United States, except in Cases of Impeachment.

---

[6]Superseded by the Twelfth Amendment.
[7]Modified by the Twenty-Fifth Amendment.

He shall have Power, by and with the Advice and Consent of the Senate, to make Treaties, provided two thirds of the Senators present concur; and he shall nominate, and by and with the Advice and Consent of the Senate, shall appoint Ambassadors, other public Ministers and Consuls, Judges of the supreme Court, and all other Officers of the United States, whose Appointments are not herein otherwise provided for, and which shall be established by Law: but the Congress may by Law vest the Appointment of such inferior Officers, as they think proper, in the President alone, in the Courts of Law, or in the Heads of Departments.

The President shall have Power to fill up all Vacancies that may happen during the Recess of the Senate, by granting Commissions which shall expire at the End of their next Session.

Section 3. He shall from time to time give to the Congress Information of the State of the Union, and recommend to their Consideration such Measures as he shall judge necessary and expedient; he may, on extraordinary Occasions, convene both Houses, or either of them, and in Case of Disagreement between them, with Respect to the Time of Adjournment, he may adjourn them to such Time as he shall think proper; he shall receive Ambassadors and other public Ministers; he shall take Care that the Laws be faithfully executed, and shall Commission all the Officers of the United States.

Section 4. The President, Vice President and all civil Officers of the United States, shall be removed from Office on Impeachment for, and Conviction of, Treason, Bribery, or other high Crimes and Misdemeanors.

ARTICLE III.

Section 1. The judicial Power of the United States, shall be vested in one supreme Court, and in such inferior Courts as the Congress may from time to time ordain and establish. The Judges, both of the supreme and inferior Courts, shall hold their Offices during good Behaviour, and shall, at stated Times, receive for their Services, a Compensation, which shall not be diminished during their Continuance in Office.

Section 2. The judicial Power shall extend to all Cases, in Law and Equity, arising under this Constitution, the Laws of the United States, and Treaties made, or which shall be made, under their Authority;—to all Cases affecting Ambassadors, other public Ministers and Consuls;—to all Cases of admiralty and maritime Jurisdiction;—to Controversies to which the United States shall be a Party;—to Controversies between two or more States;—*between a State and Citizens of another State;*[8]—between Citizens of different States;—between Citizens of the same State claiming Lands under Grants of different States, and between a State, or the Citizens thereof, and foreign States, Citizens or Subjects.

---

[8]Modified by the Eleventh Amendment.

In all Cases affecting Ambassadors, other public Ministers and Consuls, and those in which a State shall be Party, the supreme Court shall have original Jurisdiction. In all the other Cases before mentioned, the supreme Court shall have appellate Jurisdiction, both as to Law and Fact, with such Exceptions, and under such Regulations as the Congress shall make.

The Trial of all Crimes, except in Cases of Impeachment, shall be by Jury; and such Trial shall be held in the State where the said Crimes shall have been committed; but when not committed within any State, the Trial shall be at such Place or Places as the Congress may by Law have directed.

Section 3.　Treason against the United States, shall consist only in levying War against them, or in adhering to their Enemies, giving them Aid and Comfort. No Person shall be convicted of Treason unless on the Testimony of two Witnesses to the same overt Act, or on Confession in open Court.

The Congress shall have Power to declare the Punishment of Treason, but no Attainder of Treason shall work Corruption of Blood, or Forfeiture except during the Life of the Person attainted.

ARTICLE IV.

Section 1.　Full Faith and Credit shall be given in each State to the public Acts, Records, and judicial Proceedings of every other State. And the Congress may by general Laws prescribe the Manner in which such Acts, Records and Proceedings shall be proved, and the Effect thereof.

Section 2.　The Citizens of each State shall be entitled to all Privileges and Immunities of Citizens in the several States.

A person charged in any State with Treason, Felony, or other Crime, who shall flee from Justice, and be found in another State, shall on Demand of the executive Authority of the State from which he fled, be delivered up, to be removed to the State having Jurisdiction of the Crime.

No Person held to Service or Labour in one State, under the Laws thereof, escaping into another, shall, in Consequence of any Law or Regulation therein, be discharged from such Service or Labour, but shall be delivered up on Claim of the Party to whom such Service or Labour may be due.[9]

Section 3.　New States may be admitted by the Congress into this Union; but no new State shall be formed or erected within the Jurisdiction of any other State; nor any State be formed by the Junction of two or more States, or Parts of States, without the Consent of the Legislatures of the States concerned as well as of the Congress.

The Congress shall have Power to dispose of and make all needful Rules and Regulations respecting the Territory or other Property belonging to the United States; and nothing in this Constitution shall be so construed as to Prejudice any Claims of the United States, or of any particular State.

---

[9]Changed by the Thirteenth Amendment.

Section 4.   The United States shall guarantee to every State in this Union a Republican Form of Government, and shall protect each of them against Invasion; and on Application of the Legislature, or of the Executive (when the Legislature cannot be convened) against domestic Violence.

ARTICLE V.

The Congress, whenever two thirds of both Houses shall deem it necessary, shall propose Amendments to this Constitution, or, on the Application of the Legislatures of two thirds of the several States, shall call a Convention for proposing Amendments, which, in either Case, shall be valid to all Intents and Purposes, as Part of this Constitution, when ratified by the Legislatures of three fourths of the several States, or by Conventions in three fourths thereof, as the one or the other Mode of Ratification may be proposed by the Congress; Provided that no Amendment which may be made prior to the Year One thousand eight hundred and eight shall in any Manner after the first and fourth Clauses in the Ninth Section of the first Article; and that no State, without its Consent, shall be deprived of its equal Suffrage in the Senate.

ARTICLE VI.

All Debts contracted and Engagements entered into, before the Adoption of this Constitution, shall be as valid against the United States under this Constitution, as under the Confederation.

This Constitution, and the Laws of the United States which shall be made in Pursuance thereof; and all Treaties made, or which shall be made, under the Authority of the United States, shall be the Supreme Law of the Land; and the Judges in every State shall be bound thereby, any Thing in the Constitution or Laws of any State to the Contrary notwithstanding.

The Senators and Representatives before mentioned, and the Members of the several State Legislatures, and all executive and judicial Officers, both of the United States and of the several States, shall be bound by Oath or Affirmation, to support this Constitution; but no religious Test shall ever be required as a Qualification to any Office or public Trust under the United States.

ARTICLE VII.

The Ratification of the Conventions of nine States, shall be sufficient for the Establishment of this Constitution between the States so ratifying the Same.

Done in Convention by the Unanimous Consent of the States present the Seventeenth Day of September in the Year of our Lord one thousand seven hundred and Eighty seven and of the Independence of the United States of America the Twelfth In witness whereof We have hereunto subscribed our Names,

Go. Washington–*Presidt.*
and deputy from Virginia

New Hampshire	{ John Langdon Nicholas Gilman			

Delaware { Geo. Read
Gunning Bedford Jun
John Dickinson
Richard Bassett
Jaco. Broom

Massachusetts { Nathaniel Gorham
Rufus King

Connecticut { Wm. Saml. Johnson
Roger Sherman

Maryland { James McHenry
Dan of St. Thos. Jenifer
Danl. Carroll

New York   Alexander Hamilton

New Jersey { Wil. Livingston
David Brearley
Wm. Paterson
Jona. Dayton

Virginia { John Blair—
James Madison Jr.

North Carolina { Wm. Blount
Rich d. Dobbs Spaight
Hu Williamson

Pennsylvania { B Franklin
Thomas Mifflin
Robt. Morris
Geo. Clymer
Thos. FitzSimons
Jared Ingersoll
James Wilson
Gouv Morris

South Carolina { J. Rutledge
Charles Cotesworth
Pinckney
Charles Pinckney
Pierce Butler

Georgia { William Few
Abr Baldwin

[The first ten amendments, known as the "Bill of Rights," were ratified in 1791.]

AMENDMENT I

Congress shall make no law respecting an establishment of religion, or prohibiting the free exercise thereof; or abridging the freedom of speech, or of the press; or the right of the people peaceably to assemble, and to petition the Government for a redress of grievances.

AMENDMENT II

A well regulated Militia, being necessary to the security of a free State, the right of the people to keep and bear Arms, shall not be infringed.

AMENDMENT III

No Soldier shall, in time of peace be quartered in any house, without the consent of the Owner, nor in time of war, but in a manner prescribed by law.

AMENDMENT IV

The right of the people to be secure in their persons, houses, papers, and effects, against unreasonable searches and seizures, shall not be violated, and no Warrants shall issue, but upon probable cause, supported by Oath or affirmation, and particularly describing the place to be searched, and the persons or things to be seized.

AMENDMENT V

No person shall be held to answer for a capital, or otherwise infamous crime, unless on a presentment or indictment of a Grand Jury, except in cases arising in the land or naval forces, or in the Militia, when in actual service in time of War or public danger; nor shall any person be subject for the same offence to be twice put in jeopardy of life or limb; nor shall be compelled in any criminal case to be a witness against himself, nor be deprived of life, liberty, or property, without due process of law, nor shall private property be taken for public use, without just compensation.

AMENDMENT VI

In all criminal prosecutions, the accused shall enjoy the right to a speedy and public trial, by an impartial jury of the State and district wherein the crime shall have been committed, which district shall have been previously ascertained by law, and to be informed of the nature and cause of the accusation; to be confronted with the witnesses against him; to have compulsory process for obtaining witnesses in his favor, and to have Assistance of Counsel for his defence.

AMENDMENT VII

In Suits at common law, where the value in controversy shall exceed twenty dollars, the right of trial by jury shall be preserved, and no fact tried by a jury, shall be otherwise reexamined in any Court of the United States, than according to the rules of the common law.

AMENDMENT VIII

Excessive bail shall not be required, nor excessive fines imposed, nor cruel and unusual punishments inflicted.

AMENDMENT IX

The enumeration in the Constitution, of certain rights, shall not be construed to deny or disparage others retained by the people.

AMENDMENT X

The powers not delegated to the United States by the Constitution, nor prohibited by it to the States, are reserved to the States respectively, or to the people.

AMENDMENT XI [*RATIFIED IN 1795.*]

The Judicial power of the United States shall not be construed to extend to any suit in law or equity, commenced or prosecuted against one of the United States by Citizens of another State, or by Citizens or Subjects of any Foreign State.

AMENDMENT XII [*RATIFIED IN 1804.*]

The Electors shall meet in their respective states and vote by ballot for President and Vice President, one of whom, at least, shall not be an inhabitant of the same state with themselves; they shall name in their ballots the person voted for as President, and in distinct ballots the person voted for as Vice President, and they shall make distinct lists of all persons voted for as President, and of all persons voted for as Vice President, and of the number of votes for each, which lists they shall sign and certify, and transmit sealed to the seat of the government of the United States, directed to the President of the Senate;—The President of the Senate shall, in the presence of the Senate and House of Representatives, open all the certificates and the votes shall then be counted;—The person having the greatest number of votes for President, shall be the President, if such number be a majority of the whole number of Electors appointed; and if no person have such majority, then from the persons having the highest numbers not exceeding three on the list of those voted for as President, the House of Representatives shall choose immediately, by ballot, the President. But in choosing the President, the votes shall be taken by states, the representation from each state having one vote; a quorum for this purpose shall consist of a member or members from two-thirds of the states, and a majority of all the states shall be necessary to a choice. *And if the House of Representatives shall not choose a President whenever the right of choice shall devolve upon them, before the fourth day of March next following, then the Vice President shall act as President, as in the case of the death or other constitutional disability of the President.*—[10] The person having the greatest number of votes as Vice President, shall be the Vice President, if such number be a majority of the whole number of Electors appointed, and if no person have a majority, then from the two highest numbers on the list, the Senate shall choose the Vice President; a

---

[10]Changed by the Twentieth Amendment, Section 3.

quorum for the purpose shall consist of two-thirds of the whole number of Senators, and a majority of the whole number shall be necessary to a choice. But no person constitutionally ineligible to the office of President shall be eligible to that of Vice President of the United States.

AMENDMENT XIII [*RATIFIED IN 1865.*]

Section 1.   Neither slavery nor involuntary servitude, except as a punishment for crime whereof the party shall have been duly convicted, shall exist within the United States, or any place subject to their jurisdiction.

Section 2.   Congress shall have power to enforce this article by appropriate legislation.

AMENDMENT XIV [*RATIFIED IN 1868.*]

Section 1.   All persons born or naturalized in the United States and subject to the jurisdiction thereof, are citizens of the United States and of the State wherein they reside. No State shall make or enforce any law which shall abridge the privileges or immunities of citizens of the United States; nor shall any State deprive any person of life, liberty, or property, without due process of law; nor deny to any person within its jurisdiction the equal protection of the laws.

Section 2.   Representatives shall be apportioned among the several States according to their respective numbers, counting the whole number of persons in each State, excluding Indians not taxed. But when the right to vote at any election for the choice of electors for President and Vice President of the United States, Representatives in Congress, the Executive and Judicial officers of a State, or the members of the Legislature thereof, is denied to any of the *male* inhabitants of such State, being *twenty-one*[11] years of age, and citizens of the United States, or in any way abridged, except for participation in rebellion, or other crime, the basis of representation therein shall be reduced in the proportion which the number of such male citizens shall bear to the whole number of male citizens twenty-one years of age in such State.

Section 3.   No person shall be a Senator or Representative in Congress, or elector of President and Vice President, or hold any office, civil or military, under the United States, or under any State, who, having previously taken an oath, as a member of Congress, or as an officer of the United States, or as a member of any State legislature, or as an executive or judicial officer of any State, to support the Constitution of the United States, shall have engaged in insurrection or rebellion against the same, or given aid or comfort to the enemies thereof. But Congress may by a vote of two-thirds of each House, remove such disability.

---

[11]Changed by the Twenty-Sixth Amendment; the reference to "male inhabitants" may also have been by the Nineteenth Amendment.

Section 4.   The validity of the public debt of the United States, authorized by law, including debts incurred for payment of pensions and bounties for services in suppressing insurrection or rebellion, shall not be questioned. But neither the United States nor any State shall assume or pay any debt or obligation incurred in aid of insurrection or rebellion against the United States, or any claim for the loss or emancipation of any slave; but all such debts, obligations and claims shall be held illegal and void.

Section 5.   The Congress shall have power to enforce, by appropriate legislation, the provisions of this article.

AMENDMENT XV [*RATIFIED IN 1870.*]

Section 1.   The right of citizens of the United States to vote shall not be denied or abridged by the United States or by any State on account of race, color, or previous condition of servitude.

Section 2.   The Congress shall have power to enforce this article by appropriate legislation.

AMENDMENT XVI [*RATIFIED IN 1913.*]

The Congress shall have power to lay and collect taxes on incomes, from whatever source derived, without apportionment among the several States, and without regard to any census or enumeration.

AMENDMENT XVII [*RATIFIED IN 1913.*]

The Senate of the United States shall be composed of two Senators from each State, elected by the people thereof, for six years; and each Senator shall have one vote. The electors in each State shall have the qualifications requisite for electors of the most numerous branch of the State legislatures.

When vacancies happen in the representation of any State in the Senate, the executive authority of such State shall issue writs of election to fill such vacancies: *Provided,* That the legislature of any State may empower the executive thereof to make temporary appointments until the people fill the vacancies by election as the legislature may direct.

This amendment shall not be so construed as to affect the election or term of any Senator chosen before it becomes valid as part of the Constitution.

AMENDMENT XVIII [*RATIFIED IN 1919.*]

Section 1.   *After one year from the ratification of this article the manufacture, sale, or transportation of intoxicating liquors within, the importation thereof into, or the exportation thereof from the United States and all territory subject to the jurisdiction thereof for beverage purposes is hereby prohibited.*

Section 2.   The Congress and the several States shall have concurrent power to enforce this article by appropriate legislation.

Section 3.   This article shall be inoperative unless it shall have been ratified as an amendment to the Constitution by the legislatures of the several States, as provided in the Constitution, within seven years from the date of the submission hereof to the States by the Congress.[12]

AMENDMENT XIX [*RATIFIED IN 1920.*]

The right of citizens of the United States to vote shall not be denied or abridged by the United States or by any State on account of sex.
Congress shall have power to enforce this article by appropriate legislation.

AMENDMENT XX [*RATIFIED IN 1933.*]

Section 1.   The terms of the President and Vice President shall end at noon on the 20th day of January, and the terms of Senators and Representatives at noon on the 3d day of January, of the years in which such terms would have ended if this article had not been ratified; and the terms of their successors shall then begin.

Section 2.   The Congress shall assemble at least once in every year, and such meeting shall begin at noon on the 3d day of January, unless they shall by law appoint a different day.

Section 3.   If, at the time fixed for the beginning of the term of the President, the President elect shall have died, the Vice President elect shall become President. If a President shall not have been chosen before the time fixed for the beginning of his term, or if the President elect shall have failed to qualify, then the Vice President elect shall act as President until a President shall have qualified; and the Congress may by law provide for the case wherein neither a President elect nor a Vice President elect shall have qualified, declaring who shall then act as President, or the manner in which one who is to act shall be selected, and such person shall act accordingly until a President or Vice President shall have qualified.

Section 4.   The Congress may by law provide for the case of the death of any of the persons from whom the House of Representatives may choose a President whenever the right of choice shall have developed upon them, and for the case of the death of any of the persons from whom the Senate may choose a Vice President whenever the right of choice shall have devolved upon them.

---

[12]Repealed by the Twenty-First Amendment.

Section 5. Sections 1 and 2 shall take effect on the 15th day of October following the ratification of this article.

Section 6. This article shall be inoperative unless it shall have been ratified as an amendment to the Constitution by the legislatures of three-fourths of the several States within seven years from the date of its submission.

AMENDMENT XXI [*RATIFIED IN 1933.*]

Section 1. The eighteenth article of amendment to the Constitution of the United States is hereby repealed.

Section 2. The transportation or importation into any State, Territory, or possession of the United States for delivery or use therein of intoxicating liquors, in violation of the laws thereof, is hereby prohibited.

Section 3. This article shall be inoperative unless it shall have been ratified as an amendment to the Constitution by conventions in the several States, as provided in the Constitution, within seven years from the date of the submission hereof to the States by the Congress.

AMENDMENT XXII [*RATIFIED IN 1951.*]

Section 1. No person shall be elected to the office of the President more than twice, and no person who has held the office of President, or acted as President, for more than two years of a term to which some other person was elected President shall be elected to the office of the President more than once. But this Article shall not apply to any person holding the office of President when this Article was proposed by the Congress, and shall not prevent any person who may be holding the office of President, or acting as President, during the term within which this Article becomes operative from holding the office of President or acting as President during the remainder of such term.

Section 2. This Article shall be inoperative unless it shall have been ratified as an amendment to the Constitution by the legislatures of three-fourths of the several States within seven years from the date of its submission to the States by the Congress.

AMENDMENT XXIII [*RATIFIED IN 1961.*]

Section 1. The District constituting the seat of Government of the United States shall appoint in such manner as the Congress may direct:
A number of electors of President and Vice President equal to the whole number of Senators and Representatives in Congress to which the District would be entitled if it were a State, but in no event more than the least populous State;

they shall be in addition to those appointed by the States, but they shall be considered, for the purposes of the election of President and Vice President, to be electors appointed by a State; and they shall meet in the District and perform such duties as provided by the twelfth article of amendment.

Section 2. The Congress shall have power to enforce this article by appropriate legislation.

AMENDMENT XXIV [*RATIFIED IN 1964.*]

Section 1. The right of citizens of the United States to vote in any primary or other election for President or Vice President, for electors for President or Vice President, or for Senator or Representative in Congress, shall not be denied or abridged by the United States or any State by reason of failure to pay any poll tax or other tax.

Section 2. Congress shall have power to enforce this article by appropriate legislation.

AMENDMENT XXV [*RATIFIED IN 1967.*]

Section 1. In case of the removal of the President from office or of his death or resignation, the Vice President shall become President.

Section 2. Whenever there is a vacancy in the office of the Vice President, the President shall nominate a Vice President who shall take office upon confirmation by a majority vote of both Houses of Congress.

Section 3. Whenever the President transmits to the President pro tempore of the Senate and the Speaker of the House of Representatives his written declaration that he is unable to discharge the powers and duties of his office, and until he transmits to them a written declaration to the contrary, such powers and duties shall be discharged by the Vice President as Acting President.

Section 4. Whenever the Vice President and a majority of either the principal officers of the executive departments or of such other body as Congress may by law provide, transmit to the President pro tempore of the Senate and the Speaker of the House of Representatives their written declaration that the President is unable to discharge the powers and duties of his office, the Vice President shall immediately assume the powers and duties of the office as Acting President.

Thereafter, when the President transmits to the President pro tempore of the Senate and the Speaker of the House of Representatives his written declaration that no inability exists, he shall resume the powers and duties of his office unless the Vice President and a majority of either the principal officers of the executive department[s] or of such other body as Congress may by law provide, transmit within four days to the President pro tempore of the Senate and the Speaker of the

House of Representatives their written declaration that the President is unable to discharge the powers and duties of his office. Thereupon Congress shall decide the issue, assembling within forty-eight hours for that purpose if not in session. If the Congress, within twenty-one days after receipt of the latter written declaration, or, if Congress is not in session, within twenty-one days after Congress is required to assemble, determines by two-thirds vote of both Houses that the President is unable to discharge the powers and duties of his office, the Vice President shall continue to discharge the same as Acting President; otherwise, the President shall resume the powers and duties of his office.

AMENDMENT XXVI [*RATIFIED IN 1971.*]

Section 1. The right of citizens of the United States, who are eighteen years of age or older, to vote shall not be denied or abridged by the United States or by any State on account of age.

Section 2. The Congress shall have power to enforce this article by appropriate legislation.

AMENDMENT XXVII [*RATIFIED IN 1992.*]

No law varying the compensation for the services of the Senators and Representatives shall take effect, until an election of Representatives shall have intervened.

THE FEDERALIST NO. 10

James Madison

November 22, 1787

TO THE PEOPLE OF THE STATE OF NEW YORK

Among the numerous advantages promised by a well constructed Union, none deserves to be more accurately developed than its tendency to break and control the violence of faction. The friend of popular governments, never finds himself so much alarmed for their character and fate, as when he contemplates their propensity to this dangerous vice. He will not fail therefore to set a due value on any plan which, without violating the principles to which he is attached, provides a proper cure for it. The instability, injustice and confusion introduced into the public councils, have in truth been the mortal diseases under which popular governments have every where perished; as they continue to be the favorite and fruitful topics from which the adversaries to liberty derive their most specious declamations. The valuable improvements made by the American Constitutions on the popular models, both ancient and modern, cannot certainly be too much admired; but it would be an unwarrantable partiality, to contend that they have as effectually obviated the danger on this side as was wished and expected. Complaints are every where heard from our most considerate and virtuous citizens, equally the friends of public and private faith, and of public and personal liberty; that our governments are too unstable; that the public good is disregarded in the conflicts of rival parties; and that measures are too often decided, not according to the rules of justice, and the rights of the minor party; but by the superior force of an interested and over-bearing majority. However anxiously we may wish that these complaints had no foundation, the evidence of known facts will not permit us to deny that they are in some degree true. It will be found indeed, on a candid review of our situation, that some of the distresses under which we labor, have been erroneously charged on the operation of our governments; but it will be found, at the same time, that other causes will not alone account for many of our heaviest misfortunes; and particularly, for that prevailing and increasing distrust of public engagements, and alarm for private rights, which are echoed from one end of the continent to the other. These must be chiefly, if not wholly, effects of the unsteadiness and injustice, with which a factious spirit has tainted our public administrations.

By a faction I understand a number of citizens, whether amounting to a majority or minority of the whole, who are united and actuated by some common impulse of passion, or of interest, adverse to the rights of other citizens, or to the permanent and aggregate interests of the community.

There are two methods of curing the mischiefs of faction: the one, by removing its causes; the other, by controlling its effects.

There are again two methods of removing the causes of faction: the one by destroying the liberty which is essential to its existence; the other, by giving to every citizen the same opinions, the same passions, and the same interests.

It could never be more truly said than of the first remedy, that it is worse than the disease. Liberty is to faction, what air is to fire, an aliment without which it instantly expires. But it could not be a less folly to abolish liberty, which is essential to political life, because it nourishes faction, than it would be to wish the annihilation of air, which is essential to animal life, because it imparts to fire its destructive agency.

The second expedient is as impracticable, as the first would be unwise. As long as the reason of man continues fallible, and he is at liberty to exercise it, different opinions will be formed. As long as the connection subsists between his reason and his self-love, his opinions and his passions will have a reciprocal influence on each other; and the former will be objects to which the latter will attach themselves. The diversity in the faculties of men from which the rights of property originate, is not less an insuperable obstacle to a uniformity of interests. The protection of these faculties is the first object of Government. From the protection of different and unequal faculties of acquiring property, the possession of different degrees and kinds of property immediately results: and from the influence of these on the sentiments and views of the respective proprietors, ensues a division of the society into different interests and parties.

The latent causes of faction are thus sown in the nature of man; and we see them every where brought into different degrees of activity, according to the different circumstances of civil society. A zeal for different opinions concerning religion, concerning Government and many other points, as well of speculation as of practice; an attachment to different leaders ambitiously contending for preeminence and power; or to persons of other descriptions whose fortunes have been interesting to the human passions, have in turn divided mankind into parties, inflamed them with mutual animosity, and rendered them much more disposed to vex and oppress each other, than to co-operate for their common good. So strong is this propensity of mankind to fall into mutual animosities, that where no substantial occasion presents itself, the most frivolous and fanciful distinctions have been sufficient to kindle their unfriendly passions, and excite their most violent conflicts. But the most common and durable source of factions, has been the various and unequal distribution of property. Those who hold, and those who are without property, have ever formed distinct interests in society. Those who are creditors, and those who are debtors, fall under a like discrimination. A landed interest, a manufacturing interest, a mercantile interest, a monied interest, with many lesser interests, grow up of necessity in civilized nations, and divide them into different classes, actuated by different sentiments and views. The regulation of these various and interfering interests forms the principal task of modern Legislation, and involves the spirit of party and faction in the necessary and ordinary operations of Government.

No man is allowed to be a judge in his own cause; because his interest would certainly bias his judgment, and, not improbably, corrupt his integrity. With equal, nay with greater reason, a body of men, are unfit to be both judges and parties, at the same time; yet, what are many of the most important acts of legislation, but so many judicial determinations, not indeed concerning the rights of single persons, but concerning the rights of large bodies of citizens; and what are the different classes of legislators, but advocates and parties to the causes which they determine? Is a law proposed concerning private debts? It is a question to which the creditors are parties on one side, and the debtors on the other. Justice ought to hold the balance between them. Yet the parties are and must be themselves the judges; and the most numerous party, or, in other words, the most powerful faction must be expected to prevail. Shall domestic manufactures be encouraged, and in what degree, by restrictions on foreign manufactures? are questions which would be differently decided by the landed and the manufacturing classes; and probably by neither, with a sole regard to justice and the public good. The apportionment of taxes on the various descriptions of property, is an act which seems to require the most exact impartiality; yet, there is perhaps no legislative act in which greater opportunity and temptation are given to a predominant party, to trample on the rules of justice. Every shilling with which they over-burden the inferior number, is a shilling saved to their own pockets.

It is in vain to say, that enlightened statesmen will be able to adjust these clashing interests, and render them all subservient to the public good. Enlightened statesmen will not always be at the helm: Nor, in many cases, can such an adjustment be made at all, without taking into view indirect and remote considerations, which will rarely prevail over the immediate interest which one party may find in disregarding the rights of another, or the good of the whole.

The inference to which we are brought, is, that the *causes* of faction cannot be removed; and that relief is only to be sought in the means of controlling its *effects*.

If a faction consists of less than a majority, relief is supplied by the republican principle, which enables the majority to defeat its sinister views by regular vote: It may clog the administration, it may convulse the society; but it will be unable to execute and mask its violence under the forms of the Constitution. When a majority is included in a faction, the form of popular government on the other hand enables it to sacrifice to its ruling passion or interest, both the public good and the rights of other citizens. To secure the public good, and private rights, against the danger of such a faction, and at the same time to preserve the spirit and the form of popular government, is then the great object to which our enquiries are directed: Let me add that it is the great desideratum, by which alone this form of government can be rescued from the opprobrium under which it has so long labored, and be recommended to the esteem and adoption of mankind.

By what means is this object attainable? Evidently by one of two only. Either the existence of the same passion or interest in a majority at the same time, must be prevented; or the majority, having such co-existent passion or interest, must be rendered, by their number and local situation, unable to concert and carry into effect schemes of oppression. If the impulse and the opportunity be suffered to coincide, we well know that neither moral nor religious motives can be relied on as an adequate control. They are not found to be such on the injustice and violence of individuals, and lose their efficacy in proportion to the number combined together; that is, in proportion as their efficacy becomes needful.

From this view of the subject, it may be concluded, that a pure Democracy, by which I mean, a Society, consisting of a small number of citizens, who assemble and administer the Government in person, can admit of no cure for the mischiefs of faction. A common passion or interest will, in almost every case, be felt by a majority of the whole; a communication and concert results from the form of Government itself; and there is nothing to check the inducements to sacrifice the weaker party, or an obnoxious individual. Hence it is, that such Democracies have ever been spectacles of turbulence and contention; have ever been found incompatible with personal security, or the rights of property; and have in general been as short in their lives, as they have been violent in their deaths. Theoretic politicians, who have patronized this species of Government, have erroneously supposed, that by reducing mankind to a perfect equality in their political rights, they would, at the same time, be perfectly equalized and assimilated in their possessions, their opinions, and their passions.

A republic, by which I mean a government in which the scheme of representation takes place, opens a different prospect, and promises the cure for which we are seeking. Let us examine the points in which it varies from pure democracy, and we shall comprehend both the nature of the cure and the efficacy which it must derive from the union.

The two great points of difference, between a democracy and a republic, are, first, the delegation of the government, in the latter, to a small number of citizens, elected by the rest; secondly, the greater number of citizens, and greater sphere of country, over which the latter may be extended.

The effect of the first difference is, on the one hand, to refine and enlarge the public views, by passing them through the medium of a chosen body of citizens, whose wisdom may best discern the true interest of their country, and whose patriotism and love of justice, will be least likely to sacrifice it to temporary or partial considerations. Under such a regulation, it may well happen, that the public voice, pronounced by the representatives of the people, will be more consonant to the public good, than if pronounced by the people themselves, convened for the purpose. On the other hand the effect may be inverted. Men of factious tempers, of local prejudices, or of sinister designs, may by intrigue, by corruption, or by other means, first obtain the suffrages, and then betray the interest of the people. The question resulting is, whether small or extensive republics are most favorable to the election of proper guardians of the public weal, and it is clearly decided in favor of the latter by two obvious considerations.

In the first place, it is to be remarked that, however small the republic may be, the representatives must be raised to a certain number, in order to guard against the cabals of a few; and that however large it may be, they must be limited to a certain number, in order to guard against the confusion of a multitude. Hence, the number of representatives in the two cases not being in proportion to that of the constituents, and being proportionally greatest in the small republic, it follows, that if the proportion of fit characters be not less in the large than in the small republic, the former will present a greater option, and consequently a greater probability of a fit choice.

In the next place, as each Representative will be chosen by a greater number of citizens in the large than in the small Republic, it will be more difficult for unworthy candidates to practise with success the vicious arts, by which elections are too often carried; and the suffrages of the people being more free, will be more likely to center on men who possess the most attractive merit, and the most diffusive and established characters.

It must be confessed, that in this, as in most other cases, there is a mean, on both sides of which inconveniences will be found to lie. By enlarging too much the number of electors, you render the representatives too little acquainted with all their local circumstances and lesser interests; as by reducing it too much, you render him unduly attached to these, and too little fit to comprehend and pursue great and national objects. The Federal Constitution forms a happy combination in this respect; the great and aggregate interests being referred to the national, the local and particular, to the state legislatures.

The other point of difference is, the greater number of citizens and extent of territory which may be brought within the compass of Republican, than of Democratic Government; and it is this circumstance principally which renders factious combinations less to be dreaded in the former, than in the latter. The smaller the society, the fewer probably will be the distinct parties and interests composing it; the fewer the distinct parties and interests, the more frequently will a majority be found of the same party; and the smaller the number of individuals composing a majority, and the smaller the compass within which they are placed, the more easily will they concert and execute their plans of oppression. Extend the sphere, and you take in a greater variety of parties and interests; you make it less probable that a majority of the whole will have a common motive to invade the rights of other citizens; or if such a common motive exists, it will be more difficult for all who feel it to discover their own strength, and to act in unison with each other. Besides other impediments, it may be remarked, that where there is a consciousness of unjust or dishonorable purposes, communication is always checked by distrust, in proportion to the number whose concurrence is necessary.

Hence it clearly appears, that the same advantage, which a Republic has over a Democracy, in controlling the effects of factions, is enjoyed by a large over a small Republic—is enjoyed by the Union over the States composing it. Does this advantage consist in the substitution of Representatives, whose enlightened views and virtuous sentiments render them superior to local prejudices, and to schemes of injustice? It will not be denied, that the Representation of the Union will be most likely to possess these requisite endowments. Does it consist in the greater security afforded by a greater variety of parties, against the event of any one party being able to outnumber and oppress the rest? In an equal degree does the increased variety of parties, comprised within the Union, increase this security? Does it, in fine, consist in the greater obstacles opposed to the concert and accomplishment of the secret wishes of an unjust and interested majority? Here, again, the extent of the Union gives it the most palpable advantage.

The influence of factious leaders may kindle a flame within their particular States, but will be unable to spread a general conflagration through the other States: a religious sect, may degenerate into a political faction in a part of the Confederacy but the variety of sects dispersed over the entire face of it, must secure the national Councils against any danger from that source: a rage for paper money, for an abolition of debts, for an equal division of property, or for any other improper or wicked project, will be less apt to pervade the whole body of the Union, than a particular member of it; in the same proportion as such a malady is more likely to taint a particular county or district, than an entire State.

In the extent and proper structure of the Union, therefore, we behold a Republican remedy for the diseases most incident to Republican Government. And according to the degree of pleasure and pride, we feel in being Republicans, ought to be our zeal in cherishing the spirit, and supporting the character of Federalists.

PUBLIUS

THE FEDERALIST NO. 51

James Madison

February 6, 1788

TO THE PEOPLE OF THE STATE OF NEW YORK

To what expedient then shall we finally resort for maintaining in practice the necessary partition of power among the several departments, as laid down in the constitution? The only answer that can be given is, that as all these exterior provisions are found to be inadequate, the defect must be supplied, by so contriving the interior structure of the government, as that its several constituent parts may, by their mutual relations, be the means of keeping each other in their proper places. Without presuming to undertake a full development of this important idea, I will hazard a few general observations, which may perhaps place it in a clearer light, and enable us to form a more correct judgment of the principles and structure of the government planned by the convention.

In order to lay a due foundation for that separate and distinct exercise of the different powers of government, which to a certain extent, is admitted on all hands to be essential to the preservation of liberty, it is evident that each department should have a will of its own; and consequently should be so constituted, that the members of each should have as little agency as possible in the appointment of the members of the others. Were this principle rigorously adhered to, it would require that all the appointments for the supreme executive, legislative, and judiciary magistracies, should be drawn from the same fountain of authority, the people, through channels, having no communication whatever with one another. Perhaps such a plan of constructing the several departments would be less difficult in practice than it may in contemplation appear. Some difficulties however, and some additional expense, would attend the execution of it. Some deviations therefore from the principle must be admitted. In the constitution of the judiciary department in particular, it might be inexpedient to insist rigorously on the principle; first, because peculiar qualifications being essential in the members, the primary consideration ought to be to select that mode of choice, which best secures these qualifications; secondly, because the permanent tenure by which the appointments are held in that department, must soon destroy all sense of dependence on the authority conferring them.

It is equally evident that the members of each department should be as little dependent as possible on those of the others, for the emoluments annexed to their offices. Were the executive magistrate, or the judges, not independent of the legislature in this particular, their independence in every other would be merely nominal.

But the great security against a gradual concentration of the several powers in the same department, consists in giving to those who administer each department, the necessary constitutional means, and personal motives, to resist encroachments of the others. The provision for defense must in this, as in all other cases, be made commensurate to the danger of attack. Ambition must be made to counteract ambition. The interest of the man must be connected with the constitutional rights of the place. It may be a reflection on human nature, that such devices should be necessary to control the abuses of government. But what is government itself but the greatest of all reflections on human nature? If men were angels, no government would be necessary. If angels were to govern men, neither external nor internal controls on government would be necessary. In framing a government which is to be administered by men over men, the great difficulty lies in this: You must first enable the government to control the governed; and in the next place, oblige it to control itself. A dependence on the people is no doubt the primary control on the government; but experience has taught mankind the necessity of auxiliary precautions.

This policy of supplying by opposite and rival interests, the defect of better motives, might be traced through the whole system of human affairs, private as well as public. We see it particularly displayed in all the subordinate distributions of power; where the constant aim is to divide and arrange the several offices in such a manner as that each may be a check on the other; that the private interest of every individual, may be a sentinel over the public rights. These inventions of prudence cannot be less requisite in the distribution of the supreme powers of the state.

But it is not possible to give each department an equal power of self defense. In republican government the legislative authority, necessarily, predominates. The remedy for this inconveniency is, to divide the legislature into different branches; and to render them by different modes of election, and different principles of action, as little connected with each other, as the nature of their common functions, and their common dependence on the society, will admit. It may even be necessary to guard against dangerous encroachments by still further precautions. As the weight of the legislative authority requires that it should be thus divided, the weakness of the executive may require, on the other hand, that it should be fortified. An absolute negative, on the legislature, appears at first view to be the natural defense with which the executive magistrate should be armed. But perhaps it would be neither altogether safe, nor alone sufficient. On ordinary occasions, it might not be exerted with the requisite firmness; and on extraordinary occasions, it might be prefidiously abused. May not this defect of an absolute negative be supplied, by some qualified connection between this weaker department, and the weaker branch of the stronger department, by which the latter may be led to support the constitutional rights of the former, without being too much detached from the rights of its own department?

If the principles on which these observations are founded be just, as I persuade myself they are, and they be applied as a criterion, to the several state constitutions, and to the federal constitution, it will be found, that if the latter does not perfectly correspond with them, the former are infinitely less able to bear such a test.

There are moreover two considerations particularly applicable to the federal system of America, which place that system in a very interesting point of view.

First. In a single republic, all the power surrendered by the people, is submitted to the administration of a single government; and usurpations are guarded against by a division of the government into distinct and separate departments. In the compound republic of America, the power surrendered by the people, is first divided between two distinct governments, and then the portion allotted to each, subdivided among distinct and separate departments. Hence a double security arises to the rights of the people. The different governments will control each other; at the same time that each will be controlled by itself.

Second. It is of great importance in a republic, not only to guard the society against the oppression of its rulers; but to guard one part of the society against the injustice of the other part. Different interests necessarily exist in different classes of citizens. If a majority be united by a common interest, the rights of the minority will be insecure. There are but two methods of providing against this evil: The one by creating a will in the community independent of the majority, that is, of the society itself, the other by comprehending in the society so many separate descriptions of citizens, as will render an unjust combination of a majority of the whole, very improbable, if not impracticable. The first method prevails in all governments possessing an hereditary or self appointed authority. This at best is but a precarious security; because a power independent of the society may as well espouse the unjust views of the major, as the rightful interests, of the minor party, and may possibly be turned against both parties. The second method will be exemplified in the federal republic of the United States. While all authority in it will be derived from and dependent on the society, the society itself will be broken into so many parts, interests and classes of citizens, that the rights of individuals or of the minority, will be in little danger from interested combinations of the majority. In a free government, the security for civil rights must be the same as for religious rights. It consists in the one case in the multiplicity of interests, and in the other, in the multiplicity of sects. The degree of security in both cases will depend on the number of interests and sects; and this may be presumed to depend on the extent of country and number of people comprehended under the same government. This view of the subject must particularly recommend a proper federal system to all the sincere and considerate friends of republican government: Since it shows that in exact proportion as the territory of the union may be formed into more circumscribed confederacies or states, oppressive combinations of a majority will be facilitated, the best security under the republican form, for the rights of every class of citizens, will be diminished; and consequently, the stability and independence of some member of the government, the only other security, must be proportionally increased. Justice is the end of government. It is the end of civil society. It ever has been, and ever will be pursued, until it be obtained, or until liberty be lost in the pursuit. In a society under the forms of which the stronger faction can readily unite and oppress the weaker, anarchy may as truly be said to reign, as in a state of nature where the weaker individual is not secured against the violence of the stronger: And as in the latter state even the stronger individuals are prompted by the uncertainty of their condition, to submit to a government which may protect the weak as well as themselves: So in the former state, will the more powerful factions or parties be gradually induced by a like motive, to wish for a government which will protect all parties, the weaker as well as the more powerful.

It can be little doubted, that if the state of Rhode Island was separated from the confederacy, and left to itself, the insecurity of rights under the popular form of government within such narrow limits, would be displayed by such reiterated oppressions of factious majorities, that some power altogether independent of the people would soon be called for by the voice of the very factions whose misrule had proved the necessity of it. In the extended republic of the United States, and among the great variety of interests, parties and sects which it embraces, a coalition of a majority of the whole society could seldom take place on any other principles than those of justice and the general good; and there being thus less danger to a minor from the will of the major party, there must be less pretext also, to provide for the security of the former, by introducing into the government a will not dependent on the latter; or in other words, a will independent of the society itself. It is no less certain than it is important, notwithstanding the contrary opinions which have been entertained, that the larger the society, provided it lie within a practicable sphere, the more duly capable will be of self government. And happily for the *republican cause,* the practicable sphere may be carried to a very great extent, by a judicious modification and mixture of the *federal principle.*

PUBLIUS

REFERENCES

Chapter 2   The Constitution

1. John Locke, *Second Treatise of Government*, in Thomas I. Cook, ed., *Two Treatises of Government* by John Locke (New York: Hafner, 1956), esp. Chs. 1–3, 7–9.
2. Gordon S. Wood, *The Creation of the American Republic* (Chapel Hill: University of North Carolina Press, 1969). See also *Federalist* No. 49.
3. Letters of Thomas Jefferson to James Madison, January 13, 1787. In Bernard Mayo, ed., *Jefferson Himself* (Boston: Houghton Mifflin, 1942), p. 145.
4. Letter of George Washington to Henry Lee, October 31, 1787. In John C. Fitzpatrick, ed., *Writings of George Washington* (Washington, D.C.: Government Printing Office, 1939), vol. 29, p. 34.
5. *Federalist*, No. 51.
6. *Ibid.*
7. See, for example, John Hope Franklin, *Racial Equality in America* (Chicago: University of Chicago Press, 1976), Ch. 1, esp. pp. 12–20.

Chapter 3   Civil Liberties

1. Barron v. Baltimore, 7 Peters 243 (1833).
2. Chicago, Burlington, and Quincy Railroad Co. v. Chicago, 166 U.S. 226 (1897); Gitlow v. New York, 268 U.S. 652 (1925).
3. Palko v. Connecticut, 302 U.S. 319 (1937), at 325.
4. Schad v. Borough of Mt. Ephraim, 452 U.S. 61 (1981).
5. United States v. Carolene Products, 304 U.S. 144 (1938).
6. Near v. Minnesota, 283 U.S. 697 (1931).
7. Brandenburg v. Ohio, 395 U.S. 765 (1978); R.A.V. v. City of Saint Paul, 505 U.S. 311 (1992).
8. Kunz v. New York, 340 U.S. 290 (1951).
9. Hynes v. Mayor and Council of Oradell, 425 U.S. 610 (1976).
10. Nebraska Press Association v. Stuart, 427 U.S. 539 (1976).
11. *New York Times* v. Sullivan, 376 U.S. 254 (1964). But compare Time, Inc. v. Firestone, 424 U.S. 448 (1976).
12. United States v. O'Brien, 391 U.S. 367 (1968).
13. Texas v. Johnson, 109 S. Ct. 2533 (1989); Tinker v. Des Moines Community School District, 393 U.S. 503 (1969).
14. Chaplinsky v. New Hampshire, 315 U.S. 568 (1942). But compare Gooding v. Wilson, 405 U.S. 518 (1972), and Rosenfeld v. New Jersey, 408 U.S. 901 (1972).
15. Village of Skokie v. National Socialist Party, 97 S. Ct. 2205 (1977); 366 N.E. 2d 349 (1977); 373 N.E. 2d 21 (1978).
16. Henry J. Abraham, *Freedom and the Court: Civil Rights and Civil Liberties in the United States*, 3rd ed. (New York: Oxford University Press, 1977), pp. 214–215, fn. 178.
17. Concurring opinion in Jacobellis v. Ohio, 378 U.S. 184 (1964), at p. 197.
18. Miller v. California, 413 U.S. 15 (1973).
19. Reno v. American Civil Liberties Union, 521 U.S. 844 (1997); Ashcroft v. ACLU, 542 U.S. 656 (2004).
20. Renton v. Playtime Theaters, 475 U.S. 41 (1986); Young v. American Mini-Theaters, Inc., 427 U.S. 50 (1976).
21. First National Bank of Boston v. Bellotti, 435 U.S. 765 (1978); Pacific Gas and Electric Co. v. Public Utilities Commissioners, 475 U.S. 1 (1986); 44 Liquormart v. Rhode Island, 540 U.S. 93 (1996); Federal Election Commission v. Massachusetts Citizens for Life, Inc., 479 U.S. 238 (1986).
22. The campaign finance law was upheld in McConnell v. Federal Election Commission, 540 U.S. 93 (2003) but repealed in part in Citizens United v. Federal Election Commission, 08-205 (2010).
23. Hazelwood School District v. Kuhlmeier, et al., 484 U.S. 260 (1988).
24. Murdock v. Pennsylvania 319 U.S. 105 (1943).
25. Reynolds v. United States, 98 U.S. 145 (1878).
26. Jacobsen v. Massachusetts, 197 U.S. 11 (1905).
27. Faith Baptist Church v. Douglas, 454 U.S. 803 (1981).
28. Welsh v. United States, 398 U.S. 333 (1970).
29. Sherbert v. Verner, 374 U.S. 398 (1963); Wisconsin v. Yoder, 406 U.S. 207 (1972).
30. Walter Berns, *The First Amendment and the Future of American Democracy* (New York: Basic Books, 1976).
31. C. Herman Pritchett, *Constitutional Civil Liberties* (Englewood Cliffs, N.J.: Prentice-Hall, 1984), pp. 145–147.
32. Everson v. Board of Education, 330 U.S. 1 (1947).
33. Engel v. Vitale, 370 U.S. 107 (1962).
34. Lubbock Independent School District v. Lubbock Civil Liberties Union, 459 U.S. 1155 (1983).
35. School District of Abington Township v. Schempp, 374 U.S. 203 (1963).
36. Epperson v. Arkansas, 393 U.S. 97 (1968); McLean v. Arkansas Board of Education, 529 F. Supp. 1255 (1982).
37. McCollum v. Board of Education, 333 U.S. 203 (1948); Zorach v. Clauson, 343 U.S. 306 (1952).
38. Titlon v. Richardson, 403 U.S. 672 (1971).
39. Board of Education v. Allen, 392 U.S. 236 (1968).
40. Walz v. Tax Commission, 397 U.S. 664 (1970).
41. Mueller v. Allen, 463 U.S. 388 (1983).
42. Committee for Public Higher Education v. Nyquist, 413 U.S. 756 (1973).
43. Meek v. Pittenger, 421 U.S. 349 (1975).
44. Wolman v. Walter, 433 U.S. 299 (1977).
45. Agostini v. Felton, 138 L. Ed. 2d 391 (1997).
46. Zelman v. Simmons-Harris, 536 U.S. 639 (2002).
47. Lemon v. Kurtzman, 403 U.S. 602 (1971).
48. Lynch v. Donnelly, 466 U.S. 994 (1984); County of Allegheny v. ACLU, 109 S. Ct. 3086 (1989).
49. Marsh v. Chambers, 463 U.S. 783 (1983).
50. Van Orden v. Perry, 125 S. Ct. 2854 (2005); McCreay County, KY v. American Civil Liberties Union, 125 S. Ct. 2722 (2005).
51. Edwards v. Aguillard, 482 U.S. 578 (1987); Kitzmiller v. Dover Area School District, 04-2688 (2005).
52. Wolf v. Colorado, 338 U.S. 25 (1949).
53. Mapp v. Ohio, 367 U.S. 643 (1961).
54. Chimel v. California, 395 U.S. 752 (1969).
55. Washington v. Chrisman, 455 U.S. 1 (1982).
56. Oliver v. United States, 466 U.S. 170 (1984); Kyllo v. United States, 533 U.S. 27 (2001).
57. Arkansas v. Sanders, 422 U.S. 753 (1979); Robbins v. California, 453 U.S. 420 (1981).
58. United States v. Ross, 456 U.S. 798 (1982).
59. Winston v. Lee, 470 U.S. 753 (1985).

60. South Dakota v. Neville, 459 U.S. 553 (1983); Schmerber v. California, 384 U.S. 757 (1966).
61. United States v. Dunn, 480 U.S. 294 (1987); California v. Ciraolo, 106 S. Ct. 1809 (1986); California v. Carney, 471 U.S. 386 (1985).
62. O'Connor v. Ortega, 480 U.S. 709 (1987).
63. New Jersey v. T.L.O., 469 U.S. 325 (1985).
64. Skinner v. Railway Labor Executives Union, 489 U.S. 602 (1989), and National Treasury Employees Union v. von Raab, 489 U.S. 656 (1989).
65. Escobedo v. Illinois, 378 U.S. 478 (1964); Miranda v. Arizona, 384 U.S. 436 (1966).
66. Malloy v. Hogan, 378 U.S. 1 (1964).
67. Miranda v. Arizona, 384 U.S. 436 (1966).
68. Gilbert v. California, 388 U.S. 263 (1967).
69. Estelle v. Smith, 451 U.S. 454 (1981).
70. Missouri v. Seibert, 542 U.S. 600 (2004).
71. Fare v. Michael C., 442 U.S. 707 (1979).
72. United States v. Leon, 468 U.S. 897 (1984).
73. New York v. Quarles, 467 U.S. 649 (1984).
74. Nix v. Williams, 467 U.S. 431 (1984).
75. Ex parte Quirin, 317 U.S. 1 (1942).
76. Hamdi v. Rumsfeld, 542 U.S. 507 (2004); Rasul v. Bush, 542 U.S. 466 (2004).

Chapter 4   Civil Rights

1. Brown v. Board of Education, 347 U.S. 483 (1954).
2. Fullilove v. Klutznick, 448 U.S. 448 (1980); Swann v. Charlotte-Mecklenburg Board of Education, 402 U.S. 1 (1971); Regents of the University of California v. Bakke, 438 U.S. 265 (1979).
3. Green v. School Board of New Kent County, 391 U.S. 430 (1968); Swann v. Charlotte-Mecklenburg Board of Education, 402 U.S. 1 (1971).
4. Milliken v. Bradley, 418 U.S. 717 (1974); Keyes v. School District No. 1 of Denver, 423 U.S. 189 (1973); Delaware State Board v. Evans, 446 U.S. 923 (1980); Armour v. Nix, 446 U.S. 930 (1980); Crawford v. Board of Education, 458 U.S. 527 (1982).
5. Gratz v. Bollinger, 539 U.S. 244 (2003).
6. Regents of the University of California v. Bakke, 438 U.S. 265 (1978).
7. Grutter v. Bollinger, 539 U.S. 982 (2003).
8. Fullilove v. Klutznick, 448 U.S. 448 (1980); Local 28 of the Sheet Metal Workers v. EEOC, 480 U.S. 149 (1986); U.S. v. Paradise, 478 U.S. 421 (1987); Local 93, International Association of Firefighters v. Cleveland, 106 S. Ct. 3063 (1986); United Steelworkers v. Weber, 443 U.S. 197 (1979).
9. Wygant v. Jackson Board of Education, 476 U.S. 267 (1984); Johnson v. Santa Clara County Transportation Agency, 480 U.S. 616 (1987).
10. Adarand v. Pena, 515 U.S. 200 (1995).
11. Mueller v. Oregon, 208 U.S. 412 (1908).
12. Reed v. Reed, 404 U.S. 71 (1971).
13. Frontiero v. Richardson, 411 U.S. 677 (1973).
14. Stanton v. Stanton, 421 U.S. 7 (1975).
15. Craig v. Boren, 429 U.S. 191 (1976).
16. Dothard v. Rawlinson, 433 U.S. 321 (1977).
17. Cleveland Board of Education v. LaFleur, 414 U.S. 632 (1974).
18. Fortin v. Darlington Little League, 514 F. 2d 344 (1975).
19. Roberts v. United States Jaycees, 468 U.S. 609 (1984); Board of Directors of Rotary International v. Rotary Club of Duarte, 481 U.S. 537 (1987).
20. Arizona Governing Committee for Tax Deferred Annuity and Tax Deferred Compensation Plans v. Norris, 463 U.S. 1073 (1983).
21. E.E.O.C. v. Madison Community School District No. 12, 818 F. 2d 577 (7th Circuit, May 15, 1987).
22. Michael M. v. Superior Court, 450 U.S. 464 (1981).
23. Vorchheimer v. School District of Philadelphia, 430 U.S. 703 (1977).
24. Kahn v. Shevin, 416 U.S. 351 (1974).
25. Schlesinger v. Ballard, 419 U.S. 498 (1975).
26. United States v. Virginia, 518 U.S. 515 (1996).
27. Gebser v. Lago Vista School District, 524 U.S. 274 (1998); Faragher v. Boca Raton, 524 U.S. 775 (1998); Burlington Industries v. Ellerth, 524 U.S. 742 (1998).
28. Rostker v. Goldberg, 453 U.S. 57 (1981).
29. Griswold v. Connecticut, 381 U.S. 479 (1965).
30. Roe v. Wade, 410 U.S. 113 (1973).
31. Maher v. Roe, 432 U.S. 464 (1977).
32. Planned Parenthood Federation of Central Missouri v. Danforth, 428 U.S. 52 (1976); Bellotti v. Baird, 443 U.S. 622 (1979); Akron v. Akron Center for Reproductive Health, 462 U.S. 416 (1983).
33. Planned Parenthood v. Casey, 505 U.S. 833 (1992).
34. Bowers v. Hardwick, 478 U.S. 186 (1986).
35. Lawrence v. Texas, 539 U.S. 558 (2003).
36. Goodrich v. Department of Public Health, 440 Mass. 309 (2003) and 440 Mass. 1201 (2004).

Chapter 5   Federalism

1. William H. Riker. "Federalism," in Fred I. Greenstein and Nelson W. Polsby, eds., *Handbook of Political Science* (Reading, Mass.: Addison-Wesley, 1975), vol. 5, p. 101.
2. Harold J. Laski, "The Obsolescence of Federalism," *New Republic*, May 3, 1939, pp. 367–369; Riker, *op. cit.*, p. 154.
3. Daniel J. Elazar, *American Federalism: A View from the States* (New York: Crowell, 1966), p. 216.
4. United States v. Sprague, 282 U.S. 716 (1931); Garcia v. San Antonio Metropolitan Transit Authority, 105 S. Ct. 1005 (1985).
5. McCulloch v. Maryland, 4 Wheat. 316 (1819).
6. Collector v. Day, 11 Wall. 113 (1870), overruled in part in Graves v. New York, 306 U.S. 466 (1939); Pollock v. Farmers' Loan and Trust Co., 157 U.S. 429 (1895), overruled in South Carolina v. Baker, 486 U.S. 1062 (1988).
7. Texas v. White, 7 Wall. 700 (1869).
8. Wickard v. Filburn, 317 U.S. 111 (1942); NLRB v. Jones & Laughlin Steel Corp., 301 U.S. 58 (1937).
9. Kirschbaum Co. v. Walling, 316 U.S. 517 (1942).
10. New York v. U.S., 505 U.S. 144 (1992); U.S. v. Lopez, 514 U.S. 549 (1995); Printz v. U.S., 521 U.S. 898 (1997); United States v. Morrison, 529 U.S. 598 (2000).
11. Samuel H. Beer, "The Modernization of American Federalism," *Publius*, vol. 3 (Fall 1973), esp. pp. 74–79; and Beer, "Federalism, Nationalism, and Democracy in America," *American Political Science Review*, vol. 72 (March 1978), pp. 18–19.
12. Kenneth Finegold et al., *Block Grants: Historical Overview* (Washington, D.C.: Urban Institute, 2004).
13. *Congressional Record*, Vol. 126 (February 5, 1980), pp. S1009–S1013.
14. R. Douglas Arnold, "The Local Roots of Domestic Policy," in Thomas E. Mann and Norman J. Ornstein, eds., *The New Congress* (Washington, D.C.: American Enterprise Institute, 1981), p. 268.

Chapter 6   Public Opinion and Media

1. R. L. Lowenstein, *World Press Freedom*, 1966 (Columbia, Mo.: Freedom of Information Center, 1967), Publication No. 11; D. E. Butler, "Why American Political Reporting Is Better Than England's" *Harper's* (May 1963), pp. 15–25.
2. *New York Times*, March 15, 1975.
3. M. Kent Jennings and Richard G. Niemi, "The Transmission of Political Values from Parent to Child," *American Political Science Review*, vol. 62 (March 1968), p. 173; Robert D. Hess and Judith V. Torney, *The Development of Political Attitudes in Children* (Chicago: Aldine, 1967), p. 90.
4. John R. Alford, Carolyn L. Funk, and John R. Hibbing, "Are Political Orientations Genetically Transmitted?" *American Political Science Review*, 99 (May 2005), pp. 153–167.
5. Norman H. Nie, Sidney Verba, and John R. Petrocik, *The Changing American Voter* (Cambridge, Mass.: Harvard University Press, 1976), Ch. 4.
6. Alford, Funk, and Hibbing, op. cit.
7. Robert S. Erikson and Kent L. Tedin, *American Public Opinion: Its Origins, Content, and Impact*, 6th ed. (New York: Longman, 2001), pp. 189–197; Seymour Martin Lipset, *Revolution and Counterrevolution*, rev. ed. (Garden City, N.Y.: Doubleday Anchor Books, 1970), pp. 338–342.
8. Erikson and Tedin, *op. cit.*, p. 194.
9. Seymour Martin Lipset and Earl Rabb, "The Election and the Evangelicals," *Commentary* (March 1981), pp. 25–31; Erikson and Tedin, *op. cit.*, pp. 194–197.
10. Alexander M. Astin, *Four Critical Years: Effects of College on Beliefs, Attitudes, and Knowledge* (San Francisco: Jossey-Bass, 1978), p. 38; J. L. Spaeth and Andrew M. Greeley, *Recent Alumni and Higher Education* (New York: McGraw-Hill, 1970), pp. 100–110; Erland Nelson, "Persistence of Attitudes of College Students Fourteen Years Later," *Psychological Monographs*, vol. 68 (1954), pp. 1–13; Kenneth A. Feldman and Theodore M. Newcomb, *The Impact of College on Students* (San Francisco: Jossey-Bass, 1969), vol. 1, pp. 99–100, 312–320.
11. Everett Carll Ladd, Jr., and Seymour Martin Lipset, *The Divided Academy: Professors and Politics* (New York: McGraw-Hill, 1975), pp. 26–27, 55–67, 184–190.
12. U.S. Census Bureau, *Statistical Abstract of the United States, 2010.* http://www.census.gov/population/www/socdemo/educ-attn.html
13. *The Baron Report*, June 18, 1984.
14. Polls by Gallup, ABC News/*Washington Post*, and *Time*/Yankelovich, Skelly, and White, summarized in *Public Opinion* (April/May 1982), pp. 30–32.
15. Kay Lehman Schlozman and Sidney Verba, *Insult to Injury: Unemployed, Class, and Political Response* (Cambridge, Mass.: Harvard University Press, 1979), pp. 115–118.
16. David Butler and Donald Stokes, *Political Change in Great Britain* (New York: St. Martin's, 1969), pp. 70, 77; Erikson and Luttbeg, *op. cit.*, p. 184; *National Journal*, November 8, 1980, p. 1878.
17. V. O. Key, Jr., *Public Opinion and American Democracy* (New York: Knopf, 1961), pp. 122–138; Richard E. Dawson, *Public Opinion and Contemporary Disarray* (New York: Harper & Row, 1973), Ch. 4.
18. *Public Opinion* (April/May 1981), pp. 32–40, citing polls by Gallup, NORC, and ABC News/*Washington Post*; Philip E. Converse et al., *American Social Attitudes, 1947–1978* (Cambridge, Mass.: Harvard University Press, 1980), p. 109; Erikson, and Tedin, *op. cit.*, pp. 180–186.
19. Nie et al., *op. cit.*, pp. 253–256.
20. Schlozman and Verba, *op. cit.*, p. 172.
21. *Ibid.*, pp. 168, 170; *Public Opinion* (April/May 1981), p. 26, citing polls by Dresner, Morris, and Tortorello Research.
22. Nie et al., *op. cit.*, pp. 247–250.
23. *Ibid.*, p. 218.
24. Everett Carll Ladd, Jr., *Transformations of the American Party System*, 2d ed. (New York: Norton, 1978), p. 280.
25. Philip E. Converse, "The Nature of Belief Systems in Mass Publics," in David Apter, ed., *Ideology and Discontent* (New York: Free Press of Glencoe, 1964), pp. 206–261.
26. Christopher H. Achen, "Mass Political Attitudes and the Survey Proposal," *American Political Science Review*, vol. 69 (December 1975), pp. 1218–1231.
27. Nie et al., *op. cit.*, pp. 115, 129, 142.
28. John L. Sullivan et al., "Ideological Constraint in the Mass Public: A Methodical Critique and Some New Findings," *American Journal of Political Science*, vol. 22 (May 1978), pp. 233–249; George F. Bishop et al., "Change in the Structure of American Political Attitudes: The Nagging Question of Question Wording," *American Journal of Political Science*, vol. 22 (May 1978), pp. 250–269.
29. Converse, *op. cit.*
30. Seymour Martin Lipset and Earl Raab, *The Politics of Unreason* (New York: Harper & Row, 1970), Ch. 11; James A. Stimson, "Belief Systems: Constraint, Complexity, and the 1972 Election," *American Journal of Political Science*, vol. 19 (1975), pp. 393–417.
31. Stimson, *op. cit.* See also Allen H. Barton and R. Wayne Parsons, "Measuring Belief System Structure," *Public Opinion Quarterly*, vol. 41 (Summer 1977), pp. 159–180.
32. Marvin Kalb, "Get Ready for the Really Bad News," *Los Angeles Times* (July 10, 1998), p. 139.
33. Edward Jay Epstein, *News from Nowhere: Television and the News* (New York: Random House, 1974), p. 37.
34. Allen A. Barton, "Consensus and Conflict Among American Leaders," *Public Opinion Quarterly*, vol. 38 (Winter 1974–1975), pp. 507–530.
35. Paul H. Weaver, "The New Journalism and the Old—Thoughts After Watergate," *The Public Interest* (Spring 1974), pp. 67–88.
36. Near v. Minnesota, 283 U.S. 697 (1931); *New York Times v.* United States, 403 U. S. 713 (1971).
37. *New York Times* v. Sullivan, 376 U.S. 254 (1964); Miami Herald Publishing Co. v. Tornillo, 418 U.S. 241 (1974); Yates v. United States, 354 U.S. 298 (1957).
38. Branzburg v. Hayes, 408 U.S. 665 (1972).
39. Michael J. Robinson, "A Twentieth-Century Medium in a Nineteenth-Century Legislature: The Effects of Television on the American Congress," in Norman J. Ornstein, ed., *Congress in Change* (New York: Praeger, 1975), pp. 240–261.
40. S. Robert Lichter and Stanley Rothman, "Media and Business Elites," *Public Opinion* (October/November 1981), p. 44; William Schneider and I. A. Lewis, "Views on the News," *Public Opinion* (August/September 1985), p. 7; Stanley Rothman and Amy Black, "Elites Revisited: American Social and Political Leadership in the 1990s," *International Journal of Public Opinion Research*, vol. 11 (1999), pp. 169–195.
41. Michael J. Robinson, "Just How Liberal Is the News? 1980 Revisited," *Public Opinion* (February/March 1983), pp. 55–60.
42. Peter Braestrup, *Big Story: How the American Press and Television Reported and Interpreted the Crisis of Tet 1968* (Boulder, Colo.: Westview, 1977).

43. David W. Brady and Jonathan Ma, "Spot the Differences," *Wall Street Journal*, November 12, 2003; John R. Lott, Jr., and Kevin A. Hassett, "Is Newspaper Coverage of Economic Events Politically Biased?" unpublished paper, American Enterprise Institute, September 1, 2004. See also Tim Groseclose and Jeff Milyo, "A Measure of Media Bias," *Quarterly Journal of Economics*, 120 (November 2005): 1191–1237.

Chapter 7 Political Parties and Interest Groups

1. Leon D. Epstein, "Political Parties," in Fred I. Greenstein and Nelson W. Polsby, eds., *Handbook of Political Science* (Reading, Mass.: Addison-Wesley, 1975), vol. 4, p. 230.
2. Byron E. Shafer, *Quiet Revolution: The Struggle for the Democratic Party and the Shaping of Post-Reform Politics* (New York: Russell Sage Foundation, 1983), p. 230.
3. Martin Shefter, "Parties, Bureaucracy, and Political Change in the United States," in Louis Maisel and Joseph Cooper, eds., *The Development of Political Parties* (Beverly Hills, Calif.: Sage, 1978), Sage Electoral Studies Yearbook, vol. 4.
4. James Q. Wilson, *The Amateur Democrat: Club Politics in Three Cities* (Chicago: University of Chicago Press, 1962).
5. Dwaine Marvick and Charles R. Nixon, "Recruitment Contrasts in Rival Campaign Groups," in Dwaine Marvick, ed., *Political Decision-Makers* (New York: The Free Press, 1961), pp. 212–213; David Nexon, "Asymmetry in the Political System," *American Political Science Review*, vol. 65 (September 1971), pp. 716–730.
6. Samuel J. Eldersveld, *Political Parties: A Behavioral Analysis* (Chicago: Rand McNally, 1964), pp. 278, 287; Robert H. Salisbury, "The Urban Political Organization Member," *Public Opinion Quarterly*, vol. 29 (Winter 1965–1966), pp. 550–564.
7. Salisbury, *op. cit.*, pp. 557, 559.
8. Eldersveld, *op. cit.*; J. David Greenstone, *Labor in American Politics* (New York: Knopf, 1969), p. 187.
9. Seymour Martin Lipset, "The Congressional Candidate," *Journal of Contemporary Studies*, vol. 6 (Summer 1983), p. 102.
10. William Nisbet Chambers and Walter Dean Burnham, eds., *The American Party System: Stages of Political Development*, 2d ed. (New York: Oxford University Press, 1975), p. 6.
11. James Q. Wilson, *Political Organizations* (Princeton, N.J.: Princeton University Press, 1995), Ch. 12.
12. On 1972 and 1976, see Jeane Kirkpatrick, *The New Presidential Elite* (New York: Russell Sage Foundation and Twentieth Century Fund, 1976), pp. 297–315; on 1980, see *New York Times*, August 13, 1980.
13. Nelson W. Polsby, *Consequences of Party Reform* (New York: Oxford University Press, 1983), pp. 9–11, 64.
14. *Ibid.*, p. 158.
15. Michael J. Malbin, "Democratic Party Rules Are Made to Be Broken," *National Journal*, August 23, 1980; Kirkpatrick, *op. cit.*, Ch. 4.
16. Gallup Poll, various dates in 1980.
17. Norman H. Nie, Sidney Verba, and John R. Petrocik, *The Changing American Voter* (Cambridge, Mass.: Harvard University Press, 1976), p. 203; Barry Sussman, "Elites in America," *Washington Post*, September 26–30, 1976; Kirkpatrick, *op. cit.*, Tables 10-1, 10-2, 10-3, 10-7.
18. Nie et al., *op. cit.*, p. 203.
19. L. Harmon Zeigler and Hendrik van Dalen, "Interest Groups in the States," in Herbert Jacob and Kenneth N. Vines, eds., *Politics in the American States*, 2d ed. (Boston: Little, Brown, 1974), pp. 122–160; Edward C. Banfield and James Q. Wilson, *City Politics* (Cambridge, Mass: Harvard University Press, 1963); Chs. 18, 19.

20. Joseph LaPalombara, *Interest Groups in Italian Politics* (Princeton, N.J.: Princeton University Press, 1964).
21. Kay Lehman Schlozman and John T. Tierney, "More of the Same: Washington Pressure Group Activity in a Decade of Change," *Journal of Politics*, vol. 45 (1983), p. 356.
22. The use of injunctions in labor disputes was restricted by the Norris–La Guardia Act of 1932; the rights to collective bargaining and to the union shop were guaranteed by the Wagner Act of 1935.
23. Schlozman and Tierney, *op. cit.*, p. 355.
24. The distinction is drawn by Kay Lehman Schlozman and John T. Tierney, *The Mischiefs of Faction: Organized Interests in American Politics* (New York: Harper & Row, 1985).
25. Updated from Jeffrey M. Berry, *The Interest Group Society* (Boston: Little, Brown, 1984), pp. 20–21, 24, 130.
26. Gabriel A. Almond and Sidney Verba, *The Civic Culture* (Princeton, N.J.: Princeton University Press, 1963), p. 302; Derek C. Bok and John T. Dunlop, *Labor and the American Community* (New York: Simon & Schuster, 1970), p. 49; *Statistical Abstract of the United States, 1975*, p. 373.
27. Almond and Verba, *op. cit.*, p. 194.
28. *Ibid.*, p. 134.
29. Bok and Dunlop, *op. cit.*, p. 194.
30. Henry J. Pratt, *The Liberalization of American Protestantism* (Detroit, Mich.: Wayne State University Press, 1972), Ch. 12; Gerhard Lenski, *The Religious Factor* (Garden City, N.Y.: Doubleday, 1961), Ch. 4.
31. Jeffrey M. Berry, *Lobbying for the People* (Princeton, N.J.: Princeton University Press, 1977), pp. 71–76.
32. Berry, *The Interest Group Society*, *op. cit.*, p. 88.
33. *National Journal*, August 6, 1983, p. 1632.
34. Schlozman and Tierney, *The Mischiefs of Faction*, *op. cit.*
35. *Ibid.*, Table 5-4.
36. *New York Times*, December 8, 1983, p. 1.
37. Hedrick Smith, *The Power Game* (New York: Random House, 1988).
38. Michael J. Malbin, ed., *Money and Politics in the United States* (Chatham, N.J.: Chatham House, 1984), Tables A.14 and A.15, pp. 298–299.
39. Margaret Ann Latus, "Assessing Ideological PACs: From Outrage to Understanding," in Malbin, *op. cit.*, p. 143.
40. *Ibid.*, p. 144; Berry, *The Interest Group Society*, *op. cit.*, p. 163.
41. Theodore J. Eismeier and Philip H. Pollock, "Political Action Committees: Varieties of Organization Strategy," in Malbin, *op. cit.*, p. 132.
42. Malbin, *op. cit.*, Table A.8, pp. 290–291.
43. Michael J. Malbin, "Looking Back at the Future of Campaign Finance Reform: Interest Groups and American Election," in Malbin, *Money and Politics*, *op. cit.*, p. 248; James B. Kau and Paul H. Rubin, *Congressmen, Constituents, and Contributions* (Boston: Martinus Nijhoff, 1982); Henry W. Chappell, Jr., "Campaign Contributions and Voting on the Cargo Preference Bill: A Comparison of Simultaneous Models," *Public Choice*, vol. 36 (1981), pp. 301–312; W. P. Welch, "Campaign Contributions and Voting: Milk Money and Dairy Price Supports," *Western Political Quarterly*, vol. 35 (1982), pp. 478–495.
44. *National Journal*, November 19, 1977, p. 1800, quoting a study by the staff of Senator William Proxmire.
45. William T. Gormley, "A Test of the Revolving Door Hypothesis at the FCC," *American Journal of Political Science*, vol. 23 (1979), pp. 665–683; Paul J. Quirk, *Industry Influence in Federal*

Regulatory Agencies (Princeton, N.J.: Princeton University Press, 1981); Suzanne Weaver, *Decision to Prosecute* (Cambridge, Mass.: MIT Press, 1977), pp. 154–163.

46. United States v. Harriss, 347 U.S. 612 (1954).

47. Hope Eastman, *Lobbying: A Constitutionally Protected Right* (Washington D.C.: American Enterprise Institute, 1977), p. 30.

48. *United States Code*, Title 26, Sec. 501 (c)(3).

49. Wilson, *Political Organizations, op. cit.*, p. 321.

Chapter 8   Campaigns and Elections

1. Prof. Michael McDonald, *U.S. Elections Project* http://elections. gmu.edu/.

2. Sidney Verba and Norman H. Nie, *Participation in America* (New York: Harper & Row, 1972), pp. 118–119.

3. Norman H. Nie and Sidney Verba, "Political Participation," in Fred I. Greenstein and Nelson W. Polsby, eds., *Handbook of Political Science* (Reading, Mass.: Addison-Wesley, 1975), vol. 4, pp. 24–25.

4. Lester W. Milbrath and M. L. Goel, *Political Participation*, 2nd ed. (Chicago: Rand McNally, 1977), pp. 98–116; Raymond E. Wolfinger and Steven J. Rosenstone, *Who Votes?* (New Haven, Conn.: Yale University Press, 1980).

5. Nie and Verba, *op. cit.*, pp. 151–157; Milbrath and Goel, *op. cit.*, p. 120.

6. Verba and Nie, *op. cit.*, pp. 160–164.

7. The National Election Studies, 1964-2008, data compiled by Zach Courser.

8. Verba and Nie, *op. cit.*, Ch. 18.

9. Voter Education Project, Inc., of Atlanta, Georgia, as reported in *Statistical Abstract of the United States*, 1984, p. 261.

10. Congressional Quarterly, *Congress and the Nation*, vol. 3: 1969–1972 (Washington, D.C.: Congressional Quarterly Press, 1973), p. 1006; *Statistical Abstract of the United States, 1975*, p. 450.

11. Walter Dean Burnham, "The Changing Shape of the American Political Universe," *American Political Science Review*, vol. 59 (March 1965); E. E. Schattschneider, *The Semisovereign People* (New York: Holt, Rinehart, and Winston, 1960), Chs. 5, 6.

12. Morton Keller, *Affairs of State* (Cambridge, Mass.: Harvard University Press, 1977), pp. 523–524.

13. Michael P. McDonald and Samuel L. Popkin, "The Myth of the Vanishing Voter," *American Political Science Review*, vol. 95 (December 2001), pp. 963–974.

14. U.S. Bureau of Census, Current Population Survey, "Reasons for Not Voting," June 2008, table 6.

15. Donald P. Green and Alan S. Gerber, *Get Out the Vote: How to Increase Voter Turnout* (Washington, D.C.: Brookings Institution Press, 2008).

16. Alan S. Gerber, et al., "Social Pressure and Voter Turnout: Evidence from a Large-Scale Field Experiment," *American Political Science Review* 102, February 2008, p. 38.

17. Thomas E. Patterson and Robert D. McClure, *The Unseeing Eye: The Myth of Television Power in National Elections* (New York: Putnam, 1976).

18. Philip N. Howard, *New Media Campaigns and the Managed Citizen* (Cambridge: Cambridge University Press, 2006), Ch. 2.

19. *Ibid.*, 90-91.

20. Donald P. Green and Alan S. Gerber, *Get Out the Vote*, 2nd ed. (Washington, D.C.: Brookings Institution, 2008), Ch. 5 and p. 137.

21. Richard R. Lau, Lee Sigelman, and Ivy Brown Rover, "The Effects of Negative Political Campaigns: A Meta-Analytic Reassessment," *Journal of Politics*, 69 (2007): 1176-1209.

22. Angus Campbell, Philip E. Converse, Warren E. Miller, and Donald E. Stokes, *The American Voter* (New York: Wiley, 1960), p. 757.

23. Richard Wirthlin, Vincent Breglio, and Richard Beal, "Campaign Chronicle," *Public Opinion* (February/March 1981), pp. 43–49 (written by Reagan pollsters).

24. Norman H. Nie, Sidney Verba, and John R. Petrocik, *The Changing American Voter* (Cambridge, Mass.: Harvard University Press, 1976).

25. V. O. Key, Jr., *The Responsible Electorate* (Cambridge, Mass.: Harvard University Press, 1966).

26. David RePass, "Issue Salience and Party Choice," *American Political Science Review*, vol. 65 (June 1971), pp. 389–400.

27. D. Roderick Kiewit, *Macroeconomics and Micropolitics* (Chicago: University of Chicago Press, 1983), pp. 107, 126–127.

28. Morris P. Fiorina, *Retrospective Voting in American Elections* (New Haven, Conn.: Yale University Press, 1981).

29. Walter Dean Burnham, *Critical Election and the Mainsprings of American Politics* (New York: Norton, 1970), p. 10.

30. James L. Sundquist, *Dynamics of the Party System* (Washington, D.C.: Brookings Institution, 1973), Ch. 7.

31. Edward G. Carmines and James A. Stimson, "Issues Evolution, Population Replacement, and Normal Partisan Change," *American Political Science Review*, vol. 75 (March 1981), pp. 107–118; Gregory B. Markus, "Political Attitudes in an Election Year," *American Political Science Review*, vol. 76 (September 1982), pp. 538–560.

32. Rusk, *op. cit.*, pp. 1220–1238.

33. Robert Axelrod, "Where the Votes Come From: An Analysis of Electoral Coalition, 1952–1968," *American Political Science Review*, vol. 66 (March 1972), pp. 11–20; Axelrod, "Communication," *American Political Science Review*, vol. 68 (June 1974), pp. 718–719.

34. For efforts to measure the media's effect on culture, see S. Robert Lichter, Linda S. Lichter, and Stanley Rothman, *Prime Time* (Washington, D.C.: Regnery, 1994), and Shanto Iyengar and Donald R. Kinder, *News That Matters* (Chicago: University of Chicago Press, 1987).

35. Herbert Asher, *Presidential Elections and American Politics* (Homewood, Ill.: Dorsey Press, 1976), pp. 239–240 (and studies cited therein).

36. David O. Sears and Richard E. Whitney, "Political Persuasion," in Ithiel de Sola Pool, Wilbur Schramm, et al., *Handbook of Communication* (Chicago: Rand McNally, 1973), pp. 253–289.

37. Patterson and McClure, *op. cit.*; and Xandra Kayden, *Campaign Organization* (Lexington, Mass.: Heath, 1978), Ch. 6.

38. Robert S. Erikson, "The Influence of Newspaper Endorsements in Presidential Elections: The Case of 1964," *American Journal of Political Science*, vol. 20 (May 1976), pp. 207–233.

39. Maxwell E. McCombs and Donald R. Shaw, "The Agenda Setting Function of the Mass Media," *Public Opinion Quarterly*, vol. 36 (Summer 1972), pp. 176–187.

40. G. Ray Funkhouser, "The Issues of the Sixties," *Public Opinion Quarterly*, vol. 37 (Spring 1973), pp. 62–75.

41. Gary C. Jacobson, *Money in Congressional Elections* (New Haven, Conn.: Yale University Press, 1980).

42. Colorado Republican Party v. F.E.C., 518 U.S. 604 (1996).

43. McConnell v. Federal Election Commission, 124 S. Ct. 619 (2003).

44. Benjamin Ginsberg, "Elections and Public Policy," *American Political Science Review*, vol. 70 (1976), pp. 41–46.

Chapter 9   Congress

1. Wesberry v. Sanders, 376 U. S. 1 (1964).
2. H. Douglas Price, "Careers and Committees in the American Congress," in William O. Aydelotte, ed., *The History of Parliamentary Behavior* (Princeton, N.J.: Princeton University Press, 1977), pp. 28–62; John F. Bibby, Thomas E. Mann, and Norman J. Ornstein, *Vital Statistics on Congress, 1980* (Washington, D.C.: American Enterprise Institute, 1980), pp. 53–54; Thomas E. Cavanagh, "The Dispersion of Authority in the House of Representatives," *Political Science Quarterly*, vol. 97 (1982–1983), pp. 625–626.
3. David R. Mayhew, *Congress: The Electoral Connection* (New Haven, Conn.: Yale University Press, 1974); Bibby, Mann, and Ornstein, *op. cit.*, pp. 14–15.
4. Mayhew, *op. cit.*; Morris P. Fiorina, *Congress: Keystone of the Washington Establishment* (New Haven, Conn.: Yale University Press, 1977).
5. Richard F. Fenno, Jr., "U. S. House Members and Their Constituencies: An Exploration," *American Political Science Review*, vol. 71 (September 1977), pp. 883–917, esp. p. 914.
6. Richard F. Fenno, Jr., *Congressmen in Committees* (Boston: Little, Brown, 1973).
7. Bibby, Mann, and Ornstein, *op. cit.*, pp. 65–74.
8. Fiorina, *op. cit.*
9. Bibby, Mann, and Ornstein, *op. cit.*, p. 60.
10. Michael J. Malbin, "Delegation, Deliberation, and the New Role of Congressional Staff," in Thomas E. Mann and Norman J. Ornstein, eds., *The New Congress* (Washington, D.C.: American Enterprise Institute, 1981), pp. 134–177, esp. pp. 170–171.
11. Malcolm E. Jewell and Samuel C. Patterson, *The Legislative Process in the United States*, 3rd ed. (New York: Random House, 1977), p. 439.
12. Warren E. Miller and Donald E. Stokes, "Constituency Influence in Congress," in Angus Campbell et al., eds., *Elections and the Political Order* (New York: Wiley, 1966), p. 359.
13. Gary C. Jacobson, "Public Opinion and the Impeachment of Bill Clinton," in *British Elections and Parties Review*, vol. 10, ed. Philip Cowley, David Denver, Andrew Russell, and Lisa Harrison (London: Frank Cass, 2000), pp. 1–31; Jacobson, "The Electoral Basis of Partisan Polarization in Congress," paper delivered at annual meeting of the American Political Science Association (2000); David Brady and Edward P. Schwartz, "Ideology and Interests in Congressional Voting: The Politics of Abortion in the United States Senate," *Public Choice*, vol. 84 (1995), pp. 25–48.
14. Larry M. Bartels, "Partisanship and Voting Behavior, 1952–1996," *American Journal of Political Science*, vol. 44 (2000), pp. 35–50.

Chapter 10   The Presidency

1. Jean Blondel, *An Introduction to Comparative Government* (New York: Praeger, 1969), as cited in Nelson W. Polsby, "Legislatures," in Fred I. Greenstein and Nelson E. Polsby, eds., *Handbook of Political Science* (Reading, Mass.: Addison-Wesley, 1975), vol. 5, p. 275.
2. Woodrow Wilson, *Congressional Government* (New York: Meridian, 1956), pp. 167–168, 170 (first published in 1885).
3. Stephen Hess, *Organizing the Presidency* (Washington, D.C.: Brookings Institution, 1976), p. 3.
4. Walter D. Burnham, "Insulation and Responsiveness in Congressional Elections," *Political Science Quarterly*, vol. 90 (Fall 1975), pp. 412–413; George C. Edwards III, *Presidential Influence in Congress* (San Francisco, Calif.: Freeman, 1980), pp. 70–78; Warren E. Miller, "Presidential Coattails: A Study in Political Myth and Methodology," *Public Opinion Quarterly*, vol. 19 (Winter 1955–1956), p. 368; Miller, "The Motivational Basis for Straight and Split Ticket Voting," *American Political Science Review*, vol. 51 (June 1957), pp. 293–312.
5. Edwards, *op. cit.*, pp. 86–100; Douglas Rivers and Nancy L. Rose, "Passing the President's Program: Public Opinion and Presidential Influence in Congress," paper delivered at the 1981 annual meeting of the Midwestern Political Science Association.
6. Clinton v. City of New York, 118 S. Ct. 209 (1998).
7. United States v. Nixon, 418 U.S. 683 (1974).
8. Immigration and Naturalization Service v. Chadha, 103 S. Ct. 2764 (1983).

Chapter 11   The Bureaucracy

1. Charles E. Lindblom, *Politics and Markets* (New York: Basic Books, 1977), p. 114.
2. Calculated from data in *Historical Statistics of the United States: Colonial Times to 1970* (Washington, D.C.: Government Printing Office, 1975), vol. 2, pp. 1102–1103.
3. Panama Refining Co. v. Ryan, 293 U.S. 388 (1935); Hampton Jr. & Co. v. United States, 276 U.S. 394 (1928).
4. Edward S. Corwin, *The Constitution and What It Means Today*, 13th ed. (Princeton, N.J.: Princeton University Press, 1973), p. 151.
5. Bruce D. Porter, "Parkinson's Law Revisited: War and the Growth of American Government," *Public Interest* (Summer 1980), pp. 50–68.
6. See the cases cited in Corwin, *op. cit.*, p. 8.
7. *Historical Statistics of the United States*, vol. 2, p. 1107.
8. Paul C. Light, *Thickening Government* (Washington, D.C.: Brookings Institution, 1995).
9. Light, *op. cit.*, p. 11; *Statistical Abstract of the United States, 2000*, Table 537.
10. Herbert Kaufmann, *Are Government Organizations Immortal?* (Washington, D.C.: Brookings Institution, 1976), pp. 9–10, 34.
11. *Statistical Abstract of the United States, 2000*, Table 876.
12. C. Northcote Parkinson, *Parkinson's Law* (Boston: Houghton Mifflin, 1957), pp. 2–8.
13. *Statistical Abstract of the United States, 1975* (Washington, D.C.: Government Printing Office, 1975), p. 242.
14. *National Journal*, July 18, 1981, pp. 1296–1299.
15. J. Donald Kingsley, *Representative Bureaucracy* (Yellow Springs, Ohio: Antioch Press, 1944); Richard P. Nathan, *The Plot That Failed: Nixon and the Administrative Presidency* (New York: Wiley, 1975).
16. Stanley Rothman and S. Robert Lichter, "How Liberal Are Bureaucrats?" *Regulation* (November–December 1983), pp. 17–18.
17. Kenneth Meier and Lloyd Nigro, "Representative Bureaucracy and Policy Preferences: A Study of the Attitudes of Federal Executives," *Public Administration Review*, vol. 36 (July–August 1976), pp. 458–467; Bernard Mennis, *American Foreign Policy Officials* (Columbus: Ohio State University Press, 1971); Joel D. Aberbach and Bert A. Rockman, "Clashing Beliefs Within the Executive Branch: The Nixon Administration Bureaucracy," *American Political Science Review*, vol. 70 (June 1976), pp. 456–468.
18. James Q. Wilson, *Bureaucracy* (New York: Basic Books, 1989).
19. Graham K. Wilson, "Are Department Secretaries Really a President's Natural Enemies?" *British Journal of Political Science*, vol. 7 (1977), pp. 273–299.

20. Richard F. Fenno, Jr., *The Power of the Purse* (Boston: Little, Brown, 1966), pp. 450, 597.
21. John E. Schwartz and L. Earl Shaw, *The United States Congress in Comparative Perspective* (Hinsdale, Ill.: Dryden, 1976), pp. 262–263; *National Journal*, July 4, 1981, pp. 1211–1214.
22. See cases cited in Corwin, *op. cit.*, p. 22.
23. Steven Kelman, "The Grace Commission: How Much Waste in Government?" *Public Interest* (Winter 1985), pp. 62–87.

Chapter 12   The Judiciary

1. Henry J. Abraham, *The Judicial Process*, 3rd ed. (New York: Oxford University Press, 1975), pp. 279–280.
2. Robert G. McCloskey, *The American Supreme Court* (Chicago: University of Chicago Press, 1960), p. 27.
3. Marbury v. Madison, 1 Cranch 137 (1803); McCulloch v. Maryland, 4 Wheat. 316 (1819).
4. Martin v. Hunter's Lessee, 1 Wheat. 304 (1816); Cohens v. Virginia, 6 Wheat. 264 (1821); Gibbons v. Ogden, 9 Wheat. 1 (1824).
5. Quoted in Albert J. Beveridge, *The Life of John Marshall* (Boston: Houghton Mifflin, 1919), vol. 4, p. 551.
6. Dred Scott v. Sandford, 19 Howard 393 (1857).
7. Quoted in Henry J. Abraham, *Justices and Presidents* (New York: Oxford University Press, 1974), p. 74.
8. *Ibid.*, p. 75.
9. Gideon v. Wainwright, 372 U.S. 335 (1963). The story is told in Anthony Lewis, *Gideon's Trumpet* (New York: Random House, 1964).
10. Erwin Griswold, "Rationing Justice: The Supreme Court's Case Load and What the Court Does Not Do," *Cornell Law Review*, vol. 60 (1975), pp. 335–354.
11. Bernard Schwartz, *How the Supreme Court Decides Cases* (New York: Oxford University Press, 1996), pp. 50–51, 257–259.
12. Alyeska Pipeline Service Co. v. Wilderness Society, 421 U.S. 240; Maine v. Thiboutot, 448 U.S. 1 (1980).
13. Flast v. Cohen, 392 U.S. 83 (1968), which modified the earlier Frothingham v. Mellon, 262 U.S. 447 (1923); United States v. Richardson, 418 U.S. 166 (1947).
14. Brown v. Board of Education of Topeka, 347 U.S. 483 (1954).
15. Baker v. Carr, 369 U.S. 186 (1962).
16. See Louise Weinberg, "A New Judicial Federalism?" *Daedalus* (Winter 1978), pp. 129–141.
17. *Harvard Law Review*, vol. 100 (1986), p. 305.
18. A. P. Blaustein and A. H. Field, "Overruling Opinions in the Supreme Court," *Michigan Law Review*, vol. 47 (1958), p. 151; Henry J. Abraham, *The Judicial Process*, 4th ed. (New York: Oxford University Press, 1980), p. 349.
19. The Court abandoned the "political question" doctrine in Baker v. Carr, 369 U.S. 186 (1962), and began to change congressional district apportionment in Wesberry v. Sanders, 376 U.S. 1 (1964).
20. Donald J. Horowitz, *The Courts and Social Policy* (Washington, D.C.: Brookings Institution, 1977), p. 6.
21. Gates v. Collier, 349 F. Supp. 881 (1972); Lau v. Nichols, 414 U.S. 563 (1974).
22. *International Directory of Bar Associations*, 3rd ed. (Chicago: American Bar Foundation, 1973).
23. Annual Reports of the Director of the Administrative Office of the United States Courts, 1975 (Table 17) and 1983 (Table 16).
24. Warner W. Gardner, "Federal Courts and Agencies: An Audit of the Partnership Books," *Columbia Law Review*, vol. 75 (1975), pp. 800–822.
25. Anthony Partridge and William B. Eldridge, *The Second Circuit Sentencing Study* (Washington, D.C.: Federal Judicial Center, 1974).
26. Abraham, *The Judicial Process*, p. 332.
27. *Ex Parte* McCardle, 7 Wall. 506 (1869).
28. Walter J. Murphy, *Congress and the Court* (Chicago: University of Chicago Press, 1962); C. Herman Prichett, *Congress Versus the Supreme Court* (Minneapolis: University of Minnesota Press, 1961).
29. Joseph T. Tanenhaus and Walter F. Murphy, "Patterns of Public Support for the Supreme Court: A Panel Study," *Journal of Politics*, vol. 43 (1981), pp. 24–39; Gregory A. Caldeira, "Neither the Purse Nor the Sword: Dynamics of Public Confidence in the Supreme Court," *American Political Science Review*, vol. 80 (1988), p. 1213.

Chapter 13   Making Domestic Policy

1. The total national debt was over $13 trillion in mid-2010.
2. Robert S. Erikson and Kent L. Tedin, *American Public Opinion*, 5th ed. (Boston: Allyn and Bacon, 1995), 271.
3. D. Roderick Klewit, *Macroeconomics and Micropolitics* (Chicago: University of Chicago Press, 1983), Ch. 4.
4. *Statistical Abstract of the United States, 2004–2005*, Table 476.

Chapter 14   Making Foreign and Military Policy

1. Alexis de Tocqueville, *Democracy in America*, ed. Phillips Bradley (New York: Alfred Knopf, 1951), vol. 1, p. 235.
2. Compare Victor Davis Hanson, *Carnage and Culture* (New York: Anchor Books, 2002), and Hanson, *The Soul of Battle* (New York: Free Press, 1999).
3. Louis Henkin, *Foreign Affairs and the Constitution* (New York: Norton, 1972), 53, 306 n. 43; Louis W. Koenig, *The Chief Executive*, 3rd ed. (New York: Harcourt Brace Jovanovich, 1975), p. 217.
4. James C. Dobbins et al., *America's Role in Nation-Building* (Santa Monica, Calif.: RAND, 2003).
5. Updated from Louis W. Koenig, *The Chief Executive*, 3rd ed. (New York: Harcourt Brace Jovanovich, 1975), p. 217.
6. *The National Security Strategy of the United States of America*, September 2002, cover letter and p. 6.
7. The vote on the Persian Gulf War as reported in *Congress and the Nation*, vol. 8 (Washington, D.C.: Congressional Quarterly Press, 1993), p. 310; the vote on the Iraq war as reported in the *New York Times*, October 12, 2002, p. A11.
8. There were no votes on the Bosnia-Kosovo efforts, but speeches strongly supporting U.S. intervention were made by Democratic Senators Barbara Boxer, Carl Levin, and Paul Wellstone and Representative David Bonior; speeches opposing it were made by Republican Senators Don Nickles and John Warner and Representatives Robert Barr and Dan Burton. In the vote on the invasion of Iraq, each group took the opposite position.
9. James Q. Wilson and Karlyn Bowman, "Defining the 'Peace Party,'" *The Public Interest* (Fall 2003), pp. 69–78.
10. Pew Research Center for the People and the Press, November 5, 2003, survey report.
11. *The Economist*, January 3, 2004, p. 14.

GLOSSARY

Activist An individual, usually outside government, who actively promotes a political party, philosophy, or issue he or she cares about.

Activist approach (judicial) The view that judges should discern the general principles underlying the Constitution and its often vague language and assess how best to apply them in contemporary circumstances, in some cases with the guidance of moral or economic philosophy.

Affirmative action The requirement, imposed by law or administrative regulation, that an organization (business firm, government agency, labor union, school, or college) take positive steps to increase the number or proportion of women, blacks, or other minorities in its membership.

Amicus curiae A Latin term meaning "a friend of the court." Refers to interested groups or individuals, not directly involved in a suit, who may file legal briefs or make oral arguments in support of one side.

Antifederalists Opponents of a strong central government who campaigned against ratification of the Constitution in favor of a confederation of largely independent states. Antifederalists successfully marshaled public support for a federal bill of rights. After ratification, they formed a political party to support states' rights. *See also* Federalists.

Appropriation A legislative grant of money to finance a government program. *See also* Authorization legislation.

Articles of Confederation A constitution drafted by the newly independent states in 1777 and ratified in 1781. It created a weak national government that could not levy taxes or regulate commerce. In 1789, it was replaced by our current constitution in order to create a stronger national government.

Australian ballot A government-printed ballot of uniform size and shape to be cast in secret that was adopted by many states around 1890 in order to reduce the voting fraud associated with party-printed ballots cast in public.

Authorization legislation Legislative permission to begin or continue a government program or agency. An authorization bill may grant permission to spend a certain sum of money, but that money does not ordinarily become available unless it is also appropriated. Authorizations may be annual, multiyear, or permanent. *See also* Appropriation.

Benefit Any satisfaction, monetary or nonmonetary, that people believe they will enjoy if a policy is adopted.

Bicameral legislature A lawmaking body made up of two chambers or parts. The U.S. Congress is a bicameral legislature composed of a Senate and a House of Representatives.

Bill of Rights The first ten amendments to the U.S. Constitution, containing a list of individual rights and liberties, such as freedom of speech, religion, and the press.

Bipolar world A world that is militarily dominated by two superpowers, as was the case when the United States and the Soviet Union confronted each other.

Blanket primary A primary election that permits all voters, regardless of party, to choose candidates. A Democratic voter, for example, can vote in a blanket primary for both Democratic and Republican candidates for nomination.

Block grants Grants of money from the federal government to states for programs in certain general areas rather than for specific kinds of programs. *See also* Categorical grant; Grants-in-aid.

Brief A legal document prepared by an attorney representing a party before a court. The document sets forth the facts of the case, summarizes the law, gives the arguments for its side, and discusses other relevant cases.

Budget deficit A situation in which the government spends more money than it takes in from taxes and fees.

Budget resolution A proposal submitted by the House and Senate budget committees to their respective chambers recommending a total budget ceiling and a ceiling for each of several spending areas (such as health or defense) for the current fiscal year. These budget resolutions are intended to guide the work of each legislative committee as it decides what to spend in its area.

Budget surplus A situation in which the government takes in more money than it spends.

Bureaucracy A large, complex organization composed of appointed officials. The departments and agencies of the U.S. government make up the federal bureaucracy.

Cabinet By custom, the cabinet includes the heads of the fifteen major executive departments.

Categorical grant A federal grant for a specific purpose defined by federal law: to build an airport, for example, or to make welfare payments to low-income mothers. Such grants usually require that the state or locality put up money to "match" some part of the federal grant, though the amount of matching funds can be quite small. *See also* Block grants; Grants-in-aid.

Caucus (congressional) An association of members of Congress created to advocate a political ideology or a regional, ethnic, or economic interest.

Checks and balances The power of the legislative, executive, and judicial branches of government to block some acts by the other two branches. *See also* Separation of powers.

Circular structure A method of organizing a president's staff whereby several presidential assistants report directly to the president.

Civil liberties   Rights—chiefly, rights to be free of government interference—accorded to an individual by the Constitution: free speech, free press, and the like.

Civil rights   The rights of citizens to vote, to receive equal treatment before the law, and to share equally with other citizens the benefits of public facilities (such as schools).

Class-action suit   A case brought into court by a person on behalf of not only himself or herself but all other persons in the country under similar circumstances. For example, in *Brown v. Board of Education of Topeka*, the Court decided that not only Linda Brown but all others similarly situated had the right to attend a local public school of their choice without regard to race.

Client politics   A policy under which some small group receives the benefits and the public at large endures the costs.

Closed primary   A primary election limited to registered party members. Prevents members of other parties from crossing over to influence the nomination of an opposing party's candidate. *See also* Open primary; Primary election.

Closed resolution   An order from the House Rules Committee in the House of Representatives that sets a time limit on debate and forbids a particular bill from being amended on the legislative floor. *See also* Open rule; Restrictive rule.

Cloture rule   A rule used by the Senate to end or limit debate. Designed to prevent "talking a bill to death" by filibuster. To pass in the Senate, three-fifths of the entire Senate membership (or sixty senators) must vote for it. *See also* Filibuster.

Cluster structure   A system for organizing the White House in which a group of subordinates and committees all report to the president directly.

Coalition   An alliance among different interest groups (factions) or parties to achieve some political goal. An example is the coalition sometimes formed between Republicans and conservative Democrats.

Committee clearance   The ability of a congressional committee to review and approve certain agency decisions in advance and without passing a law. Such approval is not legally binding on the agency, but few agency heads will ignore the expressed wishes of committees.

Competitive service   The government offices to which people are appointed on grounds of merit as ascertained by a written examination or by having met certain selection criteria (such as training, educational attainments, or prior experience). *See also* Excepted service.

Concurrent resolution   An expression of congressional opinion without the force of law that requires the approval of both the House and Senate but not of the president. Used to settle housekeeping and procedural matters that affect both houses. *See also* Joint resolution; Simple resolution.

Concurring opinion   A Supreme Court opinion by one or more justices who agree with the majority's conclusion but for different reasons. *See also* Opinion of the Court; Dissenting opinion.

Conditions of aid   Federal rules attached to the grants that states receive. States must agree to abide by these rules in order to receive the grant.

Confederation or confederal system   A political system in which states or regional governments retain ultimate authority except for those powers that they expressly delegate to a central government. The United States was a confederation from 1776 to 1787 under the Articles of Confederation. *See also* Federal system; Federalism; Unitary system.

Conference committees   *See* Joint committees.

Congress   A national legislature composed of elected representatives who do not choose the chief executive (typically, a president).

Congressional campaign committee   A party committee in Congress that provides funds to members who are running for reelection or to would-be members running for an open seat or challenging a candidate from the opposition party.

Conservative   In general, a person who favors more limited and local government, less government regulation of markets, more social conformity to traditional norms and values, and tougher policies toward criminals. *See also* Liberal.

Constitutional court   A federal court exercising the judicial powers found in Article III of the Constitution and whose judges are given constitutional protection: they may not be fired (they serve during "good behavior"), nor may their salaries be reduced while they are in office. The most important constitutional courts are the Supreme Court, the ninety-four district courts, and the courts of appeals (one in each of eleven regions plus one in the District of Columbia).

Continuing resolution   A congressional enactment that provides funds to continue government operations in the absence of an agreed-upon budget.

Cost   Any burden, monetary or nonmonetary, that some people must bear, or think they must bear, if a policy is adopted.

Courts of appeals   The federal courts with authority to review decisions by federal district courts, regulatory commissions, and certain other federal courts. Such courts have no original jurisdiction; they can hear only appeals. There are a total of twelve courts of appeals in the United States and its territories plus one for a nationwide circuit. *See also* Constitutional court; District courts; Federal-question cases.

Critical or realigning periods   Periods during which a sharp, lasting shift occurs in the popular coalition supporting one or both parties. The issues that separate the two parties change, and so the kinds of voters supporting each party change.

Cue (political)   A signal telling a congressional representative what values (e.g., liberal or conservative) are at stake in a vote—who is for and who is against a proposal—and how that issue fits into his or her own set of political beliefs or party agenda.

Deficit The annual excess of government spending over government revenue.

Democracy Political system where the people rule.

Direct democracy Political system in which most citizens make policy, as in a town meeting.

Discharge petition A device by which any member of the House, after a committee has had a bill for thirty days, may petition to have it brought to the floor. If a majority of the members agree, the bill is discharged from the committee. The discharge petition was designed to prevent a committee from killing a bill by delaying it for too long.

Discretionary authority The extent to which appointed bureaucrats can choose courses of action and make policies that are not spelled out in advance by laws.

Dissenting opinion A Supreme Court opinion by one or more justices in the minority to explain the minority's disagreement with the Court's ruling. *See also* Opinion of the Court; Concurring opinion.

District courts The lowest federal courts where federal cases begin. They are the only federal courts where trials are held. There are a total of ninety-four district courts in the United States and its territories. *See also* Courts of appeals; Constitutional court; Federal-question cases.

Diversity cases Cases involving citizens of different states over which the federal courts have jurisdiction because at least $75,000 is at stake. *See also* Federal-question cases.

Division vote A congressional voting procedure in which members stand and are counted. *See also* Voice vote; Teller vote; Roll call.

Double tracking Setting aside a bill against which one or more senators are filibustering so that other legislation can be voted on.

Dual federalism A constitutional theory that the national government and the state governments each have defined areas of authority, especially over commerce.

Due-process clause Protection against arbitrary deprivation of life, liberty, or property as guaranteed in the Fifth and Fourteenth Amendments.

Elite (political) An identifiable group of persons who possess a disproportionate share of some valued resource—such as money or political power.

Entrepreneurial politics A policy under which society as a whole benefits while some small group pays the costs. *See also* Policy entrepreneur.

Equality of opportunities A view that it is wrong to use race or sex either to discriminate against or give preferential treatment to blacks or women. *See also* Reverse discrimination.

Equal protection clause The provision in the Fourteenth Amendment to the Constitution guaranteeing that no state shall "deny to any person" the "equal protection of the laws."

Establishment clause A clause in the First Amendment to the Constitution stating that Congress shall make no law "respecting an establishment of religion."

Excepted service Provision for appointing federal offices without going through the competitive service. *See also* Competitive service.

Exclusionary rule A rule that holds that evidence gathered in violation of the Constitution cannot be used in a trial. The rule has been used to implement two provisions of the Bill of Rights—the right to be free from unreasonable searches or seizures (Fourth Amendment) and the right not to be compelled to give evidence against oneself (Fifth Amendment). *See also* Good-faith exception.

Executive privilege A presidential claim that he may withhold certain information from Congress.

Ex post facto law A Latin term meaning "after the fact." A law that makes criminal an act that was legal when it was committed, or that increases the penalty for a crime after it has been committed, or that changes the rules of evidence to make conviction easier; a retroactive criminal law. The state legislatures and Congress are forbidden to pass such laws by Article I of the Constitution.

Faction According to James Madison, a group of people who seek to influence public policy in ways contrary to the public good.

Federalism A political system in which ultimate authority is shared between a central government and state or regional governments. *See also* Confederation; Federal system; Unitary system.

***Federalist* Papers** A series of eighty-five essays written by Alexander Hamilton, James Madison, and John Jay (all using the name "Publius") that were published in New York newspapers in 1787–1788 to convince New Yorkers to adopt the newly proposed Constitution. They are classics of American constitutional and political thought.

Federalists Supporters of a stronger central government who advocated ratification of the Constitution. After ratification, they founded a political party supporting a strong executive and Alexander Hamilton's economic policies. *See also* Antifederalists.

Federal money Money raised to support the campaign of a candidate for federal office. Amounts regulated by federal law.

Federal-question cases Cases concerning the Constitution, federal law, or treaties over which the federal courts have jurisdiction as described in the Constitution. *See also* Diversity cases.

Fee shifting A law or rule that allows the plaintiff (the party that initiates the lawsuit) to collect its legal costs from the defendant if the defendant loses.

Filibuster An attempt to defeat a bill in the Senate by talking indefinitely, thus preventing the Senate from taking action on it. From the Spanish *filibustero*, which means a "freebooter," a military adventurer.

Fiscal policy   The taxing and spending system of the government.

527s   Organizations that raise money for political campaigns that are not (yet) regulated by campaign finance laws.

Franking privilege   The ability of members of Congress to mail letters to their constituents free of charge by substituting their facsimile signature (frank) for postage.

Free-exercise clause   A clause in the First Amendment to the Constitution stating that Congress shall make no law prohibiting the "free exercise" of religion.

Gender gap   Differences in the political views and voting behavior of men and women.

General election   An election used to fill an elective office. *See also* Primary election.

Good-faith exception   Admission at a trial of evidence that is gathered in violation of the Constitution if the violation results from a technical or minor error. *See also* Exclusionary rule.

Government   The institution that, with a monopoly on the lawful use of power, can make decisions binding the whole society.

Grants-in-aid   Federal funds provided to states and localities. Grants-in-aid are typically provided for airports, highways, education, and major welfare services. *See also* Categorical grant; Block grants.

Great or **Connecticut Compromise**   A compromise at the Constitutional Convention in 1787 that reconciled the interests of small and large states by allowing the former to predominate in the Senate and the latter in the House. Under the agreement, each state received two representatives in the Senate, regardless of size, but was allotted representatives on the basis of population in the House.

Gross domestic product   The total amount of goods and services produced in a country.

Ideological party   A party that values principled stands on issues above all else, including winning. It claims to have a comprehensive view of American society and government radically different from that of the established parties.

Impeachment   An accusation against a high federal official charging him or her with "treason, bribery, or other high crimes and misdemeanors." An impeachment requires a majority vote in the House of Representatives. To be removed from office, the impeached official must be tried before the Senate and convicted by a vote of two-thirds of the members present.

Incorporation   A doctrine whereby the Supreme Court incorporates—that is, includes—many parts of the Bill of Rights into restrictions on state government actions.

Independent expenditures   Political money raised and spent by an organization on behalf of a candidate done without direction of or coordination with the candidate.

In forma pauperis   A procedure whereby a poor person can file and be heard in court as a pauper, free of charge.

Interest group   An organization of people, or a "letterhead" organization, sharing a common interest or goal that seeks to influence the making of public policy.

Interest-group politics   A policy under which one small group bears the costs and another small group receives the benefits. *See also* Majoritarian politics.

Iron triangle   A close relationship between an agency, a congressional committee, and an interest group that often becomes a mutually advantageous alliance. *See also* Client politics.

Issue network   A loose collection of leaders, interest groups, bureaucratic agencies, and congressional committees interested in some public policy.

Joint committees   Committees on which both representatives and senators serve. An especially important kind of joint committee is the *conference committee* made up of representatives and senators appointed to resolve differences in the Senate and House versions of the same piece of legislation before final passage. *See also* Select committees; Standing committees.

Joint resolution   A formal expression of congressional opinion that must be approved by both houses of Congress and by the president. Joint resolutions proposing a constitutional amendment are not signed by the president. *See also* Concurrent resolution; Simple resolution.

Judicial review   The power of the courts to declare acts of the legislature and of the executive to be unconstitutional and, hence, null and void.

Legislative court   A court that is created by Congress for some specialized purpose and staffed with judges who do not enjoy the protection of Article III of the Constitution. Legislative courts include the Court of Military Appeals and the territorial courts.

Legislative veto   The rejection of a presidential or administrative-agency action by a vote of one or both houses of Congress without the consent of the president. In 1983, the Supreme Court declared the legislative veto to be unconstitutional.

Legitimate   Political authority conferred by public opinion.

Libel   Injurious written statements about another person.

Liberal   In general, a person who favors a more active federal government for regulating business, supporting social welfare, and protecting minority rights, but who prefers less regulation of private social conduct. *See also* Conservative.

Line-item veto   The power of an executive to veto some provisions in an appropriations bill while approving others. The president does not have the right to exercise a line-item veto and must approve or reject an entire appropriations bill. *See also* Pocket veto; Veto message.

Majoritarian politics   A policy from which almost everybody benefits (or thinks they benefit) and for which almost everybody pays. *See also* Interest-group politics.

Majority leader   The legislative leader elected by party members holding the majority of seats in the House of Representatives or the Senate. *See also* Minority leader.

Mandates   Rules imposed by the federal government on the states to require that the states pay the costs of certain nationally defined programs.

Matching funds In presidential elections, money given by the national government to match, under certain conditions, money raised by each candidate.

Material incentives Benefits that have monetary value, including money, gifts, services, or discounts received as a result of one's membership in an organization.

Minority leader The legislative leader elected by party members holding a minority of seats in the House of Representatives or the Senate. *See also* Majority leader.

Motor-voter law A bill passed by Congress in 1993 to make it easier for Americans to register to vote. The law, which went into effect in 1995, requires states to allow voter registration by mail, when one applies for a driver's license, and at state offices that serve the disabled or poor.

Name-request job A job to be filled by a person whom a government agency has identified by name.

National chairman A paid, full-time manager of a party's day-to-day work who is elected by the national committee.

National committee A committee of delegates from each state and territory that runs party affairs between national conventions.

National convention A meeting of party delegates elected in state primaries, caucuses, or conventions that is held every four years. Its primary purpose is to nominate presidential and vice-presidential candidates and to ratify a campaign platform.

National debt The total amount of money that the government has spent over its history that exceeds the total amount of money that it has taken in through taxes.

Necessary-and-proper clause or elastic clause The final paragraph of Article 1, section 8, of the Constitution, which authorizes Congress to pass all laws "necessary and proper" to carry out the enumerated powers. Sometimes called the "elastic clause" because of the flexibility that it provides to Congress.

New class That part of the middle class that has college and postgraduate degrees and works in occupations that involve using symbols (such as writers and teachers). It tends to have liberal views.

New Deal coalition The different, sometimes opposed voters—southern whites, urban blacks, union workers, and intellectuals—whom Franklin D. Roosevelt made part of the Democratic party in the 1930s and 1940s.

Nullification A theory first advanced by James Madison and Thomas Jefferson that the states had the right to "nullify" (that is, declare null and void) a federal law that, in the states' opinion, violated the Constitution. The theory was revived by John C. Calhoun of South Carolina in opposition to federal efforts to restrict slavery. The North's victory in the Civil War determined once and for all that the federal union is indissoluble and that states cannot declare acts of Congress unconstitutional, a view later confirmed by the Supreme Court.

Office-bloc ballot A ballot listing all candidates for a given office under the name of that office; also called a "Massachusetts" ballot. *See also* Party-column ballot.

Open primary A primary election that permits voters to choose on election day the party primary in which they wish to vote. They may vote for candidates of only one party. *See also* Blanket primary; Closed primary; Primary election.

Open rule An order from the House Rules Committee in the House of Representatives that permits a bill to be amended on the legislative floor. *See also* Closed rule; Restrictive rule.

Opinion of the Court A Supreme Court opinion written by one or more justices in the majority to explain the decision in a case. *See also* Concurring opinion; Dissenting opinion.

Parliament A national legislature composed of elected representatives who choose the chief executive (typically, the prime minister).

Parliamentary system A government that vests power in an elected legislature that chooses the chief executive.

Party-column ballot A ballot listing all candidates of a given party together under the name of that party; also called an "Indiana" ballot. *See also* Office-bloc ballot.

Party vote There are two measures of such voting. By the stricter measure, a party vote occurs when 90 percent or more of the Democrats in either house of Congress vote together against 90 percent or more of the Republicans. A looser measure counts as a party vote any case where at least 50 percent of the Democrats vote together against at least 50 percent of the Republicans.

Per curiam opinion A brief, unsigned opinion issued by the Supreme Court to explain its ruling. *See also* Opinion of the Court.

Personal following The political support provided to a candidate on the basis of personal popularity and networks.

Pluralist theory (politics) A theory that competition among all affected interests shapes public policy.

Plurality system An electoral system, used in almost all American elections, in which the winner is the person who gets the most votes, even if he or she does not receive a majority of the votes.

Pocket veto One of two ways for a president to disapprove a bill sent to him by Congress. If the president does not sign the bill within ten days of his receiving it, and Congress has adjourned within that time, the bill does not become law. *See also* Veto message; Line-item veto.

Police powers The authority of a government to safeguard and promote public order, safety, and morals.

Policy entrepreneur A political leader who has the ability to mobilize an otherwise uninterested majority into supporting a policy opposed by a well-organized group. *See also* Entrepreneurial politics.

Political action committee (PAC) A committee set up by and representing a corporation, labor union, or special-interest group that raises and spends campaign contributions on behalf of one or more candidates or causes.

Political efficacy A citizen's sense that he or she can understand and influence politics.

Political ideology   A coherent and consistent set of attitudes about who ought to rule and what policies ought to be adopted.

Political machine   A party organization that recruits its members by dispensing *patronage*—tangible incentives such as money, political jobs, an opportunity to get favors from government—and that is characterized by a high degree of leadership control over member activity.

Political party   A group that seeks to elect candidates to public office by supplying them with a label—a "party identification"—by which they are known to the electorate.

Political question   An issue that the Supreme Court refuses to consider because it believes the Constitution has left it entirely to another branch to decide. Its view of such issues may change over time, however. For example, until the 1960s, the Court refused to hear cases about the size of congressional districts, no matter how unequal their populations. In 1962, however, it decided that it was authorized to review the constitutional implications of this issue.

Politics   The management of conflict over who shall rule and what policies shall be made.

Poll   A survey of public opinion. *See also* Random sample.

Power   The ability to give or withhold support for a course of action.

Precedent   A judicial rule that permits the court ruling settling an old case to settle a similar new one.

Presidential primary   A special kind of primary used to pick delegates to the presidential nominating conventions of the major parties.

Presidential system   A government that vests power in a separately elected president and legislature.

Primary election   An election prior to the general election in which voters select the candidates who will run on each party's ticket. *See also* Closed primary; Open primary.

Prior restraint   The traditional view of the press's free speech rights as expressed by William Blackstone, the great English jurist. According to this view, the press is guaranteed freedom from censorship—that is, rules telling it in advance what it can publish. After publication, however, the government can punish the press for material that is judged libelous or obscene.

Probable cause   *See* Search warrant.

Proportional representation   A voting system in which representatives in a legislature are chosen by the proportion of all votes each candidate (or each candidate's party) gets.

Prospective voters   Voters who vote for a candidate because they favor his or her ideas for addressing issues after the election. (Prospective means "forward-looking.") *See also* Retrospective voters.

Public-interest lobby   A political organization, the stated goals of which will principally benefit nonmembers.

Purposive incentive   The benefit that comes from serving a cause or principle from which one does not personally benefit.

Pyramid structure   A method of organizing a president's staff in which most presidential assistants report through a hierarchy to the president's chief of staff.

Random sample   A sample selected in such a way that any member of the population being surveyed (e.g., all adults or voters) has an equal chance of being interviewed. *See also* Poll.

Red tape   Complex bureaucratic rules and procedures that must be followed to get something done.

Registered voters   People who are registered to vote. While almost all adult American citizens are theoretically eligible to vote, only those who have completed a registration form by the required date may do so.

Remedy   A judicial order preventing or redressing a wrong or enforcing a right.

Representative democracy   Political system in which policy is made by officials elected by the people.

Republic   A form of democracy in which power is vested in representatives selected by means of popular competitive elections. *See also* Representative democracy).

Restrictive rule   An order from the House Rules Committee in the House of Representatives that permits certain kinds of amendments but not others to be made to a bill on the legislative floor. *See also* Closed rule; Open rule.

Retrospective voters   Voters who vote for or against the candidate or party in office because they like or dislike how things have gone in the recent past. (Retrospective means "backward-looking.") *See also* Prospective voters.

Reverse discrimination   Using race or sex as a basis to give preferential treatment to some individuals. *See also* Equality of opportunities.

Roll call   A congressional voting procedure that consists of members answering "yea" or "nay" to their names. When roll calls were handled orally, it was a time-consuming process in the House. Since 1973, an electronic voting system permits each House member to record his or her vote and learn the total automatically. *See also* Voice vote; Division vote; Teller vote.

Runoff primary   A second primary election held in some states when no candidate receives a majority of the votes in the first primary; the runoff is between the two candidates with the most votes. Runoff primaries are common in the South.)

Sampling error   The difference between the results of two surveys or samples. For example, if one random sample shows that 60 percent of all Americans like cats and another random sample taken at the same time shows that 65 percent do, the sampling error is 5 percent.

Search warrant   An order from a judge authorizing the search of a place; the order must describe what is to be searched and seized, and the judge can issue it only if he or she is persuaded by the police that good reason (probable cause) exists that a crime has been committed and that the evidence bearing on the crime will be found at a certain location.

Select committees   Congressional committees appointed for a limited time and purpose. *See also* Standing committees; Joint committees.

Selective attention   Paying attention only to those parts of a newspaper or broadcast story with which one agrees.

Studies suggest that this is how people view political ads on television.

Senatorial courtesy A tradition that makes it impossible to confirm a presidential nominee for office if a senator files a personal objection.

Separate-but-equal doctrine The doctrine, established in *Plessy* v. *Fergusson* (1896), in which the Supreme Court ruled that a state could provide "separate but equal" facilities for blacks.

Separation of powers A principle of American government whereby constitutional authority is shared by three separate branches of government—the legislative, the executive, and the judicial. *See also* Checks and balances.

Shays's Rebellion A rebellion in 1787 led by Daniel Shays and other ex–Revolutionary War soldiers and officers to prevent foreclosures of farms as a result of high interest rates and taxes. The revolt highlighted the weaknesses of the Confederation and bolstered support for a stronger national government.

Signing statements Written comments by the president about a bill he has just signed. Those that raise constitutional questions are controversial.

Simple resolution An expression of opinion either in the House of Representatives or the Senate to settle housekeeping or procedural matters in either body. Such expressions are not signed by the president and do not have the force of law. *See also* Concurrent resolution; Joint resolution.

Single-member districts Legislative districts from which one representative is chosen.

Soft money Money raised by political parties for activities other than directly supporting a federal candidate.

Solidarity An incentive that relies on friendship or sociability.

Solidary incentives The social rewards that lead people to join local or state political organizations. People who find politics fun and want to meet others who share their interests are said to respond to solidary incentives.

Sovereign immunity A doctrine that a citizen cannot sue the government without its consent. By statute Congress has given its consent for the government to be sued in many cases involving a dispute over a contract or damage done as a result of negligence.

Sovereignty A governmental unit that has supreme authority and is accountable to no higher institution.

Speaker The presiding officer of the House of Representatives and the leader of his party in the House.

Split-ticket voting Voting for candidates of different parties for various offices in the same election. For example, voting for a Republican for senator and a Democrat for president. *See also* Straight-ticket voting.

Spots (campaign) Short television advertisements used to promote a candidate for government office.

Standing A legal concept establishing who is entitled to bring a lawsuit to court. For example, an individual must ordinarily show personal harm in order to acquire standing and be heard in court.

Standing committees Permanently established legislative committees that consider and are responsible for legislation within certain subject areas. Examples are the House Ways and Means Committee and the Senate Judiciary Committee. *See also* Select committees; Joint committees.

Stare decisis A Latin term meaning "let the decision stand." The practice of basing judicial decisions on precedents established in similar cases decided in the past.

Straight-ticket voting Voting for candidates who are all of the same party. For example, voting for Republican candidates for senator, representative, and president. *See also* Split-ticket voting.

Strict constructionist approach (judicial) The view that judges should decide cases on the basis of the language of the Constitution.

Strict scrutiny The standard by which the Supreme Court judges classifications based on race. To be accepted, such a classification must be closely related to a "compelling" public purpose.

Suspect classification Classifications of people on the basis of their race and ethnicity. The courts have ruled that laws classifying people on these grounds will be subject to "strict scrutiny."

Symbolic speech An act that conveys a political message, such as burning a draft card to protest the draft.

Traditional middle class That part of the middle class that has jobs in business or farming and tends to have conservative views.

Trial balloon Information provided to the media by an anonymous public official as a way of testing the public reaction to a possible policy or appointment.

Trust funds Funds for government programs that are collected and spent outside the regular government budget; the amounts are determined by preexisting law rather than by annual appropriations. The Social Security trust fund is the largest of these. *See also* Appropriation.

Unicameral legislature A lawmaking body with only one chamber, as in Nebraska.

Unipolar world A world that is militarily dominated by one superpower, as is the case with the United States today.

Unitary system A system in which sovereignty is wholly in the hands of the national government so that subnational political units are dependent on its will. *See also* Confederation; Federalism; Federal system.

Veto Literally, "I forbid"; it refers to the power of a president to disapprove a bill. It may be overriden by a two-thirds vote of each house of Congress.

Veto message One of two ways for a president to disapprove a bill sent to him by Congress. The veto message must be sent to Congress within ten days after the president receives it. *See also* Pocket veto; Line-item veto.

Visual (campaign) A campaign activity that appears on a television news broadcast. *See also* Spots.

Voice vote A congressional voting procedure in which members shout "aye" in approval or "no" in disapproval; allows members to vote quickly or anonymously on bills. *See also* Division vote; Teller vote; Roll call.

Voting-age population (VAP) The citizens who are eligible to vote after reaching a minimum age requirement. In the

United States, a citizen must be at least eighteen years old in order to vote.

Voting-eligible population (VEP)   The VAP minus aliens and felons.

Wall of separation   A Supreme Court interpretation of the Establishment clause in the First Amendment that prevents government involvement with religion, even on a nonpreferential basis.

Whip   A senator or representative who helps the party leader stay informed about what party members are thinking, rounds up members when important votes are to be taken, and attempts to keep a nose count on how the voting on controversial issues is likely to go.

Writ of certiorari   A Latin term meaning "made more certain." An order issued by a higher court to a lower court to send up the record of a case for review. Most cases reach the Supreme Court through the writ of certiorari, issued when at least four of the nine justices feel that the case should be reviewed.

Writ of habeas corpus   A Latin term meaning "you shall have the body." A court order directing a police officer, sheriff, or warden who has a person in custody to bring the prisoner before a judge and show sufficient cause for his or her detention. The writ of habeas corpus was designed to prevent illegal arrests and imprisonment.

INDEX